Praise for *Transatlantic Trio*

In this treasure trove of literary commentary, Richard Brantley distills his decades of inquiry into the dynamic religious, scientific, and poetic forces that sustained an amazingly fruitful strain of Anglo-American Romanticism. Wordsworth, Coleridge, Blake, Keats, Tennyson, Emerson, and Dickinson play key roles in his argument, along with Locke, Wesley, Edwards, Darwin, and Brantleys of multiple generations. In their creative blendings of empiricism with evangelicalism, the writers featured here experimented with subtleties of both/and logic that challenge today's either/or reductionism. These articles, book chapters, personal writings, and reviews document energetic, sustained grappling with thinkers from the Enlightenment to the current literary scene, all treated with Brantley's characteristic insight, intensity, congeniality, and verve. As the humorous cover drawing of thirteen writer-thinkers aboard a railroading handcar suggests, Transatlantic Trio engages its readers on Brantley's adventurous scholarly excursion, "a back-and-forth that gets somewhere."

—Jane Donahue Eberwein, Distinguished Professor Emerita of English, Oakland University

Spanning almost half a century, Richard Brantley's 'ongoing project in bi-national cultural poetics' is both an erudite analysis of the history of transatlantic literary engagement and, in itself, an emblematic example of the flowering of transatlanticism as a subject of literary study. Brantley has an Emersonian talent for identifying previously unnoticed connections across space and time, tracing correspondences between empirical philosophy and evangelical faith, with coordinates ranging from Locke, Edwards and Wesley, to Blake, Dickinson and Tennyson, in a narrative that explores the complex, ambiguous subtleties of the relationships between history and literature. Brantley's scholarship does not merely tell us about the past: the forms of 'healthy skepticism' that he traces through the 17th to the 19th centuries – and which he adopts in his own readings – remain as vital as ever as antidotes to a tendency in our own times towards a 'certainty' that [. . .] 'is the enemy of decency and humanity in people who are sure they are right.'

—Chris Gair, Senior Lecturer in English Literature and American Studies, School of Critical Studies, University of Glasgow

This collection of essays and reviews provides representative examples of Richard Brantley's pioneering work in highlighting interconnections between empiricism, evangelicalism and Romanticism, and in showing the importance of positioning and connecting British and American writers, and cultural and literary movements and ideas, within a transatlantic field. Brantley's work foregrounds a productive antagonism between the experience-based epistemology of John Locke and the revivalist theology of John Wesley and Jonathan Edwards, and traces this dialectic's influence on canonical works of Anglo-American Romanticism, early and late. Moving beyond a nation-based model, Brantley offers a nuanced consideration of the ways in which British and American writers such as Wordsworth, Keats, Tennyson, and Dickinson used a comparable empirical method to authenticate and authorize the sensory experience of a physical world, while employing a similar procedure to interrogate the idea of faith in a metaphysical or supernatural realm.
—Páraic Finnerty, Reader in English and American Literature,
University of Portsmouth

Richard E. Brantley has provided, in Transatlantic Trio, *a capstone to one of the central preoccupations of his extremely distinguished scholarly career. This is the analysis of commonalities in two central but apparently divergent traditions of thought: philosophical empiricism and evangelical non-conformism. He traces the growth of British Romanticism out of the relationship between the two, attending to ways in which both traditions place emphasis on knowledge of the self through the experience of the immanent, and goes on to show how, through complex transatlantic conversations, these ideas come to form the bedrock of American intellectual and spiritual thought. As such, it gives readers both an accessibly defined account of Romanticism from a transatlantic perspective, and also offers a series of scholarly expositions of the central literary figures in the long century under view. The book does more than this, however. It also provides a fascinating overview of the subject as it has developed during the past four decades and ends with a reflection, after decades of experience, on how the consolations of pedagogy bring an enhancement of faith.*
—Matthew Scott, Lecturer in the Department of English Literature,
University of Reading

Brantley's trio, made up of empiricism, evangelicalism, and Romanticism—as spelled out in his complete title—may be thought of as a productively unresolved dialectic whereby Romanticism draws energy from the conflicting imperatives of faith and experience. In a revealing epigraph to his prologue, Brantley quotes Arthur Koestler on the generative power of opposing points of view: "Creativity arises as the result of the intersection of two quite different frames of reference." For Brantley, the "different frames of reference" are experience/empiricism/science, on the one hand, and faith/evangelicalism/religion on the other. He unites these clashing polarities at the very beginning of his prologue through the incisive chiasmus, "faith in experience and experiential Faith," that crystalizes the mutually beneficial cross-pollination that he views as the driving force of Romanticism. "British empiricism and transatlantic revivalism," he writes, "strike sparks off the literary imagination of a bi-national Romantic Movement". The poem, then, that Brantley reads across two centuries is his metaphorical celebration of these conflicting voices: "just as an antiphony is 'an opposition of sound'—'the answer made by one voice to another'—so empirical philosophy and evangelical faith alternate, or converse, in Romantic Anglo-America (OED)." Brantley goes so far as to argue that "'the harmony produced' by that 'opposition of sound,' . . . can appear on the same page of, and perhaps even as the single voice of, Anglo-American Romanticism (OED)." Such language clearly reflects Brantley's interest in presenting the great central poem of Romanticism as forward looking, and not merely a record of artistic triumph consigned to the past. He is at his most ambitious when he proposes that Romanticism is not content "just to make poetry new, but to pass it on, and perhaps even prepare the ear of readers, however unwittingly on all fronts, for the taught pleasures of the Modern-era dissonance to come." At the heart of Brantley's life's work lies his conviction that Romanticism has a crucial role to play in our present moment.

To insure that his own work meets the standard he most admires in the thinkers and artists who have long been his subject, Brantley departs from what he describes as his own tendency toward "relentless self-consistency, accentuating the positive, eliminating the negative, and reaffirming the whole" to interject an entirely "different and maybe refreshing line of auto-subversion." The key question he directs to himself in his epilogue is whether or not "human minds [his own included] rest in the mystery and doubt perhaps too glibly—or even somewhat disingenuously. . ." This willing contemplation of his own potential for superficiality ultimately leads to the most devastating of his admissions: "Who," Brantley wonders, "can deny his or her yearning for unity on some days? To see empirical vs. evangelical emerging into harmony (poetry) looks a lot like synthesis just now." Having confronted his own fears and thereby shown respect for what Jorge Luis Borges has described as the "'counter-book'" that each complete book must contain (qtd. by Brantley 615), Brantley dedicates the remainder of his epilogue to rebuilding the foundations for his argument.

The steps Brantley elaborates as most central to his method now concentrate on the emotional, affective dimension of the more narrowly intellectual approach he sketched in the prologue. His first move is to affirm the importance of ambiguity as an antidote to the allure of complacency that threatens his own scholarship as much as it does the visionary aspirations of the Romantic writers he studies. Working from the Latin roots of the term—that he translates as "to wander uncertainly"—Brantley gives particular emphasis to uncertainty as an essential byproduct of Romantic writers' determination to "search for something, they know not what." "Both/and logic," he argues, "carries the implication not just of tentativeness or open-mindedness," but the "understanding" that "those who come down hard on one side or the other can be wrong or dangerous." Brantley's next move is to present active and unceasing vigilance as the best defense against the inclination to seek final answers and succumb to single-mindedness. "The writers who have attracted the attention of the series refuse to sleep, until Jerusalem is built," but, of course, he notes, "they never sleep, for they never finish building." Here again Brantley directs attention to the forward-looking, future-oriented component of Romanticism. "Dialectical strategy," he reminds us, "proves ultimately inimical to aesthetic versatility." Continuous resistance to dialectical closure as brought about by the vigilant pursuit of an uncertain future yields the creative dynamism Brantley finds most admirable in Romantic writers, and it provides the standard he applies equally to his own published works. Brantley concludes his epilogue by asking the one question guaranteed to provoke resistance and intensify vigilance: "What next?" He concludes with a summary of his primary aims expressed in admirably plain language: "The prologue and epilogue have not just offered a master key to all these reprints and to the books, but opened the door to more investigation." We leave the epilogue with the sure sense that Brantley is already moving into the future.

—Paul Crumbley, Professor of English and
Director of the Undergraduate Studies Program,
Utah State University

In mulling nineteenth-century poetic thought in the English-speaking world, Brantley shows how empiricism and evangelicalism swept into each other and produced Romanticism. Reading the great nineteenth-century poets moves us because their poetry like the vision of John Wesley is

rich with good black earth but not earthbound. Faith arises out of sense experience.

Brantley is a fine, readable critic. His good sensible language explains Wordsworth's language of sense. Reading *Transatlantic Trio* almost enables a person to understand the blending of the spiritual and the natural that so often make us imagine that our common observations of nature are moving and uplifting.

—Sam Pickering, Professor of English, Emeritus,
University of Connecticut

These essays speak to the way Enlightenment, Romantic, and Victorian thinkers created a Venn diagram out of an opposition that still nibbles at the soul (to paraphrase Dickinson) of today's postmodern world: science vs. religion. Of the many strategies the Romantics offer us to overcome the Manichean duality that runs rampant today are the flexibility of method over the rigidity of system as well as the multiple perspectives of "both/and logic" over the singular vision of "either/or logic." In terms of literary criticism and history, these methods show us the benefits and necessity of moving beyond the single-nation formulations of Romanticism towards a comparative approach. By examining transatlantic influence and literatures as hierarchical, scholars of Transatlantic Romanticism have unwittingly embraced the very duality they are trying to deconstruct. Brantley's methodology levels these fields to remove the competitive poetics and politics that emerged in the wake of the American Revolution and still maintains a foothold. His application of these strategies to present-day Western thought expands this book beyond a work of criticism to a philosophy that overrides the binary coding of a digital age. He ties "the transatlantic trio of empiricism, evangelicalism, and Romanticism together" in new and compelling ways: the collected essays and book reviews are tesserae that together form a mosaic, a more complete scholarly picture of Anglo-American Romanticism than previously existed. The book ends with a powerful autobiographical epilogue that testifies to the transcendent methods of Anglo-American Romanticism to help us make sense of not only the 18th-to-21st centuries, but also of our own lives, the antiphony of internal and external worlds that composes our thoughts and the "music of humanity."

—Joel Pace, Professor of English,
University of Wisconsin, Eau Claire

Books by Richard E. Brantley:

Wordsworth's "Natural Methodism"
Locke, Wesley, and the Method of English Romanticism
Coordinates of Anglo-American Romanticism:
Wesley, Edwards, Carlyle, and Emerson
Anglo-American Antiphony:
The Late Romanticism of Tennyson and Emerson
Experience and Faith: The Late-Romantic
Imagination of Emily Dickinson
Emily Dickinson's Rich Conversation:
Poetry, Philosophy, Science

Transatlantic Trio:
Empiricism, Evangelicalism, Romanticism

Essays and Reviews, 1974-2017

Richard E. Brantley

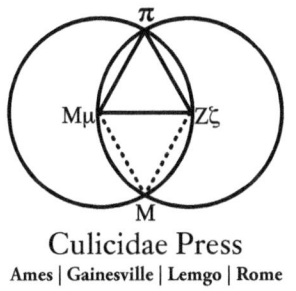

Culicidae Press
Ames | Gainesville | Lemgo | Rome

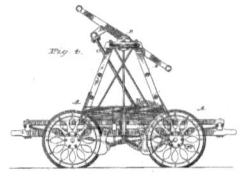

THIS IS A HANDCAR BOOK
PUBLISHED BY CULICIDAE PRESS

Copyright © 2017 by Richard E. Brantley.

All rights reserved.
No part of this book may be reproduced in any form by any electronic or mechanized means (including photocopying, recording, or information storage and retrieval) without written permission, except in the case of brief quotations embodied in critical articles and evaluations.
Every effort has been made to seek permission to reproduce those reviews whose copyright does not reside with Culicidae Press, and we are grateful to the individuals and institutions who have assisted in this task. Any omissions are entirely unintentional, and will be addressed in future editions.

For more information, please visit www.culicidaepress.com or the author's website at www.richardbrantley.com

ISBN-13: 978-1-68315-003-9

ISBN-10: 1-68315-003-1

Cover design and interior layout ©2017 by polytekton.com
Set in a digitized version of Janson, a typeface that
was created by Nicholas Kis (1650-1702).

Permissions

Grateful acknowledgment is made to the following for permission to reprint previously published material (reviews are indicated by authors' names in parentheses):

BOSTON UNIVERSITY COLLEGE OF ARTS & SCIENCES: "Wordsworth's Art of Belief," "Keats's Method," "The Empirical Imagination of Emily Dickinson," *The Obstinate Questionings of English Romanticism* (by L. J. Swingle), *The Romantic Ethic and the Spirit of Consumerism* (by Colin Campbell), *The Spiritual History of Ice: Romanticism, Science, and the Imagination* (by Eric G. Wilson), *Emerson, Romanticism, and Intuitive Reason: The Transatlantic "Light of All Our Day"* (by Patrick J. Keane), *The Story of Joy* (by Adam Potkay).

BRUNEL UNIVERSITY: "Emily Dickinson's Empirical Voice," "From Loss to Gain: Aftermath in the Late-Romantic Poetry of Emily Dickinson."

CAMBRIDGE UNIVERSITY PRESS: "Wesley and Edwards: An Anglo-American Nexus," "Empiricism and Evangelicalism: A Combination of Romanticism."

CHURCH HISTORY: *Jonathan Edwards's Writings: Text, Context, Interpretation*, edited (Stephen J. Stein).

COLLEAGUES PRESS: "Evangelical Principles of Tennyson's *In Memoriam.*"

DARTMOUTH COLLEGE: *Text as Process: Creative Composition in Wordsworth, Tennyson, and Dickinson* (by Sally Bushell).

DUKE UNIVERSITY PRESS: "Charles Wesley's Experiential Art."

THE EDWIN MELLEN PRESS: *Emily Dickinson's Experiential Poetics and Rev. Dr. Charles Wadsworth's Rhetoric of Sensation: The Intellectual Friendship between the Poet and a Pastor* (by Mary Lee Stephenson Huffer).

GEORGIA COLLEGE: *The Comedy of Redemption: Christian Faith and Comic Vision in Four American Novelists* (by Ralph C. Wood).

THE JOHNS HOPKINS UNIVERSITY PRESS: "Johnson's Wesleyan Connection," "Dickinson's Signature Conundrum," *The Evangelist of Desire: John Wesley and the Methodists* (by Henry Abelove), *Miles of Stare: Transcendentalism and the Problem of Literary Vision in Nineteenth-Century America* (by Michelle Kohler).

THE NATIONAL COUNCIL OF TEACHERS OF ENGLISH: "Sleeping with the Enemy: Communiqués from a Pedagogical Marriage."

PALGRAVE MACMILLAN: "The Wordsworthian Cast of Emily Dickinson's Romantic Heritage."

RICE UNIVERSITY PRESS: "Spiritual Maturity and Wordsworth's 1784 Christmas Vacation."

SAGE PUBLISHING: "Dickinson the Romantic," "A CCL Tribute to Robert Alter," *God, Locke, and Equality: Christian Foundations in Locke's Political Thought* (by Jeremy Waldron), *The Romantic Reformation: Religion and Politics in English Literature, 1789-1824* (by Robert M. Ryan), *William Wordsworth and the Hermeneutics of Incarnation* (by David P. Haney), *British Romantic Writers and the East: Anxieties of Empire* (by Nigel Leask), *Seeing Suffering in Women's Literature of the Romantic Era* (by Elizabeth Dolan), *Emily Dickinson's Approving God* (by Patrick J. Keane).

TAYLOR & FRANCIS: "John Wesley (1703-91)," "An Orientation to Locke, Wesley, and the Method of English Romanticism," "Locke and Wesley: An Essence of Influence," *Wesley and the Wesleyans: Religion in Eighteenth-Century Britain* (by John Kent).

UNIVERSITY OF NOTRE DAME: "The Interrogative Mood of Emily Dickinson's Quarrel with God."

To Jessica, Thomas, Justine, Chris,
Gabriel, David, Rabun, and Leif

Contents

Prologue: From Context to Text — 17

**Essays, First Series: Backgrounds of
    British and American Romanticism** — 65
1. John Wesley (1703-91) — 67
2. An Orientation to Locke, Wesley, and the Method of
English Romanticism — 89
3. Locke and Wesley: An Essence of Influence — 135
4. Wesley and Edwards: An Anglo-American Nexus — 145
5. Empiricism and Evangelicalism:
A Combination of Romanticism — 189

Essays, Second Series: British Authors — 193
6. Charles Wesley's Experiential Art — 195
7. Johnson's Wesleyan Connection — 209
8. Spiritual Maturity and Wordsworth's
1783 Christmas Vacation — 235
9. Wordsworth's Art of Belief — 245
10. Keats's Method — 267
11. Evangelical Principles of Tennyson's *IN MEMORIAM* — 287

Essays, Third Series: Emily Dickinson — 303
12. Dickinson the Romantic — 305
13. The Empirical Imagination of Emily Dickinson — 337
14. Emily Dickinson's Empirical Voice — 347
15. The Wordsworthian Cast of Dickinson's Romantic Heritage — 377
16. The Interrogative Mood of Emily Dickinson's
Quarrel with God — 397
17. From Loss to Gain: Aftermath in the Late Romantic Poetry
of Emily Dickinson — 407
18. Dickinson's Signature Conundrum — 431

Essays, Fourth Series: Miscellaneous Perspectives   459
    19. A Memorial Tribute to T. Walter Herbert 1908-1983   461
    20. Sleeping with the Enemy:
        Communiqués from a Pedagogical Marriage   469
    21. A Conference on Christianity and Literature
        Tribute to Robert Alter   477

Reviews, First Series: Books on Locke, Wesley, and Edwards   479
    22. *God, Locke, and Equality: Christian Foundations in Locke's Political
        Thought*, by Jeremy Waldron.   481
    23. *The Evangelist of Desire: John Wesley and the Methodists*,
        by Henry Abelove   491
    24. *Wesley and the Wesleyans: Religion in Eighteenth-Century Britain*,
        by John Kent   497
    25. *Jonathan Edwards's Writings: Text, Context, Interpretation*,
        edited by Stephen J. Stein   503

Reviews, Second Series: Books on British Romanticism   507
    26. *The Obstinate Questionings of English Romanticism*,
        by L. J. Swingle.   509
    27. *William Wordsworth and the Hermeneutics of Incarnation*,
        by David P. Haney   515
    28. *The Romantic Reformation: Religious Politics in English Literature,
        1789-1824*, by Robert M. Ryan   519
    29. *The Romantic Ethic and the Spirit of Modern Consumerism*,
        by Colin Campbell   537
    30. *British Romantic Writers and the East: Anxieties of Empire*,
        by Nigel Leask   543

Reviews, Third Series: Books on Transatlantic Romanticism   547
    31. *The Spiritual History of Ice: Romanticism, Science,
        and the Imagination*, by Eric G. Wilson   549
    32. *Emerson, Romanticism, and Intuitive Reason: The Transatlantic
        "Light of All Our Day"*, by Patrick J. Keane   555

33. *Text as Process: Creative Composition in Wordsworth,*
    Tennyson, and Emerson, by Sally Bushell   563
34. *Seeing Suffering in Women's Literature of the Romantic Era,*
    by Elizabeth A. Dolan; and *Emily Dickinson's Approving God:*
    Divine Design and the Problem of Suffering, by Patrick J. Keane   575

Reviews, Fourth Series: Miscellaneous Books   585
35. *Emily Dickinson's Experiential Poetics and*
    Rev. Dr. Charles Wadsworth's Rhetoric of Sensation:
    The Intellectual Friendship between the Poet and a Pastor,
    by Mary Lee Stephenson Huffer   587
36. *Miles of Stare: Transcendentalism and the Problem of Literary Vision*
    in Nineteenth-Century America, by Michelle Kohler   591
37. *The Comedy of Redemption: Christian Faith and Comic Vision*
    in Four American Novelists, by Ralph C. Wood   595
38. *The Story of Joy: From the Bible to Late Romanticism,*
    by Adam Potkay   599

Epilogue: From Credo to Credit   607

Appendix: A Range of Responses   659

About the Author   741
Cover Key   743

Edwin Graves Wilson

Prologue: From Context to Text

Clasp with thy panting soul the pendulous Earth;
As from a centre, dart thy spirit's light
Beyond all worlds, until its spacious might
Satiate the void circumference: then shrink
Even to a point within our day and night;
And keep thy heart light lest it make thee sink
When hope has kindled hope, and lured thee to the brink.
—Percy Bysshe Shelley, "Adonais" (1821), lines 417-23[1]

Creativity arises as the result of the intersection of two quite different frames of reference.
—Arthur Koestler, *The Act of Creation* (1964)[2]

. . . life is incremental, and though a worthwhile life is a gathering together of all that one is, good and bad, successful and not, the paradox is that we can never really see this one thing that all of our increments (and decrements, I suppose) add up to. "Early we receive a call," writes Czeslaw Milosz, *"yet it remains incomprehensible, / and only late do we discover how obedient we were."*
—Christian Wiman, *My Bright Abyss: Meditation of a Modern Believer* (2013) 174

Francis Jeffrey's indictment of William Wordsworth's *The Excursion* (1814) as "mystical verbiage of the Methodist pulpit"—"This will never do!"—will itself never do (Jeffrey 463, 465). Charles Lamb's praise of *The Excursion* as "natural methodism" provides a fuller, more positive clue to the historical, interdisciplinary resonance of Romanticism (Lamb 2:149). Lamb's two-word mouthful offers versatile insight, bears interpretive weight. This phrase signals how the rival traditions of empiricism and evangelicalism come together to embroider not just Wordsworth's art, but Romantic literature throughout the English-speaking world. A lower-case but not entirely secularized swerve to evangelicalism spins volumes about how 19th-century poetic faith willingly suspends disbelief: the free-wheeling swing of Romantic-era creativity proclaims interconnection.

*

The combination of "natural" and "methodism" opens a critic's pathway. British empiricism and transatlantic revivalism strike sparks off the literary imagination of a bi-national Romantic Movement. On United Kingdom/United States shores, faith in experience and experiential Faith rise inexorably to converge at the crossroads of an inspired transatlantic artistry, a prime location—and locator—of creative authority. Lamb's label pinpoints a cache of Anglo-American Romantic power. This natural methodism counts as a bi-nationally indigenous, religious as well as philosophical equivalent to M. H. Abrams's magisterially philosophical emphasis on how Continental European Natural Supernaturalism applies to British

---

[1] Quotations of British and American writers, unless otherwise indicated, are from Damrosch et al., eds., and Baym et al., eds. A shorter version of this essay appears as "Wielding Natural Methodism: Prospect's Retrospection," *The Wordsworth Circle* 47.1 (Winter 2016): 3-16. Thanks go to Marilyn Gaull for her editing—and for her encouragement. Parts of the prologue and epilogue were presented as "Dickinson and Wesley: A Comparison of Poems and Sermons" at the Emily Dickinson International Society Conference—"Experimental Dickinson"—June 24-26, 2016, Cité Internationale Universitaire de Paris, Paris, France. Gratitude is due to Jane Donahue Eberwein for organizing Panel 20: "Rewording the Word: Dickinson and the Language of Faith."

[2] Arthur Koestler's epitome of both/and aesthetics is used by Mikesch Muecke and Miriam Zach, eds., 6, to introduce the concept of creative intersection—or "resonance"—between music and architecture. Muecke and Zach build on Robert Venturi's *Complexity and Contradiction in Architecture* (1966), which re-introduced architectural history into the academy and began the post-Modern phase of architectural studies. In another, more recent publication, Annemieke Pronker-Coron pioneers a broad, yet focused, musical version of both/and aesthetics, in her book *The Bridge: Connecting Violin and Fiddle Worlds* (2015).

Romanticism (Abrams, 1971). This arc from the late 17th to the middle 19th century encompasses John Locke (1632-1704), John Wesley (1703-91), Jonathan Edwards (1703-58), and the method of Anglo-American Romanticism. This one curve of that great timeline gives meaning perhaps even to such a spontaneous overflow recollected in tranquility as the signature middle-century question asked by Emily Dickinson (1830-86) as late as 1862: "Dare you see a Soul at the White Heat?" (Poem 365, 1). For the remainder of this segment to draw out the implication of Jeffrey's negative assessment and Lamb's favorable judgment of Wordsworth's poetry is to announce that wielding natural methodism along that arc from high-to-late Romanticism of the Anglo-American world is the procedure and the concept of this essay.

Jeffrey's already-quoted words of withering condescension come from a Whig to the formerly radical but in 1814 Tory-leaning poet of middle age. Yet these terms of abuse may be conservative in that they reflect Jeffrey's neoclassical premises of literary taste. Jeffrey may disclose a way or three in which *The Excursion* does not live up to readers' expectations. Without looking for sublime thrills, sincere expression, and inventive swagger, Jeffrey nonetheless detects hot air, disingenuous formula, and crowd-pleasing convention. He assumes disconnection between religion and literature. He believes that Wordsworth could not possibly allude to Methodism, however subtly, and with however paradoxical an understanding of this simultaneously edgy and mainstream evangelical form, for any poetically proper reason. And throughout all his hostility Jeffrey makes at least one good point. Wordsworth's preachiness—his Methodist language "is repeated, till the speaker entertains no doubt that he is the chosen organ of divine truth and persuasion"—scarcely comports with the idea of art as pleasure (Jeffrey 463).

That said, Jeffrey's scathing review grinds an ax or four and makes this strangely haughty Whig British Exhibit A among those "cultured despisers" of religion whom German Romantic theologian Friedrich Schleiermacher skewers. Whether Methodism in *The Excursion* enchants the poem or merely drugs it, Jeffrey gets Methodism wrong. The savvy, sense-based reason of *ur*-Methodist Wesley, like his equally experience-oriented practice of charity, fights shy of mysticism, which, whether interior or otherworldly in its search for "union with the divine by means of ecstatic contemplation or direct reception" *(OED)*, elides embodiment, circumstance, the sensate. Each month from January, 1782, through April, 1784, in twenty-eight free-standing issues of *The Arminian Magazine,* his widely read *omnium gatherum* of free will-loving Methodist lore, Wesley abridged, annotated and popularized the truth-from-where-I-stand angle of vision celebrated throughout the perceptual epistemology of Locke's *An Essay concerning Human Understanding* (1690). The empirically evangelical, here-and-now idiom of British Romanticism in general, and the eleemosynary distinct from altruistic accent of Wordsworth in particular, ensued. Wordsworth's readers may dislike mysticism (dreamy, self-deluded, confused) and at the same time like his Romantic vernacular for its transposition of Wesley-brand non-mysticism (concrete, acute, clear-sighted) into the still, sad music of an anything but entirely anti-religious Romantic-era humanism. Just as the evangelical "spiritual sense" scarcely resembles amorphously inward, space-cadet mystery, as Jeffrey appears to scoff, but trends outer-directed instead, so Wordsworth's influential resourcefulness reinforces not just imagination of a world elsewhere or of a paradise within, but mental images of this wondrous, numinous, material world. The dubious judgment of a biased critic whom Schleiermacher would dub a defaming witling notwithstanding, Wordsworth's mysticism, to put it mildly, remains putative, at most.

Or, to dispense with Jeffrey more fairly, Wordsworth's mysticism stays under such firm control that his most characteristically religious poetry does not just intuit God, like Henry More's and Henry Vaughn's mystical writings of the 17th century, but discerns God's things through "the language of the sense" (Wordsworth, "Tintern Abbey," 1798, 108). True, Wordsworth's art of belief is very well capable of confining his faith concerns to "things hoped for," "things not seen" (Heb. 11:1; KJV). His personae, moreover, can be intent on overleaping "substance" of the former and "evidence" of the latter. Finally, his paradoxical (verbal) intimation of the apophatic (ineffable) undertow of phenomena can come across as rich and strange enough to satisfy anyone's inner (sea-changed) believer. But "subtler language" for "the deep truth" qualifies as branding for British Romantic poetry only with the stipulation that "the language of the sense" glints in the blend.[3]

---

[3] Percy Bysshe Shelley's phrases, indicative of an "imageless" (his word) ghost in the machine of metaphor-laden picture-language during the Romantic period (Shelley could be thus concrete, too, from time to time), are highlighted in Pulos; Wasserman. Image-laden language, though, perhaps even as part of Romantic religion, is acknowledged by Colin Jager, who demonstrates a self-critical "tradition of natural theology," "substantially continuous" from Hume to Blake, in which "practice" is preferred to "argument" (36-37). Describing an arc from the Enlightenment to Romanticism, Jager concludes (against legions of secularizing critics) that the "intentionality" embraced by British Romantics commits them to "divine intentionality" (224).

And Anglo-American Romanticism keeps empirically philosophical and evangelically religious language so much in play as to leave mysticism at the margin of such both/and logic. Thus the "truth" that "you shall know," and which "makes you free," can prove all the more accessible, lived, felt, or experienced, for not being remote, abstract, formulaic, or innocent (John 8:32; KJV).

In the letter to Wordsworth in which Lamb mentions "natural methodism" as what works well for *The Excursion*, he laments how William Gifford, editor of *The Quarterly*, has excised from Lamb's review its elaboration on the tagline as encomium. Did a Jeffrey-like prejudice against Methodists motivate Gifford to mute Lamb's Methodism-whispering language, consigning it to the virtual ether? Lamb makes clear to his friend that something good would have been coming Wordsworth's way: "I regret only [Lamb writes] that I did not keep a copy [of the review]. I am sure you would have been pleased with it, because I have been feeding my fancy for some months with the notion of pleasing you." It is maddening-but-tantalizing that like the *Quarterly* review (as truncated), the letter says nothing about anything Lamb might have meant by the designation, let alone about how this adjective-noun link-up hints approval. Lamb may have thought that his literary compatriot would already have known and taken pride in what natural methodism points to. What, if anything, does Lamb's veiled reference to Wordsworth's greatness signify for just how English-language Romanticism proves distinguished, too?

Does Lamb's phrase encapsulate the religious connotation as well as the philosophical denotation of Colin Clarke's classic brief (1963) for Wordsworth's "Romantic paradox" as an at once objective and subjective phenomenon? Can natural methodism epitomize the empirical connotation as well as the evangelical denotation of F. C. Gill's classic title: *The Romantic Movement and Methodism* (1937)? Is the long-running series of which this essay forms part—including not just the collection's twenty-one essays and seventeen reviews, but the six books—justified in what an anonymous University Press of Florida reader once called its "interminable lucubration" concerning Lamb's phrase? Would a Clifford Geertz agree, though, that a "thick description" of natural methodism is nonetheless desirable, or perhaps even devoutly to be wished, however incrementally or speculatively it must be accreted or induced? Answers to such questions would indicate, if only tentatively or provisionally, how Wordsworth and his fellow Romantics might welcome or even co-opt the phrase as an intellectual-*cum*-emotional descriptor of their collective work. Answers would thereby atone vicariously for Gifford's sin of omission, and would therefore placate the shades of Lamb and Wordsworth (to say nothing of scholarly curiosity). Answers, in short, would fill this gap with what the concept adds up to.

This essay, accordingly, poses, as well, the following related, yet more general, questions, all to be held in mind for both the short and long term of this cumulative, ongoing project in bi-national cultural poetics. Did the experience-framed correspondence between empirical philosophy and evangelical faith build a fire under Wordsworth's dialogical imagination? Could such an existential but mystery-laden parallel between the natural and spiritual things of earth suffice as a requisite counter-intuition for the both/and logic of any other poet worth his or her salt in that or in any other era? Did Lamb devise his locution subliminally to cry out to posterity that science and religion could once more roll into one stance, as in days not long ago? Will the creative imagination ever again make these two "quite different frames of reference" interactive enough to rediscover "similitude in dissimilitude" (Samuel Taylor Coleridge's breakthrough expression)? If the coalescence or interpenetration implied by Coleridge's enigmatic but memorable phrase is by definition rare, then it nonetheless signally obtained during the Romantic-period chapter of Anglo-American literary history.

Lamb's phrase suggests, at least, that science and religion used to converse, and did so relatively fruitfully. By contrast, interaction between evolutionary biology and post-liberal-theology evangelicalism seems out of the question now, or at any other time for the foreseeable future. Does Lamb's intimation of experience-framed correspondence between empirical philosophy and evangelical faith model both/and creativity? Regardless, high-to-late-Romantic irony was homegrown in the Anglo-American style of empiricism-*cum*-evangelicalism—and not just imported from within the both/and logic of German Romantic philosopher Friedrich Schlegel's dynamic idealism.[4] At any rate, just as the term *natural methodism* appears

---

[4] Pertinent studies of the Britain/Germany branch of 19th-century comparative literature are Garber, ed.; Mellor; Ryals; Simpson. Although binary oppositions yield irony generally, Schlegel activates double-ness in German idealism—ethics vs. complete individual freedom in *Transcendentalphilosophie* (1801); and sensual vs. spiritual love in *Lucinde* (1799). Schlegel shows that irony and unsystematic dialogues go together; that irony arises from chaos; and that all of this, on balance, is "a good thing." For an early German example of science-religion interaction, Ulinka Rublack's *The Astronomer and the Witch: Johannes Kepler's Fight for His Mother* (2015) serves well, showing, for instance, that the scientific revolution accounts not just for the end, but for the beginning, of witchcraft trials. Robert Venturi, like Schlegel, employs a slash to

to combine empirical import—*NB:* Lamb's lower-case "m," as in scientific method—with straightforward overtones of Methodism, so every crevice of Wordsworth's poetry assays natural-*cum*-spiritual ore. Just as Wesley's immersion in British empiricism and his innovation in heart religion find an experiential common denominator, so British Romantic writers live in, but are not of, this world (compare Rom. 12:2; KJV). And just as the rational empiricism of Locke suffuses the religious methodology of Wesley and Edwards, so the Locke-infused spiritual sense of "the Methodist Revolution" (Semmel) and of the First and Second Great Awakenings—triple-revival punch!—explain (without explaining away) the Anglo-American Romantic kerfuffle of intellect and emotion.

Lamb's two-word standard of knowledge-*cum*-belief, which is perhaps even his lyric measure or "criterion for tune" (to borrow a phrase from Dickinson's Poem 256), delimits a bi-national arena, and perhaps even mandates a bi-national agenda, of historical, interdisciplinary criticism. Coordinates on the arc from Locke's *Essay* to Wesley's abridgment (1773) of Edwards's *A Treatise concerning Religious Affections* (1746) to works of British and American Romanticism from William Blake's to Dickinson's spark a bi-national canon of epic proportions. The twin pioneers of transatlantic revivalism—Wesley and Edwards—are also the originating duo of such seasonally proliferating pairs of British and American writers as Thomas Carlyle and Ralph Waldo Emerson, arguably the deliberately cooperating co-founders of Anglo-American *belles-lettres,* or Alfred, Lord Tennyson and Dickinson (Brantley, 1993, 2004, 2013). High-Romantic triumvirate Wordsworth, Coleridge, and John Keats, and late-Romantic trio Emerson, Tennyson, and Dickinson—as this essay will emphasize—take the time-honored dispute between tough and tender, "Betwixt damnation and impassion'd clay," forward to the bittersweet of a latter day (Keats, "On Sitting Down," 1818, 6).

The great principle of empiricism, that one must see for oneself and be in the presence of the things one knows, applies, as well, to evangelical faith, and this prime set of interlocking contraries makes for an Anglo-American "Poetic Genius" (Blake, *All Religions Are One,* 1788, principle 3). Dickinson's

---

join and at the same time to separate "both" and "and." Venturi then places "both/and" before "logic," in order to spin reasoning toward the suspended animation—the "have your cake, and eat it, too"—brand of creativity. M. H. Abrams's incisive interpretation of William Blake's phrase *the marriage of heaven and hell* proves apropos: "the sustained tension, without victory or suppression, of co-present oppositions" (Abrams et al., eds., 2:60). Such both/and logic complicates, and enlivens, the intellectual, emotional, and literary history of the United Kingdom and the United States alike, perhaps even lending some sanction to that two-nation chronicle.

counter-intuitive but steadfast watchword, that "Retrospection is Prospect's half— / Sometimes, almost more—" pertains to how Wordsworth and other British Romantic writers hark back to the 18th century, and then blaze a trail to Emerson's "double consciousness" and Dickinson's "Compound Vision" of science vs. religion (Dickinson, Poem 1014B, 7-8; Emerson, "Fate," 1852; Dickinson, Poem 830, 9). What Emerson would call the "stupendous antagonism" between Locke and Wesley/Edwards heightens the dramatic urgency of Romantic lyricism in the English-speaking world.[5] Whether or not natural methodism goes so far as to parry the exclusionary thrust of man-unkind, this antidote to single vision nonetheless tempers the either/or excess of human-kind: Lamb's phrase bears the weight of projecting how faith in experience yields to experiential Faith, and vice versa. This progression *ad infinitum*, this "unremitting interchange / With the clear universe of things around," recycles no mere monotony of the quotidian malady but enacts, instead, a purposive interplay, a "dual" of, as well as a "duel" between, philosophy and faith (Shelley, "Mont Blanc," 1816, 39-40; Shoaf xi).

The broadly experiential, spiritual as well as natural vision of Romantic Anglo-America, in turn, sees empiricism vs. evangelicalism not just as a defining dichotomy of the English-speaking world, a non-collapsible, hard-and-fast distinction, but as a joint force liberated through creativity, a dynamic balance of the imagination. The next four segments, devoted, respectively, to high and late Romanticism and to ramification and recapitulation, will attempt to orient readers not only to these hitherto un-gathered essays and reviews (and the books), but also to the hitherto unpublished and freshly expansive epilogue. Prologue and epilogue can illustrate how collection and books are alike pitched, first, to the fit and special set of readers who can call upon esoteric backgrounds and, second, to that non-academic but gamely Googling and dictionary-loving audience who can read widely for what to do and how to live. Just what is most meaningful and truthful in this specific account of how "the new philosophy calls all into doubt"? The answer is: the will to find a way to natural methodism (what Wordsworth calls "natural piety") is the will to keep believing.

A cross-culturally central set of intertwining antinomies, then—the British and American scene of science vs. religion—informs the poetic exegesis and the donnish conversations that here follow along lines of chronological

---

[5] Eric G. Wilson discusses Emerson's "stupendous antagonisms" as generic. From the Middle Ages to Emily Dickinson, the lyric was not so much a transcendent as a history-conditioned genre (Butterfield; Jackson). The interactive relation between the 19th-century lyric and its 18th-century philosophical and religious background suggests that the lyric overlaps the dramatic.

unfolding. The prologue, in relation not just to the collection, but the series as a whole, smacks of the pastiche. In one sense, its shored fragments do profess imitation of the style and content of the series. And its parenthetical references to authors and thinkers may not necessarily seem always germane to the core idea of natural methodism. Such quotations and the many allusions here show just how this cultural poetic, a subject, now, for well over forty years, exemplifies the energy of both/and logic as a colloquial but organic whole, and appears one great poem. And finally, is the prologue not just a sequel, but a further story? Perhaps, for this impossible genre of summing up a career in a single attempt aspires to that very coherence.

*

Consider, first, a signature lyric (1802) of Wordsworth's high Romanticism:

> My heart leaps up when I behold
> A rainbow in the sky;
> So was it when my life began;
> So is it now I am a man;
> So be it when I shall grow old,
> Or let me die!
> The Child is Father of the Man;
> And I could wish my days to be
> Bound each to each by natural piety.

"Natural piety," according to Abrams, "is distinguished from piety based on the Scriptures, in which God makes the rainbow the token of his covenant with Noah and all his descendants (Genesis 9:12-17)" (Abrams et al., eds. 2:207). Distinct from an exclusively spiritual promise, "natural piety" takes tough-minded account of contingency ("When [and only when?] I behold"), of mortality ("I shall grow old, / . . . let me die!"), and of the forbidding gulf between the actual and the ideal ("I could wish..."). However, "natural piety" also turns out sufficiently tender-minded in these nine lines of near-perfect visionary summary to be characterized finally by hope. Indeed, Wordsworth here entertains the conspicuous possibility of experience-faith synthesis and, for better or worse, comes as close to attaining it as anyone could.

Freudian theory to the contrary, this text does not just emerge exclusively or narrowly from trauma, and then trend headlong deathward (Carruth). Instead, its definitive expression of Romantic-era optimism bears perennial witness to just how religiously as well as epistemologically all times and places of natural and spiritual experience re-link through "the power / Of harmony, and the deep power of joy" (Wordsworth, "Tintern Abbey," 1798, 47-48). The primacy of the visual is "seen" in the speaker's double beholding of that spiritual as well as natural rainbow, a more dual than dueling perception of outward mystery. Since Wordsworth does not write "pious nature-worship," and since "piety" receives pride of place at the end of the phrase, these two reigning words in his canny but guileless and not quite ironic quintessence of Romanticism—"natural" and "piety"—can feel less exclusively pantheistic than winningly orthodox. The possibility that a fully up-to-date version of Christianity remains both respected and in play among such so-called secular-humanist Romantic-era writers as Wordsworth is worth reconsidering, if only as part of what Stanley Fish calls the post-9/11 "return to religion" in academia.

The lower case of natural methodism notwithstanding, the phrase gels as a religio-secular as well as historically precise and formalistically glossing equivalent to the natural piety so well known to, but not necessarily always so well understood by, Wordsworth's readers. Abrams's stance, "the religious sentiment that binds Wordsworth's mature self to that of his childhood is [merely?] a continuing responsiveness to the miracle of ordinary things," is normative (Abrams et al., eds., 2:207). So is Abrams's definitive statement of Wordsworth's secularizing tendency: "The Wordsworthian theodicy of the private life translates the painful process of the Christian conversion and redemption into a painful process of self-formation, crisis, and self-recognition, which culminates in a stage of self-coherence, self-awareness, and assured power that is its own reward" (Abrams, 1971, 96). But Wordsworth scarcely secularizes everything, for, insofar as his "continuing responsiveness to the miracle of ordinary things" stays consistent with the more spiritual than natural tenor of his empirically evangelical heritage, this British Romantic poet keeps philosophically religious in temperament as well as scientifically grounded in fact (Gaull; Holmes). Insofar as Wordsworth's "wise passiveness"—his alertness or answerability to experience—persists in sync with that not un-biblical rainbow (litote-loving Wordsworth would approve of the paradoxically affirmative import of that understated phrase *not un-biblical*), his high-Romantic optimism may be difficult even for the most hard-core Deconstructionist to unravel (Wordsworth, "Expostulation and Reply," 1798, 24).

The natural methodism between religious faith and poetic faith clarifies another key passage from Wordsworth:

> Love, now a universal birth,
> From heart to heart is stealing,
> From earth to man, from man to earth:
> —It is the hour of feeling.[6]

The fervent intensity with which Wordsworth proclaims "Love," as opposed to merely dilating upon it, or thinking about it, suggests how palpably he perceives, rather than how half-heartedly he speaks about, or pays lip service to, a presence not so much disturbing or mild as exhilarating, rejuvenating, reinvigorating, and effectual. Anyone who has read Richard Crashaw recently, or Augustine, knows that when earlier poets and theologians wrote about love, they also meant fervency, and Wordsworth takes their point. But Wordsworth's stanza honors, more immediately, Charles Wesley's hymn, "Love divine, all Loves excelling," "joy of heaven to earth come down," and hence interacts with, epitomizes, the warm-hearted, born-again emphasis on *agapé* in the experiential, free-will-Arminian, and ascendant trend of 18th-to-19th-century Anglo-American evangelicalism (Brantley, 1987, 4-7).

Neither simple *eros* nor the anti-experiential, predestinarian, and waning Calvinism of that bi-national tradition seems as close as Arminian Methodism to these crucial lines of Wordsworth's twenty-eight-year-old prime. Wordsworth's proto-Dickinson dash in "—It is the hour of feeling" enacts the sharp intake of breath attendant upon, if not coterminous with, spiritual influx in the here-and-now (distinct from any passion of the purely physical kind) and perhaps even ordains (not, John Calvin-like, foreordains) Dickinson's own spirit-breathing punctuation. Wordsworth's ballad stanza (elevated in church hymns and psalms as well as bruited in tavern-karaoke) appears akin to the religious reminiscence as well as aesthetic form of Dickinson's own hymn quatrain (her *modus operandi*). However precisely Wordsworth's affirmation may parallel the politically oriented theme of brotherly love uppermost in the French Revolutionary slogan *liberté, égalité, fraternité* and implicit in Anglo-American utopianism (Jeremy Bentham's or Bronson Alcott's), his persona's temporal faith in experience nonetheless chooses the worshipful shape of spiritual spontaneity.

---

[6] Wordsworth, "To My Sister," 1798, 21-24. For "poetic faith": Samuel Taylor Coleridge, *Biographia Literaria*, 1817, chapter 14. Imagine Wordsworth reciting these lines as Thomas De Quincey said the poet typically intoned all his verse: "his voice [assumed] a methodistical drawl" (qtd. in Frances Wilson 236).

Young man Wordsworth goes so far as to subscribe to a New Testament distinct from the Platonic two-tier universe. William A. Ulmer's *The Christian Wordsworth: 1798-1805* (2001) takes hold. Ulmer's young man Wordsworth "married Christian tradition to his faith in the human mind as a spiritual power and his confidence in the spiritual joy available in nature," and retained in his "intuitive natural supernaturalism" not just an iconoclastic, but a supple or eclectic, version of mere Christianity, namely "Romantic Anglicanism" (Ulmer 16-24). Demurring, however, from *Wordsworth's "Natural Methodism"* (Brantley, 1975), Ulmer observes, as his view of the Methodist near-influence on the turn-of-the-century *Zeitgeist*: "Despite Wordsworth's support for certain Evangelical social reforms, it seems best to construe Wordsworth's spiritual intensity not as a Methodist or Evangelical legacy but as his reconciliation of Anglican traditionalism with what we can simply call Romanticism" (Ulmer 40-46). But "the Methodist or Evangelical legacy" was Anglican in origin, and remained an important and necessary, though somewhat surprising, part of Anglicanism well into the 19th century, and perhaps even thereafter (Reed).

Was the "Methodist or Evangelical legacy" in its immediate moment, its look of spontaneity in the itinerating emphasis on the outdoors, more reconcilable with the emotional hour of perambulating Romanticism than the more non-evangelical, e.g., liturgical, elements of Anglican traditionalism? Yes. Wesley never left the Church of England. Methodism did not become Dissent until 1795, four years after his death. He represented Anglican tradition and "pre-Romanticism"—a once again critical term?—in his equally retrospective and prospective composite: Methodism. The revival reconfirmed the lyrical spirit in Anglicanism that has been the point in alluding here to the strong tradition of Anglican religious poetry in the 17th and 18th centuries. The revival laid additional groundwork for that spirit, as a close background constituting continuity with, perhaps even if not necessarily prescience of, Romanticism.

Another reassessment of Wordsworth's deep-seated transcendentalism, if the adjective does not take too much away from the supernatural, is Robert M. Ryan's. *The Romantic Reformation: Religious Politics in English Literature, 1789-1824* (1997) reaffirms the influence of Protestantism and signals Ryan's respect for this religious heritage as a component of the Romantic imagination. Neither Ryan nor Ulmer indulges in any special pleading for Protestantism or Romanticism. But Ryan writes that "Wordsworth began to define in more traditionally theological terms the source of truth and grace he felt being mediated in nature" (Ryan 80-118). Ryan acknowledges that "Wordsworth's language on more than one occasion curiously, or perhaps deliberately, recalls the language of the revival." Our respective critical approaches, published together as dialogue, nudge Kant's notion of transcendentalism—as concerned with, though not derived from, experience—toward British soil, where London dwells in the possibility of the New Jerusalem (Brantley, 1999; Ryan, 1999). Ryan's book allows for transcendental happening, as though climbing over or beyond, or rising above, the world, were inherent in living.

Wordsworth's native *cogito*—I perceive naturally and spiritually; therefore, England's green and pleasant land and I are alike transfigured—corresponds to both philosophy and religion. His grasp of subject/object coalescence—"The visible scene and the observer's mind at once confront each other (preserving their distinctions) and interpenetrate deeply"—feels rich and strange enough to engender poetic enchantment (Clarke 12-13). His affinity for mystery in perception makes spirit real, and draws the numinous near. His "Romantic paradox" of mundane and otherworldly angles of vision amounts to something more than the violent juxtaposition of the "gong-tormented sea" of this world with the "silent sea" of a world elsewhere (Yeats, "Byzantium," 1930, 4; Coleridge, "Ancient Mariner," 1798, 106). His signature conundrum comes into focus as the interaction between what his strictly empirical voice calls "the world / Of all of us, the place in which, in the end, / We find our happiness, or not at all!" and the continuum joining nature to spirit (Wordsworth, *The Prelude*, 1850, 11:142-44). His "world / Of all of us" (our sub-lunar quotidian) and what his most transcendental mood calls "moments in the being / Of the eternal Silence" form hemispheres of our collective human existence, as where, to apply T. S. Eliot to Wordsworth's case, "The unstilled world still whirled / About the center of the silent Word" (Wordsworth, "Intimations of Immortality," 1807, 155-56; T. S. Eliot, "Ash Wednesday," 1917, 5:8-9).

An efficient representative of experience/faith dialogue in British Romanticism is Coleridge. His pantheistic dimension, Abrams's exclusive emphasis, is evident where the speaker celebrates

> the one life within us and abroad,
> Which meets all motion and becomes its soul,
> A light in sound, a sound-like power in light,
> Rhythm in all thought, and joyance everywhere—
> (Coleridge, "The Eolian Harp," 1796, 26-29;
> Abrams, 1984, 76-77)

Gene W. Ruoff highlights where this persona, like a Methodist, witnesses to his faith, in language warmed at the heart:

> For never guiltless may I speak of him,
> The Incomprehensible! Save when with awe
> I praise him, and with Faith that inly *feels;*
> Who with his saving mercies healèd me,
> A sinful and most miserable man.
> (Coleridge, "The Eolian Harp," 58-62; Ruoff 241-50)

Thomas McFarland, notwithstanding his primary interest in pantheism, discusses both the pantheism and the Christian elements in this very early Coleridge poem (McFarland 117-25). "The Eolian Harp" presents "the greater Romantic lyric"—Abrams's useful phrase—as edginess between Spinoza's philosophy and Wesleyan piety (Abrams, 1984, 83). "Piety," understood here not pejoratively, as unreflective adherence to religious duties and observances, but honorifically, as reverence and devotion extended thoughtfully to God and His creation, recalls Wordsworth's "natural piety." If Coleridge and his peers in the two generations of British Romantic poets are at all clarified by evangelically as well as empirically inflected interpretation, then Wordsworth's *sententiae* most often belong to this historical, interdisciplinary approach not just to British, but to Anglo-American, Romanticism (Brantley, 1984, 129-214; Brantley, 1993, 1994, 2004, 2013).

Keats's *"Negative Capability"*—his "being in uncertainties, Mysteries, doubts, without any irritable reaching after fact & reason"—stands for second-generation value (Keats, to George and Thomas Keats, December 21, 27, 1817). Keats's medical mentor Anthony Astley Cooper's serene guideline—"observe; don't speculate"—directed Keats's state-of-the-art training (Goellnicht; Ryan, 1976, 47-52). The lower-case tentativeness of his "uncertainties" and "doubts" accords, too, with the skeptical frame of his scientific mind: non-irritable "reaching after fact & reason" finds expression among this poet-doctor's thought experiments. At the heart of his skepticism, however—between uncertainties and doubts—dwells Keats's witness to upper-case "Mysteries": transcendent ineffability.

Emerson's version of negative capability commends life not just as a valley of sorrowing, of suffering, and of dying, but as what Keats calls "a Vale of Soul-Making":

> The only mode of obtaining an answer to these questions of the senses [Emerson writes], is, to forgo all low curiosity, and, accepting the tide of being which floats us into the secret of nature, work and live, work and live, and all unawares, the advancing soul has built and forged for itself a new condition, and the question and the answer are one.
>
> (Keats, to George and Georgiana Keats, February 14-May 3, 1819; Emerson, "The Over-soul," 1841)

For Emerson, Keats, and many of their precursors and contemporaries in the Anglo-American world, the supreme good of experience is often not just "a man skating," "a Woman / Combing," as Wallace Stevens would have it, but the imageless "deep truth" of Shelley (Stevens, "Of Modern Poetry," 1940, 27-28; Shelley, *Prometheus Unbound*, 1819, II.iv.16). That said, empirical perspective proves salutary, too, for these same writers, as where Dr. Keats blends the insight of upper-case (religious) Mystery with his medical knowledge of bodies-in-the-world. As indicated by his formulation of negative capability, Keats's faith in experience and his experiential Faith alike depend ironically on his being in a bearable state of suspended animation qualified by saucy doubts and fears but liberated by devout skepticism. Keats's being in the world, but not of it, opens his mind to the numinous, and prepares his imagination for self-transcending, here-and-now, soul-and-heart encounters with "the tremendous and august *mysterium*" (Rudolf Otto's "idea of the holy").

Dramatic tension, then, distinct from dream structure or power play, keeps high Romanticism trim, a force to reckon with, as these poets wrestle uncertainties and doubts; and to conjure with, as they grapple with Mystery. Notwithstanding how things just out of reach, including epistemological, theological, and hermeneutical intricacies that do not lighten "the burden of the mystery," may verge on tragedy, this cultural poetic can nonetheless fill a critical cup with the delight attendant on "The Fascination of What's Difficult" (Wordsworth, "Tintern Abbey," 1798, 38; Yeats, "The Fascination of What's Difficult," 1910). The empirically evangelical faith of Romantic Anglo-America responds like a poem to close reading insofar as this religion battens like a paradox all along the arc.[7] Distinct from anti-experiential, predes-

---
[7] Witness the scrutiny accorded by Giles Gunn, Cornel West, and Harold Bloom, 1992, respectively, to such seemingly non-literary but *lisible* sign systems as American neo-pragmatism, American race relations, and the Southern Baptist Convention. Although a thin scarf of Calvinism clothes the fundamentalist faction among Southern Baptists, the moderate wing perdures, including Jimmy Carter (though in recent years he has joined the Cooperative Bap-

tinarian evangelicalism, pro-experiential, free-will evangelicalism came into its own at the dawn of the 19th century, and reached its height around 1858, when Oliver Wendell Holmes pronounced (however prematurely) the death of Calvinism (Holmes, "The Deacon's Masterpiece," 1858; Eberwein, 2005). As the world has learned and re-learned, and as Arminian Wesley realized, "Certainty is the enemy of decency and humanity in people who are sure they are right," or, as Nietzsche put it, "Truth has never yet clung to the arm of an inflexible man" (Lewis 9; Nietzsche, *Thus Spake Zarathustra*, 1891, 79). The next segment will deem the empirical evangelicalism traceable in late Romanticism as in its own way negatively capable, too.

*

To be sure, differences show up from high to late Romanticism. For example, skepticism grows. Nevertheless, poetic faith heightens. And paradox gets curious-er. Above all, negative capability gains such traction as to keep empiricism, evangelicalism, and Romanticism a triangulation to think with: a trinity all the more redolent of the essence of Mystery.

The pellucid prologue to *In Memoriam* (1850)—Tennyson's commemoration of Arthur Henry Hallam—conceives of experience as altogether natural and spiritual. The elegist conflates empiricism with Christ-centered faith ("thee" refers to Jesus):

> We have but faith; we cannot know,
>   For knowledge is of things we see;
>   And yet we trust it comes from thee,
> A beam in darkness: let it grow.
>
> Let knowledge grow from more to more,
>   But more of reverence in us dwell;
>   That mind and soul, according well,
> May make one music as before,
>
> But vaster. (21-29)

---

tist Fellowship). This Roger Williams-pedigreed, E. Y. Mullins-reaffirmed remnant wins Harold Bloom's admiration for its intellectual as well as emotional, "soul competent," Arminian as well as Calvinist, both free will and destined, legerdemain (Mullins's term in Bloom, 1992, 198-207).

Insofar as "it" (23, 24) refers to "knowledge" (22) and to "faith" (21), empirical philosophy and experiential Faith form an identity, the "things we see" (22) the gift of God. While differing from the "things we see," "faith" seems dialectically, and appears dialogically, involved with sense experience. Both "knowledge" (25) and "reverence" (26) increase: in the experiential scheme of things, progress occurs, and in their interaction with one another, as well as in their joint interaction with, and combined effect on, the world, "mind" and "soul" (27), too, are one.

Of course, "more of reverence" could mean "more reverence than knowledge," but still, the identity put forward by Tennyson's prologue is more resonant, if not more capacious, than old cosmologies. These fifty-seven words establish the scope of *In Memoriam*. This essence of late Romanticism emerges as a philosophically state-of-the-art, theologically up-to-date *Divina Commedia*. Like the paradigm at the outset of the extended elegy, the dual methodology, and perhaps even the full antiphony, of its mastery is the continual formation of an empirical and evangelical correspondence on the hardly just contingent, evidently sacred ground of experience (Brantley, 1994, 27-152).

Dickinson's late-Romantic imagination overtakes, absorbs, survives, and succeeds her pre-Modern mode, and perhaps even her post-Modern intimation (Brantley, 2004, 116-64; Gardner). Her backward-looking Janus vision sees well. Her philosophical, religious, and literary heritage keeps her senses sharp, her faith rowdy, and her poetic faith resilient. Her concentration of mental and emotional power was Charles Darwin-tinged (Brantley, 2013, 83-92; Eberwein, 2013). But her science/religion stand-off boasts such a long cross-culture pedigree that her art of knowledge (and of belief) becomes all the more evocative.

The vital, healthy, and constructive disbelief to which Wesley subscribes compares with Dickinson's signature lyric of skepticism-plus-heart-religion: "Sweet skepticism of the Heart—" (Poem 1438). Wesley makes Locke's Cartesian method of skepticism his own: "I am as fully assured to-day [Wesley writes], as I am of the rising of the sun, that the scriptures are of God. I cannot possibly doubt of it now; yet I may doubt of it to-morrow; as I have done heretofore a thousand times, and that after the fullest assurance preceding" (Wesley, 1931, 2:92; Lee; Swingle; Wolfson). Wesley applies to traditional revelation the uncompromising skepticism whereby, after systematically searching for—and apparently discovering—what is not open to doubt, his mind, soul, and heart nonetheless remain subject to all but unthinkable possibilities: no faith, no hope, and no love. Just as his doubting method can challenge his evangelical faith, so Dickinson's skepticism proves more desirable to the speaker of her poem than the safe bet of conventional piety, and may even equate to religion as roller coaster of enthusiasm vs. terror:

> Sweet skepticism of the Heart—
> That knows—and does not know—
> And tosses like a Fleet of Balm—
> Affronted by the snow—
> Invites and then retards the truth
> Lest Certainty be sere
> Compared with the delicious throe
> Of transport filled with Fear—

The persona makes no claim to either knowing or believing. She emphasizes the coldly threatening welter of harsh existence for which the toughness uppermost in even "sweet" skepticism can scarcely be a match. However, just as the skeptical method of Wesley's heart religion makes a strangely dynamic near-ally in his quest for Methodist faith, so Dickinson's similar procedure, guileless to the end but seldom sheltered, bears this autobiographical self-projection out to the edge of doom. The poet collapses distinction between mind and heart and creates thereby an uneasy but sympathetic composite of common humanity, whether or not Wesley, the ever-growing scholarly understanding of his own audacious vantage point notwithstanding, ever went that far toward the canny and uncanny logic of empirical faith.

Despite how this miniature method of Dickinson's late Romanticism retards or denies the truth, her persona thrills with vertiginous uncertainty. She alternates philosophical rigor with religious Mystery. She cultivates a fear of God as heartfelt as implicit, as real as subtle (unless Dickinson is only poeticizing here). Distinct from sophisticated Modern, let alone paralyzed post-Modern, suspicion, Dickinson's distrust in league with trust constitutes process of knowing in concert with affinity for Mystery. Her speaker scarcely bodes just static unbelief or permanent un-decidability. Rather, her persona's experience of dreadful ecstasy entails the painfully intense, ever-intensifying joy of wisdom. Reinhold Niebuhr's "pessimistic optimism" comes across as an inadvertently shrewd retrospective complement to Dickinson's radical inter-identification of "Blank misgivings" and passionate awe (Sifton; Wordsworth, "Intimations of Immortality," 1807, 144). "Faith is *Doubt*," says Dickinson (her emphasis); for her, the reverse may be true, as well: Doubt is Faith (Dickinson, 1958, 3:830).

This doubt/faith equation contrasts with the apprehension of a gulf between "faith and unfaith" on the part of the otherwise often Dickinson-simpatico Tennyson. His lines are sung by Vivien to Merlin:

> Unfaith in aught is want of faith in all.
>
> It is the little rift within the lute,
> That by and by will make the music mute,
> And ever widening slowly silence all.
> The little rift within the lover's lute
>
> Or little pitted speck in garnered fruit,
> That rotting inward slowly molders all.
> (Tennyson, *Idylls of the King*, 1862, 6:386-92)

The two poets vary in their birthrights of both/and. Dickinson prefers throe to either/or. This difference marks her as bolder, suppler, though Tennyson's haunting lines prove delicate, feel indispensable.

Skepticism in Romantic Anglo-America far from threatens the status of experience but tends to change old-experiential doctrines into new-experiential data bases. Reminiscent of Locke more than Descartes, Carlyle's "Scepticism" is not deadening but kinetic, "not an end but a beginning" and not "the decay of old ways of believing" but "the preparation afar off for new and wider ways" (Carlyle, "Man of Letters," 1841, 251; Brantley, 1993, 43-76). Similarly, Tennyson's skepticism, like Dickinson's, lends integrity to expression of faith. An utterance famous in the Victorian debate between science and religion melds the anxiety of nervous questioning with that of religious observance:

> And falling with my weight of cares,
>   Upon the great world's altar-stairs
> That slope through darkness up to God,
>
> I stretch lame hands of faith and grope,
>   And gather dust and chaff, and call
>   To what I feel is Lord of all,
> And faintly trust the larger hope.
>
> (*In Memoriam* 55:14-20)

Authorizing the conscious dialogue of philosophy with faith, the foundationally skeptical stance of Emerson may be more systematically synthesizing than the relatively messier methods of Carlyle, Tennyson, and Dickinson (Brantley, 1993, 77-140; Brantley, 1994, 153-244; Brantley, 2013, 33-70). Emerson declares,

> The elements already exist in many minds around you, of a doctrine of life which shall transcend any written record we have. The new treatment will comprise the skepticisms, as well as the faiths of society, and out of unbeliefs a creed shall be found. For, skepticisms are not gratuitous or lawless, but are limitations of the affirmative statement, and the new philosophy must take them in, and make affirmations outside of them, just as much as it must include the oldest beliefs.
> (Emerson, "Experience," 1844, 964)

Dickinson begins to sound like that. Her "delicious throe" transports her from skepticism, un-soured incredulity, to wide-eyed influx of divine apprehension.

Between Wesley's and Dickinson's versions of healthy skepticism lies a particular comparison unsettling to anyone who assumes that Wesley could never have expressed doubt about the Bible or that Dickinson could only have doubted it. "The traditional evidence of Christianity," Wesley writes, "stands, as it were, a great way off; and therefore, although it speaks loud and clear, yet makes a less lively impression. It gives us an account of what was transacted long ago, in far distant times and places" (Wesley, "Conyers Middleton," 1746, *Works* 10:75). Dickinson's lines satirizing traditional revelation appear tough-minded enough to reflect 19th-century Higher Criticism of the Bible (Eberwein, 2013):

> The Bible is an antique Volume—
> Written by faded Men
> At the suggestion of Holy Spectres—
> Subjects—Bethlehem—
> Eden—the ancient Homestead—
> Satan—
> The Brigadier—
> Judas—the Great Defaulter—

> David—the Troubadour—
> Sin a distinguished Precipice
> Others must resist—
> Boys that "believe" are very lonesome—
> Other Boys are "lost"—
> Had but the Tale a warbling Teller—
> All the Boys would come—
> Orpheu's Sermon captivated—
> It did not condemn—
>
> (Poem 1577)

The preacher of "Orpheu's Sermon" may be the Reverend Charles Wadsworth (1814-82), Dickinson's "dearest earthly friend," who rescues her, as a late-Romantic Eurydice, from the hell of any dour theology, and if Wadsworth's sermons do not warble, they sing.[8] But Wesley, too, is such a preacher, whose thinking-plus-warm-heartedness places him in the margins of her not so much anti-biblical as pro-Arminian poem. Like Wesley, like Dickinson. Just as he associates Locke-descended persons of understanding and reflection with the Christian whose spiritual sense radiates outward, so she makes mental fight and fervency not a sentimental combination, but a tough and tender judgment.

Reminiscent of Milton, who wrote of two scriptures (inner of the mind, and outer of the text), Wesley implies that the "inward evidence" of Christian truth emerges as superior to external, scriptural evidence. He observes,

> It seems that particularly in this age, God suffers all kinds of objections to be raised against the traditional evidence of Christianity, that men of understanding, though unwilling to give it up, yet, at the same time they defend this evidence, may not rest the whole strength of their case thereon, but seek a deeper and firmer support for it. I have sometimes been almost inclined to believe that the wisdom of God has, in most later ages, permitted the external evidence of Christianity to be more or less clogged and incumbered [sic] for this very end,

---

[8] Sewall 2:452; Dickinson, 1958, 3:764. For illustrations of Charles Wadsworth's style: Brantley, 2004, 78-80. Helen Vendler identifies Dickinson's "warbling Teller" not with a preacher, but with "Sweetest Shakespeare," whom John Milton's Cheerful Man in "L'Allegro" (*ca.* 1631) hears "Warble his native wood-notes wild" (Vendler 40). Dickinson chooses "warbling" from among thirteen other adjectives.

> that men (of reflection especially) might not altogether rest there, but be constrained to look into themselves also, and attend to the light shining in their hearts.
> (Wesley, "Conyers Middleton," 1746, *Works* 10:75)

Change "men" in "men of understanding" and in "men (of reflection especially)" to "men and women" and Dickinson would be covered by these otherwise prescient words. Wesley's attitude toward the Bible comments on Dickinson's.

In the 18th and 19th centuries—so different from today in this respect—empiricism and evangelicalism were scarcely mutually exclusive. Wesley's abridgment of Edwards's *Religious Affections* evinces not just heart religion, but metaphysics and epistemology: "God has so disposed things [Wesley edits] as though every thing *[sic]* was contrived to have the greatest possible tendency to reach our hearts in the most tender part, and move our affections most sensibly" (Edwards, 1771-74, 23:317; Brantley, 1993, 7-42). This intellectual as well as emotional statement rests on the more than merely metaphorical assumption of philosophical theology: sense perception receives every good and perfect gift. In the question "What is a tender heart, but one that is easily impressed with what ought to affect it?" the abridgment displays the Locke-like buried metaphor that sense impressions write spiritually on the blank tablet of the heart (Edwards, 1771-74, 23:319). The question contains the Locke-inspired as well as proto-Wordsworth premise of "wise passiveness," for though Locke would have had trouble with sense impressions on the unthinking, un-perceiving heart, the self in Wesley's abridgment stays soul-like (albeit with remaining ambiguity about whether or not "tender heart" symbolizes receptivity to the Spirit). And insofar as evangelicals, Anglo-American or other, can still keep true to influx from without as well as from above, their un-categorical imperative of seeing for themselves, and being in the presence of, the things they know, can amount to "wise [paradoxically active] passiveness." Empirical and evangelical codes of experience join intellect to affect and the world to words through ideas and ideals of sensation, perception with grace.

Wesley's skeptical and pre-Romantic (as well as neo-apostolic) heart religion, then, defined a space-time complex of not just England, but America, from 1738, when his "heart was strangely warmed," to 1877, when Dickinson wrote "Sweet skepticism of the Heart—."[9] Religious affections might not

---

[9] Wesley writes that his conversion occurred "at a quarter to nine" on the evening of May 24, 1738, "in Aldersgate Street," London, after he had heard William Holland, a Moravian brother, read "Luther's Preface to the Epistle to the Romans" about "the change which God works in the heart through faith in Christ" (Wesley, 1909, 1:475-76).

appear to be the driving forces of heart religion, but might seem only natural causes and effects. "What cheer can the religious sentiment yield," Emerson asks, "when that is suggested to be secretly dependent on the seasons of the year, and the state of the blood?" (Emerson, "Experience, 1844, 955). For one persona in the late-Romantic period, though, the speaker of *In Memoriam* overcomes his doubt and, despite his grieving for Hallam, reaffirms his subjective experience of spiritual discovery, and renews his heart religion:

> If e'er when faith had fallen asleep,
>   I heard a voice, "believe no more,"
>   And heard an ever-breaking shore
> That tumbled in the Godless deep,
>
> A warmth within the heart would melt
>   The freezing reason's colder part,
>   And like a man in wrath the heart
> Stood up and answer'd, "I have felt."
>   (Tennyson, *In Memoriam*, 1850, 124:9-10)

These lines counter-balance the "melancholy, long withdrawing roar" of "The Sea of Faith," and reference Wesley's cross-cultural conversion (Arnold, "Dover Beach," 1851, 21, 25). Tennyson's passage reflects not just Wesley's emotion, but the warm part of Wesley's reason that unfreezes, the empirical evangelicalism that feeds his whole person. Tennyson's accessible but subtle passage stays so far from greeting-card reduction that it remembers Wesley's journey from skepticism to faith and back again, for these two stanzas hark back to empirical procedure as the chief Enlightenment underpinning of Wesley's Religious Enlightenment. And as their joint belief in prophecy would expect their searches to do, Wesley's and Tennyson's quests foreshadow and parallel, respectively, the doubt/faith engagement represented by Dickinson in her "Sweet skepticism of the Heart—," her poetic epitome of Romantic Anglo-America's method-*cum*-faith.

*

To expatiate: just as an antiphony is "an opposition of sound"—"the answer made by one voice to another"—so empirical philosophy and evangelical faith alternate, or converse, in Romantic Anglo-America *(OED)*. And just as an antiphony is also "the harmony produced" by that "opposition of sound," so empirical philosophy and evangelical faith can appear on the same page of, and perhaps even as a single voice of, Anglo-American Romanticism *(OED)*. The empirical and the evangelical languages of experience, accordingly, can complicate, and perhaps can even tend to collapse the distinction between, the tough and the tender tones of a Wordsworth and an Emerson, or of a Keats and a Dickinson. The backward-looking visage of a Janus-faced Romanticism does not just survey a bewildering range of isms, istics, and tions, from sense-based reason and the scientific method through theistic/panentheistic (distinct from Deistic/pantheistic) natural religion to traditional and immediate revelation. This Romanticism also picks and chooses among these and other elements of its heritage not just to make poetry new, but to pass it on, and perhaps even to prepare the ear of readers, however unwittingly on all fronts, for the taught pleasures of the Modern-era dissonance-to-come.

The Locke-attuned religion of the Methodist Revolution and of the First and Second Great Awakenings, in particular, model how high-to-late Romantics of the English-speaking world entertain twin concepts: that religious truth is concerned with experiential presuppositions and that experience need not be non-religious. Not just Wordsworth, Coleridge, and Keats, but Tennyson, Emerson, and Dickinson, believe in inductive reasoning—what Wordsworth's inner Locke calls "sense, conducting to ideal form"—and hold fast to the spiritual sense (Wordsworth, *The Prelude*, 1850, 14:7). The latter is passivity at first, activity at last, and the physical senses as analogues to—and as harbingers and accompaniments of—"the infinite moment" (Browning, "By the Fireside," 1855, 181; Raymond). Robert Browning's may glimpse even James Joyce's epiphany-not-so-secular. Tennyson, Emerson, and Dickinson, too, intone, at the natural extreme, their version of what Wordsworth feels as tragedy: "the heavy and the weary weight / Of all this unintelligible world" (Wordsworth, "Tintern Abbey," 1798, 40-41). At the spiritual extreme, this trinity (composed of one poet laureate and two paragons of the American Renaissance) stays free to celebrate (without dilution) what Wordsworth welcomes as comedy: "another gift / Of aspect more sublime; that blessed mood, / In which the burden of the mystery, / . . . / Is lighten'd" (Wordsworth, "Tintern Abbey," 1798, 37-39). That last word betokens the sense in which a Wordsworth and an Emerson are made lighter, and perhaps even "of a port in air," by the efficacious endowment of good spirits, and suggests the sense in which a Keats and a Dickinson are enlightened: well-instructed by, smartened-up among, natural circumstances (Stevens, "Anecdote of a Jar," 1923,

8). As though suspended in air, on what Dickinson calls the "Ether street" of buoyant possibility, such Romantics, including the late (but not-so-belated) ones among them, can fluctuate—sometimes fortuitously, and sometimes at will—between power and godsend (Dickinson, Poem 573, 12).

Anglo-American Romanticism, then, entails the birth or rebirth of faith in experience and the imagining or re-imagining of experiential Faith. Waiving the distrust of sense experience in French rationalism and German idealism, this Romanticism "sees into the life of things"; envisions "whatsoever things" are true, honest, just, pure, lovely, and "of good report"; and so embraces thick, *dinglich* living as the rich, strange means of knowing and of believing alike (Wordsworth, "Tintern Abbey," 1798, 49; Phil. 4:8; KJV). Such natural as well as spiritual "things," for this Romanticism, prove not just traditionally biblical, but immediately present, and not just available for eye-witnessing now, but worthy "of good report," in good time, through the spiritualized as well as "naturalized imagination" (Stillinger 99-119). If science and religion are "non-overlapping magisteria," as Stephen Jay Gould fundamentally claims, and if "fancy"/poetic faith cannot "cheat"/move mountains "so well / As she is fam'd to do, deceiving elf," then experience and faith can nonetheless rendezvous at Romantic Anglo-America's Uneasy Peace Intersection of Recognition Avenue and Crediting Byway (Gould 7; Keats, "Ode to a Nightingale," 1819, 73-74). Thus, with the both/and logic of natural methodism at their collective disposal, if only because such re-imagined Methodism was "in the air" at the time, no wonder Blake and a circle of his fellow Anglo-American writers think "Without Contraries is no progression" (Blake, *The Marriage of Heaven and Hell*, 1790-93, plate 3)!

"Literature," E. D. Hirsch, Jr., writes, "is everything worthy to be read, preferably the best thoughts expressed in the best manner, but above all the best thoughts."[10] This definition refreshes criticism. Hirsch subordinates "the narrower, more decadent conception of literature"—*"les belles-lettres"*—to "the grand, broad, and noble conception": *"les bonnes-lettres."* Fare like epistemology or theology belongs on the table of letters.

Wielding *bonnes* and *belles* as a two-handed engine of both/and logic, this essay suggests reciprocity between left and right brain (compare McGilchrist). If *bonnes* keeps substance in the play of letters, then *belles* helps

---

[10] Hirsch 140-42. During the 1970s, when scholar of British Romanticism and resourceful public intellectual E. D. Hirsch, Jr., penned this Matthew Arnold-like sentiment, post-Modern critical theory was in the ascendancy. Hirsch resisted what he regarded as a kneejerk, nothing-outside-the-text, hothouse-academic brand of reader-response hokum, "always already" forlorn, foregone, top-down, and grid-like, but, unfortunately, Hirsch then went to the opposite extreme: *bonnes* "better" than *belles*. Traversing the hemispheres finds them co-equal branches.

bonnes stay away from either/or. The ambiguity of belletristic Montaigne can enrich the reason/emotion dualism of bonneletristic Descartes (Bakewell; Damasio). The clarity of Descartes, in turn, can supplement the subtlety of Montaigne. And perhaps even within the realm of *les bonnes-lettres* alone, Descartes's rationalism—his regard for the mind as independent of, and superior to, sense experience—jostles Locke's sense-based reason, and vice versa, as though the French/British difference in epistemology were not just a dynamic balance, but a virtual cooperation.

To be sure, the 18th century did not cause the 19th. As a continuous present, history has no way to look forward. Nevertheless, historians of literature look back and find continuities and some influences. And the "master" figures featured here—Dickinson included (she called herself "Uncle Emily" [Dickinson, 1958, 2:449])—all signal their inklings. Their collective scientific method helps them predict. And their mutual natural methodism—remembering Methodism and its sanction of the individual believer—helps them prophesy.

Did the British Enlightenment predict how reason and the senses need pose no unsolvable dilemma for fictional personae of the long Romantic Movement whose hearts beat faster for their subject/object cleaving? And did the spiritual sense of the transatlantic revival prophesy how Romantic-era souls-in-nature would cultivate organic but hallowed ground? Are words like "anticipate" and "foreshadow" appropriate to historiography? Perhaps an academic "second naïveté" will readmit them, despite due suspicion of cause-and-effect in human affairs (Ricoeur 22). Even a Wordsworth and an Emerson, or a Keats and a Dickinson, for all their sophisticated skepticism, view time—with the wide-eyed wonder of their joint, residual guilelessness—as being not so much aimless, or even meaningless, as full of purpose (or, at least, of what Kant, intimating the relation between history and art, called *Zweckmässigkeit ohne Zweck*, purposiveness without purpose [Abrams, 1954, introduction]).

The concerted effort of this series of arguments in general, and of this collection of essays and reviews in particular, to compose a complex harmony of ideas-over-time, culminates in Emily Dickinson's inimitable, yet well-imbricated, "palpable obscurity" (Milton, *Paradise Lost*, 1674, 2:406). And with regard to the bi-national literary history following upon her poetry, Dickinson's late-Romantic, sometimes near-belated perspective hovers close to such early-Modern-era works as "The Impercipient" (1898) by Thomas Hardy and *The Education of Theron Ware* (1896) by Harold Frederick. The speaker of Hardy's poem (about post-Darwin vertigo) and the protagonist of Frederick's novel (about an Upstate New York Methodist minister who reels from unfaith) confront empiricism vs. evangelicalism with an end-time vengeance (and perhaps even with an either/or mindset). Such subject matter yet magnetizes analysis. Dickinson leads the way. She vibrates to science vs. religion. She loves a good sermon about doubt (Dickinson, 1958, 1:251, 2:502, 2:574).

Like the critical faith underlying this ongoing, cumulative project in bi-national cultural poetics, its critical method takes its rise and footing from the composite imagination of Anglo-America, especially the historical, interdisciplinary creativity of writers from Blake to Dickinson. For Locke, Wesley, and Edwards, though, as well as for belletristic precursors of "Sweet skepticism of the Heart—," natural and spiritual experience of an externalized bent signifies anew, as in: when sense-based method is connected to spiritual sense, image-ination morphs to imagination, and then manifest choosing (forget manifest destiny) blooms. How, if at all, might this collection's consideration of context and of text alike, of *bonnes*-and of *belles-lettres* together, affect further interpretation of English-language Romanticism? Another conversation among British and American pairs of authors, paying particular attention, this time, to how Romantic Anglo-America becomes *fin de siècle*, this way comes, if world enough and time ensue. Meanwhile, this prologue to these thirty-eight re-issues—this impossible genre of updating a career in an essay—has already pursued, with as much relish as the law allows, that difficult fascination. And meanwhile, too, other historical, interdisciplinary digging for the natural-*cum*-spiritual ore of Anglo-American Romanticism in general, and for the literary trace of natural methodism in particular, proceeds apace (Anderson; Barbeau; Bennett; Boyles; Campos; Cragwall; Dabundo; Farrell; Franke; Freedman; Harvey; Hsu; Jesse; Leader; Lee; Roberts; Snow).

"Have American philosophers and critics no home to go to," Denis Donoghue asks, "no intellectual tradition of their own?" (Donoghue 52). Yes, in thunder, they have, as this essay answers a question that would seem to go without asking, but which a Donoghue could pose and re-pose in the critical climate of the last fifty years. The "home" is Anglo-America, the "intellectual tradition" empiricism/pragmatism.

Heidegger, Adorno, Benjamin, Foucault, Derrida, de Man, Deleuze, Lyotard, Blanchot, and "other daunting sages" hail from France or Germany, as Donoghue points out. But you would think, perhaps even to their great credit, that they come from, say, London or New York City, the way these thinkers are often quoted there and, indeed, throughout the Anglo-American world of letters lettered by them. They are all now as Anglo-American as fish-'n'-chips plus chili-con-carne. Adorno, for one, moved from Germany to New York, and then to Los Angeles, where he wrote about, among other things, Mickey Mouse, though not, alas, about such substantially American icons as Jonathan Edwards.

Critics of any school may apply, all along the neoclassic-to-Romantic arc, the core principle of this cross-pond enterprise in comparative letters, whether *bonnes* or *belles:* not just the empiricist and the evangelical alike, but Romantics, can "see for themselves and be in the presence of the things they know" (Brantley, 1994, 1-6, 27-32). The optical proficiency, and perhaps even the optical profligacy, in both the scientific education and the evangelical upbringing of late-Romantic-era art critic John Ruskin, for example, provide the most aptly dual context for Ruskin's deep-seated *aperçu:* "The greatest thing a human soul ever does in this world [Ruskin writes] is to see something, and tell what it saw in a plain way. Hundreds of people can talk for one who can think, but thousands can think, for one who can see" (Brooks 13). Ruskin's bicameral imagination reveres the spiritual as well as natural primacy of what lies in front of his eyes (Finley). Just as "belief as sight" forms a primary figure in empirical evangelicalism, so, in that uniquely hybrid Anglophone faith, "seeing as believing" deploys physical sight itself, and does not merely rely on some vaguely analogized spiritual sense. Thus, whether interpreted actively or received out of the blue, the preeminent visual comprises a by no means entirely naturalized grace in Anglo-American Romanticism, as well.

Of course, exclusively religious highlights of the evangelical (almost) go without saying. The revealed nature of the gospel; documentary infallibility (not quite the same thing); the second coming of Christ; and the prominence of preaching (placement of pulpit, duration of sermon) (Reed): such doctrinal/ecclesiological staples stay in full view. Still, from the 18th to the 19th century, United Kingdom/United States evangelicalism metaphorically and literally itinerated out of the pulpit, and indeed well away from it, making a transcription of, and setting a record for, the experience of religion in feeling or sensation rather than—nay, in addition to—intellection. This empirical evangelicalism is not just "being in the presence" of God or of God's "things," nor is it just transcending process while going through it. It is, in addition, the partaking of life, wherein doubt and faith become balanced through transport—through immersion in, and reliance on, outward as well as inward and upward experience ("Theme this but little heard of among men—" or women [Wordsworth, prospectus to *The Recluse*, 1814, 67]).

Scholarship on affect, the history of emotions, and cognitive psychology, finally, brings in "deep time" (Dimock). During the later Middle Ages, "affective meditation on the Passion had a deceptively simple goal: to teach . . . readers how to feel" (McNamer, introduction). This tradition, Sarah McNamer adds, "marks the wide-scale shift in medieval Christian sensibility from fear of God to compassion for the suffering of Christ." McNamer wraps: "To feel compassion for Christ, in the private drama of the heart, was to feel like a woman." Wordsworth evokes this genealogy of emotions (Chandler). As late as the mid-1800s, the shift from fear to compassion ranks as religious and, by then, encompasses men. The nine male writers highlighted in this essay and in the epilogue—including Locke—take places along the arc of heart religion from medieval nuns to "the wayward nun of Amherst" (Conrad; Spellman; Tuveson; Waldron; the collection's cover image includes three additional men, also often surveyed in these introductory, and in the concluding, pages of the collection). These men and Dickinson, whether they write "craftsy" empirical and evangelical prose of the 18th century or "artsy" prose and poetry of the 19th, can recount what happens in their inward lives and say, "I feel," yet they can also spiritually comprehend their natural experience.

The transatlantic trio of empiricism, evangelicalism, and Romanticism, then—consistent with the Latin etymology of religion: *re-ligio*—tied things together again. The slip-knot of this Anglo-American interchange, however, is not a tight knot of synthesis: perhaps it is not even exclusively a matter of "the one life within us and abroad," and above us (Coleridge, "The Aeolian Harp," 1795, 26). It is, as well, and perhaps even instead (and certainly with more suspense) a back-and-forth of familiar vs. unfamiliar, and hence a subtly chthonic, reluctantly sublunary question of reenchanting, or of re-mystifying, what would otherwise appear a too-neatly-drawn triangle: the self, the world, and a world elsewhere. A Wordsworth or an Emerson, or a Keats and a Dickinson, can thereby bless the ties that bind their hearts in earthly love and, finding freedom in those very ties, "make souls" on the common ground between them and their two countries (Keats, to George and Georgiana Keats, February 14-May 3, 1819). Thus Anglo-American Romanticism validates the broadly experiential, spiritual as well as natural criterion of knowledge, belief, meaning, and truth.

*

To recapitulate: two brief but evocative responses to the poetry of William Wordsworth can best transport readers into this cultural poetic. Francis Jeffrey and Charles Lamb—two otherwise very different reviewers—assume and divergently interpret the same explanatory frame of reference: Methodism. Almost as though it were for present purposes of stout resistance to his assessment, British Romantic gate-keeper Jeffrey, the first responder to *The Excursion*, believed that evangelicalism and *belles-lettres* do not jibe. The second responder, British Romantic familiar essayist Lamb, whom Wordsworth called, with deep affection, "the frolic and the gentle," rescued *The Excursion* from Jeffrey's clutches (Wordsworth, "Extempore Effusion," 1835, 19). Lamb's praise of the poem as "natural methodism" suggests that a philosophical-*cum*-religious sign set—empirical evangelicalism—does resonate with, and enriches, the work of this Romantic progenitor. Whether or not Lamb's phrase telescopes what remains at stake throughout all critical inquiry—fluctuating answers to intractable but intriguing questions of both/and logic—the anecdotal shorthand of Lamb's letter mentioning natural methodism flashes how empiricism and evangelicalism interact in the creative imagination: through the clairvoyance of the visual.

Ocular divining remains a feature of the tradition. For example, the chapter on "Seeing" in latter-day-Thoreau Annie Dillard's *Pilgrim at Tinker's Creek* (1974) harks back to the visual as both the most acutely active and the most wisely passive sense in 18th-to-19th-century Anglo-American philosophy, religion, and literature:

> The common variety [of seeing] is active, where you strain, against the running babble of internal monologue, to pay attention to what's actually in front of you. But . . . "there is another kind of seeing that involves a letting go." You do not seek; you wait. It isn't prayer; it is grace. The visions come to you, and they come out of the blue.[11]

No matter how delightful or desirable the other senses may be, and despite the need for empirically and even evangelically oriented criticism to encompass hearing, touching, smelling, and tasting as well, "seeing," after all, "is believing" indeed. That sounds religious, and some would say mystical: seeing-is-believing can subsume the empirical and the evangelical under experience insofar as part of experience is presence—not just as religious transport, or as sacramental synesthesia, but as something else again—as something wonderful to behold in the here-and-now. Evangelical as well as empirical tradition has to

---

[11] Deresiewicz 99. William Deresiewicz quotes Annie Dillard, above.

do, by the way, with how "creation scientists" focus, like a laser beam, on the eye. The visual in their religious heritage informs their emphasis on the eye as such an improbably ingenious evolutionary development as to augur divine design. Whether or not this "proof positive" is only partial, in both senses, the Anglo-American visual can nonetheless act upon time, space, and disciplines.

To be sure, apart from its background of empirical evangelicalism, the amplitude or wholeness of English-language Romanticism ranges well beyond the visual. Relish, for example, the feast of the senses in George Gordon, Lord Byron's romance of Don Juan and Haidée in Cantos II-IV of *Don Juan* (1818-21) or in John Keats's of Porphyro and Madeline in "The Eve of St. Agnes" (1820). In both cases, the overwhelming impression of first love shows how the dominance of seeing can be suspect—indicating how the eyes rank only as first-among-sense-equals. Blake's synesthesia, moreover—whereby "the hapless Soldier's sigh / Runs in blood down Palace walls"—developed into a characteristically Romantic-era means of making full "sense" of the world (Blake, "London," 1794, 11-12).[12] Keats (and later Proust) made full use of this literary technique.[13] Perhaps even architecture, inherently under the sway of the eyes, can favor the ears and touch—as markedly as Romanticism can employ all five senses.[14] Nevertheless, vision can yet appear particularly reliable within the philosophical and religious dialogues of Romantic Anglo-America, as, memorably, where Wordsworth's heart leaps up when he beholds a spiritualized rainbow.

William Deresiewicz emphasizes that Annie Dillard's *Pilgrim* is not about a social context, or about the spirit of the times, but "about the fact of being alive, for a brief span, within the overwhelming context of the natural world" (Deresiewicz 106). Deresiewicz is a devotee of Dillard's classic. He notes, though, the absence of an ethic in the work. By contrast, the Romantic authors under survey throughout the series develop, in their various ways, that dimension, their *frisson* in the natural world notwithstanding.

In a refreshing departure from Romanticism as only nature writing, David Bromwich maps out the British Romantic intersection of the sympathetic imagination, and its feel for communal and family values, with the egotistical

---

[12] Synesthesia is a literary device that appeals to more than one sense at a time, as where color attends the sensation of sound, or when a sense (like sight) triggers another (like smell).

[13] Marcel Proust's tea-dipped, memory-producing madeleine brings senses together, capturing the triumph of synesthesia in literary history.

[14] The architectural theory and practice of Mikesch Muecke provide a case in point, as does the work of some other contemporary architects, such as Juhani Pallasmaa, Peter Zumthor, and Steven Holl.

sublime and its emphasis on personal history, revolution, energy, power, genius, and gusto. Edmund Burke, at this roundabout, begins to take on qualities of William Hazlitt, and vice versa. Bringing Wesley and Wordsworth together in the same sentences of literary criticism constitutes a similar, though a more philosophical and religious than political, means of thinking about the both/and logic, or dynamic balance, of community and self during the Romantic period. Bromwich's preference for society over self means that the imagination of community, for him, is what lies at the heart of the British Romantic legacy to social as well as literary history. And just as Wesley's soul-hood arising from his individualized spiritual biography antedates and strengthens his leadership of a transatlantic "parish"—"The world is my parish," he famously said—so Wordsworth's egotistical sublimity equally paradoxically coexists not just with his "Home at Grasmere," but within his ever-widening social circle (Page). By extension—and however markedly the series may tilt toward evangelicalism—the collection nonetheless stays sedulous to remember how the back-and-forth between empiricism (where nature survives and thrives) and evangelicalism drives a mainstream Anglo-American Romantic understanding not just of objective-subjective interpenetration, but of inter-subjectivity. Thus "Effort, and expectation, and desire, / And something evermore about to be"—psychological mediations between sheer pragmatics and as-if-eschatological purport—comprise a Romantic-era agenda for individuals and for groups alike (Wordsworth, *The Prelude*, 1850, 6:608-09; benefiting from scholarship by David P. Haney and Adam Potkay, the epilogue, too, features Wordsworth's ethics-inflected philosophy-*cum*-faith).

    The influence of German Romantic philosopher Friedrich Schlegel's both/and logic on British Romantic and Victorian irony notwithstanding, the both/and judgment of Anglo-American irony was not just Continental European in origin, but rendered in the 18th-to-19th-century transoceanic milieu. Romantic Anglo-America played within, and punned on, the experiential philosophy/experiential religion divide or détente. This creative strategy may even have worked all the better for how empiricism and evangelicalism exercised both/and logic independently of one another. Subject/object energy or spark, after all, trademarked the former, while free will/predestinarian friction or *frisson* dramatized the latter. At that bi-national cross-roads of British empiricism and transatlantic revivalism which gave a primarily 19th-century local habitation and name to a perennially English-language stripe of conundrum or paradox, Anglo-American irony arrived in style, "huge fragments vaulting like rebounding hail," or like spin-off binaries doubling and redoubling thenceforward (Coleridge, "Kubla Khan," 1798, 11). To shift the metaphor from topography/time to taste, that incongruity abounded piquantly in the English-speaking West. The contrasting realms of science and religion proved all the more constructively conversational for being antipodal. English-language Romantic irony did not just trend nihilistic, but practiced "a continual, dialogic openness, a principled rejection of settled attitudes and of finality or 'closure'" (Perkins 896). Thus the empirical/evangelical both/and gave that irony depth, energy, verve, passion, sunniness, color, exuberance, movement, and life—a full measure beyond the traditional instruction and delight.

Not just the prologue, then, but the following twenty-one essays and seventeen reviews, can yet celebrate, albeit as previously published works (newly assembled), Romantic-era logic of art and of life alike. This scholarly narrative may feel episodic, as compared with the sustained sequence appropriate to each of the series' six books. But this collection nonetheless coheres at least in showing how all these literary objects of critical analysis can live up to the criterion of accessibility-plus-subtlety. This Anglo-American Romanticism meets, as well, the both/and standard of complexity-plus-satisfaction. Thus this anthology of pieces from 1974, when "Spiritual Maturity and Wordsworth's 1784 Christmas Vacation" appeared, to 2017, when the prologue and the epilogue received their final touches, assumes a Romantic aesthetic sufficiently comprehensive, and counter-intuitive enough, to please many, and please long.

Can this transatlantic trio of sense-based method, the spiritual sense, and the poetic fancy resonate in today's oversimplified, anti-intellectual climate of polarized either/or? Not even the creative imagination can do much, it would seem, to legislate, in however unacknowledged a fashion, an end to the stand-off between science and religion "in these bad days" of arcane expertise, on the one hand, and rank know-nothing-ism, on the other (Arnold, "To a Friend," 1848, 1). However, with nice complication and fine gradation along the neoclassic-to-Romantic arc, empirical philosophy and evangelical faith interacted not so long ago, between a Locke and an Edwards, and within a Wordsworth and a Dickinson. Whether or not this prologue succeeds in girding up the approach to, and retrieving, that heritage—and whether or not the epilogue takes stock of what, if anything, "all this fiddle" of historical, interdisciplinary criticism might yet signify for the survival of reading—Romantic Anglo-America is no mere "ineffectual angel" (Marianne Moore, "Poetry," 1920, 1; Arnold, "The Function of Criticism at the Present Time," 1864). Upholding faith in experience, on the one hand, and restoring experiential Faith, on the other, this Romanticism dwells in the possibility of its afterlife:

bringing art and life back—and forth—into a workable realignment, if not, for that matter, into a mutually realized transfiguration.

In sum, this prologue names agents in a tripartite history of ideas, of affect, and of imagination. Such an otherwise motley crew as Locke, Wesley, Wordsworth, Coleridge, and Emerson work with, as well as against, one another, their folk, popular, and elite culture setting up a divergent, as well as an aggregate, readability. And Edwards, Blake, Keats, Tennyson, and Dickinson reveal, likewise, their time-as well as space-specific, collective genius for philosophical and religious give-and-take. Locke's founding of British empiricism, Wesley's and Edwards's twin pioneering of transatlantic revivalism, Wordsworth's and Emerson's as-if-premeditated co-leadership of Anglo-American *belles-lettres*, and Dickinson's final American frontier of Romanticism—all describe the upward sweep and the downward swoop of an especially formative trajectory of English-language letters. And the backstory of all that broadly experiential, spiritual as well as natural vision rivals the story.

*

Grateful acknowledgment is hereby made to publishers, who first printed these twenty-one essays and seventeen reviews (of eighteen books), which are reprinted here by permission, and which sometimes reappear here under different titles and in slightly different forms. Twelve of the essays, indicated by an asterisk, figure to varying degrees in the six books. Here is the original bibliography of the first series of essays, all five of which address backgrounds of British and American Romanticism:

"John Wesley (1703-91)." *British Prose Writers, 1690-1800: Second Series.* Ed. Donald T. Siebert. *Dictionary of Literary Biography.* Vol. 104, 271-83. Detroit: Gale Research, 1991.*

"An Orientation." *Literature Criticism from 1400 to 1800.* Eds. Marie Lazzari and Lawrence J. Trudeau. Vol. 88, 239-59. Detroit: Gale Research, 2003.*

"Locke and Wesley: An Essence of Influence." This is a condensation of "John Wesley (1703-91)."*

"The Common Ground of Wesley and Edwards." *The Harvard Theological Review* 83 (July 1990): 271-303.*

"Romanticism and Christianity." *The Cambridge Dictionary of Christianity*, 1,106. Ed. Daniel M. Patte. Cambridge: Cambridge U P, 2010.*

Here is the original bibliography of the second series of essays, all six of which examine British authors, and two of which, published forty years apart, approach William Wordsworth:

"Charles Wesley's Experiential Art." *Eighteenth-Century Life* 11 (May 1987): 1-11.
"Johnson's Wesleyan Connection." *Eighteenth-Century Studies* 10 (Winter 1976-77): 143-68.
"Spiritual Maturity and Wordsworth's 1784 Christmas Vacation." *Studies in English Literature* 17 (Autumn 1974): 479-87.*
"Wordsworth's Art of Belief." *The Wordsworth Circle* 45.2 (Spring 2014): 162-70.
"Keats's Method." *Studies in Romanticism* 22 (Fall 1983): 389-406.*
"Evangelical Principles of Tennyson's *In Memoriam*." *English Romanticism: Preludes and Postludes*, 115-26. Eds. Donald Schoonmacher and John A. Alford. A *Festschrift* in honor of Edwin G. Wilson. East Lansing, MI: Colleagues P, 1993.*

Here is the original bibliography of the third series of essays, all seven of which concentrate on Emily Dickinson, who was, to put it mildly, a leading light of the American Renaissance:

"Dickinson the Romantic." *Christianity & Literature* 46 (Spring-Summer 1997): 243-71.
"The Empirical Imagination of Emily Dickinson." *The Wordsworth Circle* 32 (Summer 2001): 144-48.
"Emily Dickinson's Empirical Voice." *Symbiosis: A Journal of Anglo-American Literary Relations* 15.1 (April 2011): 105-32.*
"The Wordsworthian Cast of Emily Dickinson's Romantic Heritage." *Wordsworth in American Literary Culture 1802-1902*, 160-76. Eds. Joel Pace and Matthew Scott. New York: Palgrave Macmillan, 2004.
"The Interrogative Mood of Emily Dickinson's Quarrel with God." *Religion & Literature* 46.1 (Summer 2014): 157-65.*
"From Loss to Gain: Aftermath in the Late-Romantic Poetry of Emily Dickinson." *Symbiosis: A Journal of Anglo-American Literary Relations* 10.2 (October 2006): 93-114.*
"Dickinson's Signature Conundrum." *The Emily Dickinson Journal* 16.1 (2007): 27-52.*

And here, finally, is the original bibliography of the fourth series of essays, a miscellaneous grouping of three—the first and third of which pay homage to scholarly individuals, and the middle of which, written with Diana R. Brantley, pertains to our mutual teaching of English composition:

"A Memorial Tribute to T. Walter Herbert." These remarks, delivered at the University of Florida on March 7, 1984, are appearing in print here for the first time.

"Sleeping with the Enemy: Communiqués from a Pedagogical Marriage." With Diana R. Brantley. *Teaching Writing in High School and College: Conversations and Collaborations,* 214-20. Ed. Thomas C. Thompson. Urbana, IL: The National Council of Teachers of English, 2002.

"A CCL Tribute to Robert Alter." *Christianity & Literature* 63.1 (Autumn 2013): 88-90. For Alter's response to his receiving the Conference on Christianity and Literature Lifetime Achievement Award, see Robert Alter, "A Life of Learning: Wandering among Fields," *Christianity & Literature* 63.1 (Autumn 2013): 91-104.

Here is the original bibliography of the first series of reviews—one of which assesses a book about John Locke, two of which evaluate books about John Wesley, and one of which sifts a collection of essays on Jonathan Edwards:

God, Locke, and Equality: Christian Foundations in Locke's Political Thought, by Jeremy Waldron. *Christianity & Literature* 54.4 (Summer 2005): 577-86. For a shorter version of the review, see *The Scriblerian and the Kit-Cats* 38.2 (Spring 2006): 334-35.

The Evangelist of Desire: John Wesley and the Methodists, by Henry Abelove. *Eighteenth-Century Studies* 25 (Winter 1991-92): 250-54.

Wesley and the Wesleyans: Religion in Eighteenth-Century Britain, by John Kent. *The Age of Johnson* (New York: AMS P, 2005): 337-40.

Jonathan Edwards's Writings: Text, Context, Interpretation, edited by Stephen J. Stein. *Church History* 67.2 (June 1998): 407-09.

Here is the original bibliography of the second series of reviews—all five of which concern British Romanticism:

The Obstinate Questionings of English Romanticism, by L. J. Swingle. *American Notes & Queries* 3 (July 1990): 142-45.

William Wordsworth and the Hermeneutics of Incarnation, by David P. Haney. *Christianity & Literature* 42.1 (Winter 1993): 355-57.

The Romantic Reformation: Religion and Politics in English Literature, 1789-1824, by Robert M. Ryan. *Christianity & Literature* 48 (Spring 1999): 349-66. For a shorter version of the review, see *Modern Philology* 99 (August 2001): 131-34. See also Ryan's reply to the review in Robert M. Ryan, "Christianity and Romanticism: A Reply," *Christianity & Literature* 49 (Autumn 1999): 81-90.

The Romantic Ethic and the Spirit of Consumerism, by Colin Campbell. *Studies in Romanticism* 29 (Fall 1990): 499-504.

British Romantic Writers and the East: Anxieties of Empire, by Nigel Leask. *JEGP* 93.3 (October 1994): 592-95.

Here is the original bibliography of the third series of reviews, all four of which concern transatlantic Romanticism, and one of which assesses not just one book, but two:

The Spiritual History of Ice: Romanticism, Science, and the Imagination, by Eric G. Wilson. *The Wordsworth Circle* 34.3 (Fall 2003): 188-90.

Emerson, Romanticism, and Intuitive Reason: The Transatlantic "Light of All Our Day", by Patrick J. Keane. *The Wordsworth Circle* 37.4 (Autumn 2006): 231-35.

Text as Process: Creative Composition in Wordsworth, Tennyson, and Dickinson, by Sally Bushell. *Review 19*: http://www.nbol-19.org (November 2009).

Seeing Suffering in Women's Literature of the Romantic Era, by Elizabeth Dolan; and *Emily Dickinson's Approving God*, by Patrick J. Keane. *European Romantic Review* 22.3 (August 2011): 527-30.

And here, finally, is the original bibliography of the fourth series of reviews: a miscellaneous quartet. The first appraises a biographical/critical study of Emily Dickinson; the second evaluates an overview of 19th-to-early-20th-century American literature; the third assesses a synoptic perspective on 20th-century American fiction; and the fourth examines a cultural poetic from ancient times to the present:

Emily Dickinson's Experiential Poetics and Rev. Dr. Charles Wadsworth's Rhetoric of Sensation: The Intellectual Friendship between the Poet and a Pastor, by Mary Lee Stephenson Huffer. Written as a Foreword (i-iv) to the book (Lewiston, NY: The Edwin Mellen P, 2007).

Miles of Stare: Transcendentalism and the Problem of Literary Vision in Nineteenth-Century America, by Michelle Kohler. *The Emily Dickinson Journal* 24.1 (2015): 112-15.

The Comedy of Redemption: Christian Faith and Comic Vision in Four American Novelists, by Ralph C. Wood. *The Flannery O'Connor Bulletin* 17 (1988): 105-08.

The Story of Joy, by Adam Potkay. *The Wordsworth Circle* 39.4 (Autumn 2008): 164-66.

These essays and reviews are laid out in a sequence that, though differing slightly from the chronological order in which they were first printed, best reveals the scholarly narrative implicit throughout these formerly scattered, yet now assembled, shorter pieces. One case—namely, "Locke and Wesley: An Essence of Influence"—compresses the collection's take not just on the British, but on the British-to-Anglo-American, milieu. At least one essay in the first series, accordingly, may be short enough for readers in a hurry. Two cases, as already specified in the bibliographical listings, re-publish only the longer of two pieces otherwise similar. Another case revises the piece in question, and changes its title from "Romanticism and Christianity" to "Empiricism and Evangelicalism: A Combination of Romanticism": this revision offers readers the quickest way to acquaint themselves with the series as a whole (books included). Establishing the broadest parameters of all the essays, a final case expands the piece and changes its title from "The Common Ground of Wesley and Edwards" to "Wesley and Edwards: An Anglo-American Nexus." All other reprints remain as they were, except for occasional clarifications and typographical corrections (for convenience in transcribing, the somewhat differing styles of citation favored among the various original publishers are retained). May readers discover only the forgivable extent of remaining infelicity!

A familiar quotation from Gertrude Stein—"A real failure does not need an excuse. It is an end in itself"—justifies preserving, warts and all, how one historical, interdisciplinary critic proceeded: one argument at a time. The record of first thoughts may be worth consolidating, if only in order to honor, from the standpoint of tranquility, spontaneous overflow, and if only to register junctures at which others began to listen. The pieces now in this gathering can henceforth have their say together, and perhaps can even resonate, as a thirty-eight-member group, with Harold Bloom's settled conviction. "All strong works of literature," including *les bonnes-lettres,* can yet "give us," Bloom concludes at age eighty-four, "the blessing of more life, whether or not they initiate a time beyond boundaries" (Bloom, 2015, 7). This spirit has infused the collection and the books alike. May the collection create interest in the books, and vice versa!

The dialogue written with Diana R. Brantley does not bear on the root of empiricism, the branch of evangelicalism, or the blossom of Romanticism. The essay is included, though, in the interests of completeness, and because its form embodies the conversational spirit of the series as a whole. "Sleeping with the Enemy" can indicate, indeed, the stylistic standards by which the books here under review are appreciated. Those eighteen volumes all pertain to this cumulative, ongoing project in bi-national cultural poetics.

*

Browsers among these essays and reviews may wish to consider whether or not British empiricism and the empirical evangelicalism of the Anglo-American world can each in its own right prove as worthy to be read for its manner as for its thoughts. Readers might also stay alert to how the confluence of empirical philosophy and evangelical faith in the neoclassic-to-Romantic imagination helps explain 19th-century authors as aficionados of the realistic and of the preternatural at one and the same time. From their varying but corresponding points of view, these thirty-eight reissues do not just examine, but dwell in the possibility of, intellectual, emotional, and imaginative re-integration. Please take to heart, again—before perusing the first essay—all three epigraphs, thereby bringing the prologue full circle. The Shelley stanza gives an important, surprising directive for anyone's natural-*cum*-spiritual experience. The Koestler statement provides a succinct, stimulating watchword for aesthetic endeavor. And the Wiman meditation bears on how a life's work ranges from the professional to the personal.

Works Cited

Abrams, M. H. *The Correspondent Breeze: Essays on English Romanticism.* New York: W. W. Norton, 1984.

―――. *The Fourth Dimension of a Poem: and Other Essays.* New York: W. W. Norton, 2012.

―――. *The Mirror and the Lamp: Romantic Theory and the Critical Tradition.* New York: Oxford U P, 1954.

―――. *Natural Supernaturalism: Tradition and Revolution in Romantic Literature.* New York: W. W. Norton, 1971.

Abrams, M. H. et al., eds. *The Norton Anthology of English Literature: Third Edition.* 2 vols. New York: W. W. Norton, 1974.

Anderson, Misty G. *Imagining Methodism in 18th-Century Britain: Enthusiasm, Belief & the Borders of the Self.* Baltimore, MD: The Johns Hopkins U P, 2012.

Bakewell, Sarah. *How to Live—Or—A Life of Montaigne in One Question and Twenty Attempts at an Answer.* New York: Other P, 2010.

Barbeau, Jeffrey W. *Coleridge, the Bible, and Religion.* New York: Palgrave Macmillan, 2008.

―――. "The Quest for System: An Introduction to Coleridge's Lifelong Project." In *Coleridge's Assertion of Religion: Essays on the* Opus Maximum. Jeffrey W. Barbeau, ed. Wilsele, Belgium: Peeters, 2006.

―――. "Romantic Religion, Life Writing, and Conversion Narratives." *The Wordsworth Circle* 47.1 (Winter 2016): 32-39.

―――. *Sara Coleridge: Her Life and Thought.* New York: Palgrave Macmillan, 2004.

Baym, Nina et al., eds. *The Norton Anthology of American Literature: Fifth Edition.* New York: W. W. Norton, 1998.

Bennett, Kelsey L. *Principle and Propensity: Experience and Religion in the Nineteenth-Century British and American Bildungsroman.* Columbia: U of South Carolina P, 2014.

Bloom, Harold. *The American Religion: The Emergence of the Post-Christian Nation.* New York: Simon and Schuster, 1992, 2006.

———. *The Daemon Knows: Literary Greatness and the American Sublime.* New York: Spiegel & Grau, 2015.

Boyles, Helen. *Romanticism and Methodism: The Embarrassment of Enthusiasm.* London and New York: Routledge, 2016.

Brantley, Richard E. *Anglo-American Antiphony: The Late Romanticism of Tennyson and Emerson.* Gainesville: U P of Florida, 1994.

———. "Charles Wesley's Experiential Art." *Eighteenth-Century Life* 11 (May 1987) 1-11.

———. "Christianity and Romanticism: A Dialectical Review." *Christianity & Literature* 48 (Spring 1999): 349-66.

———. *Coordinates of Anglo-American Romanticism: Wesley, Edwards, Carlyle, and Emerson.* Gainesville: U P of Florida, 1993.

———. *Emily Dickinson's Rich Conversation: Poetry, Philosophy, Science.* New York: Palgrave Macmillan, 2013, 2015.

———. *Experience and Faith: The Late-Romantic Imagination of Emily Dickinson.* New York: Palgrave Macmillan, 2004, 2008.

———. *Locke, Wesley, and the Method of English Romanticism.* Gainesville: U P of Florida, 1984.

———. "Wordsworth's Art of Belief." *The Wordsworth Circle* 45.2 (Spring 2014): 162-70.

———. *Wordsworth's "Natural Methodism."* New Haven, CT: Yale U P, 1975.

Bromwich, David. *A Choice of Inheritance: Self and Community from Edmund Burke to Robert Frost.* Cambridge, MA: Harvard U P, 1989.

Brooks, David. "The G.O.P. at an Immigrations Crossroad." *The New York Times*, November 14, 2015.

Butterfield, Ardis. "Why Medieval Lyric?" *ELH* 82.2 (Summer 2015): 319-43.

Campos, Isabel Sobral. "The Haunted House of Nature—Immanence's Infinity." *The Emily Dickinson Journal* 25.1 (2016): 57-82.

Carlyle, Thomas. *Thomas Carlyle: Selected Writings.* Ed. Alan Shelston. 1971. Reprint. Harmondsworth, England: Penguin P, 1986.

Carruth, Cathy. *Empirical Truths and Critical Fictions: Locke, Wordsworth, Kant, Freud.* Baltimore, MD: The Johns Hopkins U P, 1991.

———. *Unclaimed Experience: Trauma, Narrative, and History*. Baltimore, MD: The Johns Hopkins U P, 1996.

Chandler, James. "Sensibility, Sympathy and Sentiment." *William Wordsworth in Context*, 61-70. Ed. Andrew Bennett. Cambridge: Cambridge U P, 2015.

Clarke, Colin. *The Romantic Paradox: An Essay on the Poetry of Wordsworth*. New York: Barnes & Noble, 1963.

Cragwall, Jasper. *Lake Methodism: Popular Literature and Popular Religion in England, 1780-1830*. Columbus: Ohio State U P, 2013.

Dabundo, Laura S. *The Marriage of Faith: Christianity in Jane Austen and William Wordsworth*. Macon, GA: Mercer U P, 2012.

Damasio, Antonio. *Descartes' Error*. 1994. Reprint. New York: Penguin, 2005.

Damrosch, David et al., eds. *The Longman Anthology of British Literature: First Edition*. 2 vols. New York: Longman, 1999.

Deresiewicz, William. "Where Have You Gone, Annie Dillard?" *The Atlantic*, March 2016.

Dickinson, Emily. *The Letters of Emily Dickinson*. Eds. Thomas H. Johnson and Theodora Ward. 3 vols. Cambridge, MA: Harvard U P, 1958.

———. *The Poems of Emily Dickinson: Reading Edition*. Ed. Ralph W. Franklin. Cambridge, MA: The Belknap P of Harvard U P, 1999.

Dillard, Annie. *Pilgrim at Tinker's Creek*. 1974. Reprint. New York: Harper Perennial Modern Classics, 2013.

Dimock, Wai Chee. "Deep Time: American Literature and World History." *American Literary History* 13.4 (Winter 2001): 755-75.

Donoghue, Denis. "Bewitched, Bothered, and Bewildered." *The New York Review of Books*, March 25, 1993.

Eberwein, Jane Donahue. "Calvinism as Impetus to Spiritual Amplitude." *The Emily Dickinson Journal* 14.2 (2005): 12-23.

———. "Outgrowing Genesis? Dickinson, Darwin, and the Higher Criticism." *Dickinson and Philosophy*, 47-56. Eds. Marianne Noble, Jed Deppman, and Gary Lee Stonum. Cambridge: Cambridge U P, 2013.

Edwards, Jonathan. *An Extract from a Treatise concerning Religious Affections*. Abr. John Wesley. In vol. 23 of *The Works of the Rev. John Wesley*. 32 vols. Bristol, England: J. Paramore, 1771-74.

Farrell, Michael. *Blake and the Methodists*. New York: Palgrave Macmillan, 2014.

Finley, C. Stephen. *Nature's Covenant: Figures of Landscape in Ruskin*. State College: Pennsylvania State U P, 1992.

Fish, Stanley. "One University Under God?" *The Chronicle of Higher Education*, January 7, 2005: 13.

Franke, William. *Secular Scriptures: Modern Theological Poetics in the Wake of Dante.* Columbus: The Ohio State U P, 2015.

Frederick, Harold. *The Damnation of Theron Ware.* 1896. Reprint. New York: Penguin, 1994.

Freedman, Linda. *Emily Dickinson and the Religious Imagination.* Cambridge U P, 2011.

Garber, Frederick, ed. *Romantic Irony.* Amsterdam: John Benjamin Publishing Company, 1988.

Gardner, Thomas. *A Door Ajar: Contemporary Writers and Emily Dickinson.* New York: Oxford U P, 2006.

Gaull, Marilyn. "Wordsworth and Science." *The Oxford Handbook of William Wordsworth,* 599-613. Eds. Richard Gravil and Daniel Robinson. Oxford: Oxford U P, 2015.

Geertz, Clifford. *The Interpretation of Cultures: Selected Essays.* New York: Basic Books, 1973.

Gill, F. C. *The Romantic Movement and Methodism: A Study of English Romanticism and the Evangelical Revival.* London: The Epworth P, 1937.

Goellnicht, Donald C. *The Poet-Physician: Keats and Medical Science.* Pittsburgh: U of Pittsburgh P, 1984.

Gould, Stephen Jay. *Rocks of Ages: Science and Religion in the Fullness of Life.* New York: Ballantine Publishers Group, 1999.

Gunn, Giles. *Thinking across the American Grain: Ideology, Intellect, and the New Pragmatism.* Chicago: U of Chicago P, 1992.

Harvey, Samantha C. *Transatlantic Transcendentalism: Cole, Emerson, and Nature.* Edinburgh: U of Edinburgh P, 2013.

Hirsch, E. D., Jr. *The Aims of Interpretation.* Chicago: U of Chicago P, 1975.

Holl, Steven. *Intertwining: Selected Projects 1989-1995.* New York: Princeton Architectural P, 1996.

Hsu, Li-Hsin. "'The light that never was on sea or land': William Wordsworth in America and Emily Dickinson's 'Frostier' Style." *The Emily Dickinson Journal,* 25.2 (2016): 24-47.

Jackson, Virginia. *Dickinson's Misery: A Theory of Lyric Reading.* Princeton, NJ: Princeton U P, 2005.

Jager, Colin. *The Book of God: Secularization and Design in the Romantic Era.* Philadelphia: U of Pennsylvania P, 2007.

Jeffrey, Francis. "Wordsworth's Excursion." *The Edinburgh Review, or Critical Journal* 24 (November 1814) in *English Romantic Writers,* 463-467. Ed. David Perkins. New York: Harcourt Brace, 1995.

Jesse, Jennifer. *William Blake's Religious Vision: There's a Methodism in His Madness.* Lanham, MD: Lexington Books, 2013.

Keane, Patrick J. *Emerson, Romanticism, and Intuitive Reason: The Transatlantic "Light of All Our Day."* Columbia: U of Missouri P, 2005.

Koestler, Arthur. *The Act of Creation.* 1964. Reprint. New York: Penguin P, 1990.

Lamb, Charles. *The Letters of Charles Lamb to which are added those of his sister Mary Lamb.* Ed. E. V. Lucas. 8 vols. London: J. M. Dent & Sons and Methuen and Company, 1935.

Leader, Jennifer L. *Knowing, Seeing, Being: Jonathan Edwards, Emily Dickinson, Marianne Moore, and the American Typological Tradition.* Amherst: U of Massachusetts P, 2016.

Lee, Maurice. *Uncertain Chances: Science, Skepticism, and Belief in 19th-Century American Literature.* Oxford: Oxford U P, 2012.

Lewis, Anthony. "50 Years of Covering War, Looking for Peace and Honoring Law." *The New York Times,* December 16, 2001.

Lundin, Roger. *Emily Dickinson and the Art of Belief.* Grand Rapids, MI: William B. Eerdmans, 1998.

McFarland, Thomas. *Coleridge and the Pantheist Tradition.* Oxford: Clarendon P, 1969.

———. *Romanticism and the Forms of Ruin: Wordsworth, Coleridge, and Modalities of Fragmentation.* Princeton, NJ: Princeton U P, 1981.

McGilchrist, Iain. *The Master and His Emissary: The Divided Brain and the Making of the Western World.* New Haven, CT: Yale U P, 2009.

McNamer, Sarah. *Affective Meditation and the Invention of Medieval Compassion.* Philadelphia: U of Pennsylvania P, 2010.

———. "The Literariness of Literature and the History of Emotion." *PMLA* 130.5 (October 2015): 1,433-42.

Mellor, Anne K. *English Romantic Irony.* Cambridge, MA: Harvard U P, 1980.

Muecke, Mikesch and Miriam Zach, eds. *Resonance: Essays on the Intersection of Music and Architecture.* Ames/Berlin/Gainesville/Rome: Culicidae P, 2007.

Nietzsche, Friedrich. *Thus Spake Zarathustra.* Tr. R. J. Hollingdale. Harmondsworth, England: Penguin P, 1961.

Otto, Rudolf. *The Idea of the Holy.* Tr. John W. Harvey. Oxford: Oxford U P, 1958.

Page, Judith W. *Wordsworth and the Cultivation of Women.* Berkeley: U of California P, 1994.

Pallasmaa, Juhani. *The Eyes of the Skin: Architecture and the Senses.* Hoboken, NJ: John Wiley and Sons, 1996.

Perkins, David, ed. *English Romantic Writers.* New York: Harcourt Brace, 1995.

Pronker-Coron, Annemieke. *The Bridge: Connecting Violin and Fiddle Worlds.* Ames/Berlin/Gainesville/Rome: Culicidae P, 2015.

Pulos, C. E. *The Deep Truth: A Study of Shelley's Skepticism.* Lincoln: U of Nebraska P, 1954.

Raymond, William O. *The Infinite Moment and Other Essays in Robert Browning.* Toronto: U of Toronto P, 1950.

Reed, John Shelton. *Glorious Battle: The Cultural Politics of Victorian Anglo-Catholicism.* Nashville and London: Vanderbilt U P, 1996.

Ricoeur, Paul. *Freud and Philosophy.* Tr. Denis Savage. Cambridge: Cambridge U P, 1970.

Rublack, Ulinka. *The Astronomer and the Witch: Johannes Kepler's Fight for His Mother.* Oxford: Oxford U P, 2015.

Ruoff, Gene W. and Karl Kroeber, eds. *Romantic Poetry: Recent Revisionary Criticism.* New Brunswick, NJ: Rutgers U P, 1993.

Ryals, Clyde De L. *A World of Possibility: Romantic Irony in Victorian Literature.* Columbus: The Ohio State U P, 1990.

Ryan, Robert M. "Christianity and Romanticism: A Reply." *Christianity & Literature* 49 (Autumn 1999): 81-90.

_____. *Keats: The Religious Sense.* Princeton, NJ: Princeton U P, 1976.

_____. *The Romantic Reformation: Religious Politics in English Literature, 1789-1824.* Cambridge: Cambridge U P, 1997.

Schleiermacher, Friedrich. *On Religion: Speeches to Its Cultured Despisers.* Tr. John Oman. New York: Harper, 1958.

Semmel, Bernard. *The Methodist Revolution.* New York: Basic Books, 1973.

Sewall, Richard B. *The Life of Emily Dickinson.* 2 vols. 1974. Reprint. New York: Farrar, Straus, and Giroux, 1980.

Sifton, Elisabeth. *The Serenity Prayer: Faith and Politics in Times of Peace and War.* New York: W. W. Norton, 2003.

Simpson, David. *Irony and Authority in Romantic Poetry.* London: Rowan and Littlefield, 1979.

Snow, Heidi. *William Wordsworth and the Theology of Poverty.* Burlington, VT: Ashgate Publishing Company, 2013.

Spellman, W. M. *John Locke and the Problem of Depravity.* Oxford: Clarendon P, 1988.

Sperry, Stuart. *Keats the Poet.* Princeton, NJ: Princeton U P, 1973.

Stillinger, Jack. *The Hoodwinking of Madeline, and Other Essays on Keats's Poems.* Urbana: U of Illinois P, 1971.

Swingle, L. J. *The Obstinate Questionings of English Romanticism.* Baton Rouge: Louisiana State U P, 1987.

Tuveson, Ernest Lee. *The Imagination as a Means of Grace: Locke and the Aesthetics of Romanticism.* Berkeley: U of California P, 1960.

Ulmer, William A. *The Christian Wordsworth: 1798-1805.* Albany: The State U of New York P, 2001.

Vendler, Helen. "The Poet Remakes the Poem." *The New York Review of Books* 63.4 (March 10, 2016): 40-42.

Venturi, Robert. *Complexity and Contradiction in Architecture.* 1966. Reprint. New York: The Museum of Modern Art, 1977.

Waldron, Jeremy. *God, Locke, and Equality: Christian Foundations in Locke's Political Thought.* Cambridge: Cambridge U P, 2002.

Wasserman, Earl. *The Subtler Language: Critical Readings of Neoclassic and Romantic Poems.* Baltimore, MD: The Johns Hopkins U P, 1959.

Wesley, John. *The Journal of the Rev. John Wesley, A. M.* Ed. Nehemiah Curnock. 8 vols. London: Robert Culley, 1909.

———. *The Letters of the Rev. John Wesley, A. M.* Ed. John Telford. 8 vols. London: The Epworth P, 1931.

———. *The Works of the Rev. John Wesley, A. M.* Ed. Thomas Jackson. 14 vols. London: Wesleyan-Methodist Book-Room, n. d.

West, Cornel. *Race Matters.* New York: Vintage Books, 1994.

Wilson, Eric G. Review of *Emily Dickinson's Rich Conversation: Poetry, Philosophy, Science,* by Richard E. Brantley. *Review 19* (October 15, 2013): www.http//nbol-19.org.

Wilson, Frances. *Guilty Thing: A Life of Thomas De Quincey.* New York: Farra, Straus and Giroux, 2016.

Wiman, Christian. *My Bright Abyss: Meditation of a Modern Believer.* New York: Farrar, Straus and Giroux, 2013.

Wolfson, Susan J. *The Questioning Presence: Wordsworth, Keats, and the Interrogative Mode in Romantic Poetry.* Ithaca, NY: Cornell U P, 1986.

Zumthor, Peter. *Atmospheres: Architectural Environments—Surrounding Objects.* Basel, Boston: Birkhäuser, 2006.

———, and Maureen Oberli-Turner. *Thinking Architecture.* Baden: Lars Müller, 1998.

Essays, First Series:

Backgrounds of British and American Romanticism

1. John Wesley (1703-91)

John Wesley (engraving by J. Faber, after a portrait by J. Williams)

SELECTED BOOKS: *The Character of a Methodist* (Bristol: Printed by Felix Farley, 1742);

An Earnest Appeal to Men of Reason and Religion (Newcastle upon Tyne: Printed by J. Gooding, 1743);

A Farther Appeal to Men of Reason and Religion (London: Printed by W. Strahan, 1745);

Advice to the People Called Methodists (Newcastle, 1745);

Sermons on Several Occasions, volumes 1-3 (London: Printed by W. Strahan, sold by T. Trye and at the Foundery, 1746, 1748, 1750); volume 4 (Bristol: Printed by John Grabham, 1760); volume 3, enlarged (Bristol: Printed by William Pine, circa 1762-1770); volumes 5-8 (London: Printed and sold at the New Chapel, 1788); volume 9 (London: Printed by G. Story, sold by G. Whitfield, 1800);

Primitive Physick: or, An Easy and Natural Method of Curing Most Diseases (London: Printed, and sold by Thomas Trye, 1747);

A Letter to the Reverend Dr. Conyers Middleton, Occasioned by His Late Free Enquiry (London: Printed & sold by G. Woodfall, 1749);

A Plain Account of the People Called Methodists (Bristol: Printed by F. Farley, 1749);

The Complete English Dictionary, Explaining Most of Those Hard Words, which are Found in the Best English Writers (London: Printed by W. Strahan & sold by J. Robinson, T. Trye, T. James & G. Englefield, 1753; second edition, enlarged, Bristol: Printed by William Pine, 1764);

The Desideratum: or, Electricity Made Plain and Useful (London: Printed, and sold by W. Flexney, 1760);

A Short History of Methodism (London: Printed & sold at the Foundery, 1765);

The Witness of the Spirit (Bristol: Printed by William Pine, 1767);

The Works of the Rev. John Wesley, M.A., Late Fellow of Lincoln-College, Oxford, 32 volumes (Bristol: William Pine, 1771-1774);

Thoughts upon Necessity (London: Printed by W. Hawes, 1774);

Thoughts upon Slavery (London: Printed by R. Hawes, 1774);

A Concise History of England, From the Earliest Times, to the Death of George II, 4 volumes (London: Printed by R. Hawes, 1776);

A Collection of Hymns, for the Use of the People Called Methodists, by John Wesley and Charles Wesley (London: Printed by J. Paramore, 1780).

EDITIONS: *The Works of the Rev. John Wesley*, A.M., 14 volumes, edited by Thomas Jackson (London: John Mason, 1829-1831);

The Works of John Wesley, 26 volumes, edited by Frank Baker and Richard P. Heitzenrater (Oxford: Clarendon Press, 1975-1983; Nashville: Abingdon Press, 1984-).

OTHER: *A Christian Library: Consisting of Extracts from and Abridgments of the Choicest Pieces of Practical Divinity, which have been Publish'd in the English Tongue*, abridged by Wesley, 50 volumes (Bristol: Printed by F. Farley, 1749-1755);

A Survey of the Wisdom of God in the Creation: or A Compendium of Natural Philosophy, abridged by Wesley, 2 volumes (Bristol: Printed by W. Pine, 1763; Lancaster, Pa.: Hamilton, 1810);

"Extracts from Mr. Locke and Remarks upon Mr. Locke's 'Essay on Human Understanding,' " *The Arminian Magazine*, 5 (1782): 27-30, 85-88, 144-146, 190-195, 247-249, 307-310, 361-363, 413-417' 4 76-4 78, 528, 534, 585-587, 646-648; 6 (1783): 30-31, 86-89, 136-138, 197-199, 254-256, 310-312, 366-368, 418-420, 480-484, 534-536, 590-594, 650-652; 7 (1784): 32-33, 91-92, 148-149, 201-202.

John Wesley, the leader of the Methodist revival, was also an intellectual and a man of letters. His two million published words feature such marks of literary craftsmanship as grasp of narrative vocabulary, the use of familiar words and aphorisms, an especially wide range of adjectives, vivid figures of speech, and a natural assimilation of scriptural idiom. His blend of theological traditions (such as the Anglican, the Dissenting, the Puritan, the Arminian, the Calvinist, the Lutheran, the Thomistic, the Catholic, and the Anglo-Catholic) emerges from his command of theme, his resonant and forceful diction, and, above all, his mastery of such formal and informal, conventional and original genres as diaries, journals, letters, advice to the Methodists, Methodist polity and principles, polemics, appeals, open letters to exponents of religion, apologetics, expositions of doctrine, biblical exegesis, homilies, devotionals, hymns, prayers, poems, editions of fiction and biography, abridgments (of works of theology, works of philosophy, and works of natural philosophy—that is, science), a medical treatise, scientific essays, history, and, clearly not least for those interested in Wesley as a literary figure, a dictionary.

John Wesley was born on 17 June 1703 at Epworth Rectory, Lincolnshire, and he was peculiarly suited by birth to start the revival that effectively retouched the various colorations of doctrine to be found throughout the disparate kinds of English church organization. Samuel Wesley, his father, was an Anglican vicar; his mother, Susanna, was the daughter of the well-known Presbyterian divine Samuel Annesley of London. He was therefore in a position to know at firsthand about the varieties of doctrine and organization at the beginning of his century, a time when the Anglicans and the Dissenters (Congregationalists, Baptists, and Presbyterians) went their separate ways for the most part, afraid of reopening the wounds of the seventeenth-century civil war. Nurtured in both traditions, Wesley venerated the Anglican liturgy and sacraments, and at the same time responded to the covenant organization of Nonconformist ecclesiology. As a true son of the Puritans, he may well have considered himself as Susanna thought him after his rescue from the fire that destroyed the Epworth Rectory on 9 February 1709—"a brand snatched from the burning" or member of the Elect. Yet he often expressed his Anglican fear of the excesses of enthusiasm. Thus equipped to reconcile potentially opposing traditions, he seemed destined to remind England that her two religious heritages are not mutually exclusive: the Calvinism appropriated by the Puritans and their Nonconformist descendants can also be found in Archbishop Thomas Cranmer's *Book of Common Prayer* (1549). For that matter, the Augustinianism preserved in Anglican theology nurtured the thought of the well-educated Evangelical-Dissenter and Anglican alike. Wesley leavened Calvinism, finally, with Arminian free will, that is, with an emphasis on action and the practical in matters of religion.

After graduating from Christ Church, Oxford, in 1724 (John Locke was an earlier graduate) and his ordination as a deacon in the Church of England in 1725, Wesley was elected a fellow of Lincoln College, Oxford, on 17 March 1726 and was granted a master's degree in February 1727. As leader of the Holy Club (or Oxford Methodists as they came to be called) during the early 1730s, he inspired the few men in the Club to practice charity as well as to obey strict rules of study and religious observance. During a mission to Georgia (6 February 1736 - 22 December 1737), he met the German Moravians and proposed marriage to Sophia Hopkey, who refused him. His conversion, or what turned out to be the seed of his fifty-three-year itinerant ministry, occurred at a quarter to nine on the evening of 24 May 1738, in Aldersgate Street, London, where his heart was "strangely warmed"; and he began his practice of open-air preaching near Bristol on 2 April 1739, taking as his precedent the Sermon on the Mount and declaring, "the world is my parish." He dissociated himself from the Calvinism of his friend George Whitefield on 24 December 1740 (the Calvinist/Arminian controversy did not estrange him from Whitefield, but led him to found *The*

Arminian Magazine in 1778), and began his organization of lay preachers, circuit riders, class meetings (for moral and spiritual inspection), and conferences (for the expression of divergent opinions) during the 1740s. He proposed marriage to Grace Murray early in 1749, but she married instead the Reverend John Bennet (on 3 October 1749). On 19 February 1751 he married Mary Vazeille (the marriage was unhappy, and she deserted him in 1776). On 2 September 1784 he ordained Thomas Coke as a superintendent of Methodism in the United States, defying Anglican church orders and paving the way for the separation of the Methodists from the Anglican church in 1795. Wesley was also a pioneer in the protest against slavery, his abhorrence of which formed the subject of the last letter he ever wrote, to William Wilberforce on 24 February 1791.

Wesley's parents: Reverend Samuel Wesley (engraving by R. M. Meadows, after a portrait by N. Branwhite) and Susanna Annesley Wesley (engraving by Owen, after a portrait by Williams)

By himself or with his brother Charles, Wesley published twenty-three collections of hymns between 1737 and 1786. He "unawares became rich" (he said in 1789) through the sale of cheap books and tracts, but he gave his money away; his charities often exceeded £1,000 per year. Reading and writing on horseback, he traveled 250,000 miles and preached 40,000 sermons. As an endearing corollary to the Arminian belief that "Christ died for all," he entertained—rather against his usually more ironic than sentimental frame of mind—the belief in a future life for animals.

Mary Vazeile, who became Wesley's wife in 1751 (artist unknown; Methodist Church Archives and History Committee

The effects of his ministry were nothing short of astonishing. His evangelistic campaign was rapid, constant, and huge in its results. By the time of his death on 2 March 1791, he had changed both Dissent, including the radical Quakers, and Anglicanism, including the Highest Churchmen. It is sometimes suggested that Evangelicalism, binding together differing religious persuasions, helped to mold the character of the British people, who gradually showed a new humanitarian spirit—or, more precisely, an Arminian practical charity—that bore no small part in doubling the population during the eighteenth century. An awareness of the sociological as well as religious importance of the phenomenon may have led Thomas Babington Macaulay to be impatient with any earlier historian who neglected the revival. Its importance has never again been ignored. In the late nineteenth century, W. E. H. Lecky observed that Wesley's conversion "meant more for Britain than all the victories of Pitt by land and sea," and, more recently, Augustine Birrell declared that "No single figure influenced so many minds, no single voice touched so many hearts, no other man did such a work for England."

Samuel Johnson not only admired Wesley but espoused the kind of earnest faith that led his first modern editor, Birkbeck Hill, to conclude: "In his personal religion Johnson was, in the best sense, a Methodist." The next literary figures to respond to the revival were the first generation Romantics, whose formative years were passed during the period when Wesley was still active and Evangelical faith was in the flush of increasing vigor.

Because the sense of a neo-apostolic age was widespread, it is not surprising that Samuel Taylor Coleridge respected Wesley's leadership and wrote in his copy of Robert Southey's *Life of Wesley* (1820; a work in William Wordsworth's library too) that Arminian Methodism "has been the occasion, and even the cause, of turning thousands from their evil deeds, and...has made... bad and mischievous men peaceable and profitable neighbors and citizens." On the basis of both favorable and hostile reaction to Wordsworth's *The Excursion* (1814), one can ask whether Wordsworth himself consciously permitted the Methodists in particular, as well as the Evangelicals in general, to affect his literary practice. Charles Lamb praised the "natural methodism" in the poem, and Francis, Lord Jeffrey, in his notorious review, explicitly denounced Wordsworth's "mystical verbiage of the Methodist pulpit." Lord Jeffrey overstated his case for effect, and Lamb's phrase does not demonstrate any precise Methodist allegiances on Wordsworth's part. The phrase, however, was perhaps intended to suggest the poet's enthusiasm for nature—an enthusiasm to be found among many Evangelicals—or, more generally, his affinity for the larger movement. The word *methodism* also suggests the religious quality of Wordsworth's thoroughgoing reliance on one's own experience as the basis for knowing the good and the true.

Methodism, after all, besides designating the devotional exercises of Wesley's Holy Club at Oxford and besides referring to the systematic practice of one's religion (naming, somehow, whatever it was that warmed the hearts and caught the imaginations of many), connotes the induction of religious knowledge from natural as well as spiritual experience. Wesley's conversion, a spiritual watershed of English cultural life, had as much to do with place, time, and the specific circumstances of his sense experience, and as much to do with his state of mind, as with his state of spirit.

Both before and after the conversion, he derived theological method from John Locke's theory of knowledge. In 1730, intrigued by an obscure follower of Locke, Wesley abridged *The Procedure, Extent, and Limits of Human Understanding* (1728), a theologizing of Locke's empiricism by Peter Browne, Bishop of Cork and Ross during the 1720s and 1730s. In 1781 Wesley wrote annotations to Locke's *Essay Concerning Human Understanding* (1690), and published them with extracts from Locke's essay in *The Arminian Magazine* during 1782-1784.

As the result of such educational enterprises as Wesley's condensations of Browne's work, which was first published in *A Survey of the Wisdom of God in the Creation: or A Compendium of Natural Philosophy* (1763), and Locke's *Essay Concerning Human Understanding*, generations of laity were at home with Lockean categories and with Browne's appropriation of Locke for theological purposes. It is especially interesting that Wesley took women seriously as philosophical and theological discussion partners, recognizing their intellectual abilities and encouraging their literary efforts as did few of his contemporaries.

As a means of placing Wesley's works historically and of approaching them as literature, it is helpful to outline their relation to Locke's *Essay Concerning Human Understanding*, for Locke's empiricism exercised a great and lasting influence on literary theory and practice. Wesley's prose, besides being scriptural, classical, and colloquial, is pervasively philosophical, for the Lockean language of experience enabled him to raise his ineffable experience of grace to graceful, cogent, and frequent expressions of methodology. Although evangelicalism is "spiritual" and empiricism is "natural," the great principle of empiricism—that one must see for oneself and be in the presence of the thing one knows—applies to evangelical faith. Each of these two codes of human methodology operates along a continuum joining emotion to intellect, and each of these two sign systems joins externality to words through "ideas/ideals of sensation," that is, through either perception itself or grace-in-perception or both. While empiricism refers to immediate contact with and direct impact from objects and subjects in time and place, evangelicalism entertains the similarly reciprocating notions that religious truth is concerned with experiential presuppositions and that experience itself need not be nonreligious. Wesley conceived of an analogy between sense perception of natural things and "sense perception" of the divine. He thought of a continuum joining scientific method and rational empiricism to natural and revealed religion; and he succeeded in spreading this "empiricism," this peculiarly English method for understanding the "spiritual sense."

Locke's view that words correspond to things, albeit through ideas, leads him to advocate a simple style, with as little as possible of the arbitrariness of metaphor, and, though more message than intellectual treatise, Wesley's *Character of a Methodist* (1742) implies a similar view:

> The most obvious, easy, common, words, wherein our meaning can be conveyed, we prefer before others, both on ordinary occasions, and when we speak of the things of God. We never, therefore, willingly or designedly, deviate from the most usual way of speaking; unless when we express scripture truths in scripture words, which, we presume, no Christian will condemn.

This passage, describing "scripture words" as desirable, hardly excludes metaphor, but the simplicity and clarity of Wesley's writing, both here and generally, are due in part to the corollary of Locke's preference for analogy: that metaphor too easily undermines the capacity of language to communicate and represent truths whether natural or spiritual.

An Earnest Appeal to Men of Reason and Religion (1743), in its turn, is so Lockean as to suggest that Wesley had the *Essay Concerning Human Understanding* in view:

> You know ... that before it is possible for you to form a true judgment of the things of God, it is absolutely necessary that you have a clear apprehension of them, and that your ideas thereof be all fixed, distinct, and determinate. And seeing our ideas are not innate, but must all originally come from our senses, it is certainly necessary that you have senses capable of discerning objects of this kind—not those only which are called "natural senses," which in this respect profit nothing, as being altogether incapable of discerning objects of a spiritual kind, but spiritual senses, exercised to discern spiritual good and evil. ...
> And till you have these internal senses, till the eyes of your understanding are opened, you can have no apprehension of divine things, no idea of them at all. Nor consequently, till then,

can you either judge truly or reason justly concerning them, seeing your reason has no ground whereon to stand, no materials to work upon.

The sensationalist diction ("materials," "ground," "eyes," "internal senses," "spiritual senses," "natural senses," "objects," and "things") constitutes perhaps the fullest statement of Wesley's "spiritual sense." The philosophical demand for empiricism, which in Locke's case is rational as well as sensationalist, is met too in Wesley's far from antirational concept of inspiration ("reason," "understanding," "discern," "ideas," "apprehension," and "judgment"). Wesley, then, as though to maintain Lockean balance between reason and its ground, implies a more than metaphorical, far from arbitrary relation between spiritual senses and rational apprehension by the spirit. Consistent with his endorsement of *tabula rasa* as the first principle of theology, he signals his affinity for, dependence on, Lockean method.

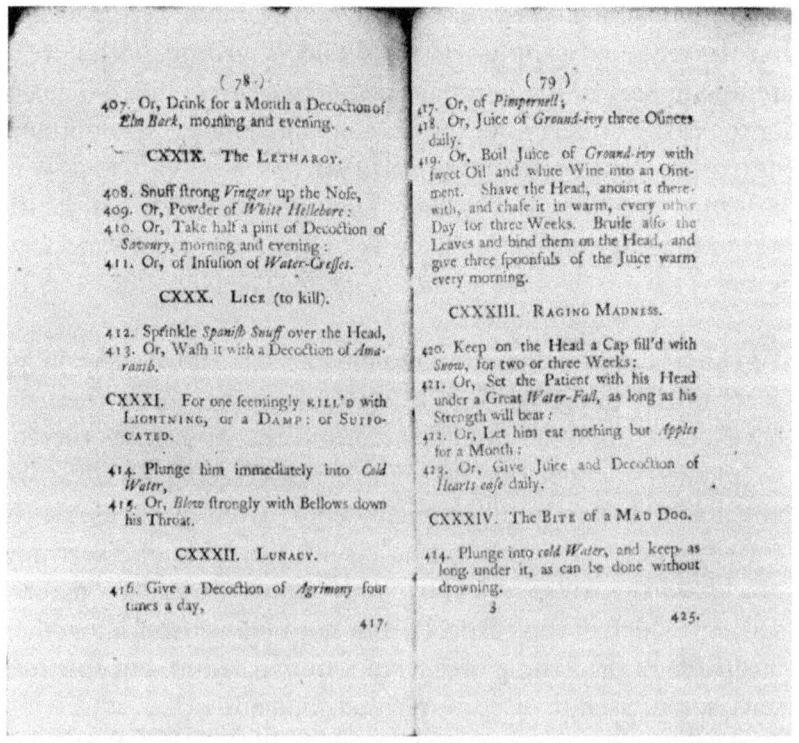

Pages from Primitive Physick, *Wesley's handbook of home remedies*

An Earnest Appeal to Men of Reason and Religion draws an analogy between faith and empirical observation: Faith "is with regard to the spiritual world what sense is with regard to the natural." This idea too is explicitly Lockean, or at least perspicuously so, for the precisely analogistic structure rests on a more than metaphorical, far from arbitrary association of faith with the natural senses. Of course, in suggesting that sense perception is related to faith, Wesley avoids implying that one ever fully knows the common ground between faith and empiricism. *An Earnest Appeal to Men of Reason and Religion*, like Locke's *Essay Concerning Human Understanding*, stresses that natural understanding cannot easily apprehend spiritual truth: "What then will your reason do here? How will it pass from things natural to spiritual? From the things that are seen to those that are not seen? From the visible to the invisible world? What a gulf is here!" Nonetheless, faith is defined not simply according to scripture, but even in accordance with a balance between the sensing and the reasoning powers:

> It is the feeling of the soul, whereby a believer perceives, through the "power of the Highest overshadowing him" [see Luke 1:35] both the existence and the presence of him in whom he "lives, moves, and has his being" [see Acts 17:28], and indeed the whole invisible world, the entire system or things eternal. And hereby, in particular, he feels "the love of God shed abroad in his heart" [see Rom. 5:5].

By *feeling*, Wesley does not mean "inner trend" so much as "faith in relation to the senses"; for on the preceding page of *An Earnest Appeal to Men of Reason and Religion* he associates faith with sight, hearing, and taste. Wesley's definition, finally, both by its diction ("whereby a believer perceives") and by its development throughout the book, intimates his view, derived from Locke, that religious feeling, like sense data, constitutes matter for the mind to work upon: faith exists, too, in relation to reason.

A Farther Appeal to Men of Reason and Religion (1745) is concerned primarily to prove that the "technical terms" of Methodism "coincide exactly with . . . the official pronouncements of the Church of England," but this appeal, like the first, is concerned as well to use the language of Lockean method. The kind of religion Wesley espouses is not "religious madness,"

> but rational as well as scriptural; it is as pure from enthusiasm as from superstition. . . . Who will prove that it is enthusiasm . . . to rejoice in the sense of [God's] love to us?

"To this day," Wesley wrote in his letters to Mr. John Smith (written in 1745-1748), "I have abundantly more temptation . . . to be . . . a philosophical sluggard, than an itinerant Preacher." ("Smith" was probably Thomas Secker, Bishop of Oxford and later Archbishop of Canterbury.) Throughout these letters, Wesley combines evangelistic goals with his evident love of "philosophical" theology, and his Lockean method is especially perspicuous, for, even to traditional revelation, he applies Lockean as well as Cartesian skepticism: "I am as fully assured to-day, as I am of the shining of the sun, that the scriptures are of God. l cannot possibly deny or doubt of it now; yet I may doubt of it tomorrow; as I have done heretofore a thousand times, and that after the fullest assurance preceding." Thus, the mind remains open even after systematically searching for, and apparently finding, what is not subject to doubt. The letters to "Smith," moreover, acknowledge both poles of Lockean method, for the sense-based nature of mind is implicit in Wesley's phraseology, "so far as men can judge from their eyes and ears." *The rise and progress of,* a phrase characteristic of eighteenth-century England, assumes the English philosophy of experience, and, where Wesley writes that "we are speaking, not of the progress, but of the first rise, of faith," he suggests, for one thing, that no more than knowledge does faith exist innately and, for another, that faith, like knowledge, must be datable by precise moments in personal history. Just as one knows what one experiences naturally, so one has faith in what one encounters spiritually: "it cannot be, in the nature of things, that a man should be filled with this peace, and joy, and love, by the inspiration of the Holy Spirit, without perceiving it as clearly as he does the light of the sun."

In *Primitive Physick: or, An Easy and Natural Method of Curing Most Diseases* (1747), Wesley's endorsement of empirical method is in his delightfully blunt praise of the ancient Greek healing art: "The Trial was made. The Cure was wrought. And Experience and Physick grew up together." He deplores much subsequent medical practice, in which "Men of Learning began to set Experience aside," but he rejoices that "there have not been wanting from Time to Time, some Lovers of Mankind ... Who have labored to explode out of [physick] all Hypotheses, and fine spun theories, and to make it a plain intelligible Thing, as it was in the Beginning: Having no more Mystery in it than this, 'Such a Medicine removes such a Pain.'" Where he asks "Has not the Author of Nature taught us the use of many ... Medicines?" he implies an undeistical, because intervenient, God of nature in the very process of scientific inquiry. Thus, *Primitive Physick* suggests that a theistical natural religion is not just consistent with, but even demanded by, empirical method.

Wesley in 1789 (engraving by W. Ward, after a portrait by George Romney)

In "The Great Privilege of Those that are Born of God" (1748), Wesley preaches that "the circumstances of the natural birth" provide "the most easy way to understand the spiritual." This sermon affirms a real correspondence between a universal, describable experience and experience that, though possible for all, would remain quite ineffable were it not for the linguistic instrument of analogy. The entire sermon teaches that the invisible world is familiar to twice-born people whose "spiritual sense" parallels the limited but sufficient *a posteriori* operation of the natural faculties. With regard to the interpenetrations of sense perception and the world of here and now, "The Great Privilege of Those that are Born of God" waxes precisely Lockean:

> no sooner is the child born into the world, than he . . . *feels* the air with which he is surrounded, and which pours into him from every side, as fast as he alternately breathes it back, to sustain the flame of life: and hence springs a continual increase

of strength, of motion, and of sensation; all the bodily senses being now awakened, and furnished with their proper objects.

In this passage the mind's wakeful involvement with sense data is just as clear as in whole sections of the *Essay Concerning Human Understanding* where Locke insists that the mind's response to sense experience is almost at one with what one needs to know about the world. The sermon's description of "senses, whereby alone we can discern the things of God" (emphasis added) bespeaks a vital interaction: what is "continually received" is "continually rendered back." At the mental level and by analogy with the senses, spiritual experience is depicted as a coalescence at least, and at most as an almost total identification, with the condescension of God. The alternation, and indeed the oscillation, between rational diction and sensationalist diction signifies, again and again, that through immediate revelation God and man are ensphered, or rather that a clear intercourse occurs not only between man as object and God as subject, but also between man as subject and God as object.

A Letter to the Reverend Dr. Conyers Middleton (1749) expresses a theology of immediate revelation:

> Traditional evidence is of an extremely complicated nature, necessarily including so many and so various considerations, that only men of a strong and clear understanding can be sensible of its full force. On the contrary, how plain and simple is this; and how level to the lowest capacity! Is not this the sum: "One thing I know; I was blind, but now I see"? [see John 9:25]. An argument so plain, that a peasant, a woman, a child, may feel all its force.
> The traditional evidence of Christianity stands, as it were, a great way off; and therefore, although it speaks loud and clear, yet makes a less lively impression. It gives us an account of what was transacted long ago, in far distant times as well as places. Whereas the inward evidence is intimately present to all persons, at all times, and in all places.

The diction here, at once sensationalist and rational, signals again the analogy between sense perception and immediate revelation, for, although Wesley is careful to manifest reticence about how much one knows even from "spiritual sense" and spiritual discernment, his relative confidence in immediate revelation is especially clear in this fully epistemological tone. Indeed, the letter to Middleton rises to an especially characteristic height where it presents experiential faith as full counterpart to a skeptical, though courageous, "empiricism":

> Is it not so? Let impartial reason speak. Does not every thinking man want a window, not so much in his neighbour's, as in his own, breast? He wants an opening there, of whatever kind, that might let in light from eternity. He is pained to be thus feeling after God so darkly and uncertainly; to know so little of God, and indeed so little of any beside material objects. He is concerned, that he must see even that little, not directly, but in the dim, sullied glass of sense; and consequently so imperfectly and obscurely, that it is all a mere enigma still.
>
> Now, these very desiderata faith supplies. It gives a more extensive knowledge of things invisible, showing what eye had not seen, nor ear heard, neither could it before enter into our heart to conceive [see I Cor. 2:9]. And all these it shows in the clearest light, with the fullest certainty and evidence. For it does not leave us to receive our notices of them by mere reflection from the dull glass of sense; but resolves a thousand enigmas of the highest concern by giving faculties suited to things invisible.

This statement, couched in the doubly "empirical" context of a telescope metaphor (for example, "resolves a thousand enigmas") and a quasi-philosophic allusion to the Bible, is more than in keeping with the *Essay Concerning Human Understanding*, for the statement epitomizes Wesley's at once spiritual and natural mode of knowing and of speaking.

During the 1740s Wesley completed his formulation of method, for he not only drew an analogy between sense perception and revelation, but also attempted to bridge the gap between natural religion and revealed religion. At once theological and philosophical, his methodology operated throughout his mind's long history: after the 1740s, to be sure, he wrote increasingly with his followers in mind; but he remained as rigorous as ever. The later works, more often sermons than not, include many non-homiletical and intellectually ambitious titles intended not only for Methodist readers but for readers in general, and these typically "public," less narrowly directed writings of his fullest literary maturity are very often either simultaneously theological and philosophical or all but exclusively philosophical. The following works, for example, are overwhelmingly philosophical, and even specifically Lockean: the preface to *The Desideratum: or, Electricity Made Plain and Useful* (1760), the preface to and the conclusion of *A Survey of the Wisdom of God in the Creation: or A Compendium of Natural Philosophy* (1763), *Thoughts upon Necessity* (1774), "Remarks upon Mr. Locke's 'Essay on Human Understanding'" (1782-1784), "The Case of Reason Impartially Considered" (1788), and "The Imperfection of Human Knowledge" (1788). *A Short History of Methodism* (1765) and *A Concise History of England* (1776), moreover, reflect an emphasis on experience reminiscent of Locke, and even of David Hume. Finally, the following sermons of Wesley's maturity are obviously pertinent to the "empirical" dimension of religion: "The Witness of the Spirit" (1767); "The Witness of our Own Spirit" (1746); 'The Means of Grace" (1746); "The Marks of the New Birth" (1748); "On a Single Eye" *(Arminian Magazine,* November-December 1790); "Walking by Sight, and Walking by Faith" *(Arminian Magazine,* January-February 1790); and, clearly not least (in view of Locke's pioneering theories in the area), "On the Education of Children" *(Arminian Magazine,* November-December 1783). Far from sacrificing quality of thought to broad appeal, Wesley's later discourse respects the common reader's intellect, for the sermons—like such mass-audience matter for the mind as the popularizations of electrical science and natural philosophy, the reviews of philosophical books, and the annotations to the *Essay Concerning Human Understanding*—reflect a consistently functioning, often explicit theologizing of Locke's empiricism.

Thus, Wesley's works disseminated empiricism as well as evangelicalism, and their influence underscores his importance in the world of letters. His determination to make challenging books available in brief and handy, yet attractive and durable form means, among other things, that he was a Mortimer J. Adler: his abridgments in particular amount to a *synopticon* of many "great books of the Western world." *A Christian Library: Consisting of Extracts from and Abridgments of the Choicest Pieces of Practical Divinity, which have been Publish'd in the English Tongue* (1749-1755) is a logical product of his prolific editorial pen; but his scientific encyclopedia for the common reader, *A Survey of the Wisdom of God in the Creation: or A Compendium of Natural Philosophy*, is also typical of him; and these collections of abridgments were read as companion sets, as an interdisciplinary *vade mecum*, for more than one hundred years.

Wesley preaching near Gwennap, Cornwall (nineteenth-century print)

Wesley, moreover, was something of a DeWitt Wallace: without diluting the works with which he challenged the common reader and while abjuring mere topicality, he otherwise anticipated *The Reader's Digest;* for by condensing a variety of works and by keeping the cost of his volumes down, he aimed for a large audience. His audience was large, even after his death, or especially then. The Methodist Episcopal church in America grew from a membership of less than ten thousand in 1780, to more than five hundred thousand by 1830. A similar pattern obtained in England; although Methodists made up only about five percent of the adult British population in I 840, they were the largest and most influential element in a much wider constituency. By 1851 there were more than two million Sunday-school scholars in England alone, six hundred thousand of whom were Methodists, and they represented seventy-six percent of working-class children between the ages of five and fifteen. The second half of the nineteenth century and at least the first part of the twentieth belonged to the evangelicals, who, even when their numbers were small, represented an especially significant Anglo-American trend, not least because their "social contract" originated in the decidedly "Lockean" as well as simply Christian "societies" that flourished among Methodists on both sides of the Atlantic during the eighteenth century. "Reading Christians," declared Wesley, "will be knowing Christians." The statement suggests a twofold ambition: first, to make the rising middle class of the Anglo-American world literate and second, to educate that class about science as well as theology. By insuring the "spiritual sense" of transatlantic culture, he insured, as well, a continuing unity of it, for epistemology and ontology, however esoteric, filter down to those who live within a worldview, distinct from those who create it (witness the analogy of "Freudians" who do not read Sigmund Freud).

Insofar as Wesley shaped an eighteenth and even nineteenth-century mode of thought and feeling, a mode in which sense perception of natural things formed the model for "sense perception" of the divine, the evangelical and the Lockean understandings of experience came together for, and in, the Anglo-American middle class. An Anglo-American character arising from the empirical as well as evangelical emphasis of the eighteenth century finds mature expression in the vital synthesis, the complex entity, of British and American letters. *Locke, Wesley, and the Method of English Romanticism* (1984) seeks to demonstrate that Wesley absorbed and spiritualized the epistemology of Locke and then, through a sometimes direct but more often indirect and rather complex process of cultural osmosis, passed on to William Blake, William Wordsworth, Samuel Taylor Coleridge, Percy Bysshe Shelley, and John Keats a method for both their natural observation and their "spiritual experience." British authors such as Thomas Carlyle, George Eliot, and Alfred, Lord Tennyson, and American authors such as Ralph Waldo Emerson, Herman Melville, and Emily Dickinson descend spiritually and intellectually from Wesley insofar as all of them theologize empiricism, ground transcendentalism in mind and world, balance religious myths and religious morality with scientific reverence for fact and detail, ally empirical assumptions with spiritual discipline, and share, above all, the simultaneously rational and sensationalist reliance on experience as the avenue to knowledge, both natural and spiritual.

LETTERS
The Letters of the Rev. John Wesley, A.M., Sometime Fellow of Lincoln College, Oxford, 8 volumes, edited by John Telford (London: Epworth Press, 1931);
Letters I-II, edited by Frank Baker, volumes 25 and 26 of *The Works of John Wesley*, edited by Baker and Richard P. Heitzenrater (Oxford: Clarendon Press, 1980).

BIBLIOGRAPHIES

Frank Baker, *A Union Catalogue of the Publications of John and Charles Wesley* (Durham, N.C.: Divinity School, Duke University, 1966);

Samuel J. Rogal, "The Wesleys: A Checklist of Critical Commentary," *Bulletin of Bibliography*, 28 (April 1971): 22-35;

Richard Green, *The Works of John and Charles Wesley*, revised edition (New York: AMS Press, 1976);

Kenneth E. Rowe, *United Methodist Studies: Basic Bibliographies* (Nashville: Abingdon Press, 1987).

BIOGRAPHIES

Robert Southey, *The Life of Wesley; and Rise and Progress of Methodism*, 2 volumes (London: Printed for Longman, Hurst, Rees, Orme & Brown, 1820); third edition, with notes by Samuel Taylor Coleridge and remarks on Wesley by Alexander Knox, edited by Charles Cuthbert Southey (London: Longman, Brown, Green & Longmans, 1846);

Luke Tyerman, *The Life and Times of the Rev. John Wesley*, 3 volumes (London: Hodder & Stoughton, 1870, 1871; New York: Harper, 1872);

V. H. H. Green, *The Young Mr. Wesley: A Study of John Wesley and Oxford* (New York: St. Martin's Press, 1961);

Martin Schmidt, *John Wesley: A Theological Biography*, 2 volumes (New York: Abingdon Press, 1961);

Richard P. Heitzenrater, *The Elusive Mr. Wesley* (Nashville: Abingdon Press, 1984).

REFERENCES

Henry Abelove, *The Evangelist of Desire: John Wesley and the Methodists* (Stanford: Stanford University Press, 1991);

Richard E. Brantley, "The Common Ground of Wesley and Edwards," *Harvard Theological Review*, 83 (forthcoming 1991);

Brantley, "Johnson's Wesleyan Connection," *Eighteenth-Century Studies*, 10 (Winter 1976/1977): 143-168;

Brantley, "Keats's Method," *Studies in Romanticism*, 22 (Fall 1983): 389-405;

Brantley, *Locke, Wesley, and the Method of English Romanticism* (Gainesville: University of Florida Press, 1984);

Brantley, *Wordsworth's "Natural Methodism"* (New Haven: Yale University Press, 1975);

Richard Carwardine, *Transatlantic Revivalism: Popular Evangelicalism in Britain and America, 1790-1865* (Westport, Conn.: Greenwood Press, 1978);

Valentine Cunningham, *Everywhere Spoken Against: Dissent in the Victorian Novel* (Oxford: Clarendon Press, 1975);

Donald Davie, *A Gathered Church: The Literature of the English Dissenting Interest* (London & Henley: Routledge, 1978);

Frederick Dreyer, "A 'Religious Society under Heaven': John Wesley and the Identity of Methodism," *Journal of British Studies*, 25 (January 1986): 62-83;

Martha England and John Sparrow, *Hymns Unbidden: Donne, Herbert, Blake, Emily Dickinson, and the Hymnographers* (New York: New York Public Library, 1966);

F. C. Gill, *The Romantic Movement and Methodism: A Study of English Romanticism and the Evangelical Revival* (London: Epworth Press, 1937);

James L. Golden, "John Wesley on Rhetoric and Belles Lettres," *Speech Monographs*, 28 (November 1961): 250-264;

A. W. Harrison, "Romanticism and Religious Revivals," *Hibbert Journal*, 31 (July 1933): 579-591;

Grace Elizabeth Harrison, *Haworth Parsonage: A Study of Wesley and the Brontës* (London: Wesley Historical Society, 1937);

F. Brompton Harvey, "Methodism and the Romantic Movement," *London Quarterly and Holborn Review*, 159 (July 1934): 289-302;

David Hempton, *Methodism and Politics in British Society 1750-1850* (Stanford: Stanford University Press, 1984);

T. Walter Herbert, *John Wesley as Editor and Author* (Princeton: Princeton University Press, 1940);

Elisabeth Jay, *The Religion of the Heart: Anglican Evangelicalism and the Nineteenth-Century Novel* (Oxford: Clarendon Press, 1979);

T. W. Laquer, *Religion and Respectability: Sunday Schools and Working Class Culture 1780-1850* (New Haven: Yale University Press, 1976);

George Lawton, *John Wesley's English: A Study of His Literary Style* (London: Allen & Unwin, 1962);

Kenneth MacLean, *John Locke and English Literature of the Eighteenth Century* (New Haven: Yale University Press, 1936);

Mark A. Noll, "Romanticism and the Hymns of Charles Wesley," *Evangelical Quarterly*, 46 (1974): 195-223;

Bernard Semmel, *The Methodist Revolution* (New York: Basic Books, 1973);

T. B. Shepherd, *Methodism and the Literature of the Eighteenth Century* (London: Epworth Press, 1940);

G. H. Vallins, *The Wesleys and the English Language* (London: Epworth Press, 1957).

PAPERS

The major collection of Wesley materials is at the John Rylands University Library of Manchester, which houses the vast Methodist Archives. Other important collections are at the British Library; Perkins Library, Duke University; Beinecke Library, Yale University; the Emory University Library; and the Southern Methodist University Library.

2. An Orientation to Locke, Wesley, and the Method of English Romanticism

Probably when our unified field theory of British Romanticism finally arrives, the materials will be somewhat nearer at hand than either the distant past of Milton or the far future of Joyce. . . . Thinking about British Romanticism primarily in connection with the eighteenth century may not taste quite so sublime to our intellectual palates; but perhaps our taste has become a bit depraved.[1]

No matter how direct the attempt at revival, the near influence is always telling. For example, Hollywood's conception of Imperial Rome fluctuates according to "modern" rather than Roman styles of costuming: compare Claudette Colbert's Cleopatra in 1932 with Elizabeth Taylor's in 1963. The buildings of Balliol College, Oxford, attempt a direct reproduction of the medieval, but are finally Victorian: their designers saw the Romanesque through neo-Georgian and "gothick" eyes. Wordsworth begins his *Prelude* in the new world atmosphere of the end of *Paradise Lost*, but he could not escape what lay between him and Milton: the near influence on the Romantic revival of far-off things is the eighteenth century. I argue here that an important aspect of that century, and hence of the near influence on Romanticism, is John Wesley's dialectic of philosophy and faith.

The founder of Methodism, of course, did not think of himself primarily as a philosopher, but, according to my point of view, Wesley (1703-91) was decidedly philosophical, or at any rate philosophically theological: his theology, if not his faith, relates clearly to the empirical philosophy in *An Essay concerning Human Understanding* (1690) by John Locke (1632-1704). By exploring the intellectual atmosphere of Wesley's formative years and by drawing out the intellectual content of his prose, I have found that the experiential emphasis of his theology derives, in large measure, from the experiential emphasis of Locke. I can show, moreover, by pointing to disseminations of his works and by pursuing his specifically philosophical (as well as otherwise intellectual) influence that writers as well as readers within his revival responded not only to his spiritual experience but also to his philosophical theology. His methodology, among some followers, served as the model for putting experience into words.

Finally, and in accord with his intellectual influence, I apply a philosophically theological perspective to British Romanticism. Specifically, I reveal that Wesley's mediation of Locke's thought is an immediate context of English Romantic poetry: Blake, Wordsworth, Coleridge, Shelley, and Keats, whatever their differences from each other, resemble each other in their formulations of experience, which echo Wesley's. His works were prominent among models of intellectual synthesis available to Romantic England, and, in consequence, I show how English Romantic poetry (and some English Romantic prose and some writers as early as Cowper and as late as the Victorians) rests on the Wesleyan (and historicist) assumption that words and concepts arise from experience both natural and spiritual.

My thesis, in short, is twofold. First, Locke's theory of knowledge grounds the intellectual method of Wesley's Methodism. And second, Wesley's Lockean thought (i. e., his reciprocating notions that religious truth is concerned with experiential presuppositions, and that experience itself need not be non-religious) provides a ready means of understanding the "religious " empiricism and the English "transcendentalism" of British Romantic poetry.

My title suggests my interest in the eighteenth century. *Locke, Wesley, and the Method of English Romanticism* conveys not only the direction of my argument, but also the centrality of Wesley thereto. Thus I hope to contribute to Wesleyan studies as well as to studies in Romanticism.

For students of Romanticism, if not for eighteenth-century scholars, I affirm at the outset Wesley's more than merely pietistic stance. By epitomizing his theology, by outlining the basis for, and urgency of, aligning him with Locke's *Essay*, by countering, specifically, the view of Wesley (especially among students of the Enlightenment) as narrow-mindedly outside the intellectual moving force of his century, and, finally, by calling attention to his language as a study in its own right, I define my terms, and orient my reader (whether "Romantic" or "neoclassical" in temperament, or whether a little of both) to my central figure.

The comprehensiveness of Wesley's understanding, if not the originality of his mind, is now well established. His thought, for example, presides over a range of doctrines, and derives from such traditions as his native Puritan, the continental Protestant, and even the Catholic.[2] Moreover, the boldly mediating quality of his "rationalist, traditionalist, and biblicist" (as well as simply "pragmatist") intellect is guided (if not determined) by the Anglican *via media* that lies between "the Scylla of Rome and the Charybdis of Wittenburg."[3] Students of Methodism have tended to see him as a significant but not significantly intellectual religious activist, but in *The Methodist Revolution* (1973) Bernard Semmel has laid to rest the assumption that Wesley's practice completely characterizes his historical contribution and his faith.[4] Wesley's religious feeling, though intuitional and in a sense distinct from his intellectual belief, is generally grounded in his spiritual discipline and particularly related to his intellectual tradition. Jacobus Arminius's theology of free will, as opposed to John Calvin's doctrine of predestination, strengthened Wesley's resolve to perform deeds of kindness. Arminius's theology of universal redemption, as opposed to Calvin's doctrine of election, generally deepened Wesley's fervor in the work of saving souls.

The force of Wesley's revival, then, derives in no small measure from the liberating energies of his thought: his strength of mind matches his work in the world. His revival remains revolutionary, of course, insofar as it reflects his sometimes anti-ecclesiastical disregard for Church order. Witness this exchange between the bold young clergy man and Joseph Butler, Bishop of Bristol:

> Butler: You have no business here. You are not commissioned to preach in this diocese. Therefore I advise you to go hence.
> Wesley: My lord, my business on earth is to do what good I can. Wherever therefore I think I can do most good, there must I stay so long as I think so. At present I think I can do most good here. Therefore here I stay.[5]

But Wesley was far from being mindlessly iconoclastic. Though his itinerant ministry led to the founding of a great world church, his thoughtful love of the Established Church kept his societies from ever formally separating during his lifetime.[6] And his love of all Christian thought steadied the momentum of his Methodism. The variety of views that all more or less insistently claim to characterize the essence of his religious thought reveals that the synthesizing range of his traditionalist imagination offered to his age not only the power and the form but also the substance of his Christian heritage.

A logical next step for the study of his theology, and the step that I am taking, is to answer the question of its philosophical dimension. "The Philosophy of Enthusiasm," by J. Clifford Hindley, links Moravian theology to Wesley's conversion but is also careful to speculate that Wesley's "philosophical studies partly supplied . . . the framework into which the teaching of the Moravians and his own experience was to be fitted."[7] Hindley's essay set me on the course I follow here.

Here, in brief, is Hindley's point, together with some pertinent history. The conversion took place at "a quarter to nine" on the evening of May 24, 1738, "in Aldersgate Street," London, where, upon hearing William Holland, a Moravian brother, read "Luther's preface to the Epistle to the Romans," Wesley felt his heart "strangely warmed"; Holland "was describing," wrote Wesley, "the change which God works in the heart through faith in Christ. "[8] Hindley argues that this experience, which was not only Wesley's conversion, but also the seed of Methodism, was facilitated by the Moravians' founding of their doctrine of assurance on Rom. 8:15:

> For ye have not received the Spirit of bondage again to fear; but ye have received the Spirit of adoption, whereby we cry, Abba, Father.[9]

But Hindley is concerned as well with whether Wesley's sudden conviction of grace was "largely determined" by the bold, but not so sudden, stroke of replacing the "metaphysical question" of knowledge of God with "the fundamentally epistemological question 'How can I know that I am saved?'" (Hindley, p. 99). "Only through experience," came the answer. What Hindley implies is that Wesley's "empiricist conditioning," if not his training in empiricism, taught him so much respect for experience as the necessary ground of knowledge that Wesley's quest for "a direct experience of the divine love" was necessarily quasi-philosophic (Hindley, pp. 107-8).

Thus, Hindley's essay announces a fresh approach to Wesley's entire career as well as to the central event of his life. His conversion has been thoroughly analyzed from exclusively theological points of view and even from the perspective of psychology.[10] Recently, a psychological approach to the entire career has proved especially fruitful: Robert L. Moore's *John Wesley and Authority* follows Erikson's *Young Man Luther* and *Gandhi's Truth* to "a psychological perspective" on the role of authority in Wesley's religious personality.[11] John Telford showed long ago that Wesley was simply expressing sincere fervor and not some psychologically based disrespect when he stood on his father's tomb and preached to more people than would fit inside the church at

Epworth,[12] but one is tempted to see in this gesture, if not something Freudian, then in Moore's terms the dynamic influence of authority on Wesley's emergent religious identity. One may be equally attracted, though, to Hindley's disciplinary emphasis, for one is led by Hindley to draw a parallel between Wesley's conversion and such resurgences of empiricism as that of A. J. Ayer, whose "verification principle" demanded that "for a proposition to have meaning we must adduce some human experience by which its truth or falsity may be tested."[13] One is intrigued, too, by Hindley's preliminary conclusion that Wesley's appeal to experience, far from being "an odd idiosyncrasy with dangerous subjective tendencies," offered "an essentially right way" to reorient theology "in the face of philosophical empiricism" and therefore amounted to "the supreme apologetic for Christian faith in eighteenth-century England" (Hindley, pp. 202, 209).

Hindley, alas, is not concerned to search out Wesley's particular responses to philosophers and so does not confront the question of direct influence, but "The Philosophy of Enthusiasm" has more than sufficed to suggest to me that Wesley's language for "that faith which none can have without knowing that he hath it" (Curnock, 1:424) is not far from the experiential language of Locke. Hindley's essay, moreover, has accompanied my research into Wesley's experiential theology. Hindley's subtitle "A Study in the Origins of Experimental Theology" connotes like *experiential theology* the particular method whereby such religious problems as the knowledge of salvation (though not, to be sure, how far predestination extends) appear to arise from (if not always to be solved at) the times and places of one's sense-oriented as well as mental life. In this connection, it is worth mentioning that the term common in both Moravian theology and one of Wesley's most characteristic doctrines is also common in the experiential English philosophy of Locke's *Essay: "Assurance"* is Locke's name for the *"highest degree of Probability" (Essay* 4.16.6; Nidditch, pp. 661-62). It is worth noting too that Wesley's sometimes antiauthoritarian stance can be seen in the light of his philosophical background: Locke argued that "a Man shall never want crooked Paths to walk in . . . where-ever he has the Foot-steps of others to follow" *(Essay* 4.20.17; Nidditch, p. 719).

Alfred H. Body, unlike Hindley, is concerned with Wesley's responses to Locke's thought in particular; Body, for example, answers why Wesley required the *Essay* in the fourth year at Wesley's Kingswood School.[14] Wesley's educational theory follows Locke's *Thoughts concerning Education* (1693) in holding that the design of education should counterbalance any bias of nature. Locke's very wording, as Body demonstrates, is reflected in Wesley's ban on holidays, his rules against play, and his insistence upon simplicity of diet and starkness of accommodation. The Lockean root of his educational theory is worthy of further examination, especially in view of *John Locke and Children's Books in Eighteenth-Century England*, in which Samuel Pickering, Jr., has recently explored *Thoughts concerning Education* in conjunction with the children's literature to which eighteenth-century evangelicalism, too, is surely pertinent; "I approached children's books," writes Pickering in his preface, "from the perspective of my earlier study of evangelicalism in the novel. Instead of finding religion on every page, however, I discovered the ideas of John Locke."[15] Finding the ideas of Locke on many pages of late eighteenth-and early nineteenth-century literature, adult if not children's, does not exclude but rather, as I hope to demonstrate, all but signals the discovery of evangelical religion on those same pages. One might look, in this connection, at David Fordyce's *Thoughts concerning Education* (London, 1745), which applies Lockean premises to religious education.

The starting point for any further discussion of Wesley's Lockean thought, educational and otherwise, is obviously his denial of innate ideas. His sermon "On the Discoveries of Faith," for example, begins thus:

> For many ages it has been allowed by sensible men, *Nihil est in intellectu quod non fuit prius in sensu:* That is, "There is nothing in the understanding which was not first perceived by some of the senses." . . . [T]his point has now been thoroughly discussed by men of the most eminent sense and learning; and it is agreed by all impartial persons, that although some things are so plain and obvious, that we can very hardly avoid knowing them as soon as we come to the use of our understanding; yet the knowledge even of those is not innate, but derived from some of our senses. (Jackson, 7:231; Yarmouth, June 11, 1788)

These sentences epitomize the main point in Book 1 of the *Essay* and indeed in the *Essay* as a whole. They make one wonder how far, and in what ways, not just this sermon but the generality of Wesley's works operates according to this particular Lockean premise and Lockean premises in general. I am concerned not with Wesley's Lockean theory of education so much as with the Lockean aspect of all of his thought. I am interested in the impact thereon of the *Essay* rather than *Thoughts concerning Education*, or, for that matter, any other works of Locke, each of which, besides being less inclusive and less important than the *Essay*, is of far less significance than the *Essay* to the history of Wesley's mind and the outpouring of his pen.

Martin Schmidt, in perhaps the broadest (and at any rate one of the most valuable) studies of Wesley's intellectual life, mentions Wesley's concurrence in Locke's denial of innate ideas.[16] And Gerald R. Cragg, in his recent edition of the two "Appeals to Men of Reason and Religion" (1743-45), observes that in the following passage from the first, "An Earnest Appeal," "Wesley 's interpretation of the senses is a part of the epistemology he derived from Locke":

> [B]efore it is possible for you to form a true judgment of the things of God, it is absolutely necessary that you have a clear apprehension of them, and that your ideas thereof be all *fixed, distinct, and determinate.* And seeing our ideas are not all innate, but must originally come from our senses, it is certainly necessary that you have senses capable of discerning objects of this kind: Not those only which are called natural senses, which in this respect profit nothing, as being altogether incapable of discerning objects of a spiritual kind; but spiritual senses, exercised to discern spiritual good and evil. It is necessary that you have the hearing ear, and the seeing eye, emphatically so called; that you have a new class of senses opened in your soul, not depending on organs of flesh and blood, to be "the evidence of things not seen" [cf. Heb. 11:1], as your bodily senses are of visible things; to be the avenues to the invisible world, to discern spiritual objects, and to furnish you with ideas of what the outward "eye hath not seen, neither the ear heard" [cf. I Cor. 2:9]. (Cragg, p. 57)

(Wesley's second "Appeal" is "A Farther Appeal." Both "Appeals" and their announcement of the doctrine of the spiritual sense are discussed in chapter 2 of *Locke, Wesley, and the Method of English Romanticism.*) The sense-based origin of ideas, then, and hence the epistemology of Locke was what Wesley evidently took for granted as the first principle of philosophy. But Cragg neglects to listen for overtones of Locke's sense-based method in any passage other than the one just quoted. And Schmidt nowhere traces the connection between Wesley's "theological biography" and his denial of innate ideas.

This is not surprising, perhaps, in view of the fact that the *Essay*, like its precursors in Greek philosophy, and like its descendants in logical positivism, is skeptical enough to seem alien to theology of any kind. Some orthodox thinkers, from its earliest reception, looked upon it as tending towards religious skepticism: Bishop Edward Stillingfleet, in "A Vindication of the Doctrine of the Trinity" (1696), attacked the *Essay* for being so general in its discussion of faith as to impugn an indispensable Christian tenet; and a sampling of titles—"The danger of corrupting the faith by philosophy" (1697) by William Sherlock; "Remarks upon Mr. Clarke's Sermons, preached at St. Paul's against Hobbs, Spinoza, and other Atheists" (1705) by William Carroll; and, on the continent, "Faith and Reason Compared . . . written . . . by a person of quality in answer to . . . theses drawn from Mr. Locke's Principles" (1713) by Metternich Freiher von Wolf—indicates how other turn-of-century polemicists-for-orthodoxy feared that religious skepticism, and even atheism, were unavoidable corollaries of what they took as Locke's failure to discern that faith and reason are drawn from distinct principles. This interpretation of Locke more or less directly anticipates the now-usual reading of the *Essay* as a determiner of secular thought in the modern world. Geoffrey Hartman, for example, in his influential study of Wordsworth, relies upon Basil Willey's still-heard argument that Locke left a demythologized world in which value and meaning had to be created.[17] Logical positivists are indeed so skeptical as to reject the claims of faith outright. Moritz Schlick, for one, in an argument reminiscent of Hume's, but even more inimical to religion, insists that since religious statements are simply expressions of attitudes, they are meaningless opinions and cannot be verified as knowledge.[18] Greek skepticism, similarly, was less than constructive with regard to faith. Pyrrho of Elis held that sense perception, since it is not known to be false, must not be distrusted on principle, but he was otherwise skeptical: he carried doubt and uncertainty to a greater extreme than either Democritus before him or Arciselaus and Carneades of the later New Academy, and as a result of traveling with Alexander the Great and observing differences between Greek religion and that of Indian fakirs Pyrrho concluded that religion and values are relative.[19]

One should bear in mind, however, that the skepticism of the *Essay* is not directed towards religion. Indeed, by founding a "knowledge" of God's perfection on the "general connexion" among "all parts of the creation," Locke shows himself in essential accord with the spirit of another philosopher, Francis Bacon, who makes the twofold observation in his essay "On Atheism" that "a little Philosophie inclineth to Atheism" but that "depth in Philosophie bringeth Men about to Religion."[20] By the same token, Locke was in agreement with Sir Thomas Browne, who came to faith as Bacon did by means of skeptical method. The *Essay*, far from insisting on religious skepticism, frequently acknowledges the Bible as source of religious knowledge and has been seen accordingly as the friend of revealed as well as natural religion. Since the *Essay* formed an element of the atmosphere in which Robert Boyle, Isaac Newton, John Ray, and Richard Bentley brought about a marriage of science and theology, it should come as no surprise that Socinians, Arians, and Deists regarded Locke as a believer in the God of natural religion. The Deist Matthew Tindal, in 1731, quotes *Essay* 4.16.10 as support for his emphasis on evidence in matters of faith; in 1713, the Deist Anthony Collins cites Locke as the authority for seeing a theological level of meaning in such terms as *evidence, understanding, judge, assent, know, proof,* and *will;* the Deist John Toland, in 1696, uses the language of Lockean epistemology to extol the concept of soul; and the compatibility between Locke and William Whiston, chief Arian and chief descendant of Socinianism, is seen in Locke's express admiration of Whiston's "New Theory of the Earth" (1696).[21] (Locke was a friend of Collins and an acquaintance of Toland.) For one who assumes that the secularist reading of Locke has always prevailed it may come as a surprise that not just proponents of natural religion, but even a proponent or two of revealed religion, were receptive to the *Essay* from the beginning. As early as 1691, for example, in "Reflections upon the Conduct of Human Life" (which incidentally was condensed and published by Wesley in 1735, just before he went to Georgia), the Anglican John Norris was drawn to the *Essay*'s denial of innate ideas; and in 1707, the Anglican Thomas Bray recommended the *Essay*, among other books, as "requisite to be perus' d . . . by the Reverend Clergy."[22]

Bishop Butler and Andrew Baxter, to be sure, are two orthodox apologists from mid-century who shared Bishop Berkeley's well-known view of Locke's philosophy as more or less explicitly materialist, but increasingly both the clergy and Christians in general summoned the *Essay* to defend the faith.[23] By 1747, when Catharine Cockburn linked her moral views to Lockean epistemology,[24] she almost had to do so since Locke was more and more assumed to be correct. Kenneth MacLean in his classic study of the *Essay*'s pervasiveness in eighteenth-century English thought and expression points out that even such conservative divines as William Law and Isaac Watts, and even the evangelical laureate William Cowper, consciously attempted to meet, in Hindley's words, "the philosophical demand for empiricism"; MacLean shows indeed that Bishop Butler, despite his Berkeleian discovery of materialism in the *Essay*, otherwise accepted its "sensational philosophy": Butler argued that the senses are "instruments of our receiving such ideas from external objects, as the Author of nature appointed those external objects to be the occasions of exciting in us."[25]

MacLean, it should be said, remains perhaps the most thorough twentieth-century definer of the *Essay*'s skepticism. It should also be said, however, that like other such definers, and despite his valuable demonstration of Locke's intellectual hegemony, MacLean leaves a somewhat biased impression of the *Essay*. He overemphasizes, or rather presents as the whole truth about Locke, Locke's admittedly major premise that, as MacLean paraphrases (p. 13), "human knowledge is limited." Locke was intent indeed upon tracing "the *cause of Obscurity* in simple *Ideas*" to "dull Organs," "weakness in the Memory," and all the other shortcomings inherent in sense perception *(Essay* 2.23.3; Nidditch, p. 363). MacLean has a sharp eye for such phrases,[26] and one may add to those he cites *Essay* 2.10.5, where Locke sounds this epistemologically elegiac note: "And our Minds represent to us those Tombs, to which we are approaching; where though the Brass and Marble remain, yet the Inscriptions are effaced by time, and the Imagery moulders away" (Nidditch, pp. 151-52). But the relentlessness of MacLean's emphasis can do scant justice to the sort of passage in which a more than expectant strain of rhapsodic optimism determines the tone of Locke's epistemology:

> Nor let any one think [simple ideas] too narrow bounds for the capacious Mind of Man to expatiate in, which takes its flight farther than the Stars, and cannot be confined by the limits of the World; that extends its thoughts often, even beyond the utmost expansion of Matter, and makes excursions into that incomprehensible Inane . . . . Nor will it be so strange, to think these few simple *Ideas* sufficient to employ the quickest Thought, or largest Capacity; and to furnish the Materials of all that various Knowledge, and more various Fancies and Opinions of all Mankind, if we consider how many Words may be made out of the various composition of 24 Letters; or if going one step farther, we will but reflect on the variety of combinations may be made, with barely one of the above-mentioned *Ideas, viz.* Number, whose stock is inexhaustible, and truly infinite: And what a large and immense field, doth Extension alone afford the Mathematicians? *(Essay* 2.7.10; Nidditch, pp. 131-32)

MacLean (p. 83) quotes the passage but does not dwell upon it. Consider also, for example, *Essay* 1.2.14 where Locke strikes an epistemologically robust note by speaking of the "very manifest difference between dreaming of being in the Fire, and being actually in it" (Nidditch, p. 537): Locke trusts sense perception to tell him of a non-illusory world. It is remarkable to find MacLean touching on the *Essay*'s incorporation into Wesley's traditional theology. In recognizing that Wesley "followed Locke in denying innate ideas," that Wesley promoted Locke's view of animals as having degrees of reason and understanding, and that Wesley adopted Locke's principle of accepting as a matter of faith only what is consistent with reason, MacLean (pp. 28, 81, 154) includes Wesley among the Anglicans who represented the growing acceptance of Locke by all stripes of religious thinkers. Horton Davies argues persuasively that Wesley's theology is so squarely in the mainstream as to have been "the bridge that crossed the chasm between . . . Anglicanism and Dissent,"[27] but no one completes the connection MacLean begins to make between Wesley's mainstream theology and the Lockean assumptions of mainstream theology. Donald Greene notes the interaction between empiricism and the Augustan Anglicans, but does not discuss Wesley among them.[28] And V H. H. Green in his study of Wesley's early life and thought recognizes Bishop Butler's attempt to establish the truths of Christianity on Lockean grounds of probability and even grants Butler's *Analogy* a significant position as "the ablest apologetic work" in Wesley's intellectual milieu, but nowhere mentions the fact that, despite Wesley's quarrel with the Bishop over Church order, Wesley fundamentally admired Butler's theology, and so could well have stood with him on its Lockean ground.[29]

MacLean, though, does not develop the parallels he points to and finally insists against his own evidence that Wesley simply "sought personal revelations of the divine will through bibliomancy and other forms of superstitious divination" (p. 154). Whenever Wesley practiced the *Sortes Liturgicae* to find out, for example, whether to go from Bristol to London, and whenever he indulged in divination by verses of the Bible, he was indeed as superstitious as when he entertained belief in ghosts and witches: all of his various forms of divination are so non-philosophical as to hark back, if not to entrail-reading, then to the *Sortes Homericae* of the ancients. His bibliomancy, on the other hand, besides relating to eighteenth-century arguments for providence in "chance" events, regards the interrespondence of mind and externality, and may therefore be said to parallel, if not Jungian synchronicity in today's scheme of things, then the eighteenth-century Lockean view that discrete and casual perceptions form individual stages in the mind's growth and progress in the world.[30] I shall have little more to say of Wesley's bibliomancy, but I suggest, in the context of what I will say of his thought, that even his bibliomancy need not be seen apart from the intellectual context of its age.

I propose, then, affirmatively to answer whether Locke's emphasis on sense perception is what is needed just now in describing the ways of Wesley's mind. Nidditch, in his introduction to his now-standard edition of the *Essay*, defines the epistemology of Locke as an experiential continuum with understanding at one pole and physical sensation at the other: Nidditch formulates, and calls "sensationalistic," the assumption underlying Locke's view of mind as *tabula rasa*—"the ultimate source of all our ideas, and the ultimate required test of all our putative knowledge and beliefs, lie within the bounds of the workings of normal sense—or inner-experience"—and Nidditch rounds out his summary of Locke's thought by observing that in his epistemology the "modest potentialities" of the senses are "circumspectly approached" and "methodically elucidated" (Nidditch, p. x). Nidditch regards the *Essay* as in no small measure "rationalistic" (p. x), but this word, suggesting the dictionary's definition of rationalism (i.e., "the theory that reason is a source of knowledge in itself, superior to and independent of sense perceptions") is sufficiently reminiscent of Cartesian philosophy to be an ill-advised description of Lockean. To be sure, Locke's distinction between beliefs and knowledge, and his accentuation of ideas, amount to an emphasis on mind as complement to the operation of the senses: the senses are prior to mind, but mind responds to sense data. True, too, that Francis Gallaway long ago popularized a blunt claim: "Locke was a rationalist to the core."[31] And V. H. H. Green, in pointing to the presence of the *Essay* in Wesley's intellectual background, labels Locke's philosophy *empirical rationalism*.[32] But words like *rationalism, rationalist,* and *rationalistic* are not finally appropriate.

Locke's philosophy teaches, first, that ideas are the mind's record of what the senses bring; second, that the mind works on these ideas to produce general propositions; third, that these propositions take their place, with ideas, as what the mind works on; fourth, that the mind applies these propositions to problems it confronts; and fifth, that solutions to these problems occur. Anyone who goes through these stages uses his reason both inductively and deductively, and may be said, therefore, to behave reasonably, rationally. But to say that he exemplifies rationalism is to speak confusingly; I have not described what Descartes said *he* thought. I hasten to add, however, that it is not only well advised, but especially necessary at present, to call attention to Locke's emphasis on reason: this emphasis has been neglected, in recent years, by critics who regard his influence on eighteenth-century writers as largely confined to his sense-oriented methodology.[33] If one thinks of

Lockean reason as sense-based, rather than independent of experience, then Gallaway's argument that Lockean reason accounts for the quality of reason in eighteenth-century England holds. *Rational empiricism*, rather than *empirical rationalism*, serves as a fuller and more accurate name for Locke's thought than *empiricism* alone. And *rational* and *reasonable*, rather than *rationalist* and *rationalistic*, are proper descriptions for an important component of his thought. While it is needful to draw a distinction between, say Shaftesbury, Francis Hutcheson, and David Hume, all of whom were sometimes nearly antirational as well as often non-rational, and such *a priori* (albeit English) rationalists as Richard Cumberland, Ralph Cudworth, and Samuel Clarke,[34] it is also needful to see that an ever-increasing (though by no means innate) strength of reason formed such an important part of Locke's empiricism that it should regularly be said to include a specific appeal thereto.

I argue, at any rate, that Locke's rational empiricism (i.e., his epistemology of sense perception attended by induction and deduction) directly informs the religious "epistemology" whereby Wesley claimed the saving faith he felt was his. *(Perception*, distinct from *sense* alone, serves to signal the mental, rational element of Locke's epistemology.) By midcentury both poles of this broadly empirical and quintessentially English philosophy had become so commonplace that they entered, directly and indirectly, non-philosophic forms of English expression: "Reason," writes Sterne, "is half of it, Sense."[35] Wesley, casually employing such phrases as "beyond all sense and reason" (e.g., Curnock, 6:6), and not so casually denouncing Rousseau's *Emile* as "grounded upon neither reason nor experience" (Curnock, 5:353), seems to think of sense-function as necessarily in concert with the distinguishing faculty of mind. The empirically rational assumption underlying these phrases could explain what Sir William Robertson Nicoll observes to be true of Wesley, namely, that while "detached" in "apostolical aloofness," he was at the same time "interested in everything."[36] Without necessarily following Hindley to his notion that empiricism engendered Wesley's conversion, I demonstrate that Wesley's Methodism derived a formal philosophic component from Locke's appeal to the senses and to reason.

This demonstration is sufficiently in line, I think, with just about all that is not ineffable regarding the conversion itself. It seems fair to say, even now, that when Wesley felt his heart warmed while thinking about the doctrine of faith, he (1) had an experience both rational and at least quasi-sensationalistic, and (2) came, then, to understand the experience along lines parallel to the Lockean view, namely, that experience is a complex process with elements each leading back to what the senses tell. I believe, in other words, that the experience of heartwarming was itself not entirely without rational as well as sense-like dimensions, and moreover that when he applied the experience in his further thinking, he was in his own view acting as a man "of reason and religion" indeed, i.e., not just as a man who in the general sense uses his mind critically and also worships God, but also as a man who, in a particular and historically appropriate sense, finds that his twice-born Christianity and his rational empiricism are strangely analogous to one other.

My view that Locke's influence on Wesley included an appeal to sense-based reason is implied only by Francis McConnell and V H. H. Green. Green, exploring Wesley's intellectual background, mentions Locke's analysis of "the natural faculties," i.e., the senses, as a central part of his philosophy, but emphasizes that reason in general, i.e., "the exercise of the intellect and an orderly, logical process of thought," and "the harmonious relationship of faith and reason" in particular, also formed important elements of the *Essay*.[37] McConnell, in his biography of Wesley, identifies Locke with "the Age of Reason."[38] But McConnell, asserting that "the Age of Reason" came "to an end" because of "the Wesleyan Movement," implies that an Age of Reason cannot also be an Age of Religion. And Green does not pursue the possibility that a reasonable as well as deeply felt faith was both a Wesleyan and a rather Lockean property. Indeed Green does not at all attempt to establish the nature of the Lockean presence in Wesley's early intellectual milieu, but my first and third chapters, especially, further acknowledge Green's otherwise useful study. No student of Wesley's intellectual life, then, has hitherto specifically realized that insofar as his spiritual experience is, to recall Nidditch, "circumspectly approached" and "methodically elucidated" by his theological argumentation, his thought is intimately related to the methodology through which Locke granted to the mind a limited license to perceive the truth and entertain belief.

Reality appears to the reader of the *Essay* as a balance between matter and mind, or rather, to borrow M. H. Abrams's words, as an "interpenetration" and "coalescence" of subject and object.[39] Wesley's exclamation that "None can have general good sense unless they have clear and determinate ideas of all things" (Telford, 6:130) does more than simply paraphrase *Essay* 3's discussion of the causes of confusion among men: Wesley surely signals, in his remark, his agreement with Locke's argument that the mind forms a link with external reality. It cannot be said that Wesley attained to the sophistication with which Coleridge, for example, was to understand objective and subjective reality:

> The groundwork, therefore, of all true philosophy [said Coleridge] is the full apprehension of the difference between . . . that intuition of things which arises when we possess ourselves, as one with the whole . . . and that which presents itself when . . . we think of ourselves as separated beings, and place nature in antithesis to the mind, as object to subject, thing to thought, death to life.[40]

But it can be said, with Hindley, that Wesley's doctrines of the "Direct Witness" and the "Witness of Our Own Spirit" amount to an understanding of subject and object, and hence to philosophical as well as theological components of his thought:

> [T]here is no . . . clear distinction in religious experience [writes Hindley] between the objective source of illumination and the subjective perception of that illumination. Insofar, therefore, as Wesley intended by "the Witness of Our Own Spirit" an immediate consciousness of God's working in the heart, we must conclude that it is empirically indistinguishable from what Wesley describes as the Witness of God's Spirit. (p. 204)

And it should be said, in line with this Wesleyan counterpart to Coleridge's "one with the whole," that Wesley was in the simultaneously "tough-minded" and "tender-minded" tradition of intellectual history. To that paradoxical tradition, William James notably assigns the *Essay*: it is "tender-minded," argues James, in being "rationalistic, intellectualistic, idealistic, optimistic, religious, free-willist, monistic, and dogmatical"; yet it is somehow also "tough-minded," i.e., "empiricist, sensationalistic, materialistic, pessimistic, irreligious, deterministic, pluralistic, and skeptical."[41]

Regardless of whether these sometimes wholly irreconcilable pairings can in every case be applied to the *Essay* (was Locke monistic? dogmatical? irreligious? pluralistic?), it can be argued here that like Locke, Wesley was constructively skeptical; and it can also be argued that though he cannot any more than Locke be described as pluralistic and irreligious, though he was certainly not any more than Locke monistic, and though he was not even conceivably either materialistic or pessimistic, he was somehow sensationalistic and empiricist and at the same time free-willist, religious, optimistic, idealistic, intellectualistic, and generally reasonable, though never quite rationalistic. Isaac Watts, incidentally, showed a similar blend of tough-mindedness and tendermindedness: his *Logic*, according to MacLean, "moderated and softened" Locke's philosophy, but it should be remembered, as MacLean points out, that in the preface to *Philosophical Essays* Watts speaks of the *Essay*'s many "truths" and emphasizes that they are "worthy of Letters of Gold."[42]

I know that my allusion to William James goes far towards implying that Locke and Wesley shared just about everything, but I run this risk of overstatement in order to cast my net as widely as possible. There is a particular need to do so, for it is the general rule that, notwithstanding such exceptions as Leslie Stephen, students of the Enlightenment don't read Wesley. Taking little or no notice of Wesleyan scholarship, they regard him as an unenlightened anachronism at worst and, at best, as a nonintellectual contrast to, and impediment of, Enlightenment thinkers.[43]

His own age, it is true, charged him with enthusiasm, or "a false pretension of an Extraordinary divine assistance"; Albert M. Lyles has amply documented the fact that Wesley-as-religious-fanatic was the polemicists' image of him.[44] But their image is wrong. "Wesley," as I have elsewhere argued, "though he conceded the occurrence of too many false claims to inspiration, defended the possibility of a 'genuine' Extraordinary witness, to be 'known by its fruits'"; and he could hardly have been both an enthusiast and a follower of John Locke: Locke's strictures against enthusiasm are well known.[45] From his congregations, to be sure, Wesley sometimes heard "loud cries," but by 1759 at least he was careful to judge such outbursts according to their measure of "love and joy" and to correct them when he found "sorrow and fear" (Curnock, 4:344). He everywhere inveighed, moreover, against the "false pretension" to "Extraordinary divine assistance"; the following instance is typical:

> I was both surprised and grieved at a genuine instance of enthusiasm. J[ohn] B[rown], of Tanfield Lea, who had received a sense of the love of God a few days before, came riding through the town, hallooing and shouting, and driving all the people before him, telling them God had told him he should be a king, and should tread all his enemies under his feet. I sent him home immediately to his work, and advised him to pray day and night to God, that he might be lowly in heart, lest Satan should again get an advantage over him.[46]

It is no wonder that Georges III and IV looked upon the revival as a force for stability. Especially when it came to political affairs and social order, Wesley rejected the extremes of Puritan fervor, despite the fact that he was affected by the character and sufferings of the Puritans: on his circuit riding, he customarily noted the destruction wrought by the "enthusiastic fury" of Cromwell's wars; Cromwell, said Wesley, was "as far from being a Christian as Henry VIII"; and, in December of 1768, because of increasing trouble in America, and because of the public outcry over the imprisonment of John Wilkes, Member for Middlesex, Wesley expressed his fears concerning "a second Cromwell" and "a field of blood."[47] Finally, I see something detached and philosophic, if not William Jamesian and scientific, in Wesley's straightforward accounts of such experiences as that of Ann Thorn, "who had been several times in trances," and "claimed" to have sojourned "in another world, knowing nothing that was done or said by all that were round about" (Curnock, 4:344).

It is an indication of my view of Wesley that the blend of English mind and religious temper with which he was endowed assured him a place in the Enlightenment of which Locke's theological as well as philosophical *Essay* was a major manifesto. In addition to the "natural faculties" of the senses and the thereby aided reason, the *Essay* includes revelation as a means of understanding, and, insofar as Wesley mastered the *Essay*, followed its principles, spread its message, reconciled it with his faith, and incorporated it into his philosophical theology, he not only participated as such an enlightened man in that Enlightenment but also contributed to it.

I am far from meaning by this sub-thesis that Wesley approved of the continental Enlightenment. At worst, he was unaware of the *philosophes*, for he nowhere mentions Kant, and at best he was ambivalent: admiring Voltaire as "a very lively writer, of a fine imagination," and respecting the "judgment" of both Voltaire and Rousseau, Wesley nevertheless denounced them because they "contributed all their labours" to "extol humanity to the skies, as the very essence of religion."[48] It is no wonder, in view of this denunciation, that in his usage *this enlightened age* was ironic and satirical.[49] The *philosophes*, as Henry May puts it, "could not get out of their systems . . . the deductive method of Descartes";[50] and Wesley's more negative than positive attitude toward Cartesian thought is farther evidence, if evidence is needed, of his distance from the continental Enlightenment. Insofar as he admired Nicolas Malebranche, who owed a debt to Descartes's deductive powers, Wesley undoubtedly recognized both those powers and, at least subconsciously, Descartes as wielder of them, but insofar as Wesley approached Cartesian thought at all, he should be said to have approached it from his English perspective: the works of John Norris, who was influenced by Descartes as well as Locke, and Berkeley's *Alciphron*, which, besides counter-interpreting Locke's *Essay*, assimilates Malebranche and hence in part Descartes, were objects of Wesley's praise.[51] Wesley, far from being in any essential sympathy with Cartesian philosophy, was finally, and from an empirical point of view, more than dubious about the results of Cartesian method, for he attacked Cartesian astronomy for being, like Ptolemaic, incapable of "solid, convincing proof" (Jackson, 13:490-91), and, by way of challenging the Cartesian view that self-knowledge, presumably "the most useful, the most necessary" kind, is certain and inevitable, he cast doubt on the *cogito* (Jackson, 13:497). (Wesley specifically scorned Descartes's notion that "the soul is lodged in the pineal gland.") Hindley is correct, then, to assert that Descartes, when present in Wesley's thinking, "is very much in the background of it" (Hindley, p. 209).

But Wesley was necessarily near the *Essay*-dominated Anglo-American Enlightenment. Though Nidditch points to important channels of the early "diffusion of Locke's epistemology in Europe," and though Peter Gay and Paul Hazard demonstrate that the *Essay* remained a staple of the continental Enlightenment until, as Hazard puts it, "Kant came on the scene,"[52] the *Essay* enjoyed a more long-lasting acceptance, and a greater one, in the English-speaking world. "Colonial readers of modern philosophy," writes May, "started with Locke's *Essay*, which they knew much better before the Revolution than his *Two Treatises on Government*"; and May points out that Locke, as representative of the "Moderate or Rational Enlightenment," continued to be admired in America well after, say, 1815, when such representatives of the "Skeptical Enlightenment" as Hume and Voltaire, and such an epitome of the "Revolutionary Enlightenment" as Rousseau, had begun to come under attack.[53] J.G. A. Pocock, for one, is not entirely comfortable with the notion of an English Enlightenment, but the *Essay*'s influence on such varied English thinkers as Isaac Newton, Anthony Collins, Bernard Mandeville, George Berkeley, Lord Bolingbroke, David Hume, Lord Kames, Adam Smith, Horace Walpole, Joseph Priestley, Edmund Burke, and Thomas Paine justifies calling Locke, if not the father of the English Enlightenment, then the progenitor of an eighteenth-century intellectual tradition at many points linked to the continental Enlightenment.[54] Without denying Gay's view of the continental Enlightenment as "the rise of modern paganism," and indeed by way of cooperating with Gay's effort to avoid "compact" definitions of the Enlightenment ("Hume's scepticism," "Diderot's vitalism," "Rousseau's passion"), I suggest in these pages that Wesley helped to assure both depth and breadth in the Anglo-American Enlightenment, which, largely because of him and Jonathan Edwards, lacked the narrow-if-not-benighted anticlericalism of the Enlightenment on the continent.[55] Insofar as a methodology of the entire Enlightenment, i.e., the Lockean, illuminates Wesley's method, he is part of the Enlightenment as generally understood, and I contend that, besides playing an essential role in the spiritual enlightenment of England (if not America) during the eighteenth century, he fostered a particularly Lockean as well as generally intellectual kind of illumination and was thus an Enlightenment figure *par excellence.*[56]

His definition of logic (he published a *Logic*) as "a proper use of deductive and inductive reasoning and of accurate evidence" (Curnock, 3:391) can serve, in advance of farther argument, to epitomize his place in the Enlightenment. The definition's element of deduction is at once distinctly continental and sufficiently Lockean. The element of induction, though distinctly Lockean, coexists with a continental spirit, for, though nothing in the *Essay* supports the *cogito* as a decent place to start, a *cogito* that follows actualities imported into the mind through, say, the eye, is warmly embraced by Locke,[57] and Lockean reason relates to Cartesian rationalism insofar as even Lockean reason, making sense of sense-data through reflection, or intuition, is of the mind's very nature. In other words, Wesley's place in the Anglo-American Enlightenment is necessarily also in, or rather quite near, the Enlightenment as a whole. Since he rejected the doctrine of innate ideas, he regarded ideas as datable impressions on the mind's white paper, but, despite doubting the *cogito*, he sympathized with a Malebranchian metaphysic and, therefore, undoubtedly (if subconsciously) entertained the notion that ideas possess what Malebranche called "a most real [i.e., Platonic] existence": they are, said Malebranche, "beings and beings spiritual."[58] For Wesley, I suggest, as for Norris and Berkeley, and even as for Locke (insofar as Locke scattered through the *Essay* tinctures of Cartesian thought), ideas are somehow both independent mental entities and the products of shaping forces. Lockean ideas, after all, not only clarify the world, but also themselves become quasi-objective, for "Ideas," in Locke's twofold understanding, are not only "Perceptions in our Minds" but also "modifications in the Bodies that cause such Perceptions in us" *(Essay* 2.8.7; Nidditch, p. 134).

My argument that Wesley's thought is at once rigorous in its conformity to Lockean criteria and important in its impact, direct and indirect, upon English life and letters entails an explicit concern with the various strengths and characteristics of his language. His tones, it is clear, are quite deliberate in their precision and their variety. George Lawton, for example, examines such topics as Wesley's adjectives, his scriptural idiom, his use of familiar speech and aphorisms, his grasp of narrative vocabulary, his figures of speech, and even his lexicography; and T. Walter. Herbert points to the "resonance and force" of the diction in Wesley's hymns and poetry.[59] Wesley's words, moreover, are carefully placed within diverse forms. Herbert goes beyond an emphasis on tone, and beyond an emphasis on the poetry and hymns, to demonstrate the grasp of genre underlying Wesley's journals, his letters, and his editions of fiction and biography. His mastery of nonreligious as well as religious genres, to say nothing, for the moment, of his virtual invention of certain genres, provides the organizing principle of the long-needed and now-in-progress *Oxford Edition of Wesley's Works*.[60] Wesley's structuring powers, like his verbal choices, form an emphasis in Samuel J. Rogal's forthcoming contribution of *The Wesleys* to the Twayne English Author Series.[61] Small wonder, in view of what is being written about Wesley's style, that he admired Swift's description of good writing as "proper words in proper places."[62]

Thus Wesley's standing as a literary figure, his words in structures, has begun to receive the attention it deserves: his two million published words reward attention to form and style as well as content. His blend of his intellectual heritages—Anglican, Dissenting, Puritan, Arminian, Calvinist, Lutheran, Thomistic, Catholic, and Anglo-Catholic— emerges not only from his command of theme but also from his richness of diction, his complexity of tone, his trenchancy, and, in general, his production of such formal and informal, conventional and original genres as diaries, journals, letters, advice to the Methodists, Methodist polity and principles, polemics, appeals, open letters to exponents of religion, apologetics, expositions of doctrine, biblical exegesis, homilies, devotionals, hymns, prayers, and poems. If not from his flexible range of genres and tones, then from my argument in *Locke, Wesley, and the Method of English Romanticism* (chapter 2), it should be clear that his language-as-language, though not the language, surely, of every writer, serenely but markedly plays with differing possibilities and so flatters even the theory of literature as paradox.

The record of his conversation, for one good example now, suggests that his language, if not paradoxical, is never quite predictable in expressing Christian truth, for his responses to his associates on August 1, 1745, at the New Room in Bristol, reveal his flair for distinctions and his sensitivity to nuance:

Q. Does not the truth of the gospel lie very near both to Calvinism and Antinomianism? A. Indeed it does; as it were, within a hair's breadth: So that it is altogether foolish and sinful, because we do not quite agree either with one or the other, to run from them as far as ever we can.

Q. Where in may we come to the very edge of Calvinism?
A. (1) In ascribing all good to the free grace of God. (2) In denying all natural free-will, and all power antecedent to grace. And, (3) In excluding all merit from man; even for what he has or does by the grace of God.

Q. Wherein may we come to the edge of Antinomianism?
A. (1) In exalting the merits and love of Christ. (2) In rejoicing evermore. (Jackson, 8: 284-85)

This language is theologically adventurous. Wesley's joy of salvation, to be sure, like his Christological reference, his emphasis on grace, and his animadversion on the natural state, is sufficiently orthodox. But his Delphic replies are not just bluntly authoritative: they evince his respect for doctrines that he usually found uncongenial (they run counter to his rather more characteristic strictures against Calvinism's "particular" redemption and the predestinarian smugness of its "irresistible grace").[63] And his joy, though hardly anything so heretical as the *fröhliche Wissenschaft* of Nietzsche, i.e., the latter-day "antinomian" headiness of seeing beyond good and evil,[64] exceeds Arminian bounds: Wesley's joy becomes a controlling and almost more than merely theological tone of his replies, which gain in energy from the exuberance of his appreciation for shades of meaning and elements of soundness in a range of doctrines. His thought, in this passage, is rich and complex; for his mind, if not exactly philosophic, is almost so in its synthesizing powers and in its discovery of truth wherever truth is to be found; and his language, though keeping to the Christian-moral interpretation of life, and expressing nothing like Nietzschean nihilism, is nonetheless sufficiently susceptible to the near-nihilistic and Nietzschean criticism whereby Deconstructionists see all modes of expression as playful and life-affirming, but amoral and anything but Christian, acts of joyful wisdom.[65] It is logical, in any case, to read this particular record of Wesley's conversation as at once an illustration of his theological, nay, even philosophic, intelligence, and a token of his primal and literary sense of the antithetical.

Students of his language, despite recognizing it as allusive, have hardly begun to listen for either his generally philosophic or his particularly Lockean voice. They are aware, of course, of his theology: Lawton establishes the conceptual referents, and conceptual resonances, of Wesley's religious vocabulary.[66] But when they focus on his vocabulary, they arc not concerned to relate it to his thought so much as to argue that it is well selected: his diction is indeed the boast of his style. Herbert, in pointing out (p. 41) that Wesley published an abridgment of the *Essay*, connects one of his most characteristic "genres" with the philosophy of John Locke: the abridgment, and Wesley's accompanying remarks on the *Essay*, form a focus of my argument. But not even Herbert specifically raises the question of Wesley's Lockean echoes. And no one has asked whether Lockean language is included among his conscious and other than exclusively religious allusions. James L. Golden acknowledges that Wesley admired Locke's style (philosophy, as Golden also notes, was part of *"belles lettres"* for Wesley);[67] but Golden overlooks the fact that the most important background to Wesley's familiarity with such "new rhetoricians" as Alexander Gerard and Hugh Blair was none other than Locke's *Essay*;[68] and no one has hitherto been in a position to see whether the timely and more than theologically intellectual component of Wesley's expression owed any of its force to the forceful accents of Locke's philosophy. Perhaps the neglect of this question is due to the fact that only one student of Wesley's language, and only a few students of his thought, have looked for his relation to any non-religious eighteenth-century disciplines whatever;[69] but for whatever reason, students of his language have not specifically asked whether either his form and diction or the concepts to which his words refer derive in part from the particularly Lockean context of his age.

It is time, then, to be specifically concerned with the form of his thought and to ask whether a Lockean idiom is central to his discourse. To Lawton's argument that "Wesley's prose is a stout three-fold cord having Scriptural, Classical, and colloquial strands interwoven" (p. 14), I add the thesis of a fourth and further reinforcing strand: the Lockean. While it is true that by the end of the nineteenth century Locke's style was considered dull, wooden, and un-elevated, rather than anything like a model of good prose, it is my contention that Wesley shared the typical eighteenth-century evaluation as represented, say, by Goldsmith, who saw as much clarity and simplicity in Locke's writing as in his understanding.[70] It is my assumption that Locke's emphasis on clarity and simplicity— "[M]ethinks those, who pretend seriously to search after, or maintain Truth, should think themselves obliged to study, how they might deliver themselves without Obscurity, Doubtfulness, or Equivocation, to which Men's Words are naturally liable, if care be not taken" (*Essay* 3.11.3; Nidditch, p. 509)—not only gave Wesley a principle for criticizing terms like legal and legality as "odd, indeterminate, troublesome, silly and unmeaning" (Telford, 5:222; Jackson, 10:369), but also provided him with a guide for avoiding equivocation (though not, to be sure, multi-vocalization) in his own prose. His predilection for similes rests on the fact that as "miniature proverbs" "their basis is the facts of experience" (Lawton, p. 132); and it is specifically Lockean language of experience, as well as experiential language in general, which I think enabled him to raise his ineffable experience of grace to graceful and cogent expressions of methodology.

Experience, of course, is in one sense preverbal. I am thinking of Theodore Roszak's recent definition: "Let me, arbitrarily then, limit experience here to that which is not a report, but knowledge before it is reflected in words or ideas: immediate contact, direct impact, knowledge at its most personal level as it is lived."[71] But Wesley verbalized his experience. And *experience*, throughout this study, is conceived as a continuum from things, through ideas, to words. This conception is in line with Hans Aarsleff's recent book, *From Locke to Saussure: Essays on the Study of Language and Intellectual History*, which argues that even so continental a principle as Saussure's structuralist distinction between signifier and signified derives from such French ideologues as Condillac and, through these French Lockeists, from Locke's "double conformity" thesis that things may conform to ideas and that ideas may conform to words.[72] Experience, in Chomsky's neo-Cartesian view, is in no sense prior to language, but Derek Bickerton's recent book, *Roots of Language*,[73] concludes that prior to language is the experience of distinguishing between the specific and the nonspecific, between state and process, between boundedness and unboundedness in events, and between the causative and the non-causative. I argue, at any rate, that John Wesley's method, if not always self-conscious, is assuredly present throughout his writings: his defenses of faith are enhanced by Locke's experiential idiom, which, though hardly so pervasive in Wesley's works as, say, his scriptural reference, is nonetheless so clearly a major feature of them as to demonstrate that besides being syncretic and steeped in tradition his theology articulates his understanding of empiricism.

I understand *literature*, then, in an inclusive sense indeed. In 1887, pursuant to arguing for English literature as a regular course of study at Oxford, Edward Dowden gave the following view of literary study in general:

> The study of literature, English or other, is not a study solely of what is graceful, attractive, and pleasure-giving in books; it attempts to understand the great thoughts of the great thinkers. To know Greek literature we must know Aristotle; to know French literature we must know Descartes. In English literature of the eighteenth century, Berkeley and Butler and Hume are greater names than Gray and Collins.[74]

Thus Dowden, though biographer of Shelley and critic of Shakespeare, seeks a broader literary canon than the works of major authors such as these, let alone such minor ones as Gray and Collins. E. D. Hirsch, Jr., distinguishing between "the narrower, more decadent conception expressed by *les belles-lettres*" and the "grand, broad, and noble conception" expressed by "*les bonnes-lettres*," quotes Dowden's remarks.[75] For Hirsch defines literature as including both conceptions and even as emphasizing *les bonnes-lettres*: "Literature," declares Hirsch, is "everything worthy to be read, preferably the best thoughts expressed in the best manner, but above all the best thoughts." Exploring *les bonnes-lettres* through the prose of Wesley and *les belles-lettres* through English Romantic poetry, I relate the poetry to the prose and describe the link between the two as not so much hierarchical (is *bonnes* "better" than *belles*?) as dialectical: Romantic poetry, in England, is sufficiently broad and hardly decadent.

With respect to Wesley's prose there is much of "best manner": unfailing readability and no little grace. But there are "best thoughts" above all: I am concerned more with what it says than with the fact that it is written well. Conveying its attractiveness, but stressing its content, I show that empiricism is both a formative influence on it and a constant presence in it. I demonstrate that *theology* is neither so inclusive nor so accurate a label for it as *philosophical theology*. And I suggest that the breadth and substance of the prose together give Wesley a place in *les bonnes-lettres* of eighteenth-century England at least as great as that of "Berkeley and Butler and Hume": Berkeley and Butler blend theology and philosophy, but Wesley is theological where Hume is not.

I propose, finally, that perhaps especially in its philosophical dimension the prose is a means of seeing the influence steadily and whole. I bring Wesley's thought, and even his manner, to bear on the manner and especially the thought of William Blake, William Wordsworth, Samuel Taylor Coleridge, Percy Bysshe Shelley, and John Keats. Thus affirming, with Dowden, that *les belles-lettres* find intellectual contexts in *les bonnes-lettres* ("To know Greek literature we must know Aristotle; to know French literature we must know Descartes"), I assume that to know English Romanticism one should know Wesley. His method, or rather the methodology of his Methodism, is traceable from its Lockean origins to its echoes in *les belles-lettres*; for I reveal that the testimonial idiom of such a representative Romantic as Coleridge coexists with, and subtly transfigures, his empirical language; and I indicate, consistent with the lasting popularity of Wesley's works, that the Wesleyan blend of philosophy and theology is not simply available to, but significantly discernible in, the aesthetic expression of all five major poets (see *Locke, Wesley*, chapter 4).

These poets have never been read against this particular background, but this particular background, surely, is the next one that they should be read against. Wesley's faith, as I contended in Wordsworth's "Natural Methodism," is more than simply prelusive to Wordsworth's theme of spiritual experience, and my essay on "Johnson's Wesleyan Connection," besides arguing that "the religious imagination for which Wesley was largely responsible relates directly to the history of Samuel Johnson's mind" (p. 144), suggests that, especially in England and conceivably in America and Germany, Romanticism is not so much "spilt religion" (in the phrase of T. E. Hulme) as religion "freely poured from renewed sources of spirituality " in the "age of spiritual awakening" (p. 168) . (This age led, say, from Wesley's first itinerant steps to the partly Wesley-inspired Oxford Movement.) Despite the fact, however, that English Romantic religion is sufficiently strong, and sufficiently precise, to have shaped the faith of Victorian England, no one has attempted systematically to characterize the collective faith of English Romanticism in both the first and second generations.[76] And no one has systematically pursued what English Romantic faith has to do with English Romantic philosophy. It is well known, of course, that the poetry of English Romanticism has to do with Lockean thought so much as to fit Robert Langbaum's label for both the Romantic and the Victorian dramatic monologue: *The Poetry of Experience*;[77] Langbaum, and a host of other scholar-critics (see chapter 4), acknowledge that the priority of experience in English Romantic poetry derives, ultimately, from Locke's *Essay*. It is time, now, to test the experiential emphasis of Wesley's thought, i.e., his philosophical theology, as a means of exploring the experiential common ground of English Romantic faith and English Romantic philosophy; I argue, in so doing, that the primarily natural experience of Locke, and the primarily spiritual experience of Wesley, not only come together in Wesley's philosophical theology, but thence inform, directly and indirectly, a central dialectic of the poets. Not only does the almost religious quality of their emotion relate to Wesley's emotional faith, but a Wesleyan blend of "spiritual sense" and *a posteriori* reason forms part of what they all retained from the century and the place in which all of them were born.

Thus Wesley's method is in these pages a sufficiently high-minded (if not always sublime) antecedent to Romanticism, for these major Romantics (if not other Romantics in England and elsewhere) reflect in their formulations of experience the Wesleyan alignment of theology with a standard philosophy of their age. Besides placing Wesley's thought in a mainstream current of Western philosophy from the late seventeenth century to the mid-nineteenth, I lay out an approach to Romanticism along lines of the following premises in their cumulative effect: the history of Wesley's mind features the philosophy of Locke; Locke's continuum from physical sensation to "human understanding" contributes method to Wesley's account of saving faith; Wesley's religious "epistemology," i.e., his philosophy of religion, helped to assure a theological as well as philosophical tone among formulations of experience in late eighteenth-and-early-nineteenth-century England; the Wesleyan mode of experience defines a criterion of truth in the most important genre of British Romantic literature; the quality of experience in English Romantic poetry is spiritual as well as natural; Wesley's philosophical theology is a satisfyingly complex, appropriately interdisciplinary, aptly inclusive, and almost only available model for the broad concept of experience everywhere implicit in English Romantic epistemology; the priority of experience in the empirical philosophy, and the importance of experience in the Wesleyan faith,[78] of eighteenth-century England provide, together, a sufficiently synoptic background to British Romanticism; English "Romantic origins" are discoverable on the Wesleyan, i.e., most broadly experiential, ground of British Romantic exemplars;[79] and British Romanticism, finally, is yet a conceivably single concept. Insofar, in sum, as I advance towards "our unified field theory of British Romanticism" by offering a perspective on English Romantic poetry at once empirical and evangelical, Wesley's place in literary history rivals his place in the history of religion and in the history of ideas.

NOTES

[1] Gene W. Ruoff and L. J. Swingle, "From the Editors." These remarks represent Ruoff's and Swingle's introduction to a special issue on British Romantic fiction.

[2] See, for example, John Murray Todd, *John Wesley and the Catholic Church*; Maximin Piette, *John Wesley in the Evolution of Protestantism*; and Robert Clarence Monk, *John Wesley: His Puritan Heritage*. See also William R. Cannon, *The Theology of John Wesley, with Special Reference to the Doctrine of Justification*; Harald Gustave Ake Lindstrom, *Wesley and Sanctification: A Study of the Doctrine of Salvation*; Arthur S. Yates, *The Doctrine of Assurance: with Special Reference to John Wesley*; Granville C. Henry, "John Wesley's Doctrine of Free Will"; and Leo George Cox, *John Wesley's Concept of Perfection*. Frederick Hunter, in view of such diversity, sees Wesley as a pioneer of ecumenical thought in his *John Wesley and the Coming Comprehensive Church*. Wesley was an eclectic traditionalist who mined the variety of Christian thought from the Middle Ages to the eighteenth century. He found time even on horseback, and indeed especially there, to express at his portable writing desk his theological perspective; see at Epworth House, City Road, London, the writing desk itself, designed to face the rear: the horse knew the circuit by heart.

[3] Frank Baker, *John Wesley and the Church of England*, p. 3. The term *Anglican*, in use only occasionally during the eighteenth century, is employed here as Baker employs it: in accordance with its current usage as a synonym for "pertaining to the Church of England."

[4] Bernard Semmel's study, *The Methodist Revolution*, emphasizes Wesley's Arminian thought. Biographies such as Luke Tyerman's *The Life and Times of John Wesley* and Richard Green's *John Wesley, Evangelist* stressed his impact on religious life. One assortment of studies was social in emphasis: see Maldwyn Lloyd Edwards, *John Wesley and the Eighteenth Century: A Study of His Social and Political Influence*; J. H. Whiteley, *Wesley's England: A Survey of Eighteenth-Century Social and Cultural Conditions*; Robert Featherstone Wearmouth, *Methodism and the Working Class Movements of England, 1800-1850*, and *Methodism and the Common People of the Eighteenth Century*.

[5] For a recent discussion of this well-known conversation, see Frank Baker, "John Wesley and Bishop Butler: A Fragment of John Wesley's Manuscript Journal, 16th to 24th August 1739."

[6] They did so in 1795. Wesley's puzzling relationship to the Anglican community is perhaps best epitomized by Joseph Beaumont: "Mr. Wesley, like a strong and skillful rower, looked one way, while every stroke of his oar took

him in the opposite direction." See Benjamin Gregory, *Sidelights on the Conflicts of Methodism*, p. 161.

⁷ J. Clifford Hindley, "The Philosophy of Enthusiasm," p. 1o6. See also Frederick Dreyer, "Faith and Experience in the Thought of John Wesley." I am delighted to find in this recent essay an ally; Dreyer, concluding that "philosophy [e. g. , that of Locke and David Hume] in the end . . . explains what [Wesley's] religion meant," is quite consistent with my own attempt to place Wesley's thought in the context of his age.

⁸ For Wesley's account of his conversion, sec Curnock, 1:475-76. Holland, though "in union with the Brethren," and though "he ranked in the Moravian Church as the first 'Congregation Elder'," was also a member of the Church of England; see Curnock's full discussion: 1:475-76n. Wesley does not identify Holland as the "one" who "was reading Luther's preface," but Curnock's argument in support of Holland is persuasive.

⁹ See Hindley, "The Philosophy of Enthusiasm," pp. 99-109, 199-210, especially 108. For Wesley's Moravian contacts (from February 7, 1738, when Peter Böhler arrived in London, to May 4, 1738, when Böhler departed for America), see Curnock, 1:436-60.

¹⁰ The following studies are classics: S. G. Dimond, *The Psychology of the Methodist Revival: An Empirical and Descriptive Study*; Umphrey Lee, *John Wesley and Modern Religion*; G. C. Cell, *The Rediscovery of John Wesley*; and J. S. Rattenbury, *The Conversion of the Wesleys: A Critical Study*.

¹¹ Robert L. Moore, *John Wesley and Authority*.

¹² John Telford, *The Life of John Wesley*, pp. 162-63.

¹³ See Hindley, "The Philosophy of Enthusiasm," p. 99, and A. J. Ayer, *Language, Truth and Logic*.

¹⁴ See Alfred H. Body, *John Wesley and Education*, especially pp. 33, 52, 56-61. Of his curriculum at Kingswood, Wesley wrote that "Whoever goes carefully through this course will be a better scholar than nine in ten of the graduates at Oxford and Cambridge" (ibid., p. 61). A. G. Ives, *Kingswood School in Wesley's Day and Since*, especially pp. 19, 240-41, 247, engagingly recasts Body's argument for the Lockean basis of Wesley's experiment at Kingswood.

Ives and Body, though making a sizable number of points concerning the relation between Wesley and Locke, do not make the Lockean background a major feature of their approaches, and each, therefore, finally resembles George Eayrs, whose *John Wesley: Christian Philosopher and Church Founder* asserts that Locke was among the authors whom Wesley "read and studied" (p. 22), but nowhere pursues the question of Wesley's debt to the *Essay*. See especially my *Locke, Wesley*, chapter 3, however, for further acknowledgment of Eayrs's otherwise useful study.

[15] Samuel F. Pickering, Jr.'s recent study, *John Locke and Children's Books in Eighteenth-Century England*, is preceded by his similarly instructive, and similarly delightful book, *The Moral Tradition in English Fiction, 1785-1850*.

[16] Martin Schmidt, *John Wesley: A Theological Biography* 2 (pt. 1): 73.

[17] See Basil Willey, "On Wordsworth and the Locke Tradition," pp. 296-309; and Hartman, *Wordsworth's Poetry 1787-1814*, pp. 33-69.

[18] Moritz Schlick, *Problems of Ethics*.

[19] Pyrrho's philosophy is known primarily through the poetical fragments of Timon of Phlius; see Leon Robin, *Pyrrhon et le Scepticisme Grec*.

[20] Alexander Campbell Fraser, in annotating *Essay* 4. 16.12, quotes Bacon's essay: see Fraser's edition 2: 381n.

[21] See, for example, the discussion in R. N. Stromberg, *Religious Liberalism in Eighteenth-Century England*, pp. 38-66. See also John Toland, *Christianity Not Mysterious*, pp. 86-87; Anthony Collins, *A Discourse of Free-thinking*, pp. 20, 25, 33, 44, 50-52, 99, 177; and Matthew Tindal, *Christianity as old as the Creation*, pp. 268, 394.

[22] See Thomas Bray's *Bibliotheca Parochialis; or a Scheme of such Theological and Other Heads, as seem requisite to be perus'd, or Occasionally consulted, by the Reverend Clergy. Together with the Books which may be profitably Read on each of these Points*, p. 40.

[23] See Andrew Baxter, *An Enquiry into the Nature of the human soul: Wherein the immateriality of the soul is evinced from the principles of reason and philosophy*; and Bishop Joseph Butler, *The Analogy of Religion, Natural and Revealed, to the constitution and course of Nature*. The word *materialism*, among many eighteenth-century English scientists and doctors, was not wholly incompatible with the notion of spirit: these materialists believed in the reality of some etherealized substance, and they distinguished between themselves and those Newtonian mechanists who explained life as exclusively physical, e.g., as a system of pulleys. See Robert E. Schofield, *Mechanism and Materialism: British Natural Philosophy in An Age of Reason*, especially pp. 91-114. Butler, Baxter, and Berkeley, clearly, worried about incompatibility between the material and the spiritual.

[24] See Catharine Cockburn, *Remarks upon the principles and reasonings of Dr. Rutherforth's Essay on the nature and obligations of virtue, in vindication of the contrary principles and reasonings inforced in the writings of the late Dr. Samuel Clarke*; see also her earlier work, *A Defence of the Essay on human understanding, written by Mr. Lock—In answer to some Remarks on that essay [by Sir Thomas Burnet]*.

²⁵ See Butler's *Analogy* 1.1.17, as quoted in Kenneth Maclean, *John Locke and English Literature of the Eighteenth Century*, p. 52. See also Hindley, "The Philosophy of Enthusiasm," p. 202, and Maclean, pp. 27, 62, 73, 101, 152, 162. Nonconformist writers as diverse, and as widely separated in time, as Thomas Tryon in his *Letters . . . Philosophical, Theological, and Moral* and Samuel Pike in his *Philosophia Sacra: or, The Principles of Natural Philosophy. Extracted from Divine Revelation* shared the Lockean attitudes of that more famous Nonconformist, Isaac Watts, and fed like him into a mainstream Christian thought that was increasingly "ecumenical" in part because of the almost universal desire to take theological account of Locke's empiricism.

²⁶ Maclean quotes, for example, *Essay* 2.23.3 (sec Maclean, *John Locke and English Literature of the Eighteenth Century*, p. 121); moreover, he quotes (pp. 96-97, 137) *Essay* 2.23.28, 32 and 4.12.10.

²⁷ Horton Davies, *Worship and Theology in England from Watts and Wesley to Maurice*, 1690-1850, pp. 143-254, especially p. 184.

²⁸ See Donald Greene, *The Age of Exuberance: Backgrounds to Eighteenth-Century English Literature*.

²⁹ For Wesley's admiration of Butler's thought, sec, for example, Curnock, 3:232; 5:265. For V. H. H. Green's comments see *The Young Mr. Wesley: A Study of John Wesley and Oxford*, pp. 10-11, 303.

³⁰ For a discerning application of this Lockean view, see Hugh Sykes Davies, "Wordsworth and the Empirical Philosophers," pp. 157-62. Compare this with the discussion of synchronicity in M.-L. von Franz, "The Process of Individuation," pp. 226-27. For Wesley's bibliomancy as a sufficiently theological guide in spiritual experience see Frederic Greeves, "John Wesley and Divine Guidance." For a recent, authoritative discussion of providential theology in the eighteenth century, see Aubrey Williams, *An Approach to Congreve*, especially pp. 31-34.

³¹ See Francis Gallaway, *Reason, Rule, and Revolt in English Classicism*, pp. 10, 25-26, 55-56, 161-62 and *passim*. Gallaway's classic study has been reprinted (New York: Octagon Books, 1965).

³² Green, *The Young Mr. Wesley*, p. 2 and *passim*.

³³ An exclusively sensationalistic empiricism, for example, is more or less explicitly assumed to comprise the entire Lockean background to *Gulliver's Travels* (1726). Irvin Ehrenpreis bases his argument that Gulliver gradually grows "irrational" on a view that the *Essay* describes man as sensationalistic rather than rational: subordinating Locke's definition of reason as man's "real essence" to his designation of "sensible shape" as man's "nominal essence,"

Ehrenpreis implies that the senses make up the more philosophically tenable, if not the more desirable and the more intended, component of Locke's epistemology. See Irvin Ehrenpreis, "The Meaning of Gulliver's Last Voyage." Ehrenpreis's interpretation of the *Essay* has been pushed further, and further applied to Swift, by W. B. Carnochan; see *Lemuel Gulliver's Mirror for Man*, pp. 118-65, especially pp. 123, 133. David B. Morris and Patricia Meyer Spacks in their studies of Pope interpret the *Essay* as primarily sensationalistic; assume that Pope thus interpreted it; and suggest that Pope, unlike Swift, embraced a primarily sensationalistic epistemology. See Spacks, *An Argument of Images: The Poetry of Alexander Pope*, pp. 42, 84, 112; and Morris, "The Kinship of Madness in Pope's *Dunciad*," especially pp. 813, 819, 831. Michael V. DePorte goes even further than Morris and Spacks in implying that among eighteenth-century English authors there was an increasing tendency to interpret and endorse Locke's philosophy as non-rational. Locke's point that irrationality is not easily cured, rather than Locke's argument that rationality can be maintained, is in DePorte's view central to Sterne's perspective in *Tristram Shandy*, which according to DePorte everywhere suggests that reason is easily lost and indeed that extreme irrationality constitutes a norm of behavior; see especially DePorte's "Digressions and Madness in *A Tale of a Tub* and *Tristram Shandy*," especially 50-52. For arguments acknowledging, if not a Lockean, then a more than rational strain in Sterne, see Arthur Hill Cash, "The Sermon in *Tristram Shandy*," p. 395; and Melvyn New, *Laurence Sterne as Satirist: A Reading of Tristram Shandy*.

[34] For a discussion of the *a priori* rationalists in England, see, for example, Robert Bernard Schuda, "A Study of Laurence Sterne's Sermons: Yorkshire Background, Ethics, and Index." William Wollaston, John Balguy, and Richard Price are also notable among the figures in Schuda's helpful analysis.

[35] "... [A]nd the measure of heaven itself," Sterne adds, "is but the measure of our present appetites and concoctions"; see Laurence Sterne, *The Life and Opinions of Tristram Shandy, Gentleman* 2:593, edited by Melvyn New and Joan New.

[36] "It is so difficult," adds Nicoll, "to feel that the fashion of this world passeth away and yet at the same time to do one's utmost in it and to care for everything"; see T. H. Darlow, *William Robertson Nicoll: Life and Letters*, p. 348.

[37] Green, *The Young Mr. Wesley*, pp. 10-11, 303.

[38] Francis McConnell, *John Wesley*, p. 326.

[39] See M. H. Abrams's "Structure and Style in the Greater Romantic Lyric."

[40] Samuel T. Coleridge, *The Friend* 3:261-62. Coleridge's statement, of course, anticipates the modern loss of balance between subject and object, i.e., the

modern victory of the subjective: see, for example, David Bleich's chapter on "The Subjective Paradigm" in *Subjective Criticism*, pp. 10-37. Modern criticism could rediscover a subject/object balance by drawing, for example, on dialectical biology, which, like Locke, attempts "to break down the alienation of subject and object"; dialectical biology, that is,

> insist[s] on the interpenetration of gene, organism, and environment. Thus, in place of the metaphor of adaptation of organisms to a preexistent environmental "niche," dialectical biology emphasizes the way in which organisms define and alter their environment in the process of their life activities. Organism and environment are both in a constant state of becoming, mutually determining each other.

See R. C. Lewontin, "The Corpse in the Elevator," p. 37, a review of *Against Biological Determinism* and *Towards a Liberatory Biology*, both edited by Steven Rose.

[41] See the concise summation in Frank Thilly, *A History of Philosophy*, pp. 1-4.

[42] See the discussion in Maclean, *John Locke and English Literature of the Eighteenth Century*, p. 15.

[43] Henry May, for example, finds in general that "people whose ultimate authority is either scripture or faith do not belong in the Enlightenment," and in particular that "Wesley, Blake, and (despite Perry Miller's arguments to the contrary) Jonathan Edwards" should be excluded; see *The Enlightenment in America*, pp. xiv, 402. Paul Hazard, assuming that Wesley was "anti-rationalist" and hence enthusiastic, asserts that he set about to end the age of reason; see *European Thought in the Eighteenth Century: From Montesquieu to Lessing*, p. 454. In "Johnson's Wesleyan Connection," pp. 146-47, I focus on the Calvinist/Arminian controversy as a means of suggesting that the differences between Wesley and George Whitefield are considerable, but students of the Enlightenment tend to lump Wesley with Whitefield, and, assuming that Wesley (like Whitefield) was not particularly intellectual, they erroneously conclude that he was un-"enlightened." Basil Willey, in *The Eighteenth-Century Background: Studies on the Idea of Nature in the Thought of the Period*, pp. 108-9, writes that "Wesley and Whitefield range[d] the world, converting their ten thousands, not by rational ethical suasion, but by impassioned appeals to the heart," but Wesley's "Earnest Appeal to Men of Reason and Religion," by the title alone, challenges Willey's assumption that appeals to emotion and the moral arguments of reason are necessarily mutually exclusive. Peter

Gay, in *The Enlightenment, An Interpretation: The Rise of Modern Paganism*, pp. 254, 346, (1) condescends to all eighteenth-century Methodists (they would have been "at home," Gay sneers, "in twelfth-century Chartres"); (2) associates Wesley with their enthusiastic excesses (neither Wesley nor Whitefield should be lumped with enthusiastic Methodists); (3) identifies Wesley, erroneously, with the strictures of Whitefield against Tillotson and the Latitudinarians; and (4) erroneously concludes that "philosophical religion" was held by Wesley, as well as Whitefield, to be "their worst enemy." Even one so proficient in the varieties of eighteenth-century religious experience as E. P. Thompson has not advanced any further than students of the Enlightenment beyond the view of Wesley as unenlightened: in his review of Donald Davie's *A Gathered Church: The Literature of the English Dissenting Interest*, Thompson declares that "the Wesleys," John and Charles, "turned their backs" upon "rational modes" and were thus "self-consciously anti-enlightenment"; see *The Modern Language Review* 75 (1980): 165. Thompson is right, of course, to take on Davie for identifying the Wesleys with Dissent; from my point of view, moreover, Thompson is right to conceive of "rational modes" in a country where the Enlightenment was chiefly Lockean. But it is worth pointing out that, in addition to the forgivable error of lumping John with Charles, whose intellectual gifts, sometimes as rich as those of John, were at no time so varied, Thompson commits the (no less forgivable) error of overlooking the self-evidently possible relation between Wesley's experience of faith and the philosophy of experience underlying the Enlightenment. For a study of an Arminian (and therefore proto-Methodist?) background to the English Enlightenment, see Rosalie L. Colie, *Light and Enlightenment: A Study of the Cambridge Platonists and the Dutch Arminians*. Wesley's "intellectual position," as set forth in his "Appeals to Men of Reason and Religion" and his lengthy treatise on "Original Sin" (1757), is mentioned in Sir Leslie Stephen's *History of English Thought in the Eighteenth Century*, 2:409. But Stephen's main points are that Wesley's "strength lies almost entirely in the sphere of practice," and that his importance, accordingly, lies in providing "the religious reaction" to the eighteenth-century emphasis on the intellect (2:409, 418-19).

[44] See Albert M. Lyles, *Methodism Mocked: The Satiric Reaction to Methodism in the Eighteenth Century*. I quote (above) the charge leveled against Wesley himself by the Rev. Thomas Church in 1744; see John Wesley, *Wesley's Standard Sermons*, edited by Edward H. Sugden, 2:84-85. A good example of the polemics, though not one cited by Lyles, is William Warburton's scorn of Wesley's

bibliomancy. Warburton, as a means of laughing at a passage from the Journal, thinks it sufficient to quote it:

> In the evening, being sent for to her again, I was unwilling, indeed afraid to go; thinking it would not avail, unless some, who were strong in faith, were to wrestle with God for her. I opened my Testament on these words—I was afraid, and went and hid my talent in the earth. [Cf. Matt. 25:25.] I stood reproved, and went immediately.

See William Warburton, *The Doctrine of Grace; or, the Office and Operations of the Holy Spirit Vindicated from the Insults of Infidelity and the Abuses of Fanaticism* 8:335.

[45] See, for example, *Essay* 4. 19 (Nidditch, pp. 697-706). See also my *Wordsworth's "Natural Methodism,"* p. 71. Wesley's *Dictionary* defines "enthusiast" as "a religious madman, one that fancies himself inspired," and "inspiration" as "that secret influence of the Holy Ghost which enables man to love and serve God."

[46] Curnock, 3:54. See also Jackson, 1:216; 3:34; 6:471-72; 8:105-6, 110, 405, 432-34, 445-68; 9:1-14, 22-28.

[47] See Telford, 5:383; Jackson, 2:49, 3:465, 503; and 4:458. See also Monk, *John Wesley: His Puritan Heritage*.

[48] Jackson, 7:271; Wesley included Hume within "the great triumvirate" of *philosophes* who preached the religion of humanity. Far from simply lumping Hume and Locke together, as empirical philosophers, Wesley distinguished between them, and, equally clearly, he preferred Locke, down to the most particular issues. For example, Wesley's pejorative phrase *the casual involuntary association of our ideas* (see Sugden, ed., *Wesley's Standard Sermons* 2:26) suggests (in the adjectives *casual* and *involuntary*) that Wesley intended to recommend association of ideas as understood by Locke rather than by Hume: Hume, like Hobbes, Dryden, Watts, and Hartley, regarded the concept positively, as an instrument for improving knowledge, whereas Locke regarded it negatively, as a detriment to judgment and as "a sort of madness" *(Essay* 2.33; Nidditch, pp. 394-401). See Chinmoy Bannerjee, "*Tristram Shandy* and the Association of Ideas"; and Maclean, *John Locke and English Literature of the Eighteenth Century*, pp. 128-30. For further discussion of Wesley's relationship to Hume, which was well informed and sometimes even implicitly positive, see my *Locke, Wesley* (chapter 2).

[49] See, for example, Telford, 2:346; 5:373.

[50] May, *The Enlightenment in America*, p. 107.

⁵¹ For Wesley 's admiration of Berkeley's *Alciphron* (1728) and the works of John Norris, see, for example, Curnock, 1:125-26, 345; 5:458; and Telford, 3:163; 5:110; and 7:228. For the interrelationship of Descartes, Malebranche, Berkeley, and Norris, see, for example, A. A. Luce, *Berkeley and Malebranche: A Study in the Origins of Berkeley's Thought*, pp. 70-75. For Wesley 's praise of *De la Recherche de la Vérité* (1674-78), see, for example, Curnock, 8:277. Scholars can welcome the following: Nicolas Malebranche, *The Search after Truth*, trans. Thomas M. Lennon and Paul L. Olscamp.

⁵² See Hazard, *European Thought in the Eighteenth Century*, pp. vi, 31, 41 -43, and Gay, *The Enlightenment, An Interpretation*, pp. 11-12; Nidditch (p. xxxvii) cites Pierre Coste's French translation of the *Essay* (1700) and Ezekiel Burridge's Latin translation (1701).

⁵³ May, *The Enlightenment in America*, pp. 38, 246-47, 337, 347.

⁵⁴ Pocock, though generally distinguishing between the continental and insular traditions, discovers one surprising interconnection: he finds eschatological patterns among the *philosophes* as well as the Puritans. See J. G. A. Pocock, "Post-Puritan England and the Problem of the Enlightenment." The broadest and most thorough demonstration of the *Essay*'s influence in England remains MacLean's *John Locke and English Literature of the Eighteenth Century*. Nidditch does not exaggerate in observing that "perhaps no other modern work of discursive prose has sold so well and steadily in the course of centuries" (p. xxxiv): the *Essay* after its first appearance went through five additional editions—in 1694, 1695, 1700, 1706, 1710—and was subsequently reprinted every three or four years until the middle of the nineteenth century.

⁵⁵ See Gay, *The Enlightenment, An Interpretation*, p. x.

⁵⁶ Going beyond a study of the Enlightenment alone, to a study of how Romanticism grew out of the Enlightenment, I shall indicate, moreover, that Wesley's age of Lockean as well as religious illumination extended to British Romanticism. Rousseau's passion, Diderot's vitalism, Hume's skepticism, Voltaire's blend of empiricism and *a priori* reason, and, clearly not least, Locke's blend of *a posteriori* reason and sense-based methodology, all form the uncompacted Enlightenment, and Wesley's transmutation of Locke's empiricism formed another, equally prophetic, element of the Enlightenment, namely, the Religious Enlightenment which, diffused throughout the atmosphere of late eighteenth-and-early-nineteenth-century England, formed in turn a condition whereby English Romanticism, uncompacted but describable, aspired to the state of its chief precursor and prime exemplar: Blake was in the world, but not of it.

[57] Consider, for example, *Essay* 4.9.3 (Nidditch, pp. 618-19):

> As for *our own Existence*, we perceive it so plainly, and so certainly, that it neither needs, nor is capable of any proof. For nothing can be more evident to us, than our own Existence. *I think, I reason, I feel Pleasure and Pain;* Can any of these be more evident to me, than my own Existence? If I doubt of all other Things, that very doubt makes me perceive my own *Existence*, and will not suffer me to doubt of that. For if I know *I feel Pain*, it is evident, I have as certain a Perception of my own Existence, as of the Existence of the Pain I feel: Or if I know *I doubt*, I have as certain a Perception of the Existence of the thing doubting, as of that Thought, which I call *doubt*. Experience then convinces us, that *we have an intuitive Knowledge of our own Existence*, and an internal infallible Perception that we are. In every Act of Sensation, Reasoning, or Thinking, we are conscious to our selves of our own Being; and, in this Matter, come not short of the highest degree of *Certainty*.

The skeptical method of this passage, calling into doubt what can be doubted, is reminiscent of Descartes, too: see his *Discourse on Method*.

[58] See the discussion in Luce, *Berkeley and Malebranche*, pp. 70-75. Locke, by contrast, gives what Luce calls "a psychology of idea," and, though Luce adds that Locke also gives "a metaphysic by means thereof," Luce concludes that Locke "attempts no metaphysic of the idea itself." Luce, in sum, distinguishes between "the reality of the idea-thing," a reality urged in Cartesian "mentalism," and psychological Lockean "ideism." Or in other words, Cartesian thought is distinct from empiricism insofar as Lockean reason is finally an *a posteriori* extension of the senses quite different in its sensuous moorings from Descartes's *a priori* brand of reasoning.

Perhaps the first modern definition of *psychology*, incidentally, is that of David Hartley, who calls it "the theory of the human Mind, with that of the intellectual Principles of Brute Animals"; see *Observations on Man, His Frame, His Duty, and His Expectations*, p. 354. At the time of Locke, the definition was linked to the myth of Psyche: "Psucologie, which Treats of the Soul," is contrasted with "Anatomy, which treats of the Body"; see Blancard's *Physical Dictionary* (2d ed., 1693), as quoted in the *Oxford English Dictionary*, s.v. "Psychology." Samuel Johnson, perhaps, was unknowingly perceiving a psychological dimension to the *Essay*, and unknowingly pioneering the psychological interpretation of it, when he referred to his own period of history as an age when, "sometimes with nice discernment" (as in the *Essay*?), "but often with idle subtilty " (as in *Observations on Man*?), "Speculation" attempts "to analyze the mind," "trace the passions to their sources," "unfold the seminal principles of vice and virtue," and "sound the depths of the heart for the motives of action"; see the discussion of Johnson's preface to the plays of Shakespeare in MacLean, *John Locke and English Literature of the Eighteenth Century*, p. 13.

[59] See T. Walter Herbert, *John Wesley as Editor and Author*, pp. 46-71; and George Lawton, *John Wesley's English: A Study of His Literary Style*.

[60] Frank Baker, general editor, *The Oxford Edition of Wesley's Works*. This edition is in the process of highlighting the various categories of Wesley's writings. The editors, devoting themselves to such topics as Wesley's poetry, not all of which is hymns, can finally be classed among students of his language; Herbert, gathering Wesley's harvest "as Editor and Publisher," is trained in the study of literature. Besides Cragg's presentation of the "Appeals to Men of Reason and Religion," Baker's edition of the early letters has appeared. Albert C. Outler's edition of the sermons, heavily annotated, is forthcoming.

[61] I am grateful to Samuel Rogal for communicating with me about his work.

[62] See the discussion in James L. Golden, "John Wesley on Rhetoric and Belles Lettres," p. 255.

[63] See Jackson, 8:300, 336-37; 10:255-58; and 11:493-95.

[64] See Friedrich Nietzsche, "European Nihilism," in Book I of *The Will to Power*, p. 7; and *Werke in Drei Bänden*, ed. Karl Schlechta, 3:881.

[65] For a Deconstructionist manifesto, see J. Hillis Miller, "The Critic as Host," pp. 217-53.

[66] See Lawton, *John Wesley's English*, especially chapter 1 ("Wesley's Vocabulary and the Evangelical Mission," pp. 15-25) and chapter 2 ("Emergence of a Distinctive Terminology," pp. 26-35).

[67] Golden, "John Wesley on Rhetoric and Belles Lettres," pp. 250-64.

[68] For the empirical assumptions of such "new rhetoricians," see Marsha Kent Savage, "Archibald Alison and the Spiritual Aesthetics of William Wordsworth"; and Byron Keith Brown, "Wordsworth's Affective Poetics: Rhetorical Theory and Poetic Revolution." See also Golden, "John Wesley on Rhetoric and Belles Lettres," pp. 263-64.

[69] See, for example, Kathleen Walker MacArthur, *The Economic Ethics of John Wesley*; Robert N. Kingdon, "Laissez-faire or Government Control: A Prob-

lem for John Wesley"; and Alfred Wesley Hill, *John Wesley Among the Physicians: A Study of Eighteenth-Century Medicine*. Herbert, in *John Wesley as Editor and Author*, discerns immediacy in Wesley's political language.

[70] See the discussion in Maclean, *John Wesley and English Literature of the Eighteenth Century*, p. 5.

[71] Theodore Roszak, "In Search of the Miraculous."

[72] Hans Aarsleff, *From Locke to Saussure: Essays on the Study of Language and Intellectual History*. See also D. W. Harding's classic study, *Experience into Words: Essays on Poetry*; and Italo Calvino's recent essay, "The Written and the Unwritten Word." Fascinated by the all but irreconcilable challenges of the writer, namely, "to use a language responsible only to itself" and "to use a language in order to reach the silence of the world," Calvino concludes:

> In a certain way, I think we always write about something we don't know, we write to give the unwritten world a chance to express itself through us. Yet the moment my attention wanders from the settled order of the written lines to the movable complexity no sentence is able to hold entirely, I come close to understanding that on the other side of the words there is something words could mean.

[73] Derek Bickerton, *Roots of Language*.

[74] These remarks form part of Edward Dowdcn's contribution to a special issue of the *Pall Mall Gazette*, as cited in E. D. Hirsch, Jr., *The Aims of Interpretation*, pp. 141-42.

[75] Hirsch, *The Aims of Interpretation*, pp. 140-42.

[76] For the relevant bibliography, see Brantley, *Wordsworth's "Natural Methodism,"* p. 175. See also Stephen Prickett, *Romanticism and Religion: The Tradition of Coleridge and Wordsworth in the Victorian Church*. I am intrigued, in this connection, by Norman Nicholson's statement that the evangelical revival "was, in fact, not so much a symptom of the Romantic Movement as the Movement itself in so far as it affected a large class and section of the population.... For these the Revival was all they ever saw or heard of Romanticism": see *William Cowper*, p. 10.

[77] Langbaum's study, *The Poetry of Experience*, is subtitled *The Dramatic Monologue in Modern Literary Tradition*.

[78] The fundamentalist absolute trust in the New Testament, of course, which is the hallmark of many evangelicals who followed Wesley, as well as of most

who did not, is incompatible with an acknowledgment of "the priority of experience," and so makes such a phrase less suitable than "the importance of experience" not only to eighteenth-century evangelicals in general, but also to Wesleyan evangelicals in particular. For the latter, however, and certainly for Wesley himself, experience was important indeed. See *Locke, Wesley* (chapter 1) for a philosophically theological perspective on, and definition of, the "evangelical faith" of which young Wesley read deeply. Wesley's own evangelical faith reflected that definition and perspective *(Locke Wesley,* chapter 2).

[79] "Romantic origins" is Leslie Brisman's phrase: see his *Romantic Origins.* Brisman argues that the various Romantic quests for origins of society, language, sexuality, and "the growth of the soul" are motivated by "the desire to know correctly a state which no longer exists, and the desire to express one's awareness of the fictionality of such a state" (p. 11); Brisman is indebted to Deconstructionist criticism. For theoretical criticism's relation to my point of view, see *Locke, Wesley* (conclusion).

SOURCES

Baker, Frank, ed. *See* Wesley, John.

Baxter, Andrew. *An Enquiry into the Nature of the human soul: Wherein the immateriality of the soul is evinced from the principles of reason and philosophy.* London: James Bettenham, 1730.

Bray, Thomas. *Bibliotheca Parochialis; or, a Scheme of such Theological and Other Heads, as seem requisite to be perus'd, or Occasionally consulted, by the Reverend Clergy. Together with the Books which may be profitably Read on each of these Points.* London: R. Wilkin and W. Hawes, 1707.

Butler, Bishop Joseph. *The Analogy of Religion, Natural and Revealed, to the constitution and course of Nature.* London: James, John, and Paul Knapton, 1736.

Cockburn, Catharine. *A Defence of the Essay on human understanding, written by Mr. Lock—In answer to some Remarks on that essay [by Sir Thomas Burnet].* London: W. Turner, 1702.

---. *Remarks upon the principles and reasonings of Dr. Rutherforth's Essay on the nature and obligations of virtue, in vindication of the contrary principles and reasonings inforced in the writings of the late Dr. Samuel Clarke.* London: J. and P. Knapton, 1747.

Coleridge, Samuel T. *The Friend: A Series of Essays, in Three Volumes, to aid in the formation of fixed principles in politics, morals, and religion, with literary amusements interspersed.* 3 vols. London: R. Fenner, 1818.

Collins, Anthony. *A Discourse of Free-thinking.* London, N.p., 1713.
Curnock, Nehemiah, ed. *See* Wesley, John.
Fraser, Alexander Campbell, ed., *See* Locke, John.
Hartley, David. *Observations on Man, His Frame, His Duty, and His Expectations.* 1749. Reprint. Gainesville, Florida: Scholars' Facsimiles and Reprints, 1966.
Jackson, Thomas, ed. *See* Wesley, John.
Locke, John. *An Essay concerning Human Understanding.* Edited by Alexander Campbell Fraser. 2 vols. Oxford: Clarendon Press, 1894.
---. *An Essay concerning Human Understanding.* 1690. Edited by Peter H. Nidditch. Oxford: Clarendon Press, 1975.
Malebranche, Nicolas. *The Search After Truth.* Translated by Thomas M. Lennon and Paul L. Olscamp. Columbus: Ohio State University Press, 1980.
Pike, Samuel. *Philosophia Sacra: or, The Principles of Natural Philosophy. Extracted from Divine Revelation.* London: J. Buckland, 1753.
Telford, John, ed. *See* Wesley, John.
Tindal, Matthew. *Christianity as old as the Creation.* London: N.p., 1731.
Toland, John. *Christianity Not Mysterious.* London: Sam. Buckley, 1696.
Tryon, Thomas. *Letters . . . Philosophical, Theological, and Moral.* London: Geo. Conyers and Eliz. Harris, 1700.
Warburton, William. *The Doctrine of Grace; or, the Office and Operations of the Holy Spirit Vindicated from the Insults of Infidelity and the Abuses of Fanaticism.* 1763. In *The Works of the Right Reverend William Warburton, D.D.* Edited by Richard Hurd. 12 vols. London: T. Cadell and W. Davies, 1811.
Wesley, John. *The Appeals to Men of Reason and Religion and Certain Related Open Letters.* Edited by Gerald R. Cragg. Vol. 11 of *The Works of John Wesley.* Edited by Frank Baker. Oxford: Clarendon Press, 1975.
---. *A Compendium of Logic: translated and abridged from Aldrich.* Bristol: W. Pine, 1750.
---. *The Complete English Dictionary.* 2d ed. Bristol: W. Pine, 1763.
---. *An Extract from Milton's* Paradise Lost: *With Notes.* London: Henry Fenwick, 1763.
---. *The Journal of the Rev. John Wesley, A.M., Sometime Fellow of Lincoln College, Oxford, Enlarged from Original MSS., With Notes from Unpublished Diaries, Annotations, Maps, and Illustrations.* Edited by Nehemiah Curnock. 8 vols. London: Robert Culley, 1909.
---. *The Letters of the Rev. John Wesley, A.M., Sometime Fellow of Lincoln College, Oxford.* Edited by John Telford. 8 vols. London: The Epworth Press, 1931.

---. *A Plain Account of the People called Methodists.* Bristol: Felix Farley, 1749.

---. *Primitive Physick: or, an Easy and Natural Method of Curing Most Diseases.* 9th ed. London: Printed by W. Strahan, 1761.

---. *Sermons on Several Occasions. First Series. Consisting of Forty-four Discourses, Published in Four Volumes, in the Years 1746 1748, 1750, and 1760 (Fourth Edition, 1787); To which Reference is Made in the Trustdeeds of the Methodist Chapels, As Constituting, with Mr. Wesley's Notes on the New Testament, The Standard Doctrines of the Methodist Connexion.* London: The Epworth Press, 1944.

---. *A Survey of the Wisdom of God in the Creation: or a Compendium of Natural Philosophy.* 1777. Reprint. Philadelphia: Jonathan Pounder, 1816.

---. *Wesley's Standard Sermons.* Edited by Edward H. Sugden. London: The Epworth Press, 1960.

--. *Letters, 1, 1721-1739.* Edited by Frank Baker. Vol. 25 of *The Works of John Wesley.* Edited by Frank Baker. Oxford: Clarendon Press, 1980.

---. *The Works of the Rev. John Wesley, A.M.* 14 vols. London: Wesleyan-Methodist Book-Room, n.d. This edition and the London 1872 edition reissued by Zondervan in 1958 are reissues of the third edition, edited by Thomas Jackson, 1829-31.

SECONDARY REFERENCES

Aarsleff, Hans. *From Locke to Saussure: Essays on the Study of Language and Intellectual History.* Minneapolis: University of Minnesota Press, 1982.

Abrams, M. H. "Structure and Style in the Greater Romantic Lyric." In *From Sensibility to Romanticism.* Edited by F. W. Hilles and Harold Bloom. New York: Oxford University Press, 1965.

Ayer, A. J. *Language, Truth and Logic.* London: V. Gollancz, 1936.

Baker, Frank. *A Union Catalogue of the Works of John and Charles Wesley.* Durham, N.C.: The Divinity School, Duke University, 1966.

---. "John Wesley and Bishop Butler: A Fragment of John Wesley's Manuscript Journal, 16th to 24th August 1739." *Proceedings of the Wesley Historical Society* 42 (May, 1980): 93-100.

---. *John Wesley and the Church of England.* Nashville: Abingdon Press, 1970.

Bannerjee, Chinmoy. "*Tristram Shandy* and the Association of Ideas." *Texas Studies in Language and Literature* 15 (1973-74): 693-706.

Bickerton, Derek. *Roots of Language.* Ann Arbor: Karoma Publishers, Inc., 1982.

Bleich, David. *Subjective Criticism.* Baltimore: The Johns Hopkins University Press, 1978.

Body, Alfred H. *John Wesley and Education.* London: The Epworth Press, 1936.
Brantley, Richard E. "Johnson's Wesleyan Connection." *Eighteenth-Century Studies* 10 (Winter 1976/77): 143-68.
---. *Wordsworth's "Natural Methodism."* New Haven: Yale University Press, 1975.
Brisman, Leslie. *Romantic Origins.* Ithaca: Cornell University Press, 1978.
Brown, Byron Keith. "Wordsworth's Affective Poetics: Rhetorical Theory and Poetic Revolution." Ph.D. diss., University of Florida, 1981.
Calvino, ltalo. "The Written and the Unwritten Word." Translated by William Weaver. *The New York Review of Books* 30 (May 12, 1983): 38-39.
Cannon, William R. *The Theology of John Wesley, with Special Reference to the Doctrine of Justification.* Nashville: Abingdon-Cokesbury Press, 1946.
Carnochan, W. B. *Lemuel Gulliver's Mirror for Man.* Berkeley and Los Angeles: University of California Press, 1968.
Cash, Arthur Hill. "The Sermon in *Tristram Shandy.*" *ELH* 31 (1964): 395-417.
Colie, Rosalie L. *Light and Enlightenment: A Study of the Cambridge Platonists and the Dutch Arminians.* Cambridge: Cambridge University Press, 1957.
Cox, Leo George. *John Wesley's Concept of Perfection.* Kansas City: Beacon Hill Press, 1964.
Darlow. T. H. *William Robertson Nicoll: Life and Letters.* London: Hodder and Stoughton, 1926.
Davie, Donald. *A Gathered Church: The Literature of the English Dissenting Interest.* London and Henley: Routledge, 1978.
Davies, Horton. *Worship and Theology in England from Watts and Wesley to Maurice, 1690-1850.* Princeton: Princeton University Press, 1961.
Davies, Hugh Sykes. *Thomas De Quincey.* Harlow, England: Longman, 1964.
---. "Wordsworth and the Empirical Philosophers." In *The English Mind: Studies in the English Moralists Presented to Basil Willey.* Edited by Hugh Sykes Davies and George Watson. Cambridge: Cambridge University Press, 1964.
DePorte, Michael V. "Digressions and Madness in *A Tale of a Tub* and *Tristram Shandy.*" *The Huntington Library Quarterly* 34 (November 1970): 43-57.
Dimond, S. G. *The Psychology of the Methodist Revival: An Empirical and Descriptive Study.* London: Oxford University Press, 1926.
Dreyer, Frederick. "Faith and Experience in the Thought of John Wesley." *The American Historical Review* 88 (February 1983): 12-30.
Eayrs, George. *John Wesley: Christian Philosopher and Church Founder.* London: The Epworth Press, 1926.
Edwards, Maldwyn Lloyd. *John Wesley and the Eighteenth Century: A Study of His Social and Political Influence.* London: G. Allen & Unwin, 1933.

Ehrenpreis, Irvin. "The Meaning of Gulliver's Last Voyage." *A Review of English Literature* 3 (July 1962): 18-38. von Franz, M.-L. "The Process of Individuation." In *Man and His Symbols,* by Carl Jung et al. New York: Dell, 1968.

Gallaway, Francis. *Reason, Rule, and Revolt in English Classicism.* New York: Charles Scribner's Sons, 1940.

Gay, Peter. *The Enlightenment, An Interpretation: The Rise of Modem Paganism.* New York: Knopf, 1967.

Golden, James L. "John Wesley on Rhetoric and Belles Lettres." *Speech Monographs* 28 (November 1961): 250-64.

Green, Richard. *John Wesley, Evangelist.* London: The Religious Tract Society, 1905.

Green, V. H. H. *The Young Mr. Wesley: A Study of John Wesley and Oxford.* New York: St. Martin's Press, 1961.

Greene, Donald. *The Age of Exuberance: Backgrounds to Eighteenth-Century English Literature.* New York: Random House, 1970.

Greeves, Frederic. "John Wesley and Divine Guidance." *London Quarterly and Holbom Review* 162 (July 1937): 379-95.

Gregory, Benjamin. *Sidelights on the Conflicts of Methodism.* London: Cassell, 1898.

Harding, D. W. *Experience into Words: Essays on Poetry.* New York: Horizon Press, 1964.

Hartman, Geoffrey. *Wordsworth's Poetry 1787-1814.* New Haven: Yale University Press, 1964.

Hazard, Paul. *European Thought in the Eighteenth Century: From Montesquieu to Lessing.* Cleveland and New York: The World Publishing Co., 1963.

Henry, Granville C. "John Wesley's Doctrine of Free Will." *London Quarterly and Holbom Review* 185 (1960): 200-204.

Herbert, T. Walter. *John Wesley as Editor and Author.* Princeton: Princeton University Press, 1940.

Hill, Alfred Wesley. *John Wesley among the Physicians: A Study of Eighteenth-Century Medicine.* London: The Epworth Press, 1958.

Hindley, J. Clifford. "The Philosophy of Enthusiasm." *The London Quarterly and Holborn Review* 182 (1957): 99-109, 199-210.

Hirsch, E. D., Jr. *The Aims of Interpretation.* Chicago: University of Chicago Press, 1975.

Hunter, Frederick. *John Wesley and the Coming Comprehensive Church.* London: The Epworth Press, 1968.

Ives, A. G. *Kingswood School in Wesley's Day and Since.* London: The Epworth Press, 1970.

Kingdon, Robert N. "Laissez-faire or Government Control: A Problem for John Wesley." *Church History* 26 (1957): 342-54.

Langbaum, Robert. *The Poetry of Experience: The Dramatic Monologue in Modern Literary Tradition.* London: Chatto & Windus, 1957.

Lawton, George. *John Wesley's English: A Study of His Literary Style.* London: George Allen & Unwin, 1962.

Lee, Umphrey. *John Wesley and Modern Religion.* Nashville: Cokesbury Press, 1936.

Lewontin, R. C. "The Corpse in the Elevator," a review of *Against Biological Determinism* and *Towards a Liberatory Biology*, both edited by Steven Rose. *The New York Review of Books* 29 (January 20, 1983): 34-37.

Lindstrom, Harald Gustave Ake. *Wesley and Sanctification: A Study of the Doctrine of Salvation.* London: The Epworth Press, 1950.

Luce, A. A. *Berkeley and Malebranche: A Study in the Origins of Berkeley's Thought.* 1934. Reprint. London: Oxford University Press, 1967.

Lyles, Albert M. *Methodism Mocked: The Satiric Reaction to Methodism in the Eighteenth Century.* London: The Epworth Press, 1960.

MacArthur, Kathleen Walker. *The Economic Ethics of John Wesley.* New York: Abingdon Press, 1936.

McConnell, Francis. *John Wesley.* New York: Abingdon, 1939.

MacLean, Kenneth. *John Locke and English Literature of the Eighteenth Century.* 1936. Reprint. New York: Russell & Russell, 1962.

May, Henry. *The Enlightenment in America.* New York: Oxford University Press, 1976.

Miller, J. Hillis. "The Critic as Host." In *Deconstruction and Criticism.* Edited by Geoffrey Hartman et al. New York: The Seabury Press, 1979.

Monk, Robert Clarence. *John Wesley: His Puritan Heritage.* Nashville: Abingdon Press, 1966.

Moore, Robert L. *John Wesley and Authority.* Missoula, Montana: Scholars Press, 1979.

Morris, David B. "The Kinship of Madness in Pope's *Dunciad*." *PQ* 51 (1972): 813-31.

New, Melvyn. *Laurence Sterne as Satirist: A Reading of* Tristram Shandy. Gainesville: University of Florida Press, 1969.

---, and Joan New, eds. *The Life and Opinions of Tristram Shandy, Gentleman.* By Laurence Sterne. 2 vols. Gainesville: University Presses of Florida, 1978.

Nicholson, Norman. *William Cowper.* London: J. Lehmann, 1951.

Nietzsche, Friedrich. "European Nihilism." In *The Will to Power.* New York: Vintage Books, 1968.

---. *Werke in Drei Bänden.* Edited by Karl Schlechta. Munich: Carl Hauser Verlag, 1966.

Pickering, Samuel F., Jr. *John Locke and Children's Books in Eighteenth-Century England.* Knoxville: University of Tennessee Press, 1981.

---. *The Moral Tradition in English Fiction, 1785-1850.* Hanover, N.H.: The University Press of New England, 1976.

Piette, Maximin. *John Wesley in the Evolution of Protestantism.* Translated by J. B. Howard. New York: Sheed and Ward, 1937.

Pocock, J. G. A. "Post-Puritan England and the Problem of the Enlightenment." In *Culture and Politics from Puritanism to the Enlightenment.* Edited by Perez Zagorin. Berkeley and Los Angeles: University of California Press, 1980.

Prickett, Stephen. *Romanticism and Religion: The Tradition of Coleridge and Wordsworth in the Victorian Church.* Cambridge: Cambridge University Press, 1976.

Rattenbury, J. E. *The Conversion of the Wesleys: A Critical Study.* London: The Epworth Press, 1938.

Robin, Leon. *Pyrrhon et le Scepticisme Grec.* Paris: Presses Universitaires de France, 1944.

Rose, Steven, ed. *Against Biological Determinism.* New York: Schocken, 1982.

---, ed. *Towards a Liberatory Biology.* New York: Schocken, 1982.

Roszak, Theodore. "In Search of the Miraculous." *Harper's,* January 1981, pp. 54-62.

Ruoff, Gene W., and L. J. Swingle. "From the Editors." *The Wordsworth Circle* 10 (Spring 1979): 130.

Savage, Marsha Kent. "Archibald Alison and the Spiritual Aesthetics of William Wordsworth." Ph.D. diss., University of Florida, 1980.

Schlick, Moritz. *Problems of Ethics.* Translated by David Ryrin. Reprint. New York: Prentice-Hall, 1939.

Schmidt, Martin. *John Wesley: A Theological Biography.* 2 vols. New York: Abingdon Press, 1961.

Schofield, Robert E. *Mechanism and Materialism: British Natural Philosophy in an Age of Reason.* Princeton: Princeton University Press, 1970.

Schuda, Robert Bernard. "A Study of Laurence Sterne's Sermons: Yorkshire Background, Ethics, and Index." Ph.D. diss., University of Wisconsin, 1975.

Semmel, Bernard. *The Methodist Revolution.* New York: Basic Books, 1973.

Spacks, Patricia Meyer. *An Argument of Images: The Poetry of Alexander Pope.* Cambridge: Harvard University Press, 1971.

Stephen, Sir Leslie. *A History of English Thought in the Eighteenth Century.* 3d ed. 2 vols. Reprint. New York: G. P. Putnam's Sons, 1927.

Stromberg, R. N. *Religious Liberalism in Eighteenth-Century England.* London: Oxford University Press, 1954.

Telford, John. *The Life of John Wesley.* London: Hodder and Stoughton, 1886.

Thilly, Frank. *A History of Philosophy.* 3d ed. rev. by Ledger Wood. New York: Holt, Rinehart, and Winston, 1957.

Thompson, E. P. Review of *A Gathered Church: The Literature of the English Dissenting Interest,* by Donald Davie. *The Modern Language Review* 75 (January 1980): 165.

Todd, John Murray. *John Wesley and the Catholic Church.* London: Hodder and Stoughton, 1958.

Tyerman, Luke. *The Life and Times of the Rev. John Wesley.* London: Harper and Brothers, 1870.

Wearmouth, Robert Featherstone. *Methodism and the Common People of the Eighteenth Century.* London: The Epworth Press, 1945.

---. *Methodism and the Working Class Movements of England, 1800-1850.* London: The Epworth Press, 1937.

Whiteley, J. H. *Wesley's England: A Survey of Eighteenth-Century Social and Cultural Conditions.* London: The Epworth Press, 1938.

Willey, Basil. *The Eighteenth-Century Background: Studies on the Idea of Nature in the Thought of the Period.* 1940. Reprint. New York: Columbia University Press, 1964.

---. "On Wordsworth and the Locke Tradition." In *The Seventeenth-Century Background: Studies in the Thought of the Age in Relation to Poetry and Religion.* 1934. Reprint. London: Chatto & Windus, 1949.

Williams, Aubrey. *An Approach to Congreve.* New Haven: Yale University Press, 1979.

Yates, Arthur S. *The Doctrine of Assurance: with Special Reference to John Wesley.* London: The Epworth Press, 1952..

3. *Locke and Wesley: An Essence of Influence*

Does the great principle of empiricism—namely, that one must see for oneself and be in the presence of the thing one knows—extend to evangelicalism? Does each of these -isms operate along a continuum joining emotion to intellect? Does one of these methodologies link the external to words through ideas of sensation as though perception were mediation? Does the other link the external to words through ideals of sensation as though grace were perception? If empiricism refers to direct impact from, and includes immediate contact with, objects and subjects in time and place, does evangelicalism entertain the similarly reciprocating notions that religious truth is concerned with experiential presuppositions, and that experience itself need not be nonreligious?

Yes, since John Locke's influence on John Wesley and Wesley's Locke's influence on Wesley's followers can constitute the twofold case in point. This nexus of thought and feeling connected the sense-based reason of British empiricism to the spiritual sense of immediate, if not traditional, revelation. This mode of philosophy and of theology morphed the analogy between sense perception and spiritual sense into experience/faith continuum, and perhaps even into experience-faith identity. Wesley spread this state-of-the-art word of natural-to-spiritual efficacy throughout his parish, the world. Thus his transatlantic revival became an experiment in life force and took on the forceful life of an experiment. His all-encompassing alignment of the Enlightenment with heart religion laid the groundwork for pro-experience heart leaps of Romantic Anglo-America, and shows to this day how different from neoclassical evangelism is its science-averse offshoot in the twenty-first-century reaches of the post-Modern world.

It may be helpful, in this essay, to summarize those previous arguments of this series that pertain to Wesley's immersion in Locke's *Essay concerning Human Understanding* (1690). Wesley, after all, will figure prominently in the series' take on how, for instance, Emily Dickinson's experience/faith dialogue favored experience at the expense of, though with continuing respect for, faith. Locke's rational empiricism galvanized Wesley to express the ineffable occurrence of sense-like grace through the language of sense-based method. It was as though natural and spiritual experience could be one and the same. Besides being scriptural, classical, and colloquial, Wesley's prose was pervasively philosophical. His rich and strange but readable hybrid, his composite thought nameable as philosophical theology, harked back to British empiricism, and leaped forward toward evangelical—and literary—practice in the nineteenth-century Anglo-American world.

Here, preliminary to the analytical as well as chronological concentration on Wesley's decisive decade of the 1740s, is a narrative overview of his empirical study. In 1730, intrigued by an obscure follower of Locke—Peter Browne, Bishop of Cork and Ross during the 1720s and 1730s—Wesley abridged Browne's *Procedure, Extent, and Limits of Human Understanding* (1728), a theologizing of empiricism. In 1763, Wesley published his condensation of Browne's work in Wesley's anthology of science, *A Survey of the Wisdom of God in the Creation: or a Compendium of Natural Philosophy*, which formed one of Wesley's many educational enterprises. In 1781, Wesley wrote annotations to Locke's *Essay*, and published them, with extracts from the *Essay*, in Wesley's serial for his followers, *The Arminian Magazine*, during 1782–1784. Thus generations of laity encountered empiricism per se, as well as empirical evangelicalism. It is especially significant that Wesley took women seriously as philosophical and theological discussion partners, encouraging their abilities as did few of his contemporaries.

Well before, long after, and as catalyst of his strange warming of the heart at a quarter to nine on the evening of May 24, 1738, in Aldersgate Street, London, Wesley was steeped in Locke's sense-based theory of knowledge. A spiritual watershed of English cultural life, Wesley's conversion had as much to do with the *tabula rasa* of Wesley's mind, and hence with the times and places of Wesley's sense experience, as with the state of his soul. Thus, besides designating the devotional exercises of his Holy Club at Oxford during the 1730s, and besides referencing the religious discipline of his followers thereafter, Wesley's intellectual as well as emotional origination of Methodism denotes their induction of knowledge from experience.

The decade to conjure with is the 1740s, when Wesley developed his Locke-derived breakthrough in the experience/faith conundrum. For example, just as Locke's view that words correspond to things through ideas led him to advocate a simple style (see the discussion of *Essay* 3 in Brantley *Locke* 31–33), so his theory of language informed Wesley's *Character of a Methodist* (1742), and turned this message into an intellectual treatise:

> The most obvious, easy, common words, wherein our meaning can be conveyed [Wesley writes], we prefer before others, both on ordinary occasions, and when we speak of the things of God. We never, therefore, willingly or designedly, deviate from the usual way of speaking, unless when we express scripture truths in scripture words, which, we presume, no Christian will condemn. (Jackson 8:340)

Of course, both Locke and Wesley recognized the fundamentally metaphorical and analogical nature of language, and hence they both acknowledged, as well, the potential for arbitrariness and imprecision in the capacity of words to represent and communicate truths, whether natural or spiritual. Still, if only at the level of diction, both the philosopher and the preacher held that simplicity and clarity of speech could augur purity, stability, reliability, and transparency of understanding.

The combination of message and intellectual treatise in *An Earnest Appeal to Men of Reason and Religion* (1743) kept not only the Bible but also Locke's *Essay* in the direct line of Wesley's central vision:

> You know [Wesley writes emphatically and at length] . . . that before it is possible for you to form a true judgment of the things of God, it is absolutely necessary that you have a clear apprehension of them, and that your ideas thereof be all fixed, distinct, and determinate. And seeing our ideas are not innate, but must all originally come from our senses, it is certainly necessary that you have senses capable of discerning objects of this kind—not those only which are called "natural senses," which in this respect profit nothing, as being altogether incapable of discerning objects of a spir-

> itual kind, but spiritual senses, exercised to discern spiritual good and evil . . .
> And till you have these internal senses, till the eyes of your understanding are opened, you can have no apprehension of divine things, no idea of them at all. Nor consequently, till then, can you either judge truly or reason justly concerning them, seeing your reason has no ground whereon to stand, no materials to work upon. (Cragg 56–57)

The sense-based word choice—namely, "materials," "ground," "eyes," "internal senses," "natural senses," "objects," and "things"—constitutes perhaps the fullest statement of Wesley's spiritual sense. The philosophical demand for empiricism, which in Locke's is rational as well as sense-based, is also met in Wesley's far from antirational concept of inspiration, which he associates with terms such as "discern," "reason," "understanding," "ideas," "apprehension," and "judgment." As though to maintain Locke's balance between reason and its ground, Wesley indicates a radically metaphorical, far from arbitrary relation between rational apprehension and the spiritual sense. Consistent with his endorsement of *tabula rasa* as the first principle of theology as well as of philosophy, he signals his dependence on, as well as his affinity for, Locke's method. The operative phrase, the heart of the matter, in Wesley's words "not those only which are called 'natural senses,'" is *natural senses*.

To be sure, in suggesting that sense perception is crucial to religion, Wesley avoids ever claiming that one can often, or even finally, stand on any common ground between experience and faith. Like *An Essay concerning Human Understanding*, *An Earnest Appeal to Men of Reason and Religion* stresses that natural understanding cannot easily, or ever clearly, apprehend spiritual truth: "What then [Wesley asks] will your reason do here? How will it pass from things natural to spiritual? From the things that are seen to those that are not seen? From the visible to the invisible world? What a gulf is here!" (Cragg 57). Nevertheless, faith is defined by Wesley not simply in accordance with scripture but even according to a balance between the sensing and the reasoning powers per se:

> [Faith] [Wesley observes] is the feeling of the soul, whereby a believer perceives, through the "power of the highest overshadowing him" [see Luke 1:35] both the existence and the presence of him in whom he "lives, moves, and has his being"

> [see Acts 17:28], and indeed the whole invisible world, the entire system of things eternal. And hereby, in particular, he feels "the love of God shed abroad in the heart" [see Romans 3:5]. (Cragg 47)

By *feeling*, Wesley does not mean "inner trend of belief" so much as "faith in relation to the senses," for *An Earnest Appeal to Men of Reason and Religion* speaks of "faith" in reference to "the eye," "the ear," and even "taste" (see, e.g., Cragg 46). Wesley's definition, finally, both by its diction ("whereby a believer *perceives*") and by its development throughout the treatise, intimates his view that religious feeling, like sense data, comprises matter for the mind to work upon. Thus the *Earnest Appeal* pays homage to Locke explicitly, or at least perspicuously. This important but surprising document of the growth of Wesley's mind during the 1740s draws an analogy between faith and empirical observation: "Faith is with regard to the spiritual world what sense is with regard to the natural" (Cragg 46). The precisely analogical structure of this breakthrough in religious epistemology rests on such far from arbitrary, if not radically metaphorical, association of faith with the natural senses that one hears here the identification of experience with faith that was to mark Methodism as a phenomenal new species of philosophical theology.

From 1745 through 1748, Wesley wrote letters to Mr. John Smith (an alias for Thomas Secker, Bishop of Oxford and later Bishop of Canterbury) in which appears such an arresting statement as this: "To this day, I have abundantly more temptation . . . to be . . . a philosophical sluggard, than an itinerant Preacher" (Telford 2:68). Throughout these letters, Wesley combines evangelistic goals with his love of philosophical theology, and especially pronounced is his Locke-derived method, for even to traditional revelation he applies Locke's as well as Descartes's skepticism. "I am as fully assured to-day [Wesley discloses to Smith], as I am of the rising of the sun, that the scriptures are of God. I cannot possibly deny or doubt of it now; yet I may doubt of it to-morrow; as I have done heretofore a thousand times, and that after the fullest assurance preceding" (Telford 2:92). Thus, the mind remains open even after carefully searching for, and apparently finding, what is not subject to doubt. The letters to Smith, moreover, acknowledge both poles of Locke's method, for the sense-based nature of mind is implicit in Wesley's phraseology "so far as men can judge from their eyes and ears" (Telford 2:44).

Rise and progress, a phrase characteristic of eighteenth-century British book titles, as in *The Rise and Progress of Religion in the Soul* (1742) by Philip

Doddridge, assumes the British philosophy of experience. When Wesley writes Smith that "we are speaking, not of the progress, but of the first rise, of faith" (Telford 2:48), he suggests, for one thing, that no more than knowledge does faith exist innately and, for another, that faith, like knowledge, must be datable by exact moments in personal history. "It cannot be, in the nature of things [Wesley tells Smith], that a man should be filled with this peace, and joy, and love, by the inspiration of the Holy Spirit, without perceiving it as clearly as he does the light of the sun" (Telford 2:64). Thus, just as one knows what one experiences naturally, so one has faith in what one encounters spiritually.[1]

In a sermon entitled "The Great Privilege of Those that are Born of God" (1748), Wesley affirms a real correspondence between universally describable experience and experience that, though possible for all, would remain quite ineffable were it not for Locke's linguistic instrument of analogy-cum-metaphor. With regard to the interpenetration of sense perception and the world of here-and-now, "The Great Privilege" sounds precisely Locke-initiated:

> No sooner is the child born into the world [Wesley teaches], than he . . . feels the air with which he is surrounded, and which pours into him from every side, as fast as he alternately breathes it back, to sustain the flame of life: and hence springs a continual increase of strength, of motion, and of sensation; all the bodily senses being now awakened, and furnished with their proper objects. (Wesley, *Sermons* 76; Wesley's emphasis)

In this passage, the mind's wakeful involvement with sense data is just as clear as in whole sections of *An Essay concerning Human Understanding* where Locke insists that the mind's response to sense experience is almost at one with what one needs to know about the world. The entire sermon preaches that "the circumstances of the natural birth" provide "the most easy way to understand the spiritual" (Wesley, *Sermons* 175)—that is, that the invisible world is familiar to twiceborn people whose spiritual sense parallels the limited but sufficient operation of the natural faculties. Wesley's description here of "senses, whereby alone we can discern the things of God" bespeaks a vital interaction—namely, what is "continually received" is "continually rendered back" (Wesley, *Sermons* 176). At the mental level, and with reference to the senses, spiritual experience is depicted throughout "The Great Privilege" as coalescence, as near-identification, with the condescension of God. Thus Wesley's alternation, or oscillation, between reason- and sense-based wording signifies, repeatedly, that through immediate revelation God and man are en-sphered, or rather that a clear intercourse occurs not just between man as object and God as subject but even between man as subject and God as object.

A Letter to the Reverend Dr. Conyers Middleton (1749), finally, expresses a paradoxically Locke-consistent theology of immediate revelation:

> Traditional evidence [Wesley admits, concerning the Bible] is of an extremely complicated nature, necessarily including so many and so various considerations, that only men of a strong and clear understanding can be sensible of its full force. On the contrary, how plain and simple is this; and how level to the lowest capacity! Is not this the sum: "One thing I know; I was blind, but now I see"? [see John 9:25]. An argument so plain, that a peasant, a woman, a child, may feel all its force.
>
> The traditional evidence of Christianity stands, as it were, a great way off; and therefore, although it speaks loud and clear, yet makes a less lively impression. It gives us an account of what was transacted long ago, in far distant times as well as places. Whereas the inward evidence is intimately present to all persons, at all times, and in all places. (Jackson 10:75–76)

The language here does not so much look down on women—see the discussion (in Brantley, *Locke*) of Wesley's proto-feminist streak—as democratically affirm the at once reason-strong and all but sensate capacity of all people to see the spiritual as well as natural object as in itself it really is. Wesley's attitude toward scripture here does not so much anticipate the Higher Criticism of the Bible during the nineteenth century as subordinate Bible-reading to near-identity between sense perception of natural knowledge and immediate revelation of the Holy Spirit's ongoing and unfolding truth.[2] Although Wesley is sedulous here to manifest reticence about just how much one can know from spiritual sense and discernment—there is no mere knowingness of self-indulgent enthusiasm in this passage—his fully epistemological tone signals his relative confidence in immediate revelation as an avenue to enlightenment.

> Is it not so [Wesley asks Middleton]? Let impartial reason speak. Does not every thinking man want a window, not so much in his

> neighbour's, as in his own, breast? He wants an opening there, of whatever kind, that might let in light from eternity. He is pained to be thus feeling after God so darkly and uncertainly: to know so little of God, and indeed so little of any beside material objects. He is concerned, that he must see even that little not directly, but in the dim, sullied glass of sense; and consequently so imperfectly and obscurely, that it is all a mere enigma still.
>
> Now, these very desiderata faith supplies. It gives a more extensive knowledge of things invisible, showing what eye had not seen, nor ear heard, neither could it enter into our heart to conceive [see I Cor. 2:9]. And all these it shows in the clearest light, with the fullest certainty and evidence. For it does not leave us to receive our notice of them by mere reflection from the dull glass of sense; but resolves a thousand enigmas of the highest concern by giving faculties suited to things invisible. (Jackson 10:74–75)

Couched in the doubly empirical context of a not-so-buried optics metaphor (notice the lens-focusing implication of "resolves a thousand enigmas") and experientially philosophical language for, and from, the Bible, this statement is more than in keeping with *An Essay concerning Human Understanding*. The avowal epitomizes Wesley's at once spiritual and natural mode of knowing and of speaking—that is, his brand of faith as less different from, than enhancing and extensive of, the senses.

Wesley not only drew an analogy between sense perception and revelation but also attempted, in an almost more than merely metaphorical manner, to bridge the gap between natural and spiritual experience. Insofar as he shaped an eighteenth- and nineteenth-century kind of thought and feeling, the empirical and the evangelical understanding of experience came together for the Anglo-American middle class. British authors as late as Thomas Carlyle and Alfred, Lord Tennyson and American authors as late as Ralph Waldo Emerson and Emily Dickinson descended intellectually as well as spiritually from Wesley insofar as all four of these writers of belletristic prose and of poetry accepted as well as theologized empiricism. This quartet grounded transcendentalism in mind and world, balanced religious myths and religious morality with scientific reverence for fact and detail, allied this-worldly assumptions with spiritual discipline, and shared the rational and sense-respecting reliance on experience as the less royal than public road to natural knowledge and divine truth alike.

NOTES

[1] One thinks here of Mark Noll's discussion of "power evangelism," "a phrase originating with Lonnie Frisbee and the title of one of [John] Wimber's best-known books, which stresses tangible signs from the Holy Spirit as the key to Christian conversion" (Noll 25).

[2] For a portrait of the Friday Masowe Apostolic Church of Zimbabwe, which has discarded the Bible in favor of direct experience of the Holy Spirit, see Engelke. The so-called "antinomianism" (John Winthrop's term) of Anne Hutchinson (during the 1630s and 1640s) comes to mind, as well.

WORKS CITED

Brantley, Richard E. *Locke, Wesley, and the Method of English Romanticism.* Gainesville: University Press of Florida, 1984.

Cragg, Gerald R., ed. *The Appeals to Men of Reason and Religion and Certain Related Open Letters.* By John Wesley. Vol. 11 of *The Works of John Wesley.* Edited by Frank Baker. Oxford: Clarendon Press, 1975.

Engelke, Matthew. *A Problem of Presence: Beyond Scripture in an African Church.* Berkeley: University of California Press, 2007.

Jackson, Thomas, ed. *The Works of the Rev. John Wesley, A. M.* 14 vols. 1829-31. Reprint. Grand Rapids, MI: Zondervan Press, 1958.

Noll, Mark. "Among the Believers" *The New Republic*, September 13, 2012, 23-28.

Telford, John, ed. *The Letters of John Wesley, A. M., Sometime Fellow of Lincoln College, Oxford.* 8 vols. London: Epworth Press, 1933.

Wesley, John. *Sermons on Several Occasions.* London: Epworth Press, 1944.

4. *Wesley and Edwards: An Anglo-American Nexus*

Commonplaces stand in need of scrutiny. The special relationship between England and the United States is more than merely political, more than merely linguistic, and even more than broadly cultural, for it is at once, and perennially, intellectual and emotional. An especially useful metaphor for this relationship is the special relationship between the Englishman John Wesley and the American Jonathan Edwards. Although they never consciously cooperated with one another, they contributed to a variety of relations between their respective lands. Wesley founded Methodist movements in both England and the United States, and Edwards joined forces with the Briton George Whitefield, who undertook the arduous journey to the colonies in order to participate in the Great Awakening. Wesley and Edwards inspired popular evangelicalism in Britain and America from the 1730s, through the American Revolution, to the end of the nineteenth century. By regarding them as emblematic, I seek to delineate an especially enduring, because still resonating, Anglo-American mode of thought and feeling. The intellectual sway and fervor of Wesley and Edwards contributed to Anglo-American experience.

Whether or not the special relationship between England and the United States rests in large part, even now, on an intellectual as well as emotional frame of reference to nature and to spirit, this frame is not only the considered construct of Wesley and Edwards but also their joint legacy to the nineteenth century. Constituting an Anglo-American *genius loci*, Wesley and Edwards express and disseminate their shared definition of feeling and thought. Through their concerted roles as social forces, through an often indirect but sometimes direct and always propitious process of cultural osmosis, they make up the very model of an Anglo-American sensibility. Their religious methodologies are not, after all, so far removed from even such early twentieth-century methods as the verification principles of the Briton A. J. Ayer and the pragmatism of the American John Dewey. Many such "representative men"[1] (one would say "representative people") participate in the same binational entity, the same "nature-culture coevolution"[2] of Anglo-American relations.

This essay, by examining the influence of Wesley and Edwards from the broadest possible perspective, and by addressing their common ground as one single subject, surveys an especially fertile ground of Anglo-American expression. I will consider them philosophically, rather than exclusively theologically, and approach them as methodologically alert, even where they thought themselves simply orthodox. I seek to demonstrate that they shared the same essentially Lockean insights that, as I have previously argued, informed much of British literature and theology from 1740 to 1840. I acknowledge differences between them, yet I discover their common ground, the full character of their two-way special relationship. The twin pioneers of transatlantic revivalism are brothers of both soul and mind in that both men appropriate Lockean empiricism for religious methodology. Indeed, the philosophical as well as religious epistemology of this charismatic duumvirate of the Anglo-American world exemplifies the Anglo-American imagination.

Edwards: An Orientation

Although recent scholarship on Edwards emphasizes his conservatism and his relation to Scottish Commonsense philosophy,[3] Locke was a formative influence on the Commonsense school. Edwards's indebtedness to Locke[4] is consistent with conservative principles in that Locke takes account of both empiricism and "a theocentric framework."[5] Terrence Erdt traces Edwards's language to its conservative source in Calvin and emphasizes the aesthetic dimension of that language; he also acknowledges that an understanding of Edwards's sense-language is central to an understanding of Edwards.[6] Roland Delattre argues that especially according to *The Nature of True Virtue* (1765) divine being is both present to humankind as beauty and known to humankind through emotion.[7] Similarly, though with explicit reference to Locke, I maintain an aesthetic-epistemological emphasis in my approach to Edwards's theology.

Sacvan Bercovitch regards with new respect the pioneering argument of Perry Miller that Edwards is a Lockean.[8] While I share this new respect, it is time to discover new complexities in the Lockean view of Edwards. As I confirm Wallace E. Anderson's conviction that Edwards "accepted Locke's view that it is a wholly contingent matter that each mind receives the sensory information it does,"[9] I consider the consensus that although Lockean ideas of sensation represent real qualities of bodies, real qualities in Edwards's works are often identified only with "the fixed order and relations of ideas."[10] Moreover, although Miller's argument is exclusively sense-oriented, my view of Locke's empiricism is that it is both sense- and reason-based, a view consistent with Edwards's immersion in the categories of sense perception and his desire for the consent of mind to mind.

Whatever the merits, then, of the labels *idealist, Platonist, scholastic, Calvinist,* and *mystic,* the labels *empiricist* and *sensationalist* are particularly apt for Edwards in his eighteenth-century context. The "radical theism" that Robert W. Jenson describes embraces what he sees as Edwards's most characteristic themes: God's relation to nature and history, religious experience, the presence of Christ, and the perfected human community.[11] But "radical theism" also includes the precisely philosophical, because specifically Lockean, theme of the here and now. Although Edwards rejects Newton's cosmology of the universe as a machine, he does not reject Locke's livelier, more down-to-earth world picture. Despite Edwards's life-long struggle with his age's Arminian tendency toward autonomous individuality, his radical theism preserves Locke-derived faith in individual experience.

Wesley and Edwards: An Overview

Charles Rogers, in his attempt to differentiate the pair, disclaims for Edwards any affinity with Wesley's views about providence in general and predestination in particular.[12] Wesley's comments about Edwards's *The Freedom of the Will* (1754) deplore its doctrines of irresistible grace and unconditional election.[13] Wesley's comments, however, approve of Edwards where Edwards posits the experiential context of the soul as a given of religious life: "The soul [quoted Wesley] is now connected with a material vehicle, and placed in the material world. Various objects here continually strike upon one or other of the bodily organs."[14] Albert C. Outler, on the basis of Wesley's published abridgments of five works by Edwards, suggests that Edwards was a formative influence on Wesley.[15] Without losing sight of Rogers's point of view, I concur with Outler's: although Edwards referred to Wesley just once, and disparagingly,[16] Wesley rejoiced in Edwards. Accordingly, I seek to establish the intellectual as well as emotional sense in which they should be linked.

Frederick Dreyer sees them as intellectual polar opposites:

> Edwards's thought was ultimately ontological and proceeded from the premise of necessary being. Wesley's was psychological and proceeded from the premise of self-consciousness. Wesley is satisfied with the apparent truths that ordinary mortals do in fact perceive. Edwards insists upon the necessary truths they ought to perceive.[17]

Except that I would substitute *epistemological* for *psychological*, I am in accord with Dreyer's estimate of Wesley, and Dreyer's estimate of Edwards rings true in that Edwards's ontological moods indeed recur. His early essay "On Being," for example, rests on a rationalistic base, the "platonic traditions of idealism";[18] and toward the end of his career, he clearly retreats from any ostensible harmony of empiricism and faith to a rather intransigent rationalism, a rationalism of the supernatural, if you will. Wesley does not follow this path, for while believing in the supernatural as much as anyone, Wesley holds to the senses and to sense-based reason.

In midcareer, however, Edwards comes close to having it both ways, as Wesley does throughout his life. Against the view of Edwards as exclusively ontological, I contend that his theology, like Wesley's, is often epistemological, and I accordingly emphasize that Lockean empiricism provides a philosophic reason for linking Wesley with Edwards. In "Wesley and Edwards: A Hypothesis," Appendix A of my *Locke, Wesley, and the Method of English Romanticism*, I suggest that Edwards derives his theological method from Locke's theory of knowledge. Wesley uses Locke's language to devise an analogy between the natural senses and the "spiritual sense"; he even conceives of a continuum joining scientific method and rational empiricism to natural and revealed religion. Edwards, too, in midcareer at least, envisions this analogy or continuum.

A Document

The shortest way to bring the pair into my field of vision is through Wesley's abridgment (1773) of Edwards's *A Treatise concerning Religious Affections* (1746). This last of Wesley's abridgments of five works by Edwards[19] culminates Wesley's thirty-year response to Edwards's works and hence constitutes Wesley's most mature judgment of those works. *Religious Affections* marks the central juncture of Edwards's development, at the midpoint of his career, and is thus the best representative of his mind and method.

Appearing in volume 23 of Wesley's collected works of 1771-74, *An Extract from a Treatise concerning Religious Affections* omits the entire preface of Edwards's work, the second, third, and fourth of the twelve major sections of part three, many shorter passages, and many words and phrases.[20] Published in 1762, the edition of *Religious Affections* that Wesley used is itself an abridgment by William Gordon.[21]

Although Gregory S. Clapper, in the only other full-length study of Wesley's abridgment, acknowledges that "Gordon's abridgment was about two-thirds of the original" and that "Wesley's was one-sixth," Clapper demonstrates that neither the "excisions and revisions" of Gordon nor those of Wesley "pervert the essential thrust of Edwards's work."[22] To compare Wesley's abridgment with Gordon's, then, is to compare it with *Religious Affections*, too. Wesley's abridgment is not only true to the original, but also "better," that is, less prolix.

Although Wesley often objected to works he carefully read,[23] and although his more than two hundred abridgments sometimes include matter with which he disagreed,[24] his abridgment of *Religious Affections* is so painstaking, polished, and selective that it indicates well his attraction to Edwards's sensibility. By analyzing the abridgment, I characterize Wesley's distillation of Edwards and hence Edwards's influence on Wesley. As occasion rises, I point to parallels between the abridgment and Wesley's works. Nothing Wesley ever wrote materially contradicts either the abridgment or any other version from Edwards's prime; indeed, what appears in the abridgment finds strikingly similar expression throughout Wesley's works.

The abridgment not only omits, but also alters, and some of the alterations are substantive.[25] As an Arminian who believes that "Christ died for *every Soul* of Man,"[26] Wesley excises Edwards's Calvinism and its doctrine of the elect. Where Edwards inveighs against the view that "mine own hands hath saved me," Wesley balks and quotes nothing,[27] thus suggesting that one bears partial responsibility for one's own salvation. Where Edwards says "the covenant is ordered in all things, and sure," Wesley is silent,[28] thus refusing predestinarian tincture. "Continuance in duty," writes Edwards, is "difficult to [one's very] nature," which is full of "blindness, deceit, self-flattery, self-exaltation, and self-confidence," and he adds, for good measure, that even "the saint . . . has sight of his own corruptions," but Wesley gives no quarter to this extreme belief in human frailty.[29]

Such omissions suggest an anti-Calvinist rationale for Wesley's numerous rejections of Edwards's harsh, uncharitable language. Where Edwards speaks of some religious affections as "false and counterfeit," Wesley calls them merely "mixed or degenerating,"[30] as though to soften the implication of hardened duplicity. Where Edwards argues that "persons may have a kind of religious love, and yet have no saving grace," Wesley, who often says that love and grace are so far from being thus mutually exclusive that they are in fact one and the same, keeps quiet.[31] Where Edwards insists on phrases like "great corruption," "strait and narrow way," "fears of hell," "the duty of self-denial," "deserved eternal burnings," "the infinitely hateful nature of sin," and "the infinitely inferior nature of men," Wesley will have none of it.[32] Indeed, Wesley will have very little Calvinist language of any kind, however innocuous, for though the word *saints*, with its overtones of the perseverance thereof, appears four times,[33] he usually goes to great lengths to avoid even this mild Calvinism. He replaces Edwards's "true saints," "eminent saints," "the character of the saints," and "the minds of the saints" with "Christians," "believers," "good men," "we," "those," or almost anything else he can think of.[34]

"The Eye altering alters all," declared William Blake,[35] which means not only that the organs of perception are creative, that the eye changes what it sees, but also that "the Eye altering" is changed by what it sees, that all is changed within. Similarly, though Wesley's emendatory powers transform some doctrines and improve the style of *Religious Affections*, his editorial eye is itself improved, his "doors of perception" "cleansed,"[36] by his encounter with and his obvious reverence for Edwards's methodology. Although Wesley's thought guides his editorial hand to the point of bias, the abridgment includes, as Wesley's Note to the Reader puts it, those "many remarks and admonitions" of Edwards's "which may be of great use to the children of God."[37]

Clapper, pointing out such parallels between *Religious Affections* and Wesley's works as reliance on Scripture and the theme of humble joy, concludes that

> if one were to give an irenic reading of their differences, one might say that Wesley and Edwards agreed about the sovereignty of God, but that while Edwards expressed this sovereignty through his Calvinist doctrines of predestination and the bondage of the will, Wesley expressed the same thing by emphasizing prevenient grace and the perfecting possibilities of the spirit.[38]

Since the agreement between Wesley and Edwards about the sovereignty of God did not prevent Wesley from rejecting Edwards's *language* of sovereignty at least three times in the abridgment,[39] one might quibble with part of Clapper's statement. But the statement rings true with regard to the abridgment as a whole, which, as Clapper demonstrates, is both careful to epitomize the four basic parts of Edwards's text and consistent with the basic tenets of Wesley's texts.

Finally, though, the abridgment represents more than the merely theological commonality of Wesley and Edwards. Although "edification was Wesley's ultimate criterion when evaluating the written word," Wesley, as even Clapper acknowledges, "shared Edwards's interest in science and philosophy."[40] Although Wesley's Note to the Reader complains that Edwards "heaps together so many curious, subtle, metaphysical distinctions, as are sufficient to puzzle the brain, and confound the intellects of all the plain men and women in the universe," that is, although the abridgment eschews Edwards's ontology, the abridgment is decidedly epistemological wherever Edwards is so.[41] Just as Lockean epistemology avoids regarding mind as superior to, or independent of, sense experience, so Wesley downplays diction that might be construed as rationalist. Where Edwards speaks of "the more vigorous and sensible exercises of the inclination and will of the soul," Wesley, by writing "the more vigorous and sensible exercises of the will,"[42] omits spiritual, mentalist elements, while he retains sense-language. Where Edwards writes, "It may be enquired what are the affections of the mind," Wesley omits "of the mind."[43] Since the fourth of Edwards's twelve distinguishing signs of "Truly Gracious and Holy Affections" asserts the intellectual component in the affections—"Gracious affections do arise from the mind's being enlightened, rightly and spiritually to understand or apprehend divine things"—it may seem strange that the intellectual Wesley omitted it, until one realizes how close it is to rationalism, that is, to a reason insufficiently involved in, or insufficiently tempered by, sense experience.[44]

In line with the fact that Edwards's reasoning is not always sense-based, an entire category of passages appears to have been altered because, although philosophical or methodological enough, they are not sufficiently empirical to suit Wesley. Where Edwards complains of those who "tell you a long story of conversion" or "a fair story of illuminations and discoveries," Wesley, who likes accounts of experiential efficacy, eliminates the complaint.[45] From Edwards's phrase "doctrinal knowledge," Wesley drops "doctrinal,"[46] as though to include natural knowledge in knowledge conducive to religion. "Ministers," writes Edwards, sometimes insist too much on "distinctness and clearness of method," for the Spirit does not "proceed discernibly in the steps of a particular established scheme, one half so often as is imagined."[47] But Wesley finds no place for this passage:[48] although his "empiricism" is not unacquainted with paradox, he likes method to be clear and distinct.[49]

Thus manipulating as well as preserving the original, Wesley's editorial procedure is motivated in decisive measure by the Lockean presuppositions of his theology. Where Edwards's theology is consistent with those presuppositions, where his theology is "empirical," Wesley tends to make it more so. Witness, for example, his twofold strategy of quoting Edwards's endorsement of experiential priorities—"Without affections, one is wholly destitute of the saving influences of the Holy Spirit"—and omitting an adjacent passage in which Edwards creates some doubt about the very affectional life he advocates: "As there is no true religion, where there is nothing else but affection; so there is no true religion, where there is no affection."[50] Where Edwards speaks of "holy desire exercised in longings, hungerings, and thirstings after God," Wesley omits "longings," as though to lessen subjectivity and so to intensify the sensationalist implications of this biblical and somehow eighteenth-century phraseology.[51]

Wesley is justified in detecting empirical assumptions and empirical language in *Religious Affections*, which is reconcilable with, and even measures up to, Wesley's own Lockean tastes and expectations, his experiential bias and, above all, his doctrine of the "spiritual sense."[52] Notably, he tampers least with passages most clearly resembling his Lockean method. These passages, totaling twenty-two of the abridgment's sixty-five pages,[53] form the focus of this essay. They constitute both a precise transformation of Lockean method and what Wesley thought was the broadest agreement between Edwards and himself. Here I consider this strain of passages both in itself and in context; I elaborate on a theological equivalent of Locke's philosophy, demonstrating the Lockean ground of both Wesley and Edwards as found in the abridgment. I enunciate a "spiritual sense" as much American as British.

Wesley's and Edwards's evangelical faiths draw in part from both the processes and the forms of late seventeenth-century empiricism, even as they laterally displace them. Wesley's editing is so thoroughly informed by Locke's *Essay concerning Human Understanding* (1690) that the abridgment emerges, without falsifying the original, as a theologizing of Locke's empiricism. To abridge is "to shorten" or even "to curtail," but the abridgment of *Religious Affections* is no mere summary, no mere abstraction, and no mere "selection of essential facts." Wesley's configuring of Edwards's "epistemology" is, in addition, a condensation that epitomizes the original without diluting it and honors the original by enhancing it. Wesley decided that *Religious Affections* is complexly but manifestly empirical, and I agree. This midpoint of Edwards's thought is indeed characterized by the same Locke-derived emphasis on experience, natural as well as spiritual, to be found in Wesley's Methodism. Wesley's abridgment, by heightening that emphasis, epitomizes the "epistemology" common to him and Edwards. Where most alike and nearest the generic level of revival imagination, they are at once methodically intellectual and in resonance with the enabling powers of empirical premises.

By the abridgment, then, I mean a bridge indeed. It is the intersection of the thought of Wesley and the thought of Edwards. The one's Arminianism and the other's Calvinism lie outside the abridgment. Wesley did not stake his theological reputation on the abridgment, nor did Edwards approve it as faithful to his thought. The abridgment contains, however, what they share, not so much the theological as the philosophical thought, the Locke-inspired emphasis on the experiential, which they then each express in their evangelical theologies and practices. So when I use the term "the abridgment" in this work, I mean the areas where the thought of Wesley and the thought of Edwards coincide.

A Reading

"Even deliberately to write against something," observes Denis Donoghue, "is to take one's bearings from it."[54] The abridgment takes its bearings from Lockean epistemology without being subsumed by it. In advocating experience as the way to knowledge, the abridgment is historically akin to and even agrees with Locke's preaching of sensation as the key to empirical knowledge. Locke, in homage to Descartes, intuits himself and deduces God:

> For nothing can be more evident to us, than our own Existence.... Thus from the Consideration of our Selves, ... our Reason leads us to the Knowledge ... That *there is an eternal, most powerful, most knowing Being.*[55]

Locke goes on to insist, however, that "the *Knowledge of the Existence* of any other thing we can have only by *Sensation,*"[56] and his epistemology of sensation is his major contribution to the ways of knowing. The abridgment, especially its twenty-two pages of Lockean method, appropriates this epistemology not only to say how one knows that natural things exist but also to indicate in what manner, and according to what similitude, one knows all spiritual things, including selves and God's own Self. Although spirit and sense would seem opposites (they can be thought of as antipodes and hence complements), the abridgment, without being either loose in applying to theology the language of sensation or glib about spiritual knowledge, attempts to locate the religious in the empirical and vice versa. Thus the abridgment suggests a way of overcoming the split between the natural and the supernatural, and indeed envisions the terms of their unification. Although the abridgment and Locke's *Essay* are not always consistent with one another, and the relation between them is one of give-and-take, they share a frame of reference and a set of methodological assumptions, a language and an interest in the same issues.

To be sure, Locke's stand against enthusiasm echoes in the abridgment. "Immediate *Revelation*," observes Locke,

> being a much easier way for Men to establish their Opinions, and regulate their Conduct, than the tedious and not always successful Labour of strict Reasoning, it is no wonder, that some have been very apt to pretend to Revelation, and to perswade themselves, that they are under the peculiar guidance of Heaven.[57]

The abridgment similarly urges caution in speaking of, and in making claims to, immediate revelation:

> The manner of the Spirit's proceeding in them that are born of the Spirit, is very often exceeding mysterious. It is oftentimes as difficult to know the way of the Spirit in the new birth, as in the first birth: "As thou knowest not what is the way of the Spirit, or how the bones do grow in the womb of her that is with child: Even so thou knowest not the work of God, that worketh all."[58]

Thus both the *Essay* and the abridgment flatly state that the Spirit's workings hardly ever come under the power of either human understanding or human observation.

Nevertheless, the abridgment proclaims the *fact* of the Spirit's proceeding, and perhaps even implies, in radical homage to Locke, that the Spirit's workings sometimes significantly come under the powers of both human understanding and human observation. Locke, on one occasion, acknowledges that God can "excite [men] to Good Actions by the immediate influence and assistance of the Holy Spirit, without any extraordinary Signs accompanying it,"[59] but Locke is primarily concerned to prevent the recurrence of mid-seventeenth-century Puritan excess.[60] His *Essay*, accordingly, though admitting the possibility of visitation, warns that people who claim it are most probably mad. The abridgment concedes that many who claim it are wrong and even that some who claim it are mad. It argues, though, that visitation is a very possible event for religious people: "How greatly," lament Wesley and Edwards, "has the doctrine of sensibly perceiving the immediate power of the Spirit of God, been ridiculed."[61] "Sensibly perceiving," highlighting Lockean language, does not just employ, but recommends for spiritual experience, a Lockean criterion that blends mind with discernment.

Almost despite itself, the same paragraph that warns that "no man can tell whence [the Spirit] came, or whither it went" (cf. John 3.8) uses empirical expression. The paragraph, though indirectly and by analogy, appeals to the powers of observation and perception in "we, as it were, hear the sound of it, the effect of it is discernible."[62] This testimony, indeed, is based on more than analogy, for "the effect of it is discernible" connotes sense perceptions as tests or validations of something prior. "We, as it were, hear the sound of it" (even with the "as it were") rings with immediacy and presence, and so stops just short of denoting the senses as preconditions for divine experience.

The abridgment often gives so much credit to Locke's experiential criteria that it entertains a thought at which Locke would be horrified, namely, the direct sensation of God's effects and presence. The following quotation, for example, places all bets on the world of sense experience: "Men will trust their God no further than they know him, and they cannot be in the exercise of faith in him one ace further than they have a sight of his fulness and faithfulness in exercise."[63] "A sight of" need not mean physical sight, but the statement implies that regarding all matters of fact and causation, including the divine, Edwards, and Wesley through him, have the courage of Locke's convictions about experiential vision.

In their evocation of Locke's trust in eyewitness accounts, moreover, Edwards and Wesley wax particularly philosophic:

> Those are very improperly called witnesses of the truth of any thing, who only declare they are of opinion, such a thing

> is true. Those only are proper witnesses who testify that they
> have seen the truth of the thing they assert.[64]

Even here, of course, ambiguities arise, for one sees not the thing, but the truth of the thing; but far from meaning only that the senses are outward analogues to inner perception, this strong statement indicates, too, the clear possibility of perceiving God and his effects directly.

Finally, in the question, "What is a tender heart, but one that is easily impressed with what ought to affect it?"[65] the abridgment evinces not only Lockean diction[66] but also, and more importantly, the entire Lockean as well as Wordsworthian premise of "wise passiveness."[67] The self in both the *Essay* and the abridgment is valued, then, insofar as it is receptive, though with a remaining ambiguity about whether "tender heart" is specifically a metaphor for receptivity to the Spirit. It mattered greatly to both the philosopher and the revivalists what is happening to us at a given time, and what acts upon us from without.

Consider, next, their telling word *impulse*. *Impulse* for Locke, Wesley, and Edwards, besides meaning "something opposed to deliberate reflection, as in the phrase 'to act on impulse,'" can indicate "a movement stirred in us from without, an influence upon the individual of some force in the outer universe."[68] Here, for example, is Locke's ambiguously subjective and objective use of *impulse*. Attacking those who claim "illumination from the Spirit of God," he observes that "whatsoever odd Action they find in themselves a strong inclination to do, that *impulse* is concluded to be a call or direction from Heaven, and must be obeyed."[69] In their own mood of attacking "self-deceivers" who claim, falsely, the "discoveries and elevations" of immediate revelation, Edwards and Wesley similarly observe that "the chief grounds of the confidence of many of them are *impulses* and supposed revelations, sometimes with texts of Scripture, and sometimes without. These *impulses* they have called the witness of the Spirit."[70] Locke for his part, and Wesley and Edwards for theirs, refuse to credit the enthusiasts' objective meaning, but the *Essay* elsewhere employs the word in its objective sense:

> How often may a Man observe in himself, that whilst his Mind
> is intently employ'd in the contemplation of some Objects; and
> curiously surveyed some ideas that are there, it takes no notice
> of impressions of sounding Bodies, made upon the organ of
> Hearing, with the same alteration, that uses to be for the pro-

ducing the Idea of a Sound? A sufficient *impulse* there may be on the Organ; but it not reaching the Observation of the Mind, there follows no perception.[71]

And Wesley and Edwards, insofar as they agree that even spiritual experience can be an external force that focuses on the individual soul and shapes it in the arena of human history, would concur in an objective usage of *impulse* such as one finds in a theological treatise published during Locke's lifetime: *Discourse of Angels, ... also Something Touching Devils, Apparitions, and Impulses* (1701).[72]

Here, with a simultaneously objective and religious meaning, albeit without the word *impulse*, is the abridgment's premise that both natural and spiritual experiences write on the mind's blank tablet:

> Indeed the witness or seal of the Spirit, consists in the effect of the Spirit of God in the heart, in the implantation and exercises of grace there, and so consists in experience: And it is beyond doubt, that this seal of the Spirit is the highest kind of evidence of our adoption, that ever we obtain: But in these exercises of grace in practice, God gives witness, and sets to his seal, in the most conspicuous, eminent and evident manner.[73]

Although the senses are in this case implicitly more proof than entry, the imagery of the stamp and the seal is not far from the metaphor of mind as *tabula rasa*, receiving the impressions of experience. This same combination of Lockean theory and spiritual theology is to be found, say, in Charles Wesley's hymns:

> Where the indubitable seal
> That ascertains the kingdom mine?
> The powerful stamp I long to feel,
> The signature of love divine.[74]

Such emphasis on faith through experience, or rather on faith *as* experience, is everywhere evident in Wesley's abridgment of Edwards's treatise. The abridgment typically declares that "the Scripture represents faith as that by which men are brought into a good estate, and therefore it cannot be the same thing, as believing that they are already in one."[75] Faith is no more innate than ideas and no less dependent than ideas on the nourishment of experience: it is far from either an inherent capacity or a blind leap. The abridgment goes on to attack those "under the notion of ... living upon Christ and not experiences."[76] Such a notion "directly thwart[s] God's wise constitution of things," for far from being mutually exclusive, Christ and experience are intimately interinvolved.

I have previously defined the epistemology of Locke as "an experiential continuum with understanding at one pole and physical sensation at the other."[77] Thus an ever-increasing though by no means innate strength of reason forms such an important part of Locke's empiricism that his empiricism should be said to include a specific appeal to this *a posteriori* brand of reasoning. Of all the works of Edwards's that Wesley might have chosen to abridge, *A Treatise concerning Religious Affections* shows perhaps the greatest balance between Edwards's immersion in the categories of sense perception and his desire for the consent of mind to mind. Of all five works of his that Wesley did abridge, *Religious Affections* offers the fullest range of Lockean "empiricism," namely, the same balance between sense and reason that characterizes Wesley's method.[78]

As for the abridgment's categories of sense perception, note, first, that "the influence of some extrinsic force upon [our] minds"[79] connotes the purely natural means whereby we passively receive impressions from without. Boldly, the abridgment often makes no distinction "between the influences of the Spirit of God, and the natural operations of our own minds."[80] This lack of difference is not so much to demythologize the Spirit as to honor experience. While Locke would separate the Spirit from natural operations, Wesley and Edwards do not. And while Locke would elevate natural operations by making them independent of "mere" faith, Wesley and Edwards elevate "mere" natural operations by relating them to, by mentioning them in the same breath as, the Spirit. "For any to expect the influence of the Spirit, without a diligent improvement of the appointed means, is presumption," declares the abridgment in obvious dialogue with Locke.[81] The abridgment adds: "To expect that he will operate upon their minds, without means subservient to the effect, is enthusiastical." So willingly, that is, does the Spirit condescend to work through the natural operations of our minds that spiritual and natural operations can be all but identical, or, to use the words of the abridgment, "It is frequently God's manner to make his hand visible."[82]

The abridgment laments the fact that such "sense perception" of the divine is often mistaken for enthusiasm: recall "how greatly has the doctrine of sensibly perceiving the immediate power of the Spirit of God, been ridiculed." Even where the abridgment speaks exclusively of the spiritual means whereby we receive impressions, it does so in empirical terms, or at least in terms that duplicate theologically the Lockean fascination with extrinsic power over the mind:

> And if persons tell of effects in their own minds, that seem to them not to be from the natural operations of their minds, but from the supernatural power of some other agent, should it at once be looked upon as a sure evidence of delusion, because things seem to them to be as they are?[83]

Between the abridgment and the *Essay*, in this regard, is a particularly striking connection. Here is the *Essay*:

> Thus we see the holy Men of old, who had *Revelations* from God, had something else besides that internal Light of assurance in their own Minds, to testify to them, that it was from God. They were not left to their own Perswasions alone, that those Perswasions were from God; But had outward Signs to convince them of the Author of those Revelations.[84]

And here is the abridgment:

> And so it was in most of the conversions of particular persons we have an account of in the New Testament: They were not wrought on in a silent, secret, gradual, and insensible manner; but with those manifest evidences of a supernatural power, wonderfully and suddenly causing a great change.[85]

Thus both Locke and Wesley/Edwards require rigorous standards of certification from the religiously inclined, but Wesley and Edwards, more broadly experiential than Locke himself, extend Lockean methods of inquiry to non-Lockean subject matter. By giving credence to "effects in their own minds" as well as to external signs, they include the internal in the catalogue of experience. They imply, thereby, that the senses can be thought of as analogous to, as indispensable for conceiving, the "sense" of inward evidence: while "effects *in* their own minds" draws a boundary around the mind, confining experience to it, "*effects* in their own minds" points to an action or impingement on the mind, such as would only occur through the avenue of the senses.

Wesley and Edwards, accordingly, seem aware that extrinsic power over the mind functions philosophically as well as religiously. The abridgment's expression of receptivity to external influence can be conventionally religious and explicitly biblical:

> I know of no reason why being affected with a view of God's glory, should not cause the body to faint, as well as being affected with a view of Solomon's glory.... My soul thirsteth for thee, my flesh longeth for thee, in a dry and thirsty land where no water is.... When I heard, my belly trembled, my lips quivered at the voice, and rottenness entered into my bones, and I trembled in myself.[86]

The following quotation, however, evinces not only heart-religion, but also, in equal measures, metaphysics and epistemology: "God has so disposed things as though every thing was contrived to have the greatest possible tendency to reach our hearts in the most tender part, and move our affections most sensibly."[87] This statement, as intellectual as it is emotional, rests on the assumption, the philosophical theology, that sense perception is blessedly constituted to receive every good and perfect gift.[88]

The abridgment, though, hardly depicts the mind as completely passive: Edwards's desire for the consent of mind to mind amounts, at times, to near rationalism, as though the mind were sufficient unto itself; and Wesley, though never himself so nearly mind-intoxicated, allows Edwards to express his desire. Whereas "passions" are the "more sudden" and "more violent" "actings of the will," such "affections" as "hope, love, desire, joy, sorrow, gratitude, compassion, and zeal" are "actings of the will" wherein the mind is more "in its own command."[89] The abridgment, then, though neither Cartesian in particular nor French in general, is, nonetheless and strangely, mentalist as well as Anglo-American.

The abridgment agrees even here, however, with Lockean reason as sense-based, for the affections, and not just the passions, are finally sense-related. Mind in the abridgment is between the extremes of active and passive, and truth in the abridgment is between the extremes of mind and matter.

Take, for example, the close interaction of mind and body. The issue is rampant in the age (it appears in medical treatises, and even in Descartes);

Locke gives it his full attention.[90] The abridgment's lengthy argument that mind affects body and vice versa is similarly experiential, similarly other-directed, and almost non-theoretical in tone. "Such are the laws of union of soul and body," declares the abridgment, "that the mind can have no vigorous exercise, without some effect upon the body." The abridgment adds: "Yea, it is questionable, whether an embodied soul ever so much as thinks one thought, or has any exercise at all, but there is some corresponding motion in some part of the body."[91] Here, mind is tacitly superior to senses, for mental experience occurs prior to, and causes, activation of the body. Yet even here, the relation between mental experience and the body is the very evidence of mind's superiority, which, according to the abridgment as well as the *Essay*, consists in a place above, but not aloof from the senses.

The mind, then, far from being independent of the senses, depends on them for its very identity, and its participation in the senses provides the evidence of God's acting in it. For when almost mind-intoxicated, and even when God-intoxicated, the abridgment comes no closer than it does at all other times, and no closer than does Locke, to the pure rationalism that views the mind's identity, and even its experience, as independent of the senses. Wesley and Edwards affirm, finally, a mind/body interaction in which body is often as active as, and sometimes even prior to, mind. After reiterating a certain primacy of mind—to wit, "Such seems to be our nature, that there never is any vigorous exercise of the will, without some effect upon the body, in some alteration of the motions of its fluids, especially of the animal spirits"—the abridgment includes the following significant addendum: "And on the other hand, the constitution of the body, and the motion of its fluids, may promote the exercise of the affections."[92] Here experience affects, and precedes, the mental, and insofar as "body promotes the exercise of the *affections*," by which the revivalists mean *religious* affections, the senses are not only receptors for divine truth but also building blocks of spiritual wisdom.

In Wesley's and Edwards's thought, as in Locke's, mind and world form a dialectic, if not a continuum and a harmonic whole. Reality appears to the reader of the *Essay* as a coalescence of subject and object: recall Locke's use of *impulse*. The abridgment, by teaching that mind extends to body and vice versa, implies that mind-body synthesis contacts external reality and vice versa.[93]

"Following the lead of the classical British experience-philosophy," wrote John E. Smith in his modern edition of *Religious Affections*, "Edwards placed primary emphasis upon first-person experience."[94] Smith does not explicitly apply this comment to *Religious Affections*, but the comment can help explain the treatise's emphasis on the practical and on action in matters of religion. The comment applies as well to that same emphasis in both the abridgment and other Wesley writings.

For the obvious reason that *his* experiential emphasis derives from British experience-philosophy, Wesley is careful to represent this aspect of Edwards's sensibility.

> The business of religion is from time to time compared to those exercises, wherein men are wont to have their hearts and strength greatly engaged, such as *running, wrestling,* and *warring.* ... And as true religion is of a practical nature, and the affections are the springs of men's actions, it must consist very much in them.[95]

Or again:

> The tendency of grace in the heart to holy practice, is direct; and the connexion close and necessary. True grace is not an inactive, barren thing, for it is, in its very nature, a principle of holy action.[96]

These statements exemplify the "epistemology" of Wesley and Edwards. The first celebrates intense experience both as analogue to faith and as precondition for it. The second, besides implying an immediate connection between spiritual influx and practical charity (recall "grace *in* the heart"), contends that the connection between spiritual and natural experience is all but unmediated, that is, that spiritual experience intersects with, superimposes itself on, and, however fleetingly, becomes one with, natural experience.

The statements are broader and more inclusive than any narrowly "scientific" epistemology: "He that has knowledge only, without affection," say Wesley and Edwards, "never is engaged in the business of religion."[97] This statement can be understood in the light of another of Smith's general remarks about Edwards, namely, that he attempted "to bring the individual back to a sense of his own individuality and to the need for a broader conception of human understanding, one that does not eliminate everything but science from its concern."[98] (By "individuality," clearly, Smith means the significance of self rather than, or in addition to, its sinfulness.) Smith points out, finally, that Edwards's emphasis on first-person experience "took the form of the new *sense* or *taste* without which faith remains at the purely notional level."[99] Wesley's abridgment includes all of Edwards's statements regarding this "spiritual sense." Here I discuss several, as they accurately appear in the abridgment.

This doctrine, first of all, is Bible-based: "The Scripture is ignorant of any faith in Christ or the operation of God," say Wesley and Edwards, "that is not grounded in a spiritual sight of Christ."[100] They add proof texts. "True faith in Christ," they write, "is never exercised any further than persons 'behold as in a glass, the glory of the Lord,' and have 'the knowledge of the glory of God in the face of Jesus Christ.'"[101] The abridgment's opening passage, concerning the persecuted Christians to whom Paul wrote, constitutes a biblically oriented announcement of the "spiritual sense":

> There was nothing visible that could induce them thus to suffer, and could carry them through such trials. But though there was nothing that the world saw, or that they themselves saw with their bodily eyes, that thus supported them, *yet* they had a supernatural principle of love to something unseen; they loved Jesus Christ, whom they *saw spiritually*.[102]

One thinks, in this connection, of John 20.29 ("Blessed are they that have not seen, and yet have believed"). Note that, even where indicating what lies beyond the grasp of sense and even where mainly quoting the Bible, the abridgment's doctrine of the "spiritual sense" employs sensate language for a distinctively historical reason. Although neither Wesley nor Edwards could avoid the Lockean hegemony, both of them exploit it. They read certain proof texts in the context of the empiricist climate, as though to enhance both the climate and the texts. Both of them reflect a sense bias in their most biblical understanding of spiritual experience, for even in that understanding, they interpret such experience in alignment with an earthly methodology: they appeal to sense experience, if only as analogue.

Their other depictions of the "spiritual sense" are more philosophical than biblical, and as much philosophical as theological. The doctrine, to the extent that it covers immediate revelation, or the Spirit's operations in the present, carries authentically Lockean implications of the senses as tests, and even as manifesters and harbingers. For purposes of consideration in this light, this tough-minded passage is worth requoting: "Men will trust their God no further than they know him, and they cannot be in the exercise of faith in him one ace further than they have a sight of his fulness and faithfulness in exercise."[103] "A sight of" intimates a not so much analogical or metaphorical as literal dimension of the "spiritual sense," for in the absence of such labels as *spiritual*, the connotation is of physical sight, as though the knowledge of God were direct or metaphysical.

In the following statement of the "spiritual sense," moreover, the abridgment shows itself fully epistemological:

> In those gracious affections which are wrought through the saving influences of the Spirit of God, there is a new inward perception or sensation, entirely different in its nature, from any thing that ever their minds were the subjects of, before they were sanctified. If grace be, in the sense above described, an entirely new kind of principle; then the exercises of it are also entirely a new kind of exercise. And if there be in the soul a new sort of exercises which it knew nothing of before, and which no improvement, composition, or management of what it was before conscious of, could produce, or any thing like it; then it follows that there is, as it were, a new spiritual sense in the mind, or an entirely new kind of perception or spiritual sensation, which is in its whole nature different from any former kinds of sensation.[104]

True, this statement tends toward the analogical, and in its insistence that God works a *new* sense into the mind-soul, it does not sound Lockean or empirical. But this "spiritual sense," though wholly unlike the physical senses, is almost consciously Lockean in its explicit adherence to *tabula rasa* and hence to the pivotal powers of experience in general. In speaking of the minds of newborn people, that is, converts, as the *subjects* of inward perception or sensation, Wesley and Edwards imply the rationalist point that mind is always ultimate, always prior to sense-like spiritual experience. Clearly, they seek the consent of mind to mind even as their language of sense perception waxes most Lockean. "Subjects *of*," however, is ambiguous. The phrase implies that minds are subjected or subordinated to spiritual sensation, which in this case, though inward, is other than, added to or prior to, mind. In spiritual experience, then, and not just in natural experience, the priority lies not in mind alone, nor even exclusively in sense-like avenues to something rich and strange, but in the interchange highlighting now one, and now the other.

Although Locke implies that immediate revelation is unlikely or even impossible, because all thought comes from sense perception rather than from the extrasensory, he argues, nonetheless, that biblical revelation is true because it showed itself in action. Wesley and Edwards, in their doctrine of the "spiritual sense," apply this argument to their brief for immediate revelation, which, if confirmed after the fact by the criteria of natural experience, is true. Wesley and Edwards, of course, hold that supernatural intakings and reshapings of the mind constitute ultimate reality, but they use Locke to defend such visitations against charges of enthusiasm. In the passage just quoted, for example, the inward perception does not exist before the natural time, and does not inhere apart from the natural place, of particular spiritual influx. This notion is Lockean insofar as it assumes that grace, like everything else, is dependent on experience. Tough-mindedly experience-oriented rather than exclusively analogistic, the passage iterates the sense-like perception of God's things as "a new sort of exercises which [the soul] knew nothing of before."

Thus Wesley and Edwards do not so much follow what Locke thinks as in their own way practice how he thinks and even how he speaks. Although they need not be labeled Lockean (their vision was their own), they do not hesitate to use Locke's distinguished epistemology. The piety of Wesley and Edwards is "natural":[105] not only do they believe in the God of nature, and not only do they think that sense experience can point to, if not include, God, but they also base their supernatural religion on experience. Not only do they assume that what happens in one's inward life is significant in the same way as what happens in one's sense experience but they also link, as their journals indicate, their sanctifications to the passage of time. They assume, in short, that what happens in one's inward life may interact with, and grow out of, what happens in one's sense experience. For them, experience both constitutes matter and mind, considered separately and together, and binds the senses to the soul.

A passage toward the end of the abridgment is perhaps most telling in suggesting this philosophical theology. It duplicates Edwards's attempt to describe faith through the language of both rational empiricism and scientific method. It not only elaborates, but also distills, the doctrine of the "spiritual sense," that is, "that sense of Divine things, which governs [our] heart and hands."[106]

> Not only does the most important part of Christian experience
> lie in spiritual practice, but nothing is so properly called by the

> name of experimental religion: For that experience which is in these exercises of grace, that prove effectual at the very point of trial, is the proper experiment of the truth of our godliness, wherein its victorious power is found by experience. This is properly Christian experience, wherein we have opportunity to see, by actual experience and trial, whether we have a heart to do the will of God, and to forsake other things for Christ, or no.[107]

By our experience, that is, we see God's prior reshapings of our hearts; but the passage indicates, too, that the range of spiritual experience can be identical with the range of natural experience. Indeed, the diction is so fully experientialist as to include an insistently scientific tenor: *by actual experience and trial, see, experiment, prove, practice*, and, not least (uncharacteristically for Wesley) the redundant uses of *experience*—all denote the particularly empirical method whereby such religious problems as the knowledge of revelation appear to be raised by and solved by one's sense-oriented as well as mental life. Wesley is more empirical than even the Edwards of *Religious Affections*. But the Edwards of *Religious Affections*, as Wesley recognizes, employs the language of actual experience and trial, and both Wesley and Edwards hold that subjectivity corresponds with and, when God-suffused, commands objective truth.

This experiential assumption informs, and may even determine, one of their most characteristic doctrines, namely, assurance. Wesley's version of it derives not just from the Moravians' emphasis on Romans 8.1—"For ye have not received the Spirit of bondage again to fear; but ye have received the Spirit of adoption, whereby we cry, Abba, Father"—but also from Locke's emphasis on "Assurance" as the label for "the highest degree of Probability" in the realm of empirical belief.[108] Wesley, therefore, has his philosophic reason for amply representing Edwards's doctrine of assurance, which, as a thoroughly experiential interpretation of the Bible, is itself a doctrine of the age of Locke. Edwards and Wesley both write:

> God, in the plainest manner, revealed and testified his special favour to Noah; Abraham; Isaac; Jacob, Moses, David, and others. Job often speaks with the greatest *assurance*. David, throughout the book of Psalms, almost every where speaks in the most positive manner of God as his God. Hezekiah appeals to God, as one that knew, "he had walked before him in truth

and with a perfect heart;" (2 Kings xx.3;) the Apostle Paul, through all his epistles, speaks in an *assured* strain, ever speaking positively of his special relation to Christ, and his interest in, and expectation of, the future reward.[109]

In sum, then, Wesley and Edwards do not subscribe to the notion of *tabula rasa* when they believe that we are born with a heavy burden of sin, but their equally characteristic emphasis on conversion admits of Lockean sanction. Conversion ascribes so much importance to what might happen, not only at inner moments but also in one's experience in the world, that whatever precedes such experiential sea-change is by comparison mere *tabula rasa*. Edwards, a Calvinist, does not assume as much responsibility as Wesley, an Arminian, does for the working out of one's own salvation. But Edwards's doctrine of "testing the spirits" gives even him, in the words of Smith, "some basis for judging the state of his own soul."[110] Although Edwards and Wesley through him warn against making "too much of [our] own doings, to the diminution of the glory of free grace," they finally ask, "Which way is it inconsistent with the freeness of God's grace, that holy practice should be a sign of God's grace?"[111] The nearest analogue to this emphasis on experience as test and not as conduit is the doctrine of good works, but the emphasis makes so much of our "own doings" that it emerges as implicitly Lockean, and the doctrine of the "spiritual sense" is where Edwards's similarity to both Locke and Wesley seems most pertinent.

I submit, now, by way of rounding off my Wesleyan-Lockean perspective on *Religious Affections*, Wesley's most Lockean statement of the "spiritual sense." The statement, from *An Earnest Appeal to Men of Reason and Religion* (1743), includes an explicit subscription to the fundamental, though only potentially theological, tenet of *tabula rasa*:

> Before it is possible for you to form a true judgment of the things of God, it is absolutely necessary that you have a *clear apprehension* of them, and that your ideas thereof be all *fixed, distinct*, and *determinate*. And seeing our ideas are not all innate, but must originally come from our senses, it is certainly necessary that you have senses capable of discerning objects of this kind: Not those only which are called natural senses, which in this respect profit nothing, as being altogether incapable of discerning objects of a spiritual kind; but spiritual senses, exer-

cised to discern spiritual good and evil. It is necessary that you have *the hearing ear,* and *the seeing eye,* emphatically so called; that you have a new class of senses opened in your soul, not depending on organs of flesh and blood, to be "the evidence of things not seen" [cf. Heb. 11:1], as your bodily senses are of visible things; to be the avenues to the invisible world, to discern spiritual objects, and to furnish you with ideas of what the outward "eye hath not seen, neither the ear heard" [cf. I Cor 2:9].[112]

This statement, formulated a scant three years before *Religious Affections* first appeared, accords with Edwards's "spiritual sense," which, whether in its analogistic dimension or in its implication that even the natural senses are visionary, proceeds, too, from Lockean assumptions. Like Wesley's *Appeals to Men of Reason and Religion* (1743-45), *Remarks upon Mr. Locke's Essay on Human Understanding* (1781), and *On Living without God* (1790),[113] Edwards's *Treatise concerning Religious Affections* teaches four points: (1) we receive an inrush of spirit and then "see" abstractions manifested in our sensible experience; (2) we walk avenues to the invisible; (3) we receive the divine from the visible; and (4) we discover the divine in the visible. Where Locke coalesces sense experience with mind, Wesley and Edwards coalesce nature with spirit. To state the conclusion another way, the "spiritual sense" of Wesley and Edwards joins rational empiricism to both theistic natural religion and immediate revelation.

A Comparison

In *Locke, Wesley, and the Method of English Romanticism,* I argue, among other things, that Wesley's abridgment (1730) of *The Procedure, Extent, and Limits of Human Understanding* (1728) by Peter Browne (d. 1735), Bishop of Cork and Ross, is a key to Wesley's thought: the abridgment demonstrates the Lockean affinity between Browne and Wesley. Wesley's access to Locke—through Browne—parallels, and serves to gloss, Wesley's access to Locke through Edwards. Since both the abridgment of *Religious Affections* and the abridgment of *The Procedure* theologize Locke's *Essay* even more thoroughly than do the originals, a brief comparison of the two abridgments can serve to reinforce my view of the Lockean agreement between Wesley and Edwards.

First, as highlighted by the abridgment of *The Procedure,* here is Browne's doctrine of analogy:

> Metaphor is mostly in Words, and is a Figure of Speech; Analogy a Similis Ratio or Proportion of Things, and an excellent and necessary Method or Means of Reason and Knowledge. Metaphor uses Ideas of Sensation to express Immaterial and heavenly Objects, to which they can bear no real Resemblance or Proportion [e.g., "I am the Good Shepherd"]; Analogy substitutes the Operations of our Soul, and notions mostly formed out of them, to represent Divine Things to which they bear a Real tho' Unknown Correspondency and Proportion [e.g., "God is love"]. In short, Metaphor has no real Foundation in the Nature of the Things compared; Analogy is founded in the Very Nature of the Things on both Sides of the Comparison.[114]

This doctrine, as I have indicated, derives from Locke's emphasis on analogy as "the only help we have in inferring unseen causes." Locke's view that a "wary reasoning from Analogy leads us often into the discovery of Truths ... which would otherwise lie concealed" (1) emphasizes the transcendent otherness of the Creator, (2) intimates, nonetheless, the accessibility of divine truth, (3) implies that just as there is unity among things above and just as there is unity among things below, so there is correspondence, if not continuity, between the natural and the spiritual worlds, (4) devalues metaphor because of the arbitrary nature of its comparisons (here, Locke is the true son of Puritans who preferred simile to metaphor), (5) proposes analogy as a nonfigurative, philosophically correct means of expression this correspondence of things, and (6) recommends analogy as our "great Rule of Probability" in theological inquiry.[115] Although thinking by an analogy of opposition that emphasizes the distance between this world and another was attacked both by skeptics such as David Hume and by such orthodox thinkers as Samuel Johnson,[116] Locke's analogy was one of proportionality. His analogy, indeed, was so far from being outmoded that it was adapted by such as Browne and Wesley, who made it the prolegomenon to all future epistemologies of faith.

No more than Locke, of course, does either Browne or Wesley wax glib about the relation between God and the world, for like Locke, both Browne and Wesley limited what could be predicated of God. But while Aquinas predicated much through "the assumption of the neo-Platonist scale of Being,"[117] Browne and Wesley predicated much through the Locke-related instrument of sense-language. With the possible exception of the attempt by the later Edwards to conceive of spirit through a congruence of abstractions and logical harmony, it is not feasible to talk about spirit except by analogy to the senses. Christ's method of parables is nothing more nor less than such analogy, as are the medieval fourfold method of exegesis and the analogies of Luther. But the version of analogy in Browne and Wesley is especially empirical in its view of the senses as providing evidence, if not as providing a source, of spiritual knowledge. Just as in Lockean terms sense perception of a human being is the only means of knowing him or her, so in terms of Browne and Wesley the feeling of love is such a good access to the nature of God that it amounts to a "spiritual sense" of him. The feeling of love, with its implication of sexual union, is at once so deep and so relational that it out-senses the senses.

Thus the abridgment of *The Procedure* delineates the analogistic dimension of the spiritual sense, but analogy in the abridgment of *The Procedure* as a whole does not so much indicate the difference between humanity and God as occupy the continuum joining nature to revelation, and such analogy of proportionality is matched by the abridgment of *Religious Affections*. Characteristically, for example, Wesley and Edwards employ that analogy's very form:

> As the affections not only belong to the human nature, but are a great part of it; so holy affections do not only belong to true religion, but are a very great part of it. . . . And as in worldly things, worldly affections are the springs of men's actions; so in religious matters, the spring of their actions is religious affections.[118]

Or again:

> As the taste of honey is diverse from the ideas men get of honey by only looking on and feeling it, so the new sense of spiritual and Divine things is entirely diverse from any thing that is perceived in them, by natural men.[119]

Here, somewhat surprisingly, the abridgment implies that, like the sense of taste, the spiritual sense renders a truth that is deep precisely because it is imageless: compare Demogorgon's "the deep truth is imageless" from Shelley's *Prometheus Unbound*. These samples of the abridgment, moreover, are so analogistic, so detached from the world, that they evince distrust of the senses. But the distrust is directed more to the sense-image world of metaphor, with its distance from the spiritual world, than toward the sense-related instrument of analogy, which describes interiority or spiritual experience according to the model of perception. Taste, after all, is a sense like seeing and hearing, albeit with an image so deep as not to resemble the images of sight and sound.

The abridgment, necessarily or not, retains sense-like criteria as the only means available to Lockean temperaments with a need to express the methods of the soul. The term *affections*, significantly, belongs to the language of sense impression and sense perception. Far from abandoning such language, Wesley and Edwards use a strange, vaguely oxymoronic, but nonetheless efficacious version of it, namely, *religious* or *holy affections*, to express a precise analogy between, if not the interpenetrations of, the spirit realm and the world of natural experience.

This doctrine, then, proportional rather than oppositional, helps Wesley and Edwards as Browne's doctrine helps him, namely, to believe that what is both felt and thought approaches, without dispelling the mystery of, what has been and is being revealed. Without quite valuing the familiar for its own sake, the doctrine of Wesley and Edwards honors the familiar as an especially faithful counterpart to what would otherwise lie entirely outside the range of human expression. The senses convince the intellect of what they have to tell. What is felt and thought, in turn, proves spiritually veridical, that is, theologically equivalent to philosophical seeing and philosophical believing.

Thus, on the relative certainty of natural knowledge, the spiritual sense of Wesley and Edwards establishes the probable truth of a theistic (distinct from Deistic or pantheistic) natural religion, and even of revelation. The twin pioneers of transatlantic revivalism search for an inclusive, intellectually current way of describing how the mind knows God, and how anyone can verify another's faith. They find that way in Lockean doctrine.

An Epitome

Although close reading, especially of Wesley's abridgment of Edwards's *Religious Affections*, recommends itself as "the fascination of what's difficult,"[120] I am concerned, here, to facilitate what is difficult, without losing the fascination of, say, philosophical theology as semiotics. I want to abstract, without diluting, the complex empiricism of Wesley and Edwards.

When teaching that mind is where divine experience takes place, the abridgment puts grace prior to the senses, which become mere physical analogues to inward spiritual experience. Insofar as the experience of Wesley and Edwards is an "experience" of God as otherworldly, a consent of being to being beyond self and senses, the abridgment demonstrates additional non-Lockean ends.

Its validation of those ends, however, its proof that spiritual experience has occurred, appeals to the senses and so amounts to a sufficiently Lockean means. Spiritual inrush, though merely analogous to sense perception, appears in a strong Lockean light, for Locke's view that impressions striking the senses are worthy guides to knowledge informs, and indeed enables, the trust of Wesley and Edwards in influxes "flooding [the] soul with glory divine."[121]

An especially intriguing trait of this philosophical theology is its implication that the senses are indispensable for an experience of the divine. The senses are secondary when they are tests for inwardness and analogies to communicate supernatural reality to a Lockean world. But the senses are primary when they are attendants on, and preconditions for, faith, that is, when natural experience not only sets the terms of, but also either becomes or combines with, spiritual experience. At "a quarter to nine" on the evening of May 24, 1738, in Aldersgate Street, London, Wesley's heart was "strangely warmed" (shades, or foreshadowing, of Blake's talking with Isaiah in the Strand).[122] This famous conversion, this spiritual watershed of English cultural life, has as much to do with time, place, and the specific circumstances of Wesley's sense experience as with his state of mind. Such a nearly empirical recipe for grace is a particular means of the abridgment, which, above all, holds to the senses.

Since Locke's tenet that one's very language depends on the senses was a given of the intellectual climate,[123] all expressions of the divine were necessarily Lockean, that is, sensuous, including the most analogistic and, for that matter, most rationalistic expressions. But the paradox of the God-centered yet sincere self is the crux in the abridgment, the sense-language of which, in accord with the abridgment's understanding of the senses themselves, is now analogue to, and now validation, manifestation, and harbinger of, spiritual experience. Whether a literal or a figurative reading of Locke, whether an uneasy attempt to incorporate senses into near-rationalism or a balance between sense perception and the consent of mind to mind, the abridgment is saturated with Lockean language. Even its consciousness of God not only submits to what Wordsworth, after Locke, calls "the language of the sense,"[124] but also arrives through that language. The very title, virtually the same as the original's, implies the Locke-derived oxymoron "spiritual sense," for *Religious Affections* ambiguously straddles the line between faith and experience.

Natural experience and spiritual experience, then, are not stark oppositions for Wesley and Edwards, whose spiritual experience, like their natural experience, is Lockean, that is, of both the mind and the senses. Just as Lockean epistemology conceives of a link between sense and reason, matter and mind, so the philosophical theologies of Wesley and Edwards, their appropriations of Locke for religious methodology, conceive of a bridge that transports us from nature to grace, returns us from grace to nature, and joins nature and grace, justifying the reality of both. This spiritual sense is even more flexible and even more up-to-date than Lockean epistemology, for it out-Lockes Locke, or carries him to his logical conclusion. It applies to the religious arena that secular trust in experience that helped the early modern mind to position itself in the natural world.

The spiritual sense of Wesley and Edwards rests, specifically, on a view of experience more inclusive, and a respect for experiential criteria greater, than Locke's. While Lockean experience is primarily natural and Lockean theology is almost entirely apart from nature, they both stress the participation of God in creation, and so enlist spirit in the catalogue of experience. The spiritual sense of Wesley and Edwards, indeed, for its part in the eighteenth century's burgeoning discipline of philosophical theology, is imaginative. For by its imaging of heavenly joy on earth, if not by its hope of earthly joy in heaven, it draws on the model of sense perception to detect, and express, a radically immanent Christianity. And by so modernizing Christianity, Wesley and Edwards lay the intellectual as well as emotional groundwork for religious expression not simply in the Anglo-American Enlightenment, but in the Anglo-American world of the nineteenth century as well.

Wesley's abridgment of Edwards's *Religious Affections*, without fudging differences or papering them over, denotes links among comparative philosophy, philosophical theology, conversion, and the leap of faith. Similarly, the abridgment links mind to mind. Just as the reader crosses the abridgment to Wesley, so the reader and Wesley cross it to Edwards. Thus a well-traveled transatlantic bridge facilitates both the intellectual overtones of evangelical zeal and the interdisciplinary character of evangelical intellect. Since the abridgment not only balances empirical and evangelical idioms but also disperses empirical and evangelical idiolects, it connotes an especially full "sense" in which the Anglo-American world is one. I will henceforth offer not simply a full, but emphatically a fully ramifying, interpretation of the abridgment. By addressing the paradox of mundane and otherworldly points of view in both England and the United States, the abridgment intimates perhaps the most inclusive sense in which British literature and American literature merge. As compendium and chief repository of Wesleyan-Edwardsean "epistemology," it forms a substantial subject in itself; as perhaps the most resonant common document of Methodism and the Great Awakening, it epitomizes and indexes, that is, quintessentially embodies, a "spiritual sense" to be found in transatlantic revivalism and hence, significantly, in the Anglo-American world; and as a background to and context for a particularly important bi-national amalgam of *les belles-lettres*, it raises the distinct possibility that just as spiritually transposed empiricism bridges empiricism per se and Enlightenment-era apologetics, so imagination bridges natural observation and Romantic-era "poetic faith."

NOTES

[1] I allude to Emerson's *Representative Men* (1850), a collection of essays on Plato, Emanuel Swedenborg, Montaigne, Shakespeare, Napoleon, and Goethe. Some of Emerson's other works, I suggest, add Wesley and Edwards to the list.

[2] I adapt the phrase "gene-culture coevolution" to my purposes. The phrase is used throughout Edward O. Wilson, *Sociobiology*.

[3] See, e.g., Norman Fiering, *Jonathan Edwards's Moral Thought and Its British Context*; William J. Wainwright, "Jonathan Edwards and the Language of God"; and Nathan O. Hatch and Harry S. Stout, eds., *Jonathan Edwards and the American Experience.*

[4] For samples of Perry Miller's argument for Edwards as a Lockean, see Miller's *Jonathan Edwards* and his "Jonathan Edwards and the Sense of the Heart."

[5] For Locke's "theocentric framework," see Richard Ashcroft, "Faith and Knowledge in Locke's Philosophy"; David Gauthier, "Why Ought One Obey God? Reflections on Hobbes and Locke"; James Farr, "The Way of Hypotheses: Locke on Method"; and W. M. Spellman, *John Locke and the Problem of Depravity*. Spellman's positioning of Locke on the Latitudinarian *via media* between Calvinism and Deism is especially persuasive. For Locke's empiricism, see, e.g., John W. Yolton, *John Locke and the Compass of Human Understanding*, and Roger Woolhouse, *Locke's Philosophy of Science and Knowledge*.

[6] Terrence Erdt, *Jonathan Edwards: Art and the Sense of the Heart.*

[7] Roland Delattre, *Beauty and Sensibility in the Thought of Jonathan Edwards: An Essay in Aesthetics and Theological Ethics.*

[8] Sacvan Bercovitch, *The American Jeremiad*, 107-8. Edwards's model of mind, according to James Hoopes, is Lockean in that it is unitary, for both Edwards

and Locke regard "mind" and "thought" as synonymous, and they do not recognize the unconscious mind. Edwards's commitment to the "way of ideas," however, out-Lockes Locke's, for while Locke's model of soul allows for spiritual substance, Edwards's "soul" is made up of ideas only. See James Hoopes, "Calvinism and Consciousness from Edwards to Beecher."

[9] Wallace E. Anderson, "The Development of Edwards' Philosophical Thought," 101-2.

[10] See the discussion in Anderson, "The Development of Edwards' Philosophical Thought," 101-2. See also Edward H. Davidson, "From Locke to Edwards"; Claude A. Smith, "Jonathan Edwards and the 'Way of Ideas'"; and Paul Helm, "John Locke and Jonathan Edwards: A Reconsideration." Michael J. Colacurcio's emphasis on Edwards's career after 1750, and especially on *The Great Christian Doctrine of Original Sin Defended*, leads to a perhaps too-narrow focus on his capacity for "idealist imagination": "what makes Edwards everywhere Edwards is some absolutely fundamental bias of imagination in favor of idealism." Edwards's career as a whole includes empiricist as well as idealist elements and is aptly summed up (if again with more idealist bias than the entire career warrants) in this observation by Colacurcio: "A capacity to suspect that reality might be very subtle, and a power to suspend belief long enough to wonder *how* subtle, may tell us more than anything else about the unity and priorities of a mind which saw spiders and thought 'teleology,' which learned of atoms and guessed 'power,' which experienced both nature and grace and leaped to 'idea,' and which ultimately contrived to hand the whole world, including its own consciousness and that of every other man, over to *God Alone.*" See Michael J. Colacurcio, "The Example of Edwards: Idealist Imagination and the Metaphysics of Sovereignty," esp. 96, 98.

[11] Robert W. Jenson, *America's Theologian: A Recommendation of Jonathan Edwards*, esp. 3.

[12] Charles Rogers, "John Wesley and Jonathan Edwards."

[13] See *The Works of the Rev. John Wesley, A.M.*, ed. Thomas Jackson, 10.463, 467, 475.

[14] Ibid., 10.460.

[15] Albert Outler, *John Wesley*, 16.

[16] See Rogers, "John Wesley and Jonathan Edwards," 36.

[17] Many thanks to Frederick Dreyer for corresponding with me about his work, which includes his "Faith and Experience in the Thought of John Wesley" and his "Evangelical Thought: John Wesley and Jonathan Edwards."

[18] The essay and Harvey G. Townsend's discussion of it are in Townsend, ed., *The Philosophy of Jonathan Edwards from His Private Notebooks*, xi-xiii, 1-20.

[19] The other four of Edwards's works abridged by Wesley are *A Faithful Narrative of the Surprising Work of God in the Conversion of many hundred souls in Northampton* (1736); *The Distinguishing Marks of a Work of the Spirit of God* (1741); *Some Thoughts concerning the Present Revival in New England* (1742); and *An Account of the Life of the Late Reverend Mr. David Brainerd* (1749). Wesley's abridgments of these works are *A Narrative of Many Surprising Conversions in Northampton and Vicinity* (1744); *The Distinguishing Marks of a Work of the Spirit of God* (1744); *Thoughts concerning the Present Revival of Religion* (1745); and *An Extract of the Life of the Late Rev. Mr. David Brainerd* (1768).

[20] See John Wesley, ed., *An Extract from a Treatise concerning Religious Affections*, in *The Works of the Rev. John Wesley*, and the discussion in *The Works of Jonathan Edwards*, ed. John E. Smith, vol. 2: *A Treatise concerning Religious Affections*, 79. My quotations of the abridgment are from a widely available reprint of it in the following collection of Wesley's abridgments: John Wesley, ed., *A Christian Library: Consisting of Extracts from and Abridgments of the choicest Pieces of Practical Divinity which have been published in the English Tongue;* see 30.308-76.

[21] See Jonathan Edwards, *A Treatise concerning Religious Affections: In Three Parts*, ed. William Gordon.

[22] Gregory S. Clapper, "'True Religion' and the Affections: A Study of John Wesley's Abridgment of Jonathan Edwards's Treatise on the Religious Affections," 418.

[23] See, e.g., Frank Baker, "A Study of John Wesley's Readings."

[24] See, e.g., T. Walter Herbert, *John Wesley as Editor and Author*, 75-79.

[25] Many of the alterations are more aesthetically motivated than pursuant to Wesley's fears about whether his readers would follow Edwards's thought. Characteristically, Wesley excises verbiage, thus clarifying Edwards's intentions and enhancing his treatise. The following instance is typical (brackets enclose Wesley's omissions): "The kindling [and raising] of gracious affections is like kindling a flame, the higher it is raised, the more ardent it is [and the more it burns, the more vehemently does it tend and seek to burn]" (Gordon's edition of Edwards, *A Treatise concerning Religious Affections*, 211, and Wesley, "An Extract from a Treatise concerning Religious Affections," in *A Christian Library*, 30.363). See also Edwards, *Treatise*, 50, and Wesley, "Extract," 334; Edwards, 54-55, and Wesley, 336; Edwards, 202, and Wesley, 359; and Edwards, 205, and Wesley, 361. Wesley's omissions of many biblical quotations constitute a major means by which he achieves economy of expression: see Edwards, 39-41, and Wesley, 329; Edwards, 42, and Wesley, 330; Edwards, 43, and Wesley, 330; Edwards, 53, and Wesley, 335; Edwards, 54,

and Wesley, 336; Edwards, 79-80, and Wesley, 344; Edwards, 81, and Wesley, 344; Edwards, 82, and Wesley, 344; Edwards, 157, and Wesley, 346; Edwards, 188, and Wesley, 353; Edwards, 199, and Wesley, 358; Edwards, 200, and Wesley, 359; Edwards, 204, and Wesley, 360; Edwards, 255-56, and Wesley, 374; and Edwards, 256-57, and Wesley, 374. Gordon, like Edwards, tolerates repetitiousness; Wesley does not: see Edwards, 17-18, and Wesley, 317; Edwards, 65, and Wesley, 342; Edwards, 74-79, and Wesley, 343; Edwards, 87-155, and Wesley, 346; Edwards, 170-71, and Wesley, 349; Edwards, 192-93, and Wesley, 355; Edwards, 202, and Wesley, 359; Edwards, 214-15, and Wesley, 363; Edwards, 217, and Wesley, 364; Edwards, 225-26, and Wesley, 366; Edwards, 237-53, and Wesley, 367; and Edwards, 244-47, and Wesley, 368. Wesley achieves his combination of brevity and fidelity to the original in part by omitting subtopics of a clearly established line of argument: for an especially notable example, see Edwards, 167-70, and Wesley, 349.

[26] I take this epitome of Arminianism from Hymn 17 of the Wesley brothers' *Collection of Hymns, for the Use of the People Called Methodists*. For a characterization of the Wesleys' Arminianism see Richard E. Brantley, "Charles Wesley's Experiential Art."

[27] See Edwards, *Religious Affections*, 33, and Wesley, "Extract," 326.

[28] See Edwards, *Religious Affections*, 53, and Wesley, "Extract," 335.

[29] See Edwards, *Religious Affections*, 55-56, and Wesley, "Extract," 336; and Edwards, *Religious Affections*, 217-21, and Wesley, "Extract," 364.

[30] See Edwards, *Religious Affections*, 38, and Wesley, "Extract," 329.

[31] See Edwards, *Religious Affections*, 38, and Wesley, "Extract," 329. See also Richard E. Brantley, *Locke, Wesley, and the Method of English Romanticism*, 53, 68, 233 n. 44.

[32] See Edwards, *Religious Affections*, 21, and Wesley, "Extract," 319; Edwards, 171-72, and Wesley, 349; Edwards, 179-80, and Wesley, 352; Edwards, 200, and Wesley, 358; Edwards, 201, and Wesley, 359; Edwards, 203, and Wesley, 360; and Edwards, 260-63, and Wesley, 376.

[33] See Edwards, *Religious Affections*, 50, and Wesley, "Extract," 334; Edwards, 53, and Wesley, 335; Edwards, 66, and Wesley, 342; and Edwards, 86, and Wesley, 345.

[34] See Edwards, *Religious Affections*, 9, and Wesley, "Extract," 314; Edwards, 24, and Wesley, 321; Edwards, 42, and Wesley, 330; Edwards, 60, and Wesley, 340; Edwards, 79, and Wesley, 343; Edwards, 85-86, and Wesley, 345; Edwards, 177, and Wesley, 351; Edwards, 204, and Wesley, 360; Edwards, 211, and Wesley, 363; and Edwards, 223-24, and Wesley, 365.

35 I refer to Blake's "The Mental Traveller" (1801-5?).
36 I refer to Blake's *The Marriage of Heaven and Hell* (1793).
37 Wesley, "Extract," 308.
38 See Clapper, "'True Religion' and the Affections," 417. "Against the encroachments of Arminian liberalism, which emphasized human reason, free will, and a benevolent Deity," wrote John Patrick Diggins (in a statement pointing to the difficulty of irenically reading Arminianism and Calvinism), "Edwards waged a rearguard defense of Calvinism's essential principles: man's utter depravity and inability to influence salvation through good works; the election of a few by a transforming grace that cannot be resisted; the uncertainty of the state of one's soul, even for the elect, hence the perseverance of the saints; and within this drama of redemption and damnation, the inscrutability of God's nature." See Diggins, "Puritans and Pragmatists," 39.
39 See Edwards, *Religious Affections*, 60-61, and Wesley, "Extract," 340; Edwards, 61-63, and Wesley, 340; and Edwards, 70-73, and Wesley, 343.
40 Clapper, "'True Religion' and the Affections," 418.
41 For a paradoxical argument that Edwards's ontology is finally epistemological, that according to Edwards's thought "dispositions and habits . . . can mediate between being and becoming, permanence and process," see Sang Hyun Lee, *The Philosophical Theology of Jonathan Edwards*, esp. 3, 115-70.
42 See Edwards, *Religious Affections*, 3, and Wesley, "Extract," 311.
43 Ibid. See also Edwards, 2, and Wesley, 310; and Edwards, 189-91, and Wesley, 354.
44 See the discussion in Clapper, "'True Religion' and the Affections," 418-19.
45 See Edwards, *Religious Affections*, 30-31, and Wesley, "Extract," 324; and Edwards, 198, and Wesley, 358. See also Brantley, *Locke, Wesley, and the Method of English Romanticism*, 15, 17, 125.
46 See Edwards, *Religious Affections*, 8, and Wesley, "Extract," 313.
47 Edwards, *Religious Affections*, 48-49.
48 See Wesley, "Extract," 333, where the passage would have appeared.
49 See Brantley, *Locke, Wesley, and the Method of English Romanticism*, 20-21.
50 See Edwards, *Religious Affections*, 18-19, and Wesley, "Extract," 317.
51 See Edwards, *Religious Affections*, 9, and Wesley, "Extract," 315. See also Edwards, 22, and Wesley, 319; Edwards, 26-27, and Wesley, 321-22; and Edwards, 33-34, and Wesley, 326-27.
52 See Brantley, *Locke, Wesley, and the Method of English Romanticism*, 15, 48-49, 61-62, 89, 100, 250 n. 31.

⁵³ For Edwards's most overt "empiricism," and for Wesley's fidelity to it, see Edwards, *Religious Affections*, 13, and Wesley, "Extract," 312-13; Edwards, 17, and Wesley, 317; Edwards, 18, and Wesley, 317-19; Edwards, 33, and Wesley, 325-26; Edwards, 43, and Wesley, 330; Edwards, 48, and Wesley, 333-35; Edwards, 58-60, and Wesley, 338-39; Edwards, 86-87, and Wesley, 345-46; Edwards, 166, and Wesley, 348; Edwards, 221-22, and Wesley, 364-65; Edwards, 224-25, and Wesley, 365; Edwards, 253-55, and Wesley, 372-73; and Edwards, 256, and Wesley, 374-75. Clapper, in "'True Religion' and the Affections," 419, recognizes "spiritual empiricism" in what the abridgment includes of the treatise's third part, but "spiritual empiricism" is scattered throughout the abridgment.

⁵⁴ Denis Donoghue, *The Third Voice: Modern British and American Verse Drama*, 18.

⁵⁵ John Locke, *Essay*, 4.9.3 and 4.10.6 in *An Essay concerning Human Understanding*, ed. Peter H. Nidditch, 618, 621. Subsequent references to this edition are abbreviated "Nidditch."

⁵⁶ Locke, *Essay*, 4.11.1; Nidditch, 630.

⁵⁷ Locke, *Essay*, 4.19.5; Nidditch, 698-99.

⁵⁸ Wesley, "Extract," 333. Cf. Eccles. 11.5.

⁵⁹ Locke, *Essay*, 4.19.16; Nidditch, 705.

⁶⁰ "God when he makes the Prophet," Locke observes, "does not unmake the Man," and Locke adds that God "leaves all Man's Faculties in their natural State, to enable him to judge of his Inspirations, whether they be of divine Original or no.... We cannot take it for a *Revelation*, or so much as for true, till we have some other Mark that it is a *Revelation*, besides our believing that it is so.... *Gideon* was sent by an Angel to deliver Israel from the *Midianites*, and yet he desired a Sign to convince him, that this Commission was from God" (*Essay*, 4.19.14-15; Nidditch, 704).

⁶¹ Wesley, "Extract," 325.

⁶² Ibid., 333.

⁶³ Ibid., 339.

⁶⁴ Ibid., 346. Cf. Locke, *Essay*, 4.18.10; Nidditch, 696.

⁶⁵ Wesley, "Extract," 317.

⁶⁶ For Locke's discussion of "constant impressions" in the mind, see Locke, *Essay*, 1.2.2-5; Nidditch, 49-51.

⁶⁷ I refer to Wordsworth's "Expostulation and Reply" (1798).

⁶⁸ See the discussion in Hugh Sykes Davies, "Wordsworth and the Empirical Philosophers." Davies focuses on Wordsworth's objective usage of *impulse*, as

in this stanza from "The Tables Turned" (1798): "One *impulse* from a vernal wood / May teach you more of man, / Of moral evil and of good, / Than all the sages can" (my italics).

[69] Locke, *Essay*, 4.19.6; Nidditch, 699 (my italics).

[70] Wesley, "Extract," 337 (my italics).

[71] Locke, *Essay*, 2.9.4; Nidditch, 144 (my italics).

[72] Richard Saunders, *A Discourse of Angels: Their Nature and Office, or Ministry; also Something Touching Devils, Apparitions, and Impulses.*

[73] Wesley, "Extract," 374.

[74] Hymn 280, Wesley and Wesley, *A Collection of Hymns, for the Use of the People Called Methodists* (1780); see the discussion in G. H. Vallins, *The Wesleys and the English Language*, 87.

[75] Wesley, "Extract," 340.

[76] Ibid., 342.

[77] See Brantley, *Locke, Wesley, and the Method of English Romanticism*, 12.

[78] See, for example, in Brantley, *Locke, Wesley, and the Method of English Romanticism*, 37-44, how Wesley's definition of faith "delineated, for the first time, revelation's inward as well as outward setting and hence its commensurability with empirical philosophy's subject/object emphasis." The other four of Edwards's works abridged by Wesley are "Lockean," too, but unlike Locke's *Essay*, as well as unlike Edwards's *Religious Affections*, they stress experience to the point of subordinating reason.

[79] Wesley, "Extract," 325.

[80] Ibid.

[81] Ibid.; cf. Locke, *Essay*, 4.19; Nidditch, 697-706.

[82] Wesley, "Extract," 326.

[83] Ibid., 325.

[84] Locke, *Essay*, 4.19.15; Nidditch, 705.

[85] Wesley, "Extract," 326.

[86] Ibid., 322. Cf. Matt. 6.29, Ps. 73.1, and Heb. 3.16.

[87] Wesley, "Extract," 319.

[88] This strain of the abridgment's experiential theology, incidentally, finds an illuminating counterpart in another "both/and" permutation of Locke by Wordsworth; here, from "Expostulation and Reply," is the full context of "wise passiveness": "The eye—it cannot choose but see; / We cannot bid the ear be still; / Our bodies feel, where'er they be, / Against or with our will. / Nor less I deem that there are Powers / Which of themselves our minds impress; / That we can feed this mind of ours / In a wise passiveness."

[89] Wesley, "Extract," 312.
[90] Locke, *Essay*, 2.10.5; Nidditch, 151-52.
[91] Wesley, "Extract," 321.
[92] Ibid., 312.
[93] Although Wordsworth, in the following lines from his "Prospectus" to *The Recluse*, does not address the issue of perception as Wesley and Edwards do, that is, although he does not on this occasion apprehend divine reality through the senses as analogues, tests, and receptors, he otherwise gets this "Wesleyan-Edwardsean," indeed this Lockean, point just right: "My voice proclaims / How exquisitely the individual Mind / (And the progressive powers perhaps no less / Of the whole species) to the external World / Is fitted;—and how exquisitely, too— / Theme this but little heard of among men— / The external World is fitted to the Mind; / And the creation (by no lower name / Can it be called) which they with blended might / Accomplish:—this is our high argument."
[94] Edwards, *A Treatise concerning Religious Affections*, ed. Smith, 46.
[95] Wesley, "Extract," 312-13.
[96] Ibid., 364-65.
[97] Ibid., 313.
[98] Edwards, *A Treatise concerning Religious Affections*, ed. Smith, 46.
[99] Ibid., 46 (my italics).
[100] Wesley, "Extract," 338.
[101] Cf. 2 Cor. 3.18; 4.6.
[102] Wesley, "Extract," 310 (my italics).
[103] Ibid., 339.
[104] Ibid., 345-46.
[105] One thinks, in this connection, of Wordsworth's "natural piety": "My heart leaps up when I behold / A rainbow in the sky: / So was it when my life began; / So is it now I am a man; / So be it when I shall grow old, / Or let me die! / The child is father of the Man; / And I could wish my days to be / Bound each to each by natural piety." These lines are thoroughly Lockean: see the discussion in Samuel F. Pickering, Jr., *John Locke and Children's Books in Eighteenth-Century England*, 160-68. The abridgment, in its Lockean dimension, is consistent with them. "Natural piety" is secularized piety, or so goes the wisdom about Wordsworth, but the phrase connotes a faith in the God of nature, and as Wordsworth responds to the rainbow, so Wesley and Edwards claim "sense perception" of God's promises.
[106] Wesley, "Extract," 373.

[107] Ibid.
[108] Locke, *Essay*, 4.16.6; Nidditch, 661-62.
[109] Wesley, "Extract," 335 (my italics).
[110] Edwards, *A Treatise concerning Religious Affections*, ed. Smith, 17.
[111] Wesley, "Extract," 375.
[112] John Wesley, *The Appeals to Men of Reason and Religion*, ed. Gerald R. Cragg, 57.
[113] See the discussion in Brantley, *Locke, Wesley, and the Method of English Romanticism*, 48-53, 99-100, 109, 113, 116, 144, 221-23.
[114] Peter Browne, *The Procedure, Extent, and Limits of Human Understanding*, 141-42.
[115] See Locke's, *Essay*, 4.16.12; Nidditch, 667.
[116] See, for example, the discussion in Leopold Damrosch's review of Brantley, *Locke, Wesley, and the Method of English Romanticism* in *Eighteenth-Century Studies* 19 (1986): 438-41.
[117] Anders Jeffner, *Butler and Hume on Religion: A Comparative Analysis*, 185.
[118] Wesley, "Extract," 313.
[119] Ibid., 346.
[120] I refer to W. B. Yeats's "The Fascination of What's Difficult" (1910).
[121] I refer to H. J. Zelley's hymn, "Heavenly Sunshine" (1898). See William J. Reynolds, ed., *Baptist Hymnal*, 472.
[122] For Wesley's account of his conversion, see *The Journal of the Rev. John Wesley, A. M.*, ed. Nehemiah Curnock, 1.475-76.
[123] See Kenneth MacLean, *John Locke and English Literature of the Eighteenth Century*, and Hans Aarsleff, *From Locke to Saussure: Essays on the Study of Language and Intellectual History*.
[124] I refer to Wordsworth's "Lines, Written a Few Miles Above Tintern Abbey" (1798).

WORKS CITED

Aarsleff, Hans. *From Locke to Saussure: Essays on the Study of Language and Intellectual History*. Minneapolis: U of Minnesota P, 1982.

Anderson, Wallace E. "The Development of Edwards' Philosophical Thought." In *Scientific and Philosophical Writings*. Vol. 6 of *The Works of Jonathan Edwards*. Edited by John E. Smith. New Haven: Yale U P, 1980.

Ashcroft, Richard. "Faith and Knowledge in Locke's Philosophy." In *John Locke: Problems and Perspectives*, edited by John W. Yolton, 194-223. Cambridge: Cambridge U P, 1969.

Baker, Frank. "John Wesley and America." *Proceedings of the Wesley Historical Society* 44 (September 1984): 117-29.

———. "A Study of John Wesley's Readings." *The London Quarterly and Holborn Review* 168 (May 1943): 237-49.

Bercovitch, Sacvan. *The American Jeremiad.* Madison: U of Wisconsin P, 1978.

Brantley, Richard E. "Charles Wesley's Experiential Art." *Eighteenth-Century Life* 11 (May 1987): 1-11.

———. *Locke, Wesley, and the Method of English Romanticism.* Gainesville: U of Florida P, 1984.

Breitenbach, William. "Piety and Moralism: Edwards and the New Divinity." In *Jonathan Edwards and the American Experience,* edited by Nathan O. Hatch and Harry S. Stout, 177-204. New York: Oxford U P, 1988.

Browne, Peter. *The Procedure, Extent, and Limits of Human Understanding.* 2d ed. London: W. Innys, 1729.

Carwardine, Richard. *Transatlantic Revivalism: Popular Evangelicalism in Britain and America, 1790-1865.* Westport, CT: Greenwood P, 1978.

Clapper, Gregory S. "'True Religion' and the Affections: A Study of John Wesley's Abridgment of Jonathan Edwards's Treatise on the Religious Affections." In *Wesleyan Theology Today,* edited by Theodore Runyon. Nashville, TN: Abingdon P, 1985.

Damrosch, Leopold, Jr. Review of *Locke, Wesley, and the Method of English Romanticism,* by Richard E. Brantley. *Eighteenth-Century Studies* 19 (1986): 438-41.

Davidson, Edward H. "From Locke to Edwards." *Journal of the History of Ideas* 24 (July-September 1963): 355-72.

Davies, Hugh Sykes. "Wordsworth and the Empirical Philosophers." In *The English Mind: Studies in English Moralists Presented to Basil Willey,* edited by Hugh Sykes Davies and George Watson. Cambridge: Cambridge U P, 1964.

Delattre, Roland. *Beauty and Sensibility in the Thought of Jonathan Edwards: An Essay in Aesthetics and Theological Ethics.* New Haven: Yale U P, 1968.

Diggins, John Patrick. "Puritans and Pragmatists." Review of *Churchmen and Philosophers,* by Bruce Kuklick. *New Republic* 194 (April 28, 1986): 38-41.

Doidge, Reginald. *John Wesley's Christian Library.* London: Epworth, 1938.

Donoghue, Denis. *The Third Voice: Modern British and American Verse Drama.* Princeton: Princeton U P, 1959.

Dreyer, Frederick. "Evangelical Thought: John Wesley and Jonathan Edwards." *Albion* 19 (Summer 1987): 177-92.

———. "Faith and Experience in the Thought of John Wesley." *American Historical Review* 88 (February 1983): 12-30.

———. "A 'Religious Society' under Heaven: John Wesley and the Identity of Methodism." *Journal of British Studies* 25 (January 1986): 62-83.

Edwards, Jonathan. *An Account of the Life of the Late Reverend Mr. David Brainerd.* Boston: D. Henchman, 1749.

———. *The Distinguishing Marks of a Work of the Spirit of God.* Boston: S. Kneeland and T. Green, 1741.

———. *The Distinguishing Marks of a Work of the Spirit of God.* Edited by John Wesley. London: W. Strahan, 1744.

———. *An Extract of the Life of the Late Rev. Mr. David Brainerd.* Edited by John Wesley. Bristol: William Pine, 1768.

———. *An Extract from a Treatise concerning Religious Affections.* Edited by John Wesley. In vol. 23 of *The Works of the Rev. John Wesley.* 32 vols. Bristol: J. Paramore, 1771-74.

———. *A Faithful Narrative of the Surprising Work of God in the Conversion of many hundred souls in Northampton.* Edinburgh: J. Oswald, 1736.

———. *A Narrative of Many Surprising Conversions in Northampton and Vicinity.* Edited by John Wesley. Boston: Felix Farley, 1744.

———. *Some Thoughts concerning the Present Revival in New England.* Boston: S. Kneeland and T. Green, 1742.

———. *Thoughts concerning the Present Revival of Religion.* Edited by John Wesley. London: W. Strahan, 1745.

———. *A Treatise concerning Religious Affections.* In vol. 2 of *The Works of Jonathan Edwards.* Edited by John E. Smith. New Haven: Yale U P, 1959.

———. *A Treatise concerning Religious Affections: In Three Parts.* Edited by William Gordon. London: T. Field, 1762.

Erdt, Terrence. *Jonathan Edwards: Art and the Sense of the Heart.* Amherst: U of Massachusetts P, 1980.

Farr, James. "The Way of Hypothesis: Locke on Method." *Journal of the History of Ideas* 48 (January-March 1987): 51-72.

Fiering, Norman. *Jonathan Edwards's Moral Thought and Its British Context.* Chapel Hill: U of North Carolina P, 1981.

Fliegelman, Jay. *Prodigals and Pilgrims: The American Revolution against Patriarchal Authority, 1750-1800.* Cambridge: Cambridge U P, 1982.

Gauthier, David. "Why Ought One Obey God? Reflections on Hobbes and Locke." *Canadian Journal of Philosophy* 7 (September 1977): 425-46.

Greven, Philip. *The Protestant Temperament: Patterns of Child-rearing, Religious Experience, and the Self in Early America.* New York: Knopf, 1977.

Hatch, Nathan O. *The Democritization of American Christianity.* New Haven: Yale U P, 1989.

———, and Harry S. Stout, eds. *Jonathan Edwards and the American Experience.* New York: Oxford U P, 1988.

Heimert, Alan. *Religion and the American Mind, from the Great Awakening to the Revolution.* Cambridge, MA: Harvard U P, 1966.

Helm, Paul. "John Locke and Jonathan Edwards: A Reconsideration." *Journal of the History of Ideas* 7 (April 1969): 51-61.

Hempton, David. *Methodism and Politics in British Society, 1750-1850.* Stanford, CA: Stanford U P, 1984.

Herbert, T. Walter. *John Wesley as Editor and Author.* Princeton: Princeton U P, 1940.

Hitchens, Christopher. *Blood, Class, and Nostalgia: Anglo-American Ironies.* New York: Farrar, Straus & Giroux, 1990.

Hoopes, James. "Calvinism and Consciousness from Edwards to Beecher." In *Jonathan Edwards and the American Experience*, edited by Nathan O. Hatch and Harry S. Stout. New York: Oxford U P, 1988.

Jeffner, Anders. *Butler and Hume on Religion: A Comparative Analysis.* Stockholm: Diakonistyrelsense bokförlog, 1966.

Jenson, Robert W. *America's Theologian: A Recommendation of Jonathan Edwards.* New York: Oxford U P, 1988.

Laquer, T. W. *Religion and Respectability: Sunday Schools and Working-class Culture, 1780-1850.* New Haven: Yale U P, 1986.

Lee, Sang Hyun. *The Philosophical Theology of Jonathan Edwards.* Princeton: Princeton U P, 1988.

Locke, John. *An Essay concerning Human Understanding.* Edited by Peter H. Nidditch. Oxford: Clarendon P, 1975.

MacLean, Kenneth. *John Locke and English Literature of the Eighteenth Century.* 1956. Reprint. New York: Russell & Russell, 1962.

Miller, Perry. *Jonathan Edwards.* New York: W. G. Sloane, 1949.

———. "Jonathan Edwards and the Sense of the Heart." *Harvard Theological Review* 41 (April 1948): 123-45.

Outler, Albert. *John Wesley.* New York: Oxford U P, 1964.

Pickering, Samuel F., Jr. *John Locke and Children's Books in Eighteenth-Century England.* Knoxville: U of Tennessee P, 1981.

Robb, Edmund W., Jr. "American Methodism at 200: The Case for Hope." *Christianity Today* 28 (December 14, 1984): 21-25.

Rogers, Charles. "John Wesley and Jonathan Edwards." *Duke Divinity School Review* 31 (January 1966): 20-38.

Rousseau, G. S. "John Wesley's *Primitive Physick* (1747)." *Harvard Library Bulletin* 16 (July 1968): 242-56.

Saunders, Richard. *A Discourse of Angels: Their Nature and Office, or Ministry; also Something Touching Devils, Apparitions, and Impulses.* London: Thomas Parkhurst, 1701.

Shaw, Peter. *American Patriots and the Rituals of Revolution.* Cambridge, MA: Harvard U P, 1981.

Smith, Claude A. "Jonathan Edwards and the 'Way of Ideas.'" *Harvard Theological Review* 59 (April 1966): 153-73.

Spellman, W. M. *John Locke and the Problem of Depravity.* Oxford: Clarendon P, 1988.

Townsend, Harvey G., ed. *The Philosophy of Jonathan Edwards from His Private Notebooks.* Eugene: U of Oregon Monographs, 1955.

Vallins, G. H. *The Wesleys and the English Language.* London: Epworth, 1957.

Wainwright, William J. "Jonathan Edwards and the Language of God." *Journal of the American Academy of Religion* 48 (December 1980): 519-30.

Wesley, Charles, and John Wesley. *Collection of Hymns for the Use of the People called Methodists.* London: J. Paramore, 1780.

Wesley, John. *The Appeals to Men of Reason and Religion.* Edited by Gerald R. Cragg. Oxford: Clarendon P, 1975.

———. *The Journal of the Rev. John Wesley, A. M., Sometime Fellow of Lincoln College, Oxford, Enlarged from Original MSS., With Notes from Unpublished Diaries, Annotations, Maps, and Illustrations.* Edited by Nehemiah Curnock. 8 vols. London: Robert Culley, 1909.

———. *The Letters of the Rev. John Wesley, A. M.* Edited by John Telford. London: Epworth, 1931.

———. *The Works of the Rev. John Wesley, A. M.* Edited by Thomas Jackson. 14 vols. London: Wesleyan-Methodist Book-Room, n. d.

———, ed. *A Christian Library: Consisting of Extracts from and Abridgments of the choicest Pieces of Practical Divinity which have been published in the English Tongue.* 50 vols. Philadelphia: Jonathan Pounder, 1819-27.

———, ed. *The Distinguishing Marks of a Work of the Spirit of God*, by Jonathan Edwards. London: W. Strahan, 1744.

———, ed. *An Extract of the Life of the Late Rev. Mr. David Brainerd*, by Jonathan Edwards. Bristol: William Pine, 1768.

———, ed. *An Extract from a Treatise concerning Religious Affections*, by Jonathan Edwards. In vol. 23 of *The Works of the Rev. John Wesley*. 32 vols. Bristol: J. Paramore, 1771-74.

———, ed. *A Narrative of Many Surprising Conversions in Northampton and Vicinity*, by Jonathan Edwards. Boston: Felix Farley, 1744.

———, ed. *Thoughts concerning the Present Revival of Religion*, by Jonathan Edwards. London: W. Strahan, 1745.

Wilson, Edward O. *Sociobiology: The New Synthesis*. Cambridge, MA: Harvard U P, 1980.

Woolhouse, Roger. *Locke's Philosophy of Science and Knowledge*. Oxford: Clarendon P, 1971.

Yolton, John W. *John Locke and the Compass of Human Understanding*. Cambridge: Cambridge U P, 1970.

Zelley, H. J. "Heavenly Sunshine" (1898). *Baptist Hymnal*, edited by William J. Reynolds, 472. Nashville, TN: Convention P, 1975.

5. Empiricism and Evangelicalism: A Combination of Romanticism

The twin pioneers of transatlantic revivalism, John Wesley (1703-1791) and Jonathan Edwards (1703-1758), absorbed and spiritualized the sensationalist epistemology of John Locke (1632-1704) and then passed along to the nineteenth century their empirical idiom of evangelical expression. As a direct as well as indirect result of this complex process of cultural osmosis, such British Romantics as William Blake, William Wordsworth, Samuel Taylor Coleridge, Percy Bysshe Shelley, and John Keats could conceive of the physical senses as portals to epiphany and not just as analogies of spiritual insight. As an illustrative Anglo-American trio of late-Romantic writers, Thomas Carlyle, Alfred, Lord Tennyson, and Ralph Waldo Emerson continued to blend what Wordsworth called "the language of the sense" with what Coleridge, anticipating the *fin-de-siècle* apprehension of art as religion, and vice versa, called "poetic faith."[1] Emily Dickinson (1830-1886), herself as much of a late-Romantic as of a Victorian-American (anti-Romantic) or pre-Modern poet, also gravitated toward the amalgamation of scientific method with the varieties of religious experience.[2] Like her precursors and contemporaries on the high-to-late-Romantic arc of literary history—the ark back and forth across the Atlantic—Dickinson grew more apt to expect truth, joy, and grace—like Locke, Wesley, and Edwards—than like Marx, Nietzsche, or Freud to suspect consciousness as false.

Thus, as distinct from Euro-continental Romanticism of either a French rationalist or a German idealist stripe, Anglo-American Romanticism generated language at once empirical and evangelical. For example, this local habitation of the long Romantic Movement from the late eighteenth to the second half of the nineteenth century perceived rather than deduced or intuited "whatsoever things" were true, honest, just, pure, lovely, and "of good report" (compare Phil 4:8). On the one hand, in a skeptical turn, this binational brand of Romanticism proclaimed a twofold imperative—namely, *Trust in Experiment! Test Religion!* On the other hand, with guileless receptivity Romantic Anglo-America also dwelt in the possibility of the spiritual sense, perhaps even reimagining as worth a try in an "age of wonder" (Holmes) the warm heart of faith. Accordingly, so radically immanent were both the philosophy and the religion of eighteenth-to-nineteenth-century Anglo-America that English-speaking Romanticism stayed grounded, for better or worse, in spiritual as well as in natural experience.

To be sure, if one may read back-in-time Stephen Jay Gould's phrase for the proper relation between science and religion in the twentieth century, the empiricism and the evangelicalism of Romantic Anglo-America can seem to be "non-overlapping magisteria." Moreover, if one may apply to the shortcomings of religion Keats's language for the limits of the creative imagination or of poetic faith, faith scarcely moves mountains "so well / As she is fam'd to do, deceiving elf" (Keats, "Ode to a Nightingale" [1819], lines 73-74). Nevertheless, Anglo-American Romantic writers anticipated that through dust and heat but for better not worse, faith in experience would lead to an experience of faith. Experience and faith emerged from this climate—this transatlantic weather—as "Contraries" that did not so much clash or meld as produce "progression" (witness Blake's dialectical terms in *The Marriage of Heaven and Hell* (1790-1793], Plate Three). Instead of nihilistic unbelief, constructive skepticism informed all that the Anglo-American century from 1770 to 1870 found resonant in "the burthen of the mystery," and in mystery itself (Wordsworth, "Tintern Abbey," line 38).

This précis, having epitomized the series-to-date, can now signal how *Emily Dickinson's Rich Conversation* (2013, 2015) differs from previous installments in this ongoing project in Anglo-American cultural poetics. Without precluding a future study of Dickinson's spiritual experience per se, that sixth volume of my historical, interdisciplinary approach to English-language Romanticism constituted a strategic drawing back from the emphasis in *Experience and Faith* (2004, 2008) on Dickinson's experience-faith fusion. Of course, her perennial human yearning for transcendence drew her toward dialectic in the first place (albeit without often getting there).[3] Still, she rarely hesitated to apply Ockham's razor to what was not absolutely required to explain the case at hand. Scarcely ever did her blessed rage for order foreclose her aesthetic choice to stick with physical evidence. She more often tended to migrate from evangelical training to empirical discipline than tried to reconcile the two on any paradoxical, counterintuitive, or oxymoronic ground of providential chance, on the one hand, or of random grace, on the other. The emphasis of *Emily Dickinson's Rich Conversation* lies less on the empirical thesis and the evangelical antithesis of her poetic synthesis (for that case, though, see Chapter 4 of *Experience and Faith*) than on the more philosophical and scientific than religious flow of her literary conversation. Thus her late-Romantic imagination engaged not so much with the destination of system as with the journey of method.

NOTES

[1] See, respectively, Wordsworth, "Lines Written a Few Miles above Tintern Abbey" (1798), line 108, and Coleridge, *Biographia Literaria* (1817), Chapter 14.

[2] The empirical/evangelical dialectic of Romantic Anglo-America can appear to foresee, though scarcely to preempt, the psychologically anthropological findings of T. M. Luhrmann. In her study of John Wimber's Vineyard Movement of evangelical churches, Luhrmann cultivates an almost more than William James-like sympathy for how these congregations school their members "to experience the supernatural with their senses," and hence to encounter or, in the vile vernacular, "friend" God personally (Luhrmann 36).

[3] Perhaps no better way exists to describe how Emily Dickinson's yearning for transcendence is a universal human trait than in the language of Oliver Sacks: "To live on a day-to-day basis is insufficient for human beings; we need to transcend, transport, escape; we need meaning, understanding, and explanation; we need to see over-all patterns in our lives. We need hope, the sense of a future. And we need freedom (or, at least, the illusion of freedom) to get beyond ourselves, whether with telescopes and microscopes and our ever-burgeoning technology, or in states of mind that allow us to travel to other worlds, to rise above our immediate surroundings" (40). The first of Sacks's three additional sentences in this vein proves equally applicable to Dickinson: "Many of us find Worthsworthian 'intimations of immortality' in nature, art, creative thinking, or religion; some people can reach transcendent states through meditation or similar trance-inducing techniques, or through prayer and spiritual exercises. But drugs offer a shortcut; they promise transcendence on demand. These shortcuts are possible because certain chemicals can directly stimulate many complex brain functions" (40).

WORKS CITED

Gould, Stephen Jay. *Time's Arrow, Time's Cycle: Myth and Metaphor in the Discovery of Geological Time.* Cambridge, MA: Harvard University Press, 1987.

Holmes, Richard. *The Age of Wonder: How the Romantic Generation Discovered the Beauty and Terror of Science.* New York: Pantheon, 2009.

Luhrmann, T. M. *When God Talks Back: Understanding the American Evangelical Relationship with God.* New York: Knopf, 2012.

Sacks, Oliver. "Altered States: Self-experiments in Chemistry." *The New Yorker*, August 27, 2012, 40-47.

Essays, Second Series:
British Authors

6. Charles Wesley's Experiential Art

Charles Wesley's regard for experience needs emphasis. Madeleine Marshall and Janet Todd, in their recent study of English congregational hymns, acknowledge on the one hand that Wesley's "cultivation of feeling" is "at odds with otherworldliness" and that for him "the world is not particularly contaminated": pains for him are "useful spurs to faith and joys are "a genuine comfort."[1] Marshall and Todd, however, since they are mainly concerned to deny "the frequently presumed" connection between Wesley's hymns and Romanticism (p. 7), see the hymns, finally, as impersonal, public, and didactic (pp. 1, 86); as "participatory religious theater" rather than "a record of common feeling" (p. 79); and as "exemplary not expressive-realistic" (p. 80). "Wesley's purpose," they conclude, "was not the expressive venting of feeling but rather the evangelical directing of feeling" (p. 79). These helpful distinctions are based on the rather tired assumptions that Romanticism is not concerned with audience and that the eighteenth century never indulged in self-expression. Wesley's poetry is often a record of common feeling.

Consider, for example, one of his most famous hymns, "For the Anniversary Day of One's Conversion":

> Then with my Heart I first believ'd,
>   Believ'd, with Faith Divine,
> Power with the Holy Ghost receiv'd
>   To call the Saviour *Mine*.[2]

The most admired Wesley hymn is surely "Wrestling Jacob" (#25), in which subjectivity and experience are more in evidence than the divine vision:

> Come, O Thou Traveller unknown,
>   Whom still I hold, but cannot see,
> My company before is gone,
>   And I am left alone with Thee,
> With Thee all Night I mean to stay,
> And wrestle till the Break of Day.

And finally:

> Ah LORD!—if Thou art in that Sigh,
>   Then hear Thyself within me pray.
> Hear in my Heart Thy Spirit's Cry,
>   Mark what my lab'ring Soul would say,
> Answer the deep, unutter'd Groan,
> And shew that Thou and I are One.
>   (#14)

Here experience and subjectivity are so nearly equivalent to grace as to anticipate the Romantic apotheosis of self. The lines, for example, seem especially pertinent to E. D. Hirsch's view of Blake's Christianity as radically immanent.[3] Martha England's observation that in Blake's poetry man was "created . . . for experience" so that he might "undergo the salvation of experience,"[4] could be said of Wesley as well.

Wesley's trust in experience, in other words, and indeed his love of it, can hardly be overemphasized. It is true that one of his best-known hymns seems pure escapism: "Jesu, Lover of my Soul, / Let me to Thy Bosom fly" (#15). But this is simply the impulse to escape, an impulse that comes precisely because the hymn's speaker is amid experience. True too that "Rapturous Height" (#73) is astonishingly otherworldly:

> I rode on the Sky
>   (Freely justified I!)
> Nor envied *Elijah* his Seat;
>   My soul mounted higher

> In a Chariot of Fire,
> And the Moon it was under my Feet.
>   O the rapturous Height
>   Of that holy Delight,
> Which I felt in the Life-giving Blood!
>   Of my Saviour possest
>   I was perfectly blest,
> As if fill'd with the Fulness of God.

Stanza 3, though, suggests that Wesley's feet are firmly on the ground: "Twas an Heaven *below* / My Saviour to know" (my italics). And the anapests, useful to memory and hence often found in popular songs, make it hard not to think of an earthly dance, especially in view of sexual implications in "Life-giving Blood," "possest," and "fill'd with the Fulness of God."

The here and now, indeed, is so important to Wesley's point of view that it overshadows theology on occasion. Upon the death of his infant daughter Martha Maria, Wesley wrote "A Short-Lived Flower," in which an inconsolable bitterness is the pertinent feature: "What was all her life below? / One sad month of fruitless woe" (#255). Upon the death of his infant son John, Wesley wrote "On the Death of a Child" (#252) in which his attempts at otherworldly consolation are overwhelmed, again, by the bitterness of his earthly but much-lamented loss:

> I bow me to the sovereign God,
>   Who snatch'd him from the evil day!
> Yet nature *will* repeat her moan,
> And fondly cry, 'My son, my son!'

These lines are worthy of the tough-mindedness in Ben Jonson's "On My First Son," in which is a similar bitterness, a similar victory of earthly love over heavenly comfort.

Charles Wesley's love for the world is much in evidence even when his love of God predominates. True, he was so worried about whether his prospective marriage to Sally Gwynne was the will of God, and whether it would interrupt His work,[5] that at one point he decided against it: "Ah! what have I to do with Peace, / Or Converse sweet, or Social Love?" (#239). Even here, though, one sees where desire lies: he did marry her, for reasons of the frankest sort. In "Hymn for April 8, 1750" (#244), written on their first wedding anniversary, Wesley follows a pious sentiment about sacrificing Sally with a less bloody but more red-blooded, and undoubtedly truer, feeling about her:

> Yet if thy gracious will consent
>   To spare her yet another year,
> With joy I grasp whom God hath lent,
>   And clasp her to my bosom here.

On her birthday, Wesley piously anticipates eternity, but even here suggests that their marriage will continue in every conceivable respect:

> There, there at his seat
> We shall suddenly meet,
> And be parted in body no more.
>   (#245)

There is no more *contemptus mundi* in Wesley's faith than in Donne's. In *Hymns for the Use of Families*, finally, Wesley wrote a series of hymns "for a woman near the time of her travail"; and, although the *Book of Common Prayer* includes a prayer for this occasion, the choice of subject matter is still rather startling, for what Marx called "the actual life process"[6] is evident even in the most explicitly religious aspect of that subject matter. Here for example is the laboring mother-to-be's almost sexual prayer:

> When my sorrows most increase,
>   Let thy strongest joys be given;
> Jesus come with my distress,
>   And agony is heaven.

Marshall and Todd hit the mark when they see Charles Wesley as an eighteenth-century man: their argument that Charles Wesley's Jesus is "a proper 'man of feeling'" proves persuasive. In Hymn 23, for example, Jesus becomes "a compassionate type who was, in much contemporary literature, the only man of virtue":

> Thy tender Heart is still the same,
> And melts the Human Woe:

> JESU, for Thee distrest I am,
> I want Thy Love to know.[7]

Another refrain, though, is: "What we have felt and seen / With confidence we tell."[8] This strain of Wesley's Methodism, this assurance, is more tough-minded than what the phrase *man of feeling* can ever quite imply. John Wesley, after all, described the 1780 *Collection of Hymns* as "a little body of experimental and practical divinity,"[9] and the word *experimental* implies something more methodical, more rigorous, than the cult of sensibility. The experiential method of John Wesley derives, as I have previously pointed out, from the experimental philosophy of John Locke,[10] and Locke's philosophy is undoubtedly a context for Charles Wesley's thought as well.

Martha England has implied as much: she regards "the position of the evangelicals" as "an outgrowth of empiricism," and both Charles and Blake, in her view, are "heirs of empiricism."[11] England's comments, though, remain assertions in need of examples and documentation. To begin with Charles Wesley's hymns, note the topical imagery of the following lines, which, as G. H. Vallins has observed, "breathes the very spirit of early Methodism":

> Touched by the lodestone of Thy Love,
>   Let all our hearts agree,
> And ever toward each other move,
>   And ever move toward Thee.[12]

Vallins goes on to say that the new electric machine had given these lines "a peculiar significance": "But the natural picture of the tiny filings moved irresistibly by the mysterious attractive power was lifted up to a spiritual plane. The people called Methodists were drawn together in sacred and mysterious fellowship because they were first irresistibly drawn by the magnet of their Master's love" (p. 88). This is close to my view that John Wesley's thought can best be understood as a continuum joining scientific method and rational empiricism to natural and revealed religion.

One finds related emphases throughout the hymns, suggesting intellectual as well as spiritual reasons for the resemblance between the two brothers. Many hymns ask the question of number 141: "How can a Sinner know His Sins on Earth forgiven?"; and this question has as much to do with epistemology, with philosophical theology, as with pure doctrine. In "Modern

Christianity" (#132), which is especially aware of the peculiar timeliness of Methodism, Charles appears to take for granted a Lockean tenet that "sense perception" of the divine, like sense perception of natural phenomena, is tantamount to knowledge:

> No fanciful Enthusiasts we
>   To look for Inspiration here,
> To dream from Sin to be set free
>   Or hope to *feel* the Spirit near,
> Or *know* our Sins on Earth forgiven,
> Or madly give up all for Heaven!

The imagery of the mold, the stamp, and the seal runs through the *Hymns*[13] and is not far from the Lockean metaphor of mind as *tabula rasa* receiving the impressions of experience.

Though not as conscious as John of Locke's importance, Charles was aware of Locke's *Essay concerning Human Understanding* (1690) as solid, substantial truth. Here are some pertinent lines from a hymn sung "at the opening of a School in Kingswood" (#105):

> Learning's redundant part and vain
>   Be here cut off, and cast aside:
> But let them, Lord, the substance gain,
>   In every solid truth abide,
> Swiftly acquire, and ne'er forego
> The knowledge fit for man to know.
>
> Unite the pair so long disjoin'd,
>   Knowledge and vital piety.

Locke's essay was required reading at the Kingswood School,[14] and since the emphasis on knowledge as limited but genuine is characteristic of Locke; since Locke regarded scholasticism as redundant learning, if not vain; since Lockean knowledge frees piety from dogma and makes it truly vital; and since Locke, therefore, was no more intent than Wesley upon separating piety from knowledge, one may detect Lockean assumptions, and Lockean language, in these lines of Charles' hymn. Indeed, the whole occasion of the hymn is reminiscent of *Some Thoughts concerning Education* (1693), in which Locke, to borrow Charles' terms, argued that knowledge may be "swiftly acquired" through guided experience. "It is true," wrote John of his brother's hymns, that "none but those who either already experience the kingdom of God within them, or, at least, earnestly desire to do so, will either relish or understand them" (*Works*, 14:339). The suggestion here, that the kingdom of God is realized in experience, transposes Locke's view that knowledge depends on experience; thus, a Lockean trust in experience underlies both Locke's pronouncement and Charles' hymns.

A Lockean view of language, moreover, underlies John's boast regarding the hymns: "We talk common sense, whether they understand it or not, both in verse and prose, and use no word but in a fixed and determinate sense" (*Works*, 14:341). Charles Wesley was a man of his times not least because of his general, eighteenth-century diction, but the "sense" of his words derives from particulars. What Hazard Adams says of Samuel Johnson, in other words, could be said of Charles Wesley: "When Johnson mentions the 'species' he seems not to be discussing some Platonic universal idea but a generalization from sense experience."[15] The sort of abstraction in which particulars have priority is characteristically Lockean, so that one wonders whether even the *Arminian* particularity of Wesley's hymns—Jesus died "For *every Soul* of Man" (#17)—is a Lockean particularity as well.

Wesley's attitudes toward music, finally, underscore the point that his poetry conveys a theology of the here and now precisely because his poetry derives from the here and now. We know, or should, that Charles was a poet indeed: we need not go so far as the boast of Bernard Manning that his *Collection* of 1780 is "elemental in its perfection" (Manning, p. 14); but we can recognize and take pleasure in his deliberate use of sophisticated literary devices throughout his 9,000 hymns.[16] We know that Charles was such an important lover of music that he all but qualifies as a musician, though, as Baker puts it, his "musical urges undoubtedly outstripped his talents" (p. 311). According to his son Samuel, Charles played the flute, "had a most accurate ear for time," and could carry a tune;[17] and it must have been pleasant for the father to think that the musical gifts of his sons, apart from being divine, came down from him.[18] What we need to realize is that the relation of Wesley the musician to Wesley the poet is a clue to the larger significance not only of Charles Wesley but of Methodism itself. The relation between his poetry and his music, between his heavenly message and the delights of sound, is a special instance of the Methodist allegiance to, and appropriation of, experience both spiritual and natural.

"The True Use of Musick" (#84A) is a case in point:
>   Listed into the Cause of Sin,
>   Why should a Good be Evil?
> Musick, alas! too long has been
>   Prest to obey the Devil:
> . . .
> Who on the Part of GOD will rise,
>   *Innocent Sound* recover,
> Fly on the Prey, and take the Prize,
>   Plunder the Carnal Lover,
> Strip him of every moving Strain,
>   Every melting Measure,
> Musick in Virtue's Cause retain,
>   Rescue the Holy Pleasure?

The language is careful, the tone well sustained. "Listed into the Cause of Sin"; "Prest to obey the Devil"—these lines establish the military metaphors of enlistment and the press-gang. It is clear from the second stanza that the hymn is addressed to soldiers: the call goes out for a military attack, for someone to "Fly on the Prey," "take the Prize" of music from the "Carnal Lover," and restore it to higher purpose.

The language, then, is general but seems to derive from particular circumstances. When Charles visited Plymouth in June 1746, "a whole army of soldiers and sailors stood behind [him] shouting and blaspheming,"[19] and Charles prolonged his stay in an attempt to restore order. It may well have been then, as Frank Baker has suggested, that he wrote this hymn, for Methodist legend has it that Charles was once

> interrupted during an open-air service in a sea-port by a company of half-drunken sailors. As he began to sing a hymn they struck up "one of their lewd songs called 'Nancy Dawson.'" Charles Wesley mastered the tune and metre, and at the following service got the people to sing new words to the sailors' tune.[20]

It is tempting to think that the "new words" were the words of "The True Use of Musick," which, as Baker first pointed out, is designed for the use of sailors or soldiers. Perhaps it was at Plymouth that Wesley wrote these verses, which were first published three years later. Baker's research reveals that a Nancy Dawson of Plymouth kept a house of ill repute, that the sailors sang a song about her, and that the song was probably sung to the tune of "Here we go round the mulberry bush."[21]

Wesley, of course, was not of the world, but he was in it; and instead of shrinking from scenes of worldliness he consciously incorporated them into his faith. His hymn retains reference not just to the senses but even to the sensual, and the horn-pipe melody to which it was evidently sung conveys, even at this late date, the degree to which he brought his vision to earth and made it dance according to the rhymes of the street. The story of this hymn suggests a continuum in Wesley's thought joining the not always verbal realm of direct physical experience to religious experience.

This hymn, as I take it, is thus representative of Wesley's poetry. "The True Use of Musick," arising from his encounter with soldiers and sailors, finds counterparts in experience-derived hymns for stoneworkers, miners, fishermen, farmers, shepherds, teachers, masons, students, cooks, cleaners, builders, and carpenters.[22] And just as "The True Use of Musick" conforms to the lilting hornpipe of "Here we go round the mulberry bush," so his poetry in general associates music with sense experience. "Jesus's Name," it is true, "is sweeter" than the harmony of musical strains: Charles Wesley would agree with Pope that "the sound must seem an echo to the sense." But music is an earthly good: its "moving Strain" and "melting Measure" are valued in themselves. By surveying Wesley's attitudes toward music as expressed in, and implied by, his verse, and in the conviction that the theme of literature and the arts finds an especially suggestive illustration in his hymns, I argue that he did not simply mean, after the manner of Dryden's two St. Cecilia's Day odes, that earthly music reflects cosmic harmony. In addition, and this is his special emphasis, he valued earthly music for itself.

His appropriation of secular music is characteristic, and is based on appreciation. To borrow the words of Martha England, Charles made "a comprehensive offer to reclaim all music for 'the Great Lover,' to make song in its entirety into a love song for Him." Here, for example, are two stanzas from his famous "Hymn for the Kingswood Colliers":

> Suffice that for the season past
>   Hell's horrid language filled our tongues,
> We all Thy words behind us cast,
>   And lewdly sang the drunkard's songs.

> But, O the power of grace divine!
>   In hymns we now our voices raise,
> Loudly our strange hosannas join,
>   And blasphemies are turned to praise!²³

Charles would not have hesitated, would indeed have delighted, to sing these lines to the tune of a drinking song. The Wesleys held Watchnight Services once a month "as a counterattraction to the ale-house roistering to which the Kingswood miners were addicted on Saturday nights" *(Representative Verse*, p. 114); and "Innocent Diversions" (#83), a Watchnight hymn, contains the remarkable testimony of colliers whose musical propensities have been as much employed as rechanneled:

> Our Concert of Praise
> To Jesus we raise,
> And all the Night long
> Continue the New Evangelical Song:
>   We dance to the Fame
>   Of Jesus's Name,
>   The Joy it imparts
> Is Heaven begun in our Musical Hearts.

No conception of the transforming power of eighteenth-century Methodism would be complete without this image of miners, innocent but still diverted.

"Sing *lustily*," wrote John Wesley in his "Directions for Congregational Singing": "Beware of singing as if you were half dead, or half asleep; but lift up your voice with strength. Be no more afraid of your voice now, nor more ashamed of its being heard, than when you sung the songs of Satan" *(Works*, 14:346). That is the point, surely, and the point is made more fully in England's modern study:

> Wesley tunes came from modern opera, popular stage shows, Handel's *Susanna*, Bickerstaffe's *Love in a Village*, Carey's song in praise of the taking of Portobello by Admiral Vernon, Arne's *Eliza*, and jigs. "Love Divine, [All Loves excelling, / Joy from Heaven to Earth Come Down]," that mixture of pure doctrine and sexuality which for decades was the wedding hymn of

> Methodism, is a parody of the curtain song from the Restoration equivalent of our musical show *Camelot*. It was sung by Venus (no less) at the close of Dryden's *King Arthur*, set by Purcell. The Wesley's used Purcell's tune .... The trail of Wesley tunes would lead one day from Lincoln Center to City Center, from Broadway to Tin Pan Alley, from the Rare Book Room of Union Theological Seminary to some very red lights indeed. (p. 96)

Even Lincoln Center is not an exaggeration; Baker, and Marshall and Todd, have built upon Eric Routley's careful study of the "operatic aria-technique" in *Hymns for the Greater Festivals* (1746).[24] The music of these hymns was edited by J. F. Lampe, a Covent Garden bassoon player converted to Methodism in 1745.

Since Charles did not write music, his use of popular song has a most practical cause, of course, and the use of well-known tunes was a big advantage in teaching hymns. His knowledge of such lore was so great, however, that it seems unthinkable he did not like it for its own sake. His joy was not just "from heaven to earth come down," but was sometimes in the first instance earthly. In "Innocent Diversions," he attacked those followers of Satan who "chaunt in a Grove to the Harpers of Hell"; it is clear that Wesley did not expect to find full joy in Vaux-Hall or Ranelagh's Gardens. And when his enemies used this line against him after his son Charles became a musician, Wesley distinguished between earthly and heavenly music: "How can I call musicians harpers of hell, yet breed my Son a Musician? I answer, there are Heavenly as well as Hellish Harpers" *(Representative Verse*, p. 115). But Wesley did not thereby condemn secular music. Despite such puritanical opposition from pious Methodists, he not only encouraged his sons in their musical ambitions (young Samuel was a prodigy, too), but even allowed them to play secular concerts in his own home.

For his hymns, then, Charles Wesley drew from secular music not just to reclaim music for the divine, but to humanize the divine with music. If he ever enjoyed a drinking song for its own sake, it must have been at a subconscious level, but consider Hymn 82, "Meet and right it is to sing." It envisions a time when earthly singers will join heavenly choirs "in full Chorus"; but meanwhile "our Voices" are "lower," and Charles is content to sing an earthly song as he waits to sing in heaven. Consider, too, the famous Hymn 64, "On the Corpse of a Believer":

> Ah! lovely Appearance of Death!
>   No Sight upon Earth is so fair:
> Not all the gay pageants that breathe
>   Can with a dead Body compare.
>
> With solemn Delight I survey
>   The Corpse, when the Spirit is fled,
> In love with the beautiful Clay,
>   And longing to lie in its stead.

These lines are ghoulishly morbid, but the anapests are rollicking, and if they do not suggest the dance hall, they participate in the animation of secular music. Thus, they are a rhythmic, even lively version of the saying that "the Methodists die well": "The genesis of the hymn," writes Baker,

> may possibly be traced to the triumphant death of a Cardiff Methodist on 13th August 1744. The preaching service on the morning following his death is thus described in Charles Wesley's *Journal:* "We had prayed last night with joy full of glory for our departing brother, just while he gave up his spirit,—as I pray God I give up mine. This morning I expounded that last best triumph of faith, I have fought a good fight, &c. ... We sang a song of victory for our deceased friend; then went to the house, and rejoiced, and gave thanks; and rejoiced again with singing over him. The spirit, at its departure, had left marks of its happiness on the clay. No sight upon earth, in my eyes, is half so lovely." *(Representative Verse,* p. 88)

"The triumph of faith," I suggest, is conveyed by the rhythm of the hymn, if not always by its diction; but even such words and phrases as "Sight upon Earth," "gay pageants," "dead body," "solemn Delight," "Corpse," and "beautiful Clay" have as much to do with Charles' tough-minded, experiential presuppositions as with morbidity.

NOTES

[1] *English Congregational Hymns in the Eighteenth Century* (Lexington: Univ. of Kentucky, 1982), p. 74. This emphasis of Marshall and Todd is reminiscent of the second part of Bernard Lord Manning's 3-part characterization of Charles' hymns: (1) "solid structure of historic dogma," (2) "passionate thrill of present experience," and (3) "glory of a mystic sunlight coming directly from another world" (*The Hymns of Wesley and Watts* [London: Epworth, 1942], p. 29).

[2] Hymn 17, *Representative Verse of Charles Wesley* ed. Frank Baker (N.Y.: Abingdon, 1962). Subsequent references to hymn numbers will be to this edn. unless otherwise indicated.

[3] *Innocence and Experience: An Introduction to Blake* (New Haven: Yale Univ., 1964), esp. pp. 27-29.

[4] Martha Winburn England and John Sparrow, *Hymns Unbidden: Donne, Herbert, Blake, Emily Dickinson and the Hymnographers* (N.Y.: New York Public Library, 1966), p. 94.

[5] See the discussion in *Representative Verse*, p. 264. Charles' courtship of Sally was filled with hesitation and uncertainty in part because of his poor financial prospects, and in part because of the age difference: he was forty, she twenty-one.

[6] I have in mind *Die Deutsche Ideologie;* see Hazard Adams, ed., *Critical Theory Since Plato* (N.Y.: Harcourt Brace Jovanovich, 1971), p. 632.

[7] See the discussion in *English Congregational Hymns*, pp. 63-64.

[8] As quoted in Manning, p. 28.

[9] Preface to *A Collection of Hymns, for the Use of the People Called Methodists* (1780), *The Works of the Rev. John Wesley* (London: Wesleyan-Methodist Book-Room, n.d.) 14:340. This edn. is a reissue of the third edn., 1829-31, ed. Thomas Jackson. Hereafter, *Works*.

[10] *Locke, Wesley, and the Method of English Romanticism* (Gainesville: Univ. of Florida, 1984).

[11] *Hymns Unbidden*, pp. 72, 85, 90, 93, 95. England acknowledges mysticism in both poets: they say, in effect, "Be still and know that I am God." But their empiricism, by which they claim "it is the here and now that matters," is a "much stronger force" in their writings. That force, specifically, is their "determination to submit dogma to the test of experience in a belief, both honest and devout, that experience was itself revelation."

[12] Vallins, *The Wesleys and the English Language* (London: Epworth, 1957), pp. 87-88. This is Hymn 721 of the 1780 *Collection of Hymns*.

[13] See, for example, Hymns 280, 572, and 713 of the 1780 *Collection.* See also the discussion in Vallins, p. 87.

[14] See Alfred H. Body, *John Wesley and Education* (London: Epworth, 1936), pp. 33, 52, 56-61; and A. G. Ives, *Kingswood School in Wesley's Day and Since* (London: Epworth, 1970), pp. 19, 240-41, 247.

[15] Adams, ed., *Critical Theory Since Plato,* p. 324.

[16] Devices such as chiasmus (ABBA): "I am [A] all unrighteousness [B]; / False and full of sin [B] I am [A]," or: "Just and holy [A] is Thy Name [B]; / Thou [B] art full of truth and grace [A]." See the literary discussion of Wesley's hymns in Manning, pp. 5-31, esp. pp. 22-23.

[17] J. T. Lightwood, *Samuel Wesley, Musician: The Story of His Life* (London: Epworth, 1937), pp. 14-15.

[18] Charles was justly proud of the younger Charles and young Samuel. When the Honorable Daines Barrington wrote an account of the two young Wesleys for *Philosophical Transactions,* Charles was moved to write a poem expressing his pleasure at Barrington's notice: see the discussion in *Representative Verse,* p. 330.

[19] The words are Charles Wesley's as quoted (but not cited) by Baker in *Representative Verse,* p. 117.

[20] Baker (p. 117) here depends on the Rev. John Kirk, *Charles Wesley, the Poet of Methodism* (London: J. Mason, 1860), pp. 44-46.

[21] The meter is unusual for Wesley, but compare Hymn 130, "Jesus, to Thee I would look up."

[22] See the discussion in England, *Hymns Unbidden,* pp. 91ff.

[23] As quoted by England; see the discussion in *Hymns Unbidden,* p. 97.

[24] See Eric Routley, *The Music of Christian Hymnody: A Study of the English Hymn Tune Since the Reformation, with Special Reference to English Protestantism* (London: Independent, 1957), p. 93; Marshall and Todd, *English Congregational Hymns,* p. 5; and *Representative Verse,* p. 82.

7. Johnson's Wesleyan Connection[1]

ON 24 MAY 1738, in Aldersgate Street, London, Wesley's heart was "strangely warmed." The Methodist revival soon ensued, continuing well into the nineteenth century and long outliving Wesley, who died in 1791. His conversion, Lecky commented in *A History of England in the Eighteenth Century* (1883), "meant more for Britain than all the victories of Pitt by land and sea," and, though the point could meet with counterpoints ("Wesley devalued tradition" and thus "fostered subjectivity," or simply "prolonged the agony of a dying myth"), historians such as Maldwyn Edwards and Robert Wearmouth have assigned him an important place in English experience, suggesting that the moral force of his revival and the spiritual progress of his followers quickened social progress in Great Britain and somewhat lessened strife.[2] Critics, notably Vineta Colby and George Landow, discovering Wesley's place in English letters, have pointed to Evangelical patterns though not much Wesleyan meaning, in Victorian prose and fiction; Wilfred Stone, in *The Cave and the Mountain* (1966), has found Evangelical echoes even later, in the life of Forster and in his novels.[3] I have suggested in *Wordsworth's "Natural Methodism"* (1975) that Wesleyan religion is not far from Romantic poetry: Wesleyan Methodism, forming part of Wordsworth's spiritual experience, lends warmth to his tone and comes strangely near the heart of his spiritual themes.[4] It is time now, in view of these studies, to ask whether Wesley influenced the literature of his own day; it is feasible, here, to explore the possibility that Wesley and his revival affected the works and life of his sometime companion Samuel Johnson. The evidence, suggesting that Johnson's temperament was often decidedly Wesleyan, shows that the religious imagination for which Wesley was largely responsible relates directly to the history of Johnson's mind. The argument for this point of view affords a glimpse of the prospect that Wesley's influence, which has only just begun to be understood in full, formed part of the continuity between "neoclassical" and "modern" expression—not simply in England but elsewhere as well; Wesley's impact upon letters is both greater and earlier than critical studies have so far indicated.

T. B. Shepherd, in *Methodism and the Literature of the Eighteenth Century* (1940), has shown that Goldsmith, Johnson, and Blake, among others, had much respect for Wesley, but Shepherd only just begins to pursue the question of Wesley's influence on their work.[5] No other student of eighteenth-century literature has followed through on any of Shepherd's leads, perhaps because of the assumption, still widespread, that Wesley's revival was not centrally important in English culture. Horton Davies, however, as a student of theology in eighteenth-century England, has demonstrated that the revival, cultivating the vast middle ground of Christian practice and tradition, was felt at all levels of society.[6]

Johnson, occupying an eminent position on the middle ground, would have recognized, nearby, the man who guided thousands—upper as well as middle and lower classes—through the mainstream currents of Christianity. It is reasonable, perhaps, to assume that Johnson could hardly have failed to recognize how important Wesley was; it seems advisable, in any case, to determine the extent of contact between a famous English writer with deep Christian faith, and the most renowned and effective preacher of the day. Wesley, like many others in England, owed much to Johnson's intellectual example, but Johnson also had things to learn: his empirical thought, his poem "On the Death of Dr. Robert Levet," his sermons, his meditations, his spirit of charity, his Establishmentarian temperament, his 1784 "conversion," and his attitudes toward topics ranging from Dissent to daily exercise, all show signs of the Evangelical feeling and thought represented best by Wesley's intellect and sincerity. It is difficult, of course, to distinguish "Evangelical feeling and thought" from all the various strands of seventeenth and eighteenth-century thought and doctrines, but it is not impossible to do so. The effort here, necessarily preliminary, can begin to supplement or modify the standard views of Johnson's Anglican faith. Johnson came to recognize Wesley's spiritual stature, and it is logical, on the evidence I present, to think that Johnson not only responded in his life and work to Wesley's spiritual leadership, but also felt the force of his faith and came to share it in some measure.

It would be well, before turning to Johnson's faith, to attempt a sketch of Wesley's. The warm heart of Wesley, an image deservedly central in Evangelical lore, symbolizes and sums up his generally pietistic outlook, his emphasis on religious feeling (grounded in spiritual discipline) as distinct from intellectual belief; but his five thousand pages of sermons, journals, and essays show his understanding of intellectual tradition and a wide range of particular doctrines. It is helpful, therefore, to think of his faith and that of his followers as a blend of syncretic thought and pietistic practice.

Wesley's piety, perhaps, needs no demonstration, but his syncretic breadth of spirit, though equally important, is less widely recognized. His spirit, for example, at once original and selective, made it possible for him to be staunchly Anglican and to reflect as well the Nonconformist background of his Presbyterian mother. He plumbed particularly the whole of Puritan covenant-making, and popularized his covenant-based modes of vowing to obey God's law. Hence Wesley could appeal to Nonconformists and Anglicans alike, and Davies, accordingly, has gone so far as to call him "the bridge that crossed the chasm between . . . Anglicanism and Dissent" (*Worship and Theology in England*, p. 184). After all, Wesleyan Methodists did not become openly Nonconformist until 1795, and Anglican Evangelicals in the Clapham Sect kept Wesley's reform, and his reformation, alive for at least thirty years after his death. His syncretic temperament, then, was strong enough to leave a legacy on which nineteenth-century non-sectarians continued to draw.

Wesley's most characteristic belief, and his chief bequeathal, was Arminian doctrine. His emphasis on free will, like that of Arminius, led him to encourage worldly involvement within Christian limits, and to make his choices especially through practical charity. (Many Evangelicals, thanks to his initiative, also became known for the power of will to do the largest and the smallest deeds of kindness.) Wesley held, moreover, to the Arminian possibility of universal redemption; he tried to make available this good news by going into all the world, an Evangelist in the most literal sense. Thus choosing to spread a message of joyful love, he preached a gospel social in emphasis and un-Calvinistically tolerant in tone. And thus at home in the world, he came to it equipped to revive the range of tradition and the heart of doctrine.

His early associate, George Whitefield, was a different sort of man from Wesley, and can serve to fill out the portrait of Wesley, and of his kind of Evangelical faith, by providing a study in contrast. Like him, Whitefield was an earnest and popular preacher. And like Wesley, too, Whitefield was Anglican. Whitefield, however, unlike Wesley, stressed the Calvinist doctrine of election, and did so narrowly enough to encourage a fanatical otherworldliness and from there a separatist impulse in the world of time and place. He unconsciously led his followers to the wilderness of proliferating sects that tended to undermine, in the next century, the ecumenical spirit of Wesley's revival. The sectarian holiness and the mood of divisiveness within the band of Whitefield bore little resemblance to the spirit of reconcilement and the unfanatical Arminian joy among Wesley's host of followers, who formed the Evangelical mainstream. Wesley, then, inspired one tone, and Whitefield quite another. The "Connexion" formed by Whitefield and his friend Selina, Countess of Huntingdon, was made up of Evangelicals who were Nonconformist temperamentally, though mainly Anglican in name. *The Wesleyan connection*, by contrast, can serve to label the central expression of late eighteenth-century faith. The faith was warm but fully able to check the impulses of separatist otherworldliness; for Wesley, Establishmentarian, Arminian, and pietistic, effectively reached and was sometimes able to unite not just Methodist-Anglicans but other Anglicans and many Nonconformists as well. Lord David Cecil must have forgotten Wesley, and must have had Whitefield in mind, when he described the Methodist revival as a "dark, melodramatic silhouette" across the pages of history.[7] Wesley's influence, though perhaps overshadowed at last by Whitefield's effect on the increasing diffuseness of nineteenth-century Evangelical faith, was greater than that of Whitefield during the revival itself, which lasted fifty years.

Johnson had a long-lasting and much-valued connection to Wesley himself, a relation more intimate than any contact practically possible for the great majority of Wesley's followers. Johnson, at least during the last dozen years of his life, was acquainted with Wesley and clearly impressed with him as well. On 15 August 1773, he praised the thoughtful quality and unpretentious sincerity of Wesley's religion, and at the same time, significantly, indicated his dislike of Whitefield's "ostentation."[8] On 6 February 1776, he wrote to Wesley and graciously thanked him for his "Commentary on the Bible" (Chapman, II, 101). In April of 1778, he expressed his enjoyment of conversations, and showed that he felt a loss whenever Wesley, the compulsive itinerant, could not stop by for discussion: "John Wesley's conversation is good, but he is never at leisure. He is always obliged to go at a certain hour. This is very disagreeable to a man who loves to fold his legs and have out his talk, as I do" (Powell, III, 230, 297). On 3 May 1779, he gave Boswell a letter of introduction to Wesley (Powell, III, 394), and, about 1781, he presented to Wesley a set of his *Lives of the Poets*.[9] In Johnson's library at the time of his death, on 13 December 1784, were several Wesleyan volumes: Charles Wesley's hymns, "Wesley's journal," "Wesley's compendium of natural philosophy" (1777), and "Wesley on the old and new testament" (1768).[10]

Small wonder then that Birkbeck Hill, editing Boswell's *Life of Johnson*, is everywhere intrigued by the relationship, and points out parallels between Johnson's attitudes and those of Wesley on a host of matters and men: Jacob Behmen, William Law, itinerant ministries, rural character, child-rearing, luxury, solitude, retirement, exercise, diet, medicine, ghosts, and witches.[11] Hill notes, of course, that Wesley and Johnson were at odds on the issue of tea-drinking (Powell, I, 313, n. 2), but the similarity in their thinking, representing a cluster of Evangelical opinions, seems hardly coincidental and in any case suggests that Johnson was close to the Evangelical Movement. His Wesleyan connection, or the manifestly spiritual dimension of his personal contact with John Wesley, shows his proximity to the revival in which Wesley was universally acknowledged to be the main influence and the chief of many gifted leaders. Time and opportunity, then, at least during the seventies and eighties, were right for Johnson's faith to take on an Evangelical coloring.

Here is Boswell, in one breath, discussing Methodism and Samuel Johnson:

> All who are acquainted with the history of religion . . . know that the appellation of Methodists was first given to a society of students in the University of Oxford, who about the year 1730, were distinguished by an earnest and methodical attention to devout exercises. This disposition of mind is not a novelty, or peculiar to any sect, but has been, and still may be found, in many Christians of every denomination. Johnson himself was, in a dignified manner, a Methodist. In his Rambler, No. 110, he mentions with respect 'the whole discipline of regulated piety;' and in his 'Prayers and Meditations,' many instances occur of his anxious examination into his spiritual state.
>
> (Powell, I, 458, n. 3)

Boswell points out that methodistical habits in Johnson were simply Christian, and puts no little distance between his subject and Methodism. In its context, moreover, his statement is clearly intended to explain away Johnson's praise of Methodist preaching, which he saw as a plain, familiar, and effective model even for "clergymen of genius and learning" (Powell, I, 459). (Johnson said this on 30 July 1763, and in so doing showed that he respected the medium of Methodism several years before his evident sympathy for Wesley and Wesleyan attitudes.) Boswell seems to have been somewhat embarrassed by Johnson's admiration, but did draw a parallel between him and the Methodists. Boswell's statement, therefore, though it can be read as a nervous response to Johnson's praise of Methodist preaching, does not disprove and seems even to recognize the possibility, implicit in the praise, that Johnson was in some sense affected by the Evangelical spirit of his day.

Recent studies of his faith specifically argue that he was in no sense so affected, and that anything seemingly Evangelical should be understood as Anglican, Thomistic, Augustinian, biblical, Christian, religious; scholars place his Anglican faith in its historical contexts of latitudinarian, utilitarian, and rational theology, but do not take into enough account the most popular Anglican expression during the last thirty years of Johnson's life.[12] Scholars seem to wince at the very idea that he could have inclined to the Methodist heart of Anglican faith, and it is not that they misunderstand Johnson's belief—they apparently misunderstand Wesley's kind of Evangelical belief. Almost everything uttered by Evangelicals from Wesley and Venn to Simeon and Wilberforce goes back, for example, to the orthodox traditions of Hooker, Aquinas, and Augustine, but the influence of Wesley, distinct from that of Whitefield, is a centrist as well as a specific and historically unique blend of practice and idea, and as such can be the model in filling out an understanding of Johnson's faith in its immediate context. Wesley's influence was at once a near spiritual context and the most widespread, and conceivably the most congenial, one available to him. It is, therefore, an influence worth testing in the search for ways that Johnson, in his spiritual experience, was a man of his time as well as master of his Christian heritage.

Take, for example, the Evangelical emphasis on conversion. It is true that Johnson, corresponding with Hill Boothby in the middle 1750s, questioned the Evangelicals' need for a precisely dated New Birth of the soul; and in 1751, in his *Life of Francis Cheynel*, Johnson seems to have thought of Methodists as belonging among the "enthusiasts of all kinds" who "imagine themselves the great instruments of salvation."[13] After the fifties, though, he gradually changed his attitude, perhaps in part because of his conversations with Wesley. Hawkins, for example, records Johnson's later interest in the individual Christian's experience of redemption,[14] as distinct from the general doctrine of salvation, and it is tempting to speculate that the change was due to his awareness of the moment or period of conversion among the ever-increasing numbers of people touched by the ministries of John Wesley and other Anglican Evangelicals. Hawkins records Johnson's own redemptive experience. On 6 January 1784, Johnson wrote to a bookseller asking for "the best printed edition of Baxter's *Call to the Unconverted*," and Hawkins gives an account of Johnson's avowed conversion soon thereafter.[15] On 19 February when he was suffering greatly from a chronic dropsical condition in his legs, Johnson told Hawkins that he feared damnation and "dreaded to meet his Saviour," but he also "declared his intention to devote the whole of the next day to fasting, humiliation, and such other devotional exercises as becomes a man in his situation." On 20 February, during these exercises, his condition was relieved "by a gradual evacuation of water to the amount of twenty pints, a like instance of which he had never experienced." Johnson's prayers and letters for the remaining ten months of his life show his growing conviction that what happened on 20 February, whatever in fact it was, was "wonderful, very wonderful" to him, and that what happened, moreover, led to what he called, at different times, "the awakening of my mind" and "the call by which [God] . . . awakened my conscience and summoned me to Repentance."[16] In a prayer, written eight days before his death on 13 December, he asked God to "accept my late conversion" (Yale, I, 417-18).

Maurice Quinlan, Chester Chapin, and Donald Greene, aware of possible Evangelical overtones of Johnson's "wonderful" experience, have nevertheless avoided the conclusion that there was anything very Evangelical about it, despite how Evangelicals recognized it as a conversion soon after it occurred, and seem even to have identified it as like their own experiences of redemption.[17] On 11 May 1784, William Cowper wrote to John Newton, "We rejoice in the account you give us of Dr. Johnson. His conversion will indeed be a singular proof of the omnipotence of Grace."

Newton and Cowper, of course, were predisposed to perceive his experience as a conversion, but the experience did include Evangelical characteristics. Johnson, for one thing, dated his conversion as precisely as Wesley dated his, and both conversions, hardly confined to an instant, took place over a somewhat protracted period. Wesley, moreover, through Arminian doctrine, saw redemption as a gift that could be freely chosen, and Johnson not only chose to read about conversion well over a month before he claimed it happened, and to read about it, besides, in a book by the Puritan forerunner of Wesley's Arminian emphasis, he also seems to have consciously set aside a day for it and through strict spiritual discipline to have willed it into being. Hawkins noted, consciously or unconsciously, an activist Arminian quality in Johnson's response to what both men regarded as the condescension of grace, for Hawkins used an Arminian diction when he remarked Johnson's "*making choice* of me for his confessor," and when he marveled "at the *freedom* with which [Johnson] opened his mind" (my italics). And finally, Johnson himself might well have placed his experience in the context of contemporary Evangelical conversion. Not only did he use words like *awakened* and *awakening*, common diction for a characteristic phenomenon of the Great *Awakening*, he also clearly wanted, less than a month before he died and at a time when the experience was a source of frequent comfort to him, to reinforce its Evangelical quality by associating daily with one whom he undoubtedly knew to be an important Evangelical figure: Johnson "spoke of his design to invite" none other than Wesley's sister, Martha Hall, "to be with him" constantly and even to occupy "Mrs. Williams's room" near his own.[18]

Scholars suggest that his experience was determined by unusual deathbed circumstances and was therefore decidedly uncharacteristic of his temperate faith, but the experience was important to him over a period of months when he felt well enough much of the time, and it is at least possible that a spiritual episode of such significance did not occur in a vacuum but rather was anticipated both by the Evangelical temper of the times and by the nature of Johnson's faith. It is demonstrable, in any case, that his faith developed along lines parallel to the Evangelical temper, or even congruent with it, so that his "late conversion" comes as no surprise. The Evangelical Movement provides an essential context for understanding his faith.

Consider, for instance, that Johnson's Establishmentarian bias, far from keeping him at a distance from the Movement, resembled Wesley's temperament and was fully consistent with mainstream Evangelical faith. It is true that Johnson blamed "some methodists" for pretending to "inner light," a "principle" "utterly incompatible with social or civil security" (Powell, II, 126), but it may be noted that he singled out "some" Methodists only, showing he knew of the others. Wesleyan Methodists, for the most part, claimed no such exclusive favor as they communed with God. Johnson's statement, suggesting that "inner light" is a socially fanatical idea, is in harmony with the viewpoint of Wesleyan Evangelicals in their spiritual restraint and in their distinctive concern for the spiritual welfare of both society and the state.[19] They shared Johnson's fear of separatist and historically dangerous otherworldliness, an antisocial and potentially tyrannical, or even anarchical, spiritual pretension that seemed, to Wesley no less than to Johnson, to be on the rise among Whitefieldian Methodists. And for that matter among American colonists: it is well known that Wesley "pirated, almost verbatim" from Johnson's *Taxation No Tyranny* (1775) his *Calm Address to the Colonies* (1775);[20] and his piracy, besides showing that Johnson sometimes influenced Wesley, is useful in suggesting that the Establishmentarian temperaments of both were strong enough, and sufficiently similar, to extend from the spiritual to the political phases of their thought; for political stability, in the views of both men, was in keeping with and in large measure grew out of a conservative ecclesiology. It is possible, given the circumstances of the time, that Johnson's temperament was Evangelical at least partially because it was, like that of Wesley, so thoroughly and so characteristically Establishmentarian. Establishmentarianism was a sufficient, and often a necessary, condition for Evangelicalism.

Johnson's temperament, certainly, was in line with the Evangelical temper of the day in so far as he made the connection, in *Idler* 4, between social well-being and charitable enthusiasm. "The present age," he wrote, "though not likely to shine hereafter, among the most splendid periods of history, has yet given examples of charity, which may be very properly recommended to imitation.... No sooner is a new species of misery brought to view, and a design of relieving it professed, than every hand is open to contribute something, every tongue is busied in solicitation, and every art of pleasure is employed for a time in the interest of virtue" (Yale, II, 14). The passage suggests that Johnson reflected, or was beginning to reflect, the Evangelical connection between an actively virtuous spiritual life and what Johnson called "civil security," for the essay was written in May of 1758, when Evangelicals were becoming known for their characteristically practical acts of charity. Their individual deeds are perhaps the nearest analogue to his unfailing kindness, practiced before and after 1758, toward friends and acquaintances as diverse and lowly as Savage, Collins, Dodd, the widow Desmoulins, Anna Williams, Frank Barber, Poll Carmichael, and old Dr. Levet; and perhaps their larger projects provide the contexts for his fight against the slave trade and his campaign for penal reform.[21] Between Johnson and Wesley is a particularly striking coincidence-a specific connection in practical charity. Wesley backed up his own campaign for penal reform by taking an interest in individual prisoners such as William Dodd, whom he visited two days before Dodd's execution; and Johnson, showing a similarly balanced interest in specific cases as well as general projects, is famous for his compassionate energy on Dodd's behalf—right up to the time of his death.[22] Another possible context for Johnson's charity, of course, is latitudinarian benevolence, but it was dominant at the beginning of the century and is probably more distantly related to his ambitious good deeds than the isolated acts of practical charity, and the socially significant ones, among most stripes of Evangelicals from the 1740s well beyond the time of Johnson's death.

Moving, now, from his life and attitudes to the kind of his writing most related to his life, consider the possibility of a link between his *Meditations* and journal writing among the Evangelicals. In 1777, to be sure, he enjoyed an article making fun of Whitefield and Wesley as "old women" who wrote "fanatick" meditations (Powell, III, 170-72). Thus, Johnson applauded like a good Establishmentarian the reviewer's scorn of fanatical tendencies among some Evangelicals (though the reviewer, like Lord David Cecil and unlike Johnson, seems to have lumped Wesley and Whitefield together). Johnson laughed as many would at the image of two famous preachers as old women, but he was laughing at himself along with Whitefield, perhaps, since the joke struck close to his own journal practice. Even Boswell saw the parallel between his anxious self-examination and Methodist devotional exercise.

Chapin places the *Meditations* in the line of Anglican piety represented by Robert Nelson at the beginning of the century.[23] A more immediate analogue, however, is the Evangelical journalism popular in Johnson's day. Nelson's meditations were grouped around festivals and fasts of the Church of England, and so, in many cases, were those of Johnson, but in his meditation and in that of the Evangelicals is a feel for the hours, minutes, and places in spiritual experience, a feeling less particularized, and less intense, in Nelson's relatively relaxed and generalized attention to a single place, the Anglican Church, and to the special days and sacred seasons of its standard year.[24] Even in Johnson's meditations based on days in the standard year, and attentive to the Church's sanctuary, there is a subjective awareness of the worldly and hourly foundations of both time and place.[25] Note, for example, his desire to move about the world, his temporal consciousness, his single reference to Easter, and his general self-examination in the Easter entry for April of 1772:

> I hope to cast my time into some stated method.
> To let no hour pass unemployed.
> To rise by degrees more early in the morning.
> To keep a journal. . . .
> I have exerted rather more activity of body. These dispositions I desire to improve.
> I resolved, last Easter to read within the year the whole Bible . . . .
> [I] finished the old Testament last Thursday.
>   (Yale, I, 147)

The entry, despite or because of its self-consciousness, sends Johnson out of self to redeem the time of his earthly place. His desire for exercise, as Hill has suggested, relates to Wesley's popular advice on health; Johnson walked both often and far. Though hardly itinerant in any spiritual way, excepting, of course, his practical charity, he wanted to be out and doing as much as the Evangelicals did, and he admired "methodist teachers" specifically for the stamina with which they traveled "nine hundred miles in a month," to "preach twelve times a week" (Powell, II, 123). He reflected in the entry and elsewhere among his meditations the spiritual method of Methodists who searched their Bibles, walked for miles to spread their message, made written and unwritten covenants to improve in every way they could, inherited the readiness as well as the covenant-making disposition of their Puritan forebears, and cultivated activist habits perhaps deriving from an Arminian exaltation of what the human will can do.

Consider, as an important final attitude in Johnson's writing and his life, his sympathy toward Dissenting practice and Dissenting faith, a sympathy made possible in large measure by the ecumenical impulse in Wesley's revival. Scholars see nothing Puritan in him, and indeed, for most of his life he regarded the Puritan heritage as a source of ignorance and, worse, of schism, but, in Hawkins's account, he came to admire the lives and learning of Puritans and their Nonconformist descendants.[26] Toward the end of the 1770s he took pains to add his "Life of Watts" to *The Lives of the Poets,* despite how Watts, though the father of Evangelical hymn writing, was not primarily a poet; he was a prolific Nonconformist theologian, and the friend of John Wesley. Johnson paid tribute to him when Wesley was making it fashionable for Anglicans to relate to their Puritan heritage and to their Nonconformist brothers and sisters, and it is therefore reasonable to infer that during the seventies, if not before, Johnson shared what he seems to have expressed in the tribute to Watts, namely, the Wesleyan spirit of Christian community. In the "Life" he wrote that Watts had early "declared his resolution to take his lot with the dissenters," but he also wrote, with a Wesleyan tolerance, that Watts was such a man "as every christian church would rejoice to have adopted" (Hill, III, 302-3). It is clear, moreover, that Johnson liked Watts for reasons based on Evangelical emphases in conduct and morality, emphases deriving as much from the Puritan heritage as from the pietistic method of Wesley's Moravian and Lutheran models. Watts, said Johnson, showed "tenderness . . . to children and to the poor," contributed a third of his income to charity, and generally searched for "the opportunities . . . of diffusing and increasing the influence of religion" (Hill, III, 307-8). His activist faith and practical charity thus rival Johnson's own deeds of kindness and, of course, his general effort to increase spiritual influence in the world at large. Watts fits, like Johnson, into the context of Christian outreach, and Johnson, in stressing the point, evidently felt that he shared with him a lively expression of morality—for which the nearest name is Evangelical practical charity.

He also admired in Watts the qualities of self-discipline and self-control, qualities deriving in part from the Puritan, and the Evangelically appropriated, heritage of covenant-making. Watts had to struggle, said Johnson, against a "natural temper" that was "quick of resentment," but through an "established and habitual practice" he conquered the passions of self and became "gentle, modest, and inoffensive" (Hill, III, 307). Johnson's "natural" temper was a melancholy indolence, or so he said. His praise of Watts's effort at self-control recalls and may well grow out of his own hope of self-mastery through the established and habitual practice of journalistic meditation. Perhaps the Evangelicals' recovery of Puritan tradition helped Johnson recognize that the covenant-making of Watts, himself an early participant in the Evangelical Movement, was part of a system of conventions and guidelines for the mastery of subjectivity and self-will; for Johnson's awareness of the covenant method of Nonconformist Evangelicals and thence of Methodist-Anglican ones is implicit in his praise of Isaac Watts and perhaps as well in his ownership of Wesley's lengthy journal.

Johnson, then, after the 1750s at least, developed practices and attitudes surrounded by and consistent with the traits and stresses of a rising and vigorous evangelical form of Christianity in eighteenth-century England; he heard, saw, and to some extent traveled the strongest current of contemporary faith. He had particularly a Puritan self-discipline, without the tincture of Calvinist doctrine, and an Arminian desire to spread at least some joy throughout his sphere of influence—he learned in his fullest maturity of spirit to enrich his Anglican faith with the variety of Christian expression in his day. His faith, moreover, like that of the Evangelicals, was grounded in his life, and his writing, therefore, like that of the Evangelicals, was often what Ian Watt, seeking an apt label for his work, has called "the literature of experience": the journal, the prayer, the diary, the private meditation.[27] These forms, it is true, show considerable self-accusation; John Wain in his recent biography has called them "pathetic" (*Samuel Johnson*, p. 225). It is well to re member, on the other hand, what Quinlan observed about them some thirteen years ago, that "the very act of writing down his shortcomings had therapeutic value" (*A Layman's Religion*, p. x). Perhaps it is best, though, to realize that the formulas of covenant-making, far from reducing Johnson to some helpless state of pulse taking, helped him get hold of himself through spiritual rather than wholly psychological means, and that he could thereby control his "modern" fear of madness most of the time. Johnson, like Wesleyan writers of spiritual autobiography, was able, indeed, to turn refreshed from covenant patterns to the world of moral action (witness, for example, his active charity at the time of writing the *Meditations*).

All these traits of his spiritual life and his private spiritual expression reflect at least indirectly the spiritual blend in Wesley's heart, mind, and sphere of influence. It is appropriate, therefore, not only to ask as occasion rises whether his acquaintance with Wesley can lead to additional direct and indirect evidence of Evangelical qualities in his faith but also, and perhaps more importantly, to be alert for Evangelical qualities in his consciously public kind of writing. The result of such alertness and of such a biographical inquiry can be, for example, an apt historical means of placing and describing philosophic aspects of Johnson's life and thought, and religious themes in the work he published for a sizable audience.

To begin such a quest, as well as to indicate its method in glances at an obvious form of his public writing and at just one of his well-known poems, consider the tribute to Levet and the sermons. Since Johnson admired Methodist preaching and its unfailing sense of audience, since he wrote sermons for John Taylor, and since, in writing to Taylor on 22 December 1774, he identified an especially "pious and orthodox" man as the friend of John Wesley, it seems desirable to investigate whether any of his sermons can be understood per Evangelical emphases in theology.[28] His general themes of vanity (VI, XII), love (XI), godliness (XVI), doubt (XX), the sacraments (X, XX), and death (XV, XXV) contain nothing exclusively Evangelical, but his sermons on repentance (II), fear (Ill), charity (IV, XIX), misery (V), and self-deceit (VIII, X) show his contribution to a province of Evangelical preaching. It is clear, moreover, that when he inveighed against "having a form of godliness" without "the power thereof" (XIII), proclaimed perfect peace (XIV), and described Christian perfection as the realizable goal of spiritual life (XIII), he practiced homiletics in admiration of Evangelical emphases, and when he addressed himself to a country parish, dealt with humble, domestic virtues, and wrote specifically for a condemned prisoner, he consciously appealed to the far-flung and often lowly audience of Evangelical preaching.[29]

It is proper, also, to hear Evangelical overtones of Johnson's elegy "On the Death of Dr. Robert Levet." The "Anglican hymn in long measure," says

Paul Fussell, is its "essential paradigm," and, since his examples are Evangelical (though not always Anglican as he implies—one is Nonconformist), here at some length is Fussell on the poem: "Its images of 'Hope's delusive mine' and 'Misery's darkest caverns' seem to remember both Toplady's cleft Rock of Ages and the 'unfathomable mines' of Cowper's *Light Shining out of Darkness*. Johnson's curious final image,

> Death broke at once the vital chain
> And freed his soul the nearest way,

seems to recall Toplady's equally curious

> When my eye-strings break in death,

as well as Isaac Watts's

> Dear Sovereign, break these vital strings
> That bind me to my clay."[30]

Such parallels suggest still others. Johnson writes, for example, that human comforts drop away "By sudden *blasts*" (Yale, VI, 314-15), and Watts, in his hymn "O God our help in ages past," seeks "shelter from the stormy *blast*" and thus expresses as Johnson does, and in the context of a faith like his and Toplady's, his wise fear of mortality and its curse (my italics). Levet, moreover, had the "power of art without the show," and in Johnson's thirteenth sermon (as well as among both Anglican and Nonconformist Evangelicals)[31] "having the form of godliness, but denying the power thereof" was the biblical way of describing spiritual emptiness (see 2 Tim. 3:5a)—Levet's remedies were by implication spiritual as much as medical in nature. In Levet's life, writes Johnson, "The modest wants of every day / The toil of every day supplied," and Wesley wrote in one of his sermons that those whose lives are spiritually imperfect spend much of their time in an anxious desire for "supplies in want" (Wesley, XI, 379). And so it is more than a matter of diction and form, for Johnson, like Arminian Evangelicals, seems to have chosen as a way of doing high honor to his friend the theme of Christian perfection and its full power to transcend—and in effect to break—the bonds of empty death. Verbal parallels—and formal ones as well, perhaps—indicate similar ideas.

Consider, finally, the possible bearing of Johnson's increasingly Evangelical faith upon his experience of philosophic development. He sought with philosophic rigor to know himself and his world, and saw spiritual dimensions in his task of epistemology whenever he engaged in introspection and moral activity, and whenever he searched in his existence for evidences of his faith.[32] He undoubtedly applied to his own mental and spiritual search the experiential emphasis in both the practical theology and the empirical philosophy of his day. Greene has argued, persuasively, that Johnson could control the tension between his empirical philosophy and his faith,[33] and he could do so in part because the tension was especially controllable—eighteenth-century faith had points in common with eighteenth-century philosophy. John Locke, observing that "Whatsoever truths we come to the clear discovery of, from the knowledge and contemplation of our own ideas, will always be certainer to us than those which are conveyed to us by traditional revelation" (Locke, II, 305), found objective truth at rarefied levels of the mind as well as somewhere on the borders between self and world, but he discovered, in saying so, a spiritual as well as an epistemological kind of truth, for he employed language explicitly theological, implying that religious truth can be known in the mind through immediate revelation. Locke, of course, like Johnson, feared fanatical subjectivity and did not credit those who claimed with Paul, and with many Whitefieldian Methodists, "that there are such things 'as eye hath not seen, nor ear heard, nor hath it entered into the heart of man to conceive'" (Locke, II, 304), but Locke, like all Evangelicals and like Johnson, valued spiritual ideas, and he seems to have wanted like Johnson and like Wesleyan Evangelicals to validate along the heart and through the doors of ear and eye the innermost and the highest intimations of hoped-for substances and unseen things.

Perhaps it can be said, then, that Johnson was both in the swift spiritual mainstream of the eighteenth century and at its intellectual center because he heard and duplicated the philosophically spiritual harmony between John Wesley his valued acquaintance and John Locke his favorite philosopher. Perhaps he knew that Locke's *Essay* received favorable treatment from Wesley; perhaps he even knew that the chief colonial exponent of Locke and hence of empirical philosophy was the leader of the Great Awakening in America, Jonathan Edwards.[34] In the "Life of Watts" Johnson praised the Nonconformist thinker for his criticism and discipleship of Locke as much as for his Evangelical quality of faith (Hill, III, 308-9), and earlier, in the *Dictionary*, he quoted epistemological passages from Watts's *Logick* (1725) and *Improvement of the Mind* (1741).[35] Leaders of the Great Awakening rested their faith in experience sometimes upon the philosophic foundation laid down by the one epistemologist who was often able to think that things exist which correspond to particular ideas in the mind, and Johnson, crediting fanatical faith no more than Locke, Watts, Edwards, and Wesley, but relying as they did upon his own means of reaching for spiritual truth, perhaps therefore saw with the Evangelicals and with Locke that immediate revelation is a theological equivalent for individual perceptions and that both ways of knowing show the true and the good.

Thus, Johnson seems to have reasoned from his awareness of the Evangelical interest in empiricism that the subject/object split in philosophy tends to be resolved by spiritual experience in the world of action and in self-examination. He surely observed that subjectivity among the Wesleyan writers of journalistic meditation was never unbridled and even yielded at last to their embrace of object and transaction in the world at large. The Evangelicals and Johnson knew and contemplated their own ideas but grounded them as Locke did in their sensations of an otherness; they were all lost as Locke was in a knowledge of things and people, aspiring as Locke sometimes did to knowledge of a power greater than the self. Johnson and the Evangelicals testified in their lives and writing to knowledge through experience. Johnson, therefore, like the Evangelicals, knew to write, and knew how to write, literature of experience, and *literature of experience* is not only an apt way to sum up the Evangelical quality of his meditative writing, it may well be an apt phrase for the way Evangelical and empirical features of his writing come together.

Wesley's impact, complex but evident, upon one major eighteenth-century author is sufficient to warrant alertness for signs of his impact upon other writers in the century's latter half; Blake and Goldsmith, two more of Shepherd's examples, are obvious ones on whom to test the applicability of a hypothetical Wesleyan influence—on the assumption, of course, that full understanding of a writer's work, even in its exclusively formalist aspects, is at least enhanced by an understanding of his spiritual life in the closest contexts of contemporary faith. Nuances of tone may depend upon spiritual vocabulary.

Wesley's impact on Johnson, extending to his empirical thought, may even be sufficient, considering the recent studies of Wesley's influence in the Romantic period (see note 3), to raise the question whether English Classicism as represented by Johnson overlaps or somehow blends into Romanticism partly because of Locke and partly because the spiritual context most available to late eighteenth- and early nineteenth-century authors was Evangelical in both message and expression. Wordsworth breathed in the Evangelical atmosphere of Anglican faith. He also stood on the ground of empirical philosophy. Disturbed by its mechanistic implications he sought in his work a way of transcendentalizing Locke and Hume;[36] in his labor to lose the self and to search out ways for the soul to rise he was often sustained not so much by neo-transcendental German metaphysics as by his own quasi-Wesleyan faith. Wesley's influence helped him discover spiritual and self-transcending sanctions for the Lockean powers of perception. Thus, drawing back from the abyss of modern solipsism, Wordsworth achieved a disciplined exaltation of spirit. Like Johnson he apprehended external sources of inner strength and truth, and *poetry of experience* in his case, like *literature of experience* in the case of Johnson, serves to suggest Evangelical as well as philosophical qualities of his writing.[37] Evangelical qualities, in both cases, absorb and tend to resolve the issues of eighteenth-century epistemology.

Since Wordsworth traveled the philosophical and spiritual mainstreams, it may be worth exploring whether other Romantics spiritualized empiricism through an Evangelical method, blending as Wordsworth did religious and empirical languages in their efforts to heighten their perceptions and mythologize their lives.[38] The Romantics were Protestant, and they knew, through their experience of self-examination, that they could rely upon only a limited range of spiritual aids and agencies. They read Hume (Coleridge and Shelley read him closely), and they felt, through their own experience of ambiguous perception, that they could hardly be sure of what they seemed to know. The Romantics, though, in so far as their spiritual reflections were grounded in their senses of a spiritual world dominated by the evangelists' efforts to impress the hearts of many, were equipped to enter the modem world, or what Keats called a "vale of Soul-making," in part because they had been reared in an increasingly Evangelical England: the tone of their modern doubt, like the soul-struggle in spiritual autobiography, was purgatorial more than infernal. It is clear, in any case, that if Wordsworth's major Romantic expression drew upon eighteenth-century spiritual strength in Britain, then Evangelical faith operated upon the emergent modern sensibility; and it is an important likelihood that Wesley's revival was the most immediate and the most widespread of all the spiritual contexts in which Romantic themes, and Romantic style, emerged from English moods of the Enlightenment.

The Wesleyan connection, in sum, forms a broad mainstream indeed. Wesley's impact on Johnson, besides suggesting the continuity of late eighteenth- and early nineteenth-century literary expression, may serve finally to suggest (especially in view of the now-charted territory of Wesley's cultural influence) that the revolutionary spiritual revival moderated the Romantic rebellion in the Anglo-American world. England avoided revolution in part because Wesley's revival had the force of one, and Robert Southey in his *Life of Wesley* (1820) devotes a lengthy chapter, based on information from Martha Hall, to the rapid rise, temperate tone, and restraining influence of Methodism in America, asserting that the revival preserved a link between America and England even during the Revolution.[39] Johnson and Wordsworth understood as many Americans did that self-government can arise from an introspective but charitable religion which trusts the authority of the conscience. Wordsworth, in lieu of a New Jerusalem in France, was content with an inner spiritual transformation nourished by precepts and inspirations in his native faith;[40] and Johnson, taking as Wesley did an establishmentarian approach to the preservation of temporal government in the colonies, held as Wesley did that religious revival could sublimate political revolution, or reduce its urgency, by effecting an utter change of power within the self. Johnson was politically at odds with most Americans, and Wordsworth came to be; but both of them seem spiritually akin to Americans from Anne Bradstreet and John Witherspoon to Jones Very and Sojourner Truth: such Americans and these particular Britons, in their particular and collective awakenings of spirit, discovered strange and rich resources in a self-consciousness tempered by the claims of charity and the claim of humility. And thus, they surpassed the limits of modem selfhood.

An awareness of Wesley's legacy, then, can point a direct way to the conclusion that Romanticism, vague as it is and variously as it has been understood in all its contexts, cultural and literary, can yet refer to a theological basis of the recognizably similar thinking in Western countries from the eighteenth century on into the twentieth; the Evangelical Movement, in its Puritan moods, at least, affected German Pietism, and Schleiermacher, for one, was aware of the subtle impact of such faith even upon the work of writers who were carefully condescending in their attitude toward popular religion.[41] It is possible, here and now, to modify the good idea of T. E. Hulme that Romanticism is "spilt religion": the religion of one English Romantic and the faith, precursive but not disjunctive, of one neoclassical writer in late eighteenth-century England, was not spilled out so much as freely poured from renewed sources of spirituality. Johnson and Wordsworth both lived in what can be called the age of spiritual awakening.

Notes

[1] Versions of this essay were delivered at the 1976 meeting of the Southeastern American Society for Eighteenth-Century Studies in New Orleans, Louisiana, and at the 1976 meeting of the American Academy of Religion in Nashville, Tennessee. Many thanks to Diana Brantley, Melvyn New, Robert Walker, and James Woolley, for their comments on the essay.

[2] See the two studies by Robert Featherstone Wearmouth: *Methodism and the Working Class Movements of England, 1800-1850* (London, 1937) and *Methodism and the Common People of the Eighteenth Century* (London, 1945); and see Maldwyn Lloyd Edwards, *John Wesley and the Eighteenth Century: A Study of his Social and Political Influence* (London, 1933). See also J. H. Whiteley, *Wesley's England: A Survey of Eighteenth Century Social and Cultural Conditions* (London, 1938); and, more recently, Bernard Semmel, *The Methodist Revolution* (New York, 1973). For Lecky's comment see William Edward Hartpole Lecky, *A History of England in the Eighteenth Century* (London, 1883), II, 521. If his view of Wesley seems hyperbolical, compare the comments of Augustine Birrell: "No single figure influenced so many minds. No single voice touched so many hearts. No other man did such a work for England." See *The Collected Essays & Addresses of the Rt. Hon. Augustine Birrell, 1880-1920* (London, 1922), I, 324-25.

[3] Stone explores, for example, Forster's relation to the Clapham Sect and argues that Forster, at the same time he "could not swallow" part of his Evangelical heritage, "revered" it nevertheless; see *The Cave and the Mountain: A Study of E. M. Forster* (Stanford, Calif., 1966), pp. 24-71. Virginia Woolf, of course, through her father Leslie Stephen, shared with Forster the Evangelical heritage; see her allusion to "The Castaway," by the Evangelical laureate William Cowper, in *To the Lighthouse*. For Evangelical patterns in Victorian fiction see the recent studies by Colby: *The Singular Anomaly: Women Novelists of the Nineteenth Century* (New York, 1970); and *Yesterday's Woman: Domestic Realism in the English Novel* (Princeton, 1974), pp. 1 45-209. Colby points out, for example, that George Eliot's early Evangelical faith had at least an indirect influence on the emotional quality of her work: "The evangelical novel reaches its artistic peak with her because she was able to distill from it those qualities of human emotion which transcend sect and dogma and penetrate to the very heart of the human condition" (*Yesterday's Woman*, p. 209). Landow, throughout his study of Ruskin's work, establishes the pervasive effect of his Evangelical upbringing; see *The Aesthetic and Critical Theories of John Ruskin* (Princeton, 1971).

⁴ See especially, in *Wordsworth's "Natural Methodism"* (New Haven, 1975), pp. 37-138. See also a number of other recent studies: Mary Jacobus has examined Peter Bell in the context of Methodist conversion narrative ("Peter Bell the First," *Essays in Criticism*, 24 [1974], 219-42); Vincent Newey has explored Wordsworth's relation to Puritan spiritual autobiography ("Wordsworth, Bunyan, and the Puritan Mind," *ELH*, 41 [1974], 212-32); and Frank D. McConnell has been aware of Methodist and Quaker backgrounds (*The Confessional Imagination: A Reading of Wordsworth's Prelude* [Baltimore, 1974]). F. C. Gill, in *The Romantic Movement and Methodism: A Study of English Romanticism and the Evangelical Revival* (London, 1937), building on earlier perceptions by William J. Courthope, Oliver Elton, William H. Hutton, A. W. Ward, A. R. Waller, Louis Cazamian, and F. Brompton Harvey, laid the groundwork for detailed exploration of what A. W. Harrison had called, in "Romanticism in Religious Revivals" (*The Hibbert Journal: A Quarterly Review of Religion, Theology, and Philosophy*, 31 [July 1933], 582), the "borderland country between Romanticism and Religion."

⁵ Shepherd also mentions the obvious example of Cowper and speculates concerning Smart and Smollett; see *Methodism and the Literature of the Eighteenth Century* (London, 1940), pp. 207-47.

⁶ See Davies, *Worship and Theology in England: From Watts and Wesley to Maurice, 1690-1850* (Princeton, 1961), pp. 143-254. See also David Spring, "Aristocracy, Social Structure, and Religion in the Early Victorian Period," *Victorian Studies*, 61 (March 1 963), 263-80.

⁷ Cecil's view is quoted in Gill, *The Romantic Movement and Methodism*, p. 13.

⁸ Whitefield, said Johnson, "sincerely meant well, but had a mixture of politics and ostentation: whereas Wesley thought of religion only"; see James Boswell, *Boswell's Life of Johnson*, ed. Hill-Powell (Oxford 1934-50), V, 35, hereafter abbreviated Powell. Other frequently cited editions are: E. L. McAdam, Jr., and Donald and Mary Hyde, eds., *The Yale Edition of the Works of Samuel Johnson* (New Haven, 1958-), hereafter abbreviated Yale; George Birkbeck Hill, *Lives of the English Poets, by Samuel Johnson, LL. D.* (1905; rpt. New York, 1967), hereafter abbreviated Hill; R. W. Chapman, ed., *The Letters of Samuel Johnson: With Mrs. Thrale's Genuine Letters to Him* (Oxford, 1952), hereafter abbreviated Chapman. References to Johnson's sermons are to the Literary Club Edition of *The Works of Samuel Johnson* (Troy, N. Y., 1903), vol. XVI.

⁹ In 1959 the Pierpont Morgan Library exhibited "Volume one of a set [of *Lives of the Poets*, 2nd ed., 1781] presented by Johnson to John Wesley ... the signature and note on the title page are by Samuel Wesley, nephew of John

Wesley, and an organist and lecturer on music." See item 64 in *Samuel Johnson, LL.D. (1709-1784): An Exhibition of First Editions, Manuscripts, Letters, and Portraits to Commemorate the 250th Anniversary of his Birth, and the 200th Anniversary of the Publication of his* Rasselas: *September 22-November 28, 1959* (New York: The Pierpont Morgan Library, 1959).

[10] As listed in the sale catalogue, which includes only a fourth of some 3,000 volumes in Johnson's library. See Donald Greene, *Samuel Johnson's Library: An Annotated Guide, English Literary Studies* (Victoria, B. C., 1975), p. 116. It is worth mentioning, as further evidence of Johnson's Wesleyan connection, that he was acquainted with Wesley's sister Martha Hall (see Powell, IV, 92), and that in his letters he often refers to Wesley; twice, in fact, he wrote to Wesley, and twice asked him or other Wesleys to dinner. In Chapman see *Letters* 195, 197, 369, 451, 541.1, 562, 612, 754.1, 896.1, 955, and 1158.

[11] See Powell, I, 46 (n. 4), 64 (n. 4), 68 (n. 2), 353 (n. 2); II, 122 (n. 6), 173, 178 (n. 3); III, 27 (n. 1), 56 (n. 2), 297, 353 (n. 5), 431 (n. 1); V, 62 (n. 5).

It is possible, on the basis of S. T. Brown's argument ("Dr. Johnson and the Religious Problem," *English Studies*, 20 [1938], 5), to conclude that similarities between Johnson and Wesley are the result not of Wesley's influence on Johnson or of their influence on each other, but of a common source in William Law. It is true that Law's *Serious Call* was an important spiritual influence on both Johnson and Wesley from the time of their Oxford days in the late 1720s. I suggest, however, that Wesley's influence on Johnson exceeds, and even subsumes to some extent, the influence of Law on Johnson.

[12] For Johnson's relation to rational, utilitarian, and latitudinarian expressions within the Anglican Church, see Paul Kent Alkon, *Samuel Johnson and Moral Discipline* (Evanston, 1967), pp. 159, 191-214; Robert Voitle, *Samuel Johnson the Moralist* (Cambridge, Mass., 1961), pp. vii-ix, 60, 63-64, 134; Chester F. Chapin, *The Religious Thought of Samuel Johnson* (Ann Arbor, 1968), pp. 70, 76, 78-80, 110, 112-15; and James Gray, *Johnson's Sermons: A Study* (Oxford, 1972), 92-114. For the view that Johnson could not have reflected Evangelical religion, a view based on an apparent assumption that the terms *Evangelical* and *Anglican* are mutually exclusive, see especially Donald Greene, "Dr. Johnson's 'Late Conversion': A Reconsideration," *Johnsonian Studies*, ed. Magdi Wahba (Cairo, 1962), 61-92; Maurice J. Quinlan, *Samuel Johnson: A Layman's Religion* (Madison, 1964), pp. 6, 50, 60, 128-31, 159-62, 185-90; Chapin, *The Religious Thought of Samuel Johnson*, pp. 29-40, 52-70; Gray, *Johnson's Sermons*, pp. 2-5.

[13] "We now observe," wrote Johnson, "that the methodists, where they scatter their opinions, represent themselves, as preaching the gospel to unconverted

nations; and enthusiasts of all kinds have been inclined to disguise their particular tenets with pompous appellations, and to imagine themselves as the great instruments of salvation." See *The Works of Samuel Johnson, LL.D.* (Oxford, 1825), VI, 417. For a discussion of Johnson's correspondence with Hill Boothby, see Chapin, *The Religious Thought of Samuel Johnson*, pp. 52-70. Johnson seems to have detected a Whitefieldian otherworldliness in Hill Boothby; he told Hester Thrale that Miss Boothby had "somewhat disqualified herself for the duties of *this* life, by her perpetual aspirations after the *next*." See George Birkbeck Hill, ed., *Johnsonian Miscellanies* (Oxford, 1897), I, 57.

[14] Hawkins records that Johnson, in the last few years of his life, "would frequently mention, with great energy and encomiums, the penitence of the man who assumed the name ... of George Psalmanazar ... who pretended to be a convert from paganism to Christianity, and, as such, received baptism. By the help of his great learning and endowments, he eluded all attempts to detect his impostures, but, in his more advanced age, became a sincere penitent, and, without any other motive than a sense of his sin, published a confession of them, and begged the pardon of mankind in terms the most humble and affecting. The remainder of his life was exemplary, and he died in 1763." On one occasion, Hawkins recalls, Johnson testified to a redemptive experience of his own: "[Johnson] said that, having reflected on the transactions of his life, and acknowledged his sins before God, he felt within himself a confidence in his mercy, and that, trusting to the merits of his Redeemer, his mind was now in a state of perfect tranquillity." See Sir John Hawkins, *The Life of Samuel Johnson, LL.D.*, ed. Bertram H. Davis (1787; rpt. New York, 1961), p. 245.

[15] See Hawkins, *The Life of Samuel Johnson*, pp. 256-58. For Johnson's letter to the bookseller, Charles Dilly, see Chapman, Letter 924.

[16] For a discussion of the prayers and letters see Greene, "Dr. Johnson's 'Late Conversion,'" p. 67. See also Hawkins, *The Life of Samuel Johnson*, p. 258.

[17] See Greene, "Dr. Johnson's 'Late Conversion,'" pp. 79-81, 88-92; Chapin, "Samuel Johnson's 'Wonderful' Experience," in Wahba, ed., *Johnsonian Studies*, 51-60; and Quinlan, "The Rumor of Dr. Johnson's Conversion," *Review of Religion*, 12 (1948), 243-61.

[18] See the "Narrative by John Hoole" in Hill, ed., *Johnsonian Miscellanies*, II, 147-48.

[19] For studies of the Evangelicals' social concern see, for example, Whiteley, *Wesley's England*, p. 331 and passim; Paul Sangster, *Pity My Simplicity: The Evangelical Revival and the Religious Education of Children, 1738-1800* (London, 1964), pp. 110-11 and passim; Reginald Coupland, *The British Anti-Slavery*

Movement (1933; rpt. London, 1964), pp. 86-111. Wesley's fear of excessive fanaticism had a restraining effect on the emotions and spiritual claims of his followers; see Thomas Jackson, ed., *The Works of the Rev. John Wesley, A. M.*, 3rd ed. (1831; rpt. London, 1872), VIII, 405-12, 423-24, 445-68. This edition is hereafter abbreviated Wesley.

[20] See William Prideaux Courtney and David Nichol Smith, eds., *A Bibliography of Samuel Johnson* (Oxford, 1968), p. 126; and items 20:45 and 20:46 in James L. Clifford and Donald Greene, eds., *Samuel Johnson: A Survey and Bibliography of Critical Studies* (Minneapolis, 1970).

[21] For a thorough and sympathetic recent study of Johnson's practical charity see John Wain, *Samuel Johnson* (New York, 1974), pp. 107-13, 122-24, 166-67, 342-44. Evangelical practical charity reached a high point in the public and private labors of William Wilberforce. See Thomas Clarkson, *History of the Rise, Progress, and Accomplishment of the Abolition of the African Slave Trade by the British Parliament* (London, 1808); and Audrey Lawson and Herbert Lawson, *The Man Who Freed the Slaves: The Story of William Wilberforce* (London, 1962).

[22] For Wesley's ministry to Dodd, see Wesley, IV, 93, 99, 103; XI, 448-56; XIII, 134.

[23] Chapin, *The Religious Thought of Samuel Johnson*, pp. 28-29.

[24] For a sampling of the Evangelical journalistic meditation see Thomas Jackson, ed., *The Lives of Early Methodist Preachers*, 2nd ed., 3 vols. (London, 1846). Nelson's style is formal and non-subjective. He employs the catechism format of question and answer in his *Companion for the Festivals and Fasts of the Church of England: With Collects and Prayers for each Solemnity*, 4th ed. (London, 1707); and his argumentation consciously addresses an audience—see *The Practice of True Devotion, in Relation to the End, as well as the Means of Religion; With an Office for the Holy Communion*, 9th ed. (London, 1725).

[25] See, for example, some of the Easter entries: Yale, I, 91-93, 95, 107-8, 131, 136, 140, 155-56, 225-26, 258, 264, 288-89, 306, 308.

[26] "It was a circumstance to be wondered at," says Hawkins (*The Life of Samuel Johnson*, pp. 242-43), "that a high-churchman, as Johnson ever professed himself to be, should be driven to seek for spiritual comfort in the writings of sectaries; men whom he affected, as well to condemn for their ignorance, as to hate for their principles; but, as his acquaintance with the world, and with the writings of such men as Watts, Foster, Lardner, and Lowman, increased, these prejudices were greatly softened. Of the early Puritans, he thought their want of general learning was atoned for by their skill in the Scriptures, and the holiness of their lives; and, to justify his opinion of them, and their writings, he

once cited to me a saying of [James] Howell in one of his letters, that to make a man a complete Christian, he must have the works of a Papist, the words of a Puritan, and the faith of a Protestant." For an explicit argument that Johnson, in his *Meditations*, was only superficially similar to the Puritans, see Chapin, *The Religious Thought of Samuel Johnson*, p. 29.

[27] Ian Watt, "Dr. Johnson and the Literature of Experience," in Wahba, ed., *Johnsonian Studies*, pp. 15-22.

[28] See Johnson's letter of 22 December 1774 (Chapman, I, 422). For Johnson's relation to Taylor, and for the establishment of the sermon canon, see Jean H. Hagstrom, "The Sermons of Samuel Johnson," *Modern Philology*, 40 (February 1943), 255-66. For the nature of Evangelical homiletics see Henry Bett, *Early Methodist Preachers* (London, 1935), and the chapters on Wesley and Whitefield in James Downey, *The Eighteenth-Century Pulpit: A Study of the Sermons of Butler, Berkeley, Secker, Sterne, Whitefield, and Wesley* (Oxford, 1969).

[29] See the discussion of Johnson's subject matter in Gray, *Johnson's Sermons*, pp. 3 ff.

[30] See Fussell, *Samuel Johnson and the Life of Writing* (New York, 1971), pp. 129-30.

[31] For the importance of this biblical text among the Nonconformist Evangelicals, see, for example, Edwin Sidney, *The Life of Rowland Hill*, 2nd ed. (London, 1834), pp. 21-22, 45. See also Wesley, VI, 80; VII, 461; VIII, 310-13.

[32] Johnson sought such evidence, for example, in his mental life. For a theological context of his search for the evidences of faith, see Robert G. Walker, "Johnson, Tillotson, and Comparative Credibility," forthcoming in *Notes and Queries*. Johnson valued testimonial evidence as a means of refuting the argument against miracles in Hume's "Essay on Miracles"; see C. S. Noyes, "Samuel Johnson Student of Hume," *Studies in English*, 3 (1962), 94.

When Johnson and Boswell staffed an imaginary university with members of the Club, Johnson went so far as to assume for himself the professorship of metaphysics (Powell, V, 1 04), and he employed a rigorous metaphysical argument in demonstrating against Soame Jenyns that the concepts of hierarchy and plenitude are mutually exclusive (Powell, I, 304, 315-16), but he was self-conscious about such uncommon sense—he feared the sin of intellectual pride. In epistemology he proceeded with a pious circumspection not unlike that of Locke, and when he delivered his famous kick to Berkeley's philosophic stone, thereby registering his awareness that epistemology can be solipsistic, he had just emerged from church where he was in the habit of submitting to a Power larger than the self (Powell, I, 471). He resembles the Evangelicals in so far as he seems to have recognized that personal piety, grounded in experience, could fully teach him spiritual things that he knew partly from a guarded epistemology but could not learn at all from the discipline of metaphysics.

[33] See Donald Greene, "Augustinianism and Empiricism," *ECS*, 1 (Fall 1967), 33-68; and *The Age of Exuberance: Backgrounds to Eighteenth-Century English Literature* (New York, 1970), pp. 100-110.

[34] Jonathan Edwards, *A Treatise Concerning Religious Affections* (Boston, 1746), contains considerable commentary on Locke, and is included in Wesley's *Christian Library*. See also Douglas J. Elwood, *The Philosophical Theology of Jonathan Edwards* (New York, 196); and Perry Miller, "Jonathan Edwards on the Sense of the Heart," *Harvard Theological Review*, 41 (April 1948), 123-45. For Wesley's essay on Locke see Wesley, XIII, 455-64; see also Wesley, I, 496; II, 390; VI, 352.

[35] For a discussion see W. K. Wimsatt, Jr., *Philosophic Words: A Study of Style and Meaning in the Rambler and Dictionary of Samuel Johnson* (1948; rpt. New York, 1968), p. 71.

[36] See, among many notable titles, Melvin Rader, *Wordsworth: A Philosophical Approach* (Oxford, 1967) and Alan Grob, *The Philosophic Mind: A Study of Wordsworth's Poetry and Thought 1797-1805* (Columbus, Ohio, 1973).

[37] The philosophical implications of the phrase are fully discussed in Robert Langbaum, *The Poetry of Experience: The Dramatic Monologue in Modern Literary Tradition* (London, 1957).

[38] It is well established that the Romantics exploited empiricist language for their various literary purposes; see the stimulating discussion, and the full bibliography, in L. J. Swingle, "On Reading Romantic Poetry," *PMLA*, 86 (1971), 974-81. I have suggested that the Evangelical Movement was a significant background to Coleridge's religious life; see *Wordsworth's "Natural Methodism,"* pp. 8, 13, 30, 38-40, 84-85, 87, 101, 109, 126, 146, 164, 178, 184, 188-90. For Byron's admiration of Dr. James Kennedy, an Evangelical convert, see the discussion in E. W. Marjarum, *Byron as Skeptic and Believer* (Princeton, 1938). One also thinks of Shelley's respect for the revival (see *The Defense of Poetry*), and of Keats's generally spiritual, and particularly experiential, diction in such later works as *The Fall of Hyperion*.

[39] Southey, after all, knew the obvious history: Wesley maintained a fifty-year concern for American spiritual health; Whitefield in 1740 brought to New England the general revival as well as his particular fervor; and he joined forces, briefly, with Edwards and the American Great Awakening; see Robert Southey, *The Life of Wesley; and the Rise and Progress of Methodism*, 2nd ed. (Lon-

don, 1820), II, 416-65. It is implicit in Southey's argument that constitutional government, newly written down in America and traditionally understood in England, was refreshed and awakened by a forceful Christianity schooled in the ways of self-government and social responsibility; eighteenth-century religion assured for the greater part of two hundred years the spiritual shapes and biases of two national characters. Edwards, with his alloy of Evangelical faith and empirical philosophy, struck a balance between the outward and the inward quests of spirit and of mind, thus contributing to a particularly Anglo-American balance.

[40] See M. H. Abrams, "English Romanticism: The Spirit of the Age," in *Romanticism Reconsidered: Selected Papers from the English Institute*, ed. Northrop Frye (New York, 1963); Abrams, *Natural Supernaturalism: Tradition and Revolution in Romantic Literature* (New York, 1971), pp. 134-40; and *Wordsworth's "Natural Methodism,"* pp. 102-10, 114, 116.

[41] In *On Religion: Speeches to its Cultured Despisers*, trans. John Oman (1799; rpt. New York, 1958), Friedrich Schleiermacher draws upon his pietist background in his attempt to recover a philosophy of religion that would be respected and used by the intellectual community in Germany; he addressed himself in particular to the disciples of Herder, Goethe, Kant, and Fichte. Goethe and Schiller responded scornfully, but the work influenced Schelling, Fichte, Hardenberg, and Harms, among others. See the discussion in Rudolf Otto's introduction to *Ueber die Religion: Reden an die Gebildeten unter ihren Verächtern*, 5. durchgeschene Auflage (Göttingen, 1926); Otto argues that Schleiermacher attempted "to lead an age weary with and alien to religion back to its very mainsprings; and to reweave religion, threatened with oblivion into the incomparably rich fabric of the burgeoning intellectual life of modern times."

Otto recognizes, moreover, the close parallel between the Methodist revival and Schleiermacher's pietist temperament, and Schleiermacher himself, though hardly an Anglophile, praised the English "popular interest in missions and the spread of the Bible" (see Oman, trans., *On Religion*, p. 23). For other evidence of British influence on German pietism see, for example, August Lang, *Puritanismus und Pietismus: Studien zu ihrer Entwicklung von. M. Butzer zum Methodismus* (Neukirchen, 1941); and Auguste Sann, *Bunyan in Deutschland: Studien zur literarischen Wechzelbeziehung zwischen England und dem Deutschen Pietismus* (Giessen, 1951).

8. *Spiritual Maturity and Wordsworth's 1783 Christmas Vacation*

The lines from *The Prelude* in which Wordsworth recalls his 1783 Christmas vacation from Hawkshead (XI.345-397, 1805)[1] have received little comment, yet they invite close examination: the passage testifies to a direct encounter with God and thus contains important religious implications. Wordsworth remembers himself as a restless and impatient youth who has scaled a crag near Hawkshead in order to discern the approach of the servant sent to bring him and his brothers home. He omits details about the servant's arrival and the vacation itself and simply announces the death of his father during the very holiday so eagerly anticipated. To him this death "appear'd / A chastisement," and he tells us that he repented of his boyish emotion:

> With trite reflections of morality,
> Yet in the deepest passion, I bow'd low
> To God, who thus corrected my desires.
> (ll. 373-375)

In annotating the passage David Perkins detects its substantially Christian content: "A sensitive boy schooled in a Christian household of the nineteenth century might conceivably take the death of his father as a punishment for his own impatience, or more generally for forgetting—despite the dreary, grim, and threatening aspects of the natural world—that earthly life is a time of sorrow and probation."[2] But the "Christian household" of Wordsworth's youth belonged to the eighteenth century, not the nineteenth; he was thirty years old at the turn of the century in which his fame began to grow. We therefore ought to remember the religious influences of his eighteenth-century childhood and early manhood: John Wesley repeatedly visited Cockermouth when

Wordsworth was a boy; Cambridge was the intellectual center of the Evangelical revival during his matriculation; Dorothy Wordsworth was an enthusiastic early participant in the Evangelically inspired Sunday-school movement; and the poet himself, indicating his sympathy for this widespread spirit of renewal, sent a complimentary copy of *Lyrical Ballads* to the Evangelical reformer William Wilberforce—with a long covering letter in which he declared himself "a Fellow-labourer with you in the same Vineyard."[3] Evangelicalism flourished in nineteenth-century households, and Wordsworth's was increasingly upright and orthodox, but his faith took root when Wesley was active and Evangelicalism in the flush of its early vigor.

Remembrance of such things in Wordsworth's past might lead us to modify the secularizing tendency in modern studies of his work, and we may yet discover Charles Lamb's reasons for describing *The Excursion* as "natural methodism."[4] The passage in question, meanwhile, speaks clearly to ears attuned to Evangelical and Wesleyan terminology. I shall argue that the passage reflects a Biblical doctrine of particular significance to Wesley and the Great Awakening: God hastens man's spiritual maturity through chastisement of pride. At the heart of this spot of time is a lesson in Christian humility, and when the passage is so understood we are less likely to be repelled by the puzzling proposition that the persona has done something for which the death of his father is a "chastisement" (it seems somewhat grotesque that God would kill a father to punish a child's impatience). Evangelical commonplaces also explain in what sense his reflections can be "trite" yet deeply religious.

Wordsworth explored the theme of pride long before he wrote *The Prelude*. In "Lines left upon a Seat in a Yew-tree," written over a ten-year period (1787-1797), he tells of a man who at first sustained his soul only "with the food of pride" but who finally acquired spiritual nourishment by "tracing . . . / An emblem of his own unfruitful life" in the "barren rocks" and "gloomy boughs" near the lake of Esthwaite (*PW*, II, 93). The moral is baldly stated:

> Stranger! henceforth be warned; and know that pride,
> Howe'er disguised in its own majesty,
> Is littleness.
>
> (ll. 50-52)

The model for such naturalized and didactic emblemology was available in Methodist spiritual autobiography—a popular feature of Wesley's *Arminian Magazine*. The Methodists, much indebted to *The Pilgrim's Progress* and *Grace*

Abounding by John Bunyan, reflected the Puritan tradition of construing the objects of nature as spiritual emblems (a spider's venom, in *Pilgrim's Progress*, is an emblem of man's sin; and a hollow tree with leaves represents the hypocrisy of those "whose outside is fair and whose inside is rotten").[5] And Wordsworth, who admired Bunyan and was undoubtedly familiar with the Methodist lives,[6] filled his own spiritual autobiography with "Apt illustrations of the moral world, / Caught at a glance, or traced with curious pains" (*Prelude* XIV.319-320, 1850). The Christmas passage is one such illustration. Its moral, unlike that of the Yew-tree poem, cannot be caught at a glance, but can be traced painstakingly— not only in the natural images but throughout the complex diction. As he reiterated his theme of pride Wordsworth increased the difficulties of interpretation without reducing the rewards and practical benefits.

The passage echoes the diction of Evangelical writers, who drew from a common fund of words to describe specific experiences in generic terms. In a hymn entitled "Religion" James Montgomery (1771-1854), whose poetry Wordsworth came to admire, associates "pride" with "guilty passions," and in "The Peak Mountains" (1812) he identifies some emotions denoting pride.[7] Like Wordsworth he is "restless" before ascending a mountain, and his frame is "fever'd"—these are symptoms of a kind of discontented "pride, the strength of manhood's prime" (II, 139-141). Though Wordsworth, for his part, never openly identifies his attitudes at Hawkshead as pride, he describes himself as "feverish, and tired, and restless" (l. 347), and thereby indicates the same kind of discontent: two of these emotional states resemble those same "guilty passions" that Montgomery associates with pride; and elsewhere in *The Prelude* the poet does associate pride with being feverish and tired. In Book II he recalls his childhood habit of prolonging summer games beyond nightfall, going to bed "feverish" and "weary" (l. 18). These adjectives seem only a realistic description of an emotional state, just as the same (or synonymous) labels, to the modern reader, seem literally and perhaps exclusively to describe the schoolboy's mood; yet Wordsworth follows this description in Book II with a seemingly unrelated conclusion: each young person, he abruptly argues, "needs a warning voice to tame the pride / . . . of virtue's self-esteem" (ll. 25-26). His high tone comes unexpectedly for any reader unfamiliar with Evangelical code-words for pride, but in fact his earlier diction has prepared for the moral comment. Such comment, then, may be implicit or even primary in the Christmas episode, for Wordsworth's terminology, with its overtones of religious meaning, suggests that the schoolboy is as much discontented in spirit as restless in mood, as much prideful in nature as "naturally" boyish.

The boy, besides being feverish, tired, and restless, is "impatient" (l. 348), and full of the "anxiety of hope" (l. 372); other lines from *The Prelude* again shed light on the meaning here. His mother, in direct contrast to his own behavior, avoids "feverish" dread (V.277), rejects unnatural "hopes" (l. 279), and never asks with "impatience" more than the "timely produce" of any season (ll. 281-282). Her contentedness with the present amounts to an admirable humility, free of such guilty or discontented passions: she

> rather lov'd
> The hours for what they are than from regards
> Glanced on their promises in restless pride.
> (ll. 282-284)

Adjectives denoting pride, while they do not apply to the mother, do characterize the schoolboy. In his restless if typically boyish impatience for the season to begin, he does not accept the timely produce of the present moment but feverishly wants to overleap the time remaining before the full enjoyment of his vacation; he wishes away some of his own life and, in a sense, some of his father's as well. On a day "Stormy, and rough, and wild"—a time when nature appears threatening—the impatient youth seems never to think of man's mortality, though the father's death is imminent even as the son stands on the "Eminence" of the crag (the horses that bear him "home," supposedly to holiday festivities, may bear his father's body "home" to the grave [ll. 349, 351-357]).

After the father's death, God assumes the paternal role of reproving the restless boy. The passage recalls the twelfth chapter of Hebrews, a chapter comparing the disciplinary function of the earthly father with the firmly paternal guidance of God:

> My son, despise not thou the chastening of the Lord, nor faint when thou art rebuked of him: For whom the Lord loveth he chasteneth, and scourgeth every son whom he receiveth. If ye endure chastening, God dealeth with you as with sons; for what son is he whom the father chasteneth not? But if ye be without *chastisement*, whereof all are partakers, then are ye bastards, and not sons. Furthermore we have had fathers of our flesh which

> *corrected* us, and we gave them reverence: shall we not much rather be in subjection unto the Father of spirits, and live?
> (5-9; my italics)

Wordsworth employs Biblical diction in describing God's paternal punishment: after the boy's uneasy sense of "chastisement" (l. 370), God "corrected" his guilty passions (l. 375). Though the prideful offense calls for stern measures, the chastisement is remedial. The God in Wordsworth's passage, like the stern "Father of spirits" in Hebrews, administers a fatherly correction both necessary and desirable; for the boy, in need of "chastisement" from an earthly father, finally achieves legitimate son-ship under the paternal love of a chastening God; and the poet pays to the Father of spirits the reverence formerly due to the father of his flesh. He thus celebrates his spiritual coming of age.

The attainment of maturity, indeed, is the specifically Evangelical theme of Wordsworth's passage, reflecting Wesley's formulation of current views of rearing children.[8] Referring to the same passage in Hebrews (Wesley, VII, 99), Wesley advises parents to punish often and severely in order to conquer the natural pride of their children, and his description of the disciplinary process resembles that of Wordsworth. Like Montgomery, he associates "pride" with "passions" (VII, 94), and, like Wordsworth, he calls these guilty passions "desires" (VII, 89). He enjoins parents to administer "timely correction" of childish desires (VII, 103), and he implies a broader faith that God Himself will "correct . . . inordinate passions" (IX, 318). This necessary chastisement effects a mature humility admired by both the poet and the preacher. After feeling God's punishment, the headstrong young Wordsworth finally "bow'd low / To God" (ll. 374-375); without punishment, warned Wesley, the strong-willed child will never "bow to God" (VII, 92). Wesley quotes from William Law (with whom Wordsworth was familiar) in order to indicate the beneficial results of strong corrective measures: firm paternal control, wrote Law, will teach the child a spirit of "humility . . . and devotion" (VII, 88).[9] The mature and now-humble Wordsworth also acquires a spirit of devotion: life's journey remains difficult, but he is strengthened by "devoutest" habits (l. 397). Nurtured in admonition, this true child of God grows into manhood and becomes, like Christian, "a Pilgrim gone/ In quest of highest truth" (ll. 392-393).

Wesley's theology helps to clarify other dimensions of the passage as well. Aware of personal guilt, the persona bows before God "With trite reflections of morality, / Yet in the deepest passion" (ll. 373-374), and these lines are puzzling, not only because passion and trite reflection seem mutually exclusive to the twentieth-century reader, but also because the boy's passion—his restless impatience—had presumably been corrected. Wesley, for his part, saw no inconsistency between a certain kind of reflection and a certain kind of passion. Concerning moral reflections, he believed that a man is disposed to "sober reflections" on the error of his ways whenever God corrects him (IX, 318). Perhaps Wordsworth's reflections spring from a similar cause. They are "trite" insofar as the lesson is an elementary one: pride is a vice, humility a virtue (there is hardly a more commonplace precept of Christian morality). The boy, however, thoroughly learns his lesson in humility for the first time. Because of God's direct teaching, he can grasp the simple truth with deep personal conviction, and his "deepest passion" is not the surface passion of pride, but rather one of zeal and certainty. According to Wesley, depth of passion implies humility. Those still burdened by "the pride of their unbroken heart" can feel "no deep repentance, or thorough conviction," can experience "no deep work in their heart" (V, 470). The "passions" of "zeal" or "fervent love," on the other hand, are consistent with humility, because this high degree of Christian love is "not puffed up" (VII, 59; cf. I Corinthians 13.4). An emotional faith without pride is therefore natural. For Wesley, the "turbulent" passions of pride— "fretfulness, discontent, impatience"—make true zeal impossible (VII, 59, 63). Wordsworth's "deepest passion," then, seems to be one of fervent love; it occurs only when God puts his impatient and restless discontent to flight. His new passion has the depth of a properly humble religious zeal, and for him a deep conviction reaffirms the validity of a basic moral truth.

The passage, indeed, emphasizes his "deep" response. The ambiguous word "trite, " though not entirely pejorative, is primarily so: superficial thoughts about morality, or even careful and sober considerations of it, are less important than *passion* (from *patere* to suffer) when passion is, as in Gethsemane and at the Crucifixion, an agony associated with total submission to God; and Wordsworth's moral reflections are trivial in comparison with his "passion," his new willingness to endure not only the threats of nature but also the chastisements of God. His former impatience, his stubborn unwillingness to suffer or bear, could hardly yield to the *topoi* of morality but does yield to loving reproof. The Evangelicals, especially the Calvinists among them, reiterated that morality was, as good deeds were, mere "filthy rags";[10] and Wordsworth's experience, like theirs, suggests that man can do little apart from external aid and agency. With such aid, however, he keeps his moral "rags" and also puts on the New Man, who submits to a Control far higher than the laws of morality.

His encounter with God recalls, moreover, Wesley's doctrine of free grace (IX, 373ff)—one cannot compel God to save but must wait patiently trusting in Him to work His will. By corollary, one is patient with the vicissitudes of life, taking every moment as the gift of God, not trying to press forward, with hectic calculation of how the present can insure the future one desires. This doctrine might almost be said to explain the structuring principle of the passage at hand, in which God's act of grace at the center (ll. 364-375) is anticipated in the first part and acknowledged toward the end. At the top of the crag the impatient youth looks toward the future, "straining [his] eyes intensely" to catch a glimpse of the servant (l. 362); he has yet to learn to accept the timing of events according to the will of God. But certain nearby objects foreshadow the remedial grace to come. The sheep on the boy's "right hand" (l. 359) seems a muted echo of Christ's invitation to the "sheep on his right hand": "Come ye blessed of my father, inherit the kingdom prepared for you from the foundation of the world" (Matthew 25.33-34). The "whistling hawthorn" (l. 360) or "blasted tree" on his "left" (l. 378) recalls the doomed and accursed goats on Christ's "left" hand (25.33) and thus may reinforce theologically the threatening aspect of the "stormy" day. The boy, in a sense, is suspended between promise and damnation but finds a makeshift refuge: he is "half-shelter'd by a naked wall" (l. 358) and thereby symbolically set apart until God corrects his desires and, in the words of a hymn by Wesley's Nonconformist friend Isaac Watts, gives full "shelter from the stormy blast." After receiving God's loving chastisement, the spiritually mature Wordsworth often remembers details from the episode—including the "single sheep," the "blasted tree," and the "old stone wall" (ll. 378-379)—and "thence ... drink[s] / As at a fountain" (ll. 384-385). His simile is a common image of grace, as Alexander Cruden's eighteenth-century Concordance suggests: not only does the fountain for "sin and uncleanness" in the Book of Zechariah (13.1) serve as a type for Christ the "matchless healing and purging Fountain" but, more generally and more importantly for this passage, symbolizes "all spiritual graces and refreshments communicated by the Spirit."[11] Wordsworth is spiritually refreshed by the memory of his encounter with God; his adolescent experience of grace, therefore, is extended to the present moment. Indeed it seems reasonable to conjecture that he regarded other spots of time, with their "efficacious spirit" (XI.269), as fountains of grace sustaining him on the pilgrimage of life.

It is possible, of course, that Wordsworth employs Evangelical diction casually, to lend authority to his narrative. But this particular passage, in which God's presence is central, suggests that a theology both traditional and vital survived in and helped to shape his new kind of verse. The theme of spiritual maturity, for instance, can also be found in other spots of time. In Book I Wordsworth remembers rowing a stolen boat "proudly," while a threatening and perhaps morally emblematic "Cliff" frightens him into returning the property to "its usual home" (ll. 375-406, 1805); the spiritual progress realized in the Christmas episode—the final spot in *The Prelude*—is thus anticipated in one of his earliest memorable moments. And we may find that these recollections of childhood, like those in Methodist spiritual autobiography, are indeed "apt illustrations of the moral world": as literal pictures in Wordsworth's mind and figurative *exempla* of his morality, they seem to constitute an emblemology deriving from his own spiritual experience and extending to that of those who duly read—"with curious pains."

NOTES

[1] References to *The Prelude* are from the following edition: *The Prelude: Or Growth of a Poet's Mind*, ed. Ernest de Selincourt, 2nd ed. rev. Helen Darbishire (Oxford, 1959); subsequent quotations, unless otherwise indicated, are from the text of 1805-1806. References to other poems are from *The Poetical Works of William Wordsworth*, ed. Ernest de Selincourt, 5 vols. (Oxford, 1940-1949), hereafter abbreviated *PW*. This essay was written with the aid of a grant from the American Philosophical Society.

[2] David Perkins, ed., *English Romantic Writers* (New York, 1967), p. 256n.

[3] Wesley visited Cockermouth eighteen times from April of 1751 to May of 1788; five of these visits occurred after Wordsworth's birth (April 7, 1770) and before his departure for Hawkshead Grammar-school (1778). See John Wesley, *The Works of the Rev. John Wesley, A. M.*, ed. Thomas Jackson, 3rd ed. (1831; rpt. London, 1872), II, 157, 159, 227, 263, 270, 284, 408, 479; III, 50, 51, 84, 184, 207, 231, 254, 275, 316, 394, 458; IV, 13, 73, 99, 101, 180, 204, 208, 271, 272, 331, 417, 486. Subsequent references to this edition appear in the text. For the Evangelical climate at Cambridge see Charles Smyth, *Simeon and Church Order: A Study of the Origins of the Evangelical Revival in Cambridge in the Eighteenth Century* (Cambridge, 1940); for evidence that Wordsworth had Evangelical friends there see Ben Ross Schneider, Jr., *Wordsworth's Cambridge Education* (Cambridge, 1957), pp. 66, 138-139, 149-150. In her Sunday-school class, Dorothy taught reading, spelling, prayers, hymns, and catechisms; see

The Letters of William and Dorothy Wordsworth, ed. Ernest de Selincourt, rev. Chester L. Shaver (Oxford, 1967), pp. 24-27. For the letter to Wilberforce (n. d.), see Shaver, p. 684.

[4] M. H. Abrams, for example, calls *The Prelude* "a secular theodicy—a theodicy without an operative *theos*"; see his *Natural Supernaturalism: Tradition and Revolution in Romantic Literature* (New York, 1971), p. 95. In a letter to Wordsworth (? early January 1815), Lamb regretted that the editor of *The Quarterly*, William Gifford, had left out Lamb's reasons for describing *The Excursion* as "natural methodism." He seemed to think that such a description would have pleased Wordsworth: "I regret only that I did not keep a copy. I am sure you would have been pleased with it, because I have been feeding my fancy for some months with the notion of pleasing you." See E. V. Lucas, ed., *The Letters of Charles Lamb to which are added those of his sister Mary Lamb* (London, 1935), II, 149. For a full discussion of Wordsworth's natural methodism, see my forthcoming book on Wordsworth's relation to Evangelical Anglicanism and Evangelical Nonconformism, soon to be published by the Yale University Press.

[5] The Methodist autobiographies were collected by Thomas Jackson in *The Lives of Early Methodist Preachers*, 3 vols. (London, 1846); for an example of the Methodists' emblematic reading of nature, see the account of Thomas Olivers, who testified that he had "often received instruction" "even from a drop of water, a blade of grass, or a grain of sand" (*Lives*, I, 208-209). For Puritan antecedents of the Methodist autobiographies see Henry Bett, *The Early Methodist Preachers* (London, 1935); J. Paul Hunter, *The Reluctant Pilgrim: Defoe's Emblematic Method and Quest for Form in* Robinson Crusoe (Baltimore, 1966); and David J. Alpaugh, "Emblem and Interpretation in *The Pilgrim's Progress*," *ELH*, 33 (1966), 299-314. For the emblems in *Pilgrim's Progress* see John Bunyan, *The Pilgrim's Progress from this World to That which is to Come*, ed. James Blanton Wharey (Oxford, 1928), pp. 212, 216.

[6] Wordsworth spoke of the "splendour" of *Pilgrim's Progress*; see William Angus Knight, *The Life of William Wordsworth* (Edinburgh, 1889), III, 356-357. During his closest association with Wordsworth, Coleridge wrote a series of letters to Thomas Poole in which he outlined his plans to write the story of his early life according to the pattern of prideful error and repentance in Methodist spiritual autobiography; there was an "honesty" in the Methodist lives, he said, which was conducive to "an amelioration of Heart." See Earl Leslie Griggs, ed., *Collected Letters of Samuel Taylor Coleridge* (Oxford, 1956-1959), I, 302; S. T. C. to Thomas Poole, February 6, 1797. Dates of the other letters are: March 1797, October 9, 1797, October 16, 1797, and February 19, 1798.

⁷ For the hymn see James Montgomery, *The Wanderer of Switzerland, and other poems* (Morristown, Pennsylvania, 1811), pp. 110-112; for "The Peak Mountains" see James Montgomery, *The Poetical Works of James Montgomery*, ed. Robert Carruthers (Boston, 1858), II, 139-141. Subsequent references to the latter edition appear in the text. In a letter to Montgomery dated November 30, 1836, Wordsworth remarked: "I cannot deny myself the satisfaction of expressing a firm belief that neither morality nor religion can have suffered from our writings; and with respect to yours I know that both have been greatly benefited by them"; see Ernest de Selincourt, ed., *The Letters of William and Dorothy Wordsworth: The Later Years* (Oxford, 1939), II, 818.

⁸ For delightful studies of Evangelical practice in rearing children see Grace Elizabeth Harrison, *Son to Susanna: The Private Life of John Wesley* (London, 1937) and Paul Sangster, *Pity My Simplicity: The Evangelical Revival and the Religious Education of Children 1728-1800* (London, 1964). References to the relevant essays by Wesley—"On the Education of Children,'" "On Obedience to Parents," and "Of the Nature and Design of our Afflictions and Mortality"—appear in the text.

⁹ Wordsworth recommended in 1808 that Christians should read Law's *A Serious Call to a Devout and Holy Life* (1728); see de Selincourt, ed., *The Letters of William and Dorothy Wordsworth: The Middle Years* (Oxford, 1937), I, 225.

¹⁰ The phrase is Isaiah's: "But we are all as an unclean thing, and all our righteousnesses are as filthy rags; and we all do fade as a leaf; and our iniquities, like the wind, have taken us away" (64.6). The controversy over this and similar texts was troublesome to Wesley. When some of his fellow-preachers became antinomian and proclaimed that morality was worthless, he rebuked them for going a bit too far. For his sympathy with antinomianism see Wesley, VIII, 284-285. For his reservations about it see Wesley, VIII, 300; IX, 101-102, 110; X, 399-401; XI, 430-432; XII, 297. For his animadversions against the antinomianism among Calvinists see Wesley, VIII, 278, 328, 336-337, 433.

¹¹ Alexander Cruden, ed., *A Complete Concordance to the Holy Scriptures of the Old and New Testament; or, A Dictionary and Alphabetical Index to the Bible*, 3rd ed. (New York, 1823), p. 219.

9. *Wordsworth's Art of Belief*

Wordsworth's image of his corpus as a "gothic church," with *The Excursion* (1814) as "the body" or nave, *The Prelude* (1805, 1850) as "the ante-chapel," and the "minor Pieces" as "the little cells, oratories, and sepulchral recesses, ordinarily included in those edifices," gives pride of place to *The Excursion*.[1] Granting the Anglo-Catholic provenance and the Anglican tenor of this extended metaphor, one may wonder if *The Excursion* constitutes the distinguishing expression of Wordsworth's High-Church Romanticism. Or, allowing the Evangelical propensity of rural Anglican churches in Wordsworth's day, one may ask how *The Excursion* embodies the best of his Low-Church Romanticism. The latter question suggests the more *avant-garde* possibility. The still, small voice of the lyrics and of *The Prelude* becomes the certain trumpet of *The Excursion*, which reverberates as the crux of Wordsworth's art of belief.[2]

Wordsworth's relation to such Dissenting as well as Anglican evangelicals as Isaac Watts, John and Charles Wesley, and William Wilberforce is sometimes direct—the near influence always telling—but more often indirect—"the power of weak ties" made manifest (Ruef 429). Wordsworth would agree with Jane Austen, who, in an 1815 letter to her niece, Fanny Knight, observes, "I am by no means convinced that we ought not all to be Evangelicals, and am at least persuaded that they who are so from Reason and Feeling, must be happiest and safest" (*Letters* 109). Wordsworth would also concur with Coleridge, who, in *Table Talk* (1835), "avow[s]" that "the Christian faith is what [John] Wesley describes": "the identity of the reason and the will, in the full energy of each, consequent on a divine rekindling."[3] Wordsworth's appeal to this evangelical background sounds similarly discerning, respectful, straightforward, and non-ironic, as though he includes among the voices of his second long poem those of such "better angels of our [religious] nature" as Wilberforce, whose reputation as an evangelical saint remains secure. Thus allying individual talent with religious tradition, Wordsworth's deuteronomic epic of biblical proportions reveals his fierce affinity for the open mind and God-warmed heart of his evangelical precursors.

Francis, Lord Jeffrey—that "cultured despiser" of religion (in German Romantic theologian Friedrich Schleiermacher's fine phrase)—condemns *The Excursion* as "mystical verbiage of the Methodist pulpit" (14). Founder Wesley's anything but mystical Methodism, however, feels deliberately grounded. "Wesley's distaste for the mystical approach to spiritual formation appears as early as 1726, when, as a college man in his early twenties, he 'began to see more and more the value of time' (*Works* I 467). Rather than cultivating a timeless inner closeness with God, Wesley recognized the importance of cultivating God's image in *time*. Understood in this way, religious self-formation is subject to the particular slowness, doubt, and hesitations that come with daily living" (Bennett 28). The Methodism of *The Excursion*, accordingly, develops temporal "closeness with God." It grows outward to others. It bears up. It stays joyful.

In an 1815 letter to Wordsworth, Charles Lamb declares that "natural methodism" (note lower case) is what makes *The Excursion* great.[4] The lower case of Lamb's low-key but intriguing and unexplained phrase could signal his approval of how Wordsworth modulates from revival liveliness to the alternative vigor of scientific procedure (Brantley, *Emily* 33-9), or for how he employs evangelical vernacular to enliven nature worship. The Methodism of *The Excursion*, however, is not "lite": neither displaced into the laboratory nor turned pantheistic, it is welcomed to speak for itself. Thus, just as the Wanderer nuances how evangelicals read Nature's Book—for its Author's good news—so the Wanderer and the Pastor build on the dual innovation of evangelical theology: immediate revelation, plus perfection in the here-and-now.[5] *The Excursion* may establish poetic *Bildungsroman* in which *Bildung* is not so much secular self-development as the *Bild* or "image" of God to which characters aspire as they live and love.[6] Wordsworth's vaulting, if in the long run rearguard, ambition to renew, as Wesley does, biblical monotheism-plus-ethics makes his Natural Methodism (note upper case) Spontaneous and Overflowing, Un-ossified and Un-self-conscious Methodism. *The Excursion* embraces not just belief in experience, but The Experience of Belief.

The Wanderer's tribute to Margaret opens a magic casement on objects-out-there, not valuing those words of God's Second Volume as "material forms ... for their own sake," but charging them as metaphors of morality and as intimations of immortality (see Wordsworth's 1798 letter to the Evangelical Anglican reformer and abolitionist Wilberforce [*Early Years* 684-5]). The spiritual reading of natural things in the 1805 *Prelude*, where "the types and symbols of Eternity" revive "the blossoms upon one tree" (VI 560-7), is of a piece with the Wanderer's subtly establishmentarian lines on how natural perception yields to the spiritual sense:

> I well remember that those very plumes,
> Those weeds, and the high spear-grass on that wall,
> By mist and silent rain-drops silvered o'er,
> As once I passed, into my heart conveyed
> So still an image of tranquility,
> So calm and still, and looked so beautiful
> Amid the uneasy thoughts which filled my mind,
> That what we feel of sorrow and despair
> From ruin and from change, and all the grief
> That passing shows of Being leave behind,
> Appeared an idle dream, that could maintain,
> Nowhere, dominion o'er the enlightened spirit
> Whose meditative sympathies repose
> Upon the breast of Faith. I turned away,
> And walked along my road in happiness.
> (*Excursion* I 942-56)

The Wanderer's sign of peace—his "plumes" as "image of tranquility"—and his symbol of new life—his "spear-grass . . . silvered o'er" by dew—illustrate his muted but winning version of the personalized emblems and types among *Lives of Early Methodist Preachers* (1846; see Jackson; Brantley, *Wordsworth's* 139-70; Brantley, *Locke* 103-28). Of the late-lamented Margaret, the Wanderer recalls that, despite her doubts, and without any recourse, on her part, to mysticism, miracle, or even conversion, she regained her spiritual sight, and hence, in however resigned a manner, recovered from her loss of husband and child:

> She learned, with soul
> Fixed on the Cross, that consolation springs,
> From sources deeper far than deepest pain,
> For the meek Sufferer.
> (I 936-9)

Based on a Hosea-to-Wesley-like grasp of faith as knowledge—"learned" here carries Locke's implication of experience as the soul of education—the Wanderer signals his refreshed (or in Blake's term cleansed) spiritual sense: "Why then should we read / The forms of things with an unworthy eye?" (I 939-40). Just as Margaret trusts the Cross, so the Wanderer finds relief from sorrow and mutability.[7] He discovers consolation in the Book of Nature, and permanence not so much in Being, as on "the breast of Faith," which, in keeping with how 17th-century Puritan sermons present the two testaments—as "the Breasts of God" (Leverenz 138-61)— connotes the Bible.

The Wanderer, then, sows a garden variety of religious experience, tends it, and brings it to harvest. Although he may foreshadow the Modern world of Marianne Moore, the "real toads" in his "imaginary garden" remain spiritual entities.[8] His types and symbols sometimes seem homegrown in "the naturalized imagination" (Stillinger 99-118), yet at other times appear calibrated to, or perhaps even incarnated from, a world elsewhere. This mode of high Romanticism retains enough earthly-to-unearthly mystery for the not-so-chthonic *Excursion* to partake of Protestant sacrament—Milton's "palpable obscure" comes to mind (*Paradise Lost* [1674] 2:406) — that is, to participate in the world, yet not be of it.

Moving from reading the Book of Nature and the Bible to experiencing God and man, the Wanderer, on the one hand, awaits divine favor, however unmerited, and so grows fascinated with the difficulties of grace. In this mood, he would agree with Milton, that "they also serve who only stand and wait" (compare "When I Consider How My Light Is Spent" [1652] with Hab 2:4). On the other hand, he values "little, nameless, unremembered acts / Of kindness and of love" ("Tintern Abbey" [1798], 34-5). In this mood, he would maintain with Milton, again, that the weariness of well-doing, the "dust and heat" of reaching for "the immortal garland," is the proper stance.[9] In effect, the Wanderer asks how the grace/deeds duel becomes a working duality, whereby being in the world coexists with, and entails, not being of it, as though—how rich and strange should this be true!—unearthliness engages loveliness, and vice versa.

Book I of *The Excursion* marks the progressive stages of the Wanderer's prophetic charisma. As a youth, he boasts conversion comparable to Wordsworth's call to poetic vocation (Brantley, *Wordsworth's* 95-100). The sight of a glorious sunrise gives the Wanderer joy and rapture and, as though divine presence dwells in the light of dawn, yields what hymn writer and Nonconformist theologian Isaac Watts identifies as "the extraordinary witness of the Holy Spirit" (Watts I 720):

> In such access of mind, in such high hour
> Of visitation from the living God,
> Thought was not; in enjoyment it expired.
> No thanks he breathed, he proffered no request;
> Rapt into still communion that transcends
> The imperfect offices of prayer and praise,
> His mind was a thanksgiving to the power
> That made him; it was blessedness and love!
> (I 197, 211-18)

In these "ecstasies," the Wanderer appears "*possessed*" (I 221; Wordsworth's emphasis), yet soon acquires the "ordinary grace" (Watts I 720) of "patience," and becomes "meek in gratitude" (*Excursion* I 236-9). Watts's hemispheres of immediate revelation, like Evangelical Anglican Wesley's Holy Spirit theology (Brantley, *Wordsworth's* 37-138), serve as glosses on the Wanderer's contrarieties of spiritual experience, as though Wordsworth's emphasis on the Spirit were as unprecedented as Wesley's. Case in point: the evangelical meaning, if not the gospel truth, of the Wanderer as a man of "graces," "filled with inward light" (I 24-5)—channel the Quaker radiance!—whose "precious gift" of communion with "the presence and the power" replaces the sublimity of sea or mountain with the Spirit's (I 135-6).

By exercising his moral faculty, the Wanderer reciprocates such favor. As though the northernmost, most Nonconformist manifestation of Wordsworth's evangelical milieu fosters the kind of child who fathers a good man, the Wanderer in his boyhood read the lives of Scottish martyrs whose "Covenant" with God and "will inflexible" supplied him with high-toned patterns of Christian behavior.[10] As a young man, led by "the stern yet kindly Spirit"—a ghostly presence attached like God on Sinai "to regions mountainous"— the Wanderer travels (like itinerant Wesley?) for the "dual purpose" of performing "kind works" and of "suffering / With those whom he saw suffer" (I 316, I 370-1, I 405). In combining the Spirit's condescension with his own love-labors, the Wanderer reaches a state of personal sanctity, of "shap[ing] his belief" "as grace divine inspired" and as "his own pure heart" "model[ed]" (I 411-2). Nor, now that he is old in the Romantic era, does he depart from his life-long, 18th-century attempt to navigate the two-lane, faith-works road to redemption: "This he remembered in his riper age / With gratitude, and reverential thoughts" (I 401-2).

The opening lines of Book IV assign equal weight to the complementary virtues of trust in God and exertion of will. Human beings, the Wanderer proclaims, must live "by faith," "Faith absolute in God" (IV 21-2). This imperative goes back to Habakkuk and Paul, or to George Whitefield and Selina, Countess of Huntingdon, who emphasize faith over works. Human beings, the Wanderer teaches, can strengthen their "boundless love" of God's "perfections," through their own precondition for perfection, their "dread / Of aught unworthily conceived, endured / Impatiently, ill-done, or left undone" (IV 21-6). Their concept of tested integrity derives from Amos and James, and favors John and Charles Wesley, who accentuate works over faith. God's indulgence preserves the possibility of human apotheosis: "By thy grace / The particle divine remained unquenched," the Wanderer concludes (IV 50-1). But he also insinuates that Romantic-era redemption is a responsibility shared between transcendent and quotidian extremes. *Re-ligio* ties monotheism back to ethics again.

As though the Third Person of the Trinity speaks to the Romantic-era heart, the Wanderer suggests that grace has been, and is being, manifested by fruits of the "all-pervading Spirit, upon whom / Our dark foundations rest" (IV 969-70). From the dawn of creation, "joy and love" were dividends of "communications spiritually maintained" between humankind and "the articulate voice / Of God," "borne on the wind" (IV 634-45). Divine influence continued to fill the earth with "hope, and love, and gratitude," throughout early recorded history (IV 660). Even "brave Progenitors" of Britain, though without the advantage of Christianity, escaped idolatry, because they knew a "spiritual presence"

>   that filled their hearts
> With joy, and gratitude, and fear, and love
> And from their fervent lips drew hymns of praise
> That through the desert rang.
>   (IV 920, 927, 929-32)

Like Watts and Wesley, the Wanderer testifies that in postbiblical times the Spirit communes with people and restores them, daily, with a "touch as gentle as the morning light" (IV 86-90).[11]

The Spirit's familiar touch illustrates the Wanderer's particular desire for the ordinary witness. True, he remembers the "fervent raptures" and the "joy exalted to beatitude" that characterize moments seemingly extraordinary, when his soul overflows with "holiest love" and all things appear full of glory (IV 119-23). Nonetheless, like Watts, he realizes that people cannot long bear such joy unspeakable: gradual dazzling prevents blindness, as Emily Dickinson would say, or as the Israelites learned from Moses's mediation. The Wanderer admits it is difficult for anyone "to *keep* / Heights which the soul is competent to gain" (IV 138-9; Wordsworth's emphasis): the Wanderer knows that people become "too dim / For any passion of the soul that leads / To ecstasy" (IV 181-3). At spiritual maturity, he is seldom "rapt" in extraordinary transport, but he savors the more dependable gifts of the Spirit—namely, "settled peace," hope, and the comforting sense of support that quells all doubt and banishes trouble (IV 187-91, 234-6). The ordinary witness suffices for him.

To be sure, the Wanderer is no enthusiast: it is scarcely feasible "to converse with heaven," 'Yet cease I not to struggle, and aspire / Heavenward; and chide the part of me that flags, / Through sinful choice" (IV 126-32). Nor is charity necessarily rewarding, yet, until their consciences mirror God's image, people should renew their vows of kindness, on "the first motion of a holy thought" (IV 216-27). The Wanderer's oscillation of aspiration and outreach, his principle of loving God and man, compares with the imagination whereby Wordsworth, in Book VI of *The Prelude*, balances guileless enchantment with salutary realism (Brantley, *Wordsworth's* 62-5). The Wanderer does not rely exclusively on grace of any kind, or entirely on the responsibilities that individuals have to others and to God, but, if he had to choose, he might conclude with Paul, despite Paul's reputation for *sola fide*, that among faith, hope, and charity, charity is greatest. After a lifetime of graces and kindness, anyone would be "glorified," ready to "dwell with God in endless love" (IV 189-90).[12]

The Solitary responds to the Wanderer's testimony. On the one hand, he hopes that "showers of grace, / When in the sky no promise may be seen," will fall "to refresh a parched and withered land" (IV 1093-5). Just as the Solitary's eye kindles, as though it were "lit by fire from heaven," so the Wanderer expects to find him restored to "peace" and "union with our God" (IV 1116-22). On the other hand, the Solitary appreciates the soul's role in salvation—he admires the sacrament of baptism in which a "dedication made" by the convert is as important as "a promise given" by God (V 289-90). This development heralds "unremitting progress" in "holiness and truth" (V 291-2).[13]

The Wanderer, then, illustrates the charitable, as distinct from the individualistic, component of Wordsworth's Low-Church Romanticism. The Wanderer's "soul competence"— recall IV 139—presages that of the Arminus- and Wesley-leaning, free will-espousing Southern Baptist thinker of the early 20th century, E. Y. Mullins (for Mullins and the Southern Baptists as offshoots of a not-so-egotistically-sublime Romantic-era subjectivity, see Bloom 198-207). The Wanderer's religious language of perfection contrasts with Godwin's philosophical version, or, in Stanley Cavell's view, with Emerson's (for Wesleyan perfection in Emerson, however, see Brantley, *Coordinates* 81-6, 91-5; Brantley, *Anglo-American* 171-2, 181-8, 228-30). The Wanderer's emphasis not just on Christian perfection, but on the Spirit at the expense of Jesus (notwithstanding Margaret's Cross), outgoes Wesley's paradoxically temporal ideal. The Wanderer's creed sharpens what is already edgy in Evangelical Anglican doctrine (as distinct from the smoother edges of late-17th-century Latitudinarianism [New 27-35]).

The Pastor triangulates not Father, Son, and Holy Ghost, but Holy Ghost, Nature (shades of the Wanderer's Nature Methodized), and the Bible. "A creature," he teaches, is empowered

> to perceive
> The Voice of Deity, on height and plain
> Whispering those truths in stillness, which the WORD,
> To the four quarters of the winds, proclaims.
> (V 990-3)

What does this Spirit impart, if not His fruits (as in Rom 5:1-5)? When the Pastor's tales are completed, the Wanderer thanks the "gracious" minister for his evangelically kerygmatic, pragmatically literary

> words of heartfelt truth,
> Tending to patience, when affliction strikes;
> To hope and love; to confident repose
> In God; and reverence for the dust of man.
> (VII 1054-7; emphasis added)

The "genuine fruits of religion" (VI 80) comprise much of what the Pastor dispenses, but, if anything, his stories belabor the exertion of moral effort, if only to make up for Spirit/Nature overbalance in his theology.

Before telling his stories, the Pastor defines "Life" as "energy of love / Divine or human" (V 1012-3), and so, with six-word efficiency, he offers a dynamic, Romantic-era version of the balance between faith and works (recall Coleridge's perception of Methodism as energy).[14] The real-life characters the Pastor presents in his modern-day parables, his pre-Modern short stories, either violate or embrace grace/deeds standards. Sometimes these personae fail to recognize the Spirit's agency, and sometimes they revel in doing so. Sometimes they fall short of individual responsibility, and sometimes they rise to the moral occasion.[15] Their stories contain some of the worthiest, most unjustly neglected, poetry in *The Excursion*. At least as firmly as *The Prelude*, the churchyard tales rest on Wordsworth's assumption that experience and death are all-too-reliable teachers. These same stories, however, also form a crucial part of Wordsworth's plan for the Solitary's redemption. They constitute objectified *exempla* complementary to Wordsworth's more personal and more well-known, yet not necessarily better-understood or entirely different, testimonies of spiritual experience, which galvanize the subjective "spots of time" scattered throughout *The Prelude* (Brantley, *Wordsworth's* 37-65).

Some tales form negative examples; an anonymous widow, for instance, proudly relies on resolution apart from grace.[16] At times, despite her poverty, she vows to support her only son, and, to her credit, she faithfully honors this covenant: she not only "resolved" to be thrifty, but also "adhered to her resolve" (VI 720). More often, though, the widow's "trust / In ceaseless pains," without appearing to realize her dependence on God, leads her to grow "slack in alms-giving," or to lose sight of charity as her lodestar (VI 721-2). Her covenant resolve remains one-sided, unsupported by grace (like Michael's misguided trust in labor: Brantley, *Wordsworth's* 135-6). In the end, she becomes intolerant, unaccountably, of "peace" (VI 732). "Gentleness" eludes her (VI 732). And the fruits of the Spirit never return to her, until she lies on her deathbed, where unmerited favor, "divine mercy," descends on her at last, and bestows the gift of "meekness" (VI 738, 771).

Prominent among the Pastor's characters worthy of emulation is the deaf dalesman.[17] Like the lily of the field (Mt 6:28), he does not work for himself, for he trusts, instead, in forces larger than his efforts, and, with wise passiveness, he turns a deaf ear, spiritually speaking, to the alluring appeals of ownership (VI 423-7).[18] Unlike the docile lily, however, he practices the good works indicative of covenant resolve, for "duteously" he pursues "the round / Of rural labours" as a *pro bono* "fellow-labourer," with his farmer brother, in fields of more than natural harvest (VII 418-9, 436). As the dalesman grows older in the selfless service of providing food for others, he reads "holy Writ" (VII 451) and, though without physical hearing, ironically sharpens his inward senses to hear the "Voice"

> Announcing immortality and joy
> To the assembled spirits of just men
> Made perfect, and from injury secure.
> (VII 452-54)

The echo (of Heb 12:23) is Wordsworth's most explicit allusion to the doctrine of perfection, in its more orthodox, otherworldly form, but the dalesman hears the Voice now, reminiscent of Charles Wesley's "joy from heaven to earth come down."[19] The dalesman's life, revered by stragglers with ears to hear the Pastor, resounds with perfection "on earth as it is in heaven." A pine tree near his grave symbolizes his "sanctity" (VII 479). After his lifetime of covenant commitment, in the world but not of it, he is gathered into the heavenly assembly, an extension of "gathered church," covenant ecclesiology (Davies 154-8), where, the Pastor believes, he joins a visionary company of the broadly elect (shades of Wesley's victory over Calvinism?).

Ellen's story, the Pastor's longest and most affecting, builds on Wesley's distinction between "covenant of grace" and "covenant of works." The former allows errant souls to "retrieve the life of God" (Wesley V 70). The latter earns "*continuance* in the favour of God," and consists of "perfect and uninterrupted obedience to every point" of God's law (Wesley V 70; Wesley's emphasis). Following her conception of a child out of wedlock, Ellen receives a covenant of grace, and then constructs her covenant of works. From the evangelical point of view, and delicately in Wordsworth's, she is lost in sin, at first, but responds to divine prompting, and gradually develops sanctity. This sinner in the hands of a merciful God works her way through to perfect love. That is, her constant communion sheds solace on her in her times of trial. And her upright dealing transfigures all that dread.

The fruit of Ellen's "shame" (VI 848) brings forth, in turn, the fruits of God's Spirit. That is, grace abounds through Ellen's child, a gift of joy and thanksgiving (VI 908, 910, 916). These graces prove signs of the mother's new birth, as dramatic as the fruits of God's Spirit, to which Wordsworth refers in his conversion call to poetic vocation. Ellen's spiritual life, like that of an evangelical, commenced at a turning-point:

> "There was a stony region in my heart;
> But He, at whose command the parchèd rock
> Was smitten, and poured forth a quenching stream,
> Hath softened that obduracy, and made

> Unlooked-for gladness in the desert place,
> To save the perishing."
> (VI 918-23)

Ellen here endorses the Old Testament passage in which God takes pity on the thirsty and spiritually arid Israelites by endowing Moses with power to extract water from the rock on Horeb. In addition to this evocation of divine condescension, Ellen's heart/stone metaphor re-mystifies such a complex of biblical covenant imagery as that of Ezekiel, who anticipates the sequence of Wesley's "covenant of grace"/ "covenant of works" distinction—unmerited favor precedes scrupulous action. The people's "stony heart," as Ezekiel writes (in Yahweh's strongest voice of ethical monotheism), is replaced with a "heart of flesh," that, with the Spirit in them, they will "walk in my statutes, and . . . keep my judgments, and do them" (Ezek 36:26-7).

God's law is now written on Ellen's heart. She finishes the labor of childbirth but undertakes spiritual labor. She makes a "covenant of works" when she makes evident, soon after her redemptive experience, her moral rededication. First, she regrets that her mother's prayers for her had been "in vain" (VI 926). Then, she moves beyond self-reproach to resolution: "Yet not in vain: it shall not be in vain" (VI 927). The good faith of this new covenant is demonstrated by her subsequent conduct. Ellen begins to feel pangs of conscience about relying too much on her mother's "slender means" (VI 940). "With dutiful content," therefore, she finds employment as a "Foster-mother," a nurse (VI 947-8).

Afflictions test Ellen. Her employers allow no visits to her child (gender unspecified). The child becomes ill and—cruel resurrection reference—dies "within three days' space" (VI 967). Ellen's strength, though, endures. With no bitterness, she mourns "her own transgressions; penitent sincere / As ever raised to heaven a streaming eye!" (VI 990-1). Because of access to the graces, she remains resilient. At her lowest point, languishing without her child, she receives the fruits of the Spirit through the Pastor's agency:

> To me [the Pastor observes]
> As to a spiritual comforter and friend,
> Her heart she opened; and no pains were spared
> To mitigate as *gently* as I could,
> The sting of self-reproach with healing words.
> (VI 1029-33; Wordsworth's emphasis)

The Pastor does the Lord's work, here, with as much respect for his female parishioner as ever occurs, say, on the 18th-to-19th-century arc of minister/protégée relationships, a set of exchanges between men and women that began with Wesley and Mary Pendarves (later Delany), and which continued until 1882 or so.[20]

As Ellen nears her death, other graces are manifested in her life. These bear witness to her realized perfection, as indicated by the Pastor's tribute: "Meek Saint! Through patience glorified on earth!" (VI 1034; emphasis added). Of course, even for evangelicals, "realized perfection" seems doctrinally unsound. Although Ellen's fictional forerunner Clarissa is also thought to be purified in her death, Richardson knows, theologically, that this is always a hope, not a certainty. Still, as oddly as this early-19th-century "fallen woman" story may strike postmodern ears, the Pastor's deportment toward her scarcely patronizes her, and with similarly Wesleyan resonance the temporality of Ellen's Christian perfection, too, comes across as Romantic. Like the dalesman (unnamed but influential), Ellen leaves the legacy of her "sanctity," which broods over her grave "till the stars sicken at the day of doom" (VI 804-5). Her story, close to Wordsworth's heart, does not just further occlude his already-veiled allusion to Annette Vallon, but grows out of his spiritual autobiography. His progress, since *The Prelude* recounts grace acquired and deeds both dared and done, adumbrates Ellen's.

The experiential theology of the Wanderer and of the Pastor alike heightens Book IX. In one paragraph (IX 206-54), the Wanderer epitomizes the conviction that he introduced and elaborated in Books I and IV, what Wordsworth (in Argument, Book VIII) calls "changes in the Country," will result from the reunification of God's Spirit and man's charity. The Wanderer expects that "the Almighty" will grant "power," "truth," "hope," and "gratitude" to each citizen, whether "proudly graced" or "meek of heart" (IX 217, 230, 233, 249). Notwithstanding how roundly Nietzsche would condemn such ordinary grace, such "meekness] of heart," and call it the impotence of slave morality, he would no doubt find something to like in "proudly graced," but could he resist reducing sturdy, grounded credo to mere master morality? Probably not, but in any case, one may hear in the Wanderer's accent, which is as far as possible from Calvinism for the few, the theological equivalent of 18th-to-19th-century political thought: "Here," the Wanderer declares, "is no boon / For high—yet not for low" but, instead, the "true equality" among souls, whereby "the smoke ascends / To heaven as lightly from the cottage hearth / As from the haughtiest palace" (IX 243-8).[21] Because of their "freedom in the will," their Arminius- rather than Calvin-comprehended "Conscience," people can know that "primal duties" are "charities that soothe, and heal, and bless" (IX 222-4, 237-9). With superhuman aid, as well as through their own efforts, people can achieve "holiness *on earth*" (IX 227; emphasis added) and, by these same tokens, can be "assured" of "heaven" (IX 228). Is the smugness of the Wanderer's moral vision here rendered less overwhelming, if not exactly more appealing, by his echo of the "blessed assurance" sung by Methodists whose unaffected joy—how pretty to think so!—would endear them to the curmudgeonly, if mellowing, "cultured despiser"?

Here is how the Pastor, at any rate, brings things to a close. He leads his wife, his son and daughter, the Wanderer, the Solitary, and the Poet to the top of a hill, where they watch a "less than ordinary" sunset (IX 591). Though the scene would appear to represent no more than a commonplace lectionary of Nature's Book, the Pastor is moved, nonetheless, to offer a prayer as ordinary and extraordinary in expression and effects as he feels the fruits of the Spirit can be. Wondering whether such common graces as "hope," "righteousness," "peace," "love," and "faith" will suffice for "triumph over sin and guilt," the Pastor asks the "Eternal Spirit! Universal God!" for fresh dispensation of His uncommon Spirit's witness:

> Almighty Lord, thy further grace impart!
> And with that help the wonder shall be seen
> Fulfilled, the hope accomplished; and thy praise
> Be sung with transport and unceasing joy.
> (IX 614, 663-5, 674-8)

The Pastor seeks here just what the political Wordsworth hopes for—that in the long years the promise, and not the Terror, of the French Revolution will prevail (the Pastor comes as close as the Solitary, here, to the revolutionary strain of *The Excursion*). In a spirit of cultivating one's garden, the Pastor's expression of "joy" and "fervent gratitude" subverts Calvinism (IX 74). His "little band / Gathered together," his "gathered-church," covenant ecclesiology, comprises the true "elect of earth," including the "very poorest," who grow "rich in peace of thought [an ordinary grace] / And in good works" (IX 729-30, 734-5; emphasis added). The Pastor concludes that he "who is endowed / With scantiest knowledge" is "master of all truth / Which the salvation of his soul requires" (IX 735-7): this religious self-sufficiency proves central to Wordsworth's Low-Church Romanticism (which honors women, too).

Wordsworth's originality after the "great decade" consists in intuiting what Emily Dickinson knows—"Retrospection is Prospect's half— / Sometimes, almost more—."[22] The bearing of the poet's religious background on the natural imagery of *The Excursion* and, at much greater length, on its neglected but central theme of spiritual experience, has been the subject matter here. Beyond Wordsworth's continuing commitment to create a new myth about the mind's role in nature, his awareness of the soul's place there, is both heightened and overmatched by his celebration of the "rise and progress of *religion* in the soul," quite apart from natural experience alone.[23] Could the saving power of faith *versus* the testimony of good works rank as the most "stupendous antagonism" Wordsworth ever contributes to Romantic-era religious contraries?[24] Yes, for the faith/works opposition of the 18th-to-19th-century Calvinist/Arminian controversy—predestination (or election) *versus* free will (or soul competence)—makes *The Excursion* breathe. Its *dramatis personae* reenact conversion, reciprocal covenant between the Spirit of God and the heart of humankind, and practical charity. Through all this updating of the evangelical tradition, the exhilarating, near-unorthodox Wesleyan strivings for Christian perfection in this life punctuate the equilibrium, set off the exalted humility, of *The Excursion*. By staging strange, yet not unreasonable holiness and familiar, yet not unthoughtful compassion, *The Excursion* takes its signature opposition from the "fine spiritual chaos" of the age, promotes that considered doublet to a profoundly theological status of classical Romanticism, and culminates Wordsworth's art of belief.[25]

The Excursion lives, then, but does it live up to Wordsworth's high opinion of it? Perhaps, if, on the ground of familiar encounter, his settled edifice houses the unseen with the seen, or embodies the spiritual by hallowing the natural. Perhaps, if *The Excursion* salves the belief/experience split. Perhaps, if, through the power of its exalted humility, this High-to-Low-Church-Romantic *tour de force* tempers hope-against-hope for the hereafter with hope-after-hope for the here-and-now. Perhaps, finally, whether or not the Christianity of *The Excursion* is too "cautious" (Bostetter 32) or too "heterodox" (Lyon 113), if *The Excursion* is as it appears—Wordsworth's most historically aware, best-thought-out contribution to the transcendental mode of Anglo-American Romanticism (see Barth; Harvey). The argument for this classic of Romanticism can thus be high. *The Prelude* is secure, of course. Still, *The Excursion* ranks well, as Wordsworth's savviest jump-start of the increasingly challenged, yet just possibly all-seasonal, divine/human dynamic.

As Jeffrey and Lamb indicate, the evangelically evocative Wordsworth harks back, in particular, to Wesley. To say little of his "heart strangely warmed" (he thought by the Holy Spirit), he mixes the loving care and stern discipline that foreshadow that very *Excursion* dichotomy. If the later Wordsworth's outward, hands-on stance tilts toward good works, as distinct from faith exclusively, then so be it, but his Natural-Methodist dialogue of epic proportions thrives. The evangelical-biblical paradox of *The Excursion* energizes its sometimes alternating, and sometimes merging, inflow and outreach. With a little help from his friends in the Religious Enlightenment, Wordsworth does not resolve, yet drives, the faith-over-works, works-over-faith rhythm of his art. In their introduction to a 1979 special issue of *The Wordsworth Circle*, on British Romantic fiction, Gene W. Ruoff and L. J. Swingle observe, "Probably when our unified field theory of British Romanticism finally arrives, the materials will be somewhat nearer at hand than either the distant past of Milton or the far future of Joyce. . . . Thinking about British Romanticism primarily in connection with the 18th century may not taste quite so sublime to our intellectual palates; but perhaps our taste has become a bit depraved" (130). Wordsworth's perspective on 18th-century evangelicalism goes well beyond Sense and Sensibility, the "Reason and Feeling" of the revival, to identify faith *versus* works as the leading variety, the oddly empirically axiomatic theorem, of Romantic-era religious experience.

 The main structure of Wordsworth's gothic church is a pretty piece of ecclesiastical sublimity, his revised standard version of Romantic scripture, and perhaps even the proof text of his own religious faith. His harking back to old-time religion and desire for the life everlasting remain in play in his de-familiarization of religious contrarieties. This combination of nostalgia and yearning depends more on the Protestant-sacramental circumstances of his evangelical heritage than on the naturalized grace of early-19th-century artistry. His individual talent hastens and would welcome the death of Calvinism, poetically announced by Oliver Wendell Holmes in "The Wonderful One-Hoss Shay" (1858). Yet he mines, for his art of belief, the Arminian faith of his evangelical fathers and mothers.

 In sum, key passages of *The Excursion* echo and reecho with the difficult but fascinating theology that forms the poet's birthright, stirs his both/and logic, and stiffens the resolve of his latter-day, yet scarcely wan, Romanticism. Such a stylistic dividend as the deliberate interplay of his didactic strengths and the deceptive simplicity of his extended parables confronts and bids fair to bridge the biblical impasse of one mode of redemption *versus* the other. The mature Wordsworth "wages peace" among such inward estrangements as fervor *versus* doubt, contests and tests for reconciliation among such outward imponderables as empathy *versus* moral demand, and converts expectation of blessing and effort of lovingkindness to absolute desire. He lets the theological conundrum of inspiration *versus* obligation deepen his poetic faith. He offers scant humor in the otherwise sufficiently complex satisfactions of his biblically comedic, un-spilled, Romantic religion. But as he broods over spiritual chaos, he achieves theistic and moral optimism. And he delays attenuated hope.

NOTES

[1] Preface to *The Excursion* in Wordsworth, *Works* V 2. Hereafter cited in the text. Many thanks go to Marilyn Gaull, David Moltke-Hansen, and Jacob Risinger for their editorial help.

[2] Lundin's title applies to Wordsworth's case. For Wordsworth's traditional belief even during the "great decade," Ryan; Ulmer. For Wordsworth as prime architect of literary Gothicism, Duggett.

[3] Qtd. in Gill 169. Coleridge adds that this Wesley-like "Faith is as real as life; as actual as force; as effectual as volition. It is the physics of the moral being." For Coleridge's interest in Methodism, Brantley, *Locke* 160-8.

[4] Lamb's letter to Wordsworth laments that the editor of *The Quarterly*, William Gifford, left out the "natural Methodism" section of Lamb's review of *The Excursion*: "I regret only that I did not keep a copy" (*Letters* II:149). Lamb tells Wordsworth how much he would have liked that now-irrecoverable characterization: "I am sure you would have been pleased with it, because I have been feeding my fancy for some months with the notion of pleasing you" (*Letters* II:149). Lamb's clue is bare, yet strangely identifying. This essay expands on, and seeks to unify, scattered views in Brantley, *Wordsworth's* 110-24, 140-2, 151-2, 156-8, 160-1.

[5] In "A Plain Account of Christian Perfection," Wesley writes: "We are to expect [Christian perfection] not at death, but at every moment: . . . now is the accepted time, now is the day of this salvation" (*Works* XI 393).

[6] Kelsey L. Bennett brings German Pietism, British Methodism, and the American Great Awakening to bear on such avatars of *Bildungsroman* as Goethe, Brontë, Dickens, Melville, and James. For *The Excursion* as a "metrical novel," Gravil. Wesley associates "purity of intention" with "renewal of the heart in the whole image of God, the full likeness of him that created it" and with "loving God with all our heart, and our neighbors as ourselves" (*Works* XI 444).

[7] Overcome by his memory of Margaret's poverty and suffering, the Wanderer overlooks the summer leaves at her abandoned cottage and sees only the

"Shrouded" cottage-yard (I 462). Fixated on a strangely memorable detail—"the useless fragment of a wooden bowl" (I 493)—he grows horrified by her broken life and remains haunted by her death. Soon remembering her spiritual strength, though, he curbs his melancholy: "How foolish are such thoughts! / Forgive them" (I 496-7). Then, for more than 400 lines of skillful blank verse, he recounts her faithful endurance (I 511-916). Does his narrative lag where it imputes to Margaret "a Christian piety which is conventional rather than deeply realized?" (Abrams, *Norton* 1.285; Abrams *Natural*). Or, is Margaret's "Christian piety" poetically functional, justifying a hope only vaguely expressed in the original version of her story (1799)? Whether Wordsworth's revision brings out a religious point of view, or merely brings one on, the Wanderer's afterword to her tale (I 917-56) suspends one's disbelief. Even one's inner atheist, among other contained multitudes, may savor the Wanderer's discovery, not just of "Christian piety," but of sacramental mediation in the Second Book of God.

[8] "Poetry" (1923) by Marianne Moore. Quotations of British authors, unless otherwise indicated, are from Damrosch et al., eds.

[9] Wesley's practical charity is the very model of such tested integrity. For the plain moral decency of every day, the weariness of earnest, steadfast well-doing, Milton's language in *Areopagitica* (1644) proves *nonpareil*. This address to Parliament (hence the Mars Hill title) on liberty of conscience anticipates the various Protestant Evangelical voices of a free-will, Arminian stripe heard, or overheard, by Wordsworth. For the influence of Jacobus Arminius's theology on Milton, see Fallon.

[10] Wordsworth writes of the Wanderer, "The Scottish Church, both on himself and those / With whom from childhood he grew up, had held / The strong hand of her purity; and still / Had watched him with an unrelenting eye" (I 397-400).

[11] "The intrinsic sufficiency of minimal experiences" (François 3) is as much a 19th-century feature of religious as of secular imagination. In the passage quoted above, the ordinary witness is more important than the extraordinary (cf. Brantley, *Wordsworth's* 81-93, 115-6).

[12] Thus, whether or not the Wanderer here puts forward the Romantic equivalent of Christian perfection on earth, Book IV advocates covenant agreement between God and man, a bond not unlike Wordsworth's metaphorically, if not actually, religious call to poetic vocation—"else sinning greatly"—during the summer of 1788.

[13] For the growing importance of the baptismal sacrament among Dissenting and Anglican evangelicals alike, see (framing "the Religious Enlightenment"

[Brantley, *Locke* 215-8]) Matthew Henry, *Baptismal Covenant* (1713) and Robert Robinson, *History of Baptism* (1790). As early as Books IV and V of *The Excursion*, the Solitary grasps I-thou fundamentals as Wesley, too, understands them (*Directions for Renewing Our Covenant with God* [1780]).

[14] The Wanderer depicts an unnamed but name-worthy Lake Country vicar of his acquaintance as a man of "resolution," "temperance," and "industry severe," in whom "all generous feelings flourish and rejoice" (VII 323-4, 328, 330). The vicar, "A labourer, with moral virtue girt, / With spiritual graces, like a glory, crowned" (VII 337-9), reverses the sequence of, yet reflects, the Wanderer's balance between reliance on grace and righteous effort. The vicar serves, as well, to introduce the Pastor. The Pastor's life reflects "the sanctity of elder times" (VI 76), and, by his light, all such perfected life will "pass, / Through shades and silent rest, to endless joy" (V 1012-16). This language, with its emphasis on perfection hereafter, is more orthodox, for once, than the temporal orientation of Wesley's most characteristic doctrine.

[15] For a contrast between Wordsworth's ethics, which emphasize personal relationships (as well as particular things), and the utilitarian norms of Mill and Bentham, see Potkay. For a comparison between Wordsworth's and Levinas's ethics, see Haney.

[16] The speaker in "Resolution and Independence" (1802) is tempted by this excess, yet waits on grace (Brantley, *Wordsworth's* 127-32). Another of the Pastor's negative *exempla* is Wilfred Armathwaite, who willfully resists redemption by grace (VI 1073-114). The Pastor's *exempla* find counterparts in the middle ages as well as in Jackson's *Lives*.

[17] The tale of a miner in search of "precious ore" (VI 217) stirs the Wanderer's desire that God would "Grant to the wise *his* firmness of resolve!" (VI 212-61, esp. 217, 261; Wordsworth's emphasis). A widower with "six fair Daughters" (VI 1129) also earns praise from the Pastor.

[18] Are Thomas Carlyle's strictures against the Goddess of Getting On evangelically tinged, as well? Brantley, *Coordinates* 45-51.

[19] Brantley, "Charles"; Brantley, *Wordsworth's* 38-41; and Brantley, *Locke* 163-8.

[20] For the intellectual as well as emotional, gender-revolutionary friendship between Wesley and Mrs. Pendarves, see Brantley, *Locke* 103-5, 111-6, 205. This focus is supplemented by Molly Peacock's account of Mrs. Delany as a collage or flower-mosaic artist. Ann Douglas offers a pioneering perspective on the "feminization" of English-language "culture" through just such minister/protégée relationships (e.g., Emerson and Margaret Fuller). One effect of this new language is the intellectual as well as emotional, poetically important

friendship between Wesley-admiring Reverend Charles Wadsworth (1814-1882) and Emily Dickinson (Brantley, *Emily* 187-99). 1882 is the date of the paradigm-ending, more-sexual-than-intellectual affair between the Rev. Henry Ward Beecher and Elizabeth Tilton (Applegate).

[21] The Arminian ascendancy in Romantic Anglo-America supplements such understandings of political development as those of Hatch and Crumbley.

[22] See the discussion of Dickinson's "This was in the White of the Year—" in Brantley, *Emily* 100, 105, 146-8, 156, 159.

[23] The above quotation is from a title (1742) by Congregational hymn writer, theologian, and educator Philip Doddridge.

[24] For Emerson's phrase for Romantic-era "Contraries" (Blake's word; Wordsworth's is "contrarieties"), see Wilson's understanding that such binaries provide psycho-social energy for balancing competing truth-claims.

[25] "Fine spiritual chaos" plays on the "fine mental chaos" that Thomas Love Peacock finds so absorbing throughout his buoyantly satirical prose (Brantley, *Experience* 12).

WORKS CITED

Abrams, M. H. *Natural Supernaturalism: Tradition and Revolution in Romantic Literature.* W. W. Norton, 1971;

---------, ed. *The Norton Anthology of English Literature: Major Authors Edition.* W. W. Norton, 1968;

Applegate, Debby. *The Most Famous Man in America: The Biography of Henry Ward Beecher.* Doubleday, 2006;

Austen, Jane. *Jane Austen's Letters.* Ed. Deirdre Le Faye. Pavilion Press, 2003;

Barth, J. Robert, S. J. *Romanticism and Transcendence: Wordsworth, Coleridge, and the Religious Imagination.* University of Missouri Press, 2003;

Bennett, Kelsey L. *Principle and Propensity: Experience and Religion in the Nineteenth-Century British and American Bildungsroman.* University of South Carolina Press, 2014;

Bloom, Harold. *The American Religion: The Emergence of the Post-Christian Nation.* Simon and Schuster, 1992;

Bostetter, Edward E. *The Romantic Ventriloquists: Wordsworth, Coleridge, Keats, Shelley, and Byron.* University of Washington Press, 1963;

Brantley, Richard E. *Anglo-American Antiphony: The Late Romanticism of Tennyson and Emerson.* University Press of Florida, 1994;

---------. "Charles Wesley's Experiential Art." *Eighteenth-Century Life* 11 (May 1987): 1-11;

---------. *Coordinates of Anglo-American Romanticism: Wesley, Edwards, Carlyle, and Emerson.* University Press of Florida, 1993;

---------. *Emily Dickinson's Rich Conversation: Poetry, Philosophy, Science.* Palgrave Macmillan, 2013;

---------. *Experience and Faith: The Late-Romantic Imagination of Emily Dickinson.* Palgrave Macmillan, 2004;

---------. *Locke, Wesley, and the Method of English Romanticism.* University Press of Florida, 1984;

---------. *Wordsworth's "Natural Methodism."* Yale University Press, 1975;

Crumbley, Paul. *Winds of Will: Emily Dickinson and the Sovereignty of Democratic Thought.* University of Alabama Press, 2010;

Damrosch, David et al., eds. *The Longman Anthology of British Literature: First Edition.* 2 vols. Longman, 1999;

Davies, Horton. *Worship and Theology in England from Watts and Wesley to Maurice, 1690-1850.* Princeton University Press, 1961;

Doddridge, Philip. *The Rise and Progress of Religion in the Soul.* J. Waugh, 1742;

Douglas, Ann. *The Feminization of American Culture.* Knopf, 1977;

Duggett, Tom. *Gothic Romanticism: Architecture, Politics, and Literary Form.* Palgrave Macmillan, 2013;

Fallon, Stephen M. "Milton's Arminianism and the Authorship of *De Doctrina Christiana*." *Texas Studies in Literature and Language* 41.2 (Summer 1999): 103-27;

François, Anne-Lise. *Open Secrets: The Literature of Uncounted Experience.* Stanford University Press, 2008;

Gill, F. C. *The Romantic Movement and Methodism: A Study of English Romanticism and the Evangelical Revival.* Epworth Press, 1937;

Gravil, Richard. "Is *The Excursion* a Metrical Novel?" *The Wordsworth Circle* 42.2 (2011): 31-6;

Haney, David P. *William Wordsworth and the Hermeneutics of Incarnation.* Pennsylvania State University Press, 1993;

Harvey, Samantha C. *Transatlantic Transcendentalism: Coleridge, Emerson, and Nature.* University of Edinburgh Press, 2013;

Hatch, Nathan O. *The Democratization of American Christianity.* Yale University Press, 1989;

Henry, Matthew. *The Celebration of Infant-Baptism among Protestant Dissenters.* W. Turner, 1747;

Jackson, Thomas, ed. *The Lives of Early Methodist Preachers.* 2d ed. 3 vols. Mason, 1846;

Jeffrey, Francis. "Wordsworth's *Excursion.*" *The Edinburgh Review, or Critical Journal* 24 (November 1814): 14;

Lamb, Charles. *The Letters of Charles Lamb.* Ed. E. V. Lucas. 2 vols. J. M. Dent, 1935;

Leverenz, David. *The Language of Puritan Feeling: An Exploration in Literature, Psychology, and Social History.* Rutgers University Press, 1980;

Lundin, Roger. *Emily Dickinson and the Art of Belief.* Eerdmans, 1998;

Lyon, J. S. *The Excursion: A Study.* Yale University Press, 1950;

New, Melvyn. Introduction, 1-44. *The Sermons of Laurence Sterne: The Notes.* Vol. 5 of *The Florida Edition of the Works of Laurence Sterne.* Ed. Melvyn New. University Press of Florida, 1996;

Peacock, Molly. *The Paper Garden: Mrs. Delany Begins Her Life's Work at 72.* McClellan & Stewart, 2010;

Potkay, Adam. *Wordsworth's Ethics.* The Johns Hopkins University Press, 2012;

Robinson, Robert. *A History of Baptism.* R. Edwards, 1790;

Ruef, Martin. "Strong Ties, Weak Ties and Islands: Structural and Cultural Predictors of Organizational Innovation." *Industrial and Corporate Change* 11 (2002): 427-49;

Ruoff, Gene W. and L. J. Swingle. "From the Editors." *The Wordsworth Circle* 10 (Spring 1979): 130;

Ryan, Robert M. *The Romantic Reformation: Religious Politics in English Literature, 1789-1824.* Cambridge University Press, 1997;

Schleiermacher, Friedrich. *On Religion: Speeches to Its Cultured Despisers.* Ed. John Oman. Harper, 1958;

Stillinger, Jack. *The Hoodwinking of Madeleine, and Other Essays on Keats's Poems.* University of Illinois Press, 1971;

Ulmer, William A. *The Christian Wordsworth: 1798-1805.* State University of New York Press, 2001;

Watts, Isaac. *The Works of the Reverend and Learned Isaac Watts, D. D.* 6 vols. Barfield, 1810-11;

Wesley, John. *Directions for Renewing Our Covenant with God.* 1780. 5th ed. W. Pine, 1790;

---------. *The Works of the Rev. John Wesley, A. M.* Ed. Thomas Jackson. 14 vols. 1829-31. Reprint. Zondervan, 1958;

Wilson, Eric G. Review of Richard E. Brantley, *Emily Dickinson's Rich Conversation. Review 19*, 2013;

Wordsworth, William. *The Letters of William and Dorothy Wordsworth: The Early Years, 1787-1805*. Ed. Ernest de Selincourt. 2d ed. rev. by Chester L. Shaver. Clarendon Press, 1967;

———. *The Poetical Works of William Wordsworth*. Eds. Ernest de Selincourt and Helen Darbishire. Clarendon Press, 1940-9.

10. *Keats's Method*

KEATS'S ATTRACTION TO COEXISTENCE BETWEEN EMPIRICISM and grace helps to account for his nostalgia for the latter and for the presence of the two in his poetry: empiricism and grace, together, make up the experiential richness of his poetic world. The next step, in other words, for those who study Keats is to explore his "skepticism" and "religion of beauty" in relation to one other.[1] Robert M. Ryan, in *Keats: The Religious Sense*, re-examines Keats's intellectual milieu and establishes, as never before, his respect and admiration for religious points of view as well as for "scientific empiricism."[2] What needs further investigation is how far Keats's allegiance to induction combines with his Methodist-like, and hence equally experiential, allegiance to the "holiness of the Heart's affections."[3] In his sensibility, I look for a Romantic version of John Wesley's theology of experience, i.e., his both/and logic of empiricism and grace. Keats was not able to reconcile, as Wesley did, the Lockean "theory of mind" with "the possibility of . . . supernatural influences on the personality,"[4] but Keats was at last like Wesley and like Locke in being alternately, or even at once, tough-minded and tender-minded.

This alternation, if not this simultaneity, is evident from the beginning of Keats's career. Consider, first, his early "naturalism," i.e., his imitation of usual natural surroundings; poetry of earth, distinct, say, from poetry of mind, or for that matter from anything else ideal, occurs in a poem at once one of his most naturalistic and one of his earliest:

> The poetry of earth is never dead:
> When all the birds are faint with the hot sun,
> And hide in cooling trees, a voice will run
> From hedge to hedge about the new-mown mead;
> That is the Grasshopper's—he takes the lead

> In summer luxury,—he has never done
> With his delights; for when tired out with fun
> He rests at ease beneath some pleasant weed.
> The poetry of earth is ceasing never:
> On a lone winter evening, when the frost
> Has wrought a silence, from the stove there shrills
> The Cricket's song, in warmth increasing ever,
> And seems to one in drowsiness half lost,
> The Grasshopper's among some grassy hills.
>   ("On the Grasshopper and the Cricket"; December, 1816)

"To My Brother George" (1817) includes among "the living pleasures of the bard" "the mysteries" not of the supernatural, but simply of nature's "night":

> ... the dark, silent blue
> With all its diamonds trembling through and through,
> Or the coy moon, when in the waviness
> Of whitest clouds she does her beauty dress,
> And staidly paces higher up, and higher.
>   (ll. 57-61, 67)

Keats adds, however, that the moon is "like a sweet nun in holy-day attire" (l. 62), and as though remembering the sky as symbol of transcendence, he stresses the thoroughly transcendental, and indeed religious, message uttered by the dying bard:

> "What though I leave this dull, and earthly mould,
> Yet shall my spirit lofty converse hold
> With after times ....
> The sage will mingle with each moral theme
> My happy thoughts sententious; he will teem
> With lofty periods when my verses fire him,
> And then I'll stoop from heaven to inspire him."
>   (ll. 71-73, 77-80)

Even "On the Grasshopper and the Cricket," balancing a faint concept of flesh as grass with a consoling (albeit natural kind of) immortality, is not without idealistic coloration.

In the early poetry, indeed, the ideal gets the better lines and hence the greater degree of Keats's involvement. Although the emphasis in "Sleep and Poetry" (1817), lies upon poetry not as mediator of otherworldly truth but rather as at once "a lovely tale of human life" (l. 110) and "a friend / To soothe the cares, and lift the thoughts of man" (ll. 246-47), it should be remembered that the latter function, at least, is as humanistic as earthly. "I Stood Tip-toe," published in 1817, is effective only when transcendental in tone; the following passage, for example, resting upon the traditional allegorization of the love between Endymion and Cynthia as "the celestial contemplation of an astronomer"[5] and containing speculations about the divine origin of that myth, is perhaps Keats's most triumphant and certainly one of his most untroubled affirmations of the ideal:

> Where had he been, from whose warm head out-flew
> That sweetest of all songs, that ever new,
> That aye refreshing, pure deliciousness,
> Coming ever to bless
> The wanderer by moonlight? to him bringing
> Shapes from the invisible world, unearthly singing
> From out the middle air, from flowery nests,
> And from the pillowy silkiness that rests
> Full in the speculation of the stars.
> Ah! surely he had burst our mortal bars;
> Into some wond'rous region he had gone,
> To search for thee, divine Endymion!
>   (ll. I 81-92)

"Full in the speculation of the stars," blending concrete with abstract diction, well represents how poets have traditionally evoked the transcendent: Douglas Bush seems right in his edition of the poems and letters when he describes the passage as a "direct statement of Keats's—and other romantic poets'—central quest, the attaining, through the imagination, of supra-human or supra-rational intuitions of spiritual reality" (p. 310). The passage's non-rational but not anti-rational tone, its references to blessing, singing, and, above all, the invisible world, bespeaks apprehension of spiritual reality, and theism is overt in the lines, elsewhere in the poem, that employ an idiom of natural religion: "For what has made the sage or poet write / But the fair paradise of Nature's light?" (ll. 125-26).

Ideal and actual find simultaneous expression in a familiar passage from *Endymion* (1817). These sixty-five lines, namely, I.777-842, "helped a little to redeem *Endymion*, in [Keats's] own opinion, as he tried energetically to turn to other writing."⁶ I quote enough of this long passage to make my point.

The ideal, therein, is expressed at times with a deliciousness all too characteristic of the early Keats. The passage's characteristically Keatsean mythological allusiveness, moreover, expresses a more Hellenic than Hebraic ideal. And the question "Wherein lies happiness?" (l. 777) is far indeed both from the traditional question of eternal life and from the then especially timely question of salvation.

Keats's answer to this question, however, is not only one of the most generally transcendental but also one of the most particularly religious passages in all his poetry:

> In that which becks
> Our ready minds to fellowship divine,
> A fellowship with essence; till we shine,
> Full alchemiz'd, and free of space. Behold
> The clear religion of heaven! ...
> Feel we these things?—that moment have we stept
> Into a sort of oneness, and our state
> Is like a floating spirit's.
>   (ll. 777-81, 795-97)

These lines, in fact, are evangelical in tone. Note, for example, Keats's emphasis on man's spiritual state, his reliance on emotion as access to faith, his use of such words as "shine," and such phrases as "religion of heaven" and "fellowship divine," and, not least, his announcement of immediate revelation: "Behold the clear religion of heaven!" Whatever "becks / Our ready minds," of course, is not anything so evangelical as the Holy Spirit. But, since "Ghosts of melodious prophecyings rave / Round every spot where trod Apollo's foot" (ll. 789-90), poetry substitutes for, if not gives access to, spiritual inspiration. And, even when Keats describes as happiness's "chief intensity" not communion with the Ghost of God so much as cultivation of such secular and humanist values as "love and friendship" (ll. 800-1), he recommends them in terms generally spiritual and specifically evangelical. "Love," for example, like graces emanating from the Spirit, sheds "influence" (l. 807), and thereby engenders "a novel sense" (l. 808) reminiscent, if not conscious, of the "spiritual sense" in Wesleyan lore.[7] "Friendship," like the Spirit and the twice-born soul, sends out "steady splendour" (ll. 804-5). And in Keats's lines on love alone—

>   . . . [I]n the end,
> Melting into its radiance, we blend,
> Mingle, and so become a part of it . . . .
> . . . [L]ove, although 'tis understood
> The mere commingling of passionate breath,
> Produce[s] more than our searching witnesseth:
>   (ll. 812-14, 835-37)

—is a particularly tender-minded sense of mystery, if not a "Wesleyan" interpenetration of subject and object: *witnesseth*, *searching*, and *radiance* suffuse with especially evangelical ideality the otherwise exclusively natural *love* of which Keats speaks.

The empirical complement to such a peculiarly English form of the transcendental is conveyed, for example, by the methodological idiom implicit in "Full alchemiz'd" (l. 780): over the notion of alchemy hovers an analogy between a supernatural "science" and experimental chemistry. Keats felt, as he wrote the sixty-five lines, "a regular stepping of the Imagination towards a Truth," and after he wrote them, he felt "set before me at once the gradations of Happiness even like a kind of Pleasure Thermometer."[8] An instrument of science, then, though not such a measure of spiritual experience as Wesley's "spiritual sense," serves metaphorically to measure something equally subjective. Keats, to be sure, favors love and friendship over the transcendental experience of "oneness" (l. 796): "But there are / Richer entanglements" (ll. 797-98). But the passage as a whole, like the thermometer-image, suggests that the contrast between supernatural mystery on the one hand, and love and friendship on the other, is of two different places along a continuum from natural to spiritual experience, rather than of two different concepts, one fruitful and one deluded.

On March 25, 1818, Keats wrote "Epistle to John Hamilton Reynolds," which, though never intended for publication, constitutes, nonetheless, a concentration of Keats's frame of mind at mid-career. Stuart Sperry is certainly right to describe Keats's final lines, in particular, as "uncompromisingly realistic and anti-romantic":[9]

>   ... '[T]was a quiet eve,
> The rocks were silent, the wide sea did weave
> An untumultuous fringe of silver foam
> Along the flat brown sand; I was at home
> And should have been most happy,—but I saw
> Too far into the sea, where every maw
> The greater on the less feeds evermore.—
> But I saw too distinct into the core
> Of an eternal fierce destruction,
> And so from happiness I far was gone.
> Still am I sick of it, and tho', to-day,
> I've gathered young spring-leaves, and flowers gay
> Of periwinkle and wild strawberry,
> Still do I that most fierce destruction see,—
> The shark at savage prey,—the hawk at pounce,—
> The gentle robin, like a pard or ounce,
> Ravening a worm,—Away ye horrid moods!
> Moods of one's mind! You know I hate them well.
> You know I'd rather be a clapping bell
> To some Kamschatkan missionary church,
> Than with these horrid moods be left i' the lurch.—
>   (ll. 89-109)

The "Epistle," though, is not entirely without an idealistic answer to the question of art's function. The realism of the lines just quoted, for example, is softened immediately thereafter: "I'll dance, / And from detested moods in new romance / Take refuge" (ll. 110-12). Earlier, in lines anticipating the nature of such "new romance" as "Isabella; or, The Pot of Basil" and "The Eve of St. Agnes," is an interplay of actual and ideal:

>   O that our dreamings all of sleep or wake,
> Would all their colours from the sunset take:
> From something of material sublime,
> Rather than shadow our own soul's day-time
> In the dark void of night. For in the world
> We jostle ....
>   (ll. 67-72)

The "Epistle," then, constitutes an inclusive version of Keats's thought.

Material sublime, as Sperry points out (p. 126), expresses "the desire of the imagination to possess the best of both worlds, the ethereal and the concrete," and this desire yields the accommodation achieved in the best of Keats's poetry. With regard to the "Epistle," of course, concrete finally outweighs ethereal: the "Epistle" is everywhere uneasy about the "drift" of art "into one-sidedness and subjectivity," i.e., about art's "continued tendency to refine away too much that is fundamental to our general awareness of life" (Sperry, p. 126). The "fullness or complexity" of Keats's "condition of awareness," writes Sperry (p. 125), "exceeds the powers of any particular work of art to harmonize or satisfy." At few points can Keats be said ever to have slighted the "wealth of human knowledge and experience that provides the substratum of all aesthetic apprehension" (Sperry, p. 125). But a species of transcendentalism is traceable even in the methodologically rigorous and intellectually uncompromising "Epistle." For Wesley's thought parallels and helps to gloss this assimilation of idealism within preponderating awareness of actuality. With regard, in other words, not only to the "Epistle," but also to the other poems, I suggest (1) that Keats's imagination was often able "to possess the best of both worlds," and (2) that the way in which it did so amounted to his version of the sufficiently transcendental, or at any rate variously ideal, and at the same time quasi-empirical "sense-perception" to be found in Wesleyan sensibility.

The point, of course, is not to claim that Methodism was a source of the poetry. Nor is it my purpose to argue that Methodism directly influenced Keats. His transcendentalism came, in part, from Plato.[10] And Keats's empiricism came from Locke. Methodism, however, was decidedly "in the air," and can be invoked not only on the side of Keats's transcendentalism, and of his empiricism, but also of them both together, on their experiential common ground. The experiential theology of Wesley, in other words, is an especially timely, especially near, and especially inclusive means of glossing the mix of tough and tender to be found in Keats's work, for Keats's point of view included not only a peculiarly English form of transcendentalism, and not only a peculiarly English form of the naturalistic, but also a peculiarly English dialectic of the two, and no one more than Wesley provides so heuristic, so close an analogue to that dialectic. Keats, in his characteristic state of Negative Capability, "when man is capable of being in uncertainties, Mysteries, doubts, without any irritable reaching after fact & reason,"[11] was in one sense further than any other romantic poet from direct contact with and sympathy for the certainties of Wesleyan fundamentalism, but, in another sense, and for the very same reason of Negative Capability, he was even closer than any other to certain aspects of Wesleyan method. Wesley showed himself capable of skeptical method, or uncertainties and doubts, precisely because *Mystery* with a capital *M*—not mysticism so much as *Mysterium Tremendum*—was for him at the center of all experience, both mental and physical, and Wesley is like Keats, too, in mastering "fact & reason" without irritably reaching after them.[12]

Consider then the "Epistle" in these terms. No one could have held the value of "jostling" in "the world" any higher than Wesley did. No one more than he could have been empirically oriented enough to insist that even the dreams of one's sleep, to say nothing of one's waking "dreams," should take on the full aspect of external reality.[13] No one more than he could have been the model for Keats's proclamatory, kerygmatic "clapping bell" of a "missionary church" near the outermost corner of the earth, in eastern Siberia on the Bering Sea. No one more than Wesley could have been as "sick" as Keats of creation's groanings from the "eternal fierce destruction" of death, since Wesley alleviated those groanings during countless waking hours. No one more than Wesley could have shared Keats's "horror of a subjective *enfer*,"[14] for no one, before Keats, asserted more than Wesley a radically Lockean, indeed a proto-Keatsean, objectivity over against, say, the "delightful fairy vision" of Addison.[15] No one more than Wesley, finally, could have managed nonetheless the sort of warmth to be found in the "Epistle"'s admixture of sublime to material.

As for the other poetry, Keats resumed, after the "Epistle," a reminiscently Methodist exploration of the "material sublime." The ideal, for example, to which Porphyro (previously all too actual, and even all too lustfully corporeal) aspires, is expressed by historically evangelical and Wesleyan (as well as generally Catholic) means:

> Ah, silver shrine, here will I take my rest,
> After so many hours of toil and quest,
> A famish'd pilgrim,—*saved* by *miracle*.
> ("The Eve of St. Agnes," ll. 337-39; my italics)

Jack Stillinger, of course, describes the pre-conversion Porphyro as "corporeal,"[16] and Stillinger suggests that in Keats's career, tough-mindedness wins out to the near-devaluation of tender-mindedness. Of the odes, for example, Stillinger states the following general view:

> Characteristically, the speaker . . . begins in the real world (A),
> takes off in mental flight to visit the ideal (B), and then—for a

variety of reasons, but most often because he finds something wanting in the imagined ideal or because, being a native of the real world, he discovers that he does not or cannot belong permanently in the ideal—returns home to the real (A1). But he has not simply arrived back where he began (hence "A1" rather than "A" at the descent), for he has acquired something—a better understanding of a situation, a change in attitude toward it—from the experience of the flight, and he is never again quite the same person who spoke at the beginning of the poem.[17]

Regarding "Psyche," at least, if not "Nightingale" and "Melancholy," "experience of the flight" is an insufficient phrase for the cause of Keats's "change in attitude." It is not just the having dared to aspire. It is also the having entertained, apart from aspiration considered as mere process, such goals of process as heaven rather than earth, immortality rather than mortality, eternity rather than time, spirituality rather than materiality, the unknown rather than the known, the infinite rather than the finite, and romance rather than realism.

Consider, to begin with, "Ode to Psyche" 's final stanza:

Yes, I will be thy priest, and build a fane
In some untrodden region of my mind,
Where branched thoughts, new grown with pleasant pain,
Instead of pines shall murmur in the wind:
Far, far around shall those dark-cluster'd trees
Fledge the wild-ridged mountains steep by steep;
And there by zephyrs, streams, and birds, and bees,
The moss-lain Dryads shall be lull'd to sleep;
And in the midst of this wide quietness
A rosy sanctuary will I dress
With the wreath'd trellis of a working brain,
With buds, and bells, and stars without a name,
With all the gardener Fancy e'er could feign,
Who breeding flowers, will never breed the same:
And there shall be for thee all soft delight
That shadowy thought can win,
A bright torch, and a casement ope at night,
To let the warm Love in!
                (ll. 50-67)

Insofar, of course, as these lines are at all religious, they are so partly at the remove of a rather too studied allusiveness to Greek mythology. But their immediate Wesleyan context is a means of explaining their peculiar modernity. For in this stanza is empiricism strikingly Wesleyan in tone. "Who can deny," asks Wesley in "Thoughts upon Necessity,"

> that not only the memory, but all the operations of the soul, are now dependent on the bodily organs, the brain in particular? . . . Our judgments . . . will and passions also . . . alternately depend on the fibres of the brain. (Jackson, X, 469-70)

It is a "working brain," similarly, and mere "shadowy thought," on which the poet must rely for the will and judgment to create the "soft delight" of passionate verse.

An at once oddly modern and oddly Wesleyan quality, likewise, governs the proximity between ideal and actual in this stanza. Its content is not so Hartleyan that it precludes the triumphantly ideal image of the window of love. That figure, in turn, notwithstanding implications of sexuality, precisely evokes the "spiritual sense" in Wesley's "Letter to the Rev. Dr. Conyers Middleton":

> Does not every thinking man want a window, not so much in his neighbour's, as in his own, breast? He wants an opening there, of whatever kind, that might let in light from eternity. He is pained to be thus feeling after God so darkly and uncertainly; to know so little of God, and indeed so little of any beside material objects. He is concerned, that he must see even that little, not directly, but in the dim, sullied glass of sense; and consequently so imperfectly and obscurely, that it is all a mere enigma still.
> Now, these very desiderata faith supplies. (Jackson, X, 74-75)

Keats's casement, in its context of the stanza's modestly empirical method, is a muted version of Wesley's hope, despite, or perhaps because of, the limits of natural perception, that a window on divine love, i.e., the "spiritual sense," will relieve the darkness and uncertainty of one's search for God. Keats's image of the mind as "untrodden region," moreover, does not so much declare Cartesian consciousness to be the subject of modern poetry as it remembers *tabula rasa.* For just as Wesley bases mind's capacity for religious knowledge not upon some innate or inherent idea of self-transcendence, but rather upon quasi-empirical acquirement of revelation, so Keats seeks to ground his faith, not in some already known capacity of mind, but rather in its potentialities. And just as Wesley, through sensuous experience in "the very world which is the world / Of all of us,"[18] finds himself not quite knowing but almost rationally persuaded of a world of the spirit, so Keats is confident of finding an ideal, if not otherworldly, "Love," despite, or perhaps because of, his collateral enterprise of writing a poetry of earth. The quasi-Wesleyan idealism of "Psyche"'s last stanza raises the possibility of immediately historical, as well as historically nostalgic, connotations of such diction as *prophet, choir, sing, holy,* and *vows* (ll. 36, 38, 43, 44, 49).

As for the other odes, I glance at their most "Wesleyan" elements, noting that their actualities even make up sufficiently "Wesleyan" as well as indispensable components of Keats's philosophically theological dialectic. "Ode on Melancholy" 's intense realism, i.e., its rejection of such dream-inducing agents as "Wolf's-bane" and "nightshade" (ll. 2, 4), is no less "Wesleyan" than Wesley's Lockean view of dreaming as unreliable access to the supernatural: Keats does not want "shade to shade" to come "too drowsily, / And drown the wakeful anguish of the soul" (ll. 9-10). This high regard for wakefulness suggests that "wake" is the desired answer to the rhetorical question with which "Ode to a Nightingale" concludes: "Do I wake or sleep?" (l. 80); the poet, I think, would not want any part of the nightingale's world were it possible to reach it only through the sleep of oblivion or even through the sleep of dreams. The poet's wakefulness, moreover, if not his quasi-Wesleyan sobriety, suggests that "a waking dream" is the desired answer to the rhetorical question comprising "Nightingale" 's penultimate line: "Was it a vision, or a waking dream?" (l. 79). It takes nothing away from the "waking dream" 's spiritually methodological status to observe that it is not a "vision" in the sense of medieval dream-vision, for in Wesley's terms one's most visionary moments are so conscious that they are recordable in journals. Keats's wakefulness, in the context of Wesley's, need not merely imply the tough-mindedness of a naturalized imagination but may signal, in addition, total concentration on some single idealism to create the impression of eternity amid time. Regarding Keats's premium on "the wakeful anguish of the soul," one thinks, on the one hand, of such a parallel as Freud's willingness to experience his cancer without benefit of pain killer, but one thinks, on the other, of the soul's wakeful anguish in Wesleyan lore, for one thinks, specifically, of Wesley's analogy in "The Great Privilege of those that are born of God," between "all the bodily senses . . . now awakened, and furnished with their proper objects" and "all the senses of the soul . . . now awake, and capable of discerning spiritual good and evil."[19] Finally, though "To Autumn" rests content, in its last stanza, with the actual rather than the ideal, Keats softens down the features of death even here with a strangely untroubled and possibly not un-"Wesleyan" series of vertical and hence semi-transcendent images:

> Where are the songs of Spring? Ay, where are they?
>   Think not of them, thou hast thy music too,—
> While barred clouds bloom the soft-dying day,
>   And touch the stubble-plains with rosy hue;
> Then in a wailful choir the small gnats mourn
>   Among the river sallows, borne aloft
>   Or sinking as the light wind lives or dies;
> And full-grown lambs loud bleat from hilly bourn;
>   Hedge-crickets sing; and now with treble soft
> The red-breast whistles from a garden-croft;
>   And gathering swallows twitter in the skies.
>   (ll. 23-33)

One may reaffirm the ideal in Keats's poetry, then, without denying its grasp of actualities. One need not veer so far from the tough-minded interpretation that one completely embraces *The Finer Tone*, in which Earl Wasserman takes a rather markedly ideal-oriented approach to the poetry.[20] Nor need one come so near Wesley's thought that one sees in Keats's work an analogical quasi-identity between perception of the natural world and receptivity to spiritual influx: the poetry, after all, never more than implies that these two ways of "knowing" are founded in the same creation, derived from the same Source, and therefore really related. On the other hand, one need not accept Stillinger's point in his essay on the odes (p. 2) that the boundary between the actual and the ideal "separates" them therein. Rather, in the odes and other poems, that boundary is a place of quasi-analogical interpenetration. Keats, like Wesley, reaffirms in no uncertain terms Locke's indication that the sense-image, as well as the thing sensed, is almost mind-independently real, so that one's experience in the natural world can hardly resemble Addisonian romance, but Keats is careful in "The Eve of St. Agnes," for example, not only to include as something incontrovertible the "haggard-seeming" (l. 344) phenomena of life and death, but also to convert such evangelical idealisms as salvation by miracle into some of the most delicious, and hence both substantial and ideal, descriptions in English poetry. In "Epistle to John Hamilton Reynolds," similarly, Keats not only trusts his impressions of nature to the point of drawing out their most painful implications, but also, and partly for that reason, solidly re-dedicates himself to a poetry of the material *sublime*.

To put the matter another way: Keats's vocabulary and his ideas are much illuminated by John Wesley's thought and language insofar as an honorific, straightforward, and non-ironic evangelical idiom coexists with and is part of Keats's empirical language. A philosophically theological dialectic lies near the heart of Keats's poetic quest insofar as his evangelical vocabulary, though frame of reference more than sign of faith, enriches his confrontation of the actual. Recent criticism emphasizes that confrontation, and is in fact so far from tender-minded that it places him among the most inflexibly empirical temperaments of the pre-Modern world; Stillinger, for example, epitomizes his argument thus:

> ... [I]n the over-all view, [Keats's] significant poems center on a single basic problem, the mutability inherent in nature and human life, and openly or in disguise they debate the pros and cons of a single hypothetical solution, transcendence of earthly limitations by means of the visionary imagination. If one were to summarize the career in a single sentence, it would be something like this: Keats came to learn that the kind of imagination he pursued was a false lure, inadequate to the needs of the problem, and in the end he traded the visionary for the naturalized imagination, embracing experience and process as his own and man's chief good.[21]

Keats indeed "came to learn that the kind of imagination he pursued was a false lure, inadequate to the needs of the problem." But he held, nevertheless, to a language of transcendence. And he was in the odd position of lending authority to his naturalized imagination by means of his nostalgia for visionary imagination. His conclusions, moreover, though hardly Wesleyan in their substance, were describable so in methodology, for he "made it new" specifically by basing his poetry, consciously, upon a tentative but satisfyingly mysterious, and not even quite merely hypothetical, spiritual "sense." His nature is the more capacious for this procedure.

Overemphasis on the actual in his poetry comes often and naturally enough from those interested in the Lockean context of Romanticism. But my approach is partly Lockean. And a faulty assumption underlies the view, widespread, that the Lockean theory of mind is in no way reconcilable with the concept of grace. This view not only misses the religious emphases within Locke's theory, but also overlooks the religious uses to which the theory was put by such as Wesley, for whom it was not often, or even ever, a question of either empiricism or grace, but rather, and distinctively, a matter of both empiricism and grace. Keats's poetry finally supports the view that he introduced the naturalized imagination, but not even of him should it be said that the naturalized imagination emerges with any great sense of either intellectual gain or broadened poetic horizons, and he was in some ways less toughminded than Wesley, whose empirical attitudes were radical.

Although the religious language of second-generation English Romantics was more attenuated than that of the first generation, even the second generation came well before religious language was often used either only casually or with little regard for its various historical nuances.[22] The religious sensibility of Keats, notably, compels consideration. Responsive, though unsponsored, his religious inclinations emerged from his milieu: Benjamin Bailey, "a student of theology and candidate for Holy Orders," was "a more impressive spokesman for orthodoxy than any other of Keats's close acquaintances," and from the beginning of his career, in his Leigh Hunt circle of friends, Keats found sympathetic access to "every major tendency in English religious life . . . from enthusiastic piety to skeptical irreverence."[23] The hallmarks of Benjamin Robert Haydon's "highly emotional religion," for example—admiration for "the abolition of African Slavery, the institution of Charities & Hospitals," and the general "amelioration of human Conditions" (Ryan, p. 90)—could only have developed from the timely evangelical enterprise of unprecedented practical charity.

On the empirical side, Ryan offers a sketch of Keats's medical teacher Astley Cooper, of whom it was said not long before his death that

> his general influence on the practice of surgery in this country has, perhaps, been most evident in the great share he has had in establishing pure induction as the only means of a just diagnosis. (*Keats: The Religious Sense*, pp. 63-64)

Ryan demonstrates that Cooper's watchword, "Don't Speculate. Observe," pertains to Keats's doctrine of Negative Capability. Keats's role of medical doctor, and thence of poetic "physician to all men" (*The Fall of Hyperion*, l. 90), is from the empiricist point of view the closest he came to being Wesleyan, since one of Wesley's chief roles was to disseminate a basic "physick" that he knew would do no harm, and which he hoped would do good to bodies, if not to minds and spirits.

The religious sense—more accurately, I think, than *material sublime*—conveys the ratio of Keats's empirical method to his religious thought: his religious thought is subordinate to—but subsumed within and consistent with—the medical orientation of his empiricism. One might explore, further, his "skepticism" and "religion of beauty" not only in relation to each other, but also in their Lockean-Wesleyan context of philosophical theology.

One might begin, for example, with "Written upon the Top of Ben Nevis":

> Read me a lesson, Muse, and speak it loud
>   Upon the top of Nevis, blind in mist!
> I look into the chasms, and a shroud
>   Vaporous doth hide them,—just so much I wist
> Mankind do know of hell; I look o'erhead,
>   And there is sullen mist,—even so much
> Mankind can tell of heaven; mist is spread
>   Before the earth, beneath me,—even such
> Even so vague is man's sight of himself!
>   Here are the craggy stones beneath my feet,—
> This much I know that, a poor witless elf,
>   I tread on them,—that all my eye doth meet
> Is mist and crag, not only on this height,
>   But in the world of thought and mental might!

Sperry, tough-minded in approach, regards this sonnet as quintessential Keats.[24] Ryan, who acknowledges in Keats strangely simultaneous degrees of the actual and the ideal, sees in these lines only the un-ideal skepticism of "metaphysical difficulties" and "helpless bewilderment."[25] Can this poem be no less "evangelical" for being tough-minded? Yes.

I suggest, in other words, that an at least nostalgic loyalty to religious ideas coexists, even here, with the almost bitterly skeptical tone. The ending, in its near-denial of the *cogito*, is not even so affirmative as solipsism. But in Keats's confident "I tread on them" is, more than a subject/object interpenetration, an ascendancy of mind in nature. And the stones he walks on seem to possess what John Crowe Ransom, for one, missed in the poetry of Shelley, namely, "thick *dinglich* substance."[26] The poem, in short, probes skeptically, but finds some solid ground. If it does not build up quite to any idea of order fully religious, neither is its state of unbelief entirely static, for its method, far from simply rejecting the Christian cosmology of heaven and hell, entertains it, rather as a doctrinal and still felt (though hardly palpable) element of a deeply felt, experiential quest for truth. The sonnet's language, in sum, is experiential theology's: though "blind in mist," Keats can say "This much I know"; and, of the "evidence" (similarly "inward") of immediate revelation, Wesley concludes "One thing I know; I was blind, but now I see" (Jackson, X, 75-76).

The progression in Keats is not so much from blindness to vision, of course, as from blindness to insight, but his various perspectives, sense-based and shifting though they are, are new, and, though not quite his substitute for immediate revelation, they ground his almost more than rational, and hence not less than ideal, methodology. His substitute for traditional revelation, of course, is poetry, but, whereas in such an early poem as "On First Looking into Chapman's Homer" (October, 1816) the written word is held to "speak out loud and bold" even when once-removed from Homer's authentic tongue, the Muse in "Written upon the Top of Ben Nevis" (June, 1818) is taunted for not "speak[ing] loud." Keats, clearly, came to expect neither the word of poetry, nor, by implication, the book of nature, to speak as "loud and clear" as Wesley told Middleton the Bible does.[27] Neither, though, was even the later Keats wholly without the "lively impression" of an "inward evidence." For the "Ben Nevis" sonnet, religious as well as philosophical, implies, like Wesley, that an inner voice is more "intimately present," and therefore more authoritative, than the evidences of both nature and the written word.

NOTES

[1] I have in mind Ronald A. Sharp's terminology in *Keats, Skepticism, and the Religion of Beauty* (Athens: The U. of Georgia Press, 1979). I supplement Sharp's non-historical approach. All quotations of Keats, unless otherwise indicated, are from Douglas Bush, ed., *Keats: Selected Poems and Letters* (New York: Riverside Editions, 1959).

[2] (Princeton: Princeton U. Press, 1976), p. 63 and *passim*. Not even Clarence Thorpe, in *The Mind of John Keats* (1926; rpt. N. Y.: Russell & Russell, 1964),

is as thorough as Ryan in unearthing materials pertinent to Keats's frame of mind. Since Ryan does not criticize the poetry systematically, one might read his volume as companion not only to the present discussion, but also to Keats, *Skepticism, and the Religion of Beauty.*

[3] Hyder E. Rollins, ed., *The Letters of John Keats, 1814-1821* (Cambridge, Mass.: Harvard U. Press, 1958), I, 184.

[4] Ernest Lee Tuveson, *Imagination as a Means of Grace: Locke and the Aesthetics of Romanticism* (Berkeley: The U. of California Press, 1960), p. 3.

[5] Douglas Bush, ed., *Keats: Selected Poems and Letters*, p. 310.

[6] David Perkins, ed., *English Romantic Writers* (New York: Harcourt, Brace & World, 1967), p. 1,146n.

[7] Here is an inclusive, and clearly Locke-derived, statement of Wesley's "spiritual sense":

> You know [writes Wesley] . . . that before it is possible for you to form a true judgment of the things of God, it is absolutely necessary that you have a *clear apprehension* of them, and that your ideas thereof be all *fixed, distinct*, and *determinate*. And seeing our ideas are not innate, but must all originally come from our senses, it is absolutely necessary that you have senses capable of discerning objects of this kind—not those only which are called 'natural senses', which in this respect profit nothing, as being altogether incapable of discerning objects of a spiritual kind, but *spiritual* senses, exercised to discern spiritual good and evil.

See Gerald R. Cragg, ed., *The Appeals to Men of Reason and Religion and Certain Open Related Letters* (Oxford: Clarendon Press, 1975), pp. 56-57. Other quotations of Wesley's works (unless otherwise indicated) are from the following edition: Thomas Jackson, ed., *The Works of the Rev. John Wesley, A. M.*, 14 vols. (1829-31; rpt. London: Wesleyan-Methodist Book-Room, n. d.).

[8] Perkins, ed., *English Romantic Writers*, p. 1,146n.

[9] *Keats the Poet* (Princeton: Princeton U. Press, 1973), p. 129.

[10] Bush, in this connection, calls Keats's Pleasure Thermometer "Platonic-Romantic." Keats "could speak, " writes Bush, "of 'the eternal Being, the Principle of Beauty' (letter to Reynolds, April 9, 1818) and of 'The mighty abstract Idea I have of Beauty in all things' (letter to George and Georgiana Keats, Oct. 21, 1818)." See Bush, ed., *Keats: Selected Poems and Letters*, p. 319.

[11] Rollins, ed., *The Letters of John Keats*, 192-93.

[12] For Wesley's easy mastery of fact and reason, see (1) the introductory and concluding essays to his encyclopedia for the common reader, *A Survey of the Wisdom of God in the Creation; or, a Compendium of Natural Philosophy* (London: Frye, 1777); (2) the "Preface" to his *Desideratum; Or, Electricity made plain and useful* (1760; see Jackson, XIV, 241-44); and (3) the "Preface" to his *Primitive Physick: or, an Easy and Natural Method of Curing Most Diseases* (1747), 9th ed. (London: Printed by W. Strahan, 1761). Wesley's open-minded faith allowed him a measure of Lockean-Cartesian skepticism with regard, even, to the Bible:

> I am as fully assured to-day, as I am of the shining sun, that the scriptures are of God. I cannot possibly deny or doubt of it now; yet I may doubt of it to-morrow; as I have done heretofore a thousand times, and that after the fullest assurance preceding. ("Letters to Mr. John Smith"; Jackson, XII, 86)

I allude, above, to Rudolph Otto's idea of the holy.

[13] Wesley's sermon "Human Life a Dream, " for example, draws upon Locke's demystification of dreams: Locke's argument that "the Dreams of sleeping Men" are "all made up of the waking Man's Ideas, though, for the most part, oddly put together" (*An Essay Concerning Human Understanding* I.i.16) is largely in accord (1) with Wesley's argument that "we are many times not able to determine" which dreams "arise from natural, which from supernatural, influence, " and (2) with Wesley's conclusion that many are due to the "constitution of the body" and the "passions of the mind" (Jackson, VII, 318).

[14] *Keats the Poet*, p. 128.

[15] For a pertinent discussion of Addisonian subjectivity, see Kenneth Maclean, *John Locke and English Literature of the Eighteenth Century* (1936; rpt. New York: Russell & Russell, 1962), pp. 93-94. Maclean (pp. 28, 81, 144, 154) includes Wesley among the moderate, rather than radical, Lockeans, but one may hear an echo of Locke's relatively untroubled realism, if not of his radical objectivity, (1) in Wesley's animadversion (*contra* Kames and Hartley) that "Wherever this argument occurs, (and it occurs ten times over,) 'The natural world is all illusion; therefore, so is the moral,'—it is just good for nothing" (Jackson, X, 471), and (2) in Wesley's more-Lockean-than-Locke (and decidedly anti-Berkeleyan) insistence that "colour is just as real as size or figure; and that all colours do as really exist without us, as trees, or corn, or heaven, or earth" (Jackson, X, 470-71).

[16] "The Hoodwinking of Madeline: Scepticism in 'The Eve of St. Agnes,'" *Studies in Philology*, 58 (1961), 533-55.

[17] "Imagination and Reality in the Odes of Keats," in Stillinger, ed., *Twentieth-Century Interpretations of Keats's Odes* (Englewood Cliffs, N. J.: Prentice-Hall, Inc., 1968), p. 3.

[18] Wordsworth's 1805 *Prelude*: x.726-27.

[19] John Wesley, *Sermons on Several Occasions* (1787; rpt. London: The Epworth Press, 1944), pp. 176-77.

[20] Wasserman's study of Keats (Baltimore: The Johns Hopkins U. Press, 1953) is subtitled *Keats's Major Poems*.

[21] "Imagination and Reality in the Odes of Keats," p. 2.

[22] I have in mind E. Leroy Lawson's *Very Sure of God: Religious Language in the Poetry of Robert Browning* (Nashville: Vanderbilt U. Press, 1974) and Ward Hellstrom's *On Tennyson's Poetry* (Gainesville: The U. of Florida Press, 1972). Hellstrom shows Tennyson's particular knowledge of Liberal Anglican thought, and Lawson shows Browning's compatibility with such thinkers as Paul Tillich, Jürgen Moltmann, and Harvey Cox. Josephine Miles, notably, puts the casual use of religious language in the 1840s: see *The Primary Language of Poetry in the 1740s and the 1840s* (Berkeley: The U. of California Press, 1950). Sharp, acknowledging my *Wordsworth's "Natural Methodism"* (New Haven: Yale U. Press, 1975) as a means of understanding Wordsworth's belief in "a reality that transcended this world," observes that "by contrast with Keats, Wordsworth is considerably more traditional": see *Keats, Skepticism, and the Religion of Beauty*, pp. 14, 169.

[23] *Keats: The Religious Sense*, pp. 71, 115. Ryan's book is flawed, somewhat, by its reduction of "Methodism and Evangelicalism" to "their emphasis on sin and guilt" (p. 80).

[24] *Keats the Poet*, p. 133.

[25] *Keats: The Religious Sense*, pp. 174-75.

[26] As quoted in Wasserman, *The Subtler Language: Critical Readings of Neoclassic and Romantic Poems* (Baltimore: The Johns Hopkins U. Press, 1959), pp. 205-6.

[27] See Jackson, x, 75-76, from which I quote, as well, in my next two sentences.

11. *Evangelical Principles of Tennyson's IN MEMORIAM*

The deeply inward yet outwardly directed and inquiring expression of faith that Alfred, Lord Tennyson (1809-92) features in the otherwise scientifically focused section 124 of his *In Memoriam: A H. H.* (1850) is matched in other passages of the poem by the elegist's emphasis on spiritual experience as the complement to natural experience. Neither from the expatiating astronomy of section 124 nor from its incisive biology would any personal discovery of the divine appear to emerge, for Tennyson declares that "I found Him not in world or sun, / Or eagle's wing, or insect's eye" (124.5-6). (All quotations of *In Memoriam* are from volume 2 of *The Poems*, edited by Ricks.) These lines, after all, undercut the bumper-sticker mentality of "I found Him!" While thus giving vent to doubts worthy of Matthew Arnold's "Dover Beach" (1867), however, Tennyson's persona overcomes his skepticism and, despite his grief over the death (in 1833) of his young friend Arthur Henry Hallam, affirms his own religious experience:

> If e'er when faith had fallen asleep,
>   I heard a voice, "believe no more,"
>   And heard an ever-breaking shore
> That tumbled in the Godless deep,
>
> A warmth within the breast would melt
>   The freezing reason's colder part,
>   And like a man in wrath the heart
> Stood up and answer'd, "I have felt."
>   (124.9-16)

These lines, echoing the conversion of John Wesley (1703-91) in Aldersgate Street, London, where, "at a quarter to nine" on the evening of May 24,

1738, the founder-of-Methodism's "heart" was "strangely warmed" (Curnock I.475-76), are more than a greeting-card version of Wesleyan conversion-passages. The lines echo, too, Wesley's eight-year journey from skepticism to faith (Brantley, *Locke* 27-47). Thus, the method of *In Memoriam* adds evangelical principles to empirical procedures. Tennyson's combination of dynamic skepticism with "post-critical naïveté" (Ricoeur *passim*) is as much Methodist as it is methodological, for 124's deeply inward yet outwardly directed and inquiring expression of faith is matched in other passages of the poem by the spiritual-experience dimension that Tennyson contributes to the natural-experience foundation of his broadly experiential vision.

Although the "thoroughgoing subjectivism" of section 124 "does not meet the difficulties raised by science, but simply bypasses them," and although "the subjectivist attitude" in *In Memoriam* has accordingly received "the severest criticism," Graham Hough, for one, finds the attitude "both honest and extremely moving" (244-45). Christopher Ricks, too, admires Tennyson's subjective faith:

> Some believers might argue that Tennyson sells Christianity short in underrating the degree to which its beliefs are susceptible of substantiation by argument; or unbelievers might argue that it is bad for people to believe things which are not susceptible of argument. But it is possible to think that Tennyson's poem offers almost all that can hereabouts be honestly offered by the Christian, and that it is hearteningly free of the heartlessness which comes from the conviction that the problems of pain, death, and evil can be dealt with by arguments. . . . Indeed the *In Memoriam* stanza (abba) is especially suited to turning round rather than going forward. To speak personally for a moment: as an atheist, I should greatly prefer Tennyson to agree with me; but I find it hard to understand the view that somehow he is stuck there in a half-complacent, half-morbid tangle from which we know—know so uncomplacently—that we have escaped.
>
> (*Tennyson* 222)

The "subjectivism" of *In Memoriam*, however, is hardly so thoroughgoing as Hough and Ricks imply. This goes even for section 124. The faith that the elegist increasingly espouses takes account of times, places, and circumstances, or of what Wordsworth calls "the world / Of all of us, the place in which, in the end, / We find our happiness, or not at all" (*The Prelude* [1850] 10.726-28). This faith even harks back to the "objectivist" patterns of experiential faith and conversion. Laid beside (if not superimposed on) the empiricism of *In Memoriam*, I argue, is its "empirical" evangelicalism.

A variety of passages besides section 124, specifically, illustrates Tennyson's advance from struggle with self-absorption to what he clearly regards as the crowning touch of his "evangelical" theology, namely, the universal efficacy that he claims for the still-"living" Hallam's Holy Spirit-like presence in the world. The most pertinent historical gloss on this theology, and hence the most powerful analogue to Tennyson's religious imagination, is the experiential, explicitly Lockean (as well as fully biblical) faith that Wesley and Jonathan Edwards (1703-58) shared and notably promulgated throughout the Anglo-American world (Brantley, *Coordinates* 36-42). The effects of the transatlantic revivalism simultaneously begun by the founder of British and American Methodism and the leader of the Great Awakening were felt long after the time of Tennyson. Sections 108, 71, 82, 28, 33, 26, the prologue, sections 36, 31, 32, 52, 7, 103, 84, 50, 110, 87, and 113, when considered in this order and from this point of view, range from Tennyson's individualistic but respectful explorations of such Christian fundamentals as the sin of selfhood, to his bold application to the here-and-now of an experientially religious as well as poetic imagination that grows out of, and is honed by, the native/bi-native, richly English-language, synthesizing, and by no means unimaginative heritage of Wesleyan-Edwardsean evangelical faith.

Apropos of Tennyson's "subjectivity," first, consider his warning against self-reflexivity or empty self-worship:

> What profit lies in barren faith,
>   And vacant yearning, though with might
>   To scale the heaven's highest height,
> Or dive below the wells of Death?
>
> What find I in the highest place,
>   But mine own phantom chanting hymns?
>   And on the depths of death there swims
> The reflex of a human face.
>   (108.5-12)

Keats's "Written upon the Top of Ben Nevis" (1818), similarly, looks both high and low for an object worthy of worship, but finding only "sullen mist" overhead and a "shroud / Vaporous" in the valley below, this sonnet discovers, too, only "mist" in "the world of thought and mental might!" Keats, presumably, would be glad to discover even such "solid ground" as solipsism is. To such a Keatsean mood of thoroughgoing doubt, Tennyson seems to prefer, if no more resounding an affirmation of faith, at least the nature-reverence at which he has proved himself adept: "I'll rather take what fruit may be / Of sorrow under human skies" (108.13-14). Referring not just to his own sorrow but to sorrow as the general condition of humankind on earth, Tennyson works his way out of selfhood to a compassionate orientation toward objects and subjects in the world below. Section 108 thus divagates from the dead-end skepticism and the extreme subjectivity of Romanticism. Tennyson's milder Romantic stance is hardly orthodox, for Christianity emphasizes joy in a world elsewhere, but his nature-reverence is experientially religious enough to be at least partially commensurate with the evangelical faith of Wesley and Edwards. Their combination of nature-reverence and this-worldly compassion forms a legendary feature of their joint legacy to the nineteenth century (Brantley, "Common Ground" *passim*).

To natural religion, though, whether Deistic, theistic, pantheistic, or chthonic, Tennyson clearly prefers an "evangelical" heart-religion, that is, an inward yet deeply engaged or experiential/other-directed faith. "Full fathom five thy father lies," writes Shakespeare in *The Tempest*, but far from being dead, "thy father" miraculously "doth suffer a sea change / Into something rich and strange" (1.2.397, 400-01), and Tennyson, while implying a rather different point, subtly alludes to these lines. Suggesting that the change is not so much from nature to another world as from natural to spiritual experience within "the world / Of all of us," Tennyson recalls that he and Hallam "talk'd / Of men and minds, the dust of *change*," reporting, significantly, that their days grew "to *something strange*" (71.9-11; my italics). Thus, even as their spirits transcended time, they remained in time. Where Tennyson affirms his faith in Hallam's afterlife—"Eternal process moving on, / From state to state the spirit walks" (82.5-6)—he means both that Hallam has passed from earth to heaven, where he continues to develop, and that amid the ceaseless activities of his life on earth, Hallam's spiritual progress occurred. During the first Christmas season after Hallam's death, Tennyson hears "the Christmas bells from hill to hill" (28.3), and despite their sing-song near-monotony—his faith is ebbing at this point—they strike his ear the more forcefully for his lack of expectation that they would strike it at all: "The merry, merry bells of Yule" touch his sorrow "with joy" (28.19). The appeal of the bells, while not fundamentally to doctrine, is evangelical enough; their kerygmatic message of hope peals out to, connects with, and begins to heal even the lowest velleities of the poet's post-traumatic experience.

In Memoriam, at least insofar as section 33 brings up short the theological liberal who feels that his open-ended faith is superior to his sister's literal creed, is classically evangelical:

> 0 thou that after toil and storm
>   Mayst seem to have reach'd a purer air,
>   Whose faith has centre everywhere,
> Nor cares to fix itself to form,
>
> Leave thou thy sister when she prays
>   Her early heaven, her happy views;
>   Nor thou with shadow'd hint confuse
> A life that leads melodious days.
>
> Her faith thro' form is pure as thine,
>   Her hands are quicker unto good.
>   0, sacred be the flesh and blood
> To which she links a truth divine!
>
> See thou, that countest reason ripe
>   In holding by the law within,
>   Thou fail not in a world of sin,
> And even for want of such a type.
>   (1-16)

Timothy Peltason's comment acknowledges that the "dignity" of the sister's "religious position" is preferred over the position of both the brother and his "hazily defined group of fellow liberals" (72). A. C. Bradley, still the most thorough commentator on *In Memoriam*, rejects the possibility that "Tennyson is thinking of himself and his sister" Emily (or Cecelia), but, nonetheless, calls the idea "plausible" (113). Tennyson may sometimes be more like the brother than like the sister, but his persona rejects the indefinite, unfixed, and indeterminate theology of the brother in favor of the sister's strong, definite, evangelical faith, which claims power as, and because, it values form. (Wesley, as I have pointed out, bases his influential emphasis on power and form on such biblical passages as I Corinthians 2.1-6; see Brantley, *Wordsworth's* 83.) Although Tennyson was intimately familiar with Liberal Anglicanism (Hellstrom *passim*), these quatrains implicitly contrast Liberal Anglicanism with Evangelical Anglicanism; the quatrains direct their satire against the former. The evangelical sister provides Tennyson with the standard by which he skewers the brother's almost rationalistic/antinomian stance, which, besides forming part of the brother's male pride, forms part of his "advanced" theology. The sister's emphasis on "flesh and blood" (33.11), by refreshing contrast, refers to the historical Jesus, the elements of communion, and all people with whom her evangelical practical charity comes in contact.

"How but in custom and in ceremony," asks William Butler Yeats, "are innocence and beauty born?" (lines 78-79 of "A Prayer for My Daughter" [1919]). Tennyson would agree with the experientially religious implications of Yeats's rhetorical question. The sister's regulated but vital experience excels by the richness of its spiritual form and content the mere *Sturm und Drang* whereby, with more Continental-Romantic than British-Romantic or British-evangelical warm-heartedness, her Liberal Anglican brother arrives at *his* truth.

What *In Memoriam* says about God can be so far from classically evangelical as to anticipate Thomas Hardy's "theology." Where Tennyson speaks of

> that eye which watches guilt
> And goodness, and hath power to see
> Within the green the moulder'd tree,
> And towers fallen as soon as built
> (26.5-8)

he rivals the sarcasm with which Hardy apprehends a possibly omniscient, but clearly indifferent, God. These lines emerge, too, as a satire against the judgmental Calvinist God of sovereignty, especially since an additional detail—"if indeed that eye foresee / Or see—in Him is no before" (26.9-10)—exposes the super-subtleties, if not the super-absurdities, of the predestinarian position. Roden Noel, in 1892, reported that "Lord Tennyson believed in 'free will' ": "When I urged the argument of Jonathan Edwards, and other more modern arguments against the popular conception of it, he replied that free will, not being subject to the law of causation, was a miracle, no doubt;

but that consciousness testifies to the fact" (Page 190). Tennyson's view is in line not only with Wesley's Arminian view, but also with the empiricist view of David Hume, for whom, in all seriousness, "free will" is a "miracle" of one's consciousness. Tennyson's dramatic monologue "St. Simeon Stylites" (1833) satirizes not just overzealous Catholics but, according to Roger S. Platizky, "the early nineteenth-century Evangelicals, whose dread of a punitive judgment and of the putridity of the flesh is similar to Simeon's" (42-43; see also Ian Bradley 23). Objection to Calvinist evangelicalism, however, leaves room for sympathy toward Arminian-Wesleyan and even toward experiential-Edwardsean (though not toward Calvinist-Edwardsean) evangelicalism. (For a study of warring paradigms in Edwards, and especially of his Lockean middle phase, see Brantley, "Common Ground" 272-82.)

Fully evangelical because Christological and quite Arminian, moreover, is another of the conceptions of Godhead in *In Memoriam*. The opening phrase of the prologue, "*Strong* Son of God" (my italics), reflects an immediate historical context, "muscular Christianity," a coinage of Charles Kingsley's. The vestiges of this Victorian form of Christianity, which led to the scouting movement for boys and girls, may still be found depicted in *Chariots of Fire*, a movie about the 1924 Olympics. Tennyson's Christ, however, is also the fundamental, decidedly evangelical Christ of traditional revelation:

> And so the Word had breath, and wrought
>   With human hands the creed of creeds
>   In loveliness of perfect deeds,
> More strong than all poetic thought.
>   (369-12)

Tennyson said that "there were, of course, difficulties in the idea of a Trinity—the Three. 'But mind,' he said, 'Son of God is quite right—that he was'" (Page 188). Tennyson's Christ is consistent with the experiential, free-willist, Arminian evangelicalism that gained ascendancy over the foreknowing, predestinate, Calvinist evangelicalism in both England and America from the eighteenth century to the nineteenth (Semmel *passim*). Arminian evangelicalism bears on Tennyson's declaration that *In Memoriam* expresses "my conviction that fear, doubts, and suffering will find answer and relief only through Faith in a God of Love" (as quoted in Ricks 212).

Consider, in the light of the Arminian-evangelical emphasis on immediate versus traditional revelation, Tennyson's recasting of the Lazarus story (cf. John 11.1-44). "When Lazarus left his charnel-cave, / And home to Mary's house return'd," his sister asked him what anyone would ask: "Where wert thou, brother, those four days?" (*In Memoriam* 31.1-2, 31.5). Bradley contrasts this question with the bland remark of Sir Thomas Browne: "I can read . . that Lazarus was raised from the dead, yet not demand where, in the interim, his soul waited" (*Religio Medici* 1.21, as quoted in A. C. Bradley 111). Tennyson, for his part, laments that "there lives no record of reply" (31.6); his disappointment is palpable: 'Telling what it is to die / Had surely added praise to praise" (31. 7-8). Although Tennyson is greatly impressed with how much the original story of Lazarus discloses to anyone willing to read it with even a minimally Protestant attention to detail—"Behold a man raised up by Christ!" (31.13)—this miracle is not finally definitive for Tennyson's account. The proponent of spiritual theology, distinct from the Bible-believer, grows dissatisfied: "The rest remaineth unreveal'd; / He told it not, or something seal'd / The lips of that Evangelist" (31.14-16). Without casting doubt on the account in traditional revelation, the poet suggests that there is room for, and a need for, immediate revelation; since he does not yet know enough, he should be given to know more, and it is not as though there is nothing else to know. The more-to-know, while lending the appeal of mystery to what is already known, awakens his appetite for, his receptivity to, further dispensations concerning not just the afterlife but, even more importantly here, other, more this-world-pertinent aspects of ultimate spiritual knowledge.

The version of the Lazarus story in *In Memoriam* 31 is thus more ambitious than other Victorian versions of it (see the discussion of Arnold's "Empedocles on Aetna" and Browning's "Epistle of Karshish" in A. D. Culler 168-69). The theology in section 31 draws imaginatively and specifically on evangelical understanding, which, like the thinking of Tennyson's persona, insists on immediate revelation and, like the thinking of Tennyson's Mary, can be starker, more "fundamentally" clear, than the Bible itself. It is almost as though Tennyson toys with a severely Protestant aesthetic whereby mediation of any kind is devalued as a most unfortunate, if necessary, distraction from the distinct, cohesive, pointblank meanings that he seeks. The poet's Mary knows three things, first that "[Lazarus] was dead," second that "there he sits," and third that "he that brought him back is here" (32.3-4); thus, she formulates with a more than biblical clarity her considerable and methodically acquired, if not hard-won, knowledge. Although Ian Bradley observes that "in the mind of Lazarus's sister," curiosity as to the state beyond death was "absorbed in love and adoration," and although A. C. Bradley sees "a blessedness" in Tennyson's Mary (110), this latter-day Mary shows such curiosity as to win her way through to a sufficiently astonishing set of religious discoveries. Not even Mary's and Lazarus's blunt, more down-to-earth than contemplative sister Martha, in Joan New's recasting of the Lazarus story (1986), shows any greater curiosity than Tennyson's Mary about what Lazarus learned on the other side, for despite deeply empathizing with Lazarus (who grieves over his sudden loss of heaven), New's Martha implores him to "Forgive me, . . . for I, / Knowing nothing else but life, choose life" (New 76). Carrying Tennyson's experiential fervor to such a narrow extreme that she leaves out Tennyson's rich-experiential desire for otherworldly knowledge, New's Martha chooses not even to inquire how the life she clings to might bear on, if not be made more abundant by (or even make more abundant), the "life" that lies ahead. Thus, even as New's poem shares in Tennyson's empirical "spirit," it skillfully, insightfully measures our distance from his spiritual "empiricism."

In view of the yearning for immediate revelation in section 31, to say nothing of the other evangelical idioms in *In Memoriam*, it may seem odd that nowhere does the elegy mention the Holy Spirit by name. Section 36, however, envisions Christ as acting in the present:

> Tho' truths in manhood darkly join,
>   Deep-seated in our mystic frame,
>   We yield all blessing to the name
> Of Him that made them *current* coin.
>   (1-4; my italics)

Thus, the evangelicals' blend of Christ and the Holy Spirit enables Tennyson's boldest theology. The poet draws on spiritual theology, as well as on Christology, to depict the continuing influence of Hallam, from whom a spirit of forgiveness Christ-like in manner and pneumatological in immediacy emanates long after his death.

Tennyson worries, to be sure, that as measured by his verses his love for Hallam must be deemed imperfect: "I cannot love thee as I ought" (52.1). After creeping "like a guilty thing" to the door of Hallam's house on hearing of his death (7. 7-8), moreover, the poet dreams that he is torn between maidens on the one hand, and Hallam's statue on the other (see section 103); Tennyson may have in mind his homoerotic feelings for Hallam. Whatever the cause of his guilt, however, Hallam's still-active spirit is graciously Arminian, for Hallam is now "the Spirit of true love" (52.6), as though the Holy Spirit and he were one. Functioning as the Comforter, accordingly, Hallam now speaks to Tennyson in explicitly Wesleyan terms of assurance:

> "Thou canst not move me from thy side,
> Nor human frailty do me wrong.
>
> "What keeps a spirit wholly true
>   To that ideal which he bears?
>   What record? not the sinless years
> That breathed beneath the Syrian blue;
>
> "So fret not like an idle girl,
>   That life is dash'd with flecks of sin.
>   Abide, thy wealth is gather'd in,
> When Time hath sunder'd shell from pearl."
>   (52.7-16)

(For the literary as well as theological importance of Wesley's doctrine of assurance, see Brantley, *Wordsworth's* 120, 133-34.) Whatever sins were committed are thus forgiven, and it is worth noting, in this connection, that the spiritual, distinct from any psychosexual, dimension of section 103 underlies the peculiar conclusion of the section, in which the statue of Hallam comes to life and, like the forgiving spirit of God, welcomes both Tennyson and the maidens into a full, a spiritual as well as physical, mutual fellowship.

Hallam's spirit, as agent/manifestation/successor of the Third Person, is not just far from dead, but even perpetually efficacious in a world to which it constitutes further dispensations of faith and divinity. Tennyson's spiritual theology carries the evangelical emphasis on the Holy Spirit to a logical extreme (for a discussion of that emphasis, see Brantley, *Wordsworth's* 66-78). Tennyson, speculating about the long life that he and Hallam might have had together, imagines that after "hovering o'er the dolorous strait / To the other shore," the two of them would have arrived at the "blessed goal" of heaven where "He that died in Holy Land" would have "reach[ed] us out the shining hand" and "take[n] us as a single soul" (84.39-44). Thus, Tennyson makes a sharp distinction between Hallam and Christ; Tennyson next asks, however, as though any hope of Christ were a weak reed compared with hope of Hallam, "What reed was that on which I leant?" (84.45). In an even bolder passage, Hallam, by the same token of earthly spiritual experience, is a still more reliable, because a still more present, Christ than Christ himself; section 50 ("Be near me when my light is low") is ultimately addressed to Hallam, type of the Christ-to-be, and while Gerard Manley Hopkins regrets that neither he nor any other priest, notwithstanding the utmost tenderness that priests regularly summon for extreme unction, can truly be "in at the end" for a dying person (I allude to Hopkins's "Felix Randall" [1880]), Tennyson, in this section, wants Hallam to perform that very god-like function for him, and thinks that he can. One is reminded, here, of Emily Dickinson's hope that, if Jesus cannot be "in at the end" of her life (I re-use Hopkins's phrase), then perhaps her good friend Susan Gilbert can (see the discussion of Dickinson's Poem 158 in Pollak 140-41). Even as Tennyson contemplates his own life's final hour, at any rate, Hallam's continuing parousial capacity puts the poet in the presence of whom he loves; Hallam as unnamed addressee of section 50 makes for an especially subtle sense of coalescence or interpenetration between Tennyson's persona and the more than human, as well as the fully human, subject of *In Memoriam*.

Hallam, then, is described evangelically. His probity, for example, proves especially infectious:

> On thee the loyal-hearted hung,
>   The proud was half disarm'd of pride,
>   Nor cared the serpent at thy side
> To flicker with his double tongue.
>   (110.5-8)

He is loved, moreover, for Christian reasons:

> I, thy nearest, sat apart,
>   And felt thy triumph was as mine;
>   And loved them more, that they were thine,
> The graceful tact, the Christian art.
>   (110.13-16)

Although he does not preach, as did his fellow-Cambridge Apostle F. D. Maurice and even as does Tennyson in his more kerygmatic moods, the Hallam of *In Memoriam* seeks to bring about a third apostolic age, the second being that of Wesley and Edwards. Exemplifying Arminian free will, the fruits of the Spirit, enthusiasm as honorifically understood, and, clearly not least, a "spiritual sense" of personal relationship with God, Hallam is quintessentially evangelical:

> A willing ear
> We lent him. Who but hung to hear
> The rapt oration flowing free
>
> From point to point, with power and grace
>   And music in the bounds of law,
>   To those conclusions when we saw
> The God within him light his face . . . ?
>   (87.30-36)

(For a study of this congeries of evangelical traits, see Brantley, "Common Ground" *passim*.) Tennyson believes that Hallam would have made his mark as a political leader, that is, as "a potent voice of Parliament" (113.11-12) or even as "a lever to uplift the earth / And roll it in another course" (113.15-16), but Tennyson's diction for the kind of social justice that Hallam would have represented is explicitly evangelical: "A life in civic *action warm*, / A *soul* on highest *mission sent*" (113.9-10; my italics).

What is commonly said about Tennyson, namely, that he was to be "the awakener of a new Albion, the poet-prophet of the good society to come" (Buckley, *Poems* xi), could be said, too, of John Wesley and, regarding America, of Jonathan Edwards. This parallel is hardly arbitrary. Entire dimensions of *In Memoriam*, and not just its portraiture of Hallam, emerge as derivations of, withdrawals from, the evangelical legacy that the eighteenth century passed on to the nineteenth. "Whatever was the immediate prompting of *In Memoriam*, whatever the form under which the author represented his aim to himself," the deepest significance of the poem, according to George Eliot, is its "sanctification of human love as a religion" (as quoted in Ricks 221). It is a short step from her view to the argument of C. F. G. Masterman that Tennyson admired Christianity primarily for its consistency with humanism and morality (210). Peltason concludes that "Tennyson's faith is not a religious faith" so much as "a faith in psychic integrity, in historical coherence, in the possibility of community" (18). These emphases on sanctification, love, good works, this-worldliness, and a balance between individualism and social consciousness, however, are especially consistent with the Arminian evangelicalism that I have sought to portray, here, as one of the headiest ingredients of Tennyson's vision at midcareer.

Other efforts than mine, of course, have historically grounded Tennyson's faith. Jerome H. Buckley, for example, describing an especially wide arc of Christianity, relates the faith of Tennyson to the faiths of Pascal, Newman, and Kierkegaard:

> [Tennyson's] faith, which . . . rests on the premise of feeling, resembles that of Pascal, who likewise trusted the reason of the heart which reason could not know. Its source, like the ground of Newman's assent, is psychological rather than logical, the will of the whole man rather than a postulate of the rational faculty. And in its development, it is frequently not far removed from Kierkegaardian "existentialism," which similarly balances the demands of the inner life against the claims of nineteenth-century "knowledge."
> (*Tennyson* 125)

Tennyson, however, is even more specifically indebted to the Broad Church theology of F. D. Maurice and others (see Mattes *passim* and Langbaum 75). Notice, for example, these latitudinarian/tolerant/"relativist" yet still Christian lines from the prologue:

> Our little systems have their day;
>   They have their day and cease to be:
>   They are but broken lights of thee,
> And thou, 0 Lord, art more than they.
>   (17-20)

Pointing to such Broad Church analogues to *In Memoriam* as John Keble's *The Christian Year* (1827), Julius and Augustus Hare's *Guesses at Truth* (1829), F. D. Maurice's *Kingdom of Christ* (1838), and even Coleridge's *Aids to Reflection* (1825), Culler comments at helpful, pertinent length:

> In *The Kingdom of Christ* Maurice distinguishes between *system* and *method*, two words which many people take to be synonymous but which seem to him "not only not synonymous, but the greatest contraries imaginable: the one indicating that which is most opposed to life, freedom, variety; and the other that without which they cannot exist." "Method" is Coleridge's

> term, in *The Friend, Aids to Reflection,* and the *Essay on Method*; "system" might be predicated of his opposite, Bentham. The terms are, indeed, useful for making distinctions throughout the century. Arnold was interested in the "method and secret of Jesus" and was criticized by Frederic Harrison for not having "a philosophy with coherent, interdependent, subordinate, and derivative principles." Maurice himself might be distinguished from Herbert Spencer as a man of method rather than system. *In Memoriam* is certainly an unsystematic poem but it is not an unmethodical one. (158-59)

These comments are fully understandable along clear lines of my interest in evangelical method.

Tennyson, after all, considered entitling *In Memoriam* "The *Way* of the Soul" (my italics). This name, like the poem itself and, for that matter, like the Broad Church Movement, harks back to *Methodism,* broadly understood as the mainstream American as well as British, experiential-Edwardsean as well as Arminian-Wesleyan evangelicalism of the eighteenth century. Tennyson's "heat of inward evidence," his knowing-beyond-reason or intuition (I refer to Tennyson's "The Two Voices" [1833], line 248), informs his poetry as early as "Armageddon" (1824), in which, at the age of fifteen, he records his "dissociation and mystical communion" (Buckley, *Poems* xi, xiii). His "religion," however, during the composition of *In Memoriam* from 1833 to 1850, that is, during the years of his greatest "soul-competency" (the term belongs to the late but still-influential Moderate of the Southern Baptist faith E. Y. Mullins), became less subjective and more orthodox, less mystical and more evangelical (for the late-late-Romantic character of Mullins's Arminian-evangelical imagination, see Bloom 198-207).

WORKS CITED

Bloom, Harold. *The American Religion: The Emergence of the Post-Christian Nation*. New York: Simon and Schuster, 1992.

Bradley, A. C. *A Commentary on Tennyson's* In Memoriam. 3rd ed. rev. London: Macmillan, 1910.

Bradley, Ian. *The Call to Seriousness: The Evangelical Impact on the Victorians*. London: Jonathan Cape, 1976.

Brantley, Richard E. "The Common Ground of Wesley and Edwards." *Harvard Theological Review* 83 (1990): 271-303.

———. *Coordinates of Anglo-American Romanticism: Wesley, Edwards, Carlyle, and Emerson*. Gainesville: University Press of Florida, 1993.

———. *Locke, Wesley, and the Method of English Romanticism*. Gainesville: University Press of Florida, 1984.

———. *Wordsworth's "Natural Methodism."* New Haven: Yale University Press, 1975.

Buckley, Jerome H. *Tennyson: The Growth of a Poet*. Cambridge: Harvard University Press, 1960; repr. 1967.

———, ed. *Poems of Tennyson*. Boston: Houghton Mifflin, 1958.

Culler, A. Dwight. *The Poetry of Tennyson*. New Haven: Yale University Press, 1977.

Curnock, Nehemiah, ed. *The Journal of the Rev. John Wesley, A. M.* 8 vols. London: Robert Culley, 1909.

Hellstrom, Ward. *On the Poems of Tennyson*. Gainesville: University Press of Florida, 1972.

Hough, Graham. "The Natural Theology of *In Memoriam*." *Review of English Studies* 33 (1947): 244-56.

Langbaum, Robert. "The Dynamic Unity of *In Memoriam*." *Modern Critical Views: Alfred Lord Tennyson*. Ed. Harold Bloom. New York: Chelsea House, 1985. 63-77.

Masterman, C. F. G. *Tennyson as a Religious Teacher*. London: Methuen, 1899; repr. Octagon, 1977.

Mattes, Eleanor B. In Memoriam: *The Way of a Soul*. New York: Exposition Press, 1951.

New, Joan. "Martha." *Seneca Review* 16 (1966): 75-76.

Page, Norman, ed. *Tennyson: Interviews and Recollections*. London: Macmillan, 1983.

Peltason, Timothy. *Reading* In Memoriam. Princeton: Princeton University Press, 1985.

Platizsky, Roger S. *A Blueprint of His Dissent: Madness and Method in Tennyson's Poetry*. Lewisburg, PA: Bucknell University Press, 1989.
Pollak, Vivian R. *Dickinson: The Anxiety of Gender*. Ithaca: Cornell University Press, 1984.
Ricks, Christopher. *Tennyson*. New York: Macmillan, 1972.
Ricoeur, Paul. *Freud and Philosophy*. New Haven: Yale University Press, 1970.
Semmel, Bernard. *The Methodist Revolution*. New York: Basic Books, 1973.
Tennyson, Alfred. *The Poems of Tennyson in Three Volumes*. Ed. Christopher Ricks. Berkeley and Los Angeles: University of California Press, 1987.

Essays, Third Series:

Emily Dickinson

12. Dickinson the Romantic

> Retrospection is Prospect's half,
> Sometimes, almost more.
> —Emily Dickinson, Poem #995

Just as Melvyn New's recent readings of Modern authors as "harbingers" of the eighteenth century bring continuities to light, just as his creative arguments for the "influence" of Marcel Proust on Laurence Sterne and of Thomas Mann on Jonathan Swift make up in cogency what might seem to be lacking in common sense (133-88), so we might well ask, if only for the sake of critical variety, what interpretive rewards await reading Emily Dickinson, the Myth of Amherst, not only in her time but also back in time. She need be none the less *our* Dickinson for such a procedure. I cannot help thinking, in this connection, of the third and fourth editions of *The Norton Anthology of English Literature* (1974, 1981), which assign the poetry of Gerard Manley Hopkins to the period of Modern literature. Although we can learn as much about Hopkins from comparing him to his modern descendant T. S. Eliot as by reading him in conjunction with his fellow-Victorian Robert Browning and his Romantic precursor John Keats, it remains more than a little odd that the editors of *The Norton Anthology* ever saw Hopkins as a twentieth-century poet; the fifth and sixth editions (1988, 1995) return him to the Victorian period. Reading nineteenth-century authors as harbingers of Modern literature in general and of Postmodern critical theory in particular persists (see Behnken, Landow, Poirier, Sinfield). What might go without saying in a different critical climate now needs emphasis. Reading Dickinson in her immediate historical context and, perhaps even more intriguingly, in conjunction with her broadly cultural heritage constitutes a more flexible means of interpreting her works than does "always already" reading them "back to the future." The sophisticated open-endedness of twentieth-century aesthetic tergiversation and lucubration, after all, can be more apparent than real, if not, indeed, precisely too clever by half.

During the all too Modern, almost all too Postmodern, horror of the Civil War, to be sure, Dickinson copied out numbers 216 through 1,066 of her 1,775 poems (Woloski). Many of her personae, accordingly, reflect the tenor of that terrible time and even anticipate the *fin-de-siècle* despair typified by Thomas Hardy in his "The Darkling Thrush" (1900):

> The land's sharp features seemed to be
> The Century's corpse outleant,
>
> ....
>
> And every spirit upon earth
> Seemed fervourless as I. (9-10, 15-16)

Some of Dickinson's personae go so far as to wonder, like Eliot's exemplum of twentieth-century paralysis J. Alfred Prufrock, whether they "dare to eat a peach" ("The Love Song of J. Alfred Prufrock" [1917] 122). Nevertheless, Dickinson's critics exaggerate when they view her as a more hopelessly fragmented than merely bravely iconoclastic poet of near-nihilism. Even Cynthia Griffin Wolff, despite the historical quality of her biographer's perspective on Dickinson's 1,775 poems, perhaps too counterintuitively registers the uncannily twentieth-century tone of the poet's "proleptic voice" (I, 8, 10, 219-37, 450, 524; see also Cameron, Dickie, Homans, Miller, Porter, Stocks). A richer legacy than either the pre-Modern mode or the Victorian-American imagination of Dickinson, specifically, is her Late, but not belated, Anglo-American Romantic imagination, which provides us with an obvious yet neglected, perhaps even an instructive yet fresh, means of realizing that her 1,775 poems mark a culmination rather than an *avant-garde*.

Although Vivian R. Pollak's conclusion that the Myth of Amherst trusted to posterity for the fame that she wanted all along but that she felt that her poetry was too experimental to bring her in her lifetime remains largely persuasive (222-50), Dickinson's innovative poetry manifests not only the "post-experiential perspective" of her pre-Modern mode (212) but also, ironically enough, her sense of tradition. No one need think of the "virgin recluse," to repeat Thomas Wentworth Higginson's rather complacently inapposite description of his friend the poet (Bingham 127), as entirely isolated from broadly cultural intersections of her present with her past. Although her more obscure than palpable "Dome of Abyss . . . Bowing / Into Solitude" exemplifies the near-imagelessness of her proto-Modernism, although neither any Modern author nor, for that matter, any Postmodern critical theorist could be any more spiritually desiccated, any more bereft of cherished illusions, than is Dickinson in her pre-Modern mode, historical influences, whether near at hand or in the rather distant past, are always telling. Her late-blooming Romantic imagination could go so far as to serve as the harbinger of a neo-Romantic age. Indeed, the rather distantly as well as quite immediately historical atmosphere of her 1,775 poems precisely counterbalances the whole sale deracination of her art by which we have tended to forget recent years that she is not so much one of us as one who tells us of more things in heaven and earth than are dreamt of in our philosophies. Although Robert Weisbuch emphasized her "uneasy" similarity to such High-to-Late-Romantic writers as Samuel Taylor Coleridge on the one hand and Ralph Waldo Emerson on the other (48-50, 151-52), her Romanticism has received little attention since the 1890s, when Higginson and Mabel Loomis Todd, despite the notorious liberties they took as her first editors, attuned their own more Late-Romantic than pre-Modern ears to the lyrical gifts of one whom they clearly regarded, albeit not in so many words, as a Late Romantic like themselves. Her most resonant writing is indeed Romantic precisely in that it constitutes the most rhapsodic as well as the most credible imagining of immanence in all of Anglo-American literature.

Wolff, emphasizing the projection of Dickinson's "proleptic voice" not so much into the twentieth century as beyond the grave, studies the poet's concern with the Victorian-American "way of death" and thus contextualizes her otherworldly concentration on end-things (219-37). I, seeking to plumb the immersion of Dickinson's 1,775 personae in the spiritual as well as natural things of this world, will attempt to determine the nature of her participation in an eighteenth- as well as nineteenth-century, British as well as American, stance on experience—namely, the effort to prove on the pulses not only knowledge of the truth but also belief in values. Hence I share much with such other approaches to Dickinson's art as that of Richard B. Sewall, who places her empirical imagination in the context of mid-nineteenth-century scientific knowledge; as that of Beth Maclay Doriani, who relates her religious imagination to the prophetic tradition beginning at least as far back as the Book of Joel in the fourth century B.C.E. (" ... and your sons and your *daughters* shall prophesy" [Joel 2:28, my emphasis; reiterated in Acts 2:17; see also Bloom, *Book of J*]); and as that of Barton Levi St. Armand, who links her aesthetic practice to an especially full, exclusively nineteenth-century range of folk, popular, and elite culture in the United States of America. Nevertheless, I assert that the eighteenth- as well as nineteenth-century, British as well as American, arc from empirical philosophy through evangelical faith to High and Late Romantic literature constitutes a telling background to Dickinson's art. Her Late, but not belated, Anglo-American Romantic imagination, her broadly experiential vision, besides projecting a great, if somewhat vague, "expectation" of "some thing evermore about to be," to quote William Wordsworth's *The Prelude* ([1850] 6.605-07), entails encounters of the spiritual as natural kind.

Critics who imply that Dickinson's art is at all Romantic, of course, tend to assume that her Late Romanticism either evinces anxiety about High Romanticism or prefigures the paralyzed skepticism of "hardcore" deconstruction (Diehl; Stonum; see also Bloom, *Anxiety*; Lehman; McFarland; Peckham; Rajan; Simpson; Wheeler). Dickinson the Romantic, on the contrary, sustains a dialectic that yields spiritually as well as naturally experiential insights of the same sort that for a quarter century I have sought to locate at the heart of British Romanticism in particular and of Anglo-American Romanticism in general. In this milieu she emerges as a more Late-Romantic than pre-Modern author, and she does so in a homegrown, English-speaking way. Even where her 1,775 personae either lament their bitter experience or call the experiential criterion of truth and of values into question, they take their bearings from their broadly experiential vision. Indeed, their more well-earned than foolish optimism is highly creative, precisely in that their combination of sensationalist epistemology and experiential faith emerges as at once more empirical in procedure than post-experiential in effect and more evangelical in principle than post-theological in tendency. Thus, regardless of whether her 1,775 poems epitomize the renewable spirit of Romanticism, a question for another treatise, they emerge as more philosophically, theologically, and aesthetically robust than, say, psychologically catatonic or politically overdetermined. Hence, even as I acknowledge the unity-in-diversity of her Late-Romantic-to-pre-Modern perspective, her experiential-to-post-experiential tonality, I choose here to highlight the backward-looking visage of her Janus-face. Dickinson the Romantic does not so much illustrate as embody the tough and tender blend of mind with soul and heart, the broadly experiential predisposition, to be found through Anglo-American culture from roughly 1770 to 1870.

I

"From about 1858 to 1864," we are told, Dickinson "made copies of more than eight hundred of her poems, gathered them into forty groups, and bound each of these gatherings together with string to form booklets." Thus the poet engaged in "a private kind of self-publication" (Oberhaus 1). Dorothy Huff Oberhaus's *Emily Dickinson's Fascicles: Method and Meaning*, building on R. W. Franklin's ground-breaking edition of Dickinson's manuscript books or "fascicles," a term first used by Todd, focuses on the final fascicle in order to indicate the relationship between all forty fascicles and the devotional tradition from Thomas à Kempis and George Herbert to T. S. Eliot and W. H. Auden. Oberhaus's contextualizing represents a broadly historical, refreshingly interdisciplinary complement to the rather narrowly biographical treatment that William Shurr brings to the fascicles on the one hand and the rather narrowly theoretical reading that Sharon Cameron brings to them on the other. Oberhaus's book, focusing on the twenty-one poems of a single fascicle, concentrates on just one phase of Dickinson's thirty-year arc of composition. The present essay, examining twenty-two poems from the beginning, middle, and end of Dickinson's career, aims to see her poetry steadily and to see it whole. Oberhaus, succeeding in a much-needed, all too rare attempt to address the poet's religious methodology, confines Dickinson's conversion theme to the meditation context of Francis de Sales and Ignatius Loyola. I, addressing the nearer Anglo-American evangelical dimension of Dickinson's religious methodology, seek a more fully interdisciplinary understanding of her "method and meaning," for I also bring Anglo-American empirical and Romantic elements to bear on her inclusively experiential vision.

Poem 1413, to be sure, bears witness not so much to natural-*cum*-spiritual experience as to thoroughgoing skepticism:

> Sweet Skepticism of the Heart—
> That knows—and does not know—
> And tosses like a Fleet of Balm—
> Affronted by the snow—
> Invites and then retards the Truth
> Lest Certainty be sere
> Compared with the delicious throe
> Of transport filled with Fear.

Nevertheless, although "Sweet Skepticism of the Heart" makes no sure claim to efficacy either as a method of knowing or as a forerunner to belief, although the speaker acknowledges, at best, only a coldly threatening welter of harsh existence, this form of skepticism, distinct from either sophisticated or paralyzed skepticism, is less a static state of unbelief and certainly less a premonition of linguistic undecidability than it is both a process of knowing and an openness to mystery. It discovers, above all, painfully intense and intensifying joy in the experiential wonders of one's encounters with phenomena-*cum*-noumenon.

Poem 1413, indeed, evinces just the sort of vital, healthy skepticism to which John Wesley, the founder of British Methodism, and Jonathan Edwards, the leader of the American Great Awakening, subscribed. This prime duumvirate of Anglo-American *bonnes-lettres* makes John Locke's Cartesian method of skepticism a strange near-ally in the dynamic of spiritual quest. It is especially intriguing, if not rather surprising, to observe that Wesley applies to traditional revelation the particularly Lockean, if not generally Cartesian, brand of skepticism whereby the mind, soul, and heart, even after systematically searching for, and apparently finding, what is not open to doubt, remain subject to such all but unspeakable, almost all but unthinkable, possibilities as no faith, no hope, and no love: "I am as fully assured today, as I am of the shining of the sun, that the scriptures are of God. I cannot possibly deny or doubt of it now; *yet I may doubt of it to-morrow; as I have done heretofore a thousand times, and that after the fullest assurance preceding*" (2:92; my italics). Thus, just as the skepticism shared between the twin pioneers of transatlantic revivalism is not only consistent with, but also conducive to, evangelical faith, so the skepticism of Poem 1413 bears faith in experience and even experiential Faith out to the edge of doom. Not only does "Sweet Skepticism of the Heart" retard/deny knowledge of truth, but such skepticism also finds grace, if you will, in the very humidity of natural-*cum*-spiritual experience. Hence, this signature lyric or miniature poetic manifesto recommends a doubting method both tough and tender in that it is both philosophically experiential in procedure and religiously/aesthetically experiential in principle. This efficaciously open-ended form of skepticism is even conducive to, as well as consistent with, a fear of God no less heartfelt for being implicit, and all the more real for being just as sweetly subtle as the strong imagination of Emily Dickinson can make it.

Poem 1071, anticipating just such a combination of tough- and tender-mindedness, recasts in Dickinson's incisive, chiseled way the British Romantic theme of natural-*cum*-spiritual perception (Clarke). Since the poem is addressed to Dickinson's sister-in-law, Susan Gilbert Dickinson, and since Emily and Sue grew apart after Sue's marriage to Emily's brother, Austin, the poet might well have in mind here the specifically experiential loss of her friend. The language of the poem, however, is simultaneously actualistic and idealistic. Although the persona knows that " Perception of an object costs / Precise the Object's loss," the very act of perception compensates for any loss of objective reality: "Perception in itself a Gain / Replying to its Price." The next lines suggest, albeit with a decidedly mixed tone of lingering uneasiness, that the absolute exists all the more indubitably for being strangely present in one's very perception of it as remote and inaccessible:

> The Object Absolute—is nought—
> Perception sets it fair
> And then upbraids a Perfectness
> That situates so far.

Thus contributing to a characteristically Anglo-American tough-mindedness, the speaker out-Humes eighteenth-century British empiricist/skeptic David Hume: she or he suggests that since the absolute is mind- or sense-dependent, it does not exist. Contributing, too, to a characteristically Anglo-American tender-mindedness, the speaker out-Berkeleys eighteenth-century British empiricist Bishop George Berkeley: she or he suggests that, since the absolute is mind- or sense-dependent, it exists. Hence the near-nihilistic doubt of the opening lines of Poem 1071 is finally, if barely, avoided through the strategic, albeit quietly desperate, introduction of a constructive, tough and tender skepticism in the closing lines of the poem, where perception out-Lockes the founder of British empiricism: it functions both as the near-equivalent of the thing and as the only proper namer/evaluator of the thing.

An at least modest confidence emerges, ironically enough, from a dynamic skepticism that leads Dickinson to the operative principle, the overall credo, of her Anglo-American Romantic imagination—namely, *I perceive; therefore, no matter how remote, inaccessible, vacuous, or nil the noumenon might seem to be, phenomena-cum-noumenon constitute "the intense inane" or "a vacancy that nevertheless holds in itself the potentiality of all that is"* (Percy Bysshe Shelley, *Prometheus Unbound* [1819] II.116; Wasserman 236). I cannot help thinking of the revelation in Eliot's "Ash Wednesday" that "the unstilled world still whirled / About the centre of the silent Word" (5.8-9). Spiritual reality, according to such lights, lies near enough at hand that, as Colin Clarke observed in his argument for Wordsworth's combination of natural perception and spiritual mystery, "the visible scene and the observer's mind," object and subject, "at once confront each other (preserving their distinctions) and interpenetrate deeply" (12-13). Thus, besides epitomizing the broadly experiential, satisfyingly complex Anglo-American Romantic dimension of Dickinson's poetry, my formulation of her operative principle or overall credo throws light on the underlying premise of her *palpably* obscure, *wonderfully* awkward concept of seeing "New Englandly":

> Because I see—New Englandly—
> The Queen, discerns like me—
> Provincially— (Poem 285)

These lines are less important for declaring Dickinson's absolute literary independence from England than for announcing her participation in an Anglo-American perceptual propensity, albeit with an American leading edge. Hence the fully experiential, satisfyingly complex Anglo-American Romantic predisposition "to see into the life of things" (Wordsworth, "Lines Composed a Few Miles Above Tintern Abbey" [1798] 49), to perceive both naturally and spiritually, is Dickinson's predisposition, too.

Dickinson's physical senses, despite, or because of, her experientially calibrated, constructively skeptical procedure, emerge as qualified enablers of her attempted syntheses of experience with faith. Whether as analogies to spiritual insight or, perhaps even more intriguingly, as harbingers or accompaniments of transcendental truth, her senses operate along the broadly experiential continuum that joins empirical philosophy at one end to evangelical faith at the other. The most exclusively spiritual given of her vision, surely, is immediate revelation or persistent immanence:

> The Infinite a sudden Guest
> Has been assumed to be—
> But how can that stupendous come
> Which never went away? (Poem 1309)

Here, too, of course, the physical senses would appear to play little or no role in the poet's confident aspiration to belief. The rigor of her spiritual epistemology, however, can be at least as empirically based as is the rigor of her natural epistemology. The speaker of Poem 185, for example, discerns perhaps most notably of all of Dickinson's personae that

> "Faith" is a fine invention
> When Gentlemen can *see*—
> But Microscopes are prudent
> In an Emergency.

What serves either to test or to supplement the spiritual sense is the perceptual extension provided only by hard science. Hence attempts at synthesis succeed at the midpoint of Dickinson's continuum by dint of Dickinson's Anglo-American Romantic will.

Dickinson desires no better way to denominate the spiritual discernment of which she is capable than to call it by the name of, even to equate it with, a particular physical sense:

> The Spirit is the Conscious Ear.
> We actually Hear
> When We inspect—that's audible—
> That is admitted—Here—
>
> For other Services—as Sound—
> There hangs a smaller Ear
> Outside the Castle—that Contain—
> The other—only—Hear— (Poem 733)

The first stanza, to be sure, can simply mean that the physical ear is only a metaphor for spirit. However, since this stanza can also mean that the physical ear is particularly active and peculiarly aware, the physical ear emerges as itself spiritual. Such a reading makes the second stanza's honorific description of the physical ear, as something that "contains" or is more inclusive than the spiritual "ear," somewhat less surprising than it might otherwise be. The biblical injunction "Who hath ears to hear, let him hear" (Matt. 13:9) would undoubtedly connote for Dickinson not so much the exclusively spiritual "ditties of no tone" to which Keats refers in his "Ode on a Grecian Urn" ([1819] 14) as the experiential common ground between the physical ear and the spiritual ear. (No more than Dickinson, of course, is Keats finally satisfied with toneless ditties.) A robust Lockean tone of confidence, accordingly, emerges from the celebratory declaration of Poem 733 that one's highly conscious ability to find out what one seeks is a spiritual as well as a natural faculty. It is as though both natural and spiritual kinds of things correspond in Dickinson's world to her ideas of sensation. It is also as though, along her broadly experiential continuum joining body to mind and mind to soul and heart, the physical senses operate spiritually and the spiritual sense operates naturally.

Common dawns, according to Dickinson's theme of natural-*cum*-spiritual perception, constitute "The Experiment of Our Lord":

> "Morning"—means "Milking"—to the Farmer—
> Dawn to the Teneriffe—
> Dice—to the Maid—
> Morning means just Risk—to the Lover—
> Just revelation—to the Beloved—
> Epicures—date a Breakfast—by it—
> Brides—an Apocalypse—
> Worlds—a Flood—
> Faint-going Lives—Their Lapse from Sighing—
> Faith—The Experiment of Our Lord— (Poem 300)

This aubade is more of a signature lyric or miniature poetic manifesto than a merely narrowly or conventionally considered love or nature poem. This comprehensively philosophical and religious sally of the imagination offers the informed, general reader a broadly experiential vision that takes account of extraordinary as well as ordinary encroachments of both the ominously godded/proleptically degodded quotidian and the normatively godded quotidian. Thus, although morning can threaten as well as beckon to one's body and one's soul, the abrupt transition of the final line, where morning reveals *parousia* (Mark 13:26-35), is decisive on behalf of hope-against-hope; the hard-won tone of optimism in Poem 300 implies that—even in the "world / Of all of us, the place in which, in the end," one is more likely to be unhappy in one's own way than to be happy in one's own way (Wordsworth, *The Prelude* 10.726-27)—one's experience of the petty pace of yet another morning yields ineluctably to the opportunity of yet another gift of dawn. Hence this gift entails, above all, the steady encouragement of the body, the sustaining enhancement of the soul, and, clearly not least, the transforming epiphany of the imagination.

Dickinson's personae embrace "The Fact that Earth is Heaven— / Whether Heaven is Heaven or not." Although this "Fact" is probably "not an Affadavit / Of that specific Spot," her high argument explores the boldly delicious paradox that even the muddle of the middle suffices to out-heaven heaven; her art of phenomena-*cum*-noumenon values the here-and-now not only for the sake of its being the best of all possible windows on a world elsewhere but also for itself (Poem 1408).

Although given points on Dickinson's broadly experiential continuum can range so far apart as to seem unrelated, her natural/spiritual dialectic, nevertheless, tends to unify her art. Poem 668, for example, identifies the physical senses with the spiritual sense:

> "Nature" is what we see—
> The Hill—the Afternoon—
> Squirrel—Eclipse—the Bumble bee—
> Nay—Nature is Heaven—
> Nature is what we hear—
> The Bobolink—the Sea—
> Thunder—the Cricket—
> Nay—Nature is Harmony—
> Nature is what we know—
> Yet have no art to say—
> So impotent our Wisdom is
> To her Simplicity.

The poet here joins natural and spiritual seeing and hearing to natural and spiritual thinking and writing. Although "nay" is often used to "express negation, dissent, denial, or refusal," the word is also "occasionally used as an introductory word, without any direct negation . . . to introduce a more correct, precise, or emphatic statement than the one first made" (*OED*); the "nays" of lines 4 and 8, accordingly, are more emphatic or ringing than negative or stuttering. Thus, from developing the "everlasting NAY" of Thomas Carlyle's *Sartor Resartus* (1836), Dickinson's "nays" signal both her "slant" or "contingent" and her "ordained" or affirmative truth-telling (Poems 1129, 1405). (More characteristic of Carlyle's vision than the "everlasting NAY" of his pre-Modern mode, incidentally, is the "everlasting YEA" of his Late-Romantic imagination, which, as I have previously tried to show, is linked inextricably to the empirical/evangelical dialectic on which Emerson, too, draws, during the 1830s and 1840s.) "What we see," albeit the literal object of physical sight, is neither contrasted with, nor undercut by, the fact that earth is heaven. Indeed, "what we see" is nothing less than precisely the participation of the literal object in spiritual vision. Spiritual perception of harmony, conversely, is of the very physical essence of hearing the bobolink. Hence, through the not-so-simple simplicity of point blank ideas that reverberate in the imagination, the satisfyingly complex, gloriously intriguing confluence of natural with spiritual perception transcends, perhaps even as it operates along, the broadly experiential continuum joining nature and the body at one extreme to wisdom and language at the other.

Donald Davie, always abreast of critical theory, laments our difficulty in maintaining the Protestant belief in direct, New Testament language: "Our yea can never be yea, nor our nay be nay, because we recognize that our language mutinously refuses to be thus univocal" (160; Matt. 5:37). Hence, Dickinson's yea can never be yea, nor her nay be nay, at least insofar as deconstruction disproves univocity. The empirical as well as Protestant goal of simplicity, however, is her goal, too. Although Poem 668 is more than sufficiently subtle to be anything but straightforward, this signature lyric or miniature poetic manifesto conceives of experience synoptically, as both natural and spiritual. Not just through the dialectic of riddle and mystery but even through the implicitly non- or preverbal (as well as through the surpassingly verbal) encounter of the divine in nature, Dickinson the Romantic all but naïvely affirms phenomena-*cum*-noumenon, and so impishly, impudently confounds *aporia*.

It might at first glance be less than clear just how Poem 657, for its contribution to the Anglo-American Romantic nexus of empirical philosophy and evangelical faith, transmogrifies experiential philosophy-*cum*-faith:

>I dwell in Possibility—
>A fairer House than Prose—
>More numerous of Windows—
>Superior—for Doors—
>
>Of Chambers as the Cedars—
>Impregnable of Eye—
>And for an Everlasting Roof
>The Gambrels of the Sky—
>
>Of Visitors—the fairest—
>For Occupation—This—
>The spreading wide my narrow Hands
>To gather Paradise—

The strictly aesthetic sense of Dickinson's art, after all, entails only autonomy or inviolable interiority: "Of Chambers as the Cedars— / Impregnable of Eye." Nevertheless, her combination of the physical senses with the spiritual sense opens literature up both horizontally— "More numerous of Windows— / Superior—for Doors"—and vertically: "And for an Everlasting Roof / The Gambrels of the Sky." Moreover, since "Monuments of unaging intellect," to use a phrase of William Butler Yeats ("Sailing to Byzantium" [1928] 8), remain accessible and, to use Dickinson's word, "breathe" (*Letters* 2:403), she, like John

Milton's Urania, "fit audience find[s], though few" (*Paradise Lost* [1674] 7.31), for her art invites "Visitors—the fairest." The "I" of Poem 657, indeed, extends an especially welcoming, precisely natural-*cum*-spiritual gesture—namely, "The spreading wide my narrow Hands / To gather Paradise." Thus, although Dickinson's personae are sometimes fictional and sometimes so difficult to identify as either male or female that they can be "gender-bending," they are also often autobiographical. If the remarkably unsuspicious persona of Poem 657 is as refreshingly close to Dickinson's voice as I think she is, then Dickinson the Romantic not only works toward the end that faith in experience will yield both ontology and doctrine but also expects that experiential Faith will realize a sacramental vision worthy of William Blake's ringing conclusion in his "The Divine Image": "Where Mercy, Love & Pity dwell / There God is dwelling too" ([1789] 19-20). Not only does her surpassingly lovely lyric remain alert both to "Effort, and expectation, and desire, / And something evermore about to be" and to "hope that can never die" (Wordsworth, *The Prelude* 6:607-09); her poem also, albeit while hardly complacent in either perceiving the truth or welcoming the influx of grace, conveys more than enough confidence of tone and of import to signal the poet's receptivity to—nay, her transformation of—whatever riddle or mystery, whatever combination of nature and the divine, might come within her ken. Hence, although "Possibility" means poetry distinct from prose, the particular kind of poetry that Dickinson implies, to borrow Robert Langbaum's phrase for the nineteenth-century dramatic monologue, is "the poetry of experience." The rich strangeness of Poem 657 illustrates Dickinson's inclusive, especially experiential stance of mind, soul, and heart.

The central "Fact" to which Dickinson the Romantic testifies through her natural-*cum*-spiritual, insistently experiential continuum is indeed "The Fact that Earth is Heaven— / Whether Heaven is Heaven or not." Precisely how her vision is thus compound becomes more than sufficiently clear from Poem 906:

> The Admirations—and Contempts—of time—
> Show justest—through an Open Tomb—
> The Dying—as it were a Height
> Reorganizes Estimate
> And what We saw not
> We distinguish clear—
> And mostly—see not
> What We saw before—

> 'Tis Compound Vision—
> Light—enabling Light—
> The Finite—furnished
> With the Infinite—
> Convex—and Concave Witness—
> Back—toward Time—
> And forward—
> Toward the God of Him—

Although "Compound Vision" means intimations of immortality, such vision also means one's practical as well as mysterious capacity to see the divine in the temporal: the speaker grasps "The Finite—furnished / With the Infinite." Although Dickinson's "flood subject" of immortality has received ample attention (Farr, Johnson, St. Armand), neither the philosophical nor the religious sense in which she is also a poet of the here-and-now has hitherto received sufficient attention; it is especially easy to overemphasize her role as a poet of futurity. Hence her "Compound Vision" ultimately encompasses the metalepsis of origins with end-things, the transumption of First and Last in midst. The "We" of the poem, the living, expatiate within a large world picture. This Late, but not belated, Anglo-American Romantic "daughter of prophecy," besides being the Sybil who ferries her readers across the Styx from life to death and from Late Romanticism to Modernism, commends the here-and-now through her mainstream, more Hebraic than Hellenic or Roman standard of natural-*cum*-spiritual synthesis.

Poem 917, significantly, albeit with no undue naïveté and even with all due sophistication, combines mathematical exactitude with methodological rigor to advance the poet's cosmologically ambitious quest for both faith in experience and experiential Faith:

> Love—is anterior to Life—
> Posterior—to Death—
> Initial of Creation, and
> The Exponent of Earth—

Love, here, is transcendence, but it is also immanence, for love not only frames, contextualizes, and authorizes but also acknowledges, intensifies, and emanates from within the world. Reality for Dickinson is so far from being entirely non- or anti-experiential as to emerge directly from appearances, for, if experience does not yield all that she needs to know of Alpha and Omega (Rev. 22:13), then life yields all that she does know of anything whatsoever, including what she understands about origins and end-things. This intellectual as well as emotional, philosophical as well as religious, quatrain comprises the entire outlook on life as well as on art of a major author careful to compound Alpha and Omega with the natural as well as spiritual pilgrimage of life, not so much to play both ends against the middle as to enlist First and Last on behalf of midst. Thus, this paean to love rivals William Shakespeare's "Let me not to the marriage of true minds," Elizabeth Barrett Browning's "How do I love thee? Let me count the ways," and the thirteenth chapter of I Corinthians. Hence the most boldly metaleptic, most efficaciously transumptive imagination in all of Western literature celebrates not only how Love transfigures midst—that is, how Word becomes event—but also, albeit with no undue naïveté and even with all due sophistication, how midst embodies First and Last—that is, how event becomes Word.

Although Dickinson never fully forswears knowledge of origins and of end-things, although no amount of contextualizing in the Victorian-American "way of death" can make her proleptic hunger to learn what, if anything, lies on the other side of life seem other than morbid, she focuses on the middle passages of life; she regards existence as more well-grounded than narrowly-constricted and as more noumenal than phenomenal. Thus, although the experientially philosophical dimension of her imagination entails epistemology, her 1,775 poems do not devalue ontology; instead, they aim at aligning nature with knowledge. Moreover, although the experientially religious dimension of her imagination entails morality, although her 1,775 poems can be understood to anticipate Emmanuel Levinas's emphasis on ethics at the expense of both ontology and epistemology (I have in mind here Levinas's Hebraizing re-mystifying of Martin Heidegger's totalizing demystifying), Dickinson's natural-*cum*-spiritual vision does not subordinate either philosophy to faith or faith to philosophy so much as it reconceives afresh a fresh experience of both knowledge and belief. She nuances method through personhood-*cum*-infinity. Hence, just as in Richard Wilbur's poem "Love Calls Us to the Things of This World" (1956), so Dickinson the Romantic calls us to the muddle of the middle, the quotidian world. Experience functions for her much as it does for Paul in Romans 5:3-5: "We glory in tribulations also: knowing that tribulation worketh patience; and patience, experience; and experience, hope; and hope maketh not ashamed." Her compression of natural with spiritual figures justifies her relish for experience on "The Hill Difficulty," in "The Slough of Despond," and throughout "Vanity Fair" (John Bunyan, *The Pilgrim's Progress* [1678]).

The present argument, then, in advance of a planned series of arguments, has so far sought to epitomize Dickinson's hope-against-hope for spiritual as well as for natural blessings in "the world / Of all of us." According to the empirical view of experience as all-important, of course, the sons and daughters of Adam and of Eve are all born as *tabulae rasae*, and Wesley, Edwards, and Dickinson agree. Their writings, however, apply this first principle of sensationalist epistemology to religion even more thoroughly than do the writings of Locke (Spellman). Not only does Dickinson's Anglo-American imagination entertain the efficacy of "Christ on the Road" as well as of "Christ on the Cross" (Bloom, *American Religion*); her art also, perhaps even more importantly, acknowledges the second Adam and Eve of experience as well as the first Adam and Eve of original sin. Although her lyrics form no system, at least in the sense of looking toward closed, predictable theory, they practice open, heuristic method; they aspire to a condition in which even spiritual experience is not only of the mind but also of the senses. Dickinson the Romantic, more than just validating spiritual insights by borrowing from sense-language, speaks literally to experience in general, including empirical observation, scientific method, and apprehension of God in nature and the Spirit. Her full measures of poetic presence constitute the "rich and strange" (Shakespeare, *The Tempest* [1609] I.ii.402) expression of a methodology by which she not only links sense to reason and matter to mind but also, perhaps even more importantly, aligns nature with grace.

Thus, insofar as an eighteenth- as well as nineteenth-century bi-national perspective on Dickinson's Late Romantic works illuminates her "both/and" logic, her methodological alertness hardly negates her "having it both ways." This last, best exponent of Anglo-American Romanticism grounds transcendentalism in the world, balances religious myths and religious morality with scientific reverence for fact and detail, allies empirical assumptions with "disciplined" spirit, and, clearly not least, holds fast, albeit somewhat desperately, to the conviction that faith in experience yields experiential Faith.

II

Since the same poet who writes that "After great pain, a formal feeling comes" (Poem 341), who "like[s] a look of Agony, / Because [she] know[s] it's true" (Poem 241), writes, too, of "rich and strange" experience, her tough and tender imagination pursues a no less than audaciously dialectical goal. Since her broadly experiential, natural-*cum*-spiritual poetics proves much more than sufficiently capacious to earn for her 1,775 poems both their characteristically robust outlook on life and their frequently rhapsodic vision of creation, her metaleptic voice blends the empirical/evangelical ebullience of the Anglo-American temperament with the past- and present- as well as future-oriented optimism of even Late Romanticism. Insofar as the satisfying complexity and the glorious intrigue of her traditional combination of palpable obscurity and ineffable mystery provide her with more than enough to know and with almost too much to believe, she recalls us to our own best heritage of emphasizing that what lies between birth and death is all we know on earth and all we need to know. Hence her poetry, despite its pre-Modern and even its proleptically Postmodern tonalities, interprets life as much more than sufficiently satisfying and even as much more than sufficiently glorious not merely to relieve but also to redirect our current twofold obsession with whether and how to be born and with when and how to die. Her "Modernism," which I place in quotation marks because I think it should be provisionally so called, far from functions only like a Sybil who ferries passengers across the Styx of the nineteenth century to the death themes of Modernism and P0stmodernism. Her "Modernism," indeed, precisely coexists with the optimism of her past- as well as present- and future-oriented, more Hebraically prophetic or bardic than merely Sybilline, Anglo-American trivium of empirical philosophy, evangelical faith, and Romantic imagination.

The more paradoxical than vertiginous, more Late Romantic than pre-Modem Poem 419, perhaps most notably of all of Dickinson's 1,775 poems, brings together the more plangently resounding than merely plaintive tone and import of her broadly experiential vision. (Thomas H. Johnson assigns the poem to the year 1862, when she was at the height of her powers.)

> We grow accustomed to the Dark—
> When Light is put away—
> As when the Neighbor holds the Lamp
> To witness her Goodbye—
>
> A Moment—We uncertain step
> For newness of the night—
> Then—fit our Vision to the Dark—
> And meet the Road—erect—

> And so of larger—Darknesses—
> Those Evenings of the Brain—
> When not a Moon disclose a sign—
> Or Star—come out—within—
>
> The Bravest—grope a little—
> And sometimes hit a Tree
> Directly in the Forehead—
> But as they learn to see—
>
> Either the Darkness alters—
> Or something in the sight
> Adjusts itself to Midnight—
> And Life steps almost straight.

"The wonderful humor of the bravest hitting a tree, directly in the forehead," declares Harold Bloom, "helps save the poem from too simplistic an allegory." Where Bloom confines the meaning to "the surmounting of our fear of the dead and so of our own death," however, he is not entirely convincing. "Dickinson," as even Bloom observes, "was no worshiper of Midnight, as Yeats was to be" (*Western Canon* 298-99). I take the humor of the poem to be the lingering lilt of Late Romanticism. The poem not only momentarily stays confusion but also lovingly dispels it. The allegory of the poem, accordingly, is not the correspondence between "fitting oneself to the dark" and "making oneself fit for the dead" so much as it is the strategic juxtaposition of the open-eyed, experientially receptive hope-against-hope characteristic of even Late Anglo-American Romanticism with the mockingly triumphant death theme prelusive to European , if not to Anglo-American, Modernism.

Poem 786, to be sure, fits Bloom's schema well:

> Severer Service of myself
> I—hastened to demand
> To fill the awful Vacuum
> Your life had left behind—
>
> I worried Nature with my Wheels
> When Hers had ceased to run—

> When she had put away Her Work
> My own had just begun.
>
> I strove to weary Brain and Bone—
> To harass to fatigue
> The glittering Retinue of nerves—
> Vitality to clog
>
> To some dull comfort Those obtain
> Who put a Head away
> They knew the Hair to—
> And forget the color of the Day—
>
> Affliction would not be appeased—
> The Darkness braced as firm
> As all my strategem had been
> The Midnight to confirm—
>
> No drug for Consciousness—can be—
> Alternative to die
> Is Nature's only Pharmacy
> For Being's Malady—

Although the speaker is busy hastening, demanding, worrying, and harassing, these activities are not so decisive as to constitute either a resolute survival strategy or "the dark night of the soul" before the dawning of a stronger faith. The suicidal implications of the final stanza, perhaps emanating from the poet's love for sister-in-law Sue or for the Rev. Charles Wadsworth or for both (Pollak, Shurr), seem closer to the tone of such a pessimistic philosophy as that of Arthur Schopenhauer than to the import of Hopkins's "terrible sonnets." Finally tough-minded to the point of either a sophisticated or a paralyzed skepticism are the tone and import of this particularly harrowing poem. The persona's experience of pain and of loss, the virtual postexperience of her form of pessimism, illustrates as well as intimates the Modernist worship of Midnight. Indeed, so mockingly triumphant are "Affliction" and "The Midnight" that the speaker is precisely hard put even to fit herself for "The Darkness," much less to make herself fit for the dead. Such pure examples of Dickinson's pre-Modern mode ("Pain—has an Element of Blank," Poem 650, is another) relentlessly sound their death themes.

Thus, no more than merely narrowly theoretical, predictably Postmodern "contextualizing" does even broadly methodological, historical contextualizing fully encompass the wonderfully "evasive poetics" of Dickinson (Forman). Nor would one wish that it could. Perhaps the more urgently for her power to elude, however, we persist in attempting to plumb her enigmas. Her 1,775 poems grow not only tantalizing to the point of mischief but also elegant to the point of entailing both subtlety and simplicity. Hence, although for its part in her delivery of a more well-earned than foolish optimism the last stanza of Poem 419 emphasizes death or Midnight with an upper-case intensity or ferocity, "Life" in the last line, with a similarly emphatic, similarly upper-case intensity or ferocity, "steps almost straight." So difficult to gainsay is the *élan*, the gaiety, of this supremely lovely, lucidly crafted signature lyric or miniature poetic manifesto that the well-tempered reader does not even wish to deny the hard-won (distinct from merely harrowing) tone of her Late but not belated Anglo-American Romantic hope-against-hope.

It is hardly as though the speaker of Poem 419, of course, were in sympathy with such "Romantics" as doctors who seek to thwart the E-bola virus or as Mother Teresa, who tilts at the windmills of saving the masses. The poem, nevertheless, gives pride of place to the distinctly Romantic possibility that the imagination can alter, even where it cannot save, the world.

Instructive enough in this regard is Song I of Heinrich Heine's *The Homecoming* (1823-24), the atmosphere of which now resembles, and now differs from, the tone and import of Poem 419.

> In my life so dark and jaded,
> Once a vision glistened bright.
> Now the vision's dim and faded—
> Once again I'm wrapped in night.
>
> In the dark a child, dissembling
> While the fearsome phantoms throng,
> Tries to cover up his trembling
> With a shrill and noisy song.
>
> I, a frantic child, am straining
> At my song in darkness here.
> What if the song's not entertaining?
> Still it's freed me of my fear.

The approaching darkness of which both Heine and Dickinson are aware, perhaps even their dim premonition of some "rough beast, its hour come round at last," slouching "towards Bethlehem to be born" (Yeats, "The Second Coming" [1919] 21-22), set both of their versions of Romanticism apart from the High Romanticism of Wordsworth and Keats. Even High Romanticism, however, is replete with the sense of lost illumination prelusive to Dickinson's growing "accustomed to the Dark." Not only does Keats announce, "Darkling I listen," and lament, "Fled is that vision" ("Ode to a Nightingale" [1819] 51, 80); Wordsworth's "visionary gleam," too, fades ("Ode: Intimations of Immortality" [1802] 56). Equally replete in the finally more compatible than incompatible imaginations of Wordsworth, Keats, and Dickinson is not only the poetic method that with however reconstructive a goal calls all into doubt but also the poetic faith that with however great a tendency to whistle past the graveyard keeps singing in the dark. Thus, Dickinson's Late Romantic imagination holds more in common with even the High Romanticism of Great Britain than with either the Late Romanticism of Heine or the Modernism of either the Continent or Anglo-America. Hence Poem 419, albeit blessedly without any of the sentimental liquidity that mars Hal Draper's translation of Heine's Song I, brings off a more Late Romantic than pre-Modern, more moment-by-moment than merely momentary, stay against confusion.

Although Song I of *The Homecoming* might put us in mind of Papageno's Glockenspiel defense against the evil spirit Monostatos in Wolfgang Amadeus Mozart's *The Magic Flute* (1791), although we might also be reminded here of Christian-existential "fear and trembling," of religious as well as philosophical dread, in Søren Kierkegaard's "anti"-epistemology, Dickinson's singing in the dark is finally more tough-minded than that of Heine. Poem 419, after all, reflects not so much the rarefied, abstract kind of hope to be found in German Romanticism as the tough and tender kind of hope-against-hope to be found in Anglo-American Romanticism. Although the tone and import of Anglo-American Romanticism is more empirically evangelical than the other way around, although Dickinson's singing is finally more tough-minded than Bard Bracy's musical defense against evil in Coleridge's "Christabel" (1816), the evangelically empirical tone and import of her Late but not belated Anglo-American Romanticism remains both tough and tender; her central theme of immortality, her "flood subject," suffices to keep both her pre-Modernism from obsessiveness concerning the death theme and her Anglo-American Romanticism from belatedness (distinct from lateness) concerning the life theme.

"Her attempt," declares Eleanor Wilner, "was imaginatively to repossess and reconstruct an old order, and if to do so, she was led to innovations which later were to serve the cause of modernism, this is historical irony, rather than intention." Wilner's classic study of Dickinson's poetics is at its best on the subject of the poet's" conservative Christian-Platonic mold of mind." Wilner demonstrates that the poet's "innovations" were more than just "precursors of a new world vision" in that they broke "the conventions of her day, in order to force the mind, not forward, but back." Wilner's conclusion, however, that Dickinson's "subjectivity is the last extreme of a dying Puritanism" is wide of the mark (145, 154).

Just as the religious consciousness of the nineteenth-century English-speaking world has less to do with the largely Calvinist-evangelical consciousness of the Puritan seventeenth century than with the gradual but ineluctable triumph of that world's Arminian-evangelical faith during the eighteenth and nineteenth centuries, so Dickinson's procedural consciousness is more remarkably resilient than severely challenged. Her imagination, moreover, is more experiential in character than anti-experiential in bias. Indeed, her broadly experiential vision is precisely empirical/evangelical in both the eighteenth-century sense of capaciousness and the nineteenth-century sense of dialectic. Thus, with more hope-against-hope of discovery-upon-discovery than with any merely complacent expectation of superimposed answers, I have begun here to suggest how Dickinson 's synthesis of form with content embodies the pastness of her presence almost to the point of making her pastness reappear before our wondering eyes. Her vision is so deeply rooted as to remain quite lively in the here and now. Her personae do not so much maintain an always already threatened, merely momentary receptivity to knowledge-*cum*-belief as they sustain a moment-by-moment, constantly renewing-and-renewable receptivity to knowledge-*cum*-belief. Hence, regardless of whether her Anglo-American Romantic voice can still resound in our minds and souls, regardless of whether her lyrical hope-against-hope can still rebound in our hearts, her liberal sense, her open-endedly receptive, empirical-evangelical temperament, represents a perennial phenomenon.

Inviting our particular attention in the context of gauging just where Dickinson's 1,775 poems belong on the arc from Romantic to Modern is Chris Snodgrass's *Aubrey Beardsley: Dandy of the Grotesque*. Just as Snodgrass's eye for the conservative side of Beardsley's Late Romantic/*fin-de-siècle* paradox constitutes perhaps the most telling perception of his book, so my eye for the backward-looking visage of Dickinson's Late Romantic/*fin-de-siècle* Janus-face suggests that her poems are no more *predictably fin-de-siècle* than are Beardsley's drawings. Although Dickinson is more of a major artist than is Beardsley, although unlike the libidinal emphases of his drawings the sexual implications of her language *liberate* rather than "limit" "viewer 'play,'" she, too, harks back imaginatively to the past; she, too, reconfigures Romantic as well as Victorian "essentialist correspondences" and "principles of noumenal truth" (130). Although Dickinson, like Beardsley, is fearful of "losing mastery, of being swallowed by illogical meaninglessness, of being reduced to the animalistic and monstrous," her grasp of realism, like his, remains more empirical than materialistic, more Romantic than Victorian; she is finally no more "swallowed by illogical meaninglessness" than is he, no more wholly "reduced to the animalistic and monstrous" than is he (161-203). Thus, just as Beardsley "oscillates" between "ontological insecurity" and "traditional authority," between "iconoclasm" and "reverence," and between the impulse to the *avant-garde* and the gift for "absorbing the canon" (13, 100, 103), so Dickinson reaffirms philosophical, religious, and imaginative authority even as she destabilizes the old order. Just as the unconscious goal of Beardsley's "stylistic defamiliarizations" is to "salvage transcendental truth" along with immanence, so the conscious goal of Dickinson's realignments of meaning is to reconstruct meaning. Although she, too, glimpses the gap between "all presumably validating sources" and "oscillating deferral of the final word," although she, too, is disturbed by such a vertiginous prospect, her "sheer joy of the game" finally exceeds the qualms that both artists suffer at the prospect of "unmasking the ultimate horror" of nothingness behind all masks. Her expectation of finding "meaning or joy in the world beyond the game," perhaps even more than does his, emerges both from faith in experience and from experiential Faith (295).

Therefore, although Dickinson is at least as concerned as is Beardsley that art be "untrammeled by preclusive meaning," she is not yet so ready as he to posit "the ultimate authority of Art" (292). Even in her loving parodies of both empirical "coherence" and "redemptive" (read: evangelical) "order," she, even more than he, desires to welcome both "an alternative coherence" and an alternative soteriology "in through the front door of art (293). That is, she is so well acquainted with the experiential stakes of philosophy and of religion that her demotically experiential-Arminian temperament contrasts with the "arcane" quality of Beardsley's "fundamentalist" (read: anti-experiential-Calvinist) temperament (282). Nevertheless, at the same time that both Beardsley and Dickinson oscillate between the more sophisticated than dynamic skeptical stance of Modernism and the more healthy than static skepticism of Romantic paradox, they both tilt, albeit in ways consistent with their two different media, toward ontology and doctrine over ontological and doctrinal insecurity and even toward reverence over iconoclasm. Hence I, like Snodgrass, am impelled to emphasize the creative energies that mid-to-late nineteenth-century authors draw from the philosophically theological dimension of their shared Romantic heritage. Indeed, Snodgrass's fresh, interdisciplinary perspective on Beardsley's aesthetics precisely reinforces my appeal to Dickinson's readers not only to gravitate toward her ontological insecurity but also to recognize her ontological-*cum*-doctrinal ambition, not only to abet her iconoclasm but also to savor her reverence, and not only to mark her perfection and control of the canon but also to cherish her loving absorption of it. I want, above all, to establish the importance of her art not just for how her poetry anticipates Modernism and Postmodernism but particularly for how it culminates a simultaneously philosophical, theological, and literary tradition that just might nourish the individual talent once again. Although her premonition of a decadent *avant-garde*, like Beardsley's, is self-fulfilling, her genius, like his, remembers the origin of the arc from Romantic to Modern.

Dickinson's 1,775 poems, then, from the standpoint of her healthy respect for experience as well as of her yearning and nostalgia for it, occur as early as 11:00 a.m. and seldom any later than noon on the arc from High Romanticism at 9:00 a.m. to High Modernism at 3:00 p.m. Her themes of selfhood, consciousness, the horrors of war, tragic memory, unrelenting trauma, a nihilistic view of the universe, and the awareness and fear of death, to be sure, are sufficiently pre-Modern. Her sense of human weakness and vulnerability, moreover, is prescient. Her more quiet than unquiet desperation, however, is sufficiently dignified to be more Thoreauvian than Kafkaesque. Although her incipient dissociation of sensibility underlies her experiments with form, although her poetry features such stylistic sallies as nonstandard, colloquial expression, figurative profusion, graphic innovations, cerebral conundrums, double-talk repetitions, lack of conventional punctuation, myriad dashes, nonrecoverable deletions, uninflected verbs, indefinite pronouns, the use of words as more than one part of speech, and the frequent inclusion in her fair copies of more one possible word choice (her readers must be active and hypertextual), such features of her backward-looking Janus-face her "impassioned expression of past remembrance," her return to nature, her return to myth, and her reaffirmation of "the ecstasy and comfort of love and the imagination" all characterize her creative dialectic at least as much as does her "Modern" mode of utterance. (I have in mind here both Cristanne Miller's analysis of Dickinson's innovative language and Warren Bargad's language for the "Romantic Modernism" of Israeli poet Amir Gilboa.) Dickinson's seldom easy but often sustained lyricism, her hard-won aesthetic of unity, and such scattered attributes of her form as ellipsis, enjambment, puns, and rich ambiguity through syntactical inversion may not simply counteract but ultimately repair both the dissonance and the fragmentation of her "Modern" aesthetics.

Thus, regardless of how Romantically or of how Modernistically Dickinson writes, she always writes "from an acute perception, whether celebrative or tragic, of human experience." Where she "refuses to write romantically," where she out-Woolfs Virginia Woolf and out-Frosts Robert Frost, she "fulfills the act" of doing so (I am again indebted to Bargad's language). Indeed, precisely because Dickinson the Romantic anticipates such distinguishing marks of Modernism as its dissociation of sensibility, its psychic-social disintegration, its ontological breakup, its theme of the death of God, and its aesthetic fragmentation, she draws the more deeply and with all the greater will, intelligence, soul, and imagination on the Anglo-American traditions of natural-*cum*-spiritual methodology on the one hand and of Romantic literature on the other. Her unsurpassed voice in Anglo-American literature might well be owing not so much to her having exhausted a ruling paradigm as to her having "wrung" changes on a relatively robust and untroubled model to the point of modulating to a minor but related key.

III

In sum, then, it is well to remember what could go without saying in a different critical climate. Dickinson speaks not so much a Modernist/Postmodernist language with the Nietzschean/Derridean accent of *aporia* as a Late Romantic language with the Wesleyan/Edwardsean accent of robust, albeit hardly unproblematical, experience. If only with more hope of having attained to a certain nuanced lucidity than from any great experience of ever having achieved such an elusively desirable tone before, I conclude now that critical understanding depends on scrutiny of the commonplace in alternation with celebration of the obvious. Regardless of whether the Myth of Amherst can ameliorate "the way we live now," regardless of whether she can clarify our broadly experiential context, the combination of subtlety and accessibility in the criticism of her works can do much to restore the public "function of criticism at the present time." Although her poetry is sufficiently *fin-de-siècle* to be read plausibly as an anticipation of Modernism and even as an intimation of Postmodernism, it is all too often read exclusively in that light. I have accordingly interpreted the broadly experiential vision of her Late but not belated Anglo-American Romantic imagination as a more satisfyingly complex and gloriously intriguing clue to the deeply mysterious riddle of her art than is the comparatively straitened and relatively short-circuited post-experiential perspective of her pre-Modern mode.

Somewhat in the spirit of George Orwell, who describes human nature as all too ready to overlook the obvious, I have argued for more far-reaching than subtle gradations of difference between Dickinson's Late Romantic imagination and full-blown Modernism. Somewhat in the spirit of William of Ockham, whose razor means that "nothing should be assumed that does not need to be assumed in accounting for a particular fact at hand" (Cox 127), I have argued for more subtle than far-reaching gradations of difference between her Late Romantic imagination and her pre-Modem mode. I have emphasized the former over the latter. Even if Dickinson somehow pre-imagines the psychic/social disintegration of Modernism, the rich, strange sea-change of tradition-*cum*-iconoclasm is nonetheless what makes her art both innovative and forceful.

Dickinson's compound, deeply as well as broadly experiential vision ends "with a bang" and not with "a whimper" the empirical/evangelical dialectic of Anglo-American Romanticism (Eliot, "The Hollow Men" [1925] 5.31). Her strong analogy between, perhaps even her near-identity of, the physical senses and the spiritual sense, to be sure, goes contrary to such relatively sense-deprived formulations of faith as that of Job 1:21, "The Lord gave, and the Lord hath taken away; blessed be the name of the Lord"; as that of Habakkuk 2:1, "I will stand upon my watch, and set me upon the tower, and will watch to see what he will say unto me"; and as that of Milton's nineteenth sonnet, "They also serve who only stand and wait." Nevertheless, her natural-*cum*-spiritual sensorium builds on the epistemological faith, the religious empiricism, that in my terms lies close to the sweet but skeptical heart, the poetic method in combination with poetic faith, of her Anglo-American Romantic heritage.

Although a given statement of identity is always a statement of faith and never of "truth" or "true knowledge," at least according to the linguistics of Ferdinand de Saussure, the "sense" in which Dickinson the Romantic writes at once from evidence and from faith relates to Modernism and to Postmodernism perhaps in the way that Jane Austen's concept of "sense" as complex but common relates to her concept of "sensibility" as excessively rarefied.

Austen is as Romantic as Neoclassical. Dickinson the Romantic claims a literary as well as a philosophical-*cum*-religious legacy from her Anglo-American tradition. The intellectual as well as emotional strength for which her poetry is now so justly admired derives from the retroleptic audacity with which she enters into and possesses, nay envelopes, her heritage. "Scorn [ing] delights" and "liv[ing] laborious days," she thus wisely invests in the "fair guerdon" of her lasting "fame" (Milton, "Lycidas" [1638] 70, 72-73). Hence, although she can appear to lack what Wesley and Edwards and even what Tennyson and Emerson appear to enjoy, natural-spiritual experience, her words for such experience all but fulfill her palpable need for blessed assurance of spiritual things as well as for certain knowledge of natural things. She rarely intimates Modernism at the expense of professing Romanticism.

It is not simply that Dickinson's Late Romantic paradigm of experience is at war with her pre-Modern paradigm of postexperience. Nor is she any more intent on breaking either paradigm apart than she is on practicing "normal science." Rather, she tests her Late Romantic model so intensely, makes such heavy demands upon it, that she transforms it. If she is not fully in control of either how the model changes or what it changes into, then neither does she ever fully abandon its twin-experiential orientations to epistemology and to belief. Never does she irretrievably forgo the natural-*cum*-spiritual frame of reference of her chosen model.

It is not just that there are two categories of Dickinson's poems, one Late Romantic and the other pre-Modern. It is, perhaps even more importantly, that a given poem often juxtaposes her Late Romantic imagination against her pre-Modern mode. Thus, a given poem often constitutes a thematic as well as a "tonal pun" on these two aspects of her art (cf. Bishop on Emerson). Neither aspect undercuts the other so much as each accords parity to the other. Her Late Romantic imagination, however, predominates.

Nietzsche, of course, recommended Dionysus over Apollo because he thought the times were too Apollonian. He would have recommended the opposite had he thought them too Dionysiac. Blake, of course, recommended imagination over reason because he thought the times were too rationalistic. He would have recommended the opposite had he thought the age too full of imagination. Were Dickinson's poetry being read as Romantic, I would recommend it as pre-Modern. I am drawn to the Late Romantic level of her layered language not only because I like it but also because it is neglected.

Thus, although the "fragments" that Eliot "shored" against his "ruins" came to him, in part, from the "frigate" of Dickinson's poems (*The Waste Land*

[1921] 431; Poem 1263), although her pre-Modern mode modulates into theories as anti-experiential as Surrealism is or, perhaps more to the point, as is the resurgent Calvinism in such manifestations of Modernism and of Postmodernism as the German theology of Karl Barth on the one hand and the American literary criticism of Ralph C. Wood on the other, her place on the arc from Romantic to Modern is a linking as well as a pivotal point. The broadly experiential vision of her Late Romantic imagination shades over into, as well as coexists with, the post-experiential perspective of her pre-Modern mode. The evangelically empirical dimension of her imagination so creatively "masters" the empirically evangelical aspect of her Anglo-American heritage that she does not so much "escape" from her tradition as she gives it life and passes it on (cf. Brooker on Eliot). Although duly "mistrustful of the cost of a re-achieved earliness," she both covets and attains to "an ever-early candor" (Bloom, *Western Canon* 295); while neither Modernism nor a pre-Modern mode fully characterizes her art, *Romantic Modernism* and even *Modernistic Romanticism* largely denominate it. While *Romanticism* largely denominates it, *Late Romanticism* perhaps best labels it. Although Dickinson the Romantic shores her share of fragments against her ruins, although she is self-conscious enough not only for irony but also for the struggle over blindness versus insight, she barely anticipates the post-twilight hour of Postmodernism. She certainly does not whimper about it.

Works Cited

Bargad, Warren. *"To Write the Lips of Sleepers": The Poetry of Amir Gilboa*. Cincinnati: Hebrew Union College P, 1994.

Behnken, Eloise M. *Thomas Carlyle: "Calvinist Without the Theology."* Columbia: U of Missouri P, 1978.

Bingham, Millicent Todd. *Ancestors' Brocades: The Literary Debut of Emily Dickinson*. New York: Harper, 1945.

Bishop, Jonathan. *Emerson and the Soul*. Cambridge: Harvard UP, 1964.

Bloom, Harold. *The American Religion: The Emergence of the Post-Christian Nation*. New York: Simon & Schuster, 1992.

———. *The Anxiety of Influence: A Theory of Poetry*. New York: Oxford UP, 1973.

———. *The Book of J*. New York: Grove Weidenfeld, 1990.

———. *The Western Canon: The Books and School of the Ages*. New York: Harcourt, 1994.

Brantley, Richard E. *Anglo-American Antiphony: The Late Romanticism of Tennyson and Emerson*. Gainesville: UP of Florida, 1994.

———. *Coordinates of Anglo-American Romanticism: Wesley, Edwards, Carlyle, and Emerson*. Gainesville: UP of Florida, 1993.

———. *Locke, Wesley, and the Method of English Romanticism*. Gainesville: UP of Florida, 1984.

———. *Wordsworth's "Natural Methodism."* New Haven: Yale UP, 1975.

Brooker, Jewel Spears. *Mastery and Escape: T. S. Eliot and the Dialectic of Modernism*. Amherst: U of Massachusetts P, 1994.

Cameron, Sharon. *Choosing Not Choosing: Dickinson's Fascicles*. Chicago: U of Chicago P, 1992.

Clarke, Colin. *Romantic Paradox: An Essay on the Poetry of Wordsworth*. New York: Barnes & Noble, 1963.

Cox, John D. "Nominalist Ethics and the New Historicism." *Christianity and Literature* 39 (1990): 127-39.

Davie, Donald. "Nonconformist Poetics: A Reply to Daniel Jenkins." *Literature and Theology* 2 (1988): 160-73.

Dickie, Margaret. *Lyric Contingencies: Emily Dickinson and Wallace Stevens*. Philadelphia: U of Pennsylvania P, 1991.

Dickinson, Emily. *The Letters of Emily Dickinson*. Ed. Thomas H. Johnson and Theodora Ward. 3 vols. Cambridge: Harvard UP, 1958.

———. *The Poems of Emily Dickinson*. Ed. Thomas H. Johnson. 3 vols. Cambridge: Harvard UP, 1955.

Diehl, Joanne Feit. *Dickinson and the Romantic Imagination*. Princeton: Princeton UP, 1981.

Doriani, Beth Maclay. *Emily Dickinson: Daughter of Prophecy*. Amherst: U of Massachusetts P, 1996.

Farr, Judith. *The Passion of Emily Dickinson*. Cambridge: Harvard UP, 1992.

Forman, Douglas. "Dickinson's Poetry of Evasion." University of Florida Ph.D. diss., 1996.

Franklin, R. W. *The Manuscript Books of Emily Dickinson*. 2 vols. Cambridge: Harvard UP, 1981.

Heine, Heinrich. *The Complete Poems of Heinrich Heine: A Modern English Version*. Trans. Hal Draper. Boston: Suhrkamp/Insel, 1982.

Homans, Margaret. *Women Writers and Poetic Identity: Dorothy Wordsworth, Emily Brontë, and Emily Dickinson*. Princeton: Princeton UP, 1980.

Johnson, Greg. *Emily Dickinson: Perception and the Poet's Quest*. University: U of Alabama P, 1985.

Landow, George P. *Elegant Jeremiahs: The Sage from Carlyle to Mailer.* Ithaca: Cornell UP, 1986.

Langbaum, Robert. *The Poetry of Experience: The Dramatic Monologue in Modern Literary Tradition.* London: Chatto and Windus, 1957.

Lehman, David. *Signs of the Times: Deconstruction and the Fall of Paul de Man.* New York: Poseidon, 1991.

McFarland, Thomas. *Romanticism and the Forms of Ruin: Wordsworth, Coleridge, and Modalities of Fragmentation.* Princeton: Princeton UP, 1981.

Miller, Cristanne. *Emily Dickinson: A Poet's Grammar.* Cambridge: Harvard UP, 1987.

New, Melvyn. *Telling New Lies: Seven Essays in Fiction, Past and Present.* Gainesville: UP of Florida, 1992.

Oberhaus, Dorothy Huff. *Emily Dickinson's Fascicles: Method and Meaning.* University Park: Pennsylvania State UP, 1995.

Peckham, Morse. *Romanticism and Ideology.* Greenwood: Penkeville, 1985.

Poirier, Richard. "The Question of Genius: The Challenge of Emerson." *Modern Critical Views: Ralph Waldo Emerson.* Ed. Harold Bloom. New York: Chelsea House, 1985. 167-85.

Pollak, Vivian R. *Dickinson: The Anxiety of Gender.* Ithaca: Cornell UP, 1984.

Porter, David. *Dickinson: The Modern Idiom.* Cambridge: Harvard UP, 1981.

Rajan, Tilottama. *Dark Interpreter: The Discourse of Romanticism.* Ithaca: Cornell UP, 1980.

St. Armand, Barton Levi. *The Soul's Society: Emily Dickinson and Her Culture.* New York: Cambridge UP, 1984.

Sewall, Richard B. *The Life of Emily Dickinson.* 2 vols. New York: Farrar, 1974.

Shurr, William H. *The Marriage of Emily Dickinson: A Study of the Fascicles.* Lexington: U of Kentucky P, 1983.

Simpson, David. *Romanticism, Modernism, and the Revolt against Theory.* Chicago: U of Chicago P, 1993.

Sinfield, Alan. *Alfred Tennyson.* Oxford: Basil Blackwell, 1986.

Snodgrass, Chris. *Aubrey Beardsley: Dandy of the Grotesque.* Oxford: Oxford UP, 1995.

Spellman, W. M. *John Locke and the Problem of Depravity.* Oxford: Clarendon, 1988.

Stocks, Kenneth. *Emily Dickinson and the Modern Consciousness: A Poet of Our Time.* New York: St. Martin's, 1988.

Stonum, Gary Lee. *The Dickinson Sublime.* Madison: U of Wisconsin P, 1990.

Wasserman, Earl R. *The Subtler Language: Critical Readings of Neoclassic and Romantic Poems*. Baltimore: Johns Hopkins UP, 1959.
Weisbuch, Robert. *Emily Dickinson's Poetry*. Chicago: U of Chicago P, 1975.
Wesley, John. *The Letters of the Rev. John Wesley, A.M.* Ed. John Telford. 8 vols. London: Epworth, 1931.
Wheeler, Kathleen M. *Romanticism, Pragmatism, and Deconstruction*. Oxford: Basil Blackwell, 1993.
Wilner, Eleanor. "The Poetics of Emily Dickinson." *ELH* 38 (1971): 128-54.
Wolff, Cynthia Griffin. *Emily Dickinson*. New York: Knopf, 1986.
Woloski, Shira. *Emily Dickinson: A Voice of War*. New Haven: Yale UP, 1984.

13. *The Empirical Imagination of Emily Dickinson*

"We'll finish an education sometime, won't we?" asked Emily Dickinson of Abiah Root on February 23, 1845. "You may then be Plato," Dickinson added, "and I will be Socrates, provided you won't be wiser than I am" (Johnson and Ward I:10). Thus, at fourteen, Dickinson showed herself to be philosophically precocious, recognizing the distinction between Plato and his persona and anticipating her role as gadfly. On October 10, 1851, she wrote to her brother, Austin, "I had a dissertation from Eliza Coleman a day or two ago—dont know which was the author—Plato, or Socrates—rather think Jove had a finger in it" (Johnson and Ward I:147). Hence at twenty, with ambivalence about whether philosophy should trump theology, Dickinson indicated the philosophical nature of her correspondence with Eliza, through whom, incidentally, she met the surprisingly philosophical Reverend Charles Wadsworth, her "dearest earthly friend" (Johnson and Ward III:764; Leyda I:lxxvi-lxxviii). The mature poet, among all her protean shapes, assumes the guise of a philosopher indeed, not so much of a "transcendental realist" kind, as David Van Leer understands Plato to be, or of a "transcendental idealist" kind, as Van Leer understands Ralph Waldo Emerson to be (8), as of a rational empiricist kind, I understand Emerson to be, albeit in precise dialectic with his experiential faith (Brantley *Coordinates passim*; Brantley *Antiphony passim*). Dickinson's sense-based reason, I argue, without exactly demonstrating that she is some sort of scientist, evolutionary or other, makes all the difference to her image-making power. Her 1,789 personae, as though they were so many amateur epistemologists of sensation, follow her imperative not so much to "*finish* an education," if I may again quote schoolgirl Dickinson, as to carry it forward from strength to strength.

The extent of Dickinson's reading in British empiricism, to be sure, is unknown. For what it is worth to my argument, though, she tracked her brother's progress through the writings of David Hume: on January 23, 1850, she wrote to Jane Humphrey that "Austin was reading Hume's History...—and his getting through was the signal for general up roar" (Johnson and Ward I:83). Dickinson's access to empirical philosophy, I believe, was through the Scottish Common Sense School, which was well represented in her father's library. Her Prose Fragment 68, after all—"Common Sense is almost as omniscient as God" (Johnson and Ward III:922)— distills British empiricism. It signifies that truth emerges slowly, yet surely, from the sense-based means of knowing, and perhaps even that sense-based knowing is the *avenue* to truth. As Dickinson wrote to Thomas Wentworth Higginson in November 1871, "Truth like Ancestor's Brocades can stand alone—" (Johnson and Ward II:491). Truth, that is, grows sturdier, as though wisdom, like love, were as strong as death.

What Richard B. Sewall identifies as Dickinson's "voice of seasoned skepticism" in Poem 1181 ("Teaching" 34), specifically, is in my view the anything but destructively skeptical stance, if not exactly the robustly untroubled outlook, of all her empirical procedures:

> Experiment escorts us last—
> His pungent company
> Will not allow an Axiom
> An Opportunity— (Franklin II:1024)

That the open-ended inquiry of Dickinson's empirical procedures could both begin and end in *religious* skepticism, to be sure, is understood by John Robinson to lie at, or near, the heart of this signature lyric or miniature poetic manifesto of her faith in experience. "We do not know," as Robinson paraphrases the poem, "what the final experience, death, will bring...so we cannot establish doctrines because they may not take account of this experience" (89). In a letter to Higginson, written about October 1870, Dickinson included these very lines and introduced them by means of her reference to the doubts of Jesus Himself: "...[E]ven in Our Lord's [']that they be where I am,' I taste interrogation" (Johnson and Ward II:481; cf. John 17:21). Nevertheless, I take the focus of the poem to be what L. J. Swingle calls the "radical skepticism" of empirical, as well as Cartesian, philosophy (39). Even Robinson, after all, observes that the skepticism of Dickinson's quatrain "has its origins as much in a feeling about life as in her eschatology" (89; my italics). The *religious* element of her empirical understanding per se is nothing more, or less, than her veneration for "Experiment."

Poem 1181, to be sure, could be construed as a pejorative characterization of the scientific method, for "Pungent," connoting the sweaty, the overwrought, is by no means an entirely flattering descriptor, and "Experiment," personified, would seem to behave all too much like the possessive, jealous lover in not allowing "an Axiom," personified, "An Opportunity—" to compete for intellectual favor in the world of thoughts and things. Moreover, Dickinson's alternative reading for "escorts us" is, remarkably enough, "accosts us" (Franklin II:1024), as though the poet were bent on suggesting, albeit at the bottom of her fair copy (on a sub-textual level), that both the certainty and the serenity of Euclidean rationalism (recall: "an *Axiom*") might be preferable, in the long run, to the constant impingement of undifferentiated sense impressions from what Wordsworth rather ominously calls "the world / Of all of us, the place in which, in the end, / We find our happiness, or not at all" (*The Prelude* [1850]: X:726-29).

Finally, however, I concur in Sewall's regard for the face-value of this poem, for "escorts us," suggesting not so much, say, the salaciousness of escort services as the honor and protection bestowed by loving friends and friendly lovers, is the poet's primary choice here for her opening predicate, and "Last—," for that matter, means not so much "belatedly—," or "perfunctorily—," and not so much "*at* Last—" (translation: "it's about *time—*") as, instead, "faithfully out to the edge of doom," or "by our sides even after all our other intellectual props have fallen into abeyance and, especially like the predilection for axioms itself, proven chimerical all along." This signature lyric or miniature poetic manifesto of Dickinson's "naturalized imagination," if I may adapt to my purposes here Jack Stillinger's phrase for Keats's "poetry of earth" (99-118), emphasizes honorific language, denoting that empirical procedures in general and the scientific method in particular are not only the reliable and steadfast friends of truth but also, despite being seductive and despite doing violence, on occasion, to humankind's sense of its importance in the universe, the alert and forceful enemies of all our logical justifications for hermetic systems.

I cannot help thinking, in this connection, of *The Enquirer* (1797), by William Godwin, who, four years after the appearance of *An Enquiry concerning Political Justice* and at a time when he had begun to turn away from French rationalism (or the belief that mind is independent of and superior to sense impressions) and back toward British empiricism, taught, above all, that "We proceed most safely when we enter upon each portion of our process, as it were, *de novo* . . . . There is danger, if we are too exclusively anxious about consistency of system, that we may forget the perpetual attention we owe to experience, the pole-star of truth" (v, viii). This passage, in my judgment, is the best of all possible glosses on the sensationalist epistemology of Romantic Anglo-America in general and of the Myth of Amherst in particular. The acute, keen companionship of the scientific method, in part because of the poet's love for botany and for geology, and despite her adeptness at mathematics (Sewall *Life* II:336-64), helps her spurn the advances, and perhaps even resist the blandishments, of pure logic alone, which relies all too heavily and all too complacently for her developing taste on the glibly applied doctrine and the downright spurious attraction of "self-evident" truth, inadvisedly so called.

Poem 359, perhaps, receives the most dramatically urgent commentary of all Dickinson's poems with an evolutionary twist:

> A Bird came down the Walk—
> He did not know I saw—
> He bit an Angleworm in halves
> And ate the fellow, raw,
>
> And then he drank a Dew
> From a Convenient Grass—
> And then hopped sidewise to the Wall
> To let a Beetle pass—
>
> He glanced with rapid eyes
> That hurried all around—
> They looked like frightened Beads, I thought—
> He stirred his Velvet Head
>
> Like One in danger, Cautious,
> I offered him a Crumb
> And he unrolled his feathers
> And rowed him softer home—
>
> Than Oars divide the Ocean,
> Too silver for a seam—
> Or Butterflies, off Banks of Noon
> Leap, plashless as they swim. (Franklin I:383)

Debate centers on whether the poem belongs primarily to the bird or to the speaker: whereas the "masculine" bird, according to Darryl Hattenhauer, represents the "freedom and ease denied to . . . nineteenth-century women of proper Massachusetts society" (54-55)—and whereas Anthony Hecht asks, "might not this be a shy and modest allegory of human possibility?" (4)— Lynn Keller and Cristanne Miller conclude, "By the end of the poem, we are more interested in the observer than in what she sees . . . . [T]he real drama of such a poem seems to lie in its speaker's idiosyncratic mental processes" (546-7). Nancy Walker, too, sides with the speaker, remarking, "Instead of raising herself to the level of nature, [the speaker] lifts it to her own superior level" (60). Other critics, while acknowledging the bird/speaker split, do not see the speaker as the symbol of a socially/scientifically superior human being but regard the bird as the token of an alternately intriguing and threatening, but always mysterious, evolutionary otherness: "The truth" of the poem, in Jerome Loving's view, "is that nature is a nice place, a pastoral scene until man blunders on the stage with the full weight of his past and future," so that "any suggestion of danger comes when the human narrator offers the bird a crumb" (55-56, 62). Lisa Paddock, even more ominously, speaks of "the cleavage between man and nature which is the subject of the poem" (73). For Bettina L. Knapp, the poem "depicts the voracity of nature as well as its beauty and cyclicality," so that the otherness of nature is finally more disturbing than comforting (106). For Jonnie G. Guerra, the otherness of nature is more neutral than disturbing: "Initially, the speaker's choice of verbs seems to express a desire to anthropomorphize the bird; however, in the final stanzas, verbs that reflect the speaker's recognition of the bird's separateness from the human world create the poem's thematic climax" (29). Cynthia Griffin Wolff, similarly, observes that "Oddly, although the speaker fails in her attempt to comprehend and describe the bird's nature, the poem itself does not fail to the same degree, for the use of these inadequate social categories to deal with the activities of an essentially unknowable bird serves nicely to highlight nature's impenetrable enigma" (523).

The insight closest to my own view is that of Douglas Anderson, who remarks of Poem 359 that "Presence is elusive and, in a small way, dangerous here . . . but it is also deeply captivating" (221). E. Miller Budick, too, strikes just the right note in declaring that the poem resists "the dangerous distortion of both natural and theological truths which can occur when biological happenstance is promulgated as divine gospel" (209). I would add, however, that the speaker implicates herself as well as the bird in the biological happenstance that constitutes natural, if not theological, truths. Her tone celebrates the scientific sense in which both she and the bird share common ground. Thus, regardless of whether "Like One in danger, Cautious," refers to the speaker or to the bird—the line, after all, is syntactically ambiguous—the speaker in the *final* lines seems to derive fellow-feeling—does the bird *take* the crumb?—as well as positive, progressive aspiration from a creature that, as distinct, say, from tending downward on however extended or dignified wings, soars in triumph and with a natural grace. Hence, is there a suggestion of grace in the bird's letting the "Beetle pass—"?

Dickinson, then, does not skew evolutionary science in a human-centered direction, but she does hold that the poet participates in, and perhaps even best represents, the conscious stillness at the apex of evolutionary progress. She offers her own Late Romantic version of what Keats calls the "egotistical sublime" (Oct. 27, 1818). Thus, although the speaker of Dickinson's Poem 912 complains that "Creation seemed a mighty Crack— / To make me visible—" (Franklin II:845), and although these lines imply that, as Greg Johnson paraphrases them, "the speaker attempts to escape some outer, hostile perception" (60), the lines affirm that "What the speaker longs for is not privacy taken as secrecy so much as invisibility" (Benfey 100). I would go further and declare that what many of Dickinson's not-*so*-invisible personae long for, and what they characteristically achieve, is the quiet authority of speaking with the voice of Charles Darwin's sense-based truth. The role that the hard sciences play in her empirical outlook on life, if I may cross over from her personae to Dickinson the Romantic herself, rises, on occasion, if not to the height of her practicing the scientific method itself, then to the level of her solid scientific knowledge as she goes about her business in the world of thoughts and things, where her thumb, famously, is green. The poet is a sensationalist epistemologist *par excellence*, and, at her empirically Romantic best, she is filled with wonder even at what Lord Alfred Tennyson, in not so Romantic a mood, calls "Nature, red in tooth and claw / With ravine" (*In Memoriam* [1850] 56:15-16).

The last two stanzas of Poem 1433 epitomize the transatlantically Romantic, tough-and-tender character of Dickinson's empirical imagination. They strongly imply, for example, that the scientist should strive to match the humility of even the most reverent worshiper:

> But nature is a stranger yet;
> The ones that cite her most

> Have never passed her haunted house,
> Nor simplified her ghost.
>
> To pity those that know her not
> Is helped by the regret
> That those who know her, know her less
> The nearer her they get. (Franklin III:1254)

Kenneth Stocks, to be sure, observes that these lines express "a recovered unity with nature at a high level of human awareness and understanding, the poet fulfilling her role as nature's consciousness and tongue" (71) . Stocks's insight, however, gives more credit to the poet's comprehension of nature than she does herself. John Reiss is closer to the mark: "There is no cause to pity those who do not understand the spirit of nature, because that spirit is almost completely unknowable. For most who cite nature, nature reflects their own image. Those who can penetrate nature's reflection see the abyss" (28-29). "Abyss," though, might be too strong, for this is a poem, in the end, about "a willingness to forego certainty and knowledge" (Benfey 66). Shades, or retrolepsis, of Keats's "Negative Capability," whereby, if I may conflate his renowned definition of Romantic epistemology with Dickinson's own signature phrase for it, the well-tempered Romantic learns to "dwell in Possibility—" indeed (Franklin I:483; Poem 466)—that is, precisely to abide in "uncertainties, Mysteries, doubts, without any irritable reaching after fact & reason" (Dec., 1817). Locke would approve of such a modest way of carrying one's education forward—that is, by re-externalizing quest-romance on the road toward what will suffice.

In the final analysis, then, Locke's *Essay concerning Human Understanding* (1690), underlies the emphasis on natural experience to be found not only in British High Romanticism— for example, in "My Heart Leaps Up" (1804), by Wordsworth—but also in Anglo-American Romanticism, including Dickinson's Late Romantic art. Thus, just as Wadsworth's sermons define an idea of sensation (after the manner of Locke) as "the image, or form, of a thing in the mind," so that "a complete idea must therefore be the image of a whole thing, and not merely one of its parts" (*Sermons* [1869] 23)—shades, or retrospection, of Bishop George Berkeley's clusters, or bundles, of thoughts (Brantley *Locke* 9, 18-19, 72-73)—so too does the empirical imagination of Emily Dickinson hold fast, regardless of any misgivings on her part about the mere *means* of knowing, to the efficacy of sensationalist epistemology in general. Hence, just as Wadsworth's sermons define education (in Locke's terms) as "simply *education*, a *drawing-forth*, or development; not knowledge or erudition *forced into* the mind, but the mind itself quickened, strengthened, trained unto thoughtful, practical activity" (*Sermons* [1905] 231), so too does Dickinson's empirical imagination cherish, regardless of any misgivings on her part about the mere means of *knowing*, the integrity of the scientific method in particular.

Here, for purposes of recapitulating Dickinson's interplay between perceiving and imagining, is the subtly humorous Poem 1779:

> To make a prairie it takes a clover and one bee,
> One clover, and a bee,
> And revery.
> The revery alone will do,
> If bees are few. (Franklin III:1521)

Suzanne Juhasz paraphrases these lines as follows: "The mind's idea of a given object creates it, makes it, insofar as, through the act of perception, mind provides object with meaning. And, since the mind can also think of an object that is unperceived, in that sense it creates the object before perception" (24-25). Juhasz's gloss on "revery" is excellent for its understanding of the Romantic imagination, but "revery" works not so much in isolation from, as in interaction with, clovers, and perhaps even some bees, so that the strangeness of empirical perception, or the mystery of subject-object coalescence and interpenetration, remains a crucial part of Dickinson's *image*-ination. Witness Budick's conclusion that "the philosophical system that informs the symbolic logic of [this poem] . . . is perhaps most usefully thought of as material-idealism, the coexistence of reality's constituent phases in total equality of status and in absolute separateness" (179). I would only italicize "*material-idealism*" and "*coexistence*" and mute (or place in parentheses) "and in absolute separateness." "*I think*," reveals Dickinson in Poem 1295, "that the Root of the *Wind* is *Water*" (Franklin III:1123, my italics). The fact that *she thinks* so not only makes it all the more *true*, as far as Dickinson the Romantic is concerned, but also, and no less in the spirit of *Anglo-American* Romanticism, does not make it any less *independently* true. In *her* world of Romantic Anglo-America, mind is all the more *imaginatively* thoughtful for being thoroughly *grounded* in "All things both great and small" (cf. Samuel Taylor Coleridge, "The Rime of the Ancient Mariner" [1797/1817] VII:615).

Works Cited

Anderson, Douglas. "Presence and Place in Emily Dickinson's Poetry," *New England Quarterly* 57 (1984), 205-24;

Benfey, Christopher. *Emily Dickinson and the Problem of Others.* 1984;

Brantley, Richard E. *Anglo-American Antiphony: The Late Romanticism of Tennyson and Emerson.* 1994;

———. *Coordinates of Anglo-American Romanticism: Wesley, Edwards, Carlyle and Emerson.* 1993;

———. *Locke, Wesley, and the Method of English Romanticism.* 1984;

Budick, E. Miller. *Emily Dickinson and the Life of Language: A Study in Symbolic Poetics.* 1985;

———. "The Dangers of the Living Word: Aspects of Dickinson's Epistemology, Cosmology, and Symbolism," *ESQ: A Journal of the American Renaissance* 29 (1983), 208-24;

Dickinson, Emily. *The Letters of Emily Dickinson*, eds. Thomas H. Johnson and Theodora Ward. 1958;

_. *The Poems of Emily Dickinson*, ed. Ralph W. Franklin. 1998;

_. *The Years and Hours of Emily Dickinson*, ed. Jay Leyda. 1960;

Godwin, William. *The Enquirer.* 1797;

Guerra, Jonnie G. "Dickinson's 'A bird came down the walk,'" *The Explicator* 48 (1989), 29-30;

Hattenhauer, Darryl. "Feminism in Dickinson's Bird Imagery," *Dickinson Studies* 52 (1984), 54-57;

Hecht, Anthony. "The Riddles of Emily Dickinson," *The New England Review* 1 (1978), 1-24;

Johnson, Greg. *Emily Dickinson: Perception and the Poet's Quest.* 1985;

Juhasz, Suzanne. "'To Make a Prairie': Language and Form in Emily Dickinson's Poems about Mental Experience," *Ball State University Forum* 21 (1980), 12-25;

Keller, Lynn, and Cristanne Miller. "Emily Dickinson, Elizabeth Bishop, and the Rewards of Indirection," *New England Quarterly* 57 (1984), 533-53;

Knapp, Bettina L. *Emily Dickinson.* 1989;

Loving, Jerome. *Emily Dickinson: The Poet on the Second Story.* 1986;

Paddock, Lisa. "Metaphor as Reason: Emily Dickinson's Approach to Nature," *Massachusetts Studies in English* 8 (1981), 70-79;

Robinson, John. *Emily Dickinson: Looking to Canaan.* 1986;

Sewall, Richard B. *The Life of Emily Dickinson.* 1974; reprinted 1994;

———. "Teaching Dickinson: Testimony of a Veteran." In *Approaches to Teaching Dickinson's Poetry*, eds. Robin Riley Fast and Christine Mack Gordon. 1989;

Stillinger, Jack. "Imagination and Reality in the Odes of Keats." In *The Hoodwinking of Madeline, and Other Essays on Keats's Poems*. 1988;

Swingle, L. J. *The Obstinate Questionings of English Romanticism*. 1987;

Van Leer, David. *Emerson's Epistemology: The Argument of the Essays*. 1986;

Wadsworth, Charles. *Sermons*. 1905;

———. *Sermons*. 1869;

Walker, Nancy. "Emily Dickinson and the Self: Humor as Identity," *Tulsa Studies in Women's Literature* 2 (1983), 57-68;

Wolff, Cynthia Griffin. *Emily Dickinson*. 1988.

14. *Emily Dickinson's Empirical Voice*

Does empirical language out-resound, however barely, the evangelical expression that echoes, as well, throughout Romantic Anglo-America? Perhaps so, for, in the spirit of palinode and for heuristic purposes, this essay takes its cue from the lower-case usage of Charles Lamb's epistemological as well as revival-like label for the poetry of William Wordsworth—"natural methodism."[1] As my case in point, the quite possibly more philosophical than religious letters and poems of Emily Dickinson (1830-86) distill the naturalizing rather than spiritualizing kind of "methodism" to which I now believe that Lamb might well have had unwitting—and witting—primary reference.[2] Insofar as such "natural methodism" drives a force, and perhaps even animates the forms, of Romantic Anglo-America, this philosophical trait of Anglo-American "sense," as distinct from some theological wind of Anglo-American doctrine, accounts in spades for the substance of Dickinson's Late Romantic thought, the poet's tender-minded choice of hymn-like form notwithstanding. Thus her "natural methodism" can serve to resist the Euro-Continental drift that comprehends even English-language Romanticism as German-idealism-induced "natural supernaturalism" rather than British-empiricism-inspired faith in up-from-the-grass-roots experience.[3]

Let me expand, first, on the historical, interdisciplinary, and biographical terms of my critical analysis to follow (in segments 2 and 3 of this essay). I can see the British empiricism of John Locke (1632-1704) filtering through to Dickinson's slant truth-telling by surviving intact in a) the British Methodism of John Wesley (1703-91) and b) the American evangelism of Dickinson's "dearest earthly friend," the Locke- and Wesley-influenced Charles Wadsworth (1814-82).[4] This leap across space and time could seem anachronistic, but the Anglo-American "sense" for which I have previously argued that Locke and Wesley qualify as prime movers proves a much subtler near influence on Wadsworth and Dickinson than his Presbyterian allegiance and her Congregational affiliation put together do.[5] Thus, although the religious preoccupations of Wesley and Wadsworth color any discussion of their works and overlap manifold manifestations of Dickinson's own spiritual interests and concerns, this study underscores natural philosophy as it burgeons from Locke's *An Essay concerning Human Understanding* (1690) to all three of these master-figures of Anglo-American culture. Wadsworth's enthusiasm for expressing his faith as Wesley did, in the proto-scientific language of Locke, and hence for advocating experience as the best means of knowing what is naturally and spiritually true, can justify my choice here to focus on the empirically philosophical, broadly scientific ramifications of his link to Dickinson. Theirs, in my view, was a "marriage of true minds," and just as some have drawn convincing theological parallels between Wadsworth's sermons and Dickinson's poems—I aspire to join, someday, this very conversation[6]—so too do I meanwhile make philosophical comparisons between their respective canons. Although I will consider such other founts of Dickinson's empiricism as her scientific education, I will emphasize Wadsworth throughout this essay, as perhaps the only remaining unstudied source of, or analogue to, the sense-based reason practiced throughout her poetic "thought experiments." In any case, the eighteenth- to nineteenth-century, philosophical as well as scientific sounding-board for her empirical voice—Wadsworth's sermons ring loudest in her ears—can supplement/broaden the tendency to align both her expression and that of her peers/coevals (e.g., Walt Whitman's) with the immediately mid-nineteenth-century progress of science per se.[7]

Literary history, moreover, can add "volume" to Dickinson's empirical voice and hence belletristic sonority to my intellectually and culturally historical "audition" of it, for Anglo-American Romanticism's empirical and scientific idiom, distinct from its Christian and evangelical inflection, *also* glosses the philosophical woof, distinct from the religious warp, of Dickinson's weblike connections with other writers.[8] Thus, just as eighteenth-century Wesley thought of himself as "more . . . philosophical sluggard, than . . . itinerant Preacher" (Telford 2:68) so nineteenth-century Dickinson became both poet and philosopher. Now wittingly, and now unwittingly, her thinking holds in equipoise, keeps in play, and improves upon the natural philosophies of Locke, Wesley, and Wadsworth, on the one hand, and the scientific predilections and break-throughs of such High-to-Late-Romantic Anglo-American authors as

Wordsworth, Thomas Carlyle, and Ralph Waldo Emerson, on the other. As a result, her art can mediate the evangelical- and Romantic-era controversy between philosophy and religion.

An arc of empirical philosophy and even of science, then, extends from Locke and Wesley to prose writers and poets of Anglo-America's first water, notably prose stylist Wadsworth and lyric master Dickinson. This pair, as historic as Locke and Wesley, seldom flinches from religion-challenging, poetry-disenchanting tough-mindedness, reveling, even, in the claim-testing swagger of constructive skepticism. To restate Dickinson's importance on the intellectual, cultural, and literary arc of history, her disciplined devotion to sense-based reason and even her zealous veneration of science cap the Locke-derived "philosophy of enthusiasm" ascendant in Wesley's and Wadsworth's spiritual experience and in such English-language Romanticism as that of Wordsworth and company.[9] True, her letters and poems entertain mind over matter, resembling, thereby, the German-idealist or French-rationalist stripe of Euro-Continental Romanticism, but her language also celebrates—"Theme this but little heard of among men" (albeit resonant with British Empiricism and American Pragmatism alike)—matter over mind.[10]

I have finished sketching, now, the Dickinson-centered group portrait that for the remainder of this essay I will fill out as a composite, presiding, inward, and outward genius of her not-*so*-solitary existence. *Words*worth and company (make no mistake about it) loomed as vividly present in Dickinson's life and art as *Wads*worth and company ever did (and perhaps even more often so).[11] I have announced in advance of my full exploration here, as well, the foundational topic of Dickinson's "*rich* . . . conversation" (L54) with these others—namely, the recommended epistemological means, and perhaps even the sure-fire scientific method, of seeking the truth. Just as *rich* "conversation" comprised the "innovation" that "marked the [British Royal] Society out for success" ("Their way of making knowledge was mainly to talk about it"), so Dickinson's correspondence-energized-by-her-colloquial-imagination honored not "abstract reasoning" nor "complicated mathematics" nor belief alone so much as group-effort toward "dogged aggregation of phenomena."[12] Whether she encountered minds, souls, and hearts face-to-face, on the page, or "inner than the bone" of her bi-national DNA (cf. Fr334, line 14), she favored, as they did (and reinforced some of them to sanction) the explanatory powers of experiential philosophy over the relative merits (like testimonial witness) of experiential faith.[13]

I

As a very young woman, Emily Dickinson showed herself to be philosophically well informed, though not necessarily empirically vociferous just yet. At fourteen, writing to her chum Abiah Root, she recognized the distinction between Plato and the chief persona of his dialogues: "We'll finish an education sometime, won't we? You may then be Plato, and I will be Socrates, provided you won't be wiser than I am" (L5). Thus, the schoolgirl anticipated the adult poet's role as an assertively philosophical gadfly. At twenty, writing to her brother, Austin, and replaying the pairing of Socrates with Plato, Dickinson spoke of philosophy and religion (or of philosophy and mythology) in the same breath: "I had a dissertation from Eliza Coleman a day or two ago—I don't know which was the author—Plato, or Socrates—rather think Jove had a finger in it" (L57). Whatever else this rather obscure comment might mean, it satirizes Coleman for favoring religion over philosophy, and perhaps even for betraying Dickinson's trust in her as a philosophical discussion partner. Despite Dickinson's own interest in religion, which figures in this essay as a leitmotif, the empirical leanings of the poet's educational training call the plays of her "fine mental chaos," to borrow a phrase from British Romantic novelist Thomas Love Peacock.[14] This segment's run-up to my practical criticism (in the next two) epitomizes how Locke's *Essay* hovers in the background of Dickinson's sense-based reasoning. Thus, in a spirit of review, yet with increasing reference to Dickinson, this segment over-views the pertinent intellectual and cultural history.

The founding document of British empiricism contends that simple ideas or ideas of sensation form the mind's account of what the senses bring and then give rise to general propositions that yield solutions. Thus, Locke's set of intellectual stages presents the opposite of French rationalism (or the mind's independence of, and superiority to, sense impressions); for the *Essay*, after all, grounds mind in sense-data. At the same time, however, Locke's masterwork savors just how much more the mind can comprehend than even his own view of its limitation by the senses might ever seem to allow. Consider, for instance, this important passage from *Essay* 2: "Nor let anyone think [simple ideas or ideas of sensation] too narrow bounds for the capacious Mind of Man to expatiate in, which takes its flight farther than the Stars, and cannot be confined by the limits of the World; that extends its thoughts often, even beyond the utmost expansion of Matter, and makes excursions into that incomprehensible Inane."[15] Dickinson, for her part, captures this expansive thought (of fifty-nine words) in seven: "The Brain—is wider than the Sky—" (Fr598, line 1).

Despite the inherent modesty of its inductive reasoning, the *Essay* venerates the mind's engagement in, and perhaps even worships its lordship over, the universe. Locke can soar, as in the passage just quoted, to the point of world-transcendence. On the other hand, his rational empiricism contrasts with the pure rationalism of Plato and of René Descartes. Locke's philosophy also differs from the sense-suspicious German idealism of Immanuel Kant. The reasoning emphasis in Locke's sensationalist epistemology jibes with experience-driven cerebrations concerning sense-based or sense-related interrogatives like whether, how, and what one knows, believes, or both.

Locke's faith in experience as the means of knowing what is true forms the prelude to John Wesley's experience of faith. From June 5, 1782, through June 30, 1784, in thirty issues of his middlebrow serial, *The Arminian Magazine*, Wesley devoted ninety-one pages to his extracts of twenty-eight passages from Books 1 and 2 of Locke's *Essay*. He gave six pages to his remarks on twenty-four excerpts from Books 3 and 4 (see Brantley *Locke* 224-25). This is as if the Reverend Rick Warren were to edit for his flock, and expect it to read, the Martin Heidegger-transmogrifying ethics of Emmanuel Levinas!

In his resounding reconfirmation of the sometimes recessive but stubbornly re-assertive empirical tradition, Wesley observes,

> For many ages, it has been allowed by sensible men, *Nihil est in intellectu quod non fuit prius in sensu*. That is, 'There is nothing in the understanding which was not first perceived by some of the senses.' ... [T]his point has now been thoroughly discussed by men of the most eminent sense and learning, and it is agreed by all impartial persons, that although some things are so plain and obvious, that we can hardly avoid knowing them as soon as we come to the use of our understanding, yet the knowledge even of those is not innate, but derived from some of our senses. (Jackson 7:231)

Locke's presiding idea of *tabula rasa* falls from the lips of the *über*-Methodist. And Wesley reported on Locke's ideas of sensation to his "parish," "all the world" (qtd. in Hurst 141).

Wesley's Locke-derived season of the empirical tradition runs the course from Wesley's sense-based reasoning to his educational theory and practice. Regarding the former, he concludes,

> No sooner is the child born into the world, than he . . . feels the air with which he is surrounded, and which pours into him from every side, as fast as he alternately breathes it back, to sustain the flame of life: and hence springs a continued increase of strength, of motion, and of sensation; all the bodily senses being now awakened, and furnished with their proper objects. (Wesley *Sermons* 176)

As for his educational ideas, Wesley follows Locke's *Some Thoughts concerning Education* (1693), for this preacher, in homage to this philosopher, holds that the design of an ideal pedagogy counterbalances the bias of nature. Locke's very wording appears in the written rules for Wesley's Kingswood School, an empirically philosophical experiment in Christian education—specifically, in Kingswood's ban on holidays, in its injunction against play, and in its insistence on simplicity of diet and starkness of accommodation (Body 56-61).

In the fourth year of Wesley's curriculum there, he required Locke's *Essay*, which, as I have previously maintained, underlies Wesley's experience-oriented, sense-analogized, and even sense-tested heart religion.[16] The Locke-derived foundation of Wesley's experiment at Kingswood School merits further attention in light of Samuel Pickering's *John Locke and Children's Books in Eighteenth-Century England* (1981). That root grew educational stem and flower in the nineteenth century, with Dickinson's theme of intellectual development a prominent blossom. To borrow Locke's phrase, her fourteen-year-old "thoughts concerning education," in her letter to Abiah Root, are ultimately Locke-relevant, as well as possibly Plato-centric.

Just as Wesley preaches ideas of sensation to his flock, so too, finally, does Charles Wadsworth evoke them in sermons. "Sensations," Wadsworth writes, "are the image, or form, of a thing in the mind" (Wadsworth *Sermons* [1869] 23). He even recalls, or appears to, the arcana of empirical philosopher (and Bishop) George Berkeley. Like Berkeley, Wadsworth holds that "a complete idea must also be the image of a whole thing, and not merely one of its parts."[17] To put it mildly, he feeds his sheep a more substantial fare than the typical message of such a Postmodern-era evangelical as the Reverend Joel Osteen, whose Jesus finds parking spaces for shoppers!

At times, Wadsworth seems anti-professorial at best, and anti-intellectual at worst. This Presbyterian evangelical, after all, views "[s]cholarship, by a dread necessity, as predestined to be valetudinarian." "Nay," he continues, a scholar "must be a creature of the delicate frame-work and the unbronzed check and the lily fingers, and . . . like heavy ordinances, such an intellectual will recoil on its mounting and shatter a puny frame-work" (Wadsworth *Sermons* [1884] 231, 232). One thinks, in this connection, of Theodore Holland, the son of Dickinson's friends Elizabeth and Josiah Gilbert Holland, who probably served as intermediaries for Dickinson's correspondence with Wadsworth.[18] When Dickinson hears that Theodore has passed his oral examination at Columbia University Law School, she remarks, "I am glad if Theodore balked the Professors—Most such are Mannikins, and a warm blow from a brave Anatomy, hurls them into Wherefores—" (L901).

Just as Dickinson agrees with Wadsworth on the superiority of robust men to effete academics, so she concurs with his theory of education in general. Wadsworth defines "*education*" in Locke's terms, as "simply a *drawing-forth*, a development, not knowledge or erudition *forced into* the mind, but the mind itself, quickened, strengthened, trained unto thoughtful, practical activity" (Wadsworth *Sermons* [1905] 231). In a manner reminiscent of Dickinson's teen-aged aspiration to "finish an education sometime," Wadsworth declares that " [t]here is none whose education is [or by his implication ever should be] finished." He proclaims that "[e]very man to whom God hath given an intellect should have enough self-knowledge to understand thoroughly its peculiar powers." Consonant with Dickinson's views, he laments that " [m]any men practically ignore their intellectual faculties," that "[s]ome . . . never think at all," and that these "live among feelings," "prefer[ring] to buy thought as they buy groceries, second-hand and diluted" (Wadsworth *Sermons* [1869] 331, 114, 114-15). "How do most people live without any Thoughts[?]" asks Dickinson of her literary preceptor Thomas Wentworth Higginson, adding, "There are many people in the world (you must have noticed them in the street)[.] How do they get strength to put on their clothes in the morning[?]" (L342a; see also Wineapple). Thus, in 1870, a year after Wadsworth had lambasted people who purchase their thought second-hand, Dickinson advocated earning thought first-hand.[19] She surely appreciated the rhetorical flair that comes across in Wadsworth's conclusion: "So [writes Wadsworth] the popular press roars and foams a grand Niagara of sentiment and water!" (Wadsworth *Sermons* [1869] 115).

Dickinson's readers can gain a clear sense of the kind of empirical thought that attracted her by comparing her writings to those of philosophically sage, empirically savvy, Reverend Wadsworth, whom she undoubtedly met through her philosophical discussion partner and his parishioner Eliza Coleman.[20] Dickinson subscribed to Wadsworth's Wesley-like standard for clergy and laity alike—that is, up-to-date knowledge of philosophy and faithful subscription to sense-based reasoning. In part because of the welcome extended to empiricism by such simultaneously normative and trendsetting proponents of religious values as Wesley and Wadsworth, Dickinson's down-to-earth, downright empirical, instructors taught her well. At Amherst Academy and Mount Holyoke Female Seminary, and perhaps even at Amherst College, where she might have attended lectures by Dickinson family friend and important Professor of Natural History and Divinity Edward Hitchcock, Dickinson, like other young women of her day, benefited from scientific training.[21] Thanks to the legacy that her teachers of science inherited from the empiricism of Locke (as well as due to their own strengths and virtues), these preceptors of the poet-to-be eschewed pedantry, intellectual pride, overly refined game-playing, and, not least, the ascetic, sterile, will-o'-the-wisp or bugbear of mind/body dualism. As a result, Dickinson's education never ceased, nor did she ever lessen her respect for empirical procedures. To say little here of the other pole of her Late Romantic exposition (or expedition)—namely, the experiential faith that she struggled constantly to maintain—her experiential philosophy made a crucial difference to her image-making power, distinct from her spiritual sense foreshadowed by her sense-based reason.

A sample of Dickinson's personae, accordingly, carries education forward step by step, advancing, thereby, from strength to strength. As exalted as the long Romantic Movement could inspire them to be, yet as humble as Anglo-American Romanticism could also model, Dickinson and her dramatic monologists venture "out opon [sic] Circumference—" of selfhood, world, and universe, like "a speck opon a Ball—" (Fr633, line 7). Then, they come back down to earth (cf. Robert Frost, "Birches" [1916]). These Late Romantic excursions exhibit the exuberance, in combination with the modesty, shown by Locke and Percy Bysshe Shelley. In a clear allusion to Locke's *Essay* (the passage I quoted earlier), Shelley boasts of "darting [his] spirit's light / Beyond all worlds" and into the "intense inane."[22] Shelley thought of *inane* as the "vacancy that nevertheless holds in itself the potentiality of all that is" (Wasserman 209). Locke might have approved of Shelley's down-to-earth, downright empirical, endorsement of his "panting soul"'s "Clasp" of "the pendulous Earth."[23] Like the empirical imaginations of Locke, Wesley, and Wadsworth, on the one hand, and like those developed in their wake by such

High-to-Late-Romantic mavens as Wordsworth and Emerson, on the other, Dickinson's, too, underwrites, cherishes, and propels epistemology's sense-based means and the sense-driven method of science.

II

Without losing tender-minded overtone, as in Platonic or French rationalism, German idealism, or the evangelical faith embedded in her bi-national context, Dickinson's empirical voice demonstrates the richest payoff of her experience-laden worldview—namely, her almost scientifically tough-minded tone. Her spirit of experiment prevails even on the inter-subjective plane of her existence. Her poetically reasoned transposition from sense-based means to sense-driven method transforms her ideas of sensation and reflection into "finely explicit" models of reality or poeticized hypotheses for physical and life sciences.[24] Thus reaching back to Locke, the Late Romantic paragon of Anglo-American letters does not simply "dwell in Possibility—" of empirical truth (Fr466, line 1). She also realizes the facsimile of scientific knowledge. Of the "Anglo-Saxon" age in which he and Emily Dickinson thrived, Charles Wadsworth exclaims, "We live in the harvest time of mind and thought," adding, "The development of the mental follows the law of material development." In his celebration of mechanical inventiveness, accordingly, Wadsworth expresses his view that the telegraph, in particular, "has demonstrated the great possibility. And to Anglo-Saxon thought, a great possibility is a great certainty" (Wadsworth *Sermons* [1869] 292, 293-94). Wadsworth's down-to-earth (as well as ethnocentric) philosophical optimism suggests that Dickinson's words "I dwell in Possibility—" can refer to the pause between an idea of sensation or reflection and the thing it produces, as in how the Romantic-era imagination is believed to yield the thing imaged.

According to this brash duo's politically incorrect reading of history, in any case—and despite how quaintly this bi-national, cultural bias now strikes the ear—"a great possibility is a great *certainty*" in England and the United States—for better not worse. Do the words "I dwell in Possibility—" signal merely "totally self-contained experience" (Walker 21)? Does this signature sentence imply the either/or choice between existence and aesthetics, as though Dickinson's imagination were "deadlocked" and her life/art dilemma "irresolvable"? Does this saying of hers struggle between "a Poeian constriction"—"I *dwell* in Possibility—" and "an Emersonian expansion"—"I dwell in *Possibility*—" (Robinson 34, 29)? If "Paradise" (in line 8 of the poem "I dwell in Possibility—") is "the farthest space conceivable" and if the poet's "mind can expand to include it" (Juhasz 19-20), then her not-*so*-enclosed earthly garden can also encompass the Anglo-American setting for human advancement in both knowledge and wellbeing. Perhaps even more incisively than does the mordant Wadsworth, Dickinson thinks that tidy-to-untidy realms of observation and reflection might well render superfluous the "pure serene,"[25] the tender-minded excess, of axiomatic rationalism. With something of Wadsworth's near-triumphal spirit of Anglo-America, Dickinson revels in steam technology, nor can even too-far-down-to-earth geology and evolutionary biology so much as materially spoil her Anglo-American mind's epistemological brio or fatally reduce her more-than-merely-sky-wide brain's place in nature.[26]

Wadsworth's praise of steam technology, first of all, sounds unmistakably like Dickinson's. At the same time, however, his tribute serves to throw her genius for substantive and stylistic condensation into especially bold relief. "Steam—that fantastic shape that played aerial and useless before the eyes of old dreamers—" has become, in Wadsworth's modern vein, "man's Titanic servant everywhere: chained in the dark caverns of the earth, fettered to the wheels of great machinery." Wadsworth marvels, in particular, at steam "harnessed on the thoroughfares of traffic; rushing through the valleys; leaping on the mountains; marching on the seas—God's own wingèd wind unto man's chariot, bearing him over all the brute forces and forms of nature, in imperial dominion conquering and to conquer" (Wadsworth *Sermons* [1869] 293). Dickinson's twelve-word paean to all kinds of steam power similarly envisions virile engineering. Her persona fairly and appropriately *hisses* the message of fire-generated energy (her *f*'s and *l*'s also embody licking flame): "For*c*e Flame / And with a Blonde pu*sh* / Over your impotence / Flit*s s*team" (Fr963, lines 9-12; emphasis added). In Dickinson's enthusiasm for steam power here, as in Wadsworth's everywhere, there can be little or no anticipation of the post-Titanic-disaster irony that marks the hubris, and perhaps even the nemesis, of the Modern world.

Of course, there can be more than a touch of such complexity in Dickinson's ode to the train and its steam-engine:

> I like to see it lap the Miles—
> And lick the Valleys up—
> And stop to feed itself at Tanks—
> And then—prodigious step

> Around a Pile of Mountains—
> And supercilious peer
> In Shanties—by the sides of Roads—
> And then a Quarry pare
>
> To fit its sides
> And crawl between
> Complaining all the while
> In horrid—hooting stanza—
> Then chase itself down Hill—
>
> And neigh like Boanerges—
> Then—prompter than a Star
> Stop—docile and omnipotent
> At its own stable door— (Fr383)

Still, if Dickinson's train threatens danger, then her liking of it nonetheless comes through. Despite the faintly satirical edge to this lyric (the speaker's social consciousness, after all, signifies that the train docs not necessarily equal progress), the honorific tone rings. *Words*worth's praise of "Steamboats, Viaducts, and Railways" (1841) is a particularly intrepid sonnet that late in his career similarly welcomes—as its name alone implies—the products of humankind's industrial imagination into Romantic Nature's visionary company. Perhaps even more closely than does Wordsworth's somewhat divided attention, Emerson's "Nature" (1836) apples to the subject matter of "I like to see it lap the Miles—": "What new thoughts are suggested [writes Emerson] by seeing a face of country quite familiar, in the rapid movement of the railroad car!" (Murphy 1:845-46). Dickinson's empiricism can take the form of her more than merely Wadsworth-related interest in the rise, trials, tribulations, and, above all, progress of the Industrial Revolution.

"I Like to see it lap the Miles—", finally, signals the poet's strikingly Wadsworth-related pride in her father, Edward, who, as Director of the Amherst and Belchertown Railroad, brought the world to Amherst and vice versa (L72). Wadsworth's comparison of a man like Edward Dickinson with a train like the one in Dickinson's poem applies to her industrial art:

> *Patience and earnestness, conservation and progress* [writes Wadsworth]. These must be found together in the character of the

> truly successful man. These qualities arc not opposites; they are only different manifestations of perseverance. They answer respectively to the steam power and the brakes of a train. Without the first *life* has no movement at all; without the *last* it moves only to disaster and destruction. (Wadsworth *Sermons* [1905] 182)

The fact that Dickinson's train *moves*, has more to do with the earnest and progressive spirit of her father and of the Industrial Revolution than with the "sexual advance" of the "male" (Philip 74-75). The fact that Dickinson's train *halts*, has more to do with the patient conservatism of her father and of his Whig Party's stop-and-start, slow-but-sure plans for moderate American expansion than with the "symbolized ... journey of death" (Downey 28). "I like to see it lap the Miles—" might be "about poetry and about itself" or might concern "the differences in traditional masculine and feminine consciousness in the nineteenth century," for dominating "locomotive" versus "landscape subject" comes through, and might even further complicate Dickinson's rich conversation with Wadsworth (Freedman 31; Martin 134-35). This well-known poem, however, can perhaps best be understood as addressing straightforward, sturdy, and robust values of the nineteenth century, or what Wadsworth would call "different [antiphonal more than opposing] manifestations of perseverance" (be they progressive, conservative, personal, or cultural.)

If Edward Hitchcock influenced Dickinson's interest in the new science of geology (Sewall *Life* 2:235-65), then Wadsworth also wrote about geology, in ways equally parallel to Dickinson's views of this edgy, proto-evolutionary subject matter. With Wadsworth's help, indeed, she balanced the vast reaches of geological time with the pressing needs o f her brief span of life, for, without diluting the facts of this physical science, she came to terms with, and made the best of, its harshly impersonal force.

In a surprisingly tough-minded, refreshingly prescient grasp of geological issues, Wesley had already asked, "What is at the center of the earth?" and "What, for that matter, does one know of its surface?" (Jackson 13: 492-93). Wadsworth builds on this empirical interrogative posed by his religious forebear. Dickinson's "dearest earthly friend" asks and answers other geological questions:

> For tell me where, either in creation or Providence, God thus hurries to conclusions? How many ages were consumed in the slow progress whereby this planet became fitted for human

habitation? Why, the very fuel consumed in your houses is the slow product of countless years. And the tiny gem of your adornment was crystallized only in an immensity of generations! Jehovah's law of work is no hurrying and headlong progress. He wins slowly, and in circles of immense sweep! A thousand years arc but as a day in the majesty of his movements. And in all this quiet and slow progress how truly Godlike he seems! (Wadsworth *Sermons* [1869] 14)

Dickinson's "Business" of "Circumference" (L268), it turns out, is in part to explore, albeit without quite as much overtly divine reference as Wadsworth indulges in, the "circles of immense sweep" wherein earth takes time to crystallize gems.

Here is a poem in which Dickinson, like Wadsworth, suggests that "later is better" over the vast reaches of geological time, partly for spiritual reasons:

> The Day that I was crowned
> Was like the other Days—
> Until the Coronation came—
> And then—'twas Otherwise—
>
> As Carbon in the Coal
> And Carbon in the Gem
> Are One—and yet the former
> Were dull for Diadem—
>
> I rose, and all was plain—
> But when the Day declined
> Myself and It, in Majesty
> Were equally—adorned—
>
> The Grace that I—was chose—
> To me—surpassed the Crown
> That was the Witness for the Grace—
> 'Twas even that 'twas Mine— (Fr613)

The second stanza of this poem parallels a passage in which Wadsworth's geological language supplies him with an analogy to spiritual life: "The value of a gem is not in its composition, but in its crystallization. Even the diamond is composed mainly of carbon, and differs from the black coal of our furnaces only in this mysterious transfiguration.... But the spiritual man has through gracious crystallization become a gem, reflecting Divine light, and thus fitted for a diadem" (qtd. in Sewall *Life* 2:452-53). The poem, in line with Wadsworth's spiritual analogy, engages in a more than simply geological colloquy with his prose. For instance, one recognizes in the poem "ritualism reminiscent of New England baptism" (Jones 40). For both the preacher and the poet, moreover, just as carbon changes into diamond, so plainness *becomes* the beauty of holiness.

Thus, just as "later is better" for the earth in their joint view, so too, in their respective judgments, does plainness become the beauty of *love*, perhaps even between Wadsworth's self-projection here and Dickinson's persona. Although Dickinson's speaker values inner social meaning more highly than she rates the external symbols and trappings of her new bond, this poem's focus entails a now alternately, now simultaneously, religious and romantic attachment. Meanwhile, geology hovers nearby, as secular seal. "The Day that I was crowned," therefore, seems scarcely "the heretical assumption of autonomous being" (Keller *Only* 290). The psychosocial, and perhaps even the psychosexual, tinge to this lyric's contribution to geological-and-spiritual discussion is unmistakable. Regardless of whether this speaker entertains a simple idea or (perish the thought) an idea of sensation concerning Wadsworth, she "was chose—" as much by human as by spiritual agency (though only in the realm of virtual reality). In light of the poem's geological imagery, this detail signals how, for Dickinson's self-projection here, the personal is not the religious (or political) so much as it is the philosophical and scientific. Dickinson can understand science, in fact, as rather tender-minded.

What is the poet's attitude toward how human beings fit into natural selection? Her lyrics run the gamut of emotions from bemused hope to precariously controlled insouciance to despair to calm acceptance. First of all, however, in the manner of John Wesley and Charles Wadsworth, Dickinson could meditate on evolutionary biology as a species of rather surprisingly joyful wisdom. As participant-observers in Methodist heritage know, yet as no academic historians, to my knowledge, have recognized, Wesley prepared ground for Charles Darwin's theory (Collier 34-35; Barber 74-77). Thus, in the run-up to *On the Origin of Species* (1859), Wesley's natural philosophy figures more prominently than one otherwise might expect it to, perhaps even for such a scientific evangelical as he turns out to be. Wesley's concretizing, Anglicizing abridgment of Charles de Bonnet's *Contemplation of Nature* (1764) emphasizes, like Darwin (except for Wesley's religious reference), that God gradually but progressively develops nature through organic and human forms. Part-time student of science Wadsworth's attitude toward evolutionary biology, similarly, traces back "New Englandly" to Wesley's proto-evolutionary (as well as simply Christian) theism and sounds blithe (cf. Dickinson's phrase in Fr256, line 15). Adopting a relaxed, humorous tone, Wadsworth pauses in his defense of Christianity long enough to joke—shades of the Huxley-Wilberforce exchange during the 1860s—that "If any man will continue to believe that he is only an improved beast, we will not quarrel with his genesis, but only wish him joy of his grandmother" (Wadsworth *Sermons* [1884] 2).

Mark Twain made a point of hearing Wadsworth preach, and "the humor that pleased [Twain] was close to the 'roguery'" that Dickinson also "cherished" in Wadsworth "and often indulged in" (Sewall *Life* 2:451-52). Dickinson, accordingly, observes that "Science is very near Us—I found a megatherium on my strawberry" (L3:926-27). Since a megatherium is a "huge extinct sloth" (L3:927n.1), this Wadsworth-like squib familiarizes Darwin's theory and implies that (the disappearance of the megatherium notwithstanding) a gigantic, almost identical sloth survives! Thus Dickinson's empirically philosophical tone can sound anything but worried or concerned about evolutionary biology. In her book, even the tough-minded science of Darwin can prove a nonthreatening, if not exactly an intimate, presence.

The speaker of "A science—so the Savans say," as a case in point, remains no less sweetly lyrical for having "surely learned her lesson" in the proto-evolutionary science of "geology and fossil findings" from Edward Hitchcock (Wolff 196-97):

> A science—so the Savans say,
> "Comparative Anatomy"—
> By which a single bone—
> Is made a secret to unfold
> Of some rare tenant of the mold—
> Else perished in the stone—
>
> So to the eye prospective led,
> The meekest flower of the mead
> Upon a winter's day,
> Stands representative in gold

> Of Rose and Lily, manifold,
> And countless Butterfly! (Fr 147)

"*Countless* Butterfly," like "the meekest flower of the mead," tempers the tough tone of the poem as established by its first stanza. As the poem progresses, the speaker turns her eye toward *living* species, for the "representative flower (perhaps herself) stands, after the Emersonian manner of each and all, as typal synechdoche of the whole of nature" (Keller "Alephs" 310-11). This monodrama, despite its Darwinian method, feels as lyrical as any other Dickinson poem.[27] To add to the name of Hitchcock, I evoke those of Wesley and Wadsworth. Their lessons of an evolutionary kind disturbed no one's equilibrium, owing ultimately, in my terms of analysis, to the robust epistemology, and perhaps even to the constructive skepticism, of British empirical philosophy. Just as Wesley *anticipates* the truths of evolutionary biology with sangfroid, and just as Wadsworth *contemplates* them with nerve, though scarcely with a light and lyrical heart, so too does the Dickinson of "A science—so the Savans say" remain at once evolution-minded and carefree. For this speaker, it is as though the age of Darwin can coexist with Late Romantic lilt, and perhaps even as though the latter can withstand the former.

Dickinson, however, can also recoil from Darwin's science. She can become alarmed by, and can struggle with, what Alfred, Lord Tennyson's tough-minded interpretation of Robert Chambers's proto-Darwinian *Vestiges of the Natural History of Creation* (1844) discovers at the core of evolution's harsh particulars—namely, "Nature, red in tooth and claw / With ravine" (Tennyson, *In Memoriam: A H. H.* [1850] 56.15-16). Dickinson's cry that "Darwin docs not tell us" "*Why* the Thief ingredient accompanies all sweetness" tells us *that* it does so, for reasons of Darwin's science (L2:485; emphasis added). Darwin's views by no means turn out entirely irreligious (Brown). Darwin's science, however, reduces God at best and, in the form of natural selection, applies Ockham's razor to God's very existence.[28]

The cryptic, caustic comment that Dickinson makes to her late-life love-interest Judge Otis P. Lord, with whom she shares a skeptical streak (Guthrie *Emily*), leaps to mind: "Mrs Dr Stearns called to know if we didn't think it very shocking for [former Union General and candidate for Massachusetts Governor Benjamin F.] Butler to 'liken himself to his Redeemer,' but we [Emily and Austin] thought Darwin had thrown 'the Redeemer' away" (L3:728). Thus if, as the result of evolutionary biology, God is dead, then Butler's apotheosis of himself, though only in the heat of political campaigning, represents the sole kind of "divinity" still feasible in the Late Romantic period, no matter how much this development might scandalize "Mrs Dr Stearns." To mention General Butler's Civil War occupation of New Orleans, he played God there egregiously enough to earn himself the nickname "Beast," so far exceeding what the law allowed that he might have frightened even other Late Romantic self-divinizers (Sandburg 246-47, 468-70, 512-3, 613). In any case, to paraphrase Fyodor Dostoyevsky, without God all is permitted, and Dickinson might have agreed, for no matter how waggishly she and Austin enjoyed Darwin's discard of Jesus as divine, they do not seem likely on the other side of their sarcastic coin to have done so lightly.

The notion that Darwin spells the death of God and the end of Redemption shocks Emily Dickinson and marks her poems. This Darwin-haunted speaker, for example, faces galling disenchantment:

> The missing All—prevented Me
> From missing minor Things.
> If nothing larger than a World's
> Departure from a Hinge—
> Or Sun's Extinction, be observed—
> 'Twas not so large that I
> Could lift my Forehead from my work
> For Curiosity. (Fr995)

To say nothing of species, the disappearance of worlds here seems bad enough. The extinction of God, however, looms worse still. Even wholesale loss would feel less cataclysmic.[29]

The poet's nonchalance masks her undertone of gallows humor, thereby intimating her horror at vacuum. "The missing All," with lower-case "m" and upper-case "A," occupies limbo between insignificance and awe. Hollowness, however, intensifies if gerund "missing" belongs to the speaker's lassitude. The deliberated, upper-case importance of "Me," in the phrase "prevented Me," disturbs the reader's peace because of the capitalized pronoun's self-apotheosizing, "Beast"-Butlerizing connotation.

If the persona, like Butler, arrogates godhead, substituting her own creativity for that of a God now gone or dead and buried with the fossils, then she does so not with pride but with discreet, touching gesture, averting her glance from cosmic disaster. Such stance, however plucky or full of aplomb, lands "The missing All, prevented Me" 180 degrees away from Wesley's death-bed *mot*, "The best of all is, God is with us" (qtd. in Hurst 141). The hindering absence of Dickinson's *Deus Absconditus*, or Deity Moribund, makes all lower-case absences of no consequence whatsoever. What I have previously designated as Dickinson's "acquiring grace," seeks balance between choosing and being chosen, but grace, fitfully evident in "The Day that I was crowned," seldom leavens Dickinson's poems of evolutionary biology, which perplex and retard any prevenient grace of Wesley's always-already-present God (Brantley "Dickinson's" 49).

Darwin's "Nature, red in tooth and claw / With ravine" relegates Dickinson's lyric impulse to bittersweet. Does she entertain the likelihood that Darwin bears as much responsibility for the decline of poetic as of religious faith (as he himself might have acknowledged)? In Dickinson's view, as in Darwin's, species just are, at least while they last. This considerable body of her knowledge comes to seem "all / [She] know[s] on earth,"[30] though not by a long shot all she desires to learn.

For Dickinson, natural law defeats human measures against, say, the rodent kind. Even the despised rat, in nature's scheme, occupies the dignity of place. Dickinson's poetic laboratory report, accordingly, forbears to punctuate rat's equilibrium (Cf. Gould): "Hate cannot harm / Foe so reticent— / Neither Decree prohibit him— / Lawful as Equilibrium" (Fr1369, lines 7-10). A species so alienated from, and so much at enmity with, humankind as the detestable, rebarbative fly, moreover, fails to alter Dickinson's brave acceptance of scientific reality as more ultimate for differing from any human-centered concept of rightness or fairness. "Of their peculiar calling," she declares of flies (in subtly attenuated Calvinist terms), "Unqualified to judge," adding, "To Nature we remand Them / To justify or scourge—" (Fr1393, lines 13-16). Thus Dickinson describes species as meticulously, and with as little regard for human agendas of interpretation, as Darwin depicts the objects of his attention on Galapagos, or as David Hume critiques causation. Or as Wesley, the follower of Locke as well as of Jesus, shows his all but Darwin-like, yet by now not-*so*-surprising, reverence for the exacting procedures of the scientific method.

Here follows the most striking passage of an empirically philosophical kind that John Wesley ever wrote:

> I endeavour [writes Wesley] not to account for things, but only to describe them. I undertake barely to set down what appears in nature; not the cause of those appearances. The facts lie

> within the reach of our senses and understanding; the causes are more remote. That things are so, we know with certainty; but why they are so, we know not. In many ways, we cannot know; and the more we inquire, the more we are perplexed and entangled. God hath so done his works, that we may admire and adore; but we cannot search them out to perfection. (Jackson 14:301. Cf. Ecclesiastes 3:11)

These words anticipate Dickinson's Darwin-informed worldview. They also rebuke, *avant la lettre*, the fuzzy anti-intellectualism of much twenty-first-century American evangelical/creationist discourse (there being no such British expression to speak of any more). Like Wesley, as well as like Darwin, Dickinson writes things down, respects them, and reaches non-irritably for their causes, yet without grasping causation. Thus, though Locke, Wesley, Wadsworth, the other Romantic-era Anglo-American writers, and she acknowledge the perplexity, viscosity, and entanglement of truth, they know it "will hold—" (Fr343, line 10). "The Truth," as she tells it slant but whole, "is Bald—and Cold—" (Fr343, line 9), but she takes the violent mutability *and* the plodding sameness of the world in stride. Casting her objective eye on life, on death, she passes on, starts all over again. Precisely because she knows the truth will set her readers free, she provides salubrious, as well as unflinching, example of courageous intellect *and* heroic imagination.

III

The stress of this essay, perhaps, has fallen more on the optimistic, pre-Civil War atmosphere of Edward Hitchcock's Amherst than on the post-Civil War, post-Darwin tone of incipient pessimism that other scholars emphasize.[31] My approach here, however, can still apply to Dickinson's whole career. She and her fellow authors, and perhaps even Locke, Wesley, and Wadsworth to some extent, encounter seeds of pessimism on their industrial, geological, and biological forays not so much into "the incomprehensible Inane" or "out upon Circumference—" as anti-prophetically into "the malady of the quotidian."[32] Even the constructive skepticism of Locke, Berkeley, Hume, and Shelley-influencing William Drummond becomes destructive in the nihilism of Dickinson's pre-modern mode or postmodern intimations. On the other hand, the heart of her constructively skeptical tradition sustained her Late Romantic imagination, for the poetic personae interpreted in this discussion, far from vegetating in some static state of unbelief, display in their pursuit of truth animated measures of both realism and hope.

"We proceed most safely," declares Romantic-era philosopher William Godwin, "when we enter upon each portion of our process, as it were, *de novo*," adding, "There is danger, if we are too exclusively anxious about consistency of system, that we may forget the perpetual attention we owe to experience, the pole-star of truth" (Godwin *Enquirer* vi, viii). Thus, four years after espousing French rationalism in his *Enquiry concerning Political Justice* (1793), Briton Godwin turned back toward British empiricism in his *Enquirer* (1797). His dramatic palinode, or revival, as it were, of his philosophical birthright, serves as commentary on the sensationalist epistemology, and hence on the scientific inclination, of such a trio of Anglo-American writers as his wife, Mary Wollstonecraft, his daughter, Mary Shelley, and his intellectual descendant (and theirs), Emily Dickinson.[33] To recall Keats's Doctrine of Negative Capability—namely, "the condition of being in uncertainties, Mysteries, doubts, without any irritable reaching after fact & reason"[34]—and to reiterate the signature phrase for Dickinson's Late Romantic epistemology, to "dwell in" the "Possibility—" of empirical findings is to eschew overconfidence in predicting them. By the same token of her philosophical modesty, however, thus to "dwell in Possibility—" is also to enhance the likelihood of discovering the truth.

"We cannot hope for truth, only for ever richer (humanly created) meanings," declares Clifford Geertz, adding, "indeed, an embarrassment of meanings; for, such is the indeterminacy of the signs we use, uncontrollably proliferating meanings are present in the slightest, least considered utterance" (qtd. in Tallis 3). Entertaining, by contrast, the robust, untroubled idea of "a fundamental attunement between the human mind and the universe," Raymond Tallis asks of Geertz, "What is the truth status of the assertion that truth has dissolved into meaning?" (Tallis 4). Emily Dickinson might have answered, "Dubious, at best." Adjustment of mind to the universe, and perhaps even the promise of this relationship's refinement, arises from her and her dramatic monologists' experiences as tests of stable or dynamic truth, not as records of teeming meanings. This Dickinson's brand of philosophical optimism grows wise or well-earned, not foolish or cock-eyed. Side-stepping naïveté, yet "march[ing] breast forward," she strives, thrives, and fights on.[35]

NOTES

I thank Diana Brantley, Burton John Fishman, Melvyn New, and Marianne Noble for their invaluable suggestions concerning just how Emily Dickinson might count as poet-philosopher. Earlier versions of this article were delivered to the June 2009 Symbiosis Conference in Boston, Massachusetts, and to the August 2010 Emily Dickinson International Society Conference in Oxford, England.

[1] In a letter to William Wordsworth, probably written in early January 1815, Charles Lamb regretted that the editor of *The Quarterly*, William Gifford, had omitted from Lamb's review of Wordsworth's *The Excursion* (1814) Lamb's argument for Wordsworth's poetry as "natural methodism." Lamb thought that Wordsworth would have liked such an interpretation of his works: "I regret only that I did not keep a copy. I am sure you would have been pleased with it, because I have been feeding my fancy for some months with the notion of pleasing you" (Lamb 2:149). See Brantley *Wordsworth's* 8, 135, 142, 174, and passim.

[2] My career-long stake in the rather large claim that Lamb's identification of Wordsworth's poetry as "natural methodism" can apply to Romantic-era prose and poetry of Anglo-America in general, has proceeded too much, perhaps, as though the first *m* of Lamb's word *methodism* were upper case. I hereby acknowledge that this paradoxical phrase grows epistemological as well as revival-like, and perhaps even more the former.

[3] Whereas Abrams relates the "natural supernaturalism" of Thomas Carlyle to German idealism (see also Cazamian).

[4] Second only to Brooklyn Congregational Reverend Henry Ward Beecher in national clerical renown, Philadelphia Presbyterian Reverend Charles Wadsworth inspired in Dickinson a range of honorifics from her embarrassingly deferential "My Clergyman" to her playfully allusive "My Philadelphia" (cf. Antony to Cleopatra: "My Egypt") to her superlatively heartfelt "my dearest earthly friend" and "my closest earthly friend" (Applegate; Finnerty; L750; L765; L790; L807; Sewall *Life* 2:451-52). Although Wadsworth and Dickinson, as far as one knows, met only twice, in 1860 and 1880, some speculate about the emotional tinge, and perhaps even the passionate character, of their relationship (Habegger; Pollak *Anxiety*; Shurr; Strickland). I am persuaded by Habegger's carefully understated argument for Wadsworth as the addressee of the three (sexually charged) "Master Letters" (L187; L233; L248). If Habegger is correct, then these letters are the only ones surviving from Dickinson

to Wadsworth. An undated one from Wadsworth to Dickinson (undoubtedly the first in their series) consists only of perfunctory pastoral counseling and is the sole known correspondence from him to her (L248a). Their friendship, like that between, say, George Bernard Shaw and Ellen Terry, stayed largely an epistolary embodiment. Their letters, however, might have enclosed sermons and poems. My phrase *slant truth-telling*, above, alludes to one of Dickinson's most familiar poems, "Tell all the truth but tell it slant—" (Fr1263).

[5] For the influence a) of Locke on Wesley, see Brantley *Locke* 27-102; b) of Locke and Wesley on the leader of the American Great Awakening, Jonathan Edwards, see Brantley *Coordinates* 7-42; and c) of Locke, Wesley, and Edwards on Anglo-American Romanticism, see Brantley *Coordinates* 54-140 and Brantley *Anglo-American* 27-244. For Wadsworth's praise for the scientific aspect of Wesley's practice as a lay physician, see Wadsworth *Sermons* (1905) 169. For Dickinson's similarly empirical medical views, see Brantley *Experience* 48-50.

[6] Huffer; Lease; Miller; Sewall *Life* 2:449-54.

[7] For Whitman's immersion in the scientific thought of his day, see Scholnick. For Dickinson's relation to mid-nineteenth-century scientific progress, see Peel.

[8] For a lively study of the immediately scientific (in preference to the long-range empirically philosophical) context of Romantic Britain's theme of sense-based reason, see Holmes. For Romantic Britain's Dissenting and Anglican overtones, see Harding, Mee, Daniel E. White, Ulmer, and Ryan. Brantley *Wordsworth's* focuses on one British Romantic's evangelical voice.

[9] "The Philosophy of Enthusiasm," by J. Clifford Hindley, links Moravian theology to Wesley's famous conversion (on May 24, 1738, in Aldersgate Street, London), yet includes, as well, intriguingly philosophical speculation (hence my emphasis, above, on Hindley's word *Philosophy*). Wesley's "empiricist conditioning," Hindley observes, taught him so much respect for experience as the necessary ground of knowledge that his distinctive quest for "a direct experience of the divine love" was in the first instance, and perhaps even ultimately, quasi-philosophic (Hindley 107-08).

[10] I adapt for my purposes, above, the words of Wordsworth in Prospectus to *The Recluse* (1814), in which his "voice proclaims / How exquisitely the individual Mind / (And the progressive powers perhaps no less / Of the whole species) to the external World / Is fitted—and how exquisitely, too— / Theme this but little heard of among men— / The external World is fitted to the Mind" (lines 62-68). Quotations of British and American authors, unless otherwise indicated, are from Damrosch et al., eds., and Baym et al., eds.

[11] For the concept of Dickinson's conversing with such precursors as Wordsworth, I am indebted to Beer's characterization of Charles Darwin's procedure: "Darwin's reading is always a process of conversation, marked by ripostes scribbled on the page as well as ruminative notes recorded alongside. And beyond that, he engages in the active silent dialogue in which the reader slides into the place of the writer and yet presses back into his or her own person too (something close to what he calls 'double consciousness as . . . ideal argument held in one's own mind' [Barrett 90])" (Beer 8).

[12] I quote, in the sentence above, a) from James Gleick's opening essay in Bryson's edited collection on "the story of science and the Royal Society" and b) from Lea's review of Bryson's collection (Lea 22).

[13] For Dickinson, the sight of the face is sufficient but not necessary for ethical exchange. Prose/poetic personae, for her (hers and those of other writers), can represent visitation, first disclosure, and trans-cultural moment. Verbal masks for her do not so much belie/deny/militate against as enact ethics. Cf. the discussion in Wieseltier.

[14] Qtd. in Swingle 71. Although religious specifics in Dickinson's poetry are well established (Eberwein; Keane; Lundin; McIntosh; Oberhaus), this study suggests that her empirical procedure, or faith in experience, trumps her evangelical yearning, or experience of faith.

[15] Locke *Essay* 2.7.10 (Nidditch 131).

[16] Body 33; Brantley Locke 27-102. For other studies of Locke's influence on Wesley, see Dreyer and Hindley.

[17] Brantley *Locke* 72-73, 202-03. See also Wadsworth *Sermons* (1869) 23.

[18] For an overview of Dickinson's friendship with Wadsworth, including the facilitating importance of Elizabeth and Josiah Gilbert Holland, see Sewall *Life* 2:444-62, 2:729-41. See also Reynolds 31 and Lease 4, 6.

[19] Besides Wadsworth, two ministerial candidates for intellectual compatibility with Dickinson are Horace Bushnell and Edwards A. Park (Habegger 311-13).

[20] For the argument that Eliza Coleman brought Emily Dickinson and her sister, Lavinia, to hear Charles Wadsworth preach (perhaps philosophically, who knows?) at his Arch Street Presbyterian Church in Philadelphia, in March 1855, see, for example, Leyda 1:lxxvi-lxxvii.

[21] Sewall, *Life* 2:262-68; Leyda 1:29, 1:37, 1:323, 2:33.

[22] Percy Bysshe Shelley, "Adonais" (1821), line 417; Shelley, *Prometheus Unbound* (1819), act 3, scene 1, line 204.

[23] Shelley, "Adonais" (1821), line 418. Cf. Frost, "To Earthward" (1923).

[24] I refer to Bloom's watchword for criticism: "to make the implicit finely explicit" (7).

[25] John Keats, "On First Looking into Chapman's Homer" (1816), line 7.

[26] For Dickinson's somewhat less Wadsworth-related mastery of mathematics, chemistry, botany, ornithology, entomology, and the healing arts, see Brantley *Experience* 35, 45-50, 55-62, 90-93, 96-102. For Dickinson's ethnocentrism, see Erkkila.

[27] According to Gravil, Tennyson's monodrama *Maud* (1855) forms a major influence on Dickinson's forty fascicles, or manuscript books.

[28] As Emerson laments, with a proto-Dickinson blend of sarcastic blasphemy and sorrowful anger, "Providence has a wild, rough, incalculable road to its end, and it is of no use to try to whitewash its huge, mixed instrumentalities, or to dress up that terrific benefactor in a clean, white shirt and white neckcloth of a student in divinity" ("Fate" [1852] in Whicher 333).

[29] "The distinctive feature of this poem," writes Cameron of "The missing All, prevented Me," "is its impersonality, the largesse with which departure characterizes not only psychological reality but also physical and natural fact" (170-71). I would replace "largesse" with "chill." "The real subject of the poem," as McClave affirms, "is the continuing sense and the definitive act of *missing*" (4). "Clearly," she adds, "this is what sets the terms of [the speaker's] existence, so that the mind has some choice in the drama of happen stance" (5). The choice that the mind has, however, yields cold comfort. To conflate Dickinson's words with those of Dylan Thomas, after the near-explicit death of "the missing All," "there is no other" death ("A Refusal to Mourn the Death, by Fire, of a Child in London" [1937] line 16).

[30] Cf. Keats, "Ode on a Grecian Urn" (1819), lines 49-50.

[31] Lundin; Menand; Howe in Pollak "Neither" 19; Benfey *Summer*;Wineapple.

[32] Wallace Stevens qtd. in Keane *Emily* 140.

[33] For a recent study of the scientific imaginations of Mary Wollstonecraft, Mary Shelley, and Charlotte Smith, see Dolan.

[34] Keats to George and Thomas Keats, December 21, 27 [?], 1817.

[35] Robert Browning, "Epilogue to *Asolando*" (1890), lines 11, 19.

WORKS CITED

The following abbreviations are used to refer to the writings of Emily Dickinson:

Fr *The Poems of Emily Dickinson*. Ed. R. W. Franklin. 3 vols. Cambridge, MA: Harvard University Press, 1998. Citation by poem number.

L *The Letters of Emily Dickinson*. Ed. Thomas H. Johnson and Theodora Ward. 3 vols. Cambridge, MA: Harvard University Press, 1958. Citation by letter number.

Abrams, M. H. *Natural Supernaturalism: Tradition and Revolution in Romantic Literature*. New York: W. W. Norton, 1971.
Allen, Mary. *Animals in American Literature*. Urbana: University of Illinois Press, 1983.
Applegate, Debby. *The Most Famous Man in America: The Biography of Henry Ward Beecher*. New York: Doubleday, 2006.
Barber, Frank Louis. *The Philosophy of John Wesley*. Toronto: The Ryerson Press, 1923.
Barrett, Paul H., ed. *Metaphysics, Materialism and the Evolution of Mind: Early Charles Darwin*. With a Commentary by Howard E. Gruber. Chicago: University of Chicago Press, 1980.
Baym, Nina et al., eds. *The Norton Anthology of American Literature: Fifth Edition*. New York: W. W. Norton, 1998.
Beer, Gillian. "Darwinian Romanticism." *The Wordsworth Circle* 41.1 (Winter 2010): 3-9.
Benfey, Christopher. *Emily Dickinson and the Problem of Others*. Amherst: University of Massachusetts Press, 1984.
___. *A Summer of Hummingbirds: Love, Art, and Scandal in the Intersecting Worlds of Emily Dickinson, Mark Twain, Harriet Beecher Stowe, and Martin Johnson Heade*. Harmondsworth, England: Penguin Press, 2008.
Bloom, Harold. *Shakespeare: The Invention of the Human*. New York: Rivershead Books, 1998.
Body, Alfred H. *John Wesley and Education*. London: The Epworth Press, 1936.
Brantley, Richard E. *Anglo-American Antiphony: The Late Romanticism of Tennyson and Emerson*. Gainesville: University Press of Florida, 1994.
___. "The Common Ground of Wesley and Edwards." *Harvard Theological Review* 83 (July 1990): 271-303.
___. *Coordinates of Anglo-American Romanticism: Wesley, Edwards, Carlyle, and Emerson*. Gainesville: University Press of Florida, 1993.
___. "Dickinson's Signature Conundrum." *The Emily Dickinson Journal* 16.1 (2007): 27-52.
___. *Experience and Faith: The Late-Romantic Imagination of Emily Dickinson*. 2004. Reprint. New York: Palgrave Macmillan, 2008.
___. *Locke, Wesley, and the Method of English Romanticism*. Gainesville: University Press of Florida, 1984.
___. *Wordsworth's "Natural Methodism."* New Haven, CT: Yale University Press, 1975.
Brown, Frank Burch. *The Evolution of Darwin's Religious Views*. Macon, GA: Mercer University Press, 1986.

Bryson, Bill, ed. *Seeing Further: The Story of Science and the Royal Society*. San Francisco: Harper Press, 2010.

Cameron, Sharon. *Lyric Time: Dickinson and the Limits of Genre*. Baltimore, MD: The Johns Hopkins University Press, 1979.

Cazamian, Louis. *Carlyle*. Translated by E. K. Brown. 1912. Reprint. Hamden, CT: Archon Books, 1966.

Collier, Frank Wilbur. *Back to Wesley*. New York: Methodist Book Concern, 1924.

Damrosch, David et al., eds. *The Longman Anthology of British Literature: First Edition*. 2 vols. New York: Longman, 1999.

Deppman, Jed. *Trying to Think with Emily Dickinson*. Amherst: University of Massachusetts Press, 2008.

Diehl, Joanne Feit. *Dickinson and the Romantic Imagination*. Princeton, NJ: Princeton University Press, 1981.

Dolan, Elizabeth A. *Seeing Suffering in Women's Literature of the Romantic Era*. Aldershot, England; Burlington, VT: Ashgate, 2008.

Downey, Charlotte. "Emily Dickinson's Appeal for a Child Audience." *Dickinson Studies* 55 (1st Half 1985): 21-31.

Dreyer, Frederick. "Faith and Experience in the Thought of John Wesley." *The American Historical Review* 88 (February 1983): 12-30.

Eberwein, Jane Donahue. "'When—Omnipresence—Fly?' Calvinism as Impetus to Spiritual Amplitude." *The Emily Dickinson Journal* 14.2 (2005): 12-23.

Erkkila, Betsy. "Emily Dickinson and Class." *American Literary History* 4 (Spring 1992): 1-27.

Finnerty, Paráic. *Emily Dickinson's Shakespeare*. Amherst: University of Massachusetts Press, 2006.

Freedman, William. "Dickinson's 'I Like to See It Lap the Miles'." *The Explicator* 41 (Spring 1982): 30-32.

Godwin, William. *The Enquirer*. London: J. Johnson, 1797.

___. *An Enquiry Concerning Political Justice, and Its Influence on Morals and Happiness*. 1793. Reprint. Toronto: University of Toronto Press, 1946.

Gould, Stephen Jay. *Time's Arrow, Time's Cycle: Myth and Metaphor in the Discovery of Geological Time*. Cambridge, MA: Harvard University Press, 1987.

Gravil, Richard. "Emily Dickinson (and Walt Whitman): The Escape from 'Locksley Hall'." *Symbiosis: A Journal of Anglo-American Literary Relations* 7.1 (April 2003): 56-75.

Guthrie, James R. *Emily Dickinson's Vision: Illness and Identity in Her Poetry*. Gainesville: University Press of Florida, 1998.

Habegger, Alfred. *My Wars Are Laid Away in Books*. New York: Random House, 2001.

Harding, Anthony John. "An Ethics of Reading: A Conflicted Romantic Heritage." *Keats-Shelley Journal* 57 (2008): 45-65.

Hindley, J. Clifford. "The Philosophy of Enthusiasm." *The London Quarterly and Holborn Review* 182 (1957): 99-109, 199-210.

Hirsch, E. D., Jr. *The Aims of Interpretation*. Chicago: University of Chicago Press, 1975.

Holmes, Richard. *The Age of Wonder: How the Romantic Generation Discovered the Beauty and Terror of Science*. New York: Pantheon Books, 2008.

Howells, Richard. "Resinking the *Titanic*: Hubris, Nemesis, and the Modern World." *Symbiosis: A Journal of Anglo-American Literary Relations* 1 (October 1997): 151-58.

Huffer, Mary Lee Stephenson. *Emily Dickinson's Experiential Poetics and Rev. Dr. Charles Wadsworth's Rhetoric of Sensation: The Intellectual Friendship between the Poet and a Pastor*. Lewiston, NY: Edwin Mellen Press, 2007.

Hurst, J. F. *John Wesley, the Methodist*. 1904. Reprint. Whitefish, MT: Kessinger Publications, 1999.

Jackson, Thomas, ed. *The Works of the Rev. John Wesley, A M*. 14 vols. 1829-31. Reprint. Grand Rapids, MI: Zondervan Press, 1958.

Johnson, Greg. *Emily Dickinson: Perception and the Poet's Quest*. University: University of Alabama Press, 1985.

Jones, Rowena Revis. "'A Royal Seal': Emily Dickinson's Rite of Baptism." *Religion and Literature* 18 (Fall 1986): 29-51.

Juhasz, Suzanne. *The Undiscovered Continent: Emily Dickinson and the Space Within*. Bloomington: Indiana University Press, 1983.

Keane, Patrick J. *Emily Dickinson's Approving God: Divine Design and the Problem of Suffering*. Columbia: University of Missouri Press, 2008.

Keller, Karl. *The Only Kangaroo Among the Beauty: Emily Dickinson and America*. The Johns Hopkins University Press, 1979.

———. "Alephs, Zahirs, and the Triumph of Ambiguity: Typology in Nineteenth-Century American Literature." In *Literary Uses of Typology from the Late Middle Ages to the Present*, ed. Earl Miner. Princeton, NJ: Princeton University Press, 1977.

Kher, Inda Nath. *The Landscape of Absence: Emily Dickinson's Poetry*. New Haven and London: Yale University Press, 1974.

Kimpel, Ben. *Emily Dickinson as Philosopher*. New York and Toronto: Edwin Mellen Press, 1981.

Lamb, Charles. *The Letters of Charles Lamb*, ed. E. V. Lucas. 2 vols. London: J. M. Dent & Sons and Methuen & Co., 1935.

Langbaum, Robert. *The Poetry of Experience: The Dramatic Monologue in Modern Literary Tradition*. London: Chatto and Windus, 1957.

Lease, Benjamin. *Emily Dickinson's Reading of Men and Books: Sacred Soundings*. Basingstoke, England: Macmillan, 1990.

Lea, Richard. "Lightning Rods." *TLS* (June 4, 2010): 22.

Leyda, Jay, ed. *The Years and Hours of Emily Dickinson*. 2 vols. New Haven, CT: Yale University Press, 1960.

Locke, John. *An Essay Concerning Human Understanding*. 1690. Edited by Peter H. Nidditch. Oxford: Clarendon Press, 1975.

___. *The Reasonableness of Christianity. As Delivered in the Scriptures*. London: A. and J. Churchill, 1695.

___. *Some Thoughts Concerning Education*. London: A. and J. Churchill, 1693.

Lundin, Roger. *Emily Dickinson and the Art of Belief*. Grand Rapids, MI: William B. Eerdmans, 1998.

McClave, Heather. "Emily Dickinson: The Missing All." *Southern Humanities Review* 14 (Winter 1989): 1-12.

McIntosh, James. *Nimble Believing: Dickinson and the Unknown*. Ann Arbor: University of Michigan Press, 2000.

Maddox, Randy L. *Responsible Grace: John Wesley's Practical Theology*. Nashville, TN: Kingswood Books, 1994.

Manning, Susan. *Fragments of Union: Making Connections in Scottish and American Writing*. London: Palgrave Macmillan, 2002.

Martin, Wendy. *An American Triptych: Anne Bradstreet, Emily Dickinson, Adrienne Rich*. Chapel Hill: University of North Carolina Press, 1984.

Matthews, Rex D. *"'Religion and Reason Joined': A Study in the Theology of John Wesley."* Th.D. diss., Harvard University Press, 1986.

Mee, Jon. *Romanticism, Enthusiasm and Regulation: Poetics and the Policing of Culture in the Romantic Period*. Oxford: Oxford University Press, 2003.

Menand, Louis. *The Metaphysical Club*. New York: Farrar, Straus, and Giroux, 2001.

Miller, Paul M. 'The Relevance of the Rev. Charles Wadsworth to the Poet Emily Dickinson." *Higginson Journal* 6 (First Half 1991): 1-69.

Morey, Frederick L. "Dickinson-Kant: The First Critique." *Dickinson Studies* 60 (2nd half 1986): 1-70.

Murphy, Francis, and Herschel Parker, eds. *The Norton Anthology of American Literature: Second Edition*. 2 vols. New York: W. W. Norton, 1985.

Nidditch, Peter, ed. *An Essay Concerning Human Understanding*. 1690. By John Locke. Oxford: Clarendon Press, 1975.

Oberhaus, Dorothy Huff. *Emily Dickinson's Fascicles: Method and Meaning*. University Park: Pennsylvania State University Press, 1995.

Peel, Robin. *Emily Dickinson and the Hill of Science*. Madison, NJ: Fairleigh Dickinson University Press, 2010.

Philip, Jim. "Valley News: Emily Dickinson at Home and Beyond." In *Nineteenth-Century American Poetry*, ed. A. Robert Lee. Totowa, NJ: Barnes and Noble, 1985.

Pickering, Samuel F. *John Locke and Children's Books in Eighteenth-Century England*. Knoxville: University of Tennessee Press, 1981.

Pollak, Vivian R. *Dickinson: The Anxiety of Gender*. Ithaca, NY: Cornell University Press, 1984.

___. "Neither Even Nor Odd." *Emily Dickinson International Society Bulletin* 13 (November/December 2001): 19.

Pulos, C. E. *The Deep Truth: A Study of Shelley's Skepticism*. Lincoln: University of Nebraska Press, 1954.

Reynolds, David S. *Beneath the American Renaissance: The Subversive Imagination in the Age of Emerson and Melville*. Cambridge, MA: Harvard University Press, 1988.

Ricoeur, Paul. *Freud and Philosophy*. Translated by Denis Savage. Cambridge: Cambridge University Press, 1970.

Robinson, Douglas. "Two Dickinson Readings." *Dickinson Studies* 70 (Bonus 1989): 25-35.

Ryan, Robert M. *The Romantic Reformation: Religious Politics in English Literature, 1789-1824*. Cambridge: Cambridge University Press, 1997.

Sandburg, Carl. *Abraham Lincoln: The Prairie Years and the War Years*. 1954. Reprint. New York: Harcourt, 1982.

Schiller, Friedrich von. *Letters on the Education of Man*. In *Critical Theory Since Plato: Revised Edition*, ed. Hazard Adams. San Diego: Harcourt Brace Jovanovich, 1992.

Scholnick, Robert. "'The Password Primeval': Whitman's Use of Science in 'Song of Myself'." *Studies in the American Renaissance* (1986): 385-425.

Sewall, Richard B. *The Life of Emily Dickinson*. 2 vols. 1974. Reprint. New York: Farrar, Straus, and Giroux, 1980.

Shurr, William H. *The Marriage of Emily Dickinson: A Study of the Fascicles*. Lexington: University Press of Kentucky, 1981.

Stillinger, Jack. "Imagination and Reality in the Odes of John Keats." In *The Hoodwinking of Madeline, and Other Essays on Keats's Poems*. Urbana: University of Illinois Press, 1971.

Strickland, Georgiana. "Emily Dickinson's Philadelphia." *The Emily Dickinson Journal* 13.2 (2004): 79-115.

Swingle, L. J. *The Obstinate Questionings of English Romanticism*. Baton Rouge: Louisiana State University Press, 1987.

Tallis, Raymond. "The Truth about Lies: Foucault, Nietzsche, and the Cretan Paradox." *TLS* (December 21, 2001): 3-4.

Telford, John, ed. *The Letters of the Rev. John Wesley, A.M.* 8 vols. London: The Epworth Press, 1931.

Ulmer, William A. *The Christian Wordsworth: 1798-1805*. Albany: State University of New York Press, 2001.

Wadsworth, Charles. *Sermons*. Brooklyn: Eagle Bookland Job Printing Co., 1905.

___. *Sermons*. New York and San Francisco: A . Ronan & Company, 1869.

___. *Sermons*. Philadelphia: Presbyterian Publishing Co., 1882.

___. *Sermons*. Philadelphia: Presbyterian Publishing Co., 1884.

Walker, Julia M. "Emily Dickinson's Poetic of Private Liberation." *Dickinson Studies* 45 (June 1983): 17-22.

Wasserman, Earl. *The Subtler Language: Critical Readings of Neoclassical and Romantic Poems*. Baltimore: The Johns Hopkins University Press, 1959.

Wesley, John. *Sermons on Several Occasions*. London: Epworth Press, 1944.

___, ed. *A Survey of the Wisdom of God in the Creation: or a Compendium of Natural Philosophy*. 1777. Reprint. Philadelphia: Jonathan Pounder, 1816.

Whicher, Stephen E., ed. *Selections from Ralph Waldo Emerson: An Organic Anthology*. Boston, MA: Houghton Mifflin Company, 1957.

White, Daniel E. *Early Romanticism and Religious Dissent*. Cambridge: Cambridge University Press, 2010.

Wieseltier, Leon. "Faces and Faiths." *The New Republic*, August 12, 2010, 40.

Wilson, Eric G. *The Spiritual History of Ice*. New York: Palgrave Macmillan, 2009.

Wineapple, Brenda. *White Heat: The Friendship of Emily Dickinson and Thomas Wentworth Higginson*. New York: Knopf, 2008.

Wolff, Cynthia Griffin. *Emily Dickinson*. Reading, PA: Addison-Wesley, 1988.

15. The Wordsworthian Cast of Dickinson's Romantic Heritage

Anglo-American Romanticism runs the gamut from rational empiricism and the scientific method, through theistic rather than Deistic natural religion, to immediate distinct from traditional revelation.[1] For example, such an Anglo-American triptych of Late Romantic writers as Carlyle, Tennyson, and Emerson at once emphasizes inductive reasoning—what Wordsworth's most strictly empirical mood calls 'sense, conducting to ideal form' (*TP*, 1850, XIV, 76)—and highlights the spiritual sense. I have previously described the latter as 'passivity at first, activity at last, the physical senses as analogies to spiritual insight, and, most intriguingly perhaps, the physical senses as both harbingers and accompaniments of at once transcendent and immanent truth' (*Anglo-American Antiphony*, 230). Now, my philosophical and religious contextualizing of Anglo-American writers shades into reading the poetry of Emily Dickinson (1830-86). Her High-to-Late-Romantic forebears and contemporaries, without being culpably particular, take both their sensationalist epistemology and their testimonial heart-religion straight, at least by comparison with the slant truth-telling[2] to be found throughout her Late Romanticism. (They even gravitate towards the goal of synthesis, as distinct from remaining true to their best standard of intellectual, spiritual, and imaginative receptivity—namely, 'being in uncertainties, Mysteries, doubts, without any irritable reaching after fact & reason'.[3]) Dickinson does not so much simply cultivate '*Negative Capability*' as choose to 'dwell' within the positive 'Possibility—' (Dickinson, 466, 1) of the synthesizing process itself. Still, she is not all that 'anxious' about Wordsworth, I argue[4]—instead, the spiritual as well as natural vision of her chief precursor nurtures her wisest tone, and perhaps even inspires her most optimistic import. Her art is the more accessible, and perhaps even the subtler, for this constructive influence.

Dickinson, specifically, 'see[s] into the life of things' (*LB* 'Tintern Abbey' 50)—that is, again to apply the words of Wordsworth to her case, she exercises her spiritual as well as natural vision in 'the world / Of all of us, the place in which, in the end, / We find our happiness, or not at all' (*TP*, 1850, X, 725-7). The triangle of empirical philosophy, evangelical religion, and Romantic literature informs all that the Anglo-American century from 1770 to 1870 found resonant not only in what Wordsworth elegizes as 'the *burden* of the mystery' (*LB* 'Tintern Abbey', 39; emphasis added) but also in what he praises as mystery itself. Carlyle, Tennyson, and Emerson, on the one hand, intone their Late Romantic version of what Wordsworth feels as tragedy— that is, as 'the heavy and the weary weight / Of all this unintelligible world' (*LB* 'Tintern Abbey', 40-1). On the other hand, they celebrate their Late Romantic experience of what Wordsworth receives as comedy—that is, as 'another gift, / Of aspect more sublime; that blessed mood, / In which the burden of the mystery, / . . . / Is *lighten'd*' (*LB* 'Tintern Abbey', 37-9, 42; emphasis added). Similarly, insofar as Dickinson earns for herself the vocabulary of her 1,789 personae, this poet of flesh and blood is as much a lyricist of comedy and of tragicomedy as a maker of satire or a bard of tragedy. Her poetry, modulating from epistemology (narrowly so called) to the twin-experiential realms of philosophy and religion, realizes both natural and spiritual progress towards all manner of other-ness. She does not so much suspect 'false' consciousness, after the manner of Marx, Nietzsche, or Freud,[5] as expect truth, grace, and joy, like Locke, Wesley, and Edwards. Her achievements of truth-seeking, and perhaps even her wisely passive (*LB*, 'Expostulation and Reply', 24) receptivity to the influxes of grace and the surprises of joy, are more than merely modest in that her still-imitable combination of watchfulness with openness enhances the 'high argument' ('Prospectus' to *The Recluse*, 71), the innovative, communitarian sublimity, of her more than merely Miltonic imagination.

As a consequence, just as Dickinson's 'obscurity' can be 'palpable',[6] so too can her mystery be urgent. Her love-producing, as well as simply awe-inspiring, collapsing of nature into spirit, and vice versa, on her pilgrimage of art, if not of life, 'calls us to the things of this world',[7] which, from her Late Romantic perspective, include such 'fruits of the Spirit'[8] as faith, hope, grace, and joy. Thus, although 'the lady whom the people call the *Myth*'[9] remains so subjective as to seem solipsistic, and although she can be so reclusive as to seem isolated,[10] the paradox of her solitude is, nevertheless, that she sets herself apart from the world in order to apprehend it. She participates, thereby, in the Anglo-American Romantic colloquy of experience and faith. As I fill in some of the background to her 1,789 poems, and as I develop readings, I name or allude to Wordsworth in each one of my paragraphs. It is not so much that Dickinson works with his very words and phrases as that she breathes in the atmosphere to which he gives his expression, and which, for that matter, bears his signature. Building, in particular, on the spiritualized as well as 'naturalized imagination'[11] that I have consistently endeavoured to locate among such High-to-Late-Romantic writers of the Anglo-American world as Wordsworth and Emerson, Dickinson absorbs, Alters, and distills their broadly experiential dialectic. The Anglo-American Romantic tenet that sense-based reason is not only analogous to spirit but also part of it primes Dickinson's 'soul-competency',[12] which, in turn, underlies her more Late Romantic than premodern art.

I

Harold Bloom, who comments on everything, has pronounced: 'She had the best mind of all our poets, early and late'.[13] But Dickinson had the best heart of all our poets, too. What her first reviewer, Arlo Bates, admires as her *emotional thought* is what Richard B. Sewall, her most thorough biographer, praises as her 'ideas felt on the pulses, in the bloodstream'.[14] Sewall echoes Wordsworth's 'sensations sweet, / Felt in the blood, and felt along the heart, / And passing even into my purer mind, / With tranquil restoration' (*LB*, 'Tintern Abbey', 29-31), thus suggesting that the emphasis on both *mind* and *heart* that defines British Romanticism must also energize Dickinson's 'upheavals of thought'.[15] I would only add that she contributes all her strength of mind, *soul*, and heart to Romantic Anglo-America, as well as simply to what Bloom calls 'the Western canon'.[16] Her fusion finds perhaps its most inclusive antecedent in such *spiritual* phrasings as Wordsworth's 'sensations *sweet*', '*purer* mind', and 'tranquil *restoration*' (*LB*, 'Tintern Abbey', 28, 30, 31; emphasis added).

Wordsworth, specifically, hovers near Dickinson's dramatic as well as lyrical combination of the spirit of sceptical counter-interpretation with a heart-felt sense of traditional presence. Wordsworth's most strictly sceptical mood, on the one hand, actually prefers 'the world / Of all of us' to the blandishments of any transcendental realm. Dickinson, similarly, positively celebrates 'The Fact that Earth is Heaven— / Whether Heaven is Heaven or not' (Dickinson, 1435, 1-2). On the other hand, Wordsworth's most strictly transcendental mood declares that 'trailing clouds of glory do we come / From God, who is our home' ('Ode: Intimations of Immortality', 64-5). Similarly, Dickinson's homebody-ness reflects a certain *contemptus mundi* of her own.

Most characteristically, perhaps, just as Wordsworth bares his 'Romantic Religion'[17] on the *tabula rasa* of his poetry, so too does Dickinson quite thoroughly subscribe to the broadly experiential criterion of both truth and value. Thus following Blake to 'cleanse the doors' of her 'perception'[18] of both a world elsewhere and 'the world / Of all of us', she cultivates, without necessarily valuing process over results, Wordsworth's most thoroughly idealistic mood of 'Effort, and expectation, and desire, / And something evermore about to be' (*TP*, 1850, VI, 608-9). Dickinson's personae, accordingly, as though they were so many amateur 'Scientist[s] of Faith' (Dickinson, 1261, 12), put the very doctrine of immortality to the test of their experience, which, somewhat after the manner of Wordsworth's 'intimations' of immortality, offers a muted, yet reasonable, hope-against-hope for the afterlife.

Let me show, as an initial reading harking back to Wordsworth's 'Ode: Intimations of Immortality' (1802-04), just how experience and faith operate in such a signature lyric or miniature poetic manifesto of Dickinson's Late Romantic imagination as Poem 373, which, above all, attests to everlasting life:

> This World is not conclusion.
> A Species stands beyond—
> Invisible, as Music—
> But positive, as Sound—
> It beckons, and it baffles—
> Philosophy, don't know—
> And through a Riddle, at the last—
> Sagacity, must go—
> To guess it, puzzles scholars—
> To gain it, Men have borne
> Contempt of Generations
> And Crucifixion, shown—
> Faith slips—and laughs, and rallies—
> Blushes, if any see—
> Plucks at a twig of Evidence—
> And asks a Vane, the way—
> Much Gesture from the Pulpit—
> Strong Hallelujahs roll—
> Narcotics cannot still the Tooth
> That nibbles at the soul—

Debate centres on whether the persona's faith survives her experience. Cynthia Griffin Wolff observes 'the systematic way [the poem] examines the leakage and finally the loss of faith'.[19] Christopher Benfey suggests that the poem 'could almost be a gloss on Emerson's "Montaigne; or, The Skeptic"' (1846).[20] Jane Donahue Eberwein, with particular pertinence to my interests here, emphasizes how 'the hope of immortality [in these lines] finds insufficient supports in [such] human wisdom' as science, philosophy, and theology.[21] Lawrence Buell goes so far as to conclude that the persona of Poem 373 'is just as aware of the precariousness of doctrinal structures as Emerson, but she feels the problems and possibilities of her position more keenly because she sees these structures both as all-important and as bankrupt'.[22] David Porter, similarly, thinks that the poem illustrates 'the absence of a controlling design'.[23] Nevertheless, Ben Kimpel finds that 'this poem in every respect is ... a parallel of Augustine's *Confessions*. . . . Basic to this poem is a confident affirmation that there is an order of reality which is other than the world, and is transcendent of it in the sense that it is "beyond" it'.[24]

The insight closest to my own view is that of Daniel J. Orsini, who observes, 'Obviously, the poem never proves the narrator's initial thesis, but it does at least spare her religious beliefs, since the evidences of the senses, of science, appear no more conclusive than her lofty spiritual yearnings'.[25] What the poet elsewhere calls 'Sweet skepticism of the Heart' (Dickinson, 1438, 1) equates here to experience that includes both doubt and faith. The persona's *un*systematic questioning is not so much the 'leakage' of faith as the *true sign* thereof. Absence, for her, does not so much signify that God is dead as reveal that the Unknowable *is* God. If it is too much to speak of the persona's 'confident affirmation', then her religious beliefs are surely more than merely 'spared'. 'The evidences of the senses' and of 'her lofty spiritual yearnings', after all, are alike inconclusive and conclusive—that is, not so much clouded as enriched by her experience. It is as though, for her, 'the meanest flower that blows' (*WP*, 'Ode: Intimations of Immortality', 202) can give more moment-by-moment than merely momentary 'Intimations of Immortality'.

Thus, despite the faintly satirical, constructively sceptical edge to Poem 373, its outlook stands as guardedly optimistic, if not, for that matter, as relatively robust and untroubled. Although scholarship here is of little avail against enigmas of the spirit, and although philosophy here is of no avail in solving the riddle of immortality, the humble, sense-based reason of inductive, sensationalist epistemology is, nevertheless, of considerable avail here in all matters of experiential faith, including 'intimations' of immortality. 'Faith' that 'Plucks at a twig of Evidence— / And asks a Vane, the way—' is not just analogous to, but even fully employs, the physical senses. 'Faith' that 'slips—' but 'laughs, and rallies—' is schooled in contingencies, as well as simply sustained by grace. The very hope of heaven takes its rise and footing, as well as simply its bearings, from experience, for, just as the 'Species . . . beyond—', though 'Invisible', remains 'positive, as Sound—', so too does it beckon, or remain positive, as vision. Therefore, although the persona is not so certain of either truth or value as rationalists are of the mind's lordship, she is, nevertheless, at least as confident of the quasi-Darwinian, as well as simply heavenly, 'Species' as logical positivists are of empirical knowledge. (After all, just as she 'hears' loved ones who have crossed over, so too does her Darwinian language for life after death suggest continuing 'sight' of them, as well.) Accordingly, since not even institutional religion (called the opiate of the masses) can calm her spiritual insistence, the ache of her painful desire for transcendence constitutes not so much her passionate inference of God as her clamorous longing for eternity. She holds both tough- and tender-mindedly, as well as simply nostalgically, not only to the High Romantic 'faith that all which we behold / Is full of blessings' (*LB* 'Tintern Abbey', 134-5) but also to High Romantic 'Intimations of Immortality'.

II

The Wordsworthian cast of Dickinson's Romantic heritage undergirds the constructive scepticism whereby her poetic method gives rise to the almost more than merely natural apperceptions of her poetic faith. This faith, if not the genuine religion in her faith per se, emerges from her Late Romantic imagination as an unscathed prop, and perhaps even as an unattenuated mainstay, of her mind, soul, and heart. Although her premodern mode toughens her tone, and although her postmodern intimations undermine her import, her doubt/faith dialectic draws energy from, and perhaps even abides in, the broadly experiential, spiritual as well as natural vision of Anglo-American Romanticism. Her art, in my judgment, centres on a point closer to High Romanticism than to High Modernism, notwithstanding her prescience. Her intimations of *immortality*, after all, are a far cry from both the midnight-worshiping *death*-theme of her premodern mode[26] and the outright nihilism of her *postmodern* intimations.

Dickinson's 'post-experiential perspective',[27] to be sure, is a riddle for her readers to puzzle over, if not exactly to be diverted by. Aftermath, for her, can seem like dissolved sugar, or like a bird either featherless or too fat to fly: 'Too happy Time dissolves itself / And leaves no remnant by— / 'Tis Anguish not a Feather hath / Or too much weight to fly—' (Dickinson, 1182). The poet, moreover, has learned enough from her experience not only to articulate 'Proverbs of Hell'[28] but also to substitute them for the outmoded, greeting-card-like sentimentality of such received wisdom as 'Time heals all wounds':

> They say that "Time assuages"—
> Time never did assuage—
> An actual suffering strengthens
> As Sinews do, with Age—
> Time is a Test of Trouble—
> But not a Remedy—
> If such it prove, it prove too
> There was no Malady— (861)

The speaker here, in the middle stages of her post-experience, does not claim to know much, and she conveys ambiguity concerning whether human suffering merely gets worse, or whether we get stronger the worse our suffering becomes. Without a doubt, however, she is sentient enough, if I may apply to her case the words of Shelley, 'to repeal / Large codes of fraud', if not of 'woe'[29]—that is, to defamiliarize cliché by means of 'craft or sullen art'.[30] It is as though she knows, with Hopkins, that her own 'cries' have become 'a chief / Woe, world-sorrow',[31] or that they have matured, like those of Wordsworth, into 'Thoughts that do often lie too deep for tears' (*WP* 'Ode: Intimations of Immortality', 203). It is almost as though she would now no longer even want the merely facile consolation of nostrums about the passage of time. It is as though she would exclaim with Wordsworth, and in a vein of self-correction similar to his, 'Through what power, / Even for the least division of an hour, / Have I been so beguiled as to be blind / To my most grievous loss!' (*WP* 'Surprised by Joy', 6-9).

Within the walls of Dickinson's post-experiential prison, notwithstanding her suffering there, 'moments of escape' (Dickinson, 360, 11) testify to the persisting possibility that love will continue to sustain her, perhaps even after she has apparently lost it. That is why 'A Prison gets to be a friend—', or 'A Geometric Joy—', to the point that 'The Liberty we knew' is 'avoided—like a Dream—' (Dickinson, 456, 16, 29-30). Or, as Wordsworth puts it, 'Nuns fret not at their convent's narrow room' ('Prefatory Sonnet', 1). I have in mind here, moreover, the freedom that exists, paradoxically enough, because of the prison walls of Byron's 'Prisoner of Chillon', or of Beethoven's *Fidelio*. This kind of freedom, in the case of Dickinson, is the choice to do something, anything, in defiance of post-experiential despair, and on the assumption that the fact of doing trumps whether action is effectual:

> At leisure is the Soul
> That gets a staggering Blow—
> The Width of Life—before it spreads
> Without a thing to do—
>
> It begs you give it Work—
> But just the placing Pins—
> Or humblest Patchwork—Children do—
> To Help it's Vacant Hands— (683)

These lines concern not so much 'the woman in her dealings with Power'[32] as the woman poised for action, no matter how unspectacular.

Dickinson's broad concept of experience, then, remains crucial to her aesthetic procedures and principles. Regardless of whether any close correlation obtains between her life and her art, her personae are other-directed. Somewhat after the manner of Wordsworth's 'Love of Nature Leading to Love of Man' (*TP*, VIII), one of her speakers confesses, 'I thought that nature was enough / Till Human nature came / But that the other did absorb / As Parallax a Flame—' (1269, 1-4). Thus the impersonal yields to the personal. The personal, in turn, grows towards the Other: 'Of Human nature just aware / There added the Divine' (5-6). This speaker joins nature to God.

Roger Lundin, to be sure, in his account of *Emily Dickinson and the Art of Belief* (1998), contrasts 'the muteness of nature [in Dickinson's poetry] with the talkative role it had long assumed in romantic thought'. Whereas Emerson had taught that 'the ancient, "Know thyself" and the modern precept, "study nature", become at last one maxim', Dickinson, for her part, 'struggled to believe that mind and nature were knit together as Emerson had said they were, but she could not do so'.[33] Such lines as 'We pass, and [nature] abides, / We conjugate Her Skill / While She creates and federates / Without a syllable—' (Dickinson, 798, 5-8) reveal the poet's larger fear that 'nature', as Lundin puts it, 'goes on with her business, saying nothing intelligible to us, even as we labor to interpret her' (153). Nevertheless, as indicated by Dickinson's Prose

Fragment 119, the poet entertains alternately, if not at once, the difficulty and the possibility of knowing Nature well:

> We must travel abreast with Nature if we want to know her, but where shall be obtained the Horse—A something overtakes the mind—we do not hear it coming[34]

The first insight implies that we lack the means of satisfying our desire for intimacy with Nature. The second suggests that nature herself, whenever she comes abreast of us in her own good time and way, supplies that very intimacy. The two insights, taken together, suggest that Dickinson not only rises to the challenge of solving Nature's riddle but also cultivates the 'wise passiveness' (*LB* 'Expostulation and Reply', 24) of leaving the riddle unsolved. Her latter strategy, paradoxically enough, is a no less efficacious means of acquiring natural knowledge and of strengthening spiritual belief.

On one occasion, as though Dickinson were announcing the divorce of seeing from knowing, she declares that 'Not seeing, still we know—' (Dickinson, 1566, 1). Thus, in an echo of I Peter 1:8 ('Whom having not seen, ye love; in whom, though now ye see him not, yet believing, ye rejoice with joy unspeakable and full of glory'), the poet 'is now able to accept belief in an afterlife without proof'.[35] On almost all occasions when she is *not* referring to the afterlife, however, and perhaps even on some occasions when she *is*, she reveals that, as far as she is concerned, there can be no substitute for *seeing*—that is, for being in the presence of the thing one knows. Consider, if you will, the opening lines of Poem 1028, which, arguably enough, operate along a continuum joining nature to spirit: 'Who *saw* no Sunrise cannot say / The Countenance 'twould be— / Who *guess* at seeing, guess at loss / Of the Ability' (emphasis added). (The wistful implication here is that seeing will be believing even in 'that great getting-up morning bye and bye'.) '*Intimations* of Immortality', albeit necessarily at the lowest possible threshold of experience, whether of the natural or of the spiritual kind, or whether of both kinds at once, offer more comfort in the here-and-now than any merely abstract doctrine of immortality could ever begin to provide. Meanwhile, 'What we see we know somewhat / Be it but a little - / What we don't surmise we do / Though it shows so fickle' (Dickinson, 1272, 1-4). This poem 'discusses the conflict between empiricism and supposition, but supposition's daring, even criminal procedure is the subject'.[36] 'Even criminal' is overstated, perhaps, since Dickinson might well be willing to forgive the all too human tendency to act as though we see, whether we see or not.

As soon after *On the Origin of Species* (1859) as 1865, to be sure, Poem 995 takes God to task:

> The missing All, prevented Me
> From missing minor Things.
> If nothing larger than a World's
> Departure from a Hinge
> Or Sun's Extinction, be observed
> 'Twas not so large that I
> Could lift my Forehead from my work
> For Curiosity.

The speaker here, depicting a more preventing God of extinctions than any Wesleyan God of prevenient grace, suggests that 'The missing All' is Himself extinct, but she only feigns indifference to the absence, or to the death, of God. Just as a range of thinkers from Coleridge and Emerson to Max Weber, Paul Ricoeur, and Richard Rorty feels deeply the loss of the external world as the language of God, so too does Dickinson attempt, yet fail, to break the silence of Being and of God (Lundin 43-7). Poems as early as numbers 340 and 347, and as late as numbers 610, 778 and 1072, as Lundin points out, lack Wordsworth's confidence in hearing 'this mighty sum / Of things for ever speaking' (*LB* 'Expostulation and Reply', 24). Nature, in Dickinson's time, becomes, if not what Lundin calls an 'endless play of signs without design', then, surely, what he phrases as 'a mere trope of human desire', as distinct from a clear type of God's loving intentions (151-3). Nevertheless, while both Darwin's science and the Civil War were undoubtedly the necessary, if not sufficient, conditions for the force with which Dickinson foretold both modernism and postmodernism, her recognition of the split between science and religion was of long standing. It included the same sort of creative tension, as distinct from antipodal opposition, that produced the rich strangeness of her lifelong 'art of belief'.

Dickinson's 'art of belief', I suggest, comes not so much despite, as because of, her disbelief. As she declares, 'We both believe and disbelieve a hundred times an Hour, which keeps believing nimble—' (*Letters of Emily Dickinson*, III, 728).[37] I maintain, indeed, that her oscillation between, if not her dialectic of, poetic method and poetic faith obtains at any given moment of her career, whether before or after the *Origin of Species*, or whether before, after, or during the Civil War. She never stops 'dwell[ing] in Possibility—' of synthesis, in large measure because she resists all attempts to *disenchant* 'the world / Of all of us'.

Poem 1475, written about 1878, is perhaps the most explicit case in point. Here Dickinson pits all the sweetness of her Late Romantic imagination against her chief postmodern premonition—namely, the overweening proclivity of 'man-unkind' to debunk whatever comes within his ken:

> Whoever disenchants
> A single Human soul
> By failure or irreverence
> Is guilty of the whole—
>
> As guileless as a Bird
> As graphic as a Star
> Till the suggestion sinister
> Things are not what they are—

Thus, although I yield to no one in my admiration for the bravery with which Dickinson contemplates nothingness ('"Tis so appalling it exhilarates', 341, 1), I spurn, nevertheless, the temptation to focus too exclusively on poems like no. 1581, which, haunting Lundin, nags at his efforts to establish Dickinson's belief (4, 34, 78, 134, 149):

> Those—dying then,
> Knew where they went—
> They went to God's Right Hand—
> That Hand is amputated now
> And God cannot be found—
>
> The abdication of Belief
> Makes the Behavior small—
> Better an ignis fatuus
> Than no illume at all—

The insufficiently emphasized final four lines suggest that even the foolish fire of combustible marsh gas might yield to what Wordsworth would call 'light that never was, on sea or land' (*WP* 'Elegiac Stanzas: Suggested by a Picture of Peele Castle', 15)—that is, inward illumination.

Dickinson's persona appears, by corollary, to believe that experience keeps her ideals trustworthy, and perhaps even her goals true. If, towards the end of the poet's career, she does not exactly maintain so positive a view of empirical procedures that they emerge as her necessary and sufficient basis for progress in the world, then her poems, at any rate, never quite renounce her faith in experience. If she comes, at last, to fear that Experiment would not be Faithful, or that natural religion would be unavailing, then her poems hold out hope, none the less, for an experience of faith. Regardless of whether she wants to 'Ring in the Christ that is to be',[38] or to 'forge in the smithy of [her] soul the uncreated conscience of the race',[39] she poises herself, as Wordsworth does, between nature and spirit. Regardless of whether she effects her version of Tennyson's, or of de Chardin's, enterprise of reconciling, however vaguely, and in however anachronistic a fashion, evolution with religion,[40] she stakes out, in any case, her opposing positions, and perhaps even gropes towards synthesis through the spiritual sense.

Mediating, then, between Dickinson's premodern tone and her Late Romantic import, I seek to tilt the balance of critical emphasis in favour of the latter. I cannot help thinking, in this connection, of the last stanza of Frost's 'Neither Out Far Nor In Deep' (1936), which, insofar as it is more post-Romantic than High Modern, applies instinctively to Dickinson's poetry: 'They cannot look out far. / They cannot look in deep. / But when was that ever a bar / To any watch they keep?' Randall Jarrell, in an anti-Romantic mood of reading this stanza, observes that 'it would be hard to find anything more unpleasant to say about people'. Along Romantic lines, however, and against the quasi-postmodern notion of Frost as a curmudgeon, Brad Leithauser queries, in answer to Jarrell, 'Isn't [Frost] saying that, as seekers after the truth, we're to be commended for our immoderate appetites, rather than damned for our modest achievements?'[41] Thus, even the 'Great Old Modern' admits of Romantic interpretation, for 'Neither Out Far Nor In Deep' seems finally consistent with Blake's perception that 'More! More! Is the cry' of Man and that 'less than All cannot satisfy'.[42] For her part, Dickinson the Romantic out-quests other Romantics. Like Wordsworth, who recognizes that, 'As it sometimes chanceth, from the might / Of joy in minds that can no further go, / As high as we have mounted in delight / In our dejection do we sink as low' (*WP* 'Resolution and Independence', 22-5, 114), she grasps the manic-depressive proximity of happiness to sadness. Her 'hope', however, perhaps even stronger than his, is almost never 'unwilling to be fed' (*TP*, 1850, VI, 605-7).

Dickinson's hope in Poem 314, perhaps most notably, not only endures against all odds but also poises itself to soar:

> "Hope" is the thing with feathers—
> That perches in the soul—
> And sings the tune without the words—
> And never stops—at all—
>
> And sweetest—in the Gale—is heard—
> And sore must be the storm—
> That could abash the little Bird
> That kept so many warm—
>
> I've heard it in the chillest land—
> And on the strangest Sea—
> Yet—never—in Extremity,
> It asked a crumb—of me.

These lines, if they do not exactly speak of the persona's happiness, express nothing more pessimistic than hope-against-hope. They remain sufficiently Romantic at least and, at most, quintessentially so, for 'the thing with Feathers—' is 'perhaps ... even every human's potential for music and poetry, brave stays against the brooding dark' (Wolff 478). (Standing 'behind Dickinson's famous poem' is a pictorial emblem 'available to her at the time', which, shades of Coleridge, shows a drowning man clinging to an albatross.)[43] According to my Romantic interpretation, the spiritual sense of Dickinson's 1,789 personae blends their knowledge with their faith. Their more moment-by-moment than merely momentary stay against confusion— that is, their natural/spiritual dialectic of experience—helps their unbelief. Indeed, their Wordsworthian hope-against-hope is for spiritual as well as natural *blessing* from 'this mighty sum / Of things for ever speaking'. Dickinson's 'something evermore about to be', therefore, is not primarily in the nature of either an *avant-garde* or a heavenly reward. Instead, her great, if somewhat vague, 'expectation' is of 'something' both subtly and simply in synchrony with the rich and strange auspices of the here-and-now.

III

'Lyric poetry', declares Adam Kirsch, should not so much 'cede narrative and drama' to 'an acute ability to consider consciousness' as 'attempt to force the mind's half-tones and shadows out into the bright light of art'. It is as though 'nothing can have any value as art that is not rigorously retrieved and patterned, and thereby brought back into the world' from whence art comes in the first place.[44] Dickinson, notwithstanding her fey sobriquet as 'the lady whom the people call the *Myth*', is by no means so single-minded in her focus on her consciousness as either to neglect the narrative and dramatic aspects of her art or to overemphasize her mind's half-tones and shadows. Indeed, the patterns of her poems are culturally powerful in part because they arise from the well-grounded stuff of her life, whether 'Felt in the blood, and felt along the heart', or whether 'passing even into [her] purer mind / With tranquil restoration'. The naturally experiential 'world / Of all of us' and spiritually experiential 'moments in the being / Of the eternal Silence' (*WP* 'Ode: Intimations of Immortality' 155-6) inform the synthesizing imagination of the Myth of Amherst.

Dickinson's 'Compound Vision—' (Dickinson, 830, 9)—that is, her co-ordination of the physical senses with the spiritual sense—'Distills amazing sense/ From Ordinary Meanings—' (Dickinson, 446, 3-4). The reader expects different capitalization here—namely, 'Amazing Sense / From ordinary meanings—'. Dickinson, however, reverses expectations. She suggests that, far from having to transmogrify the ordinary in order to render it amazing, she finds it so. To apply the words of Wordsworth to her case, 'meadow, grove, and stream, / The earth, and every common sight' seem 'Appareled', for her, 'in celestial light', and perhaps even suffused, for her, with 'The glory and the freshness of a dream' (*WP* 'Ode: Intimations of Immortality', 2, 4-5). The supernal seems accessible to her, and, to 'dwell in Possibility—' indeed, the commonplace and the miraculous seem able at any given point on her pilgrimage of art, if not of life, to interpenetrate both deeply and well.

Dickinson's personae, accordingly, 'burn' not so much with the 'hard, gem-like flame' of a decadent, premodern sensibility[45] as with her own Late Romantic desire for the 'obscure', yet 'palpable', consummation of the here-and-now with the noumenon. She is not so much enamoured of philosophical conundra nor so much given to ideas of sensation as intent on the ideals thereof whereby she emerges, on balance, as both 'impatient .. . to share the transport' of everyday grace and 'Surprised by joy' thereof (*WP* 'Surprised by Joy', 1-2). If only by dint of her preternatural effort on grounds of her Spartan, yet intense, existence, and perhaps even of her strenuous, yet abundant, experience, her personae all but reconcile their knowledge with their belief. They are especially self-consistent where they do not so much value destination, whether despaired of, wished for, supposed, hoped for, or finally trusted in, as pilgrimage itself.

Dickinson's 'Compound Vision—', then, is not so much *mazed* by her way of knowing as *a*mazed by her way of believing. Although she tempers the hard drive towards synthesis that such an Anglo-American pairing of Late Romantic writers as Carlyle with Emerson favours, and although she is more apt to keep her epistemological rigor and her spiritual autobiography in play than to harmonize them, her personae compound, nevertheless, method with faith. The poet adds one part sensationalist epistemology and one part theological free will to one part synthesizing imagination. It is as though Keats's faith in life's relevance to art were uppermost in Dickinson's mind: 'I am certain of nothing [writes Keats] but of the holiness of the Heart's affections and the truth of Imagination—'.[46] Dickinson's art, therefore, is in creative tension with Anglo-American Romanticism. Her 'Effort, and expectation, and desire' are aimed not so much at generating mere meaning-after-meaning as at discovering truth, grace and joy.

Modern painter Piet Mondrian, according to Jed Perl, not only entrusts 'the spare language of an ascetic' to his 'unsparing, unsentimental canvases' but also 'shapes his overflowing romantic emotions'. Thus, just as Mondrian exhibits 'stand-alone individuality and emotional complexity' at the same time that he effects his version of Prufrockian withdrawal from experience,[47] so too do the broadly experiential vision of Dickinson's Late Romantic imagination and the post-experiential perspective of her premodern mode coexist. If l am reading her poems aright, they are every bit as deeply rooted in her bi-national past as justly ascendant in our present. They are ascendant in our present, indeed, *because* they are rooted in her past. Her premodern mode is every bit as demythologizing as F. C. McGrath claims Modernism is.[48] Her Late Romantic imagination, moreover, can be as iconoclastic as Bloom claims High Romanticism is.[49] Nevertheless, her art can be as *tender* as I claim the art of Wordsworth, or of Emerson, can be. And since her poetry flourishes on the British as well as American ground of a *rigorous* as well as hopeful, *empirical* as well as expectant Romantic method, her Late Romantic imagination is no less Romantic for being as *tough* as I claim Anglo-American Romanticism can be.

'Not the fruit of experience, but experience itself', Walter Pater observes, 'is the end of life'.[50] For Dickinson, the point of living is not so much to achieve synthesis as to practise dialectic, with experience as her polestar of both truth and value. It is not so much that she gives due weight to the experience of doubting the validity of experience itself as that she is willing to engage with the actual and 'Surprised by joy' of the ideal. Her poems not only acknowledge 'all the unhealthy and o'erdarkened ways / Made for our searching'[51] but also bear witness to the grace of our becoming.⁵² Her personae, perhaps even where they cannot hold on to their experience of faith, never altogether lose their faith in experience. Indeed, if only by corollary with what I have described as 'the empirical/evangelical dialectic of Anglo-American Romanticism', her poetry progresses at once towards more truth than falsehood and towards more joy than sorrow. With the both/and logic of her Late Romantic imagination, she resists the nothing-comes-of-nothing mentality of her premodern mode, and perhaps even trumps the anti-experiential propensity of her postmodern intimations.⁵³ Her more wise and well-earned than merely foolish optimism wins out in her art, if not exactly in her consciousness moment-by-moment.

Dickinson's more Late Romantic than premodern art, above all, not only still bears 'the burden of the mystery'—that is, 'the heavy and the weary weight / Of all this unintelligible world'—but also still resonates with mystery. She can still inspire, thereby, her readers to declare, as Wordsworth inspires her to believe, 'And I have felt / A presence that disturbs me with the joy / Of elevated thoughts; a sense sublime / Of something far more deeply interfused' (*LB* 'Tintern Abbey', 38-40, 93-6). Thus, although Wordsworth testifies that presence disturbs as well as elevates him, his sublime imagination gravitates, nevertheless, towards mystery. Dickinson's poetry, too, is no less tough for being tender, and vice versa. Just as Wordsworth blends thought and style to construct the High Romantic argument that experience is the last, best hope for knowledge-with-belief, so too does Dickinson's life of writing include her essentially Late Romantic theme of natural and spiritual experience. Her broadly experiential vision, as distinct from the post-experiential pessimism of her premodern mode, re-envisions idealism for us, not as warm, fuzzy feeling, nor even necessarily as deep feeling, and certainly not as sentimentality, but, instead, as a deliberately imprecise, practically messy, yet abidingly un-cynical and fully moral hope-against-hope. Without either oversimplifying intellectual problems or underestimating spiritual dilemmas, and certainly without betraying any merely wishful thinking on her part, she remains sufficiently close to her experiential ground of both knowledge and belief to engage the minds, souls, and hearts of her readers. She calls upon us to contemplate whatever problems of epistemology, religious methodology, or aesthetics might lie near to our hands.

In sum, 'the fascination of what's difficult'⁵⁴ about the historical and critical interdisciplinary study to which I remain committed climaxes in the study of Dickinson's art. I have attempted here to apprehend anew the philosophical, religious, and literary triangle that I have previously tried to delineate. I have asked here, above all, just how Dickinson the Romantic stands on the broadly experiential common ground between sensationalist epistemology and testimonial heart-religion. She stands there quietly, yet sturdily, with no rigidity. She stands there resolutely, yet resourcefully, after the manner of wily Odysseus, or of resilient Jeremiah, or of both. And, as though her stance there were far and away the most captivating purport of her entire life of writing, she stands ready to move, albeit with more of 'honest doubt' than of 'creeds',[55] and if only in speech acts, toward truth, grace, and joy. Her 'wise passiveness', to reinforce the Wordsworthian cast of Dickinson's Romantic heritage, makes her as much Wordsworth's prime legatee as Whitman's 'self-reliance' makes him Emerson's.

NOTES

[1] See Richard E. Brantley, *Coordinates of Anglo-American Romanticism: Wesley, Edwards, Carlyle, and Emerson* (Gainesville: UP of Florida, 1993) and Brantley, *Anglo-American Antiphony: The Late Romanticism of Tennyson and Emerson* (Gainesville: UP of Florida, 1994). See also Brantley, *Wordsworth's 'Natural Methodism'* (New Haven, CT: Yale UP, 1975); and Brantley, *Locke, Wesley, and the Method of English Romanticism* (Gainesville: UP of Florida, 1984).

[2] Cf. Emily Dickinson, Poem 1263, line 1. Quotations of Dickinson's poems are reprinted by permission of the publishers and Trustees of Amherst College from *The Poems of Emily Dickinson*, ed. Ralph W. Franklin (Cambridge, MA: Belknap Press of Harvard UP, 1998). Copyright © 1998 by the President and Fellows of Harvard College. Copyright © 1954, 1955, 1979 by the President and Fellows of Harvard College. Hereafter cited parenthetically in the essay by referring to the number of the poem followed by the line number.

[3] John Keats to George and Thomas Keats, 21, 27 December 1817.

[4] For a different view, see Joanne Feit Diehl, *Dickinson and the Romantic Imagination* (Princeton, NJ: Princeton UP, 1981). See also Harold Bloom, *The Anxiety of Influence* (New York: Oxford UP, 1973).

[5] Paul Ricoeur, *Freud and Philosophy*, trans. Denis Savage (Cambridge: Cambridge UP, 1970), 27.

[6] John Milton, *Paradise Lost* (1674), II:406.

[7] Richard Wilbur, 'Love Calls Us to the Things of This World' (1955).

[8] Gal. 5:22; Eph. 5:9. Quotations of the Bible are from the King James Version.

[9] Mabel Loomis Todd as quoted in Emily Dickinson, *The Years and Hours of*

Emily Dickinson, ed. Jay Leyda (2 vols, New Haven, CT: Yale UP, 1960), II, 357, 376.

[10] I have in mind, in particular, Dickinson, Poem 1696: 'There is a solitude of space / A solitude of sea / A solitude of Death, but these / Society shall be / Compared with that profounder site / That polar privacy / A soul admitted to itself—'.

[11] Jack Stillinger, 'Imagination and Reality in the Odes of Keats' in *The Hoodwinking of Madeline, and Other Essays on Keats's Poems* (Urbana, IL: University of Illinois Press, 1971), 99-119.

[12] I adapt to my purposes the chief latter-day Protestant doctrine of early twentieth-century Southern Baptist master figure E. Y. Mullins, as discussed in Harold Bloom, *The American Religion: The Emergence of the Post-Christian Nation* (New York: Simon & Schuster, 1992), 164-83.

[13] Harold Bloom, *The Western Canon: The Books and School of the Ages* (New York: Harcourt Brace, 1994), 300.

[14] See Richard B. Sewall, 'Teaching Dickinson: Testimony of a Veteran' in *Approaches to Teaching Dickinson's Poetry*, eds. Robin Riley Fast and Christine Mack Gordon (New York: Modern Language Association, 1989). See also Richard B. Sewall, *The Life of Emily Dickinson*, 2 vols. (New York: Farrar, Straus & Giroux, 1980).

[15] I allude to Martha C. Nussbaum, *Upheavals of Thought: The Intelligence of Emotion* (Cambridge: Cambridge UP, 2001). I have in mind, as well, the emphasis on *emotional intelligence* in both the philosophy and the fiction of Iris Murdoch.

[16] Bloom only half-whimsically includes Dickinson among the 26 most authoritative writers in all of western history. See Bloom, *Western Canon*, 291-311.

[17] I conflate the pairing in Stephen Prickett's title, *Romanticism and Religion*. His subtitle is *The Tradition of Coleridge and Wordsworth in the Victorian Church* (New York: Cambridge UP, 1976).

[18] William Blake, *The Marriage of Heaven and Hell* (1793), plate 14.

[19] Cynthia Griffin Wolff, *Emily Dickinson* (Reading, PA: Addison-Wesley, 1988), 269-70, 440.

[20] Christopher Benfey, *Emily Dickinson and the Problem of Others* (Amherst, MA: University of Massachusetts Press, 1984), 14, 16.

[21] Jane Donahue Eberwein, *Dickinson: Strategies of Limitation* (Amherst, MA: University of Massachusetts Press), 227-8.

[22] Lawrence Buell, *New England Literary Culture: From Revolution through Renaissance* (Cambridge: Cambridge UP, 1986), 133-4.

[23] David Porter, *Dickinson: The Modern Idiom* (Cambridge, MA: Harvard UP, 1981), 106-7.

[24] Ben Kimpel, *Emily Dickinson as Philosopher* (New York: Mellen, 1981), 228-31, 277.

[25] Daniel J. Orsini, 'Emily Dickinson and the Romantic Use of Science', *Massachusetts Studies in English* 7.4-8.1 (1981): 57-69, esp. 63-4.

[26] I have in mind, in particular, Bloom's insight, 'Dickinson was no worshiper of Midnight, as Yeats was to be' (*Western Canon*, 299).

[27] Vivian R. Pollak, *Dickinson: The Anxiety of Gender* (Ithaca, NY: Cornell UP, 1984), 212.

[28] Blake, *The Marriage of Heaven and Hell*, plates 7-10.

[29] Percy Bysshe Shelley, 'Mont Blanc' (1817), lines 80-1.

[30] Dylan Thomas, 'In My Craft or Sullen Art' (1946), line 1.

[31] Gerard Manley Hopkins, 'No Worst, There is None' (1885), lines 5-6.

[32] Dorothea Steiner, 'Emily Dickinson: Image Patterns and the Female Imagination', *Arbeiten aus Anglistik und Amerikanistik* 6.1 (1981): 57-71, esp. 65.

[33] Roger Lundin, *Emily Dickinson and the Art of Belief* (Grand Rapids, MI: William B. Eerdmans, 1998), 153. Lundin quotes from Ralph Waldo Emerson, 'The American Scholar' (1837).

[34] Emily Dickinson, *The Letters of Emily Dickinson*, eds. Thomas H. Johnson and Theodora Ward (3 vols., Cambridge, MA: Harvard UP, 1958), III, 929.

[35] Virginia H. Oliver, *Apocalypse of Green: A Study of Emily Dickinson's Eschatology* (New York: Lang, 1989), 86-7.

[36] Suzanne Juhasz, *The Undiscovered Continent: Emily Dickinson and the Space of the Mind* (Bloomington, IN: Indiana UP, 1983), 136-8, 140-1, esp. 137.

[37] *Letters of Emily Dickinson*, 111, 728. See also James McIntosh, *Nimble Believing: Dickinson and the Unknown* (Anne Arbor, MI: University of Michigan Press, 2000).

[38] Alfred, Lord Tennyson, *In Memoriam* (1850) 106:32.

[39] I adapt to my purposes the presiding idea of Stephen Dedalus in James Joyce, *Portrait of the Artist as a Young Man* (1908).

[40] See Graham Hough, 'The Natural Theology of *In Memoriam*', *Review of English Studies* 33 (1947): 244-56. See also Eugene R. August, 'Tennyson and Teilhard: The Faith of *In Memoriam*', *PMLA* 84 (1969): 217-26.

[41] Brad Leithauser, 'Great Old Modern', *New York Review of Books* 43 (8 August 1996): 42.

[42] Blake, *There Is No Natural Religion* (1788), plate b7.

[43] Barton Levi St Armand and George Monteiro, 'Dickinson's "'Hope' is the thing with feathers"', *The Explicator*, 47, no. 4 (Summer 1989): 34-7. See also

St Armand and Monteiro, "The Experienced Emblem: A Study of the Poetry of Emily Dickinson' in *Prospects: The Annual of American Cultural Studies*, ed. Jack Salzman (New York: Burt Franklin, 1981), VI, 187-280.

[44] Adam Kirsch, 'The Trouble with Lively', *New Republic* (13 July 1999): 39.

[45] Walter Pater, 'Conclusion' to *Leonardo da Vinci* (1873).

[46] Keats to Benjamin Bailey, 22 November 1817.

[47] Jed Perl, 'Absolutely Mondrian', *New Republic* (31 July 1995): 27-32, esp. 27.

[48] F. C. McGrath, *The Sensible Spirit: Walter Pater and the Modernist Paradigm* (Gainesville: UP of Florida, 1986).

[49] Harold Bloom, *Ruin the Sacred Truths* (Cambridge, MA: Harvard UP, 1989).

[50] Pater, 'Conclusion' to *The Renaissance* (1868).

[51] Keats, *Endymion: A Poetic Romance* (1817) 1:10-11.

[52] I have in mind, in particular, Poem 401: 'Dare you see a Soul at the White Heat? / Then crouch within the door— / Red— is the Fire's common tint— / But when the vivid Ore / Has vanquished Flame's conditions, / It quivers from the Forge / Without a color, but the light / Of unanointed Blaze. / Least Village has it's Blacksmith / Whose Anvil's even ring / Stands symbol for the finer Forge / That soundless tugs— within— / Refining these impatient Ores / With Hammer, and with Blaze / Until the Designated Light / Repudiate the Forge—'.

[53] I have in mind, in particular, Poem 760: 'Pain—has an Element of Blank / It cannot recollect / When it began—Or if there were / A time when it was not— / It has no Future—but itself— / It's Infinite contain / It's Past—enlightened to perceive / New Periods—Of Pain'.

[54] William Butler Yeats, 'The Fascination of What's Difficult' (1910).

[55] Tennyson, *In Memoriam*, 96: 11-12.

16. *The Interrogative Mood of Emily Dickinson's Quarrel with God*

Darwinism challenged Emily Dickinson to construct a theodicy. For her, evolutionary biology did not mean that there was no God, but that her individual talent, her Charles Darwin-inflected voice of poetic justice, should shift tradition away from justifying, and toward raising skeptical concerns about, the ways of God to man.[1] The late-romantic-to-pre-modern Miltons or Jobs among Dickinson's lyrical speakers, accordingly, offer a truncated, edgy, and not-so-lyrical version of this profoundly theological conundrum. This subset of Dickinson's art does not address the problem of suffering by locating systematic solutions: rather, these personae direct their subtle, yet near-blasphemous, questions to the dynamic, yet unloving, God of natural selection. Will He answer? wonders the Myth of Amherst.

According to Patrick J. Keane, the signature poem offering Dickinson's perspective on "divine design and the problem of suffering" appears "less hopeful than many readers . . . would seem to prefer":[2]

> Apparently with no surprise
> To any happy Flower
> The Frost beheads it at its play—
> In accidental power—
> The blonde Assassin passes on—
> The Sun proceeds unmoved
> To measure off another Day
> For an Approving God— (*Fr* 1668)

This poem resists "any facile conception of either a painless natural theology or a providential Design" (130). "By the breath of God," declares Job, "frost is given" (Job 37:10); if Dickinson thinks of the beautiful "blonde Assassin" as doing the work of divinity, she nevertheless takes a dim view of this frost-God as a pale rider, ash blonde, "an agent of the destruction of beauty" (129, 140). The speaker of the poem remains appalled that God would sanction such waste. Whereas Jesus's theodicy interprets a grain of wheat in the ground as a metaphor for earthly death that leads to heavenly fruit (John 12:24), Dickinson can find no such divine purpose in the natural death of "any happy Flower." "By making the symbolic 'victim' of violence floral rather than human" (28), she takes a cosmic view. She rejected such human-centered theodicy as the claim that people suffer a) when they abuse the divine gift of free will or b) as part of God's omelet-creating but egg-breaking plan of ultimate redemption.

In "Apparently with no surprise—" the speaker sarcastically gives up on God and triumphantly spurns him without denying that he existed in the past or waiving the right to speak with him again. Keane's close reading brings Dickinson's word *accidental* (from *accidens*, a befalling or falling-to) from its theological connotation of fortunate fall to the nineteenth-century denotation of randomness or chance (121). One thinks of Emerson's characterization of his son Waldo's death as "caducous" and of the "Crass Casualty" in Hardy's "Hap." Dickinson's poetry would appear to include more of Blake's "dull round" or of Stevens's "malady of the quotidian" than of any coherent plan, "genuine dialectical change," or "Kantian or Darwinian purposiveness without purpose" (140). As Richard Gravil argues in *Romantic Dialogues*, Dickinson's relation to her high-to-late-romantic precursors and contemporaries remains conversational rather than invariably antagonistic.

Like Wordsworth, for example, she keened a romantic song of suffering in her poems and letters on theodicy. Dickinson twice alluded (*L* 315, *L* 394) to Wordsworth's "Elegiac Stanzas" and developed what Keane calls her own Wordsworth-like "poetic realization of the inevitability and universality of loss and suffering mingled with hope" (190). Still, the stubbornness of her questioning lacked the insouciance of pre-Darwinian theodicy, and her late-romantic form of questioning proved less hopeful and more tragic than Wordsworth's darkest songs of suffering. Darwin could find no room for the benign theism of Wordsworth's *Excursion*, in which "darts of anguish" "*fix* not" in the Wanderer's flesh (Keane 183-6). Neither could Dickinson; "Heavenly Hurt" had wounded her too deeply and permanently:

> We can find no scar,
> But internal difference—
> Where the Meanings, are— (*Fr* 320)

Dickinson parted company with the Wanderer's stoicism (paradoxically on the residually Calvinist grounds of "Heavenly Hurt").

Although the "romantic crisis" concerns "the dichotomy between the world of scientific laws—cold, indifferent to human values—and man's inner world," Dickinson's perspective on suffering as a variety of religious experience calls for a rearguard "defense of divine holiness and justice in respect to the existence of evil."[3] She sings "the dark under-song of Romanticism" by lamenting not only "the cleavage between the human and the natural" (Milosz 125) but also the sundering of the human and the divine. Whereas Wordsworth huffs and puffs that "I must think, do all I can," that "there was pleasure" in the flower ("Lines Written in Early Spring"), Dickinson grows sure that (*pace* Wordsworth) *not* "every flower / Enjoys the air it breathes" ("Early Spring"). What Coleridge called Wordsworth's "poetic faith" was more pantheistic than theistic, but Dickinson's questioning remained theistic even as she asked whether this was the best of all possible worlds or the worst of all godless universes. Her poetic effort to complete a theodicy for her time corresponds to various efforts by Wordsworth, Emerson, and other romantic poets and transcendentalists, but it gives evidence of more theological rigor than their substitution of hope-without-an-object for God.

In one sense, Dickinson agreed with Thomas Jefferson's characterization of the early-nineteenth-century God of Calvinism as nothing more than "a daemon of malignant spirit."[4] In this sense, she joined Shelley's attack on this God in *Queen Mab*, and as she confronted her tormentor-God, she became, in the words of Keane, less thankful and more "dismayed or denunciatory" (40). At the same time, she could not embrace Jefferson's conclusion that "it would be more pardonable to believe in no God at all" than to acknowledge the existence of such a malignant daemon.[5] The deadening God who haunts her poetry is the inscrutable Calvinist Deity whom she "alternately believed in, questioned, quarreled with, rebelled against, caricatured, even condemned, but never ceased to engage" (36). If Dickinson did not exactly believe in this God, she nonetheless brought her case before him and appealed to his nobler nature. And like Job, she also brought her case against him:

> "Heavenly Father"—take to thee
> The supreme iniquity
> Fashioned by thy candid Hand
> In a moment contraband—
> Though to trust us—seem to us

> More respectful—"We are Dust"—
> We apologize to thee
> For thine own Duplicity— (*Fr* 1500)

Such bold if not wickedly irreverent poems as "'Heavenly Father'—take to thee" (the deflating quotation marks are heavily ironic) turn back on God God's prejudgment of human beings as guilt-ridden dust (Gen 3:19), worms (Job 25:2-6), and embodiments of sin or depravity (Exod 20:5).

Dickinson's riposte to Paul's rhetorical question, "If God be for us, who can be against us?" (Rom 8:31) is bitter: "but when he is against us, other allies are useless—" (*L* 746). According to Paul's theodicy, "the whole creation" has been groaning "until now" (Rom 8:22), yet as Patrick Keane argues, such divine delivery from suffering failed to assuage the poet: "Dickinson's omnipresent deity is personal, though more likely to be an antagonist than a friend, exercising his power unpredictably and often cruelly" (74). Dickinson's Calvinist God remained more inscrutable than personal and stood back so far from solving suffering as to constitute the problem.[6]

Dickinson's sympathetic portrait of Jesus as fellow-sufferer came as close to a finished theodicy as she ever got, but from her vantage point she was unable to achieve a theological closure even in her Christological reflection. "To be human," she writes, "is more than to be divine, for when Christ was divine, he was uncontented till he had been human" (*L* 519). She admits that Jesus existed "before Abraham was" (John 5:58) but honors his flesh and blood, and since her Jesus is no longer God, his suffering complicates and renders futile the religious approach to the problem. Dickinson's Jesus echoes Schopenhauer's as the emblem of suffering humanity and parallels Nietzsche's crucified Christ. Dickinson reasons that the exclusively human agony of Jesus speaks well for him, as the spiritual song declares:

> Nobody knows the trouble I've seen,
> Nobody knows but Jesus,

and his passion, from *pati*, to endure, has appealed to the suffering ages.

In Dickinson's view, however, the sorrow of Jesus does nothing to solve the problem of theodicy. "The resurrection was to Dickinson testimony of the humanity of Jesus," writes Keane, and "Christ's suffering and death registered [with her] more powerfully than the resurrection" (93). As the poet proclaims—"'Twas Christ's own personal Expanse / That bore him from the

Tomb—" (*Fr* 1573)—Jesus is remembered not as an agent of God's salvation but as one who lived courageously, through toils and snares (experience, from *ex* + *periculum*, means going all the way through danger to its other side). For her, both the extravagant claim of Jesus as God and the modest concept of him as God's surrogate fail to pass the empirical test, and she "raises a possibility never dreamed of " even by liberal theologian Henry Ward Beecher, namely, that "Darwin had thrown 'the Redeemer' away" (Keane 36-37; *L* 750).

For Darwin and Dickinson alike, the game of cat and mouse imaged, epitomized, the theodicean's all-but-insurmountable dilemma. Consider Darwin's 1860 letter to his friend and fellow-scientist Asa Gray, for whom evolutionary biology and intelligent design remained commensurate.

> I had no intention [Darwin discloses] of writing atheistically. But I own that I cannot see as plainly as others do, and as I should wish to do, evidence of design and beneficence on all sides of us. There seems to me too much misery in the world. I cannot persuade myself that a beneficent and omnipotent God would have designedly created the Ichneumonidae [assassination wasps] with the express intention of their [larva] feeding within the living bodies of Caterpillars, or that a cat should play with mice.[7]

For her part in this mid-nineteenth-century dialogue between science and religion, Dickinson also signaled her acknowledgment of, and horror at, cat-and-mouse cruelty:

> The Cat reprieves the mouse
> She eases from her teeth
> Just long enough for Hope to teaze—
> Then mashes it to death— (*Fr* 485)

As Keane observes of Dickinson's stance, she, like Ivan Karamazov,

> was no atheist but a challenger who, in her own oblique way, never ceased asking the same questions: Why does evil strike so meaninglessly? Why do the innocent suffer? How can a purportedly omnipotent and loving God approve of such an apparently random, brutally violent process? (72)

Just as no "divine resolution" can in Dostoyevsky's judgment justify "the tears of a single tortured child" (Keane, 72), so answers elude the faith-attracted interrogations of Dickinson.

For Darwin, suffering is clarified as the fallout of natural selection and need not represent a mystery to be explored in relation to God's tender ways or mercies towards humankind. Nevertheless, just as Darwin yearned for such an understanding, so Dickinson struggled towards one. She refused to take refuge in agnosticism, as Darwin did, and neither let God off the hook nor let him up off the mat. For, like Jacob with the angel, she vowed, "I will not let thee go except thou bless me" (Gen 32:26). Her quarrel with God was based on Darwin's science but also harked back to Job's struggle with the Almighty. Of course, her impassioned and intelligent stab at the problem of evil arose from the "upheavals" of her philosophically inclined and scientifically grounded "thought" (Nussbaum's terms). Still, her quest for a theodicy faced its greatest challenges in theology rather than in evolutionary biology. Even her scientific investigation found more faith in honest doubt than in half the creeds.

Dickinson's challenge to God never received an answer either directly in the form of theophany (as in Job 38-41) or indirectly through the vatic voice of romanticism (contrast the declaration of divine authority in *Paradise Lost* to Milton's own godlike utterance throughout his epic, sometimes proto-romantic theodicy). Because Darwin's science called Dickinson's religious frame of reference into doubt, her theodicean imperative can feel less full-throated than that of the less Darwin-haunted Hopkins in *The Wreck of the Deutschland* or in his "terrible sonnets." Dickinson's poetry of suffering and cerebral God-talk, however, looks forward in search of those for whom shoring fragments against their ruin remains their first-aid means of survival. "Better an ignis fatuus," she tells them, "Than no illume at all—" (*Fr* 1581), but better still, she would say, to brave the bald, cold truth that holds (*Fr* 341). It is not that Dickinson's perspective on theodicy, and hence her severe reservations about it, made her in any way an irreligious poet. On the contrary, for her, "Faith is *Doubt*" (*L* 912), and in her skeptical questioning she kept God as hearer of something like her prayer. Perhaps her "Flood subject" of "Immortality" (*L* 319) was not so much about pie in the sky as about her coming day in God's court of justice, where she would be less a criminal in the dock than a plaintiff expecting an award of heavy damages. "Then call, and I will answer; or let me speak, and do thou reply to me," Job pleads as he imagines speaking to God after death (Job 13:22). The result of such an exchange, for Dickinson, would be "Some new Equation, given—" (*Fr* 403) by God to satisfy "Man that is born of a woman" (Job 14:1)—that is, everyone—with why the unjust and the just alike must endure affliction on this earth. Who knows, for no traveler has ever returned from that bourn, but her hope for an explanation and an exculpatory judgment might, just might, have proved adequate to fill this failed theodicean with a faith in the prospect of her vindication.

Emily Dickinson, then, tried to reconcile good and evil on complex but satisfying grounds of theology, yet she could not do so and at the same time remain intellectually honest. She asked, in effect, how "he who made the Lamb" also made "the Tyger" (Blake), but she could not harmonize the weal with the woe of God (Isa 45:7), nor, in religious terms, could she either officiate at "the marriage of heaven and hell" (Blake) or "extricate bliss from its neighbor pain" (Keats). Just as the interrogative mood of Emily Dickinson's quarrel with God paralleled the misgivings of Wordsworth's not always buoyant empiricism—his "obstinate questionings / Of sense and outward things" ("Ode: Intimations of Immortality," lines 140-42)—so the stubborn doubts of Dickinson's struggling faith scarcely squared (as Tennyson's efforts did) Jesus's "immortal Love" with "Life in man and brute."[8] Thus, she pursued the questioning/answering dialectic of theodicy, yet she emphasized the skepticism of this theological genre. *Is* God's eye on the sparrow? she wondered (contrast Matt 10:29).

If Dickinson's Job-like protest that "the missing All" (*Fr* 995, line 1) loved beetles more than people had gotten God's attention, or even God's goat, then she would have felt somewhat vindicated, but the God of Moses himself, after all, can appear equally self-veiling, similarly un-reciprocating.[9] Dickinson would have appreciated Kipling's satirical needling: "Do you use a little g / When you write of God?"[10] She respected the grammar, parsed the Logos, of God as Word, and, insofar as she never put scare quotation marks around the word God, she never dispraised this Holy Name. Contrast, by the way, Dickinson's straightforwardly reverent capital letter for divinity (recall: "the missing All") with her coy, ambivalent presentation of the word-of-all-work *nature*: the debunking punctuation of "'Nature' is all we see—" (*Fr* 721) ironizes this signifier, notwithstanding the "N."[11] Dickinson would think of God—to apply the evolutionary idiom of Dylan Thomas to her case—as "the force that through the green fuse drives the flower" and that "drives (her] green age" (with the stipulation, though, that she might naturally deploy upper-case *force*). If Dickinson did not rediscover the powerful, loving God, she nonetheless believed, for better or worse, in the prolific but devouring, residually Calvinist God of natural selection, albeit only to challenge this God by well representing extinct species, as in: "The Perished Patterns murmur—" (*Fr* 747, line 9). Dickinson's lament that "God cannot be found" (*Fr* 1581, line 5) was not the same as her saying, in her heart, what the fool said in his— namely, that God does not exist. This poet did not so much contemplate a godless universe, or hear the bare, ruined choirs of godless science, as accept, and bridle at, the bald, cold truth of God's science.

In sum, the difficult fascination of justifying the ways of God to humankind assured the exquisite perplexity of Emily Dickinson's perspective in the age of Darwin. Can M. H. Abrams's description of Blake's progression of contraries as "the sustained tension, without victory or suppression, of co-present oppositions" pertain just as aptly to Dickinson's nervous set of stupendous antagonisms, her mental chaos all the finer for being both a phenomenal and a numinous dynamic of inquiry?[12] Was there some justice, some reduction of evil and tyranny, or some alleviation of suffering in *her* progression of contraries, *her* concept of their resolution that is the more luminescent for its being understated? Did the Myth of Amherst, in however tenuous a manner, go "beyond good and evil," as though, like Nietzsche, she suspected that these two categories of ultra-ethics were too human-centered, insufficiently imperative, to be taken entirely at their religious or transcendental face value? Whatever the settlement of these and other such issues of literary and intellectual history, and no matter how secularizing their nineteenth-to-twentieth-century trend, Dickinson's unfinished attempt at theodicy was an all the livelier work-in-progress for forthrightly depicting her retrospective, up-to-date, and prospective struggles and dilemmas of the theological kind. Her obstinate questionings not so much of "Nature, red in tooth and claw / With ravine" as of the God of natural selection entailed some expectation of renewal and no little experience of beauty—even if her God of nature signified (more exclusively than Tennyson's) immanent agency alone (*In Memoriam* 56: 15-16). This lingering hope and this aesthetic pluck of Dickinson's lent more than a modicum of guileless enchantment to the otherwise most thoroughly tough-minded outlooks of her personae. If God's eye had never been, or was no longer, on the sparrow, then Dickinson's saw the beauty of such an individual or species in its very impermanence, and, as for Jesus's love, nothing else came as close as that did to this poet's ideal of endurance.

NOTES

[1] Emily Dickinson's poems and letters will be cited parenthetically. For the poems, the citation will include an abbreviation for the edition used—*Fr* for Franklin—followed by the poem number in that edition; for the letters, the abbreviation (*L*) will be followed by the number assigned to the letter in the Johnson and Ward edition. Quotations of British authors are from Damrosch et al., eds.

[2] Keane, *Dickinson's Approving God*, 30. Hereafter cited parenthetically by page number.

[3] Milosz, *Ulro*, 94.

[4] Jefferson, quoted in Taylor, *Secular Age*, 804n59.

[5] Ibid.

[6] Brantley, *Experience and Faith*, 19-20, 162-63, 197-98.

[7] Darwin, *Life and Letters*, 2:105.

[8] Tennyson, *In Memoriam*, lines 1, 6.

[9] Brisman, "On the Divine," 112.

[10] Qtd. in Logan, "Imperial Rhymes," 16.

[11] See Katz, "Deconstructing Dickinson's Dharma," 48.

[12] Abrams, *The Norton Anthology*, Vol. 2, 60.

BIBLIOGRAPHY

Abrams, M. H. et al., eds. *The Norton Anthology of English Literature: Fifth Edition*. 2 vols. New York: Norton, 1991.

The Bible: Authorized King James Version. Oxford: Oxford UP, 1998.

Brantley, Richard E. *Experience and Faith: The Late-Romantic Imagination of Emily Dickinson*. New York: Palgrave Macmillan, 2004, 2008.

Brisman, Leslie. "On the Divine Presence in Exodus." In *Exodus: Modern Critical Interpretations*, edited by Harold Bloom, 105-22. New York: Chelsea House, 1987.

Damrosch, David et al., eds. *The Longman Anthology of British Literature*. 1st ed. 2 vols. New York: Longman, 1999.

Darwin, Charles. *The Life and Letters of Charles Darwin*. Edited by Francis Darwin. 2 vols. 1887. Reprint, New York: Basic, 1959.

Dickinson, Emily. *The Letters of Emily Dickinson*. Edited by Thomas H. Johnson and Theodora Ward. 3 vols. Cambridge, MA: Belknap Press of Harvard UP, 1958.

———. *The Poems of Emily Dickinson: Variorum Edition*. Edited by R. W. Franklin. 3 vols. Cambridge, MA: Belknap Press of Harvard UP, 1998.

Diehl, Joanne Feit. *Dickinson and the Romantic Imagination*. Princeton, NJ: Princeton U P, 1981.

Gravil, Richard. "Emily Dickinson (and Walt Whitman): The Escape from 'Locksley Hall.'" *Symbiosis: A Journal of Anglo-American Literary Relations* 7, no. 1 (2003): 56-75.

———. *Romantic Dialogues: Anglo-American Continuities 1776-1862*. New York: St. Martin's, 2000.

Homans, Margaret. *Women Writers and Poetic Identity: Dorothy Wordsworth, Emily Brontë, and Emily Dickinson*. Princeton, NJ: Princeton U P, 1980.

Katz, Adam. "Deconstructing Dickinson's Dharma." *The Emily Dickinson Journal* 22.2 (2013): 46-64.

Keane, Patrick J. *Emily Dickinson's Approving God: Divine Design and the Problem of Suffering*. Columbia: U of Missouri P, 2008.

Logan, William. "Imperial Rhymes." *The New York Times Book Review* (December 1, 2013): 16.

Milosz, Czeslaw. *The Land of Ulro*. Translated by Louis Iribarne. New York: Farrar, 1984.

Nussbaum, Martha C. *Upheavals of Thought: The Intelligence of Emotions*. Cambridge: Cambridge U P, 2001.

Taylor, Charles. *A Secular Age*. Cambridge, MA: Belknap Press of Harvard U P, 2007.

17. *From Loss to Gain: Aftermath in the Late Romantic Poetry of Emily Dickinson*

'Did we not find (gain) as we lost,' declares Emily Dickinson (1830-86) in Prose Fragment 71, 'we should make but a threadbare exhibition after a few years.'[1] Thus, our loss and our gain become concomitant phenomena, if not one and the same. David Porter, as though Dickinson's art were a record of pure loss, describes her 'poetry of aftermath' as pessimistic.[2] By contrast, and in keeping with the balance between loss and gain in Prose Fragment 71, I regard her concept of aftermath—namely, that 'After great pain, a formal feeling comes—' (Poem 371, line 1)[3]—as less despairing, and as broader, than it at first appears. Just as her Late Romantic faith in experience rarely wanes—I argue this in my most recent study of the broadly experiential, spiritual as well as natural vision of Romantic Anglo-America[4]—so, paradoxically, her 'post-experiential perspective'[5] yields, and yields to, optimism of a distinctively experience-based, Anglo-American kind.

Prose Fragment 49 further prepares Dickinson's reader for historically interpreting her poetry of aftermath as a tipping of the balance between loss and gain in favor of progress from the former to the latter:

> Tis a dangerous moment for anyone when the meaning goes out of things and Life stands straight—and punctual—and yet no content(s) (signal) come(s). Yet such moments are. If we survive them they expand us. If we do not, but that is Death, whose if is everlasting. (*J* 3:919)

The first two sentences, it is true, far from underestimating, or taking lightly, the devastation of aftermath, acknowledge the threat that post-experience poses to our very sanity. The second part of the fourth sentence, moreover (the sentence begins 'If we do not') suggests that each loss threatens us with death, the ultimate aftermath. Experience can thus seem ineffectual, unimportant. Nonetheless, Dickinson's third sentence, 'If we survive [dangerous moments] they expand us,' speaks of hope, or at least of hope-against-hope. One thinks, in this connection, of Friedrich Nietzsche's well-known notion that what does not kill us only makes us stronger.[6] Since, for Dickinson, 'the meaning of things' never entirely 'goes out of things,' and since her survival can 'expand' her, her poetry of aftermath *includes* her experience, as distinct from simply entailing it, and as opposed to merely lamenting the loss thereof. In the end, her post-experiential perspective renews her lease on life, if not exactly the full-blown experience of faith that, as I have previously tried to show, she shares with her precursors and coevals on the High-to-Late-Romantic arc of Anglo-American literature.[7]

I offer, then, a partial palinode, a strategic drawing-back from delineating Dickinson's contribution to the well-earned optimism of Romantic Anglo-America. *Experience and Faith: The Late Romantic Imagination of Emily Dickinson* (2004) pays too little attention, perhaps, to what everyone knows—namely, Dickinson's reputation as a recluse—and too much heed, undoubtedly, to Richard B. Sewall's cultural contextualization of Dickinson's art as socially engaged enough to approximate the outlook of a Rotarian.[8] Her post-traumatic stress, according to Roger Lundin, attends her concerns about Darwinian science and the American Civil War.[9] Her withdrawal from the social life of Amherst, Massachusetts, around 1860, moreover, in Vivian R. Pollak's view has to do with her flawed relationships with her sister-in-law, Susan Huntington Dickinson (wife of Austin), and her 'dearest earthly friend,' the Reverend Charles Wadsworth.[10] Still, as James R. Guthrie demonstrates, her reclusive tendency also derives, more optimistically, from the spiritual and aesthetic dedication with which she makes a virtue of the necessity of her Teiresias-like, Homeric, and Miltonic eye-trouble.[11] Even more importantly—and herein lies the emphasis of my palinode *only* partial, my drawing-back *merely* strategic—I look within Romantic Anglo-America for a tough-minded, yet hopeful, explanation of Dickinson's withdrawal. Over her poetry of aftermath, when all is said and done, presides such an idea of post-experience as that of William Wordsworth, for whom 'abundant recompense' proves the quintessentially British-Romantic phrase for rich reward in, and for, loss of 'splendor in the grass' and of 'glory in the flower' (see, respectively, Wordsworth, 'Lines Written a Few Miles above Tintern Abbey' [1798], line 88; and Wordsworth, 'Ode: Intimations of Immortality from Recollections of Early Childhood' [1807], line 180).[12]

'Emerging from an Abyss, and reentering it—that is Life, is it not, Dear?' asked Emily of Sue, in 1885 (*L* 3:893). The pessimistic dimension of this rhetorical question compares with Percy Bysshe Shelley's High Romantic version of aftermath—for instance, his tragic vision of modern love in 'When the Lamp Is Shattered' (1824):

When the lips have spoken,
Loved accents are soon forgot....
From thy nest every rafter
Will rot, and thine eagle home
Leave thee naked to laughter,
When leaves fall and cold winds come. (Lines 7-8, 29-32)

These lines, relentless in their harsh detail, find their Late Romantic match in Ralph Waldo Emerson's equally horrific, deterministically slanted essay on 'Experience' (1844): 'Every roof is agreeable to the eye, until it is lifted; then we find tragedy and moaning women, and hard-eyed husbands, and deluges of lethe, and the men ask, "What's the news?" as if the old were so bad.'[13] 'Our relations to each other,' Emerson perceives, 'are oblique and casual' ('Experience,' 947). He concludes that 'the plaint of tragedy which murmurs' from the vain search 'in regard to persons, to friendship and love' derives from the futile quest for a 'lasting relation' between 'intellect' and 'thing' ('Experience,' 947). The pointed quality of Dickinson's rhetorical question—that is, its sarcasm—suggests the troubled nature of her relationship with Sue,[14] as well as the threat of her final illness, during which she composed the letter (she died on May 15, 1886, at the age of fifty-five).

On the other hand, if Dickinson's question scarcely balances pessimism with optimism, it does more than merely negate her experience. She emerges from, as well as reenters, 'an Abyss.' As Denis Donoghue has observed, 'Even to write against something is to take one's bearings from it.'[15] Like the bulk of Shelley's verse and of Emerson's prose, and like most other Anglo-American Romanticism as I have perennially attempted to define it,[16] Dickinson's poetry of aftermath draws on her Late Romantic imagination to negotiate the strait between the Scylla of experience and the Charybdis of faith. As L. J. Swingle paraphrases the British Romanticism from which Dickinson, like Emerson, derives her ability to generate spiritual hope from subjective despair, 'It is only by touching the abyss that the soul comes to recognize its power.'[17]

Emerson, to be sure, far from always writing autobiography as the genre most compatible with experiential expectations, can offer instead, and in a manner prelusive to the obvious pessimism in Dickinson's poetry of aftermath, a precisely anti-experiential reason for not doing so: 'Our life looks trivial, and we shun to record it' ('Experience,' 943). The only *sensationalist* epistemology to which Alfred, Lord Tennyson's *In Memoriam: A. H. H.* (1850) at first lays any claim, similarly, equates to his persona's 'awful *sense* / Of one mute Shadow watching all,' as distinct from any *spiritual* sense whatsoever (30:7-8; emphasis added). Thus death, as though it were the only reality, can dominate life, and can fill all perception. 'Nothing is left us now,' declares Emerson, 'but death,' and he adds, 'We look to that with grim satisfaction, saying, there at least, is reality that will not dodge us' ('Experience,' 945). Nevertheless, in keeping with the lighter mood of Tennyson and of Emerson—that is, the 'soul-competency' of their Anglo-American Romanticism[18]—the not-so-obvious but finally decisive role of optimism in Dickinson's poetry of aftermath aspires to the lyrical lilt of her Late-Romantic imagination, as distinct from the movement of her pre-Modern mode 'downward to darkness' (Wallace Stevens, 'Sunday Morning' [1915], line 120). This yearning, if it does not quite reconstitute experience for this reclusive poet, constitutes, in any case, a finally less troubled than surprisingly robust means by which Dickinson the Romantic 'dwell [s] in Possibility—' (Poem 466, line 1).

In 1869, to be sure, Emily grimly wrote to Sue of absence, and hence of aftermath as pessimism: 'The things of which we want the proof are those we knew before' (*L* 2:464). Now, insofar as *want* means 'lack,' whatever we used to possess has simply disappeared without a trace. Loss looms so inevitably, in fact, that even what we still have seems, practically speaking, already gone. Nevertheless, since *want* can also mean 'desire,' we rarely give up on whom we greatly yearn for, and we scarcely forfeit that for which we yet seek evidence. We rejoice, from the perspective of our aftermath, 'that in our embers / Is something that doth live, / That nature yet remembers/ What was so fugitive!' (Wordsworth, 'Ode: Intimations of Immortality,' lines 129-32).[19] Thus, the British-Romantic progress from loss to gain applies in Dickinson's case. No sooner does she cry, with John Keats, 'Fled is that music,'[20] than in her own way, and at almost the same time, she utters for the very reason of her loss the post-traumatic, but far from either paralyzed or ascetic, quadrilateral value of Wordsworth—namely, 'Effort, and expectation, and desire, / And something evermore about to be' (see, respectively, Keats, 'Ode to a Nightingale' [1819], line 80; and Wordsworth, *The Prelude* [1850] 6:608-09).

*

Poem 576, make no mistake about it, descends to the lowest point of Dickinson's aftermath:

> The difference between Despair
> And Fear—is like the One
> Between the instant of a Wreck—
> And when the Wreck has been—
>
> The Mind is smooth—no Motion—
> Contented as the eye
> Opon the Forehead of a Bust—
> That knows—it cannot see—

Despair, it is true, finds an alert style here—namely, 'the complexity that analogy and parallelism often achieve.'[21] Nonetheless, the first sentence of Prose Fragment 49, 'Tis a dangerous moment for anyone when the meaning goes out of things and Life stands straight—and punctual—and yet no content(s) (signal) come(s),' seems worth repeating in this context. Poem 576 enunciates the principle that, at its worst, aftermath equates to numbness. The emphasis lies on the danger of a moment when, in the absence of the beloved, the speaker waits, in effect, on Godot. Emily sent the poem to Sue about 1864.

Poem 1055, just two lines long, constitutes, accordingly, an anti-aubade: 'To Whom the Mornings stand for Nights, / What must the Midnights—be!' Instead of substituting for, or replacing, nights, and instead of compensating for loveless nights by eliminating, or by reducing to just proportions, the intense darkness thereof, this speaker's mornings *symbolize* loveless nights. In fact, her mornings *become* such nights; *any* morning that follows nights of no lovemaking, by her implication here, scarcely exceeds the most loveless nights imaginable.

Poem 388, Dickinson's fullest statement of post-experiential pessimism, merits complete quotation and thorough discussion:

> It would never be Common—more—I said—
> Difference—had begun—
> Many a bitterness—had been—
> But that old sort—was done—

> Or—if it sometime—showed—as 'twill—
> Opon the Downiest—morn—
> Such bliss—had I—for all the years—
> 'Twould give an easier—pain—
>
> I'd so much joy—I told it—Red—
> Opon my simple Cheek—
> I felt it publish—in my eye—
> 'Twas needless—any speak—
>
> I walked—as wings—my body bore—
> The feet—I former used—
> Unnecessary—now to me—
> As boots—would be—to Birds—
>
> I put my pleasure all abroad—
> I dealt a word of Gold
> To every Creature—that I met—
> And Dowered—all the World—
>
> When—suddenly—my Riches shrank—
> A Goblin—drank my Dew—
> My Palaces—dropped tenantless—
> Myself—was beggared—too—
>
> I clutched at sounds—
> I groped at shapes—
> I touched the tops of Films—
> I felt the Wilderness roll back
> Along my Golden lines—
>
> The Sackcloth—hangs opon the nail—
> The Frock I used to wear—
> But where my moment of Brocade—
> My—drop—of India? (Poem 388)

Joanne Feit Diehl's hunch that the poem qualifies as 'paradigmatic expression'[22] bears fruit in Maryanne Garbowsky's deft placement of it at, or near, the centre of Dickinson's 'poems of aftermath.'[23] Cristanne Miller, too, addresses the lyric's meta-poetical dimension: 'The poem,' she argues, 'tells a Cinderella story in which the speaker is her own fairy godmother. She turns herself from a "Common" woman into a poet, and her magic gift and husband Prince are all words.'[24] Shira Wolosky and Alice Fulton stress the meta-poetical, as well, but, by contrast with Miller, they highlight the poet's fall from, rather than her access to, verbal power. 'This poem,' offers Wolosky, 'perhaps merely describes the passing of poetic inspiration.'[25] Fulton, for her part, contends that here 'a woman confronts literary effacement.'[26]

Cynthia Griffin Wolff's reading of Poem 388, perhaps most comprehensively of all these negative perspectives on the meta-poetical dimension of Dickinson's aftermath, emphasizes the ebb and flow of the speaker's verbal power. 'The ever-shifting balance of power between the creative forces and the forces of destruction,' declares Wolff, 'swings against the poet, and the effort to impose order must begin again.'[27] Thus, like other works of art, Poem 388 concerns itself with itself, and with how it came to be; like Wolosky, Fulton, and Wolff, I emphasize the speaker's fall from verbal power. Although the poem stands as an illustration of Miller's point that this woman, however 'Common' she might have seemed, ranks high as a poet, Dickinson ends on a note of aesthetic timidity. Since the final line laments the loss of her 'drop—of India'—that is, her thick, black ink for the lettering of her art—the reader senses that, for the moment, at least, the poet's pen has run dry.

Poem 388, to be sure, resembles many poems of aftermath in which, as Benjamin Kimpel puts it, Dickinson describes 'occasions in her life out of which her *religious* response occurred' (emphasis added).[28] Emily Miller Budick, too, sees the poem as religious, or as otherworldly, and hence as idealistic, if not optimistic. Nevertheless, as Budick also makes clear, the poet's criterion of experience *qualifies* her religious response. 'The attempt to characterize heaven in ordinary symbolic language,' writes Budick, in paraphrase of Dickinson's argument here, 'can only result in a disappointment and loss that are both proximate and ultimate.'[29] The third, fourth, and fifth stanzas of the poem, by this light, evince such miraculous ideality that they have nowhere else to go but toward a correspondingly intense, post-lapsarian tone in the sixth, seventh, and eighth stanzas. Poem 388, in consequence, comes across as more naturally than spiritually experiential, and therefore as more realistic, or actualistic, than idealistic, or optimistic.

One of the most skillful effects of Poem 388 concerns the poet's use of dashes in the sixth stanza to mark the transition from first love to forlorn devastation.[30] In the seventh stanza, where the speaker reports that she 'felt the Wilderness roll back / Along my Golden lines—' Dickinson psychologizes the New England/Puritan 'Errand into the Wilderness.'[31] The myth of the golden age, as Shelley dilutes it in 'The World's Great Age Begins Anew' (1822) and as Joni Mitchell also attenuates it in 'We've Got to Get Ourselves Back to the Garden' (1971), proves equally apropos. Thus, although Dickinson's persona in the final stanza puts behind her the 'Sackcloth' of bitterness, her 'Frock' of young love's hope and promise recedes, too. She stands alone, in a daze, looking backward, and wondering what hit her.

Poem 371, similarly, explores how aftermath—that is, the 'formal feeling' that comes after 'great pain'—stays so far from functioning as a palliative that it can, and probably will, kill the sufferer:

> The Feet, mechanical, go round—
> A Wooden way
> Of Ground, or Air, or Ought—
> Regardless grown,
> A Quartz contentment, like a stone—
> This is the Hour of Lead—
> Remembered, if outlived,
> As Freezing persons, recollect the Snow—
> First—Chill—then Stupor—then the letting go—
>   (Poem 371, lines 1, 5-13)

As Jane Marston observes, 'The event that has caused pain is not named; thus, pain may be understood as either loss or physical pain, the one prefiguring grief, the other, death . . . . The speaker cares about effect, not cause—about what it is like to live out the aftermath of pain.'[32] 'The poem,' Garbowsky writes, 'suggests the panic attack where the individual is numbed with anxiety and fear, feeling as if death has come.'[33] Pollak's insight, no less tough-minded, qualifies as equally psychological—namely, that Dickinson's 'pain signifies a loyalty to frustrated aspirations which is both heroic and dysfunctional.'[34]

Formalistic understanding of Poem 371 and of its pre-Modern tinge emerges from John Robinson's conclusion that the 'orderly and analytic' message of the poem 'is dramatically enacted in terms which challenge that control and even threaten the message.'[35] A. R. C. Finch, in a historically aware as well as formalistically sophisticated insight, observes that 'as the meter of the past poets overtakes the poem, the poet uses iambic pentameter to present an image of helpless, frozen stupor.'[36] Wolff drops the formalistically radical, almost Postmodern bombshell that the poem's 'themes of violation and disorder' mean that Dickinson's poetry itself 'has been fatally wounded by the pain of its creator.'[37] Thus Dickinson anticipates such High Moderns as William Butler Yeats, T. S. Eliot, Robert Frost, and Wallace Stevens. As Linda J. Taylor puts it, Poem 371 helps 'to establish a place for [Dickinson] in the mainstream of...post-romantic poetry in England.'[38]

The poem helps, moreover, to establish Dickinson's place in High-to-Late-Romantic literature. The tough-minded side of Anglo-American Romanticism provides a solid model for the pain of her aftermath's 'formal feeling.' 'In the death of my son [Waldo], now more than two years ago,' writes Emerson, in his own Late-Romantic version of aftermath,

> I seem to have lost a beautiful estate,—no more.... [I]t does not touch me: some thing which I fancied was a part of me, which could not be torn away without tearing me, nor enlarged without enriching me, falls off from me, and leaves no scar. It was caducous. I grieve that grief can teach me nothing, nor carry me one step into real nature. ('Experience,' 944)

This attitude, as Barbara Packer observes, comes across as both 'self-lacerating' and filled with 'casual brutality.' 'We can imagine a voice that says all these things with bitter irony,' she writes, but we can also imagine 'a voice as toneless and detached as that of a witness giving evidence in a war crimes trial.'[39]

An additional analogy to the latter voice, Packer continues, inheres in the 'wasted and suffering' discharged soldier whom Wordsworth questions in Book 4 of *The Prelude* (1850): 'In all he said / There was a strange half-absence, as of one / Knowing too well the importance of his theme / But feeling it no longer' (lines 442-45). Packer concludes that 'the casual brutality of the sentence in which Emerson introduces the death of his son as an illustration is unmatched by anything I know of in literature, unless it is the parenthetical remark in which Virginia Woolf reports the death of Mrs. Ramsay in the "Time passes" section of *To the Lighthouse* [1927].' Packer thinks, too, of Sir Thomas Browne's *Hydrotaphia* (1681)'—'There is no antidote,' writes Browne, 'against the *Opium* of time.' Finally, and significantly, Packer instances Dickinson's 'After great pain, a formal feeling comes.'[40]

On the other hand, Aliki Barnstone offers a more hopeful reading of Dickinson's aftermath in general and of 'After great pain' in particular—namely, that the poet evinces 'the Nirvana principle of abandonment to nothingness, which is a release and a liberation, the necessary state for revelation.'[41] This observation, it is true, might seem too optimistic, too spiritual, to suit the poem entirely. Nonetheless, Barnstone's argument adds religious dimension to the poet's psychological insight. Her poem, along the lines of Barnstone's exegesis, enunciates a strangely positive truth—that is, that even the worst of aftermath constitutes spiritual discipline for, as well as survival training in, what Keats, in a letter to his brother George and his sister-in-law Georgiana, calls 'a World of Pains and troubles' (February 14-May 31, 1819). To this extent, at least, 'After great pain' seems more Late-Romantic than pre-Modern.

Consider, in this regard, Edward Fitzgerald's objection to the lowest moments of Tennyson's *In Memoriam*: 'I felt that if Tennyson had got on a horse and ridden 20 miles, instead of moaning over his pipe, he would have been cured of his sorrows in half the time. As it is, it is almost 3 years before the Poetic Soul walks itself out of darkness and Despair and into Common Sense.'[42] As James R. Kincaid has pointed out, Fitzgerald undervalues the sense in which Tennyson's hope '*comes from* darkness' (Kincaid's emphasis).[43] Even the empirical voice of *In Memoriam*, to say nothing of its voice of faith, transcends, as I have elsewhere argued,[44] the poet's despair over the death of Arthur Henry Hallam. This voice lends vitality, if not exactly untroubled robustness, to Tennyson's Late-Romantic version of aftermath. The speaker of 'After great pain,' in any case, exemplifies spiritual discipline. Instead of ever having backed off, with an attitude of 'Do I dare to eat a peach?,' the persona has welcomed 'frequent sights of what is to be borne!,' and sustains, accordingly, a strangely liberating abandonment to nothingness: recall 'then the letting go—' (see, respectively, T. S. Eliot, 'The Love Song of J. Alfred Prufrock' [1910-11], line 122; and Wordsworth, 'Elegiac Stanzas' [1807], line 58).

Despite, or perhaps because of, being hard-won, moreover, the optimism in Dickinson's theme of aftermath reflects survival training, as distinct from defense mechanism. The 'Languour,' or 'Drowsiness,' which equates to 'Pain's Successor—,' it is true, 'Envelopes [Dickinson's] Consciousness—' (Poem 552, lines 1, 3, 5, 7). Her aftermath turns out an even more ominous portent of her death, the logical conclusion of her post-experience, than her first sharp outcry of pain:

> The Surgeon—does not blanch—at pain—
> His Habit—is severe—

> But tell him that it ceased to feel—
> The Creature lying there—
>
> And he will tell you—Skill is late—
> A Mightier than He—
> Has ministered before Him—
> There's no Vitality[.] (Poem 552, lines 9-16)

Nonetheless, as psychologically and linguistically acute as Dickinson's most pessimistic perspective on aftermath can be, she understands that even the worst of it serves at least the pre-Modern purpose of generating defense mechanism. At most—and more importantly—her aftermath fulfills the dually Late Romantic function of survival training and of spiritual discipline.

Dickinson's hope, paradoxically, *comes from* the darkness that sometimes encompasses her. Thus, if her poetry of aftermath includes the near-suicidal mood of Gerard Manley Hopkins's 'No Worst, There Is None' (1885), or of the third chapter of the Book of Job, then it also encourages her efficacious reemergence. She implies that trancelike aftermath helps her forget her suffering. She facilitates, thereby, her living, as distinct from merely attaining to the state of sleep-walking, and as opposed to simply obtaining oblivion:

> There is a pain—so utter—
> It swallows substance up—
> Then covers the Abyss with Trance—
> So Memory can step
> Around—across—opon it—
> As One within a Swoon—
> Goes safely—where an open eye—
> Would drop Him—Bone by Bone— (Poem 515)

Pollak grasps the strangely positive function of such affliction and of its lingering effects. 'Extreme pain,' she writes in paraphrase of Dickinson's Poem 515, 'destroys the memory of its occasion.... The soul cannot bear too much reality and commands a variety of amnesiac responses which blank out pain, all of which prefigure the ultimate amnesiac, death.'[45] Garbowsky, albeit heavy-handedly—her rather clinical interpretation of Dickinson's poetry as agoraphobic borders on single-mindedness—goes further than Pollak, at any rate, in capturing the ameliorative properties of these lines. 'This description of the trancelike effect of depersonalization brought on by the panic attack,' writes Garbowsky, 'accurately describes its release function and the protective purpose it serves. By cutting the victim's feelings off, depersonalization prevents him or her from a more serious breakdown.'[46]

What might seem denial, then, turns out another, more positive, defense mechanism. I refer to the naturalized grace of Dickinson's recuperative powers:

> A Doubt if it be Us
> Assists the staggering Mind
> In an extremer Anguish
> Until it footing find—
>
> An Unreality is lent,
> A merciful Mirage
> That makes the living possible
> While it suspends the lives. (Poem 903)

No longer does pain simply envelope Dickinson's consciousness. Barbara Mossberg sums up the poem. 'While the voice of the poet is anguished, it is operative.'[47]

Poem 522, the most autobiographical among Dickinson's more hopeful poems of aftermath, merits, like Poem 388, complete quotation and full consideration:

> I tie my Hat—I crease my Shawl—
> Life's little duties do—precisely—
> As the very least
> Were infinite—to me—
>
> I put new Blossoms in the Glass—
> And throw the Old—away—
> I push a petal from my Gown
> That anchored there—I weigh
> The time 'twill be till six o'clock—
> So much I have to do—
> And yet—existence—some way back—
> Stopped—struck—my ticking—through—

> We cannot put Ourself away
> As a completed Man
> Or Woman—When the errand's done
> We came to Flesh—opon—
> There may be—Miles on Miles of Nought—
> Of Action—sicker far—
> To simulate—is stinging work—
> To cover what we are
> From Science—and from Surgery—
> Too Telescopic eyes
> To bear on us unshaded—
> For their—sake—Not for Our's—
>
> Therefore—we do life's labor—
> Though life's Reward—be done—
> With scrupulous exactness—
> To hold our Senses—on— (Poem 522)

Aftermath, it is true, appears grim enough here. 'Life is represented as fury corning to terms with sexuality, and both are subject to the efforts of repression.'[48] While Dickinson's reader might identify with her uncharacteristically pejorative use of an empirical metaphor—'Dickinson's fear that the inner world would be looked into is surely connected with the development of science, particularly the telescope'[49]—her desire to keep the unconscious repressed might strike him or her as unhealthy. Nonetheless, as Garbowsky recognizes, 'The speaker's admission that the bomb is calm now reveals that the panic attacks are in remission, and although the bomb is still intact, she is in a state of relative ease, trying to appear normal.'[50]

Although 'time is meaningless to [Dickinson]' at a subjective level, 'objectively, it continues to organize her behavior.'[51] Poem 522, in other words, concerns 'a life in which control is the only meaning and meaning the only control.'[52] The poem 'allows us a sight of Emily Dickinson presenting herself to the eyes of other people and sustaining herself by the fact of that observation.'[53] Here, accordingly, her aftermath contributes further survival training and more spiritual discipline to her formalistic technique. She not only 'speaks of the trivial duties that must be done even though "Existence" has effectually ended,' but also 'remains in firm control of her poem, choosing figures that, far from exaggerating, seem to understate her dilemma.'[54]

Dickinson's style of firm control through understatement harks back, incidentally, to the eighteenth-century genre of abridgment, to which John Wesley contributed his characteristic litotes.[55] *To abridge* is 'to shorten,' or even 'to curtail' (*OED*), but Dickinson's 'abridgments' prove no mere summary, no mere abstraction, and no mere 'selection of essential facts' (*OED*). Her condensations of her experience epitomize the original without diluting it and honor the original by enhancing it. Her characteristic understatements extend her experience to the present and deliver it to the future.

*

The Dickinson of aftermath, to be sure, *dwells* on the past. Her doing so, for that matter, emerges as a desirable, as well as an inevitable, result of losing what she cherishes most. Poem 276 quite rightly deplores the leopard's loss of her native land:

> Pity—the Pard—that left her Asia!
> Memories—of Palm—
> Cannot be shifted—with Narcotic—
> Nor suppressed—with Balm— (Poem 276)

Nevertheless, as Rebecca Patterson points out, the leopard remains 'somehow involved in the central idea of love as tropical heat, vitality itself.'[56]

The speaker of Poem 261, by corollary, looks back with the bitter-sweetness of nostalgia, as well as in anger:

> I held a jewel in my fingers—
> And went to sleep—
> The day was warm, and winds were prosy—
> I said "Twill keep'—
>
> I woke—and chid my honest fingers,
> The Gem was gone—
> And now, an Amethyst remembrance
> Is all I own— (Poem 261)

Although blankness here means 'Dickinson's fear of losing her ability to create,'[57] and although 'jewels appear often in Dickinson's imagery as emblems for the poet's self, or more specifically, for her artistic genius,'[58] her pet-name for her 'dearest earthly friend,' the Reverend Wadsworth (*L* 3:764), was 'Dark Gem' (*L* 3:745). Jeffrey E. Simpson strikes close to the mark, therefore, where he concludes that Dickinson uses the 'gem metaphor to heighten the sense of the preciousness of her friends.'[59] Although Albert Gelpi might go too far in claiming that this poem defines poetry as 'the reclamation or repossession of absence,' his point—namely, that the poem exemplifies poetry as 'the owning of loss,' or 'the owning up of loss'—sounds right.[60] I would only add that the poem has more to do with the latter, than with the former.

Poem 158, to epitomize this category of Dickinson's poetry, offers a blueprint of her aftermath's balance of meaning:

> Where I have lost, I softer tread—
> I sow sweet flower from garden bed—
> I pause above that vanished head
> And mourn.
>
> Whom I have lost, I pious guard
> From accent harsh, or ruthless word—
> Feeling as if their pillow heard,
> Though stone!
>
> When I have lost, you'll know by this—
> A Bonnet black—A dusk surplice—
> A little tremor in my voice
> Like this!
>
> Why I have lost, the people know
> Who dressed in frocks of purest snow
> Went home a century ago
> Next Bliss! (Poem 158)

This early lyric poses the where, who, when, and why of parting in general and of bereavement in particular. As the poet would later observe, 'Parting is all we know of heaven, / And all we need of hell' (Poem 1773, lines 7-8). To the extent that Poem 158 can*not* answer these journalistic questions, it merely owns up to loss as life's defining anti-experience. Only those who now see face to face could explain *why* she has lost. Her funereal sorrow *when* she loses proves *her* only certainty. To the extent that the lyric *can* answer such questions, however, it *owns* loss. It represents, thereby, experience within aftermath.

The fact that William H. Shurr nowhere mentions Poem 158, despite his argument that the Reverend Wadsworth inspired Dickinson's love poetry, seems surprising, since the poem laments the loss of Charles perhaps even more than that of Sue.[61] Consider the parallel between the second stanza of Poem 158, just quoted, and the fourth and fifth stanzas of the more familiar Poem 764, 'My Life had stood—a Loaded Gun—':

> And when at Night—Our good Day done—
> I guard My Master's Head—
> 'Tis better than the Eider Duck's
> Deep Pillow—to have shared—
>
> To foe of His—I'm deadly foe—
> None stir the second time—
> On whom I lay a Yellow Eye—
> Or an emphatic Thumb— (Poem 764, lines 13-20)

The metaphor of the speaker's life as correspondent with a gun confirms Margaret H. Freeman's view of this lyric as Dickinson's signature employment of 'cognitive poetics'—that is, since metaphor is a product of the *embodied* mind, 'knowledge of the world is *formed* by an experience of the world' (Freeman's emphasis). The gun's projected life, according to Freeman, is 'impoverished and inadequate,' but the speakers of both poems, notwithstanding 158's emphasis on aftermath and 764's on jealousy, claim that the mind puts the world together. Dickinson's 'so-called abstract images,' Freeman concludes, 'are grounded in her physical and intellectual *experience* of ... the universe around her' (emphasis added).[62] In any case, the continued loving on the part of the speaker of Poem 158, as distinct from her softer treading, characterizes her ongoing existence, regardless of whether 'Next Bliss! ' shades over from hope into envy. The *experience* of aftermath, to inflect the phrase, conveys the poet's resilient, rather than defeatist, stance.

*

Dickinson's withdrawal, then, does more than merely signal either her post-traumatic stress of one kind or another or, for that matter, some fugitive, cloistered, or un-praiseworthy virtue on her part. Her reputation as a recluse signifies, as well, fullness of time—that is, lesson learned, gist grasped, intense concentration, ongoing readiness, unwearied watchfulness, and, not least, imaginative receptivity. Even faded friendship and lost love, for her and for her 1,789 poetic personae, open heartfelt access to the divine, as opposed to merely exacerbating destructive skepticism, on the one hand, and paralyzed aporia,[63] on the other. 'The lady whom the people call the *Myth*'[64] remains, thereby, a recluse with experience, as distinct from the simple 'experience' of her being a recluse. Thus, her aesthetic self-projections at their lowest moments of distress and hopelessness manage to salvage, against all odds, the constructive skepticism, if not exactly the lyrical lilt, of their poet's Late Romantic imagination. The 'perpetual attention' that Dickinson's poetry of aftermath pays 'to experience, the pole-star of truth,'[65] accordingly, glosses the sensationalist epistemology, if not exactly the experiential Faith, of Romantic Anglo-America.

Dickinson's post-experiential perspective, specifically, has more to do with Wordsworth's 'wise passiveness'—that is, his transition from survival training to spiritual discipline—than with defense mechanism ('Expostulation and Reply' [1798], line 7). Dickinson's poetry of aftermath proves equally consonant with Keats's *'Negative Capability,'* as distinct from nihilism. Her poetry, like his, fosters the condition 'of being in uncertainties, Mysteries, doubts, without any irritable reaching after fact & reason' (Keats to George and Thomas Keats, December 21, 27 [?], 1817).

Dickinson's persona resonates more strongly with Thomas Carlyle's, moreover, than with T. S. Eliot's Prufrock. According to 'The Hero as Man of Letters' (1841), Carlyle's 'scepticism is not an end but a beginning,' not 'the decay of old ways of believing' but 'the preparation afar off for new and wider ways.' Pertinent to hearing High and Late Romanticism in Dickinson's combination of pessimism with optimism, in other words, is Carlyle's hard-won definition of doubt as *constructive* skepticism. 'Doubt,' as he puts it, represents 'the mystic working of the mind, on the subject it is *getting* to know and believe.'[66] Thus, the aftermath of Late Romanticism retains access to purposive process. Herein lies the importance of Dickinson's placing of an engraving of Carlyle, along with likenesses of Elizabeth Barrett Browning and George Eliot, on the wall of her room.[67]

Dickinson's assimilation of the open quality of Tennyson's skepticism, furthermore, obtains. Except for the God-talk, *In Memoriam* can sound remarkably Dickinsonian:

> And falling with my weight of cares
> Upon the great world's altar-stairs
> That slope through darkness up to God,
>
> I stretch lame hands of faith and grope,
>   And gather dust and chaff, and call
>   To what I feel is Lord of all,
> And faintly trust the larger hope. (*In Memoriam* 55:14-20)

Dickinson's absorption of the radically skeptical, yet eminently constructive, stance of Emerson, finally, proves equally apropos. Emerson declares, 'Out of unbeliefs a creed shall be formed.' He adds, 'For, skepticisms are not gratuitous or lawless, but are limitations of the affirmative statement, and the new philosophy must take them in, and make affirmations outside of them, just as much as it must include the oldest beliefs' ('Experience,' 955).

The poet whose persona goes 'White—unto the White Creator—,' to be sure, would scarcely seem to have relied on experience as a means of growing in either wisdom or grace (Poem 788, line 7). *White*, after all, connotes, besides issues of race and class, the 'blankness' of John Locke's *tabula rasa*, which, far from representing the way to round off a life, properly applies at birth only. What Susan Manning calls Dickinson's *candor*, accordingly—from *candidus* ('white')—signals the poet's 'guilelessness,' 'openness,' 'sweetness of temper,' and 'purity of mind.'[68] Nevertheless, 'frankness,' 'directness,' and 'straight-forwardness' apply to Dickinson's art, as well. Her poetry arises from her tough-minded wisdom, as opposed to any naïve inexperience on her part.

Dickinson's *candor*, in my view, means her 'incandescence'—that is, the 'glow' with which her poetic personae retain, rekindle, the white-hot heat of their experience. Even their post-experience constitutes, if not their 'spontaneous overflow of powerful feeling,' then, in any case, their 'emotion recollected in tranquility,' and makes, thereby, 'internal difference— / Where the Meanings, are—' and where, for better or for worse, life continues to 'burn with a hard, gem-like flame' (see, respectively, Wordsworth, Preface to *Lyrical Ballads* [1798]; Dickinson, Poem 320, lines 7-8; and Walter Pater, Conclusion to *Leonardo da Vinci* [1873]). The whiteness of Dickinson's aesthetic self-projections—their presence-of-all-color, as distinct from either the stainlessness of their purity or the bleakness of their nihilism—signifies their ongoing, existential authenticity. They align themselves with what Shelley means by 'Mont

Blanc' (1817)—namely, 'a vacancy that nevertheless holds in itself the potentiality of all that is'[69]—as distinct from Captain Ahab's apprehension of void in the whiteness of the whale, or Arthur Gordon Pym's of horror in the whiteness of Antarctica.[70] The whiteness of Dickinson's poetic personae denotes the further, fresh experience, the dynamic possibility (recall: 'I dwell in Possibility—' [Poem 466, line 1]), of aesthetic/cinematic white-out, of near-death experience, and, for that matter, of 'the white radiance of Eternity' (Shelley, 'Adonais' [1821], line 463).

In sum, Dickinson's poetry of aftermath does more than merely illustrate the post-experiential perspective of her pre-Modern mode and the anti-experiential bias of her Postmodern intimations. In addition, if only for a glimmering moment, this strain of her art reactivates, like her Late Romantic imagination generally, the natural/spiritual dialectic of Anglo-American Romanticism. Her *experience* of post-experience, illustrating, among other things, the ongoing role of friendship and of love in her 'internalized quest romance,'[71] turns straw into gold, as well as loss into gain. This post-experiential perspective turns out consonant with my previous, against-the-mainstream characterization of Dickinson's art as 'the poetry of experience.'[72] Her concept of *aftermath*, besides equating to 'disastrous consequences,' entails 'outcome,' auguring, thereby, 'further harvest' (*OED*).

Notes

Quotations from Dickinson's poetry are reprinted by permission of the publishers and the Trustees of Amherst College from *The Poems of Emily Dickinson*, Ralph W. Franklin, ed. (Cambridge, Mass.: The Belknap Press of Harvard University Press), copyright 1998 by the President and Fellows of Harvard College. Copyright 1951, 1955, 1979 by the President and Fellows of Harvard College. Quotations from Dickinson's letters are reprinted by permission of the publishers from *The Letters of Emily Dickinson*, Thomas H. Johnson and Theodora Ward, eds., Cambridge, Mass.: The Belknap Press of Harvard University Press, copyright 1958, 1986 by the President and Fellows of Harvard College.

[1] *The Complete Poems of Emily Dickinson*, ed. Thomas H. Johnson, 3 vols. (Cambridge, Mass.: Harvard University Press, 1955): 3:923, hereafter abbreviated *J*.

[2] David Porter, *Dickinson: The Modern Idiom* (Cambridge, Mass.: Harvard University Press, 1981), 9-24.

[3] Quotations of Dickinson's poetry are from *The Poems of Emily Dickinson: Variorum Edition*, ed. Ralph W. Franklin, 3 vols. (Cambridge, Mass: Harvard University Press, 1998).

⁴ See chapter 1 ('Experimental Trust') of Richard E. Brantley, *Experience and Faith: The Late-Romantic Imagination of Emily Dickinson* (New York: Palgrave Macmillan, 2004), 31-77. See also Brantley, *Coordinates of Anglo-American Romanticism: Wesley, Edwards, Carlyle, and Emerson* (Gainesville: University Press of Florida, 1993); and Brantley, *Anglo-American Antiphony: The Late Romanticism of Tennyson and Emerson* (Gainesville: University Press of Florida, 1994).

⁵ Vivian R. Pollak, *Dickinson: The Anxiety of Gender* (Ithaca: Cornell University Press, 1984), 202.

⁶ For a recent survey of Friedrich Nietzsche's standard ideas, see Robert C. Solomon, *Living with Nietzsche: What the Great 'Immoralist' Has to Teach Us* (New York: Oxford University Press, 2003), esp. 3-18.

⁷ See chapter 4 ('Romantic to Modern Arc') of Brantley, *Experience and Faith*, 116-64.

⁸ See Brantley, *Experience and Faith*, x, 7, 15, 59, 61, 63, 71-72, 92, 116, 179, 208, 214 n. 6, 234 n. 50. My former student William Bowers, as part of his recent emphasis on Dickinson's psychological scars, tactfully pokes some good clean fun at my classroom emphasis on her poems as, for all practical purposes, rough drafts of speeches by the ebullient Theodore Roosevelt. See Bowers, 'Freaks! Poetry! Anguish and Triumph at a Community College,' *Oxford American* 43 (January/February 2003): 14-23, esp. 17. See also Richard B. Sewall, *The Life of Emily Dickinson*, 2 vols. (1974; reprint: New York: Farrar, Straus, and Giroux, 1980).

⁹ See Roger Lundin, *Emily Dickinson and the Art of Belief* (Grand Rapids: William B. Eerdmans, 1998). See also Louis Menand, *The Metaphysical Club* (New York: Farrar, Straus, and Giroux, 2001); and Brantley, *Experience and Faith*, 78-79, 142-45.

¹⁰ See chapters 2 ('Susan Gilbert'), 3 ('Master'), 5 ('Sisterhood'), and 6 ('The Wife without the Sign') in Pollak, Dickinson: The Anxiety of Gender, 59-104, 133-89. See also *The Letters of Emily Dickinson*, ed. Thomas H. Johnson and Theodora Ward, 3 vols. (Cambridge, Mass.: Harvard University Press, 1958) 3:764, hereafter abbreviated *L*.

¹¹ See James R. Guthrie, *Emily Dickinson's Vision: Illness and Identity in Her Poetry* (Gainesville: University Press of Florida, 1998). See also Brantley, *Experience and Faith*, 222 n. 43, 227 n. 73.

¹² Quotations of British and American writers, unless otherwise indicated, are from *The Longman Anthology of British Literature: First Edition*, ed. David Damrosch, 2 vols. (New York: Longman, 1999); and *The Norton Anthology of American Literature: Fifth Edition*, ed. Nina Baym, 2 vols. (New York: W. W. Norton, 1998).

[13] *The Norton Anthology of American Literature: Second Edition*, ed. Francis Murphy and Herschel Parker, 2 vols. (New York: W. W. Norton, 1985) 1:943-44.

[14] *Open Me Carefully: Emily Dickinson's Intimate Letters to Susan Huntington Dickinson*, ed. Ellen Louise Hart and Martha Nell Smith (Ashfield, Mass.: Paris Press, 1998).

[15] Denis Donoghue, *The Third Voice: Modem British and American Verse Drama* (Princeton: Princeton University Press, 1959), 18.

[16] See, besides my *Coordinates of Anglo-American Romanticism* and my *Anglo-American Antiphony*, my *Wordsworth's 'Natural Methodism'* (New Haven: Yale University Press, 1975) and my *Locke, Wesley, and the Method of English Romanticism* (Gainesville: University Press of Florida, 1984).

[17] L. J. Swingle, *The Obstinate Questionings of English Romanticism* (Baton Rouge: Louisiana State University Press, 1987), 77.

[18] For a discussion of 'soul-competency,' see Harold Bloom, *The American Religion: The Emergence of the Post-Christian Nation* (New York: Simon and Schuster, 1992), 111-43. See also Brantley, *Anglo-American Antiphony*, passim.

[19] For those of a certain age and with a knowledge of aftermath, it may prove bittersweet to recall that in the summer of 2005, an actor read the above-quoted lines at the wedding of Charles, Prince of Wales, and Camilla Parker Bowles.

[20] 'For Poets—I have Keats—and Mr and Mrs Browning,' declared Dickinson to Thomas Wentworth Higginson, on April 25, 1862 (*L* 2:404).

[21] Suzanne Juhasz, '"To Make a Prairie": Language and Form in Emily Dickinson's Poems about Mental Experience,' *Ball State University Forum* 21.2 (Spring 1980): 12-25, esp. 16-17.

[22] Joanne Feit Diehl, '"Ransom in a Voice": Language as Defense in Dickinson's Poetry,' in *Feminist Critics Read Emily Dickinson*, ed. Suzanne Juhasz (Bloomington: Indiana University Press, 1983), 156-75, esp. 170-72.

[23] Maryanne Garbowsky, *The House without the Door: A Study of Emily Dickinson and the Illness of Agoraphobia* (Rutherford: Fairleigh Dickinson University Press, 1989), 128-29, 138.

[24] Cristanne Miller, 'How "Low Feet" Stagger: Disruptions of Language in Dickinson's Poetry,' in *Feminist Critics Read Emily Dickinson*, ed. Juhasz, 134-55, esp. 147-49, 151.

[25] Shira Wolosky, *Emily Dickinson: A Voice of War* (New Haven: Yale University Press, 1984), 155-57.

[26] Alice Fulton, 'Her Moment of Brocade: The Reconstruction of Emily Dickinson,' *Parnassus: Poetry in Review* 15.1 (Spring 1989): 9-44, esp. 43.

[27] Cynthia Griffin Wolff, *Emily Dickinson* (Reading: Addison-Wesley, 1988), 217-19, 383, 529.

²⁸ Benjamin Kimpel, *Emily Dickinson as Philosopher* (New York: Mellen, 1981), 245.

²⁹ Emily Miller Budick, *Emily Dickinson and the Life of Language: A Study in Symbolic Poetics* (Baton Rouge: Louisiana State University Press, 1985), 71-73.

³⁰ For a study of Dickinson's dashes, see Paul Crumbley, *Inflections of the Pen: Dash and Voice in Emily Dickinson* (Lexington: University Press of Kentucky, 1997).

³¹ See Perry Miller, *Errand into the Wilderness* (Cambridge, Mass.: Harvard University Press, 1956). See also Edmund Morgan, *Visible Saints: The History of a Puritan Idea* (Ithaca: Cornell University Press, 1965).

³² Jane Marston, 'Metaphorical Language and Terminal Illness: Reflections upon Images of Death,' *Literature and Medicine* 5 (1986): 109-21, esp. 112-13, 114.

³³ Garbowsky, *The House without the Door*, 134-35.

³⁴ Pollak, *Dickinson: The Anxiety of Gender*, 199, 206-11.

³⁵ John Robinson, *Emily Dickinson: Looking to Canaan* (London: Faber, 1986), 114-16, 126.

³⁶ A. R. C. Finch, 'Dickinson and Patriarchal Meter: A Theory of Metrical Codes,' *PMLA* 102.2 (March 1987): 166-76, esp. 173.

³⁷ Wolff, *Emily Dickinson*, 154, 468-70, 589.

³⁸ Linda J. Taylor, 'Form, Process, and the Dialectic of Self-Construction: "After Great Pain" and Three Modern Poems,' *University of Dayton Review* 19.1 (Winter 1987-88): 91-101, esp. 93. See also Mordecai Marcus, 'Dickinson and Frost: Walking Out One's Grief,' *Dickinson Studies* 63 (1987): 16-29; and Brantley, *Experience and Faith*, 142-54. For overviews of the Romantic to Modem arc, see George Bornstein, *Transformations of Romanticism in Yeats, Eliot, and Stevens* (Chicago: University of Chicago Press, 1976); and Carlos Baker, *The Echoing Green: Romanticism, Modernism, and the Phenomena of Transference in Poetry* (Princeton: Princeton University Press, 1984).

³⁹ Barbara Packer, *Emerson 's Fall: A New Interpretation of the Major Essays* (New York: Continuum, 1982), 117-21.

⁴⁰ Packer, *Emerson 's Fall*, 122-48.

⁴¹ Aliki Barnstone, 'Houses within Houses: Emily Dickinson and Mary Wilkins Freeman's "A New England Nun,"' *Centennial Review* 28.2 (Spring 1984): 129-45, esp. 130, 139, 142-43.

⁴² As quoted in Christopher Ricks, *Tennyson* (New York: Macmillan, 1972), 214.

⁴³ James R. Kincaid, *Tennyson's Major Poems: The Comic and Ironic Patterns* (New Haven: Yale University Press, 1975), 83-84.

⁴⁴ Brantley, *Anglo-American Antiphony*, 33-50.

⁴⁵ Pollak, *Dickinson: The Anxiety of Gender*, 209.

⁴⁶ Garbowsky, *The House without the Door*, 122, 123, 139, esp. 123.
⁴⁷ Barbara Mossberg, *Emily Dickinson: When a Writer Is a Daughter* (Bloomington: Indiana University Press, 1982), 29.
⁴⁸ Sharon Cameron, '"A Loaded Gun": Dickinson and the Dialectic of Rage,' *PMlA* 93.3 (May 1978): 423-37, esp. 431, 434.
⁴⁹ Hiroko Uno, 'Optical Instruments and "Compound Vision" in Emily Dickinson's Poetry,' *Studies in English Literature* (English Literary Society of Japan) 64.2 (January 1988): 227-43, esp. 238-40.
⁵⁰ Garbowsky, *The House without the Door*, 125-28, esp. 126.
⁵¹ Pollak, *Dickinson: The Anxiety of Gender*, 204.
⁵² Margaret Dickie, 'Dickinson's Discontinuous Lyric Self,' *American Literature* 60.4 (December 1988): 537-53, esp. 552.
⁵³ Robinson, *Emily Dickinson: Looking to Canaan*, 96-99, esp. 97.
⁵⁴ Rebecca Patterson, *Emily Dickinson's Imagery*, edited and introduced by Margaret H. Freeman (Amherst: University of Massachusetts Press, 1979), 98, 111-12, 147, esp. 112.
⁵⁵ Wesley understates the style of Jonathan Edwards, for example, in his abridgment (1773) of Edwards's *A Treatise concerning Religious Affections* (1746). See Brantley, *Coordinates of Anglo-American Romanticism*, 7-42.
⁵⁶ Patterson, *Emily Dickinson's Imagery*, 151, 152-53, 161, 170, esp. 151.
⁵⁷ Mossberg, *Emily Dickinson: When a Writer Is a Daughter*, 171-72.
⁵⁸ Wendy Barker, *Lunacy of Light: Emily Dickinson and the Experience of Metaphor* (Carbondale: Southern Illinois University Press, 1987), 169-70.
⁵⁹ Jeffrey E. Simpson, 'The Dependent Self: Emily Dickinson and Friendship,' *Dickinson Studies* 45 (June 1983): 35-42, esp. 38.
⁶⁰ Albert Gelpi, 'Emily Dickinson's Word: Presence as Absence, Absence as Presence,' *American Poetry* 4.2 (Winter 1987): 41-50, esp. 44.
⁶¹ William H. Shurr's omission of Poem 158 from his otherwise thorough discussion of the presence of the Reverend Charles Wadsworth in Dickinson's poetry constitutes the exception that proves the rule of Shurr's thoroughness. See Shurr, *The Marriage of Emily Dickinson: A Study of the Fascicles* (Lexington: University Press of Kentucky, 1983).
⁶² Margaret H. Freeman, 'A Cognitive Approach to Dickinson's Metaphors,' in *The Emily Dickinson Handbook*, ed. Gudrun Grabher et al. (Amherst: University of Massachusetts Press, 1998), 258-72, esp. 262, 267.
⁶³ William Harmon and Hugh C. Holman define *aporia* (a presiding idea of Deconstruction) as 'a point of undecidability, which locates the site at which the text most obviously undermines its own rhetorical structure, dismantles,

or deconstructs itself.' See Harmon and Holman, *A Handbook to Literature: Seventh Edition* (Saddle River, NJ.: Prentice Hall, 1996), 36.

[64] Mabel Loomis Todd, as quoted in *The Years and Hours of Emily Dickinson*, ed. Jay Leyda, 2 vols. (New Haven: Yale University Press, 1960), 2:357, 2:376.

[65] See William Godwin, *The Enquirer* (London: J. Johnson, 1797), vi, viii. See also Swingle, *The Obstinate Questionings of English Romanticism*, 41-44; and Brantley, *Experience and Faith*, 34.

[66] Thomas Carlyle, 'The Hero as Man of Letters' (1841), as quoted in *Thomas Carlyle: Selected Writings*, ed. Alan Shelston (1971; reprint: Harmondsworth: Penguin, 1986), 253.

[67] Polly Longsworth, '"The Latitude of Home": Life in the Homestead and the Evergreens,' in *The Dickinsons of Amherst*, ed. Christopher Benfey et al. (Hanover: University Press of New England, 2001), 49.

[68] I am indebted to conversations with Susan Manning and Melvyn New concerning François-Marie Arouet de Voltaire's *Candide* (1759) and Samuel Johnson's *Dictionary* (1755). The latter calls on John Dryden to illustrate the meaning of *candid* ('white'): 'The box receives all black: but, pour'd from thence, / The stones come candid forth, the hue of innocence.'

[69] Earl Wasserman, *The Subtler Language: Critical Readings of Neoclassic and Romantic Poems* (Baltimore: The Johns Hopkins University Press, 1959), 236.

[70] For discussions of Herman Melville and Edgar Allen Poe, see Eric G. Wilson, *Coleridge's Melancholia: An Anatomy of Limbo* (Gainesville: University Press of Florida, 2004), 140-45; and Wilson, *The Spiritual History of Ice: Romanticism, Science, and the Imagination* (New York: Palgrave Macmillan, 2003), 151-57.

[71] In 2003, Harold Bloom remarked, 'I suspect my central essay on Romanticism is "The Internalization of Quest Romance" in *Romanticism and Consciousness* [1970].' Bloom had argued, therein, that the Romantics psychologize the love, desire, and enchantment found in medieval Christian romance. See Judith W. Page, *Imperfect Sympathies: Jews and Judaism in British Romantic Literature and Culture* (New York: Palgrave Macmillan, 2004), 188-94, esp. 192. For parallels between Dickinson as a paradoxically engaged recluse and her father Edward's canny withdrawal from politics, see Coleman Hutchison, '"Eastern Exiles": Dickinson, Whiggery and War,' *The Emily Dickinson Journal* 13 (2004): 1-26.

[72] I refer to Robert Langbaum, *The Poetry of Experience: The Dramatic Monologue in Modern Literary Tradition* (London: Chatto and Windus, 1957).

18. *Dickinson's Signature Conundrum*

Hope and despair define the human condition. For example, Emily Dickinson lamented "the hollowness & awfulness of the *world*" (Leyda 1:213) but testified that "I find ecstasy in living—the mere sense of living is joy enough" (L342a). These opposing stances of her life express themselves—and dramatize one another—in her art; the optimism of her poetic personae celebrates their pessimism, and vice versa. Dickinson's despair, I argue, paradoxically lets her "choose life" (Deuteronomy 30:19). Thus, her canon can reclaim an affirmation lately appropriated by the chief "culture war" of the United States.

Notwithstanding the widespread view of Dickinson's life and work as static, her recurring pessimism contains a seed of her perennial resilience. One thinks, in this connection, of a lyric (1814) by George Gordon, Lord Byron:

> They say that Hope is happiness—
> But genuine Love must prize the past;
> And Mem'ry wakes the thoughts that bless:
> They rose the first—they set the last.
>
> And all that mem'ry loves the most
> Was once our only hope to be:
> And all that hope adored and lost
> Hath melted into memory.
>
> Alas! It is delusion all—
> The future cheats us from afar:

> Nor can we be what we recall,
> Nor dare we think on what we are.¹

Dickinson's despair rarely sinks this low. In fact, it yields, before it yields to, her hope, and such complexity excels that of pure oscillation, on the one hand, and of predictable synthesis, on the other. Her despair out-hopes hope, since, in isolation, or as a half-binary, simple hope bestows only chaste satisfaction. Dickinson's very despair entertains un-cloistered, sturdy, and engaged, though muted, or subtle, hope *as* happiness.

Scant joy, to be sure, would seem to remain to Dickinson's hopeless love for her "dearest earthly friend" (L807), the Reverend Charles Wadsworth (1814-82), and for her sister-in-law, Susan Huntington Dickinson, wife of Austin.² The sort of discipline with which Dickinson learned to do without Wadsworth (did he know how much she loved him?), and perhaps even a whiff of her despair over "love's alternate joy and woe" (Byron, "Maid of Athens, Ere We Part" [1810], line 7), mirror Wadsworth's Presbyterian doctrine of self-denial: "The grand secret of contentment is found, not in increasing our supplies—but in diminishing our necessities" (266). Wadsworth's use of a dash (are *Byron's* dashes, too, proto-Dickinsonian?) represents another Dickinson-like element of his homiletical aphorism. Nevertheless, the modest goal of contentment set forth by Wadsworth's instruction contrasts with Dickinson's signature conundrum of "*sumptuous* Destitution- " (Fr1404; emphasis added). The poet's rich less proves more. As novelist Kathryn Harrison has aptly observed in quite another context, "Desiring to not desire, after all, is itself a new form of desire" (22).

Dickinson's signature lyric of "sumptuous Destitution - " epitomizes her hope, as well as her despair, and intimates the interpenetration, or coalescence, of these, and of such other paired stances as sorrow and joy:

> In many and reportless places
> We feel a Joy -
> Reportless, also, but sincere as Nature
> Or Deity –
>
> It comes, without a consternation -
> Dissolves - the same -
> But leaves a sumptuous Destitution -
> Without a Name -

> Profane it by a search - we cannot -
> It has no home -
> Nor we who having once inhaled it -
> thereafter roam.
> (Fr1404A; variant line 11: waylaid it)

The upper-case "Destitution - " that exemplifies Dickinson's use of adjective-noun phrases to address the enigma of life recognizes "the hollowness & awfulness of the *world*." This speaker forgoes her joy no more willingly than she loses either her natural anchor or her divine guidance, for the absence of either of these components of her theism *constitutes* her joylessness. Any effort on her part to rediscover joy, whether personal or religious, would reduce the mystery of the original experience, but her having *had* joy equates to her *still* having it, *if* she receives back what she resigns. Thus, to say nothing of Dickinson's "ecstasy in living," her "mere sense of living is joy enough," because, though at one remove from "living," the "sense" thereof counts (through imagination) as life. "Joy's sincerity," according to Jean McClure Mudge's ironic reading, "parallels Nature's and God's; that is, it is untrustworthy, for both cosmic forces betrayed [Dickinson]" (223-4). The speaker's happiness, however, leaves by degrees and never quite dissipates, for the poet's lack of consternation eases her transition from joy to "sumptuous Destitution -," and her never-fully-alloyed joy, explicit in "sumptuous," stays genuine.

To modify mainstream terms for Dickinson's pessimism, the "postexperiential perspective" (Pollak 202) of her "poetry of aftermath" (Cody *After Great Pain*) emphasizes her post-traumatic despair but coexists with, and includes, hope as "the thing with feathers - " (Fr314), "a strange invention - " (Fr1424), and "a subtle Glutton - " (Fr1493). Such a signature lyric of her aftermath as "After great pain, a formal feeling comes" (Fr372) begins to look less like Dickinson's outcry over disastrous consequences and more like her witness to the sort of outcome that augurs further harvest. At the risk of smoothing out her three-steps-forward, two-steps-back progress (Job's, too, looks ragged), I sample these poems out of sequence, the better to highlight Dickinson's power to *resume* her optimism. If she forgets that "the thing with feathers" is "perhaps . . . every human's potential for music and poetry, brave stays against the brooding dark" (Wolff 478), then she remembers in the dark. The ongoing renewal of hope among her speakers of aftermath, and not just the persistence of their hope after hope, or of their hope against hope, demonstrates the upholding strength of Dickinson's own "Columnar Self - " (Fr740). Their pluck discloses as much about her as about her artistry.

Although the role of Dickinson's poetry of aftermath in psychobiographical approaches to her art concerns me greatly, the relation between her postexperiential perspective and the spiritual as well as natural vision of Romantic Anglo-America interests me even more.[3] If the forward-looking, pre-Modern visage of Dickinson's Victorian-American Janus-face looks on trauma, whether individual or collective, as her thematic prescience, then her backward-looking, Late-Romantic visage beckons her cultural heritage to overcome both her personal past and the cultural crisis of her Victorian-American limbo. Her Late-Romantic negotiation of her aesthetic dilemma as a Victorian-American poet gives positive new meaning to the "postexperiential perspective" of her "poetry of aftermath." I allude to and quote, accordingly, parallel Anglo-American writers of prose, fiction, and poetry.

As explicitly as possible, yet in the shorthand manner of Matthew Arnold's "touchstones," my procedure for indicating Dickinson's more Late-Romantic than either Victorian-American or pre-Modern place on the arc from Romantic to Modern resembles the method of Nicholson Baker's homage to John Updike (*U and I* [1991]). Just as Baker's closed-book, self-administered testing of his loving memory of Updike's novels alludes to, and quotes, only what he recalls, so too do I draw here only on such scattered bits of Anglo-American literature as spring to my mind when I read Dickinson. Thus, at the risk of betraying density, I aim at a pastiche, and perhaps even at a mosaic, of allusive argument, in my conviction that the best-written, most substantial literature lodges in the mind (Frost "The Figure a Poem Makes" [1939]). My borrowing rarely demonstrates how well Dickinson knew this literature, but my repeated references suppose that she conned it well enough,[4] and, in any case, they contextualize the copious resonance of her poetry of aftermath. In paying homage to Dickinson, I suggest how the genius of her own form and content lodges where it will be hard to get rid of, in the mind, soul, and heart of her reader.

I indirectly maintain here that even Dickinson's poetry of aftermath, like her canon in general but more subtly, participates in Late Romanticism, with particular affinities for William Wordsworth. For this body of her work, as for much of his, language and interiority remain integral to, and part of, experience. Thus even her postexperiential perspective expresses her Late-Romantic hope. Her signature conundrum of "sumptuous Destitution - ," to apply to her case the words of Wordsworth, resolves itself into her "joy! that in

[her] embers / Is something that doth live." Those of a certain age, or with knowledge of aftermath, or both, might find it bittersweet to recall, in this connection, the summer of 2005, when an actor read these very words of Wordsworth's into the rather sweet, but vaguely postlapsarian, atmosphere at the wedding of Charles, Prince of Wales, and Camilla Parker Bowles. Dickinson's poetic personae of "sumptuous Destitution - " go beyond mere intuition of familiar near-nihilism and aspire to the more than simply "poetic" faith espoused among the most optimistic of her speakers. Her Late-Romantic, anti-Victorian art differs from Arnold's anti-Romantic, High-Victorian "Wandering between two worlds, one dead, / The other powerless to be born." Her postexperiential perspective revives one world in order to grace the other's "growing gloom" (Thomas Hardy, "The Darkling Thrush" [1900], line 24).

Dickinson's poetry of aftermath, in my occasionally ironic, yet never anti-Romantic, reading of it, sometimes nearly regains the very paradise that her more fully tender-minded singing almost never loses. Her pre-Modern mode, and perhaps even her Postmodern intimations, overlap her Late-Romantic imagination at the point in her Victorian-American limbo where her faith in experience restores her experience of faith.

Her "*formal* feeling" of "great pain" (Fr372, emphasis added), besides connoting closed-system, nothing-outside-the-text nihilism, denotes the slough of her pre-modern despond wherein, metaphorically speaking, she wonders stiffly whether to eat a peach. Her larger confession of this feeling pre-sounds "the atonal banshee of the emerging egomania called The Modern" (Wilson 12), if not the modern to postmodern cry of Sisyphean futility. On the other hand, to inflect her phrase a different way, the "formal *feeling*" that follows her "great pain" might, just might, relieve it, as well as constitute the heartache, uncertainty, doubt, and silence thereof. Her larger confession of *this* feeling, according to my hearing of it in the set pieces of her aftermath, plays again, or re-sounds, the High-Romantic song of love, joy, and hope. Thus her postexperiential perspective defamiliarizes the quotidian.

Although Dickinson's poetic personae of "sumptuous Destitution - " suffer from loss, absence, and rejection, and although they scarcely win their way through to gain, presence, and embrace, they seldom settle quietly into either mere contentment or desperation. On the contrary, they frequently lead lives of strenuous abundance. Reeling from, yet still able to speak after, their initial throes, they proceed by stops and starts toward their intellectual, spiritual, and imaginative solutions to the kinds of problems faced generally by humankind, as well as by themselves (like Job's advancement from self-absorption to empathy). As befits their origins in joy, and by way of perpetuating it, these speakers learn from, as distinct from just dwelling on, or coping with, their past experiences of abandonment and deprivation. Thus, through their post-traumatic perspective, they arrive at cognition. Moreover, in keeping with the tacit magnificence of their way of living, they accumulate spiritual wealth. With splendor in appearance, self-expression, and representation of the world, they "redeem the time" of their post-traumatic existence—that is, they "glory in tribulations" (Ephesians 5:6; Colossians 4:5; Romans 5:3). They do this despite, or in part because of, the forlorn state of their having been forsaken, deserted, and robbed, for, in setting off their hope, their despair aspires to the glory, as well as to the muddle, of experience.

An early poem of aftermath, to be sure, sounds entirely hopeless:

> I breathed enough to take the Trick -
> And now, removed from Air -
> I simulate the Breath, so well -
> That One, to be quite sure –
>
> The Lungs are stirless - must descend
> Among the cunning cells -
> And track the Pantomime - Himself,
> How numb, the Bellows feels!
> (Fr308)

Nevertheless, Dickinson revels in clarity here. Compare her procedure with the well-known section 54 of Alfred, Lord Tennyson's *In Memoriam: A. H. H.*, which begins, "O, yet we trust that somehow good / Will be the final goal of ill" (all quotations of Tennyson are from *In Memoriam*). At this "grim center of *In Memoriam*," observes Timothy Peltason, "we are characteristically given no single moment of greatest despair, but a pattern of related moments, a virtuosity and variety of despair. And this despair, like the charged and changing grief of earlier lyrics, is both the evidence and the cause of imaginative activity, an incitement to us to rechart the poem's course" (84). The first-hand, almost scientific language of "I breathed enough to take the Trick - ," in keeping with Tennyson's implication that virtuosity of despair somehow yields the good, advances a by no means entirely hopeless proposition—namely, that airlessness, or lunglessness, comprises the working model, or metaphysical conceit, of suspended animation. "If we place the agoraphobic syndrome at the center" of "I breathed enough to take the Trick - ," declares Maryanne Garbowsky, "we gain a deeper insight into the physical discomforts the poet documents, as well as into the nature of the psychic disturbances that fueled them" (89). This criticism proves more helpful than narrowly expert, or reductively clinical. I would blend Garbowsky's language, however, with that of Peltason. Dickinson's unflinching understanding of her "psychic disturbances" and of her "physical discomforts" constitutes "a virtuosity and variety of despair" that signify "imaginative activity," and hence hope.

Dickinson's postexperiential perspective poses a riddle for her reader to puzzle over, as well as to be diverted by. *Residue* of happiness can seem, by turns, like dissolved sugar, or like a bird either newly featherless or grown too heavy to leave the ground:

> Too happy Time dissolves itself
> And leaves no remnant by -
> 'Tis Anguish not a Feather hath
> Or too much weight to fly -
> (Fr1182)[5]

The poet, moreover, has learned enough from her experience to articulate what William Blake calls "Proverbs of Hell," on one hand, and to substitute them, on the other, for the outmoded, greeting card-like sentimentality of such conventional wisdom as "Time heals all wounds":

> They say that "Time assuages" -
> Time never did assuage -
> An actual suffering strengthens
> As Sinews do, with Age –
>
> Time is a Test of Trouble -
> But not a Remedy -
> If such it prove, it prove too
> There was no Malady -
> (Fr861)

The speaker here, in the middle stages of her postexperience, claims to know little, and she conveys ambiguity concerning whether her suffering gets worse or whether she grows stronger the worse her trial becomes. To apply to Dickinson's case the language of Percy Bysshe Shelley and of Dylan Thomas, she remains sentient enough "to repeal / Large codes of fraud," if not of "woe"—that is, to defamiliarize cliché by means of her "craft, or sullen art."

To read between the lines of "They say that 'Time assuages' - ," and to interpret the poem as a dark-night-of-the-soul phase of Dickinson's spiritual autobiography, she knows, as does her coeval Gerard Manley Hopkins, that, to use Hopkins's words, her own "cries" have become "a chief / Woe, world-sorrow." Like the world-sorrow of Dickinson's precursor Wordsworth, moreover, if I may take "Too happy Time dissolves itself" and "They say that 'Time assuages' - " together, as companion pieces, her own "chief woe" has matured in "Thoughts that do often lie too deep for tears." In fact, she might now pore over, and assimilate, Wordsworth's own vein of fierce self-correction—namely,

> Through what power,
> Even for the least division of an hour,
> Have I been so beguiled as to be blind
> To my most grievous loss!—

Thus Dickinson the Late-Romantic poet of aftermath would no longer even *want* the facile consolations of nostrums about the passage of time.

The apathy, or, at best, the aimless, obscure searching, of Dickinson's aftermath can appear more corrosively cynical than either ironic or straightforward:

> From Blank to Blank -
> A Threadless Way
> I pushed Mechanic feet -
> To stop - or perish - or advance -
> Alike indifferent –
>
> If end I gained
> It ends beyond
> Indefinite disclosed -
> I shut my eyes - and groped as well -
> 'Twas lighter - to be Blind -
>   (Fr484)

Kenneth Stocks emphasizes the historical importance of this poem, which "extends beyond the purely personal and subjective into the consciousness of the age" (97). This consciousness, according to Douglas Novich Leonard, proves to be pre-Modern: "The absurdity of life, the unknowableness of its purpose, and sheer fatigue overwhelm the speaker and leave her in a state of spiritual apathy" (337-38). Cynthia Griffin Wolff expresses the poem's nihilistic implications: "'Blank' is almost a totemic word in Dickinson's work to identify a course of human affairs that has been stripped of larger significance. Now ... there are no defined beginnings or endings to be acknowledged or rejected. Even the structure that the drive toward death had imposed has been lost" (473). Shira Wolosky, too, acknowledges the pessimism of "From Blank to Blank": "When space has no definition, [seeing and not seeing] become functional equivalents—except that blindness raises no doomed expectations. Blindness is therefore chosen, but as a darkness which remains itself: an incomplete dialectic unsynthesized into any all-inclusive divine light" (23-24). Still, Wolosky emphasizes the continued deliberation, if scarcely the robust activity, of the speaker. "The very blankness of the poem," as even Leonard acknowledges, "becomes a kind of vision, its own reward for the heroic seeker after light" (338).

Thus, again within the stark confines of Dickinson's postexperiential perspective, and with no "irritable reaching," on her part, after renewed experience, her poetry shows itself capable of more than tenebrous, if not clear-sighted, cognition. For example, to assume a psychobiographical dimension to a lyric that looks back on summer, this persona of "sumptuous Destitution - " so vividly remembers "the affairs of June - " (shades of a lost beloved) that she treasures new felts of love ("The Violin – in Baize – replaced – "):

> Like Some Old fashioned Miracle -
> When Summertime is done -
> Seems Summer's Recollection -
> And the affairs of June -
> . . . .
> Her Memory - like Strains - enchant -
> Tho' Orchestra be dumb -
> The Violin - in Baize - replaced -
> And Ear, and Heaven - numb -
> (Fr408A, lines 1-4, 13-16)

"We learn in the Retreating," declares another speaker, "How vast an one / Was recently among us - " (Fr1045); she then adds, with exquisite paradox,

> A Perished Sun
>
> Endear in the departure
> How doubly more
> Than all the Golden presence
> It was - before -

Dickinson's postexperience seems itself able to advance understanding of Charles, or of Sue, or of both.

The poems I discuss have gone largely unnoticed, perhaps because, notwithstanding their emphasis on loss, even *they* sound too upbeat for postmodern taste. In the subtlest, if not most profound, of them, Dickinson suggests in keeping with the laws of optics that her clear vision of one departing—perhaps a beloved—depends on his or her moving out of her sight:

> By a departing light
> We see acuter, quite,
> Than by a wick that stays.
> There's something in the flight
> That clarifies the sight
> And decks the rays
>   (Fr1749)

Thus "None can experience stint / Who Bounty - have not known - " (Fr870). At the same time that such lines do not necessarily clarify whether the relation between then and now is good or bad, Wolosky seems right to observe of "By a departing light" that "*Recompense* is posited here" (82; emphasis added). "Decks," after all, could mean "adorns," as well as "covers," or "floors." Wordsworth's positing of "Abundant recompense" as the payoff of his own postexperience comes to mind.

Dickinson's postexperiential perspective proves capable of *joyful* cognition. Although the horror of living in prison never entirely dissipates, and although this horror rivals that of a Modernist author like Joseph Conrad, it coexists with rich moments of release, freedom, and ecstasy:

> The Soul has Bandaged moments -
> When too appalled to stir -
> She feels some ghastly Fright come up
> And stop to look at her –
>
> Salute her, with long fingers -
> Caress her freezing hair -
> Sip, Goblin, from the very lips
> The Lover - hovered - o'er –
>
> Unworthy, that a thought so mean
> Accost a Theme - so - fair –
> The soul has moments of escape -
> When bursting all the doors -
> She dances like a Bomb, abroad,
> And swings opon the Hours,
>
> As do the Bee - delirious borne -
> Long Dungeoned from his Rose -
> Touch Liberty - then know no more -
> But Noon, and Paradise –
>
> The Soul's retaken moments -
> When, Felon led along,
> With shackles on the plumed feet,
> And staples, in the song,
> The Horror welcomes her, again,
> These, are not brayed of Tongue -
>   (Fr360)

Such language as "the very lips / The Lover - hovered - o'er - " appears more than merely spiritually autobiographical. Still, if "The Lover" may refer to the Wadsworth of Dickinson's imagination, then there occurs no more joyous an expression of Dickinson's redeeming esteem of him than in stanzas three and four. These match any other passage of sustained optimism in her canon; I cannot agree that "here Emily Dickinson uses the traditional distinction between female powerlessness and male aggression" (Wendy Martin 120). The aggressor, surely, is not "The Lover," whether male or female, but the usurping Goblin of death, and, to say the least, the speaker's feeling for "The Lover" remains powerful and empowering.

The similarly suspicious reading of Joan Burbick feels more nuanced, more telling: "The ability of the speaker's 'Soul' to flip between images of lover and goblin is unnerving. To depict desire as always vulnerable to control by death equates desire with threat" (374-5). Not even "threat," however, can take away the *jouissance* of stanzas three and four. Most instructively, Jane Donahue Eberwein concludes: "The tone of these stanzas on manic release overpowers even the reader's judgment to the point that one regrets the psychological bomb's forced return to captivity and horror" (*Strategies of Limitation* 125). I would replace manic with ecstatic. One's regret registers the power in the poem's idiom of release.

To modulate from "The Soul has Bandaged moments - " to other surprisingly hopeful poems of Dickinson's aftermath, her "moments of escape" within the walls of her postexperiential prison testify to the persisting possibility that her love will continue to sustain her long after she has seemed to lose it. That explains why "A Prison gets to be a friend - ," or even "A Geometric Joy - ," to the point that "the Liberty we knew" of is "Avoided - like a Dream - " (Fr456). As Wordsworth puts it, "Nuns fret not at their convent's narrow room." Freedom also appears to exist only within, if not because of, the prison walls of Byron's "The Prisoner of Chillon," as well as of Ludwig van Beethoven's *Fidelio*. Dickinson's four citations of Byron's "Prisoner" (L233; L249; L293; L1042), including one in a "Master" letter (L233), make this hopeful poem of High-Romantic aftermath the most-mentioned Romantic work in all of her letters and prose fragments.

Freedom, in Dickinson's definition, emerges as her choice to do something, anything, on the assumption that the fact of her doing trumps, within the penumbra of her aftermath, the question of whether her doing grows effectual:

>At leisure is the Soul
>That gets a staggering Blow -
>The Width of Life - before it spreads
>Without a thing to do –
>
>It begs you give it Work -
>But just the placing Pins -
>Or humblest Patchwork - Children do -

> To Help it's Vacant Hands -
> (Fr683; variant: "To still it's noisy hands")

These lines, according to Dorothea Steiner, concern "the woman in her dealings with Power" (65), but the woman in quest of, and with no little residual faith in, the abiding power of action, however unspectacular, speaks here, as well. "At leisure is the Soul" suggests, by corollary, that the fact of doing constitutes faith, even if the doing appears ineffectual. Tennyson, too, reports this insight—that is, that going through the motions, or simply staying busy, fills in for faltering faith:

> Yet go, and while the holly boughs
> Entwine the cold baptismal font,
> Make one Wreath more for Use and Wont.

Dickinson's intimation in "At leisure is the Soul" that the fact of doing trumps the question of whether language proves effectual ("the Soul / That gets a staggering Blow - " says nothing) resonates with Thomas Carlyle's preference for deeds over speech: "The cloudy-browed, thick-soled, opaque Practicality, with no logical utterance, in silence mainly, with here and there a low grunt or growl, has in him what transcends all logic-utterance: a Congruence with the Unuttered. The Speakable, which lies atop, as a superficial film, or outer skin, is his or not his: but the Doable, which reaches down to the World's centre, you find him there!"[6] This still High-Romantic passage explains, in part, why a portrait of Carlyle (along with one of Elizabeth Barrett Browning and one of George Eliot) hangs on Dickinson's bedroom wall. The tension between Tennyson's "practice . . . expert / In fitting aptest words to things" and his logic of silence comes to mind; what makes Tennyson more Late-Romantic than either High-Victorian or pre-Modern is the almost High-Romantic force of his preference for life over art—that is, his faith in experience. Thus I concur with Harold Bloom's conclusion that "the Tennyson who counts for most" is "certainly a Romantic poet, and not a Victorian anti-Romantic resembling the [belated] Arnold of 'Merope' or the straining Hopkins of *The Wreck of the Deutschland*" (9). Tennyson, Bloom adds (with telling, if amusing, redundancy), is "a major Romantic poet." Ralph Waldo Emerson's Late-Romantic faith in experience, likewise, parallels the preference, ironically *stated*, for deeds: "Central Unity is . . . conspicuous in actions. Words are finite organs of the infinite mind. They cannot cover the dimensions of what is in truth. They break, chop, and impoverish it. An action is the perfection and publication of thought. A right action seems to fill the eye, and to be related to all nature."⁷ This passage suggests, in particular, that the relation between Dickinson's laconic style and what Emerson says here (though not the typically voluble way in which he says it) constitutes a sense in which his imagination haunts hers.

To refocus on the postexperience of Dickinson's poetic personae is to summon a presiding idea of Friedrich Nietzsche: what fails to kill them makes them stronger. Their power, in fact, resembles the acquired strength of Atlas:

> Give Balm - to Giants -
> And they'll wilt, like Men -
> Give Himmaleh -
> They'll carry - Him!
> (Fr312)

"Here," writes Suzanne Juhasz, Dickinson "identifies power with pain, because, by means of one's own discipline, one can possess it" (58). "Here," adds Wolff, "Dickinson explicitly argues against accepting any surrogate: permit no one to suffer in your behalf, the poem entreats, for when you seek to evade sorrow, you only relinquish the means to strength. Even God's mercy can be castrating" (214-5). John Cody reinforces the point; he observes of "I can wade Grief - " that, whereas "prosperity debilitates and renders ordinary," "pain strengthens and provides a stimulus to extraordinary action" (15). Thus pain, in Dickinson's view—besides preceding and continuing in aftermath *as* pain—proves tantamount, therein, to acquiring naturalized, "responsible grace"—and perhaps even to constituting that grace.⁸

The fact that action turns out to be possible "after," and in part because of (as well as during) "great pain," yields sublime, transcendent nobility:

> Superiority to Fate
> Is difficult to gain
> 'Tis not conferred of any
> But possible to earn
>
> A pittance at a time
> Until to Her surprise
> The Soul with strict economy
> Subsist till Paradise.
> (Fr1043)

Here, it is true, Dickinson "challenges the idea of having objectives and seeking to reach them, of judging life by targets which are or are not attained. Such purposefulness . . . makes someone vulnerable to circumstance, whereas her hope . . . is that someone who manages in different terms may be liberated" (John Robinson 22). Nonetheless, besides feeling oddly embedded in the past, as opposed to sounding forward-looking, the quality of Dickinson's hope lingers in the presence of difficult circumstances.

Lest we go too far toward imputing stoical, static stance to the speaker of "Superiority to Fate," Douglas Leonard reminds readers that: "The poem is faithful, even in its equivocation, to Emerson's concept of self-reliance . . . . The paradox still intrigues her: fate, necessity, and chance are present and inescapable, yet the soul can achieve its own will by constant striving" (340-41). The poem modulates from philosophical to religious language, for the Calvinist/Arminian controversy of the eighteenth and nineteenth centuries, like the theological tendency of "Superiority to Fate," pits predestination against free will, and perhaps even tilts toward the latter.[9] The "arminianized Calvinism" of Dickinson's day "softened the fundamental Calvinist dogma asserting depraved man's total dependence on God for salvation by allowing for a person's cooperation in the work of salvation through exercise of free will" (Eberwein review 98).

"Paralysis - ," declares Dickinson, comprises "our Primer - dumb - / Unto Vitality!" (Fr284A). On one hand, postexperience represents death-in-life, for it is "*dumb* - / Unto Vitality!" On the other, postexperience equates to a schoolbook for life, for, to inflect the phrase a different way, it is "dumb - / *Unto Vitality!*"

The species of vitality specific to Dickinson's aftermath proves at once natural and spiritual:

>Before I got my eye put out
>I liked as well to see -
>As other Creatures, that have Eyes
>And know no other way –
>
>But were it told to me - today -
>That I might have the sky
>For mine - I tell you that my Heart
>Would split, for size of me –

> The meadows - mine -
> The Mountains - mine -
> All Forests - Stintless Stars -
> As much of Noon as I could take
> Between my finite eyes –
>
> The Motions of The Dipping Birds -
> The Morning's Amber Road -
> For mine - to look at when I liked -
> The News would strike me dead –
>
> So safer Guess -
> With just my Soul opon the Window pane -
> Where other Creatures put their eyes -
> Incautious - of the Sun -
>   (Fr336A)

One would not want to overestimate the optimistic outlook of this poem, whether residually sense-based or increasingly quasi-intuitional. Dickinson's chief loss here, in Rebecca Patterson's view, remains "the faithless beloved" (44). Equally downbeat, the interpretation of Sandra Gilbert and Susan Gubar suggests that Dickinson's "metaphorical (and perhaps occasionally literal) blindness in this poem" functions, à la Sophocles, "as a castration metaphor" (595-6). By implication, the speaker sorely misses the direct physical sight of whom she once knew and still loves. However, while the poet implies here that "the superiority of insight over visual sight is [a] given in the claim that she now sees more when blinded than she did sighted" (Robinson 65-6), she saw much before, whether naturally or spiritually, and she continues to see near-naturally, as well as spiritually.

Thus the "sublimities of the household seer" come across as "more authentic" than the sublimities she knew before (Daniel O'Hara 176-8); the "two kinds of perception" implied by "Before I got my eye put out"—namely, the experiential visual and the non-experiential intuitive—emerge as "ambiguities deliberately left unresolved" (Johnson 8-9). Despite, or in part because of, the conditional mood of the middle stanzas, their intensity illustrates the poet's new dispensation of spiritual experience. These thirteen lines, moreover, virtually restore her world of sense experience.

The best paraphrase of Dickinson's "sumptuous Destitution - ," to my mind, has come from Douglas Anderson, who understands that Dickinson's postexperience is well attuned to natural and spiritual vitality. With special sensitivity to "Before I got my eye put out," he argues that "the condition of perception that Dickinson describes... is both something less and something more than ordinary human power" (220-21). To clinch his balanced view, Anderson concludes: "To maintain its poise between the remembered fact and the present miracle of memory is the poem's chief objective" (222). I must add that the chief glory of the poem—its hopeful tone—grows out of, and depends on, the perennial miracle of memory.

Dickinson's poems that follow upon her loss of Charles, or of Sue, or of someone else (such as William Smith Clark [Jones], or of Judge Otis Lord [Guthrie]), or of something equally momentous (natural religion? faith in God?), evince a tendency in emotion quite like happiness, if not beatitude. "Transport's mighty price is no more than he is worth - " (L359): Dickinson implies here that ecstasy grows more valuable for its fleeting quality and that residue thereof substitutes for the experience. As Keats would say, since joy ever bids adieu, bursting its grape can extend its savor. Dickinson's Keats-like philosophy of aftermath excels Frost's later nostalgia-inducing view that happiness makes up in height what it lacks in duration. Dickinson's postexperience by no means starves her, and perhaps even sustains her. If what remains to her proves to be only a strategy of survival, or of spiritual discipline, then this plan transcends any mere defense mechanism against manic depression.

Dickinson's close encounters of this important kind revive her Late-Romantic soul, extending, in the process, the almost High-Romantic, "Superior instants," when her heart, like Wordsworth's, leapt for joy (Fr630). From moment to moment, and not simply from time to time, her poetic personae of "sumptuous Destitution - " illustrate the paradox of their post-traumatic hope. Though fallen from the grace of experience, they expect the world to lie all before them anyway. Thus they bear the resonance—that is, they aspire to the animated suspension between despair and hope—of John Milton's postlapsarian couple.

The lingering effects—or aftermath—of Dickinson's love (or loves) equate to an emphatically abundant recompense for her loss. As her coeval Tennyson declares, "'Tis better to have loved and lost / Than never to have loved at all." "Quoted by now into meaninglessness," observes Peltason of these lines, they "evidence an important new understanding. The end of experience is not the sum of experience or the only source of meaning. The poet has loved and he has lost, but the second of these has not canceled out the first" (61). The epilogue to *In Memoriam* rejoices that "love is more / Than in the summers that are flown." Tennyson adds, "I myself with these have grown / To something greater than before." Thus, even the Tennyson who has loved and lost, and not just Tennyson in his ecstasy, assumes the efficacy of natural and of spiritual experience. In like manner, even the Dickinson of aftermath, and not just the Dickinson whose heart leaps up cultivates the faith that time and experience define character and make us know our selves, as Wordsworth says, in

> the world
> Of all of us, the place in which, in the end,
> We find our happiness, or not at all.

Dickinson's poems about postexperiential perspective, in short, *include* experience. George Bernard Shaw, significantly, had an answer for those bemused by the fact that his love of actress Ellen Terry consisted entirely of his twenty-five years' worth of letters to her: "Let them . . . remember that only on paper has humanity yet achieved glory, beauty, truth, knowledge, virtue, and abiding love." Dickinson's poetry of aftermath contributes a greater degree of dramatic urgency than of either/or logic to the perennial debate between art and life. Her ongoing life, as evidenced in her letters and prose fragments, as well as in her poems, stays far from being merely unalloyed grimness; it becomes, instead, an overrunning cup.

The physical absence of Charles and of Sue, on the evidence of the set pieces of Emily's aftermath, enhances their spiritual presence in her imagination. Notwithstanding Pollak's view that Emily's loss of the two great relationships of her life creates an "awful Vacuum" in her art (Fr887; Pollak 190-221), I conclude that her ongoing, if only imaginary, experience of Charles and of Sue proves partly positive, and perhaps even more than metaphorical. All manner of others and of otherness abide in her imagination, not just as anticipation, or sustaining memory, but even as presence, or revivifying force. An *Awe*-filled Vacuum signifies, if not the fulfilled potential of her optimism, then the mysterious possibility held in reserve for her by her hope.

Dickinson's "sumptuous Destitution - ," like her Late-Romantic imagination, resounds with her mimetic, as well as expressive, conviction that, as Emerson metaphorizes it in his own blend of the actual and the ideal, "My book should smell of pines and reverberate with the hum of insects." If Emerson's "smell of pines" were to apply to Dickinson's "old house under the pines" (Bianchi 27), then the rich strangeness of this aroma could serve to evoke the nonverbal, or preverbal, aspect of Dickinson's ongoing experience. If Emerson's "hum of insects" were to reverberate as the "spectral Canticle" of Dickinson's lines entitled "My Cricket" (Fr895E), then this entomological music could signal the verbal and aesthetic character of her ongoing experience. Such ongoing immersions of her life and her art in other lives and other arts compensate for whatever Wordsworthian "fallings from us," whatever "vanishings," she might seem previously to have incurred, including her strained, yet enduring, friendships and her star-crossed love for Charles, or for Sue, or for both. The poet whose life appears to have passed her by goes on and enjoys her life.

Dickinson's signature conundrum of "sumptuous Destitution - ," contrary to the growing pessimism of her times (Lundin, Menand, Wilson) and of modernism and postmodernism (Porter, Cameron), views the external world as more than merely a window on her soul. As an objective *correlative* to her desire, and as an *objective* correlative to her cognition, the world fills her more Late-Romantic than either Victorian-American or pre-Modern imagination. Jed Deppman's formulation of Dickinson's link to Postmodernism strikes a balance between comparison and contrast: on one hand, he writes, "To read Dickinson as a postmodern thinker and writer is . . . to explore the ways postmodern theory makes visible important aspects of her work and . . . to see how her poetry exemplifies and illuminates central postmodern predicaments." On the other hand, as he wisely adds, "Dickinson played more seriously, engaged more sharply with her culture's vocabularies, and had more all-around faith in the agency of the writer than does your average postmodern" ("Trying to Think with Emily Dickinson" 87). Dickinson's postexperiential perspective hardly prevents her from re-expressing the perennial Western belief that life proves well worth living, and perhaps even quite full of promise. Her poetry of aftermath, by re-opening her personal access to otherness through others, re-vamps the foundational strategy whereby the naturalized and spiritualized imagination of her poetry in general grasps the mystery of "all in all."

Despite, or in part because of, whatever traumas of fading friendship, flawed epistemology, challenged faith, or aesthetic crisis have crossed her mind, soul, and heart, Dickinson's paradox that less of one thing means more of another resonates with, and re-sounds, the ultimate Western conundrum of *felix culpa*. Her strangely maximal minimalism—that is, the harder her fall, the more her grace—emerges from, entails, and augurs her experience as well as that of the thirty-four poetic personae presented here. Dickinson's art of aftermath bids scant farewell to her life, notwithstanding such destructively/

deconstructively skeptical poems in this category as "I like a look of Agony" (Fr339) and "Severer Service of myself" (Fr887). The Dickinson of aftermath "see[s] by glimpses now," with Wordsworth, but "the hiding-places of [her] power / Return upon [her]," "enshrining, / Such is her hope, the spirit of the Past / For future restoration." Dickinson's harking back links her present to her past, and her present and her past to her future. Her definition of "Retrospection" as "Prospect's half, / Sometimes, almost more - " (Fr1014) fits the larger concept of her poetic definitions, to borrow from Deppman's "definition" of them, as "the universal, structural, and essential aspects of an experience" ("'I Could Not Have Defined the Change'" 53). By implication, Dickinson's underlying experience of a given definition represents her outward circumstance, as well as expresses her inward life, and does not confine itself to "the consciousness of the one involved in the experience" whether Dickinson herself, her aesthetic self-projection, or her reader.

The lyric in which Dickinson's language of prospective retrospection most explicitly occurs proves conclusive with regard to her own experience and that of her social circle:

> This was in the White of the Year -
> That - was in the Green -
> Drifts were as difficult then to think
> As Daisies now to be seen –
>
> Looking back, is best that is left
> Or if it be - before -
> Retrospection is Prospect's half,
> Sometimes, almost more -
>   (Fr1014)

Dickinson sent this poem to her Norcross cousins in 1865. It probably refers to the deaths of their father and mother. The poem scarcely glosses over the challenge posed by pessimism. As Grace Sherrer writes, "The *d* alliteration and the short syllables suggest the difficulty which her thought strives to express, and the auxiliaries are used for their contribution to the effect she is expressing" (40). On the other hand, Dickinson's definition of "Retrospection" allows the cousins a natural and spiritual, as well as a psychological, consolation. The earthly lives of their parents foreshadow their parents' afterlives, if only by the freezing thoughts of the cousins' stupefying grief, or—in hope—by the green thoughts of green shades that the poet invites these and other readers to entertain as a means of drawing solace from spring following winter. The cousins and other readers might gather from the intimations of immortality in this poem of prospective retrospection full-blown hope of parents "pinnacled dim" in Shelley's "white radiance of Eternity."

To return to Wadsworth's homiletical aphorism, with which I began, such an idea would appall, as well as appeal to, Emily Dickinson, to be sure. Nevertheless, her signature conundrum of "*sumptuous* Destitution - " alleviates her misgivings of Wordsworthian "blank desertion," and her choice of renunciation cultivates her deep hopefulness. Although Dickinson's arrival at "Quartz *contentment*, like a stone - " (Fr372, emphasis added) reflects Wadsworth's modest goal, the signature lyric of aftermath in which these words occur—namely, "After great pain, a formal feeling comes"—does so boldly, and more imaginatively than in Wadsworth's language. The pessimism of this poem makes only a reluctant, uneasy peace with Wadsworth's strict injunction against self-indulgence. The optimism of an otherwise similarly destitute poem of aftermath, moreover, belongs to the hopeful dimension of "sumptuous Destitution - ," for "I felt a Funeral, in my Brain" envisions "Finished," or accomplished/perfected (as well as truncated), knowledge at the end of life (Fr340). Although Dickinson's "dearest earthly friend" counseled his congregation that straitened less *should* mean less, her counterintuition that less of one thing, whether chosen or unwelcome, signifies expected, imminent/present, more of another, reveals that her unfulfilled need leads to paradoxical compatibility between her physical/material desire and her spiritual/moral abundance. As philosopher Gaston Bachelard has concluded, "The attainment of the superfluous causes a greater spiritual excitement than the attainment of necessities. Man is a creature of desire and not a creature of need" (as quoted in Donoghue 91). As opposed to merely illustrating the experience of being a recluse, the "lady whom the people call the *Myth*" embodies experience (Mabel Loomis Todd, as quoted in Leyda 2:357, 2:376).

Dickinson's definition of "Retrospection" as "Prospect's half, / Sometimes, almost more - "—her gnomic equivalent to High-Romantic inference of intimation from recollection—means that looking backward is looking forward not only personally but also culturally. Her faith in human progress deepens as her looking backward yields both a sense of historical immediacy and prophetic foreknowledge. Not even her speakers of aftermath, aware of collective human experience, commit pure nostalgia, the enemy of hope; their "historiography" out-historicizes G. W. F. Hegel. Thus Dickinson avoids the nemesis of cyclical monotony, for, to echo Thomas Hobbes, as well as Hegel, she, too, understands time and experience as both naturally inexorable and spiritually efficacious. This Dickinson appears all the more dynamically paradoxical for her becoming Anglo-American Romantic in hindsight, as well as pre-Modern in foresight.

Dickinson's most prescient poems, then, prove remnants saved by her Late-Romantic hope, as much as anti-Romantic signs of Victorian-American belatedness, or ominous fragments shored against her pre-Modern ruins. "The poetry of experience," to quote Robert Langbaum's classic phrase for the nineteenth-century lyric zenith, paradoxically jibes with Dickinson's poetry of aftermath. Her poetic personae of "sumptuous Destitution - " play on, and keep in play, the philosophical and religious poles of her art. Although the best moments of these speakers hardly rival the "Superior instants - " of Dickinson's more fully Late-Romantic personae, they earn the not-*so*-muted optimism of hope. Thus aftermath means outcome that augurs further harvest, for Dickinson's great, though vague, "expectation" of Wordsworth's "something evermore about to be" includes her heavenly reward, as well as just her auspicious engagement with past and present. Updike's similarly "Late-Romantic" exhilaration comes to mind—namely, "What we seek, gropingly, in fiction, is enlargement, a glorification of the furtive and secret and seemingly trivial, a valorization of human experience" (108).

Although the double perspective of her Late-Romantic imagination achieves her strongest combination of natural models with spiritual metaphors, and although this counterintuition champions both the androgynous ideal of her nineteenth-century feminism and her belief in immortality, Dickinson's postexperiential perspective, too, riddles with special skill, including a grasp of oxymoron. Her poetic personae of "sumptuous Destitution - ," notwithstanding the decidedly *un*-sumptuous enervation of their pre-modern mode and the relentlessly *anti*-sumptuous anomie of their postmodern intimations, reap rich harvest from their creator's Late-Romantic hope. Without fully sharing her experiential Faith, or abundant life (John 10:10), or without always engendering for all seasons her more Late-Romantic than either Victorian-American or pre-Modern dialectic of joyful wisdom with spiritual wealth, the personae "dwell in Possibility - " (Fr466).

In sum, Dickinson's friends and loved ones, her literary precursors and coevals, her literary beneficiaries, and her aesthetic self-projections define the possibility of personal access to otherness through others. She forms no "party of one," like Milton's solipsistic, antinomian Abdiel; she rarely "parties" alone. Her "Soul selects her own Society - " (Fr409), made up of multitudes that she contains and many real people besides. Like the speaker of "The Soul selects," Dickinson "Choose[s] One" *society*, not one *person* (Fr409, line 10). Just as *society* pertains to John Locke's *social contract* and to John Wesley's *Societies* alike, so too does this key word denote Dickinson's minimum adult daily requirement of intellectual, spiritual, and imaginative *communion*.

Notes

For reasons of aesthetic preference and argument, I choose among the versions and variant lines in Franklin's three-volume variorum edition of Dickinson's poems; where I do not choose his final version of the complete poem, I mark the version A, B, etc. or note any variant lines adopted. Otherwise the version cited is that which also appears in Franklin's reading edition.

[1] Quotations of British and American writers, unless otherwise indicated, are from Damrosch et al., eds.; and Baym et al., eds.

[2] William H. Shurr grapples with the presence of Presbyterian preacher Charles Wadsworth in Emily Dickinson's forty fascicles (see also Habegger; Lease; Paul M. Miller; and Strickland). Martha Nell Smith focuses on the role of Susan Huntington Dickinson (see also Hart and Smith, eds.; and Bennett). Vivian R. Pollak addresses the centrality of Charles and of Sue alike (see also Sewall *The Life of Emily Dickinson*). Judith Farr demonstrates the influence of Samuel Bowles, editor of *The Springfield Republican*, but many "Poems for Master" (Farr's phrase) address a minister and employ Presbyterian diction (Shurr). Pollak suggests that the geographical distance between Emily and Charles—the Wadsworths lived, for a time (1864-7), in San Francisco—and the emotional distance between Emily and neighbor Sue—so near, yet so far—contributed narrative tension and dramatic conflict to Dickinson's love poetry. "Poems for Master" and "Poems for Sue" (Farr's phrases) emerge from Pollak's psychobiographical criticism as more tragic than many readers might expect love poetry to be. Dickinson's philosophy of friendship rivals and resembles her poetic faith.

[3] The context of Dickinson's postexperiential perspective in the experiential philosophy and in the faith-experience of eighteenth-to-nineteenth-century Anglo-America forms a subtext of my emphasis here on literary history. Although the focus of John Locke (1632-1704) on inference contrasts with that of John Wesley (1703-91) on direct knowledge, Locke and Wesley alike cher-

ish assurance and access. For an insightful, Bloomian account of Dickinson's relation to her literary precursors and coevals, see Diehl.

[4] Among the master figures of High-to-Late-Romantic Anglo-America on whom I have previously focused, and to whom I continue to refer, William Blake, Samuel Taylor Coleridge, Percy Bysshe Shelley, and Thomas Carlyle receive no mention, quotation, or allusion in Dickinson's 1,049 letters and 124 prose fragments. However, these letters and prose fragments quote Wordsworth three times (L96, L315, L394), Byron three times (L233, L249, L293), Alfred, Lord Tennyson four times (L353, L486, L506, L801), and Ralph Waldo Emerson five times (L436, L794, L823, L1004, PF116). They mention Tennyson four times (L23, L243, L320, L616) and Emerson eight times (L30, L330, L353, L457, L481, L486, L750, L962). They allude to Wordsworth once (L400), Byron once (L1042), and Emerson twice (L269, PF10; see also MacKenzie and Capps).

[5] I am indebted to Sewall's reading of "Too happy Time dissolves itself" ("Teaching Dickinson: Testimony of a Veteran").

[6] See the quotation and discussion of Thomas Carlyle's *Past and Present* (1843) in Ikeler 6-7. See also Brantley, *Coordinates of Anglo-American Romanticism*, 43-76.

[7] See the quotation of Ralph Waldo Emerson's "Nature" (1836) in Murphy et al. 1:843. Subsequent references to this volume appear in the text. See also Brantley, *Coordinates of Anglo-American Romanticism*, 97-117.

[8] I refer to Wesley's central doctrine, which, as Randy L. Maddox argues, reconciles divining grace (Eastern Christianity), free grace (Lutheran tradition), sovereign grace (Reformed tradition), co-operant grace (Arminian tradition), sanctifying grace (radical Reformed tradition), and mediated grace (Catholic tradition). Dickinson's acquiring grace, in my view a delicate balance between choosing and being chosen, boasts in common with Wesley's "responsible grace" "the fascination of what's difficult" about experience (William Butler Yeats, "The Fascination of What's Difficult" [1910]).

[9] For the Arminian (free-will) tendency of Dickinson's thought and practice, see Brantley, *Experience and Faith*, 15, 90-93, 139, 198, 237 n.25, and passim. For Dickinson's Calvinist (predestinarian) strain, see Eberwein "'Where - Omnipresence - fly?' Calvinism as Impetus to Spiritual Amplitude." For political implications of the Arminian ascendancy during the increasingly democratic nineteenth century, see Nathan Hatch. My series of arguments for the empirical/evangelical dialectic of Romantic Anglo-America consistently describe the Calvinist/Arminian controversy and the Arminian ascendancy as

glosses on eighteenth-to-nineteenth-century literary development; see also Brantley *Wordsworth's "Natural Methodism."* The life of Henry Ward Beecher, whose "gospel of love" resists father Lyman's doctrine of depravity, illustrates the triumph, for better or worse, of Arminianism (Applegate).

WORKS CITED

The following abbreviations are used to refer to the writings of Emily Dickinson:

Fr *The Poems of Emily Dickinson.* ed. R.W. Franklin. 3 vols. Cambridge, MA: Harvard UP, 1998. Citation by poem number.

L *The Letters of Emily Dickinson.* ed. Thomas H. Johnson and Theodora Ward. 3 vols. Cambridge, MA: Harvard UP, 1958. Citation by letter number.

Anderson, Douglas. "Presence and Place in Emily Dickinson's Poetry." *New England Quarterly* 57.2 (1984): 205-24.

Applegate, Debby. *The Most Famous Man in America: The Biography of Henry Ward Beecher.* New York: Doubleday, 2006.

Baker, Nicholson. *U and I: A True Story.* New York: Random House, 1991.

Baym, Nina et al., eds. *The Norton Anthology of American Literature: Fifth Edition.* New York: W. W. Norton, 1998.

Bennett, Paula. *Emily Dickinson: Woman Poet.* Iowa City: U of Iowa P, 1992.

Bianchi, Martha Dickinson. *The Life and Letters of Emily Dickinson.* Boston, MA: Houghton Mifflin, 1924.

Bloom, Harold, ed. *Modern Critical Views: Alfred Lord Tennyson.* New York: Chelsea House, 1985.

Brantley, Richard E. *Coordinates of Anglo-American Romanticism: Wesley, Edwards, Carlyle, and Emerson.* Gainesville: UP of Florida, 1993.

_____. *Experience and Faith: The Late-Romantic Imagination of Emily Dickinson.* New York: Palgrave Macmillan, 2004.

_____. *Wordsworth's "Natural Methodism".* New Haven, CT: Yale UP, 1975.

Burbick, Joan. "Emily Dickinson and the Economics of Desire." *American Literature* 58.3 (1986): 361-78.

Cameron, Sharon. *Choosing Not Choosing: Emily Dickinson's Fascicles.* Chicago, IL: U of Chicago P, 1992.

Capps, Jack L. *Emily Dickinson's Reading: 1836-1886.* Cambridge, MA: Harvard UP, 1966.

Cody, John. *After Great Pain: The Inner Life of Emily Dickinson*. Cambridge, MA: Harvard UP, 1971.

———. "Dickinson's 'I Can Wade Grief.'" *The Explicator* 37.1 (1978): 15-16.

Damrosch, David et al., eds. *The Longman Anthology of British Literature: First Edition*. 2 vols. New York: Longman, 1999.

Deppman, Jed. "'I Could Not Have Defined the Change': Rereading Dickinson's Definition Poetry." *The Emily Dickinson Journal* 11.1 (2002): 49-80.

———. "Trying to Think with Emily Dickinson." *The Emily Dickinson Journal* 14.1 (2005): 84-103.

Diehl, Joanne Feit. *Dickinson and the Romantic Imagination*. Princeton, NJ: Princeton UP, 1981.

Donoghue, Denis. "The Discreet Charm of the Bourgeoisie: Taste and Middle-Class Values." *Harper's*, February 2006, 89-94.

Eberwein, Jane Donahue. *Dickinson: Strategies of Limitation*. Amherst: U of Massachusetts P, 1985.

———. Review of *Experience and Faith: The Late-Romantic Imagination of Emily Dickinson*, by Richard E. Brantley. *The Emily Dickinson Journal* 15.1 (2006): 96-100.

———. "'Where - Omnipresence - Fly?' Calvinism as Impetus to Spiritual Amplitude." *The Emily Dickinson Journal* 14.2 (2005): 12-23.

Farr, Judith. *The Passion of Emily Dickinson*. Cambridge, MA: Harvard UP, 1992.

Garbowsky, Maryanne. *The House without the Door: A Study of Emily Dickinson and the Illness of Agoraphobia*. Rutherford, NJ: Fairleigh Dickinson UP, 1989.

Gilbert, Sandra M., and Susan Gubar. *The Madwoman in the Attic: The Woman Writer and the Nineteenth-Century Literary Imagination*. New Haven, CT: Yale UP, 1979.

Guthrie, James R. *Emily Dickinson's Vision: Illness and Identity in Her Poetry*. Gainesville: UP of Florida, 1998.

Habegger, Alfred. *My Wars Are Laid Away in Books*. New York: Random House, 2001.

Harrison, Kathryn. "I Am, Therefore I Want." *The New York Review of Books*, November 6, 2005, 22.

Hart, Ellen Louise, and Martha Nell Smith, eds. *Open Me Carefully: Emily Dickinson's Intimate Letters to Susan Huntington Dickinson*. Ashfield, MA: Paris P, 1998.

Hatch, Nathan O. *The Democritization of American Christianity*. New Haven, CT: Yale UP, 1989.

Ikeler, A. Abbott. *Puritan Temper and Transcendental Faith: Carlyle's Literary Vision*. Columbus: Ohio State UP, 1977.

Johnson, Greg. "Emily Dickinson: Perception and the Poet's Quest." *Renaissance: Essays on Value in Literature* 35.1 (1982): 2-15.

Jones, Ruth Owen. "'Neighbor - and friend - and Bridegroom - ': William Smith Clark as Emily Dickinson's Master Figure." *The Emily Dickinson Journal* 11.2 (2003): 48-85.

Juhasz, Suzanne. "Reading Doubly: Dickinson, Gender, and Double Meaning." In *Approaches to Teaching Dickinson's Poetry*. Eds. Robin Riley Fast and Christine Mack Gordon. New York: The Modern Language Association of America, 1989. 85-94.

Langbaum, Robert. *The Poetry of Experience: The Dramatic Monologue in Modern Literary Tradition*. London: Chatto and Windus, 1957.

Lease, Benjamin. *Emily Dickinson's Reading of Men and Books: Sacred Soundings*. Basingstoke, England: Macmillan, 1990.

Leonard, Douglas Novich. "Emily Dickinson's Religion: An 'Ablative Estate.'" *Christian Scholar's Review* 13.4 (1984): 333-48.

Leyda, Jay, ed. *The Years and Hours of Emily Dickinson*. 2 vols. New Haven, CT: Yale UP, 1960.

Lundin, Roger. *Emily Dickinson and the Art of Belief*. Grand Rapids, MI: William B. Eerdmans, 1998.

MacKenzie, Cynthia, ed. *Concordance to the Letters of Emily Dickinson*. Boulder: UP of Colorado, 2000.

Maddox, Randy L. *Responsible Grace: John Wesley's Practical Theology*. Nashville, TN: Kingswood Books, 1994.

Martin, Wendy. *An American Triptych: Anne Bradstreet, Emily Dickinson, and Adrienne Rich*. Chapel Hill: U of North Carolina P, 1984.

Menand, Louis. *The Metaphysical Club*. New York: Farrar, Straus, and Giroux, 2001.

Miller, Paul M. "The Relevance of the Rev. Charles Wadsworth to the Poet Emily Dickinson." *Higginson Journal* 61 (First Half 1991): 1-69.

Mudge, Jean McClure. *Emily Dickinson and the Image of Home*. Amherst: U of Massachusetts P, 1975.

Murphy, Francis et al., eds. *The Norton Anthology of American Literature: Second Edition*. 2 volumes. New York: W. W. Norton, 1985.

O'Hara, Daniel T. "'The Designated Light': Irony in Emily Dickinson." *Boundary 2: An International Journal of Literature and Culture* 7.3 (1979): 175-98.

Patterson, Rebecca. *Emily Dickinson's Imagery*, ed. Margaret H. Freeman. Amherst: U of Massachusetts P, 1979.

Peltason, Timothy. *Reading* In Memoriam. Princeton, NJ: Princeton UP, 1985.

Pollak, Vivian R. *Dickinson: The Anxiety of Gender*. Ithaca, NY: Cornell UP, 1984.

Porter, David. *Dickinson: The Modern Idiom*. Cambridge, MA: Harvard UP, 1981.

Robinson, John. *Emily Dickinson: Looking to Canaan*. London: Faber, 1986.

Sewall, Richard B. "Teaching Dickinson: Testimony of a Veteran." In *Approaches to Teaching Dickinson's Poetry*. Eds. Robin Riley Fast and Christine Mack Gordon. New York: The Modern Language Association of America, 1989. 30-38.

———. *The Life of Emily Dickinson*. 2 vols. 1974. Reprint. New York: Farrar, Straus, and Giroux, 1980.

Sherrer, Grace B. "A Study of Unusual Verb Constructions in the Poems of Emily Dickinson." *American Literature* 7.1 (1935): 37-46.

Shurr, William H. *The Marriage of Emily Dickinson: A Study of the Fascicles*. Lexington: UP of Kentucky, 1983.

Smith, Martha Nell. *Rowing in Eden: Rereading Emily Dickinson*. Austin: U of Texas P, 1992.

Steiner, Dorothea. "Emily Dickinson: Image Patterns and the Female Imagination." *Arbeiten aus Anglistik und Amerikanistik* 6.1 (1981): 57-61.

Stocks, Kenneth. *Emily Dickinson and the Modern Consciousness: A Poet of Our Time*. New York: St. Martin's, 1988.

Strickland, Georgiana. "Emily Dickinson's Philadelphia." *The Emily Dickinson Journal* 13.2 (2004): 79-115.

Updike, John. "Novel Thoughts: Four Fiction Writers with Metaphysics on their Minds." *The New Yorker* (August 21 and 28, 1995): 105-14.

Wadsworth, Charles. *Sermons*. New York and San Francisco: A. Roman & Company, 1869.

Wilson, A. N. *God's Funeral*. New York: W. W. Norton, 1999.

Wolff, Cynthia Griffin. *Emily Dickinson*. Radcliffe Biography Series. Reading, England: Addison-Wesley, 1988.

Wolosky, Shira. *Emily Dickinson: A Voice of War*. New Haven, CT: Yale UP, 1984.

Essays, Fourth Series: Miscellaneous Perspectives

T. Walter Herbert (1908-1983)

19. *A Memorial Tribute to T. Walter Herbert 1908-1983*

(Remarks Delivered at the University of Florida, March 7, 1984)

I was Walter Herbert's colleague in the English Department. For fifteen years, I knew him well. I observed how this good old fashioned professor balanced the scholar's study with the classroom. In this man old enough to be my father I discovered not just an authority figure, but a friend. He remains not just a name for us to conjure with, but a presence.

John Wesley as Editor and Author, Princeton University Press, 1940, holds a special place in my affections. My sentiments concerning Walter's first book are exactly those of President Henry N. Snyder of Wofford College, Walter's *alma mater* (Spartanburg, South Carolina). In a letter to Walter, written on January 27, 1940, President Snyder told just how spellbinding he found the hot-off-the-press hardcover debut of a very promising young scholar:

> Your father had sent me a copy of your book for the Library. However, I couldn't resist reading it. I began it in my office rather early in the morning, and except for necessary interruptions, did not put it down until I had finished it at eleven o'clock that night. You have done an exceptionally fine piece of work and in a manner that has in it distinction and charm. Your interpretation of the literary aspect of Wesley's amazing career seems to me the best that has yet been done. I was particularly pleased that you managed to keep me from hearing the rattling of the bones of fact, though every now and then I did turn to the appendix to take a view of the skeleton. From this I got an appreciation of the scholarly research which lay behind a certain lightness of touch in the body of your book. I am mighty proud of this achievement of yours!

My own absorbed reading of this book, which has not yet been bested in the field, resulted in my attempts to build on Walter's work, namely *Wordsworth's "Natural Methodism"* (Yale University Press, 1975) and *Locke, Wesley, and the Method of English Romanticism* (University Press of Florida, 1984). These titles merely elaborate Walter's bold and original point: in an important and surprising sense the founder of British and American Methodism made philosophical and literary, as well as religious, history. I am still simply excavating the mine opened, owned, and operated by T. Walter Herbert, proprietor.

Walter was not falsely modest about recommending this first fruit of his labor. From old correspondence we find that Princeton wanted to charge $2.00 for *John Wesley as Editor and Author*. Trying to persuade the publicity department to price the three hundred copies at just $1.75 apiece, Walter adopted an at once self-deprecating, droll, edgy, and barbed tone: "I see no objection to getting rid of the edition as expeditiously as possible without appealing to the department of sanitation." Walter made a good point here. He had received, after all, a letter from a Methodist preacher, saying that, while the book was wonderful in every way, the Methodists could nonetheless afford to pay only $1.00! In these letters, now more than forty years old, Walter's desire to share his work with the very people from whom it sprang, and for whose sake, in one sense, he always generated such democratically appealing prose, comes across as anything but mercenary. I covet Walter's almost eighteenth-century-satirical lack of sentimentality, his tough-mindedness salutary not just in the epistolary exchange from which I have been quoting, but throughout his signature professional composition.

Walter's recent volume, *Oberon's Mazèd World*, Louisiana State University Press, 1978, strengthens my conviction that our profession would be better off if it were possible, which it is not, for untenured professors to take twenty years rather than five or nine to write a book. Walter's sustained, painstaking, and lovingly languid attention to a single play by Shakespeare notably paid off in this well-deserved, visibly-placed encomium in the otherwise often downright acerbic, and perhaps even the sometimes notoriously dyspeptic, *TLS:*

> This book is impossible to dislike, at least for anyone who regularly reads the output of the Shakespeare industry. It is the product of a generous imagination and a dedicated scholarly intelligence. The staple of its prose . . . has a lightheartedness and a vivacity that would not disgrace the epithet Elizabethan. . . . Professor Herbert gives a vivid sense of the simultaneous

> operation of [the Elizabethan period's] contending intellectual and emotional loyalties. . . . The richly nutty flavor of this book will linger pleasurably in the memory long after more conventionally worthy Shakespearean exercises are forgotten. (May 12, 1978)

TLS implies, here, pointedly and quite rightly, that "conventionally worthy Shakespearean exercises" are just too quickly produced, nowadays, to qualify as those all-too-rare labors of love for which we look, and which we crave. Walter's book, at any rate, will henceforth embody his genius, whether for scrutinizers at the Folger or skimmers at the beach.

His fictionalized persona of a skeptical Cambridge graduate and still-young Elizabethan playgoer (whose recall of Shakespeare's happy play proves total) ranks as nothing short of nifty. Nor does it much matter that, whatever else he may succeed at, this playgoer reflects throughout his language and manner the unmistakable speech and accents of our very own T. Walter Herbert! In accordance with critical theory (as well as in the light of common sense), the interpreter is in the final analysis not just unavoidably, but properly, thinly veiled. Walter's book about Shakespeare reads like an impeccably historical first-person-narrative novel. Such praise can celebrate the lifetime achievement of a complete man of letters, who once said to me, "When a work of scholarship takes as long as it needs, it is then a work of art, as well."

President Snyder's noun "charm" describes Walter's last creation: an essay on Wesley's editorial efforts. Written as the introduction to a volume in the modern edition of Wesley's works, now forthcoming from Oxford University Press, this piece won immediate acceptance by the General Editor, Frank Baker. In September of 1983, five weeks before Walter's death, Baker wrote: "This is carefully and charmingly done, and would indeed stand on its own as a separate article." The essay engagingly makes the complex case that the redactional brio of Wesley's life-long series of 200-plus abridgments for a popular audience, including editions of Milton, Locke, and the chemist Charles de Bonnet, as well as of religious thinkers like Thomas à Kempis, yielded *Reader's Digest*-like innovation in publishing. Thus Walter brought his career full circle.

What, exactly, was Walter Herbert's method? When his son Walt was in town for the funeral, he stated, "In the best sense, my father lacked system." If I may borrow Walter's favorite quotation from the Romantic period, he possessed, in handy measure, what John Keats called *Negative Capability:* "being in uncertainties, Mysteries, doubts, without any irritable reaching after fact & reason." As the preacher of the funeral concluded, Walter embodied "the English tradition of open mind and warm heart." To invoke the literary theory of public intellectual E. D. Hirsch, Jr., what Walter knew was "not already theory-laden," like criticism at its worst, for *how* Walter knew, was as flexible as imagination at its best. If, again to apply Hirsch's language to Walter's criticism, Walter's books and articles were inevitably "imprinted with foreknowledge," then his essay-like writing nonetheless displayed, at key moments, not calculated interpretation, but a given guilelessness. If received wisdom tells us that thoughts come faster than the words that stand for them, then literary theory touts the reverse, and Walter's prose, like his hesitant but ingratiating talk, which made us lean forward, kept pace with his unwavering mental procedure. Less abstractly, on our common ground here in Gainesville Walter's scholarship has adorned the humanities at this university, from its auspicious early days of research emphasis, right on up through the present moment of its institutional ambition.

I remember a theory-driven conversation that occurred among some of us Gator-heaven critics. It was two or three years ago, when Hirsch had come down to lecture, and, at one point in the discussion, Hirsch turned to Walter, who had been holding his peace, and kindly asked, "And where are you, theoretically?" Quick was Walter's reply: "In left field." This incident speaks to Walter's modesty, yet puts him in no fringe light. The case for Walter's near-theoretical sophistication can alone rest on his Elizabethan playgoer, provided we understand this perspicuous figure aright, as a lively embodiment not just of Walter's difficult fascination with Shakespearean drama, but of his pure delight in criticism. In the current vernacular, he was no one's "epigone." Instead, he developed models based on induction, and that is why his books and articles will stay fresh.

Walter Herbert could "pause a while from letters to be wise." On one hand, he was positively capable of saying, "A book is a miracle!" On the other, with a scholar's version of negative capability, he exhibited the sanity of a most attractive non-bookishness. Hear, for instance, the final sentence of his proposal, submitted last summer to the American Philosophical Society, to complete his essay on Wesley's editorial prowess: "I should very much like to have the grant I request, but without it I shall betake myself to activities less scholarly, perhaps less useful, but no less enticing." I, for one, would have funded this project, on the very basis of that paradoxically throwaway clincher. Perhaps even now, I would raise neither eyebrow at his arch exit line. Would you?

Walter the teacher found the classroom enticing, useful, and scholarly. The minister at the service was spot-on to stress this man's passion for instruction, for gladly would Walter explain, clarify, inculcate, and instill, and gladly would he learn, thereby. Did you know that Walter Herbert wrote *marginalia* and cover statements for each of those final exams that no undergrad I know of ever came back to pick up? How greatly would those students have benefited, had they only done so! Walter's philosophy of education is contained, I think, in the lavish glory of his Shakespeare book's subtitle, so please sit back, now, while we are thinking about Walter's teaching, to get this whopping Renaissance mouthful of thoroughly pedagogical implication: *A Judicious Young Elizabethan contemplates* A Midsummer Night's Dream *with a Mind Shaped by the Learning of Christendom Modified by the New Naturalist Philosophy and Excited by the Vision of a Rich, Powerful England.* Whew: my point in again referring to *Oberon's Mazèd World* is that Walter Herbert wanted his students to be like his playgoer: learned in the Arts and Sciences, and hence in the range of disciplines necessary for admission into Phi Beta Kappa and High Honors. Perhaps Walter even wished for his young scholars to become rich and powerful, though I hasten to stipulate that the only part of the rich and powerful world Walter allowed himself was that string of very non-English-professor-like white Cadillacs he owned and called "Moby Dick." These guzzlers were his lone, comfortable vice, of which the donkey-riding Jesus would scarcely approve, yet which we would permit our mutual friend to have, for we know he would quote Shakespeare on the subject: "Reason not the need."

For the practical purpose of my survival as a professor at the University of Florida, I belonged among Walter Herbert's students. At my own expense, and to his credit, I confirm, here, just how he taught me. I had thought to burn the early draft of a book he helped me with—anything to cover embarrassing tracks!—but among us fellow-teachers I nonetheless bring to light his *marginalia*, and hence the quality of his teacher's mind, illustrating his Blake-like principle that "opposition is true friendship." I confess, there were times when I wished, from him, less of that particular kind of rapport. If only for whatever admonitory functions his redoubtable precepts may yet perform for rising junior professors, here or elsewhere, I offer, now, a sample of his comments on my prosaic *juvenilia*.

Savor the brogue of the man, as he speaks to us throughout the following set of his scholastic strictures, an eighteen-item concatenation that I would hereby like to enter into the Walter Herbert teaching legend:

- By George! I didn't know this. Is it indeed unequivocally so?
- This goes without saying.
- This seems to me a bit enthusiastic.
- Not quite the point is it?
- You don't need to put a metaphor inside quotation marks.
- Is this the *mot juste*?
- Is this a sort of mixed metaphor?
- Oh-oh.
- Surely this exaggerates.
- This cries out to be instanced.
- I suppose you are really going to say this kind of thing.
- Is this word ok by you?
- That sounds fine, but I don't know what it means.
- Ouch
- Is it really so?
- Jiminy
- Alas for me, I didn't know this and I am not persuaded.
- Oh Lordy I thought 1 and 2 meant the same thing. Cuss my Webster.

A lot of what Walter objected to was the young scholar's love of jargon, and this young scholar, believe me, wondered, upon seeing this red ink, whether or not he was ever going to be able to buy shoes for that baby of his back at home. Regarding my unguarded observation that "philosophical theology spoke of a faith to transform the world," Walter remonstrated: "People talk like this. But the world includes the Afghan rebels. It is not yet certain that they are about to be transformed by philosophical theology, whatever that is." Or again, he pleaded: "When I say that I can't make out what you are talking about I suppose I merely exhibit my own ignorance. But aren't people like me proper readers of your book?" And finally, he protested: "I think the point you are making is important, if I follow you. But I have trouble with 'represents quintessentially subjectivist,' for example. By *represents* do you mean *is*? Does *subjectivist* refer to a common and easily understandable philosophical position I don't know about?" Such commentary can only be called what Jean Herbert, Walter's wife, called it—"a Walter Herbert acid bath," but this senior colleague knew how to befriend me in the world of publish or perish: through tough love.

In the nick of time, Walter knew when to throw me a lifeline of hope, if only to offer just enough positive reinforcement to motivate going back to the drawing board. Consider this threefold sub-set that gives, takes away, and gives again, framing fault with grace:

- This seems ok to me.
- I don't see that.
- I do see that.

My heart leapt up when I beheld two favorable observations in a row:

- That's fair enough.
- A good paragraph.

I was ready to go and sin no more, when I read the following effusive praise: "That, now, is right as rain."

The manuscript Walter helped me with became *Locke, Wesley, and the Method of English Romanticism*. Walter was so happy about its acceptance that he brought champagne to my house. This editor of works by Wesley; this author of a book on Wesley's leadership, witting and unwitting, in the realm of letters; and this grandson, son, brother, and father of Methodist ministers ended our revels, that night, in imperfect sobriety. This *ur*-Methodist bracketed his Methodism just this once. His *marginalia* yet comprise the lesson that keeps on teaching.

No wonder, Jean, that you have been up sometimes until one or two in the morning, reading and replying to an astounding outpouring of correspondence from friends dating back to the '30s, and before, and from places as widely separated as Holland and India. The preacher memorably exulted that "Walter's watermark of quality lives in the pages of his sons." I have known Walt longer than I knew Walter; I look forward to knowing Linton and Carlisle better. But fullness of time crowns Walter's life: that I know for sure, and in that I will rejoice.

T. Walter Herbert was a close influence on us, and his close influence is always telling. Perhaps even as he believed in me when I did not believe in myself, so I believed in him, to the point of believing what he believed: I hazard that his knowledge-with-life, his English major's both/and logic, keeps us all from single vision. I can hear him, now, in his horse-of-instruction voice, saying, "I mean to be understood," and this intention of his was fulfilled in spades. I can hear him acknowledging absurdity and unease as friend to friend, saying, "While I am *in compos mentis*," yet of course he was always of sound mind. The steady health of his whole mental nature stood before us in the pre-eminence of his joy.

Our mutual grieving for our loss of his companionship, then, stays the more acute for our philosophic mind toward death. We well know how Walter would stand by us, so let us value our mutual commemoration of one whom life in its array beguiled. Jean said Walter was the luckiest person she knew, and his luck held out in the manner of his going, when he came in from tennis, lay down on his bed, and did not rise. Grateful for your life, Walter, we ask you for the rest of ours just how in the world you ever managed to defeat the pride implicit in the virtue of humility, yet you did. May these remarks, refuting "the rest is silence," re-echo homage to the scholar, teacher, and friend you were—and are.

20. *Sleeping with the Enemy: Communiqués from a Pedagogical Marriage*

Richard E. Brantley, University of Florida
Diana R. Brantley, Eastside High School

Although Richard and Diana work with the same materials, try to teach similar skills, and encounter the same students as year follows year, he teaches college and she teaches high school and it is an unacknowledged truism that high school English teachers and professors of English in colleges and universities have all too little to say to one another. In this chapter, they consider formally the relationship of college and university professors of English to high school teachers of the same subject, for their more than thirty-year marriage has spanned that divide on a daily basis.

Richard: To avoid a senior professor's rut of specialization, I want to experiment with how I teach writing. Sheridan Baker's *The Practical Stylist*, though, has always served me well. I distribute watchwords: "Get black on white" (De Maupassant); "Put proper words in proper places" (Swift); and "Translate time into space" (Brantley). I cherish Emerson's advice: "The way to write is to throw your body at the mark when your arrows are spent." And Pope's: "Snatch a grace beyond the reach of art." I tell my students, undergraduates and graduates alike, that it is better to write for a very bright ten-year-old than for lovers of academic jargon.

Diana: Nowadays I work with an international baccalaureate program as an assistant principal, which has pulled me away from composition per se. Nevertheless, the past year has been the occasion for that wonderful advantage called hindsight, or at least for some modest perspective on the role that the teaching of writing has played, and may even continue to play, in my career.

Richard: We met at Wake Forest University, where we were both English majors. I came to English through the example of the late Judson B.

Allen, a beloved professor of medieval literature; Diana came to it kicking and screaming but giving in to its universality. We shared such mentors as Allen and Edwin G. Wilson, the first of whom emphasized a sense of rigor and the second of whom inspired a sense of wonder. We came to love language and literature as the means of bringing the disciplines together and of helping students find their own humane ways.

Ours, in other words, has been a rather old-fashioned experience. Our careers have been unusually traditional. In the uproarious sixties, we were sedately in grad school, watching from the sidelines. If that also means that we are now a bit out of date, then we're so far out we're coming back in. We remain, at any rate, enthusiastic about the discipline and its ever-changing variations. We are both lucky and blessed to be doing what we enjoy.

Diana: It is sad and ironic that teachers and professors of English choose the profession because we love working with beautiful language, yet we thereby spend a lifetime reading terrible student prose. Only F. Scott Fitzgerald's "infinite hope" can keep us going. But our jobs and our relationship have survived the paradox. Indeed, our most fruitful and happy times seem to come when we're discussing reading, writing, and pedagogy. Believe it or not, we do not actually diagram sentences at the dinner table (though our children may say differently). I must say that I did not want to teach school. I've found in this traditional career, however, an opportunity for professional independence, even in Gainesville, Florida, the complete company town. In this context, I must add another mentor, Christine Croft, who taught me in high school that the field of English mixed hard work with pleasure. We learn how to teach by modeling our former teachers, after all.

Things We Do That Are Similar

Diana: Since we think of ourselves as political "radiclibs," we recognize with a shock that our profession is in many ways conservative at its core. When it comes to the rules of usage, we are hardliners, not in a political or moral sense, but more as a question of good manners for good communication. Perhaps it is not entirely healthy for us to fight the lost cause rearguard action of traditional usage with such relish. The "lie/lay" and "different from/different than" distinctions are gone. The selection of cases to use in personal pronouns seems to have become a matter of individual preference. Perhaps this attention to language detail is the thing about English teachers that causes strangers to fall silent when we tell them what we do.

Richard: We recognize that language constantly changes as time passes, but at what point do we capitulate to the ongoing flux of written usage? How much consistency is necessary for effective (and beautiful) communication? Horace said that studies serve both to instruct and to delight. Jonathan Swift's bees bring both "sweetness and light." If we bear down on the enlightenment of students, we risk obscuring delight at any level of instruction. High schoolers are often as mature as college students, and undergraduates are often as callow as any high schooler. Diana might lean a bit toward E. D. Hirsch's notion of inculcating a type of "cultural literacy"; I might lean a bit toward Howard Gardner's progressivist focus on depth and understanding and his call for a curriculum based on the ancient categories of the good, the beautiful, and the true. But the two of us agree that we are trying to teach our students not only to think and write clearly but also to apply a broad model of aesthetic appreciation to a multiplicity of times, genres, and cultures.

Diana: I might frame the topic a little differently, placing "cultural literacy" advocates over against those who endorse "critical thinking skills." Phrases like these highlight arguments about politics, money, and hot-button topics, including such egregious shams as the "Nation at Risk" movement. But, finally, we enjoy working with students, we love the subject matter, and we care about clear and imaginative thinking reflected in good writing.

Things We Do That Are Different

Richard: Our jobs are structured differently day by day. We all assume professors are writing away in an inaccessible ivory tower, free to set an independent daily schedule. We all assume high school teachers are constantly harried and in danger of being shot dead at any moment.

Diana: We are judged by different sets of expectations, frequently nowadays as a result of collective bargaining and political rhetoric.

Richard: We relate to students differently: classroom management is not a big topic in university English departments, and deep discussions of critical theory do not happen in high school. High school teachers worry more and more about competency testing of students, and university professors worry about attracting majors and placing graduates in the job market.

Diana: We have different relationships with our subject matter. Works that live high in high school are rarely studied elsewhere: when was the last time the average college professor read *A Tale of Two Cities*, *Julius Caesar*, or *To Kill a Mockingbird*? The ongoing update of the literary canon among universities has been widely and invigoratingly discussed, even in the media. The high school canon makes the news mainly because of questions about banned books.

Richard: Our status in society is different. A salary comparison is merely the most obvious way of making this point. But the difference in remuneration reflects a difference in mindset. A professor works hard for an initial credential, usually a doctorate, and tenure, but then it is assumed that each professor is a professional who can maintain currency in the field.

Diana: Teachers' initial credentials and tenure are not enough to ensure their professionalism, apparently, since they must continually update their certification and receive "inservice" instruction on topics from ESOL to IDEA and other alphabet soup.

Richard: All these differences make communicating difficult. We have years of resentment, condescension, isolation, and ignorance to bridge. As it is, we too often badmouth each other. I read Diana's poetry, when she lets me, but she doesn't read my stuff as often as she used to.

Diana: Except for the first four or five paragraphs, which I read about a thousand times while he's revising. Besides, my education is dated, and I don't dabble in hermeneutics.

Richard: A spouse who lives with a high school teacher learns not to hassle him or her. I don't make demands on her time. Across such gaps silence falls.

Diana: The problem is illustrated in the way we went about writing this. It's like the money conversation that couples have. It was the same conversation again and again, with little or no advancement from one conversation to another.

Richard: I would ask, "Don't you think we'd better start writing?" Diana: And I would reply, "Don't worry, it'll be all right."

Richard: You can see which one had more time on his hands. Yet by picking around the assignment, and by picking at it, we began to get somewhere as the deadline approached. After all, we acknowledge that some of the best times of our marriage were when we mutually expressed our shared love of the discipline. Some of the best times were when we discussed each other's writing despite the pain entailed by such discussion. So I try to take a leaf from Diana's book. . . .

Diana: . . . and I try to take a leaf from his. Each tries to cultivate respect for what the other is doing.

Richard: And in that spirit of mutuality, together we offer some concrete suggestions to help us all appreciate our colleagues who teach at different grade levels.

Suggestions for Making Things Better

Diana: We need to talk to one another, whatever the forum; for instance, the reading held for advanced placement examinations offers an opportunity to discuss standards and works, and to be paid for the privilege. Both NCTE and MLA, not to mention such newly formed groups as the Association of Literary Critics and Scholars, need to encourage communication between teachers and professors by programming specific sessions to make such discussion happen.

Richard: One result of such discussion could be a formal method for speeding up a kind of sharing that happens informally and by osmosis now. Diana and I and our older daughter, who is a new teacher of English, have found that our discussions of pedagogical technique have been fruitful on all sides. We enjoyed exploring how a thesis should be both "important" and "surprising." I have received at least as many ideas for improving my classroom style as I've given.

Diana: A wonderful contribution that professors could make would be to help K-12 teachers enrich what we do. As it is, we spend more and more time teaching to tests such as Florida's FCAT, which does a disservice to most of our students. Classroom time is spent going over basic-level skills rather than plunging into the wealth of cultures that we claim as our traditional subject matter. We don't begin to bring theory or criticism to the students. But we should. One concrete way to further this effort would be to offer a college course that considers state-adopted standard high school English textbooks. Furthermore, we need professors to help us convince politicians and the public that schooling should be more than drilling in minimal-level skills aimed at the lowest common denominator. All students deserve opportunity.

Richard: This kind of collaboration would bring to colleges better students from a wider selection of the population. The state of Florida, for instance, does provide a place on professors' annual activities reports for us to indicate "service to high schools," but the traditional way of visiting—a one-period presentation—is inadequate. One of my colleagues, who is at the forefront of theory and technology, plans to merge his undergraduate class with a high school class in order to conduct studies of the local area using the Web. This kind of project could eliminate the problem of reaching high school students who do not live close to a college.

Diana: Co-teaching between school and college might be a radical but useful idea. Richard could take over one of my classes; I could teach one of his. That way we would learn more about each other's worlds, and the exchange would give both the high school and the university faculties a good idea of our common pool of students.

Richard: The state might find it difficult to support a professor for a semester at a high school, but we just might contrive to support him or her with grants at the grassroots level. Would such an exchange fit in to Gainesville's acute town-versus-gown awareness nowadays? Could such exchanges blossom throughout the state?

Diana: Could summer retreats work? Say, over a weekend? Professors and teachers could discuss two selected books on theory or criticism. I went to an informal beach retreat sponsored by a new school board member a few years ago. The intense discussion and brainstorming about ways of improving the school system have led to concrete changes in the local district. As Wordsworth says, we can "build up great things from least suggestions." An idea starts with an individual.

Richard: Book groups have exploded in popularity; what about putting together professors and teachers? No one has time for more reading, but we always do what is important to us. Groups could be held not only in college towns but also in outlying communities. The book groups would have nothing to do with certification; they would not be about jumping through hoops. If they were fun, they would bloom.

Diana: What is my perspective after two years as an assistant principal for curriculum? Ordering books is not the relationship I ever wanted to have with them. Yet ordering textbooks, in the present scheme of things, is my reward for twenty-five years of successful teaching. What else might the reward for teaching be? Sabbaticals. At present, fifteen yearly sabbaticals are offered for the more than two thousand teachers in my district, but nowhere near that many are given out, because the year is at half pay; because takers have to write a report of the year's activity; and, worst of all, because takers have to be going to school in order to receive a sabbatical. Sabbaticals should be a means of offering a professional person an opportunity for independent research, for undertaking a focused reading program to develop curriculum, for writing/painting/composing/building a contribution to our national culture.

Richard: To help any proposals along these lines come to fruition, individual teachers and professors need to initiate a change in the way their institutions relate to each other. That means principals need to confer with chairs of departments, deans with superintendents. Some crises of numbers are coming: many future forecasters predict a shortfall of both teachers and professors as the baby boomers retire. People who grew up in the technological revolution, who anticipate spending their careers at dot-coms, who think that a virtual human interaction will do, will be sorely pressed to educate their children if the humanity of teaching disappears at any level. To attract good people to this highly interactive, deeply personal, and labor-intensive profession, we need to make changes, to train a new generation, and to talk to one another.

21. *A Conference on Christianity and Literature Tribute to Robert Alter*

Emeritus Professor of Hebrew and Comparative Literature at Berkeley, Robert Alter is the author of twenty-three books on such subjects as Stendhal, Kafka, Benjamin, Scholem, the picaresque novel, the theory of narrative, and various novelists' takes on urban experience. More important from CCL's point of view are his criticism and translation of, and his commentary on, the Hebrew Bible. Just as Professor Alter received the National Jewish Book Award for Jewish Thought, so he wins CCL's Award for Lifetime Achievement. This "most accomplished Jewish humanist in America," as Leon Wieseltier has called him, ranks among the most accomplished humanists in the world, for Robert Alter has advanced Jewish/Christian conversation about the golden realm of letters. He gives vital meaning to how Blake refers to the Bible we all share—as "the Great Code of Art."

As anyone "of a certain age" well knows, courses in the Bible as Literature were drowning in the alphabet soup of JEDP until Professor Alter came along, to shift biblical scholarship from source criticism to reading the whole text as it appears before us on the page. In his own words, his goal is "not to promote the Hebrew Bible, but simply to register a crucial fact about its formal status"; he adds, "If you want to read [the Bible] competently even with an intended focus on it as a set of religious documents, you have to follow closely its literary articulations." Robert Alter understands the Scriptures as dynamic and multi-layered and shows how language that might not be literally true approximates deep truth nonetheless. Just as John Updike's fiction locates the beautiful in the mundane, the redemptive in the descriptive, so Robert Alter's Bible finds saving grace, "a momentary stay against confusion" and hence "clarification of life" (Frost's language), in the conflicts, perplexities, unfathomability, vividness, and revelatory dialogue of ever-changing character both human and divine.

By giving his readers credit for literacy, Professor Alter performs the difficult but fascinating task of translation, rendering into English with no diminution of "concrete directness" the "strongly cadenced" as well as "beautifully compact" Hebrew (Alter's language). Not for Robert Alter the fashionable version of the creation account that tells plants to "Green up!" or of the Lord's Prayer that asks for "three square meals" rather than for "daily bread." Where the Jewish Publication Society translates the psalmist's "soul" thirsting for God, Alter's image, closer to the Hebrew and rooted in the challenges of desert subsistence, is of the poet's "throat" thirsting for God. As Adam Kirsch has recently observed, Professor Alter's "ongoing translation of the Hebrew Bible into a new, more accurate and forceful English version is one of the most ambitious literary projects of this or any age." CCL's Alan Jacobs rejoices that Robert Alter's "climb up the sheer face of the pentateuchal mount resembles some of the great monuments of humanistic scholarship more than the work of the rabbis."

Professor Alter, finally, writes commentary, and so he regards the Book he is commenting on as a *master* work. He presumes that "the biblical authors knew what they were doing, which in turn allows him to exert his considerable critical skills to imagine what that might have been" (Jacobs). His "commentary is as useful as the translation itself," as when he points out that Qoheleth's words—"For the fate of the sons of men and the fate of the beasts is a single fate" (Alter's translation)—"are a direct repudiation of Genesis" (Kirsch). "Here," as Kirsch aptly remarks, "is the Bible itself making the same disenchanting argument" as Darwin. Thus Robert Alter can save Judaism and Christianity from themselves, for he returns abstraction to text. Kierkegaard said that doctrine merely defends the Church against the Bible's "coming too close" and that theology tries vainly to restrain "this confounded book which would, one, two, three, run us down if it got loose." For his part and in this very spirit of Kierkegaard, Robert Alter shows no such "interest in 'protecting' us from the biblical text" (Jacobs). He reminds us, above all, that no one can be even a good devotional reader of Scripture without being in constant contact with one's inner English major.

Thank you, Professor Alter, for giving us our heritage in the most faithful terms by which its significance may be understood. You have recently remarked that it is "basically an actuarial question" whether you will translate the entire Hebrew Bible. But you have already advanced Jewish/Christian dialogue. You are leading us across the bridge from living symbol to life itself, for, to adapt to your case Emily Dickinson's not-*so*-lapsed Congregationalist grasp of the Bible, "every page" of your Hebrew Scriptures is "a Pulse" that—precisely by "elud[ing] stability"—"instills, incites, infatuates—blesses and blames."

Reviews, First Series:

Books on Locke, Wesley, and Edwards

22. *God, Locke, and Equality: Christian Foundations in Locke's Political Thought*, by Jeremy Waldron

Cambridge: Cambridge University Press, 2002.
ISBN 0521810019 (hardcover); 0521890578 (paper).
Pp. xii + 263. $65.00 (hardcover); $22.00 (paper).

In 1982, at the Carlyle Lectures in Oxford, Jeremy Waldron heard Alasdair Macintyre observe that "the arguments of John Locke concerning basic equality and individual rights were so imbued with religious content that they were not fit, constitutionally, to be taught in the public schools of the United States" (44). Accordingly, in a paper that Waldron "had the good sense" not to attempt to publish, the Columbia University law professor endeavored to isolate "a defensible *secular* conception of equality" in Locke's thought (44; emphasis added). He failed. Eventually, in the 1999 Carlyle Lectures, Waldron argued that "we are not able to bracket off the theological dimension of Locke's commitment to equality" (44). Moreover, in Waldron's considered judgment, we should not even try

Thus *God, Locke, and Equality* represents a palinode. "I actually don't think it is clear," Waldron declares, "that we—now—*can* shape and defend an adequate conception of basic human equality apart from some religious foundation" (13). This breakthrough in the understanding of Locke's philosophy in general, as well as of his *Two Treatises of Government*, inspires, in turn, a reconsideration of Locke's relation to Christian and to political history, though it scarcely forms part of Waldron's purpose to say so. In the end, *God, Locke, and Equality* carries implications, again unwittingly, for Locke's influence on literature, as well.

Waldron, to begin with, excels at spelling out just how his view of Locke as an "equality-radical" advances scholarly conversation (50). Asking in what sense Locke's theory is "ours," he aligns Locke with such political philosophers as Bernard Williams, John Rawls, Ronald Dworkin, and Amartya Sen (8). Obsessively, yet persuasively, Waldron resists Peter Laslett's time-bound tendency to contextualize Locke's *Two Treatises* in such detail that they seem completely different from all of Locke's other works (50, 52, 62, 68, 160-61, 190, 193, 241, and *passim*). Thus Waldron "has some fun with some of the sillier manifestations of Cambridge-style historicism" (11), which, in eschewing timelessness, might drive one to the opposite extreme—namely, Harold Bloom's dictum that a work is eternal, or it is nothing.

John Dunne, in "the standard theological reading of Locke's politics," assumes Locke's faith in A. O. Lovejoy's hierarchical "Great Chain of Being" (55), but Waldron reveals Locke's near-egalitarian belief in "Species . . . linked together, and differ[ing] but in almost invisible degrees" *(An Essay Concerning Human Understanding,* as quoted in Waldron, 55). Waldron's eye for all that Locke says about equality scrutinizes such vivid, yet neglected, passages as the following extended implication of crossovers, or even oneness (a principle of *e pluribus unum*), among species:

> Nor let any one say, that the power of propagation in animals by the mixture of Male and Female . . . keeps the supposed real *Species* distinct and entire . . . for if History lie not, women have conceived by Drills [mandrills]; and what real *Species*, by that measure, such a Production will be in Nature, will be a new Question; and we have Reason to think this is not impossible. I once saw a Creature, that was the issue of a Cat and a Rat, and had the plain Marks of both about it; wherein Nature appeared to have followed the Pattern of neither sort alone, but to have jumbled them both together. *(An Essay,* as quoted in Waldron, 65)

"The members of the laboring class," C. B. Macpherson's reading of Locke asserts, "do not and cannot live a fully rational life" (Macpherson, as quoted in Waldron, 85), but, in Waldron's words, Locke insists on "the fundamental adequacy of even the meanest intellect" (87). Waldron, correspondingly, refutes Macpherson's narrow understanding of Lockean "property" as tangible possessions (126): Locke's concept, in Waldron's highlighting of it, features life, liberty, and labor (173-75).

Locke, as Waldron understands him, "believed it was possible to use human reason—*ordinary* human reason—to sift through the customs of the world and determine at least for some of them whether or not they were in conformity with the requirements of natural law" (168; emphasis added). Thus Waldron shows how "Locke's opposition to innateism does not lead him to relativism" (168). The *Essay*, as Waldron quotes it, teaches that the poorest have souls: "No Man is so wholly taken up with the Attendance on the Means of Living, as to have no spare Time at all to think of his Soul, and inform himself in Matters of Religion" (87). The *Essay*, in fact, gives no great respect to their putative betters: "For, notwithstanding these learned Disputants, these all-knowing Doctors, it was to the unscholastick Statesman, that the Governments of the World owed their Peace, Defence, and Liberties; and from the illiterate and contemned Mechanick (a Name of Disgrace) that they received the improvements of useful Arts" (as quoted in Waldron, 91). The *Second Treatise*, therefore, assumes that laborers prove worthy of their hire (cf. Luke 10:7): "The Ploughman's Pains, the Reaper's and Thresher's Toil, and the Baker's Sweat, is to be counted into the Bread we eat; the Labor of those who broke the Oxen, who digged and wrought the Iron and Stones, who felled and framed the Timber employed about the Plough, Mill, Oven, or any other Utensils, which are a vast Number, requisite to this Corn, from its being feed to be sown to its being made Bread, must all be charged on the account of Labor" (as quoted in Waldron, 174).

Whereas the "modern liberal theory" of Allen Buchanan regards charity as a duty, Locke's theory, as grasped by one of Waldron's most original sub-theses, regards charity as "a matter of right" (180). The upshot of Locke's forceful argument against Sir Robert Filmer, according to Waldron's startling, yet persuasive, interpretation of the *Two Treatises*, is that "neither the rich nor civil society on their behalf is entitled to *resist* the poor when the poor attempt to seize their surplus goods for themselves" (185). Locke, by reputation, extended his personal acts of charity to anyone who worked (186); throughout his writings, more radically, God grants the right of charity to everyone. The *First Treatise* puts this right in the strongest possible terms:

> God the Lord and Father of all, has given no one of his Children such a Property, in his peculiar Portion of the Things of this World, but that he has given his needy Brother a Right to the Surplusage of his Goods; so that it cannot justly be denied him, when his pressing Wants call for it. As *Justice* gives every Man a Title to the Product of his honest Industry, and the fair Acquisitions of his Ancestors descended to him; so *Charity* gives every Man a Title to so much out of another's Plenty, as will keep him from extream want, where he has no means to subsist otherwise. (As quoted in Waldron, 178-79)

"Lockean government," Waldron continues, "may have to be continually interfering to redistribute surplus goods from the rich to the most needy" (178-79). Thus, though scarcely separated from the state, on the one hand, and though obviously far from the party-affiliated brand of conservative Christianity now dominant in the US, on the other, Locke's Christianity feels spiritually communitarian (as distinct from temporally socialist).

Waldron's paraphrase of Locke's notes on Romans 13:1-5, on obeying "the powers that be," rings true. "If reason shows that some *de facto* ruler is *not* exercising legitimate authority," writes Waldron, "then Romans 13 gives the ruler no support. But if reason shows that a *de facto* ruler *is* expressing legitimate authority, then the fact that some of his subjects are Christians (while the ruler perhaps is not) does not detract from his authority" (197). Waldron's paraphrase of Locke's notes on I Corinthians 7:20-23, about slaves obeying their masters, proves telling. "*If* slavery is legitimate," writes Waldron, "then Christians may be slaves; and then they should obey their masters on account of its legitimacy, not on account of Christian quietism. But if slavery is illegitimate, then Christians, like everyone else, may not be slaves and need not and probably should not obey their *de facto* masters" (198). Although Locke's monetary investment in "plantation enterprises" suggests that people often fail to put their money where their mouths are, and although Waldron risks sounding feebly apologetic for Christianity's acquiescence in black slavery, Waldron reminds his readers that

> the symbolic politics familiar to us—the politics of disinvestment, conscientious refusal, and righteous dissociation—are not unproblematically available as an ahistorical matrix on which we can infer what Locke must have thought from the company he kept and the investments he made. (205)

Locke, in Waldron's estimation, slips "some distinctly Lockean ideas" into *The Fundamental Constitutions of Carolina* (1669)—for instance, freedom of worship for the slave population there (205). The *First Treatise* thunders "No!" to slavery, as though the peculiar institution were the last abuse on earth ever likely to win the approval of the Magna Carta's heirs, of whatever class: "Slavery," proclaims Locke, "is so vile and miserable an Estate of Man, and so distinctly opposite to the generous Temper and Courage of our Nation; that 'tis hardly to be conceived, that an *Englishman*, much less a Gentleman, should plead for't" (as quoted in Waldron, 199).

Waldron contests, at the outset of his book and as a persistent motif, Lorenne Clark's verdict that Locke's theory displays "unequivocally sexist assumptions" (23). As Waldron sums up Locke's view, "If we have sinned, that is true of Eve [and of Adam] only [and not necessarily of all other women and men]. If Eve was subordinated to her husband by her greater transgression, that is true of Eve only [and not necessarily of all other wives] " (27). For more than six pages in the *First Treatise*, after all, Locke elaborates on the fifth commandment's inclusion of mothers. For instance:

> For no body can deny but that the Woman hath an equal share, if not greater, as nourishing a Child a long time in her own Body out of her own Substance. There it is fashion'd, and from her it receives the Materials and Principles of its Constitution. And it is so hard to imagine the rational Soul should presently Inhabit the yet unformed Embrio, as soon as the Father has done his part in the Act of Generation, that if it must be supposed to derive anything from the Parents, it must certainly owe most to the Mother. (As quoted in Waldron, 39)

Waldron's ear for Locke's "logic of contractarianism" hears Locke acknowledging women's parental authority, their property, and even their marital partnership (123). Thus Waldron makes good use of Melissa Butler's pioneering essay, "Early Liberal Roots of Feminism: John Locke and the Attack on Patriarchy" (1978). His perspective on Locke's close reading of biblical passages, moreover, brings to mind the feminist hermeneutics of Bible scholars Phyllis Trible and Mieke Bal. As Waldron points out, Locke praised a 1696 sermon by Rebecca Collier and observed that "women had the honour first to publish the resurrection of the Lord of Love" (41-42).

"The scriptural character of Locke's writing," Waldron admits, "might suggest that he is doing something different from philosophical argumentation" (191). "In fact," however, "Locke is trying to give the world a lesson in the difference between arguing from scriptural revelation and simply assembling [as Filmer does] various verses and catch-phrases in an opportunistic tract" (191). Thus Waldron, like Locke, gives "serious consideration" to the possibility that "basic equality *must* be grounded in a religious conception" (14). Against Rawls's conclusion that "citizens may not appeal to their religious convictions in voting or in arguing for particular political positions" (237), Waldron juxtaposes the Lockean view that "a commitment to human equality is most coherent and attractive when it is grounded in theological truth" (236). Dunne writes that one "cannot conceive of constructing an analysis of any issue in contemporary political theory around the affirmation or negation of anything which Locke says about political matters" (as quoted in Waldron, 241). By contrast, in what seems (from the perspective of 2005 America) a stunning understatement, Waldron concludes that "we should not be too quick to congratulate ourselves on having left the religious issues behind us" (241). For his part, Waldron finds it no "offense against historical propriety" to bring Locke's "reflections about religion and the basis of political morality" to bear on the present (241).

Waldron's book, his fifth, reflects most of the strengths, and some of the weaknesses, of a law professor's strategy. As for flaws, he is constantly announcing what he will do, as opposed simply to doing it: "I am going to take up," "I shall postpone," "I will talk," etc. (21; see also 48, 49, 84, 86, 101, 116, 118, 141, 180, 224, and *passim*). What Waldron himself calls a "long and complicated" discussion of real *versus* nominal essences, moreover, glazes the eyes, for even Locke calls this distinction "pudder" (55-57, 67). With all due respect for Waldron's fondness for algebraic symbols, finally, this gambit does not work for him, for it bounces off the frontal lobes of most laypersons, as in:

> There is a difference between saying that the truth of a descriptive statement (a has property D) implies a prescription (a ought to be treated in manner D), and saying that P supervenes upon D. Supervenience implies that if a is to be treated differently from b, then there must be some other difference between a and b on which that prescriptive difference supervenes. (And so on; see 68-69; see also 156-58)

But on the other hand, jargon such as "anti-speciesist," "contractarianism," "physicalist," and "interpretive heuristic" (for "thesis"?) proves relatively rare (63, 123, 129, 152). And one welcomes Waldron's frequent candor: "I have no tidy resolution to offer" (40; see also 115, 143, 158, and *passim*). Thus, if Waldron loses sight, on occasion, of his religious theme ("This, at last," he remarks after a long, religion-free discussion of "corporeal rationality," "is where the religious argument comes in" [78]), one can only admire, on the whole, his skillful, latter-day emulation of Locke's own lawyerly strategy—namely, "resisting each step in his opponent's argument, by showing successively that even if the previous step is conceded, the next step does not follow, and so on" (178).

Waldron's Locke, then, emerges clearly enough from the unforced force of Waldron's better argument, and stands with the Christian Locke of John Yolton and W. M. Spellman. Locke's exclusion of atheists from public life, it is true, constitutes his least admirable position. Nonetheless, this very stance makes Waldron's point, offering yet another proof, if proof were needed, of Locke's continuing influence. No atheist, for better or worse, could ever be elected President of the United States. Waldron's emphasis, however, lies on the "equality-radical" of Locke's "Christian Foundations," as opposed to Christianity's exclusionary strain.

The payoff of *God, Locke, and Equality*, for the present age of faith-based politics, resides in realizing that the phrase *liberal Christianity* need prove no mere oxymoron. If Locke's "equality-radical" Christianity strengthened the Late-Enlightenment-to-Early-Romantic fight against the slave trade, led by liberal-evangelical William Wilberforce, then Locke's concern for the rights of the poor resurfaces, too, among such now-ascendant, moderate-to-liberal evangelicals as Barry Hankins, Ron Sider, Rich Cizik, Darren Cushman Wood, and Jim Wallis. These, unlike Jerry Falwell, Pat Robertson, James Dobson, Ralph Reed, and Richard Land (notice the strange absence of women from such lists), are moving away from preoccupation with sexual sin, and toward concern for practical charity, environmentalism ("creation care"), terrorism, the Gaza Strip, HIV/AIDS, the IMF, and the World Bank.

Waldron's Locke, for example, epitomizes the intellectual ancestry of Hankins's moderate-Baptist exploration of the conservative-Baptists' fudging of their liberal-Baptist roots—namely, *Uneasy in Babylon: Southern Baptist Conservatives and American Culture* (2002). In effect, moreover, Waldron's Locke haunts Sider's "old"-evangelical indictment of "new"-evangelical hypocrisy in *The Scandal of the Evangelical Conscience* (2004). This Locke, likewise, informs Cizik's already-influential pamphlet, "For the Health of the Nation: An Evangelical Call to Civic Responsibility" (2004). This Locke, furthermore, underlies Wood's Methodism-saturated reaffirmation of basic human equality—namely, *Blue Collar Jesus: How Christianity Supports Workers' Rights* (2004). Waldron's Locke, finally, hovers near Wallis's progressive journal, *Sojourners*, and his runaway bestseller, *God's Politics: Why the Right Got It Wrong and the Left Doesn't Get It* (2005). Thus, if this Locke lays down the "radical-equality" principle of liberal evangelicalism, from neoclassical to postmodern times, then Waldron's Locke clearly resonates in ways that

Locke, despite widespread recognition of his enormous influence, has seldom resonated before.

Consider briefly, in this regard, the eighteenth and nineteenth centuries. The Lockean assumption of John Wesley's thought leads not only to Wesley's quasi-epistemological doctrine of the "spiritual sense" but also to the egalitarian basis of his respect for the poor and of his practice of charity. His encouragement of women preachers harks back to Locke's praise for Rebecca Collier, as well as to biblical standards of fairness. Locke's conviction that "poor, ignorant, illiterate men" *(The Reasonableness of Christianity*, as quoted in Waldron, 192) "could be relied on simply to report what they were told" about Jesus (Waldron's words, 192) resounds in Ralph Waldo Emerson's aesthetic that "every man should be so much an artist, that he could report in conversation what had befallen him" ("The Poet" [1841]). Locke's "college made up, for the most part, of ignorant, but inspired fishermen" *(The Reasonableness*, as quoted in Waldron, 100) sets the Christian standard of Emily Dickinson's satire, which judges both "freckled Human Nature" and "A Fisherman's—Degree—" as morally and intellectually superior to the "Brittle Lady" of Victorian-American high society (Poem 675 [1863]). Locke's premonition that "the taking away of God, tho' but even in thought, dissolves all" *(A Letter Concerning Toleration*, as quoted in Waldron, 228) comes true not just in Fyodor Dostoevsky's well-known apprehension that without God, all is permitted. It bears, as well, on Dickinson's horrified realization that "The abdication of Belief / Makes the Behavior small—" (Poem 1581 [1882]), and perhaps even on her resigned conclusion—namely, "Better an ignis fatuus / Than no illume at all" (Poem 1581).

One question one would raise with Waldron, I think, is whether Locke uses Christianity to support his political views—or, rather, lets Christianity appear when it does not contradict his views. He does insist on his Christianity, but he also came under attack from his contemporaries, who found him *un*-Christian. Somehow, with or without Locke, the world of the eighteenth century became increasingly secular. If Locke did not contribute to this trend, is the line direct from Thomas Hobbes to David Hume and the French Revolution? Were the *philosophes* mistaken in reading Locke as framer of the non-Christian state? Is their *égalité* just a Christian notion also? If Christianity takes the credit for liberty, freedom, equality, etc., should it not take credit as well for ushering in modern secularism in general, and if it should, then does this possibility complicate the notion of "secular" as a process of thought emerging, but not separated, from Christianity?

In sum, Waldron's Locke reverberates far beyond the boundaries of this book. *God, Locke, and Equality*, regardless of how one might answer the questions just posed, teaches that the connection between, say, Locke and Wesley proves even more important, though somewhat less surprising, than it had seemed before. If the Christian as well as empirical Locke, and the empirical as well as Christian Wesley, inspire the natural-to-spiritual autobiography that, as I have argued for more than thirty years (please hear my full disclosure), forms a strain of Anglo-American Romanticism, then so be it. In any case, Waldron's Locke makes it henceforth imprudent for scholars to rest content with the secularized Locke of much nineteenth-to-twentieth-century Lockean study. Waldron's Locke provides just the impetus for full reconsideration of the links between Anglo-American sensibility in general and Lockean sense in particular, even if such religious and political reassessment renders Locke unfit, constitutionally, to be taught in the public schools of the United States. As a result, in my view, Locke will emerge as more praiseworthy than ever for having developed the most reliably democratic values that English-language culture has ever offered the world. Even now, readers of *Christianity and Literature* can learn from Waldron to think of Locke's trinity of religion, politics, and philosophy as central to his legacy, as well as of Locke's compound of religion and politics as foundational to his philosophy.

WORKS CITED

Bal, Mieke. *Death and Dissymetry: The Politics of Coherence in the Book of Judges*. Chicago: U of Chicago P, 1988.

Bloom, Harold. *Where Shall Wisdom Be Found?* New York: Penguin, 2004.

Buchanan, Allen. "Justice and Charity." *Ethics* 97 (1987): 558-75.

Butler, Melissa. "Early Liberal Roots of Feminism: John Locke and the Attack on Patriarchy." *American Political Science Review* 72 (1978): 135-50.

Clark, Lorenne M. G. "Women and Locke: Who Owns the Apples in the Garden of Eden?" *The Sexism of Social and Political Theory: Women and Reproduction from Plato to Nietzsche*. Eds. L. M. G. Clark and L. Lange. Toronto: U of Toronto P, 1979. 16-40.

Dunne, John. *The Political Thought of John Locke: An Historical Account of the Argument of the Two Treatises of Government*. Cambridge: Cambridge UP, 1969.

Dworkin, Ronald. *Sovereign Virtue: The Theory and Practice of Equality*. Cambridge: Harvard UP, 2000.

Hankins, Barry. *Uneasy in Babylon: Southern Baptist Conservatives and American Culture.* Tuscaloosa: U of Alabama P, 2002.

Laslett, Peter. Introduction. *Two Treatises of Government.* By John Locke. Ed. Peter Laslett. Cambridge: Cambridge UP, 1988. 3-126.

Lovejoy, A. O. *The Great Chain of Being.* Cambridge: Harvard UP, 1974.

Macintyre, Alasdair. *Whose Justice? Which Rationality?* Notre Dame: U of Notre Dame P, 1988.

Macpherson, C. B. *The Political Theory of Possessive Individualism: Hobbes to Locke.* Oxford: Oxford UP, 1962.

Rawls, John. *Political Liberalism.* New York: Columbia UP, 1993.

Sen, Amartya. *Collective Choice and Social Welfare.* Amsterdam: Elsevier, 1969.

Sider, Ronald J. *The Scandal of the Evangelical Conscience: Why Are Christians Living Just Like the Rest of the World?* New York: Baker, 2004.

Spellman, W. M. *John Locke and the Problem of Depravity.* Oxford: Clarendon, 1988.

Trible, Phyllis. *God and the Rhetoric of Sexuality.* Philadelphia: Fortress, 1988.

Wallis, Jim. *God's Politics: Why the Right Gets It Wrong and the Left Doesn't Get It.* San Francisco: HarperCollins, 2005.

Williams, Bernard. *Problems of the Self: Philosophical Papers 1956-1972.* Cambridge: Cambridge UP, 1973.

Wood, Darren Cushman. *Blue Collar Jesus: How Christianity Supports Workers' Rights.* Santa Ana, Calif.: Seven Locks, 2005.

Yolton, John W. *Two Intellectual Worlds of John Locke: Man, Person, and Spirits in the "Essay".* Ithaca: Cornell UP, 2004.

23. *The Evangelist of Desire: John Wesley and the Methodists,* by Henry Abelove

Stanford: Stanford University Press, 1990. Pp. 136. $25.

In 1977, following two years of negotiations between the University of Manchester and the Methodist Conference, the Collection of the Methodist Archives and Research Centre moved from the modest facilities at Epworth House, London, to the John Rylands University Library of Manchester. Cataloguing of material relating to Wesley and others is making autograph letters, diaries, journals, minutes, pamphlets, periodicals, hymnbooks, class tickets, circuit plans, and brochures fully accessible. As a result of mining the Rylands Collection's 26,000 printed works and 600 shelving feet of manuscripts, Henry Abelove considers such important but hitherto neglected items as the journals and memoirs of James Chubb, Richard Treffrey, and Richard Burdsall. The bibliography alone is worth the price of Abelove's *The Evangelist of Desire: John Wesley and the Methodists.*

The jacket blurb reads as follows: "This study goes beyond the usual modes of explanation in religious and intellectual history (which have traditionally relied on the abstract appeal of ideas . . .) to open up a space for the body, for the play of desire, and for erotic forces." Since my own explanation of Wesley's appeal relies on the "usual modes" of "religious and intellectual history," Abelove calls my work "a different view" (p. 95). If I "came to scoff," however, I "remained to pray," for *The Evangelist of Desire* does not disappoint an expectation of fresh, as well as deeply founded, insights into Wesley's influence.

John Donne's lines—". . . for I / Except you enthrall me, never shall be free, / Nor ever chast, except you ravish mee."—serve as the epigraph for Abelove's argument that Wesley's influence is based upon a combination of deference to, and love for, the evangelist himself. "If Wesley was successful in attracting to himself a long-staying following," contends Abelove, it was not because he was a good organizer and not because he offered a particularly appealing set of doctrines, but because he was "both seductive and monopolistic" (pp. xi-xii).

Abelove's Wesley, first, was a "gentleman" whose followers were "plebeians." His gown, cassock, bands, silk, gold, silver, hair, servants, London house, country touring, retinue, horses, carriage, and riches were all "the appurtenances of gentility" (p. 10). It was a "genteel function," too, for him to give away money and to "doctor people without charge" (pp. 8-9). Thus Abelove's method smacks of Foucault's. It offers the new-historicist, if not neo-Marxist, slant on relationships of class and power within the Methodist Movement.

Abelove's method makes use, too, of Lacan and Freud. Abelove understands Wesley as a "therapist" who "seduces" his followers. Wesley's absence of systematic theology, for Abelove, is Wesley's means of becoming "all things to all men"—and women. According to the dynamics of transference, all therapists get the response of love from their patients, and since Wesley's people loved him for the proto-"shock therapy" that he administered to them through his electrical apparatuses, he was no exception. Just as members of groups might put "one and the same object in place of their ego ideal" and then identify themselves "with one another in their ego" (Freud, as quoted by Abelove, p. 45), so, according to Abelove, the Methodists felt themselves to be united with Wesley and then felt a strong sense of union with one another. Whereas Jonathan Edwards never took his eyes off the bell-rope above his pulpit, Wesley, in Abelove's view, maintained eye contact with his followers for the purpose of "seducing" them.

Some of his helpers really did seduce women. Such incidents led to the jokes in Tobias Smollett's *Humphrey Clinker*. But Wesley married Mary Vazeille to stop the gossip about him. She was jealous of him, "opened his mail, spied on him, forbade him to meet his women followers in private, beat him, and eventually, after seven years of marriage, left him" (p. 37). Actually, as Abelove recognizes, the monogamous Wesley engendered the love of his followers because of his financial charity and his offering up of universal Arminian salvation.

George Orwell points out the difficulty of seeing what is in front of our eyes, and this may be Abelove's shortcoming. He gives too little credit to Wesley's religion. Some of his conclusions—for example, "[Wesley] eclipsed his colleagues and even God Almighty in the hearts of his followers" (p. 40) or "The Methodists organized themselves entirely on their own initiative" (p. 48)—seem overdrawn. Surely, Wesley meant for his people to love God, and not just John Wesley. As even Abelove admits, Wesley's last request was for his sermon on "the love of God" to be generally distributed.

"A sense that the individual man was infinitely valuable, merely from the fact of his humanity," writes T. Walter Herbert in *John Wesley as Editor and Author* (1940), "was an integral and dominating part of the religious conviction which furnished the driving force of [Wesley's] whole life." Abelove does not succeed in revising such a standard view. Moreover, he does not adequately explain how Wesley's desire for deference squares with his lifelong willingness to endure scoffers' threats of violence. He skims over the fact that Wesley rendered himself "déclassé" by his willingness to marry his servant Grace Murray. (Wesley was dissuaded from doing so only by the strong insistence of his brother, Charles, and others.) He argues that Wesley's revival was "uniquely continuous" (p. 43), but the Second Great Awakening in America "continued" Edwards's Great Awakening. Charitable practices were not widespread among the aristocracy until the nineteenth century (and then largely because of Wesley), yet Abelove implies that Wesley took his cue to practice charity from the gentry, not the Bible.

The method of *The Evangelist of Desire* is by no means entirely self-consistent. Arguing, for example, that Edwards's revival was "finished by 1742, or 1744 at the latest" (p. 42), Abelove overlooks what one might expect him to admire, namely, Edwards's later mission to the Housatonics. Abelove's inaccurate remark that when Wesley was eighty-one, he was "too old obviously to know what exactly was going on" (p. 103), leaps off the page. Wesley's sermons and active life show that until he died at age eighty-eight, he "obviously" knew "exactly" what was going on. Abelove's repeated use of the word *plebeian* (pp. xii, 6, 23, 24, 33, etc.) grows irritating. Since it comes from E. P. Thompson's distinction between "Patrician Society" and "Plebeian Culture," Abelove's diction, if not his method, seems all too derivatively Marxist. Any reader from either plebeian or patrician stock begins to feel stereotyped.

Most importantly, Wesley's enduring sway has a great deal to do with his intellectual influence. He was concerned not so much with psychological dominance, e.g., "seducing" or "monopolizing" women, as with educating everyone. Ready to establish with all women the Freud-fraught but still intellectual relationships he enjoyed with his mother Susanna and his first romantic attachment, Mary Granville Pendarves, he was one man who took the intellects of women seriously. Had Abelove given more play to the "abstract appeal of ideas," he would have heightened the dramatic urgency of his argument. He emphasizes that the Methodists resisted their master's prohibitions against tea, snuff, dirt, and play, but Abelove might better remember how the Methodists followed Wesley in the larger matters of mind as well as heart. Wesley's intellectual as well as emotional influence was more positive than negative, and much more long lasting than even his long life.

In a barn filled with "Cotigers," Wesley asked rhetorically: "You will say, how can we know when we love God? I ask you, men, how do you know when you love your wives? Ye wives, how do you know when you love your husbands?" His non-rhetorical answer was, "I feel it" (p. 38). Abelove understands this account (from James Barritt's autobiography) according to the various idioms of bodily desire, but the diction of Wesley's question—*how* can we *know?*—contributes to, as well as derives from, eighteenth-century epistemological language.

Abelove's book, even if not uniformly well argued, is cumulatively persuasive. We can learn much by delving, as Abelove does, beneath the religious and intellectual approaches to Wesley and his Method. No "historian of sex," until Abelove, "has noticed just how extreme Wesley's position actually was" (p. 51). *Thoughts on Marriage and a Single Life* (1743) requires that every believer stay single and celibate, and although *Thoughts on a Single Life* (1765) reduces this requirement to a desideratum, even the later treatise emphasizes how a single person is "exempt from the numberless Occasions of Sorrow and Anxiety" with which parents "who have sickly or weak, or unhappy, or disobedient children" are "intangled" (p. 52). Accordingly, Wesley segregated congregations by sex and rejected Moravianism in part because of what Abelove calls its "pro-sex" attitudes (p. 54). Too, Wesley performed "very few" marriages; for him, an appealing fringe benefit of itinerancy was that he did not have to perform them (p. 56). Abelove even makes the intriguing case that Wesley inspired Shaker celibacy.

Methodists, then, "found sanction in what Wesley said for devaluing and even breaking the family ties that troubled them; for releasing same-sex sexual feeling; and possibly also for practicing abstinence, within marriage, at the wife's insistence, as a means of birth control" (p. 63). For women particularly, "Methodism presented a unique opportunity to modify the family obligations that they felt to be oppressive" (p. 64). Prayer meetings, class meetings, lovefeasts, and watchnight services provided escape from household drudgery. In fact, one of the most destructive anti-Methodist riots, at Wednesbury, Staffordshire, was sparked by a woman's "temporary disappearance" from home; she was found a week later, "at one of the [Methodist] Class-houses" (p. 64). We may now add "long-term conjugal abstinence at the wife's insistence" to such eighteenth-century means of family planning as coitus interruptus, coitus reservatus, abortion, infanticide, and child neglect (p. 70).

Abelove's new-historicist strategy of starting chapters in an unstructured way, with what he takes to be significant "tableaux" (p. 40), is an especially engaging aspect of his style. It may seem a distortion to focus on such works as Wesley's *Thoughts on the Sin of Onan* (1767), but these works are sufficiently characteristic, as well as inherently interesting, and they have hitherto been suppressed. At any rate, we now have a context for the odd beliefs of Wesley (and Samuel Tissot) that drinking milk helps to prevent masturbation and that the milk of the human female is "generally believed to be the most strengthening" kind (Wesley, as quoted in Abelove, p. 54).

Above all, Abelove brings us nuggets from the mother lode of primary material. We relish the accents of John Nelson, a Yorkshireman who describes the "blessed morning" when he first heard John Wesley preach: "Soon as he got upon the stand, he stroked back his hair, and turned his face towards where I stood, and I thought fixed his eyes upon me" (p. 25). Although this account supports Abelove's theory of seduction, both it and many other incidents surmount his theory, too. His method, in the main, is neither predictable nor unduly predetermined, for even if Abelove himself does not resist the seductively reductive framework of postmodernism, his procedure remains, paradoxically enough in these days, essentially label-free.

24. *Wesley and the Wesleyans: Religion in Eighteenth-Century Britain*, by John Kent

Cambridge: Cambridge Univ. Press, 2002. Pp. 229.

Over the course of a distinguished career, John Kent has addressed such ambitious topics as the development of theology since 1700, the relation between historiography in general and church history in particular, and the triangle of church, state, and society in Britain from 1880 through 1950. This Emeritus Professor of theology at the University of Bristol, England, remains the chief taxonomist, as well as the prime anatomist, of Victorian revivalism. He occupies a good position, therefore, from which to generate fresh perspective on Methodism. His fifth book does just that. His *Wesley and the Wesleyans*, indeed, constitutes a bombshell dropped on the ground of Wesleyan studies, which have tended to be hagiographical.

Kent, for example, will have none of the Elie Halévy thesis, stating that the evangelical revival "saved [the British people] from the tempting freedoms of the French Revolution" (p. 1). Kent, for his part, "starts from the assumption that the many drives which constantly go to produce religious behaviour would have operated in eighteenth-century England even if the 'revival' had not taken place" (pp. 48–49). He concludes, "There was no question of Methodism preventing revolution. Revolution was never possible" (p. 100). He countermands, thereby, Bernard Semmel's view, which, as Kent contends, "translated the Wesleyan-Arminian stress on theological freedom much too easily into a radical political doctrine" (p. 215; see Semmel, *The Methodist Revolution* [New York: Basic Books, 1973], pp. 70–79]).

Kent, moreover, will have none of a more recent argument—namely, that John Wesley became a "religious empiricist" (pp. 37, 218, and passim; see my *Locke, Wesley, and the Method of English Romanticism* [Gainesville: Univ. Press of Florida, 1984], and Frederick Dreyer, "Faith and Experience in the Thought of John Wesley," *American Historical Review*, 88 [1983], 12–30). "Hanoverian

Methodism," according to Kent, boasted "no equivalent" of such "Dissenting intellectuals" as Thomas Paine, Joseph Priestley, and Richard Price (p. 4). Thus Wesley, in Kent's view, stayed as far away from the Enlightenment as possible.

Kent, in the end, grants Wesley almost no historical importance. "Wesleyanism," for Kent, was such a "communal" creation that "too much attention can be paid to the Wesleys themselves"—that is, to John and his hymn-writing brother, Charles (p. 59). John comes across here as not only unenlightened but also self-regarding, egoistic, self-satisfied, dogmatic, uncritical, bigoted, and all but stupid—or, as Kent typically remarks, "Wesley's analysis missed the point of what was happening" (pp. 4, 25, 29–30, 42–43, 56, 65–66, 79). Wesley gets no credit, remarkably, for inspiring the widespread participation of women in his movement, or even for contributing to the reinvigoration of the Anglican Church.

The heart of Kent's argument—and his greatest contribution—lies in his emphasis on "the primary religious impulse," which, as he carefully defines it, tries "to seek some kind of extra-human power, either for personal protection, including the cure of diseases, or for the sake of ecstatic experience, and possibly prophetic guidance" (pp. 1–2). Thus communal Wesleyanism—beyond the awareness of the Wesleys—derived its significance from perennial religious behavior rather than from such Wesleyan doctrines as holiness and perfection. Religion, in this light, reduces personal anxieties, resolves practical problems, increases self-approval, and creates space for development; Kent, by corollary, understands the "so-called" evangelical revival as a psychological rather than theological phenomenon (pp. 1–2). In so doing, he owes more to Van A. Harvey's *Feuerbach and the Interpretation of Religion* (Cambridge: Cambridge Univ. Press, 1995) than to the writings of the Wesleys. "A subculture of tears and cries and of 'the powers of the world to come'; this, not abstract beliefs and doctrines," Kent insists, "reflects . . . Feuerbach's understanding of the power of the small community to *generate its own* religious images, rites, and music" (p. 51; emphasis added).

All of these insights seem fair enough, and they certainly prove intriguing. "Institutionalised theologies," Kent declares, "are imposed on the primary level of religion," but "the primary level, with its basic belief in intrusive supernatural power, survives at all times" (p. 7). "Thus both George Whitefield—a Calvinist, and therefore technically with no use for human free will—and the Wesleys—Arminian, and therefore anxious to preserve a meaning for free will, however abstruse and qualified—took it for granted that what mattered in the activities in which they were taking part was the speculative theology they used to understand and control events" (p. 7). But they were wrong, Kent asserts, because "They did not suspect that what counted much more than doctrine was the freedom which primary religious aspirations found for at least two generations in the social frameworks which the various Methodist leaders devised" (p. 7).

Wesley and the Wesleyans highlights important, yet neglected, primary material. Chapter 5 ("Anglican Responses"), for example, draws on Thomas Hobbes, Edmund Gibson, Richard Graves, Henry Fielding, Thomas Secker, John Berridge, William Warburton, Conyers Middleton, Thomas Turner, Alice Miller, William Wilberforce, and Hannah More to argue that—far from renewing Anglicanism—Methodism frightened Anglicans with the specter of political intolerance (pp. 140–86). Archbishop Secker assumed that the Methodist emphasis on holiness and perfection—that is, on faith without works—would return England to seventeenth-century religious radicalism (p. 167). One thinks, however, of Wesley's most famous quotation, emblazoned on my favorite coffee mug: "Do all the good you can, by all the means you can, in all the ways you can, in all the places you can, at all the times you can, as long as ever you can." No one accomplished more works of practical charity than did John Wesley, and Kent's censure of him for caring more about a beggar-girl's soul than about the ragged state of her clothing seems— in the context of Wesley's career as a whole—quite unfair (pp. 184–85).

Wesley and the Wesleyans, unfortunately, treats scholars with cavalier haste. Dreyer's argument, for example, deserves a point-by-point refutation, yet it receives only a passing mention. Leonard I. Sweet's evocation of the philosophical background to Methodism, like Nathan O. Hatch's brief for the Arminian flavor of Anglo-American democracy, makes no appearance in Kent's skimpy bibliography. The reader of *Wesley and the Wesleyans* should supplement it by examining such proponents of Wesley's intellectual and social significance as Henry Abelove, Dee E. Andrews, Richard Heitzenrater, David Hempton, H. D. Rack, Martin Schmidt, and Michael Watts.

The present reviewer, after years of studying the cultural osmosis between Wesley and literary history, scarcely shares Kent's impatience with Wesley's speculative theology. I remain impressed by Wesley's empirical idiom as found in his "On the Discoveries of Faith" (1788)—

> For many ages, it has been allowed by sensible men, Nihil est in intellectu quod non fuit prius in sensu. That is, "There is

nothing in the understanding which was not first perceived by some of the senses." . . . This point has now been thoroughly discussed by men of the most eminent sense and learning, and it is agreed by all impartial persons, that although some things are so plain and obvious, that we can hardly avoid knowing them as soon as we come to the use of our understanding; yet the knowledge even of those is not innate, but derived from some of our senses. (*The Works of the Rev. John Wesley, A. M.*, ed. Thomas Jackson, 14 vols. [London: Wesleyan-Methodist Book-Room, n.d.), VII, 231)

—and in his "Human Life a Dream" (1761):

> How advisable, by every possible means, to connect the ideas of time and eternity! so to associate them together, that the thought of one may never recur to your mind, without the thought of the other! It is our highest wisdom to associate the ideas of the visible and invisible world; to connect temporal and spiritual, mortal and immortal being. (*Works*, VII, 324)

Such topics as astronomy, Berkeley, causation, education, Edwards, experience, experiments, geology, Higher Criticism, Hume, Locke, medical science, natural religion, Newton, philosophical theology, skepticism, and the spiritual sense pervade Wesley's widely disseminated, astonishingly prolific works, and help to contextualize such literature as the poetry of Emily Dickinson (see my *Experience and Faith: The Late-Romantic Imagination of Emily Dickinson* [New York: Palgrave Macmillan, 2004], pp. 17–18, 31–36, 42, 46–48, 57, 60–64, 68, 74, 117–18, 123–35, 159, 166–68, 193, 200). The bridge between Wesley the unwitting facilitator of primary religion and Wesley the religious empiricist spans, in effect, the exciting argument of Emily Walker Head, who, with more scope than I have attempted, places Wesley within, and at the forefront of, the empirical/evangelical dialectic of Romantic Anglo-America (see Head, "Flutters, Feeling, and Fancies: John Wesley's Sentimental Sermons and the Spirit of the Age," *Christianity and Literature*, 53 [2004], 141–62; see also Candy Gunther Brown, *The Word in the World: Evangelical Writing, Publishing, and Reading in America, 1789–1880* [Chapel Hill: Univ. of North Carolina Press, 2004]).

I wish that *Wesley and the Wesleyans* had been available for my investigation, over the years, of Locke, Wesley, and Edwards as precursors to Blake,

Wordsworth, Coleridge, Shelley, Keats, Carlyle, Tennyson, Emerson, and Dickinson. Students of Anglo-American culture must henceforth take Kent's revisionist argument into account. His perspective, besides offering a refreshing view of the terrain, charts territory. Besides necessitating strategic refinements in Wesleyan studies, it should occasion some partial palinodes. To end on the positive note with which I began, *Wesley and the Wesleyans* will accompany my ongoing efforts to assess the quality of Wesley's influence, and students of the eighteenth century in general will want to include it on their short list of required reading.

25. *Jonathan Edwards's Writings: Text, Context, Interpretation,* edited by Stephen J. Stein

Bloomington: Indiana University Press, 1996. xix+ 219 pp. $39.95 cloth.

These twelve essays, indirectly testifying to the continuing presence of Jonathan Edwards's theology even at the turn of millennium three, reconfirm the fundamental relationship between his thought and practice, on the one hand, and eighteenth- and nineteenth-century Anglo-American church history, on the other. Indeed, *Jonathan Edwards's Writings* goes so far as to indicate Edwards's precise centrality to Anglo-American sensibility in general.

The first four essays, written by four generations of scholars, establish the importance of Edwards's unpublished manuscripts. Ava Chamberlain, demonstrating that Edwards "had both a pastoral and a speculative purpose in choosing to write his first sermon series on the parable of the wise and foolish virgins," concludes that even before the Great Awakening, he had developed "the views that would establish his position as a moderate New Light in the upcoming years" (4-5). Christopher Grasso, focusing on manuscript sermons written "during and after the communion controversy," asks "what Edwards perpetuated and what he discarded in the image of New England as 'God's New Israel'" (21). Grasso answers that Edwards "emphasized the experience of the people's religious revival rather than the legal fact of their covenantal status" (29). Gerald R. McDermott shows that although Edwards was usually willing to learn from non-Christian traditions, his "denunciations of Muhammad's tribe were unusually vitriolic because he considered Islam to be a foil for one of Reformed Christianity's most dangerous enemies: deism" (39). Kenneth P. Minkema, focusing on the "precise scriptural exegesis" of Edwards's 500-page manuscript, "the harmony of the old and new Testament in three Parts," argues that although Edwards "emulated Locke's methodology," he "was intent on demonstrating that revealed religion was not merely a 'republication' of natural religion" (52-53, 55).

The middle essays develop historical perspectives on Edwards's published works. Paul R. Lucas, observing that "[Solomon] Stoddard's legacy, as much as Edwards's, anticipates and helps explain the religious revivalism of the nineteenth century," demonstrates that Stoddard, Edwards's grandfather, embraced "the Christian imperialism and nationalism" of seventeenth-century English lawyer and activist William Prynne and of seventeenth-century Scottish Presbyterians John Knox and Samuel Rutherford (69-70). Lucas argues that Stoddard influenced Edwards to project "the evangelical 'church militant'" through such works as *The Life of the Rev. David Brainerd* as well as through his "missionary work among the Indians" (79). William K. B. Stoever, exploring "continuities" between seventeenth-century New England antinomian controversialist Thomas Shepard and Edwards "respecting evidence of a godly estate," contextualizes the viewpoint of Edwards's *Charity and Its Fruits*—namely, that "true converts" are few (85, 96). Richard A. S. Hall, arguing for "continuities of thought between Edwards's *Nature of True Virtue* and Berkeley's *Alciphron* with respect to their common critique of the moral sense theory," concludes that "both men agreed" that virtue was not so much an "accident of taste" as part of "the very purpose and nature of the universe (100-101). Wayne Proudfoot, believing that Edwards's *Religious Affections* is" "a more sophisticated" treatise than William James's *Varieties of Religious Experience*, devalues perception and intuition and contends that Edwards's "practice of moral appraisal" derives, instead, from "complex and reflexive self-consciousness" (123).

Jonathan Edwards's Writings, finally, reassesses Edwards's impact on the nineteenth century. Douglas A. Sweeney, focusing on Nathaniel W. Taylor, the Dwight Professor of Didactic Theology at Yale University from 1822 to 1858, argues that Taylor was "neither an Arminian nor an Old Calvinist" but a neo-Edwardsian (139-40). Sweeney concludes that Taylor made Edwards's "distinction between moral and natural ability," his insistence that we are not sinful before we actually sin, a ruling paradigm of American religious experience (147-48). Allen C. Guelzo, too, argues for the influence of Edwards's *Freedom of the Will*. Guelzo maintains that despite the experiential dimension of transatlantic revivalism, the expectation of perfection among such Oberlin revivalists as Charles G. Finney derives less from the "privatized and sentimental" leanings of "Wesleyan holiness" than from the "visible and public" character of Edwardsian "natural ability": "Human liberty," wrote Finney, "does not consist in a self-determining power in the will," but exclusively in "the power which a moral agent possesses, of choosing in any direction, in view of motives" (160-61, 163, 170). Genevieve McCoy, investigating how far Edwards's influence "urged Christian women to be both actors and acted upon," observes that "in their dependent and subordinate position," women "could more easily than men accept . . . a perplexing theology and wield its contingent power" (179-80). Joseph Conforti, arguing that the mid-century's "most prolific interpreter of Edwardsian theological tradition" was Andover Seminary's Edwards A. Park, concludes that Park not only sought to reconcile "divine sovereignty and human accountability" but also reflected both Edwards's emphasis on inherently sinful "taste" or "relish" on the one hand and his even greater emphasis on "exercises of the heart" or "sensible exercises of the will" on the other (193-94, 197).

The discipline of church history, then, reemerges as foundational to Anglo-American studies. Lucas and McCoy, after all, go so far as to locate Edwards's thought and practice in the political, psychological, and sociological history of Anglo-America. Minkema, Hall, Proudfoot, and Guelzo place his theology in Anglo-American intellectual history. Guelzo's essay, incidentally paralleling my recent efforts to relate the Lockean theologies of John Wesley and of Edwards to the broadly experiential vision of Anglo-American Romanticism, specifically recognizes Wesley and Edwards as twin pioneers of the recondite, yet resonant, inter-discipline of Anglo-American philosophical theology. Be that as it may, however, *Jonathan Edwards's Writings* leads us all to "fresh woods, and pastures new." Indeed, this more than welcome florilegium of essays precisely constitutes the more than merely heuristic prolegomenon to all future Edwardsian inquiry.

Reviews, Second Series: Books on British Romanticism

26. *The Obstinate Questionings of English Romanticism*, by L. J. Swingle

Baton Rouge and London: Louisiana State Univ. Press, 1987. 211 pp. $28.00

In English Romanticism, the "obstinate questionings / Of sense and outward things" ("Intimations of Immortality," lines 142-43) are not so much "something to be dispelled," in L. J. Swingle's view, as "the warmth of life itself" (5). Against the complacent view of Jerome J. McGann and others that "doctrinal structures" of the Romantics are "well known" ("Informed persons," insists McGann, "do generally agree on what is comprised under the terms Romantic and Romantic Movement"), Swingle argues that Romantic writers "assert and undercut assertion in the same breath" (8). He understands this phenomenon not according to Deconstruction, but historically: "Reasonable analysis of Romantic questioning is probably better served by employing a more familiar historical approach that pays attention to such contemporaries of the phenomenon as Thomas Paine and William Godwin, and that seeks a style of analysis that would be amenable to Samuel Johnson's common reader" (10). Swingle's book, by showing how the English philosophy of radical skepticism informs English Romantic writing, makes a lasting contribution at once to studies in Romanticism and to philosophical studies.

Chapter 1, "The Romantic Situation: The Ground of Romantic Questioning," does not identify Romanticism with either a list of attributes ("revolutionary fervor," "love of nature," "celebration of imagination") or a problem to be solved ("order out of chaos," "subtler language" out of "cosmic syntax"), but rather with "the propensity to see . . . polarities as differing so fundamentally at the axiomatic level that each becomes not merely a viable system unto itself but also a nearly unsolvable mystery to systems beyond itself" (39). "The specter of enthrallment to single-minded perception," Swingle continues, "haunts Romantic literary art" (49), and he adds that "The literary artifact is designed to move the reader, in company with the artist, toward a free mental space beyond or between enthrallments through simultaneous invocations of competing enthrallments" (52).

"Can you make fast, / After due search," asks Byron in *Don Juan* (Canto 14, lines 7-8), "your faith to any question?" The implied answer, according to Swingle (18-19), is "No." Keats's famous letter on "Soul-making" proposes "a faint sketch of a system of Salvation," and Swingle diagnoses the hesitancy of "faint sketch" as "the recurring Romantic dis-ease about system" (19n.9). Pope's "One truth is clear, 'Whatever *Is*, is *Right*'" yields to such revolutionary formulas as "We hold these truths to be self-evident" (others, by implication, hold other truths): Romanticism, then, lines up systems in competition with one another (Swingle 24-25).

Between the inducements of We and They is a middle ground: hence "Wordsworth's early drama *The Borderers*, for example, and Walter Scott's Waverly novels, which reflect a preoccupation with life on the border" (Swingle 31). Swingle's skeptical ideal is perhaps best expressed by the positive tone of Mr. Flosky in Peacock's *Nightmare Abbey*: "[L]et society only give fair play at one and the same time . . . to my system of metaphysics, and Scythrop's system of politics, and Mr. Listless's system of manners, and Mr. Toobad's system of religion, and the result will be as fine a mental chaos as even the immortal Kant could ever have hoped to see; in the prospect of which I rejoice" (as quoted in Swingle 37).

Kant, though, is not the context that either Flosky or Swingle has in mind. The English context pointed to by Swingle is skepticism from Hume to Drummond, a tradition represented best, for Swingle's purposes, not by the William Godwin of the French-inspired *An Enquiry Concerning Political Justice* (1793), but by the fully-English Godwin of *The Enquirer* (1797).

"We proceed most safely," states *The Enquirer*, not when we lay down "one or two simple principles" and then develop them, but "when we enter upon each portion of our process, as it were, *de novo* . . . there is danger, if we are too exclusively anxious about consistency of system, that we may forget the perpetual attention we owe to experience, the pole-star of truth" (as quoted in Swingle 41). In English Romanticism, according to Swingle, there was no substitute for "incessant recurrence to experiment and actual observation" (the words are from *The Enquirer*). Just as *The Enquirer* attempts "only a short excursion at a time" and then "set[s] out afresh upon a new pursuit," so Wordsworth's *Excursion* does not "announce a system" (see his preface to the poem) but offers instead (again see the preface) "clear thoughts, lively images, and strong feelings" (as quoted in Swingle 42).

Some of the most important lines in *The Excursion*, from Swingle's point of view, amount to a verse version of Mr. Flosky's playfully skeptical prose-principle: the Wanderer announces,

> If tired with systems, each in its degree
> Substantial, and all crumbling in their turn,
> Let him build systems of his own, and smile
> At the fond work, demolished with a touch.
> (Book 4, lines 603-06; qtd. in Swingle 42)

This English attitude underlies Los's proclamation that "I must Create a System, or be enslav'd by another Mans" (*Jerusalem*, Plate 10): *Create* receives more emphasis than *System*. Blake's procedure for "freeing the mind," according to Swingle (53), is *that* one creates: Blake does not so much care *what* one creates.

Whereas Michael G. Cooke defines Romanticism as "acts of inclusion," i.e., strivings for "both/and" rather than "either/or" reasoning, Swingle (admirably consistent with himself) points out that Romantics do not necessarily exclude even "either/or": Shelley's "Lines Written Among the Euganean Hills" entertains the possibility of "a single ideology, a party program, a remote isle in 'the deep wide sea of Misery' that is indeed The Way" (35). Romantic skepticism, as Swingle also recognizes (35), includes doubt about skepticism itself: "We murder to dissect." "It has been popular," writes Swingle, "to propose that Romanticism invokes tests of experience as a means of resolving questions of truth and value" (44), but Swingle cites titles twenty years old, and his discussion might acquire additional drama, if not more urgency, in dialectic with my view respecting the subject/object subtleties of the English Romantics, namely, that their experiential epistemology opens questions of truth and value. I view English Romanticism against the twofold background of Methodism, i.e., experiential faith, and experience-philosophy, i.e., British empiricism. Although Locke was no stranger to skepticism (neither was Wesley, for that matter), Locke's methodology, like Wesley's, was relatively robust, and Locke's conspicuous absence from Swingle's group of English philosophers makes the group rather too unrepresentative. Swingle holds that the Romantics' view of experience was "problematic" (45), but their view was not problematic either to the extent or in the way that an age of Deconstruction would have experience to be.

The virtues of "The Romantic Situation: The Ground of Romantic Questioning" are also in "Romantic Poetic Strategy: The Means and Ends of Questioning" (chapter 2). Swingle's precisely stated sentence-guides to Romanticism, for example, recur, striking me, again, as perennially helpful: "Perhaps it is best to say that while the Romantics were cautiously supportive of many of our most traditional, fundamental human values, and while they were inclined to grant or at least explore sympathetically various clusters of provisional truths, nevertheless their minds generally continued to harbor an element of nagging uneasiness or suspicion . . . . Obstinate questionings of sense and outward things let spirit and inward things emerge . . . . It is only by touching the abyss that the soul comes to recognize its power" (72, 77). Test cases, as before, linger in the mind: "We are invited," writes Swingle, to stand with Childe Harold "in the middle" of the Bridge of Sighs "and to adopt a perspective that maintains its distance from the traps that lie at either end" (58); the Mariner's dropping "Below the lighthouse" amounts to Coleridge's investigation of "what ground, if any, [such] beacons rest upon" (61); and the principle that "the Romantics tend to arrive at an 'I' from which nothing further seems to follow of necessity" is starkly illustrated by John Clare's blunt *cogito*, "now I only know I am—that's all" (72).

In "Wordsworth's Silent Thought: The History of an Encounter with Romantic Questioning" (chapter 3), Swingle traces Wordsworth's development from the "gentle invitation" of the early poetry, through the "stern control" of the poetry immediately following the crisis of the mid-1790s, to the "dramatic voice" of the mature poetry, a voice "caught up in qualifying conditions of particular times, places, and circumstances" (88-89). The concluding image of Matthew in "The Two April Mornings," "his bough / Of wilding in his hand," is by no means obvious in its meaning, but as a qualifying condition of Matthew's time and place, it tempts the reader to construct interpretations (see the discussion in Swingle 93). In "Romantic Questioning and the Novelists of the Romantic Period" (chapter 4), Swingle focuses on Scott and Austen by bringing the poetry to bear on them, e.g., "As Keats uses the mind's encounter with the strange syntax of a Grecian urn to illumine the values of our distinctively human nature, so Austen uses the strangeness of one character to another in her novels to mark boundaries between parties or species of thought and values within humanity itself, revealing fundamental divisions in human nature" (158).

Swingle's conclusion, referring to as many as five works in two pages (e.g., 170-71), is perhaps a too-sweeping survey of Victorian literature, but this chapter, aptly entitled "From the Romantic Gleam to the Victorian Game," earns its place in the book. It aptly distinguishes, for example, between the

Romantic and the Victorian modes of skepticism: "To reach a free space between the claims of competing ideologies is not to discover the creative power of our distinguishing human nature; instead, it is to risk falling either into a state of almost metaphysical paralysis or into a state of perverse activity that seems antagonistic to humanistic impulses" (188). The abyss, for the Victorians, is a danger "hiding either nothing or Mr. Hyde," and they seek, accordingly, to "hold the monster in check" by (1) diverting the reader, (2) telling tales of wonder, and (3) "showing us possibilities . . . of game in experience" (193-95). "The beauty of a line from Tennyson," Swingle observes, is so far from "mindless" as to be "mind-transcending": any line of Tennyson's, as far as Swingle is concerned, is "the product of a writer who perceives the need to divert the mind with beauty" (194).

This welcome study, more than sixteen years in the making (three chapters have appeared earlier), is the fruit of deep consideration. Swingle's approach is the more effective for his low-key style, e.g., the throwaway wit in his remark (10n.8) that David Simpson "acknowledges the need to ground Romantic irony in a historical context, and regrets that he lacks space in his study [of *Irony and Authority in Romantic Poetry*] to address that issue." *The Obstinate Questionings of English Romanticism* does credit, finally, to the issuing press: refreshingly error-free, the text is handsomely produced.

27. *William Wordsworth and the Hermeneutics of Incarnation,* by David P. Haney

University Park: Pennsylvania State University Press, 1993.
ISBN 0-271-00911-X. Pp. xiii+ 269. $35.00.

David P. Haney explores Wordsworth's hope-against-hope, his implicit belief, that language embodies thought. Haney argues that "Wordsworth's incarnational poetics does not simply secularize a Christian concept in the service of a theory of representation, but rather pursues a critical, nonrepresentational, historically engaged, concrete hermeneutic of both thought and language" (2). Thus he scores against Frances Ferguson, who, while analyzing the "self-consuming rhetoric" of Romanticism, oversimplifies or simply dismisses "the theological, historical, and ethical side of Wordsworth's thought" (3).

Haney believes that Wordsworth's "hermeneutics of incarnation" resembles Augustine's, although "the intervention of British empiricism" orients Wordsworth "even more ... toward process, event, and materiality (rather than representation of presence)" (25). What Louis Marin calls "the complex and unitary space of the eucharistic model" dissolves the binary oppositions of representational logic into "a mysterious unity" (qtd. 15). As Haney puts it, "the celebration of the Eucharist is not simply a representation of Christ's action, but a repetition of that event, with an efficaciousness of its own, in which God is not represented but presented" (97-98). Or again, "Incarnation is not an ideal effacement of the difference between word and referent, but rather a process of spirit becoming event, a process by which (by analogy with Jesus entering the world) words move from the ideality of thought to become—for better and for worse—things and events in the world" (19). Thus Haney recognizes "the dark underside of the Christian incarnation." Although God became man and "the infinite entered the finite," Jesus died. Wordsworth's incarnational language involves "not only a living connection to the infinite but also the death of the infinite in the finite, of thought in language" (39).

Haney says Wordsworth "offers an alternative to semiotic representation" (31), whether of the Enlightenment variety (Locke's sign and idea) or of the more problematic modern/postmodern variety (Saussure's signifier and signified). Haney says that Wordsworth must move about "in a world that Kant has made unrealizable"; his incarnational rather than representational rhetoric, therefore, emphasizes "troth" rather than "truth" (67). Charles Taylor's emphasis on the importance of moral frameworks to our constructions of ontologies and epistemologies, Stanley Cavell's emphasis on "acknowledgment" of the object rather than "knowledge" of it, and Emmanuel Levinas's preference for "the realm of the ethical"—that is, "the conversation with the other that constitutes infinity"—over the "totality" of the theoretical enable Haney to pursue "the relation between the ethical and the epistemological in Wordsworth's incarnational thought" (36-37). Haney uses Cavell and Levinas to argue that Lucy's death is "unthinkable" not from a representational and epistemological standpoint but from an incarnational and ethical one (45). Focusing on Books 11 through 13 of *The Prelude*, Haney explores the incarnational model in Wordsworth's assertion of the absolute individual's dependence on inaccessible sources.

The most welcome contribution of Haney's book is his view of *The Excursion*. Declaring that the universe is "a shell" to "the ear of Faith," the Wanderer adds that "there are times, / I doubt not, when to you it doth impart / Authentic tidings of invisible things" (*The Excursion* 4.1142-44). These lines best support Haney's reading. Whereas "vision is not a transcendence," declares Levinas, hearing is (qtd. 153). Haney says "we choose what to look at," so that vision exerts "the tyranny of the subjective eye upon the separate objective world." Hearing, he adds, "chooses us," so that "we are taken up into a trans-subjective dialogue" (154). Whereas vision, then, is "highly representational," hearing is "the realm of living incarnational communication" (160). The Solitary, accordingly, "feels better not because of any concepts represented to him but because of the give-and-take of conversation itself":

> While question rose
> And answer flowed, the fetters of reserve
> Dropping from every mind, the Solitary
> Resumed the manners of his happier days.
>   (*The Excursion* 8.524-27)

Haney thinks that "the concept of instrumental reason inherited from Descartes and developed by Locke and others into a system of arbitrary tool-like signs has attempted to jettison its moral sources" (199). Such students of Locke as Richard Ashcroft, Frederick Dreyer, James Farr, and W. M. Spellman, however, argue that in the writings of Locke moral sources and instrumental reason coexist. What Haney sees as Locke's "separation of word and thing" (31) I see as Locke's sensationalist continuum joining thing, idea, and word. Where Haney concludes that "theories of knowledge should serve the ethical, not the other way around" (191), I agree. The ethical in Wordsworth, however, is not always independent of, or prior to, epistemological method. Wordsworth's adherence to the *tabula rasa* ("The Child is Father of the Man") means, among other things, that ethics, like all else, takes its rise and footing here—that is, from the very experience that ethics *a posteriori* transcends. "The mind's repose / On evidence," declares the Wanderer, "is not to be ensured / By act of naked reason," and "moral truth"

> Is no mechanic structure, built by rule;
> And which, once built, retains a steadfast shape
> And undisturbed proportions; but a thing
> Subject, you deem, to vital accidents;
> And, like the water-lily, lives and thrives,
> Whose root is fixed in stable earth, whose head
> Floats on the tossing waves.
> (*The Excursion* 5.560-69)

When Haney acknowledges interrelations, he is at his best: "The ethical is seen as united from the start with epistemological representation: the ethical is not an alternative to representation so much as it is the ground of representation" (186-87).

Although Haney recognizes the Wanderer's "iconoclastic Calvinist heritage" (174), he is silent about the Arminian idiom that also pervades Wordsworth's religious language: the very experiential idiom that he finds so appealing in the poetry harks back not only to Lockean empiricism but also to the Arminian doctrine of partial responsibility for one's own salvation. "Anglicanism," he declares, "is not to be blamed for any decrease in [Wordsworth's] poetic power," for "Anglicanism's middle ground between Catholicism and Evangelicalism can uniquely support rhetorical and even theological heterodoxy" (173). This is fair enough, but Haney might want to consider the pertinence of *Evangelical* Anglicanism. If, as I have argued elsewhere, John Wesley is the conduit from Locke to the Romantics, there is not as sharp a break between the Enlightenment and Romantic "hermeneutics of incarnation" as Haney thinks.

Haney's book, then, illuminates a wide range of data, from Wordsworth's call for words to be of importance "not only as symbols of the passion, but as things, active and efficient, which are of themselves part of the passion" (qtd. 24), to De Quincey's own version of "the hermeneutics of incarnation" (see 18). Haney's emphasis on "the dark side of Christian incarnation," to be sure, makes Wordsworth's poetry seem more tragic than it really is. Because of Haney's shrewd awareness that "the celebrity status of modern literary theorists" undermines their attempt to erase subjectivity from theory (147), moreover, a greater measure of subjectivity from Haney himself would be in order. He places in memorably sharp relief, however, the difference between Wordsworth ("Now, I know of no book or system of moral philosophy written with sufficient power to melt into our affections, to incorporate itself with the blood and vital juices of our minds") and Kant ("The ground of obligation here must not be sought in the nature of man or in the circumstances in which he is placed but *a priori* solely in the concepts of pure reason") (qtd. 184-85). Where Cavell argues that "the Romantic project . . . replace[s] religion with an interaction between philosophy and poetry" (qtd. 103), Haney discovers an incarnational rhetoric emerging from that very interaction. Studies in Romanticism, accordingly, should henceforth require replacing the axis of philosophy and literature with the triangulation of philosophy, religion, and literature. Haney's resistance to hermeneutical suspicion, at any rate, although it is hardly a naïve, respectful reading grounded in wonder, is a quite refreshing departure from today's self-conscious professionalism—that is, the intellectual pride that masquerades as skeptical doubt.

28. *The Romantic Reformation: Religious Politics in English Literature, 1789-1824*, by Robert M. Ryan

Cambridge: Cambridge University Press, 1997. Pp. ix + 292.

Robert M. Ryan's "Old Historicist" alignment of new-line Protestant faith with British Romantic art triangulates religion, politics, and literature: William Blake, William Wordsworth, Lord Byron, John Keats, and the Shelleys enter the brave new world of Nonconformist religion, reform-movement politics, and transformed/transforming imagination. "British Romanticism's historical milieu," declares Ryan, "was at least as intensely religious in character as it was political" (10). A more nuanced subtitle might read "Political Religion in English Literature, 1789-1824." All six of Ryan's Romantic Reformers depend for their significance on being understood along lines of their Christian socialism or, better yet, their socialist Protestantism. Thus Ryan's triangle is isosceles, the short leg of which provides the subversive and progressive common denominator of his Christian and Romantic emphases.

The Romantic Reformation reminds us, specifically, that "a commitment to orthodoxy is *compatible* . . . with political insubordination" (46; my emphasis). Ryan's refreshingly unattenuated perspective on British Romantic art as fully Protestant in both tone and import counteracts, first, the New Historicist, all too hegemonic assumption of Jerome J. McGann and others that even major British Romantic authors are not political enough (or not sufficiently politically correct). The six major authors under Ryan's consideration, to the contrary, are the more boldly political for being anything but formulaically proto-Marxist after the manner of timidly post-Marxist New Historicism. I cannot help thinking in this connection of Baptist-born antislavery reformer and "Late Romantic" prophet William Lloyd Garrison, who, while anything but Marxist, was decidedly subversive and progressive in his idealistic social vision. Ryan's Romantic Reformers, similarly, are the more fundamentally religious for out-doing Marx—that is, for regarding social being as not only materialistically but also sacredly dialectical. Ryan's reliably detailed new guide to the strange borderland country of Christianity and Romanticism counteracts, moreover, the widespread, all too standard assumption of M. H. Abrams and others that British Romantic authors are major if, and only if, they are anything but Christian. Blake, Wordsworth, Byron, Keats, and the Shelleys, in the light of Ryan's strong premise, are the more genuinely Christian for being richly Protestant after the manner of, say, the politically insubordinate, formidably courageous, and by any measure highly admirable sect of one—namely, the Lutheran pastor and the defier of Hitler—Dietrich Bonhoeffer. Their proto-Hegelian thought, by which their contradictions merge into a higher truth that comprehends them, and through which their opposites are continuously unified, dares frame their fearful symmetry—that is, bravely attempts a synthesis of their solicitous concern for the material well-being of all with their hope-against-hope for universal salvation.

Thus, just as Jacobus Arminius, Roger Williams, and John Wesley, if not Martin Luther, John Calvin, and Jonathan Edwards (whose politics are relatively covert), exploit the creative tension of *their* "religious politics," so too do all six of Ryan's Romantic Reformers fight the good Protestant fight for social justice in their time and place. I cannot help thinking here of the central optative of Amos— namely, to "let justice roll down like waters, and righteousness like a mighty stream" (RSV 5:24). Just as Amos evinces millennial earliness as well as apocalyptic belatedness, so do all six of Ryan's Romantic Reformers not only fear the time when, as Wordsworth puts it, "the light of sense goes out" but also entertain the hope that, as Percy Shelley has it, "the world's great age begins anew." Carefully, to be sure, Ryan's Romantic Reformers espouse the pure Christianity that they all find specifically inherent in their otherwise diverse interpretations of the Judeo-Christian ethic. Their ideal of social progress, therefore, eschews mere iconoclasm on the one hand and the mere spinning of false prophecy's wheels-within-wheels on the other; for, at the same time that they all describe progress as individual, natural, and incremental, they all delineate it as collective, spiritual, and sure. Even their subversive tempers strengthen their faiths. All six of Ryan's fighters of the good fight *keep* the faith, not so much by brandishing it, nor even so much by transforming it from within, as, instead, by reforming it along messy, practical lines of the here and now, what Wordsworth in a more than merely skeptical mood calls "the world / Of all of us, the place in which, in the end, / We find our happiness, or not at all."

Hence my review will focus not so much on what Ryan says about imagination of the transformed/transforming kind, nor even so much on what he emphasizes concerning politics of the reform-movement kind, as on what his sophisticated new contribution to studies in Romanticism has to teach us about religion of the Nonconformist kind. I will also draw out his implications concerning skepticism of the constructive kind. Blake, Wordsworth, Byron, Keats, and the Shelleys, according to Ryan's exciting new study, do not so much reach irritably after political order alone as subordinate the dialectical materialism of their political process to the relatively open-ended method of their Protestant/aesthetic interface. Ryan's thesis that the Christian/Romantic dialogue in England pays off in politics remains both important and surprising, but the most impressive achievement of *The Romantic Reformation*, to my mind, rests on its yield of poetic *faith*, emphatically so called.

I

"A man is the most perfect Protestant," declares Edmund Burke, "who protests against the whole Christian religion." Burke's "ironic remark," as Ryan calls it (46), means that the logical extension of Protestantism is atheism; Protestantism, after all, entails doubt. Ultimately, however, Ryan interprets Burke's witticism as the straightforward observation that any Protestant faith worth its salt rejects "a corrupt and spurious Christianity" and even that "an extreme form of Protestantism" constitutes "radical Christianity" (46). Thus, the thoroughgoing skepticism of the Romantic movement, which looks like atheism to some, appears to Ryan as simply (or not so simply) part of the Romantic Reformation—namely, its Protestant heritage of doubt attendant on faith. In Ryan's terms, British Romantic art is all the more subversively, progressively political, but no less Christian, for being at once a protest movement and a genuine outgrowth of the Protestant Reformation itself.

With the aid of Ryan's perspective, certain cruxes of British Romanticism become clear. In *A Vision of the Last Judgment*, Blake proclaims that "He who is out of the Church & opposes it is no less an Agent of Religion than he who is in it. [T]o be an Error & to be Cast out is a part of Gods design" (qtd. in Ryan 79). Thus Blake protests against institutional Christianity. Wordsworth, deeply engaged in the religious/political dialectic of the early 1790s, concludes like a good "Dissenting Republican" (Leslie Chard's phrase) that subversive, progressive causes arise from, and are indissolubly linked to, the first principles of faith. Hence the Solitary in *The Excursion* "from the pulpit zealously maintained / The cause of Christ and civil liberty, / As one; and moving to one glorious end" (qtd. in Ryan 29). Lord Byron, in Ryan's view, writes reverently as well as sardonically. *Don Juan*, specifically engaging the doubt/faith dialectic, explores, perhaps most rigorously of all of Byron's works, "Those holier mysteries, which the wise and just / Receive as gospel, and which grow more rooted, / As all truths must, the more they are disputed" (qtd. in Ryan 151). Percy Shelley, protesting against Christianity with the express purpose of purifying it, retains a persistent spirit of the Protestant Reformation. Even *The Triumph of Life*, notwithstanding its reputation for nihilism (fostered by Jacques Derrida's deconstruction of this Romantic set-piece), tends to free the faith from taint. Ryan suggests that this is so by virtue of its skepticism, not despite it. All the more Protestant for being skeptical, this poem laments the unfortunate historical fact that, with their sullied faith, Jesus' followers all too often "rose like shadows between Man and god / Till that eclipse, still hanging under Heaven, / Was worshipped by the world o'er which they strode / For the true Sun it quenched" (qtd. in Ryan 222). Such history, from the standpoint of Shelley's subversive, progressive Protestantism, entails neither too much predestination on the one hand nor too much irremediableness on the other. Such history is nothing if not eminently formable and reformable, and especially such a highly skeptical man of letters as Shelley cultivates the "honest doubt" (Tennyson's phrase) that includes faith.

David McCracken's review of *The Romantic Reformation* concludes that Ryan's "tracing of Shelley's evolving ideas about religion, from disgust at Christianity to admiration of Jesus' unrealizable ideals, makes him a credible protagonist in a Romantic spiritual reformation" (115). I would change "credible" to "central." Shelley, despite his youthful reputation for atheism, which he did affect at Oxford, makes Ryan's case for "religious politics in English literature, 1789-1824." "We owe the great writers of the golden age of our literature," declares Shelley in his preface to *Prometheus Unbound*, "to the fervid awakening of the public mind which shook to dust the oldest and most oppressive form of the Christian religion" (qtd. in Ryan 13). Although Ryan does not address the rather blatant anti-Catholicism of this passage, the passage nicely poses the chief question asked throughout *The Romantic Reformation*: When Protestant faith and English literature come together, can subversive, progressive politics be far behind?

The Protestant Reformation spirit of Shelley's "religious politics" is explicit in *A Philosophical Review of Reform*, where he frames his conviction that during the English Reformation, "The exposition of a certain portion of religious imposture drew with it an inquiry into political imposture and was attended with an extraordinary exertion of the energies of intellectual power.

Shakespeare and Lord Bacon and the great writers of the age of Elizabeth and James the 1st were at once the effects of the new spirit in men's minds and the causes of its more complete development" (qtd. in Ryan 41). What Shelley believes of the English Renaissance, he envisions concerning his own age. The subversive, progressive politics of British Protestant culture advances toward synthesis in British Romantic literature, with especially momentous consequences for, and especially millenarian contributions from, the Romantic Reformation that now is plain for all to see because of Ryan's book.

As Ryan first delineates it, then, the Romantic Reformation constitutes both a blessed rage for sacred truths and a mental fight for the New Jerusalem. "While Wordsworth and Blake were able to reach an accommodation with orthodoxy," declares Ryan, "[Percy] Shelley and Keats decisively repudiated the Christianity of their time as incorrigibly dishonest and pernicious. But they all adopted as their goal the spiritual and moral rehabilitation of their society, a renovation that presupposed an alteration in the national religious consciousness" (4). Samuel Taylor Coleridge seldom appears in Ryan's pages, implicitly because Ryan recoils from the plagiarisms of this major British Romantic author (196-201) and explicitly because a proper argument concerning this important theologian, political thinker, poet, and philosopher "would require at least another volume the size of this one" (10). Byron and Mary Shelley, for their parts in Ryan's "comprehensive survey of the major [British Romantic] authors as participants in a common religious enterprise," are all the more Protestant in both letter and spirit for having hovered between orthodoxy and repudiation (4, 236).

To paraphrase Ryan's high-serious interpretation of Burke's *bon mot*, finally, an author is the most perfect British Romantic writer whose genius thrives not only on dissenting politics but also on Dissent itself. Blake, Wordsworth, Byron, Keats, and the Shelleys are in Ryan's terms all the more thoroughly Christian because their triangulation of dissenting religion, reform-movement politics, and transformed, transforming imagination, out-protests Protestantism. The subversive, progressive politics of Blake and of Wordsworth constitute the most formative feature of the Romantic Reformation that Ryan brings into focus here. The deliberately Protestant disavowals of these master figures, for example, not only derive from but also contribute to and enhance the especially radical Christianity of early 1790s Nonconformity. Ryan's historical, interdisciplinary method, above all, gives new meaning to Blake and Wordsworth as the twin pioneers of British Romanticism, by showing that their Romanticism not only reflects the Protestant Reformation but extends it. Thus, if the doubt/faith dialectic of the Protestant tradition does not exactly compose the British Romantic mind, then it does energize, nonetheless, the British Romantic imagination. Hence the more than merely iconoclastic Reformation of which Ryan writes does not so much "ruin the sacred truths" (in Harold Bloom's phrase borrowed from Andrew Marvell) as tie them back together again after the manner of a truly Protestant *re-ligio*, a sufficiently self-doubting, yet highly individualistic, reforming zeal.

II

Ryan is at his best, perhaps, in his delineation of British Romantic Calvinism. Blake "comes very close to Calvinism," for example, in *Milton*'s prophecy that "the Elect shall say to the Redeemed. We behold it is of Divine Mercy alone! of Free Gift and Election that we live. Our Virtues and Cruel Goodnesses have deserv'd Eternal Death" (qtd. in Ryan 50). Blake prefigures the neo-Calvinism of Karl Barth, who preaches that mistaken "man uses his religious activities as a means of justifying and sanctifying himself instead of letting God do it by grace" (74). The Calvinist "Religion of Generation" in Blake's *Jerusalem* emphasizes sin, atonement, and "moral conformity" (75).

Concerning the Calvinism of Wordsworth's *The Excursion*, Ryan points out that "in a quite orthodox, even Calvinistic prayer," the Pastor invokes the Eternal Spirit as a "Power inaccessible to human thought, / Save by degrees and steps which thou hast deigned / To furnish ... to the infirmity of mortal sense" (qtd. in Ryan 106). The Solitary, fully subscribing to the doctrine of original sin, seeks, without much hope of finding, what Ryan calls "the gratuitous mercy of Calvin's unappeasable God" (108).

The second-generation Romantics are equally Calvinist in Ryan's view. Just as "Calvin accentuated the Bible's insistence on the awful omnipotence of an all-seeing God," so too does Byron surrender to something mysterious, terrible, and wholly other—namely, to what Ryan calls "the *mysterium tremendum et augustum* that Rudolf Otto has associated with the idea of the holy" (125). "In what could be considered another manifestation of his Calvinist tendencies," Byron in *The Vision of Judgment* permits George III to be "saved by the inscrutable mercy" of a God of justice "whose ways are past finding out" (146). Without approving of either the content of Calvinism or its forms, Mary Shelley's *Frankenstein* discloses her knowledge of its power. Just as the "Genevan ghost, John Calvin," haunts Victor Frankenstein's "role of punishing divinity," so too does Victor's particularly Calvinistic treatment of the Monster as "totally depraved" appear more than sufficiently cruel to turn this Monster-victim into a quite sympathetic character (185). Thus, as Ryan's ingenious interpretation of this quintessentially British Romantic novel makes clear, the language of second-generation Romanticism is the more persistently Calvinist just where it attacks Calvinism. "Even to write against something," as Denis Donoghue observes in another context, "is to take one's bearings from it" (17).

From the standpoint of their Calvinism, then, the six major Romantics explore justification by grace, not by works; the doctrine of the elect; a doctrine of atonement based on the payment of debt, not on the giving of love; the transcendent sovereignty of God; the innate depravity of man; a God of wrath and of judgment; a God of deep, holy mystery; and a God whose mercy is unsearchable at best, and unforthcoming at worst. "The most widely read essayist of the time," after all, "was not Hazlitt, Hunt, or Lamb, but John Foster, a Calvinist Baptist whose collected essays, published in 1804, ran to eighteen editions in his lifetime" (225). Calvinist poet laureate William Cowper, significantly, was a near-contemporary of the six major authors under Ryan's consideration (108, 225).

If anything, Ryan accords Romantic Arminianism even more space than Romantic Calvinism. His decision to do so, incidentally, is consistent with my own findings in *Coordinates of Anglo-American Romanticism: Wesley, Edwards, Carlyle, and Emerson* and *Anglo-American Antiphony: The Late Romanticism of Tennyson and Emerson* that the High and Late Romantic theology of Anglo-America entails Arminian import as well as Calvinist tone. Ryan's six Romantics, at any rate, forcefully entertain criteria of poetic faith not only the more optimistic for being unattenuated but also no less unattenuated for being quite un-Calvinistic. In Ryan's view they are all not just Calvinist in mood but Arminian in tendency; their faith is primarily experiential.

Although Ryan does not use the term "Arminian," he should. He describes Blake's doctrine of atonement as an emphasis on love and on John 3:16, rather than on the mere satisfaction of debt (49-50). He discusses "the spirit of forgiveness and the imaginative freedom that Blake understood as essential elements of true Christianity" (76). He analyzes the social gospel in *Jerusalem* and in *The Excursion* (72-73, 113). He demonstrates that Keats increasingly reflected Benjamin Robert Haydon's "Evangelical" polemic against the neglect of the poor in Leigh Hunt's "Greek religion" (162-63). He traces Percy Shelley's threefold theme of charity, mercy, and forgiveness in both *Prometheus Unbound* and *Hellas* (211-12). He recognizes that *A Philosophical*

View of Reform favors Christian missions as the social, collective equivalent to individual, moral responsibility (206). And he acknowledges that *A Defense of Poetry* gives the lion's share of credit to Christianity for both "the abolition of personal and domestic slavery" and "the emancipation of women from a great part of the degrading restraints of antiquity" (qtd. in Ryan 211).

Hence Ryan's Reformers explore, above all, an Arminian doctrine of free will that constitutes nothing less than "soul-competency." I have in mind here Bloom's portrait of the more Arminian than Calvinist Baptist master figure and American "Late Romantic" E. Y. Mullins. These six, after the manner of Arminian Protestantism, and again as Ryan frequently points out, issue their serious calls for the widespread emulation of divine mercy, cultivate their hopes that practical charity is not so much the avenue to salvation as simply what one does with one's free will, and give their assurances of political progress through the social gospel.

I take Ryan's point, implicit though it remains, that the Calvinist/Arminian controversy forms a large part of the religious/political oscillation of British Romanticism. Arminian Baptist preacher Robert Hall, for example, not only repudiated "Burke's efforts to sanctify the counter-revolution" but also showed "in his 1791 tract *Christianity Consistent with a Love of Freedom* that religious zeal could be recruited equally well on the radical side" (30). Like Hall, incidentally, the British Romantic Reformers inherited their Arminian legacy primarily from Arminius-inspired John Wesley, a Protestant master figure much more immediate than, and at least as influential as, the "Genevan ghost, John Calvin." The six major authors discussed by Ryan take a progressive, yet stable, *via media* between the Calvinist possibility of tyrannical repression and the Arminian possibility of too much freedom. This *via media* accounts, perhaps, for the relatively nonviolent, salutary tone of "religious politics in English literature, 1789-1824." The least creative tension of the Protestant tradition, after all, is its violence, which is insufficiently self-doubting to be either Protestant or, for that matter, Christian at all. "I beseech you in the bowels of Christ," expostulates exasperated alpha-Protestant Oliver Cromwell to his bloody, moralistic followers, "think it possible you may be mistaken" (qtd. in Brantley, *Anglo-American Antiphony* 183). The Calvinist/Arminian dialectic of the British Romantic imagination necessitates neither stasis nor cataclysm so much as it leads to hope-against-hope for a thousand years of peace. The tension of British Romantic "religious politics" is the more creative for being millennial, not apocalyptic; the Romantic Reformation resists cheerlessness, however brilliant, by means of its emphasis on the here and now.

Ryan's Reformers suggest for a rare time in human history that faith can *be* experiential, for they specifically exploit the creative tension between Calvinist salvation by faith and Arminian salvation by works. "Won't you make a decision for Christ?" asks the upstart Arminian. "I think He's very well capable of making that decision for Himself, thank you," answers the old-line Calvinist. This hypothetical exchange, suggested to me by Ralph C. Wood, epitomizes the high stakes not only of the Calvinist/Arminian controversy but also of British Romanticism—namely, complete dependence on grace (or on what Wordsworth calls "wise passiveness") versus full responsibility for "Soul-making" (to use Keats's term). What Ryan calls the "common religious enterprise" of the major British Romantic authors remains both Calvinist enough to restrict the human condition and Arminian enough to celebrate spiritual experience. Although Ryan does not refer to "My heart leaps up when I behold / A rainbow in the sky," this article of Romantic faith means in its Arminian sense that the spiritual as well as natural well-being of Wordsworth's persona depends on what happens to him as the result of his own choice: ". . . *when I behold* / A rainbow in the sky." On its Calvinist sublevel, moreover, the article suggests that the spiritual as well as natural well-being of this persona depends also on what happens to him not so much as the result of his own action or of mere circumstance (as though the Romantic universe were somehow a random occurrence) as of the unmerited grace that lightens upon him from both nature and the Bible: ". . . when I behold / *A rainbow in the sky*" (cf. Gen. 9:12-17). Those many moments when the heart of even a Romantic writer does *not* leap up are still as spiritually complex and intriguing as, and certainly more Calvinistically inscrutable than, those few moments, relatively speaking, when the heart of especially a Romantic writer *does* leap up. Unsearchable mystery, indeed, precisely obtains not only in the richly experiential Arminian dimension of British Romantic art—that is, in its robustly confident spiritual import—but also in its strangely anti-experiential Calvinist component—that is, in its passively or scantly experiential, nay, its sometimes non-experiential, spiritual tone.

Thus, just as the Calvinist/Arminian controversy seeks to balance predestinarian sensibility with theological openness, just as this dialectic seeks to reconcile reverence with soul-competence, and tends to eschew the univocal, either/or thinking of Calvinistic and Arminian totalizing alike, so too does it flatter the theory of literature as paradox, forming and informing both/and logic with rich ambiguity. The six major Romantics considered by Ryan triumphantly exploit the creative tension that they all discover between transcendent Power and aspirant yearning, or between humbling sublimity and heady imagination. Hence, if anything tragic should inhere in dour Calvinism (I have in mind the tragic overtones of the Book of Ecclesiastes, a Calvinist proof-text) and if anything comic should inhere in sunny Arminianism (I have in mind Dante's sense of "divine comedy"), then the Calvinist/Arminian dialectic of British Romantic art, especially if one assumes its slight Arminian edge, entails tragi*comedy*. Calvinists, of course, could be progressive; Arminians could be morally conforming. Calvinists were both interested in social justice and aware of God's love; Arminians were not only respectful of justice but also hungry for grace. Nevertheless, in just such areas of overlap, in just such exceptions that prove the rule, the Calvinist/Arminian dialectic of the six major Romantics finds much of its drive toward synthesis.

Ryan especially well indicates that even the Calvinist element of this dialectic remains more than sufficiently strong to enliven, dramatize, enhance, and complicate the Anglo-American world-picture well into the nineteenth century. I cannot help thinking in this regard of the distinction between the covertly political Calvinist Baptist Billy Graham, on the one hand, and the overtly political Arminian Baptist Jesse Jackson, on the other. If I may follow Ryan's lead and analogize further the relation between Baptist Christianity and Romanticism, just as today's Southern Baptists include "moderates" as well as "fundamentalists" among their more than sixteen million members, so too are Ryan's Romantic Baptists (Foster and Hall) characterized by the Calvinist/Arminian controversy of all Evangelical faiths during the late eighteenth and early nineteenth centuries. (Thus the Baptist/Romantic dialectic accounts in part for the Romantic Reformation's Calvinist/Arminian controversy.) In the Anglo-American long run, of course, Arminianism won out. I have in mind here not only the death-throes of old-line Calvinism in Oliver Wendell Holmes's "The Deacon's Masterpiece; or, the Wonderful 'One-Hoss Shay'" (1858) but also the drum-beating for new-line Arminianism in Harriet Beecher Stowe's *Uncle Tom's Cabin; or, Life among the Lowly* (1852). Nevertheless, the slight Arminian bias of Ryan's six authors does not close off British Romantic art, and with Edwards' Calvinism as a continuing presence of Evangelical faith even in the nineteenth century, Ryan's awareness of a Calvinist/Romantic dialectic takes on whole new bi-national meaning. Thanks in part to Ryan's skillful evocation of Romanticism's Calvinist sub-rubric, I am persuaded that the astringent streak of Late Romantic poet Emily Dickinson (1830-86) is due, above all, to her tough-minded Calvinist birthright, as distinct, say, from the sweetness and joy of her tender-minded Arminian evolution. Hence, not least because *The*

Romantic Reformation neither neglects the Calvinist tone of English-language Romanticism nor overemphasizes the Arminian import thereof, I hail Ryan's advance toward a unified field theory of Romanticism.

III

The Romantic Reformation picks some especially juicy bones with the twin obsessions of postmodern critical theory: first, evaluating literature according to its latencies of money, power, and the id; and second, overselling *aporia*, the site at which any text undermines itself. Three of Ryan's antideconstructionist points make for especially good reading. The first involves Tilottama Rajan's criticizing "the absence in the first-generation Romantics of 'that radical irony which makes it impossible to turn back to illusion.'" Ryan retorts, "But a truly radical irony would have to allow for the possible truth of apparent 'illusion'—and the possibility that irony itself might not be the most appropriate response to the condition of the world. This I think was Byron's position." In a second and related point Ryan persuades us that Anne K. Mellor's "account of the ideological basis of artistic irony" is not "especially relevant to Byron" (128). And third, in the spirit of Ryan's refusal to traffic in semantic hare-chasing, surely the most relentlessly impersonal tic of deconstruction, he straightforwardly announces, "I do not concur with [Jerrold E.] Hogle's central thesis—that Shelley's apparent theism is only a metaphor for an unceasing process of linguistic transference" (264). The knowing tone of New Historicism raises Ryan's particular ire. Concerning McGann's sweeping comment that Shelley "overturns and denies the whole of *Hellas*" in its last six lines, for example, Ryan icily observes, "A less self-assured reader might have hesitated before attributing such an inconsistency to such an artist" (216).

Although Ryan credits New Historicist Romanticists with restraining the tendency of Romanticists in general to court the danger of all inquiry—namely, that of working too much from within the phenomenon that one is supposedly analyzing as *spectator ab extra*, he will have none of this fashionable methodology's cookie-cutter formulations. "In recent years," he sighs, "the Romantic poets have been reproached for withdrawing from engagement with political and economic realities" and for "taking refuge in poetry that deliberately distanced itself from the social crises of the time" (1). Whereas the New Historicists beat up on the Romantics with their club of politics, Ryan keeps the Romantics' politics but eliminates the beating. His Romantics merely take their lumps from him. His heuristic triangle of religion, politics, and literature so ruthlessly exposes the pseudoscientific predictabilities of New Historicist methodology that *The Romantic Reformation* brings at least some hope to our recent critical experience. Only Thomas McFarland, to my knowledge, has similarly shown how far this narrow historicism still has to go before its heavy-handed, yet strangely timid, form of Marxism yields, at last, to the finesse of methodological maturity. Ryan's finesse is so little apt to allow any one of his analytical terms to undercut either one of the other two that all three remain in play as parts of his elegant whole.

Ryan's tone, collegial enough, is rarely neutral. The very victims of his corrective gaze, I expect, will take pleasure in his skillful skewering. To Leopold Damrosch's predictable, twofold conclusion that "Blake's religion was never that of the orthodox," and that "to the end of his life [Blake] continued to assert the humanity of Jesus as the only God," Ryan pointedly objects: "Damrosch intended the second clause . . . to support the first, but the fact is that it was possible in Blake's time to assert the humanity of Jesus as the only God and still be well inside the vaguely drawn boundaries of Protestant orthodoxy" (48). Consistent with Ryan's demonstration that "it was not necessary for Wordsworth to leave his 'pantheism' at the door when he resumed his pew in the Church," Ryan not only disposes of Coleridge's objection to Wordsworth's "Janus-head of Spinoza and Dr. Watts," but also gainsays the still-too-prevalent view of Wordsworth's descendant, Jonathan Wordsworth—namely, that "in [Wordsworth's] hands the One Life lost any connection with formal Christianity" (94-95). "The poet," Ryan concludes, "does not in fact seem to have acknowledged any need to dissociate the two" (94). One of Ryan's most characteristic refrains—"Generations of critics have followed one another in assuming that . . ." (see, for example, 126)—is also one of his most telling motifs. His examined assumptions, anything but lemming-like, lead him to fresh woods and pastures new.

Although Ryan should have engaged the mature arguments of my more recent studies, he fairly faults my 1975 book, *Wordsworth's "Natural Methodism,"* for finding "little else" than "Evangelicalism in Wordsworth's religious background" (237). He modestly includes himself among the axe-grinders by acknowledging that his *Keats: The Religious Sense* argues for the "lifelong theism" of a poet in whose works Ronald A. Sharp's *Keats, Skepticism, and the Religion of Beauty*, equally plausibly, finds only lifelong skeptical humanism (10, 237). Ryan, by "examining the public articulation rather than speculating on the private content of the poets' creeds," hopes to avoid "falling too often into special pleading" (10-11). His hope is fulfilled. "I am aware," he declares, "that discussion of religion in literature creates rich opportunity for grinding personal axes; critics are never more likely to pursue their own hidden, even unconscious agendas than when reading religion into their favorite poets" (10). A statement of the relationship between his argument, on the one hand, and his religious background, on the other, might have clarified Ryan's assumptions, and perhaps even have strengthened his case in these confessional times.

Although Ryan forthrightly credits my *Locke, Wesley, and the Method of English Romanticism* with counterweighting Abrams's rather Whiggish regard for modern secularism as the British Romantics' only "standard of metaphysical authenticity" (31, 236-37), he might have highlighted Methodism as a prime inspiration of the neo-Reformation 1790s in which he is primarily interested. He never says exactly how his work complements the huge, already well-established scholarly conversation concerning "the Evangelical Revival" that he does recognize as a prominent feature of the British Romantic landscape. While focusing on "the campaign for religious liberty being waged throughout the country by Protestant Dissenters," he neglects "the remarkable nationwide rebirth of Christian faith and piety that became known as the Evangelical Revival" (18).

Ryan wisely perceives that the Evangelical Anglican reformer William Wilberforce and the anticlerical Deistic protester Thomas Paine, despite their many differences, "resembled each other in their understanding of the need for a purification of the national religion of England and in the belief that their own time was ripe with opportunity for such a reformation." Ryan, however, should elaborate on his recognition that Wilberforce and Paine were "worlds apart in their vision of what a future society should look like" (17). He is unaccountably more interested in the figuratively Protestant-Reformation Paine than in the literally Protestant-Reformation Wilberforce, thereby sidestepping the *Ding an Sich* of his momentous subject matter. Although he duly recognizes the political importance of Wilberforce's religious views, he never sufficiently ponders the fact that Methodism is itself fraught with political significance, as Henry Abelove has demonstrated in *The Evangelist of Desire: John Wesley and the Methodists*.

"Critics," declares Ryan, "have always acknowledged and usually honored the Romantics' tendencies toward skepticism." Ryan promises something different: "I will argue here that what made them important figures in our intellectual history was not their skepticism but their belief" (7). Ryan's logic should be both skepticism and belief. British culture of the eighteenth and nineteenth centuries encourages a rich, strange coexistence between philosophical skepticism and religious orthodoxy. Thus, just as Wesley's skeptical legacy from John Locke (as well as Descartes) assumes that there is something to know (including religious as well as political truth), so too does the philosophical as well as religious skepticism of the six major authors under Ryan's consideration enter into a mutually enhancing interchange with their poetic faith. Yet Ryan does not explicitly say so. Hence, just as Ryan's review of my *Locke, Wesley, and the Method of English Romanticism* taught me to regard historical materials not as glosses and influences, but as dramatic elements of a *Kulturkampf,* and just as *The Romantic Reformation* now teaches me that the Christian/Romantic dialectic entails subversive, progressive politics, so too do I call to Ryan's attention the fact that the religious/literary dialectic in which he and I are both interested entails, as well, the experiential common denominator between empirical epistemology and evangelical "methodism." The Christian/Romantic dialectic of England forms part of a larger, still more interdisciplinary dialectic—namely, Romantic Britain's (and, for that matter, Romantic Anglo-America's) creative tension between empirical philosophy and evangelical faith. The constructive skepticism of the Romantic Reformation is flexible, because not only Wesley, but also Locke, contributed to it.

Notwithstanding my mild demurrals, I hasten to emphasize how much I welcome Ryan as a full-fledged, if not quite charter, member of a band of scholars who "have attempted a comprehensive survey of the major [British Romantic] authors as participants in a common religious enterprise" (236). He instructs these few—John Middleton Murry, Hoxie Neale Fairchild, James Benziger, John Clubbe, Ernest Lovell, and me—how we all should have broadened the shared religious/literary focus of our surveys still further: "Insofar as modern critics have taken the poets seriously as religious thinkers, they have most commonly been treated as creative metaphysicians articulating private intuitions of a noumenal order rather than as active participants in the public life of their times" (8). This remonstrance is fair enough. Although I still do not wish to lose sight of the poets' "private intuitions" of the noumenon, I am quite happy, nevertheless, to balance my all too narrow focus on religion and literature alone, not only with philosophy of the empirical kind, but also with my new, Ryan-derived, appreciation for the phenomenal "public life" of the poets. Unlike much of my work, and perhaps even unlike some of what the "happy few" have argued, Ryan's exciting new guide to the strange borderland country of Christianity and Romanticism rarely courts the danger of underestimating either the political complexity or the political scope of the

Christian/Romantic dialectic of England, in which he is deeply interested and about which he is widely informed. "Participants" in the "common religious enterprise" of the British Romantic Reformation turn out to be just as Ryan says they are—"active," subversive/progressive "participants" in the "religious politics" of "English literature, 1789-1824."

IV

In sum, *The Romantic Reformation* throws new light on the British Romantic drive toward synthesis. Subversive/progressive politics constitutes an important, influential element common to Christianity and Romanticism. Although religion may trump politics in Ryan's scheme of things, Blake, Wordsworth, Byron, Keats, and the Shelleys emerge from Ryan's new guide as deliberate exponents of a politically meliorist, as well as Protestant Reformation-inflected, imagination. Whereas Romanticists have tended to assume that British Romantic authors are political rather than religious, or more political than religious, or too political to be religious, or not political enough, or not religious at all, Ryan discerns that these six authors emerge from their time and place as subversive and progressive for decidedly and decisively Protestant reasons. Ryan's sometimes ironic but usually optimistic concept of the Romantic Reformation serves as nothing less than a prolegomenon to further study. His concept serves paradoxically as an already *classic* marker in our not so quixotic and in any case ongoing quest for a unified field theory of *Romanticism*.

All six Reformers, of course, were nominally or fully Anglican. Ryan might have said more about the influence of "state religion" Anglicanism. Stephen Prickett's tracing of a direct line of descent from the Anglican imagination of Wordsworth and of Coleridge to the Victorian renewal of faith and experience comes to mind. Ryan, for that matter, might have included Prickett, and Bernard M. G. Reardon, as members of the scholarly band. Anglicanism judged Dissent to be guilty of excess. It does not immediately appear just where the *un*-Dissentingly Protestant influence comes into the Romantic Reformation. Would Ryan agree that Anglicanism, like Dissent, generates faith from the skeptical suspension of alternatives? Regardless, this "state religion" was itself so caught up in the larger Evangelical Revival that it exerted transforming, almost Dissentingly Protestant, influence on the six Romantics whose work Ryan discusses. Wesley and his Calvinist-Evangelical lieutenant George Whitefield, significantly, were not only fathers of 1790s Dissent, but also lifelong Anglicans.

The most striking implication of the Romantic Reformation is that "real toads" live in British Romantic "gardens." Strange as it might sound to say in these hermeneutically suspicious times (when latency gives rise to the first principles of criticism), even the most tough-minded among the major Romantics emerge as Reformers for patently Christian reasons. Byron and Mary Shelley, after all, oscillate between orthodoxy and repudiation. If they do not exactly keep the faith, then neither do they entirely lose their faiths. In their willingness to risk faith, they receive it back again. Wesley models such alternation: "I am as fully assured to-day, as I am of the shining of the sun, that the scriptures are of God. I cannot possibly deny or doubt of it now; yet I may doubt of it to-morrow; as I have done heretofore a thousand times, and that after the fullest assurance preceding" (qtd. in Brantley, *Locke, Wesley* 53). Yet Wesley's hermeneutical circle ends where it begins, in experiential Faith. And so does the circle of Ryan's Reformers.

How richly does *The Romantic Reformation* deserve the Conference on Christianity and Literature's 1997 Book of the Year Award! Ryan's thesis is sturdy and flexible enough to explain British Romantic works, without explaining them away. At some point, the Romantic Reformation includes too much, but I have not reached that point. Although Ryan's modulation of the religious and literary into the religious, political, and literary might seem muddy, his dialectic is lively, his triangle clear. What C. E. Pulos accomplished for Shelley and skepticism, *The Romantic Reformation* achieves for the Christian/Romantic conversation in England—namely, confirmation of the "religious politics" rubric for our sessions of sweet silent thought about literary history. Just as we can no longer consider Shelley apart from David Hume, so too are we no longer able to survey British Romanticism, Shelley's works included, apart from the Protestant Reformation dating all the way back to Luther. The world of Romantic scholarship cannot long thrive without taking Ryan's important yet neglected topic into account (and the sub-rubric of Catholicism and British Romanticism, or of Judaism and British Romanticism, now beckons). To say the least, *The Romantic Reformation* provides us with a store of insights; to say the most, it teaches us that, since all six Reformers do not suspect false consciousness after the manner of Marx, Nietzsche, or Freud, so much as they expect truth, grace, and joy like Calvin, Arminius, and Wesley, they all qualify as peerless questers on their timebound, yet timeless, spiritual course between the Scylla of paralyzed skepticism and the Charybdis of revolutionary violence. How else will Ryan deliver us from our academic routines?

WORKS CITED

Abelove, Henry. *The Evangelist of Desire: John Wesley and the Methodists.* Stanford: Stanford UP, 1990.

Abrams, M.H. *Natural Supernaturalism: Tradition and Revolution in Romantic Literature.* New York: Norton, 1971.

Barth, Karl. *Church Dogmatics.* Trans. G. T. Thomson and Harold Knight. New York: Scribner, 1955-56.

Benziger, James. *Images of Eternity: Studies in the Poetry of Religious Vision from Wordsworth to T. S. Eliot.* Carbondale: Southern Illinois UP, 1962.

Bloom, Harold. *The American Religion: The Emergence of the Post-Christian Nation.* New York: Simon, 1992.

———. *Ruin the Sacred Truths: Poetry and Belief from the Bible to the Present.* Cambridge: Harvard UP, 1989.

Brantley, Richard E. *Anglo-American Antiphony: The Late Romanticism of Tennyson and Emerson.* Gainesville: UP of Florida, 1994.

———. *Coordinates of Anglo-American Romanticism: Wesley, Edwards, Carlyle, and Emerson.* Gainesville: UP of Florida, 1993.

———. "Dickinson the Romantic." *Christianity and Literature* 46 (1997): 243-71.

———. *Locke, Wesley, and the Method of English Romanticism.* Gainesville: UP of Florida, 1984.

———. *Wordsworth's "Natural Methodism."* New Haven: Yale UP, 1975.

Chard, Leslie. *Dissenting Republican: Wordsworth's Early Life and Thought in Their Political Context.* The Hague: Mouton, 1972.

Clubbe, John, and Ernest Lovell. *English Romanticism: The Grounds of Belief.* DeKalb: Northern Illinois UP, 1983.

Damrosch, Leopold. *Symbol and Truth in Blake's Myth.* Princeton: Princeton UP, 1980.

Derrida, Jacques. "Living On." Trans. James Hulbert. *Deconstruction and Criticism.* Ed. Harold Bloom. New York: Seabury, 1979. 75-176.

Donoghue, Denis. *The Third Voice: Modern British and American Verse Drama.* Princeton: Princeton UP, 1959.

Fairchild, Hoxie Neale. *1780-1830, Romantic Faith.* Vol. 3 of *Religious Trends in English Poetry.* New York: Columbia UP, 1949.

Hogle, Jerrold E. *Shelley's Process: Radical Transference and the Development of His Major Works.* New York: Oxford UP, 1988.

McCracken, David. Rev. of *The Romantic Reformation: Religious Politics in English Literature, 1789-1824,* by Robert M. Ryan. *Christianity and Literature* 48 (1998): 113-16.

McFarland, Thomas. *William Wordsworth: Intensity and Achievement.* Oxford: Clarendon, 1992.
McGann, Jerome J. *The Romantic Ideology: A Critical Investigation.* Chicago: U of Chicago P, 1983.
———. "The Secrets of an Elder Day: Shelley after *Hellas.*" *Keats-Shelley Journal* 15 (1966): 25-41.
Mellor, Anne K. *English Romantic Irony.* Cambridge: Harvard UP, 1980.
Murry, John Middleton. *Keats and Shakespeare.* 1935; rpt. London: Oxford UP, 1958.
Otto, Rudolf. *The Idea of the Holy.* New York: Oxford UP, 1958.
Prickett, Stephen. *Romanticism and Religion: The Tradition of Coleridge and Wordsworth in the Victorian Church.* Cambridge: Cambridge UP, 1976.
Pulos, C. E. *The Deep Truth: A Study of Shelley's Skepticism.* Lincoln: U of Nebraska P, 1954.
Rajan, Tilottama. *Dark Interpreter: The Discourse of Romanticism.* Ithaca: Cornell UP, 1980.
Reardon, Bernard M. G. *Religion in the Age of Romanticism.* Cambridge: Cambridge UP, 1985.
Ryan, Robert M. *Keats: The Religious Sense.* Princeton: Princeton UP, 1976.
———. Rev. of *Locke, Wesley, and the Method of English Romanticism,* by Richard E. Brantley. *The Wordsworth Circle* 16 (1985): 182-85.
———. *The Romantic Reformation: Religious Politics in English Literature, 1789-1824.* Cambridge: Cambridge UP, 1997.
Sharp, Ronald A. *Keats, Skepticism, and the Religion of Beauty.* Athens: U of Georgia P, 1979.
Wordsworth, Jonathan. *The Music of Humanity.* New York: Harper, 1969.

29. *The Romantic Ethic and the Spirit of Modern Consumerism,* by Colin Campbell

Oxford: Basil Blackwell, 1987. Pp. 301. $24.95

The Romantic Ethic and the Spirit of Modern Consumerism, though "not a detailed scholarly work, " is "a broad-ranging and fundamentally speculative attempt," i.e., an essay (13), and, though no book-length essay should be excused from scholarly industry and though Colin Campbell is no Montaigne (he is Senior Lecturer in Sociology at the University of York) one does make fresh connections as the result of his germinal work.

Campbell's book, as its title indicates, parallels *The Protestant Ethic and the Spirit of Capitalism* (1930) by Max Weber, for, while Weber focuses on "rational and ascetic" features of Protestantism, Campbell emphasizes that the "sentimental Pietistic" side of Protestantism contributed, too, to modem economics (9, 11). By extending Weber's "historical dateline" of 1720, Campbell argues that both the Protestant ethic and the consumer ethic fed into "the predominantly middle-class character of the Romantic Movement" (5, 8--9, 11).

Since "productionist economic bias" pervades most social science, Campbell seeks, first, a "satisfactory theory of modem consumerism" (6). Although neither history nor anthropology supports the idea that human beings share a "natural" tendency to display "insatiable wanting," the idea of man as "a consuming animal with boundless appetites, capable of driving the economy to new levels of prosperity," arose during the eighteenth century (29, 39). The Spanish Conquistadors lusted after gold; and Don Juan lusted after women; but far from having a single focus, the insatiability of the modem consumer is characterized by "the inexhaustibility of wants themselves, which forever arise, phoenix-like, from the ashes of their predecessors" (37). The "spending orgy" in England during the 1760s and '70s was "aided and abetted" by salesmen, sales promotion, and advertising, but the consumer revolution in textiles, beer, crockery, buckles, buttons, pins, cutlery, toys, cosmetics, novels, and women's journals signified "a wider cultural revolution, a change in values and attitudes" (9, 24-25).

Campbell wonders what motivates modem consumerism. He rejects Abraham Maslow's "instinct," since people will override physiological urges for the sake of "prestige" or "self-respect" (45). He rejects simple "need," since "yesterday's luxuries become today's necessities" (59). He does not like either Thorstein Veblen's "emulation of the upper classes" or Vance Packard's "subliminal techniques" that introduce a "want" into "the blood stream of consumers" (19, 46). After toying with simple "gratification" or "satisfaction" of "desire" (60-61), he concludes that consumer behavior is motivated by "the imaginative pleasure-seeking to which the product image lends itself " (89): "Viewed in this way," he adds, "the emphasis upon novelty as well as . . . insatiability . . . become[s] comprehensible." He even claims that "the distinctively modern faculty is the ability to create an illusion which is known to be false but felt to be true" (78).

Campbell contends, next, that Protestantism played an especially crucial role in the development of modem hedonism. Although the symbols of Protestantism "counteract experientially induced emotion," they "induce emotions in the absence of any discernible environmental stimulus" (74), and Arminian theology in particular, with its "free will" as "codeterminant of salvation" and its attendant emphasis upon "charity and the associated feelings of pity and sorrow," "justified" the "emotional pleasure-seeking" of hedonistic consumerism (109-10, 113).

Finally, Campbell contends that "the self-determination of emotional experience" in both Puritanism and modem consumerism led to that "literacy in conjunction with individualism" which created the audience of romantic art (72): "Belief dependent" rather than "event dependent" emotionality, first evident in graveyard poetry and the Gothic novel, frightens even the consumer-reader who no longer fears the devil, sin, and damnation, so that "puritan" and "romantic," thanks to "sociological understanding," need not be seen as "cultural polar types" or "stark cultural alternatives" (9, 74-75, 217).

One welcomes Campbell's twofold conclusion that "the Romantic Movement assisted crucially at the birth of modern consumerism" and "has continued" (witness the "close correspondence" between "periods of creative consumer boom" and outbreaks of Bohemianism in the 1890s, the 1920s, and the 1960s) "to provide a renewed impetus to the dynamic of consumerism" (206). One finds useful his definition of "Romanticism" as "the cultural laboratory for modern society, as crucial in connection with consumption as science and technology is [*sic*] for production" (201). He can carry his approach to its logical, if unsubtle, extreme: "It seems only too likely that romantic poems, novels and music will be employed as little more than the raw material for a leisure and recreation industry; with dreams used less to raise the vision of an imaginatively apprehended ideal world with which to counter this one, than to overcome boredom and alienation" (216). He can recognize satisfying complexities: the interchange between romanticism and modern consumerism, he observes, is "ironic"; for through the same "cunning of reason" by which people often "intend one thing but actually attain something quite different," "romantic idealists" may promote "a self-seeking hedonism"; and "the self-illusory pleasure-seeker" may tend, unwittingly, toward "an idealistic commitment" (209-10). One thinks of *Sehnsucht*, and the heightened subjectivity of romanticism, upon reading that "modern hedonism," with its "little reliance" on "real stimuli," is "covert" and "self-illusory" (does Campbell mean "self-deluding"?), and Campbell adds that "although one must always desire something, one can long for . . . one knows not what" (77, 87). To Blake's "Less than all cannot satisfy," one is tempted to respond that not *even* all can satisfy, for Campbell's point that the consumer is "permanently exposed to the experience of wanting, something which is only periodically and briefly interspersed with 'soon-to-be' disillusioned consummations of desire" (195), is well taken. "No other person," writes Campbell, "is in such a good position to provide pleasurable stimulation as the hedonist himself" (68), and, with just this hint from him, one may think of the autoerotic dimension of romantic psychosexuality. When one reads that "the cycle of desire-acquisition-use-disillusionment-renewed-desire is a general feature of modern hedonism, and applies to romantic interpersonal relationships as much as the consumption of cultural products such as clothes and records" (90), one thinks that the restless psychosexual attentions of Byron and Shelley, not to mention numberless latter-day romantics, may be consumption-related.

"As the consequence [of Arminianism]," writes Campbell, "the previous emphasis upon God's grace was replaced by that on God's love" (112), and one thinks, naturally enough, of Wordsworth's "Love, now a universal birth, / From heart to heart is stealing" (though one thinks, too, of his "grace" in "Resolution and Independence"). When one reads that the Puritan "is not characterized by the absence of emotion but by the presence of very powerful emotions of particular kinds" (e. g. , loneliness, dejection, self-doubt, fear of damnation, and, not least, the desperate need for reassuring signs of election, 123) one may think of *Sturm und Drang* or the romantic agony. Though Campbell does not establish historical links between Puritanism and romanticism, he does suggest a psychological link: "[A]ttempts to raise children as 'puritans', by encouraging deferred gratification and emotional restraint, may actually give rise to both day-dreaming and suppressed passion, thereby providing the conditions necessary for the development of a romantic personality" (222).

Seldom, however, does Campbell make such connections himself. Opportunity knocks, for him, more than once.

At the beginning of chapter 4, he quotes Xerxes ("I will offer one thousand gold pieces to any man who can show me a new pleasure") and Keats ("Heard melodies are sweet, but those unheard / Are sweeter") but nowhere pursues how pleasure-oriented consumer-theory might apply to Keats or anyone else. He mentions Keats three times, Blake four, Byron two, Coleridge two, and Shelley four, and, though he allots ten references to Wordsworth, he quotes only the Preface to *Lyrical Ballads* at any length and offers no evidence at all for the startling but unnuanced conclusion that Wordsworth articulates "the essential features" of "modern, rationalized hedonism" (182-83, 187-92). He quotes William Cobbett's observation of one yeoman family that "they had long been in command of sufficient income to acquire new possessions, but only now felt compelled to do so" (18) and Jeremy Bentham's definition of utility as that which produces "pleasure" as well as "benefit, advantage, good, or happiness" (60) but nowhere dwells on these or any such primary materials as the economic context of romantic texts. The subtitle of Cobbett's *Rural Rides—With Economical and Political Observations—*beckons the historical researcher but does not beckon Campbell.

Campbell, faulting Weber for regarding Arminian Methodism as "a variant" (rather than "a further development") of Protestant thought, asks whether John Wesley (1703-91) "exerted any significant influence upon the nature of economic conduct; a question which turns, in particular, upon whether it is correct to characterize the Enlightenment as an unequivocally 'secularizing' influence" (104-5); but nowhere does he answer his own question. He devotes a paragraph (184-85) to *The Romantic Movement and Methodism* (1937) by F. C. Gill but ignores the economic implications of Gill's work and does not even cite the work of Bernard Semmel, whose *The Methodist Revolution* (1971) documents the triumph of Arminianism in the early decades of the nineteenth century. Though aware that Arminian theology enjoyed the ascendancy over an increasingly defensive Calvinism, Campbell does not sufficiently distinguish between "Arminianism" on the one hand and "Puritanism" or "Calvinism" on the other, and, though interested in "the practical consequences of theology" for Latitudinarian Protestants of the eighteenth century (117), he seems indifferent to the practical consequences of theology for Arminian evangelical Protestants from, say, 1780 to 1830. Such consequences, surely, pertain to his "consuming" interest in romanticism, and they have received attention in the scholarship following in Gill's wake: I recommend, besides Semmel's scholarship, *The Confessional Imagination: A Reading of Wordsworth's Prelude* (1974) by Frank D. McConnell. "It is clear," writes Campbell, "that we have now arrived at the point of being able to conclude, with [John W.] Draper, that what happened to Puritanism between 1660 and 1760 was that 'the middle classes reinterpreted Protestantism on a Sentimental, rather than a Calvinistic basis'" (134-35): the revealing phrase, here, is "with Draper"; for despite giving the impression of making a contribution, Campbell does not do so; and similarly, he rehashes Weber's book at too-great length (e. g., 125-31), extensively quotes (136) and uncritically accepts (150) H. N. Fairchild's biased study of *Religious Trends in English Poetry* (1939-49), beats a dead horse in a long attack on Veblen (49-57), and reinvents and spins historical wheels in old arguments concerning Shaftesbury, Hutcheson, Hume, Gerard, Burke, Kames, Blair, Reynolds, and Alison (150-60).

Clogged, unwieldy phrases ("modern autonomous imaginative hedonism" 77) and numbing transitions ("The second significant feature of the consumer revolution of the eighteenth century which research has revealed concerns..." 25) abound. Unparsable sentences bounce off the frontal lobes: "Whilst, in that context, this argument was employed to advance scepticism concerning the suggestion that the writings of such advocates of consumption as Dudley North or Adam Smith could be credited with making middle-class consumers consider it morally right to purchase luxury goods, it has now, in the light of the preceding discussion, taken on the character of a seemingly even-stronger objection against the contention that modern consumerism is dependent upon a form of hedonism" (100; see also 23, 30, 36, 77, 212, and *passim*).

Sentence fragments (28, 33, 34, 39, 43, 132, 153, 176, 177, 179, 188, 196, 211) make for an especially egregious solecism. Though my aversions to comma splices (80, 183), "quote" for quotation (91 and *passim*), "refer back" for refer (3), and subject-verb disagreement (89, 201) may be teacherly bigotry, Campbell's use of nouns as adjectives ("ideal type solutions" 56; "fashion emulation explanation" 106) and his annoyingly abstract tongue-twisters ("maximization of satisfaction" 68) will put all of his readers (and not just the "horses of instruction" among them) in mind to follow W. H. Auden's command in "Under Which Lyre": "Thou shalt not sit / With statisticians nor commit / A social science."

Lack of proofreading (let's regard "the principal of individual autonomy," 108, as such) is shockingly evident. One encounters errors on 5, 19, 26, 45, 46, 48, 68, 80, 85, 108, 121, 136, 162, 183, 197, 216, and 219, and, by the time one gets to 136, where three errors occur in one sentence, one struggles to attend to a book unaccountably abandoned, in its hour of need, by both author and publisher.

Campbell's sin of unreadability, to say nothing of his reliance on dated secondary sources, makes the extraction of his "sociology of romanticism" (4) exceedingly problematic, and, since he never applies his expertise to examples, he shirks the central task of any project such as this. He has the right idea; and his title is inspired parallelism; but did Weber omit research? did Weber write bad prose? We do not have, yet, the companion to Weber's book that Campbell's tries to be. However pioneering, and however bold, "a fundamentally speculative attempt" cannot make the intellectual triple play of economics, religion, and romanticism, and not even Montaigne would have indulged in a book-length essay. Someone needs to get it right; maybe Campbell will.

30. *British Romantic Writers and the East: Anxieties of Empire,* by Nigel Leask

Cambridge: Cambridge University Press, 1992.
Pp. xvi+ 266; 9 illustrations. $54.95.

In 1950, Raymond Schwab argued that the late eighteenth-century "discovery" of ancient "oriental" languages bears the same relationship to Romanticism as the "discovery" of classical humanist texts bears to the Renaissance. In his 1978 *Orientalism* Edward Said emphasized "complicities" between the Enlightenment and Western imperialism in Asia. Now, in *British Romantic Writers and the East*, Nigel Leask focuses on "anxieties and instabilities rather than positivities and totalities in the Romantic discourse of the Orient" (p. 2). At a time when "discussion of the history and ideology of nationalism is a very urgent concern," and when "Romantic studies more than Renaissance studies in Britain have been slow to address the imperial components of the culture," Leask argues that the imperialist politics of Shelley, Byron, and De Quincey are "constitutive" of their works (p. 11).

This is a very large claim. But Leask is dead serious about it: while he acknowledges that Byron's *The Island* and Shelley's *Prometheus Unbound* "rethink the relations of power and desire," he emphasizes that "the compulsive pursuit of an elusive (and figuratively female) oriental ideal is a form of self-destruction" for Romantic writers (p. 10). Since he uses fetish-object psychoanalytic theory, Bakhtin's category of hybridization, and Lacan's concept of mimicry, Leask can state his thesis in a fashionably theoretical way: "The Same cannot emerge except in relation to the Other; in a diachronic scale, the varieties of Otherness are successively incorporated into the Same by the ongoing displacement of the site of the Other" (p. 86). This book is not easy to read.

Byron, Leask writes, regarded Greece as the "lost source" of European civilization "smothered beneath the blanket of the Ottoman Empire"; Byron's emphasis on the Levant in his *Eastern Tales*, accordingly, is "to some extent complicit in the jealous gaze of British policy" (p. 23). The predicament of

Selim in *The Bride of Abydos* reflects the dilemma of the Whigs after 1812, when they were "caught between the devil and the deep blue sea of Tory triumphalism and the growing tide of unacceptable plebeian radicalism" (p. 39). The association of the active heroine in *The Corsair* with democratic politics opens the poem up to "a revolutionary potential"; the conclusion of the poem, however, retreats from that potential (p. 53). In *Lara*, "Asiatic values" threaten to "swamp the West" (p. 61). Only in *The Island* does Byron place his hopes in a single family of humankind.

Thus, while Byron's attitudes are far from the opportunistic monopolism of Tory imperialism, they are also far from being radically anti-imperialistic. His political philosophy, Leask thinks, is never more liberal than the Whig combination of free trade and colonialism, and his Whig conception of liberty is based on "an autocratic classical republicanism quite distinct from the democratic ideology of contemporary 'rights of man' radicalism" (p. 37). The notes to *Childe Harold* declare, revealingly, that "the Greeks will never be independent; they will never be sovereign as heretofore, and God forbid they ever should! but they may be subjects without being slaves. Our colonies are not independent, but they are free and industrious, and such may Greece be hereafter!" (as quoted in Leask, p. 23).

Leask's chapter on Shelley focuses on how *The Assassin, The Revolt of Islam*, and *Alastor* are "specifically interested in the question of British India" (p. 72). Shelley's answer to the "Asiatic despotism" of Islam is an idealized Hellenism, not a rejuvenated Hinduism. His anxiety about the East—both his assumption of superiority, and his fear of instability and absorption—is no different from the anxiety displayed by the East India Company. "I want to maintain," declares Leask, "that Shelley's metaphors for the dichotomy reason/imagination were loaded with the weight of material history (imperialism and patriarchy), rather than generated by some disinterested epistemological decision" (p. 121). Anyone who thinks that Shelley is a "Prophet against Empire" is mistaken (p. 79). (Leask alludes to David Erdman's argument concerning Blake.) Shelley, though no belligerent jingoist, is quite the "civilizing" missionary (p. 79).

Leask's final chapter, "Autobiography, Opium and Empire in 'Confessions of an English Opium Eater' and 'Biographia Literaria'," argues that "De Quincey represented the pleasures and pains of opium upon his sensitive nervous system as a metaphor (or a symbol, in the Coleridgean sense) for the effects of capitalism, in its newly developed imperialist phase, upon the body politic" (p. 171). "To be an English opium-eater," Leask declares, "was to consume (although maybe . . . to be consumed by) the East" (p. 208). Leask concludes that De Quincey's "literature of power," like British Romantic literature as a whole, is "complicit with a Eurocentric cultural hegemony" (p. 212).

The subtext of the "Romantic quest," Leask believes, is "a nineteenth-century epic of empire" (p. 162). The subtext of "Romantic idealism," similarly, is "imperial heroism" (p. 162). The Romantics, to be sure, were not "manifest imperialists," for they did not support the slave trade, mercantilist monopoly, or the military subjugation of non-European peoples (p. 92). But they were "covert imperialists": they never questioned "the expansion of the norms of European civilization over the whole globe" (p. 92). Leask, while admitting that *Prometheus Unbound* "attempts to rethink binary stereotypes," emphasizes that the poem bases "the liberation of men and women on the premise of imperial domination" (p. 122). Hence Shelley in no way achieved "a balancing act in the constitution of a symmetrical, integrated humanism" (p. 121).

Leask's scholarly "thick descriptions" are in the best traditions of the new historicism. One might wish, however, for less hermeneutical suspicion, if not for some integrated humanism. Leask's Romantics verge on being so politically incorrect that he might want to eject them from the canon. We might temper his rather predictable methodology with the refreshing recantation of new historicism by Stephen Greenblatt, who questions "the academic left's current dream—my dream, too, for a very long time—that history will somehow save one from the complacencies of humanism, that it is better to confront the historical roots of conflict than to comfort oneself with the fraudulent fantasy of a shared humanity, that 'difference' and 'otherness' are more progressive, more hopeful, than 'the illusory goal of wholeness'": "But why should we believe any of this? How can the dream of redemptive historical difference survive the end of the Cold War and linger on in the murderous age of ethnic hatreds? Why should we imagine that if we grasp more firmly the 'historical' roots of conflict we will then choose the morally preferable alternative?" (Stephen Greenblatt, "Kindly Visions," *The New Yorker*, 11 October 1993, pp. 112-20, especially p. 119). One is reminded of Matthew Arnold's definition of greatness: "That is what I call living by ideas: when one side of a question has long had your earnest support, when all your feelings are engaged, when you hear all around you no language but one, when your party talks this language like a steam engine and can imagine no other--still to be able to think, still to be irresistibly carried, if so it be, by the current of thought to the opposite side of the question, and, like Balaam, to be unable to speak anything but what the Lord has put in your mouth" (*The Function of Criticism at the Present Time*, 1864). It is feasible, at any rate, to resist Leask's "postcolonial," "modern 'unromantic'" reading of Romanticism (pp. 222-23). Regardless of whether "shared humanity" is our only hope, the will to power does not fully define human nature, and the integrated humanism that informs Romantic ideology is as defensible as any agenda of difference.

Reviews, Third Series:

Books on Transatlantic Romanticism

31. *The Spiritual History of Ice: Romanticism, Science, and the Imagination,* by Eric G. Wilson

Palgrave Macmillan, 2003, viii + 278 pp. $39.95

Eric G. Wilson's *The Spiritual History of Ice* does for ice what Marjorie Hope Nicolson's *Mountain Gloom and Mountain Glory* (1963) did for mountains—and more. The book assimilates a staggering number of primary sources and secondary references and strikes a balance between theoretical abstraction and practical criticism. It offers the anatomy as well as the history of crystals, glaciers, and poles that "blanch the earth into a corpse" and "translucently reveal life's vital core" (2). *Spiritual History* includes an apology for the "ecological inflection" of this "Romantic mode of seeing" (3). It constitutes Wilson's best book yet.

Crystallography in Emerson and Thoreau, glaciology in the Shelleys and Byron, and polar exploration in Coleridge and Poe translate "the data of science into literary dreams" (4). These authors agree on what ice means—namely, that "the world is double—local and global, same and other, pattern and abyss" (86). Whereas the crystal "powerfully discloses a self-organizing universe and the glacier notably opened into a cosmos of infinite regression," the poles prove "more likely to explode their beholders into an apocalyptic vista of the eternal *terra incognita*" (192). This argument stays alert to the spiritual in the scientific, as where magi from Zoroaster and Hermes, through Ficino and Pico, to Paracelsus are said to consent to, rather than to violate, nature's laws (96-97). Emerson's "The Snow-Storm" introduces "the poetics of crystal" (29). "The Mer de Glace, like all glaciers, stuns the observer into the vertigo of infinite regress—origins that have origins that have origins, ad infinitum, and ad infinitum, ends that point to ends that open to more ends" (127). The "unmapped spaces" of polar regions inspire exhilarating "spiritual sublimities," as in Coleridge's "The Rime of the Ancient Mariner," or pernicious "mental systems," as in Poe's *The Narrative of Arthur Gordon Pym*

(141-3). The explanatory power of Wilson's approach to nineteenth-century literature extends to authors beyond his scope; for instance, Emily Dickinson's snow-crystal riddle ("It sifts from Leaden Sieves—"), her psychologizing of geological time ("Retrospection is Prospect's half— / Sometimes, almost more—"), and her "polar privacy," her healthy and unhealthy, sublime and bipolar interior world, come to mind (Poem 291, line l; Poem 995, lines 7-8; Poem 1695, line 6).

Wilson's readings advance the scholarly conversation. The "transparent eye-ball" in Emerson's "Nature" must henceforth serve to reveal the Romantic self as "a crystal, a transpicuous lens through which infinite forces oscillate" (33). Wilson's attention to ice-lore pays off in Emerson-criticism:

> Different and indifferent, transpicuous and dense, uncircumscribed and spherical, Emerson as glassy ball, as shew-stone, is not pellucid. Duplicitous, conflicted, he clusters cosmic poles. Yet, in turning into a surreal *coincidentia oppositorum*, he is not aberrant but a convoluted part of a torqued whole. In his landscape, numerous contraries coincide. The common is slushy, liquid and solid. The time is twilight, day and night. The sky obscure and clear, is cloudy yet opens to infinite space. The blithe air, spirit, bathes, as matter. Emerson turned crystal simply finds his place in a crystalline cosmos. (34)

The twenty-four-page interpretation of Coleridge's "Rime" (168-92) answers why the Mariner embraces the ice: he "converts from the single vision—phenomena as either one thing or the other—to a double science: events are polarized" (176). Wilson identifies both/and logic as the presiding agent of Romantic change and as the principal guarantor of Romantic redemption.

In the beginning was the Romantic word. Goethe "first imagined miraculous glacial powers almost a decade before Louis Agassiz offered empirical evidence for the shaping actions of 'God's great plough[s]'" (73). Thus Wilson regards Romanticism as a sudden break. Humphrey Davy's focus on crystals, James Hutton's on glaciation, and James Cook's on the Antarctic Circle for the first time emphasized that "ice is not evil matter to be transcended or bland material to be commodified"; it is, rather, from about 1800 on, "a vehicle and revelation of vital energy" (4). In a more important sense, though, Wilson instructs students of Romanticism about various intellectual and historical continuities, for, without losing a sense of how the Romantic period represents a departure, *Spiritual History* boasts thousand-year overviews. The section on glaciers surveys occult, magical origins dating back to Saxo Grammaticus and earlier, as well as science from Horace de Saussure, through Hutton, to Agassiz (74). Mountain theology from Abraham and Moses, through Jesus, Zoroaster, and Mohammed, to Shelley, Byron, Nietzsche, and Mann lends credibility to a major conclusion of this magisterial book—namely, that the "salubrious craft" of white magic recognizes and expresses "a spiritual flow . . . always present yet hidden in all things" (83). If some readers chafe at finding little explication of the canon before page 30, they will admire the resonance achieved when the pattern of background leads to exquisite interpretation of *belles-lettres*.

Romantic method goes beyond dialectic, or synthesis. It becomes oscillation, or suspension. "Thoreau's way of seeing [in *Walden Pond*] is, like the crystal itself, a middle way, between object and subject, fact and imagination, visible and invisible" (44). The interpretation of the uncanny in the snow-puddle passage is theoretically refined (49). So too is the similar reading of the thawing-bank sequence in the "Spring" chapter (55).

After fourteen pages with no mention of ice (102-16), the following question comes none too soon: "What do these digressions on fate and freedom, matter and mind, evil and good have to do with glaciers and 'Mont Blanc'?" (116). Some of the most brilliant passages of Wilson's book, however, appear in the section on freedom and fate; page 108, notwithstanding the icelessness of it, rivets attention. *Spiritual History* remains cogent even as it refuses thesis-ridden argumentation. Again, twelve pages can seem long without ice (178-90), but the use of Blake to understand the Mariner supplements Wilson's polar contextualizing. The Mariner, in effect, learns how "Blake's holarchical hermeneutic restores Urizenic machines to vigorous manifolds" (187). Blake's works gloss those of other Romantics under consideration. The proverb of hell—"Where man is not, nature is barren"—clarifies the concluding question of "Mont Blanc"—"And what were thou, and earth, and stars, and sea, / If to the human mind's imaginings / Silence and solitude were vacancy?" (125). If the discussion of "Mont Blanc" leans toward paraphrase (121), the procedure nonetheless gives new meaning to Shelley's acknowledgment of the exterior world.

The issue of Shelley's problematic belief in necessity acquires sharp focus: "The question is not 'Are we fated or free?' but 'How are we fated *and* free'?" (103). The thirty-four-page reading of "Mont Blanc" (94-128) rivals such other "thick descriptions" of the poem as that of Earl Wasserman and reconfirms Shelley's signature statement as a miniature poetic manifesto of Romanticism. "Awed beyond the concepts of empiricism," Wilson argues, "Shelley grasps for magic" (105). Shelley finds in John Frank Newton "a stimulating interlocutor on Zoroastrianism" (97): his view of Newton as paraphrased by Wilson offers the best Zoroastrian perspective on "Mont Blanc." "If Shelley's Ahrimanes is strict fate," Wilson writes, "then his Ormuzd is limited freedom. If Ahrimanes is a line, Ormuzd is a slight bend. If Ahrimanes is blind matter, Ormuzd is conscious mind" (106).

Wilson guards against reinventing the wheel. Such classical scholars as Stephen Whicher, M. H. Abrams, C. E. Pulos, and John Livingston Lowes receive their due. This quotation from Kathleen Raine could serve as the epigraph: "To the alchemists spirit and matter, active and passive, light and darkness, above and below are, like the Chinese yin and yang, complementary principles, both alike rooted in the divine. The *deus absconditus* is hidden and operating in matter, no less than He is to be found in the spiritual order" (*Blake and Tradition* [1968] 118, as quoted in Wilson, 262). From one point of view, *Spiritual History* legitimates new direction for Western alchemy!

Individual sentences lodge in the mind: "The creeping Alpine ice is earth poet, the globe-maker of the past, present, and future, troping (turning) the raw earth to fit its cold ideas of form and function" (73). Or again: "The frozen crystal, the Alpine glacier, the snowy pole constitute sacred technologies that make spiritual travel less arduous" (85). Distinctive idioms ring: "Pym is a hylic, a dupe of the demiurge's legerdemain" (208). The definition of "geological dynamics" as "the globe's own Bildungsroman" tells (72). Such diction and phrasing as *scrying, lubricious,* and *kaleidoscopic fulgurations* sound precise and delicious, rather than pedantic and bombastic.

Insights abound. Schelling's *On The World Soul*—"all nature is a vast crystal"; "crystals are early humans"; "humans are advanced crystals"—underlies science in Christian Samuel Weiss's demonstration that "direction," not the geometrical atom, "is the primary characteristic of crystal types" (29). *Spiritual History* alters views of individual Romantics (for example, Emerson's crystal transparency "heals the rift between Emerson the 'transcendentalist' and Emerson the 'pragmatist' " [39]) and provides the means of making distinctions between them (for example, whereas Thoreau was versed, like Emerson, in theories of the crystal, he "valued experience over authority" [41]). Thoreau as crystal gazer, optical thinker, physicist, chemist, and biologist—in short, "a scribbling magus, a scientist armed with tropes" (41)—comes to life. Familiar passages appear in a new light, as where these words from *Walden Pond*—"We inhabitants of New England live this mean life that we do because our vision does not penetrate the surface of things"—emerge as Thoreau's lament over an absence of scrying (51). The single-paragraph critique of Percy Shelley's *Prometheus Unbound* could fuel a teaching-unit (114). If the analysis of Mary Shelley's Victor and Byron's Manfred strays at times from glaciers, the commentary on their "submission to fate" as an "egocentrically magical violation of necessity," rather than as a "cosmologically magical" respect for it, enhances the understanding of them as negative examples of Romanticism (131). Some of the best criticism of Poe lies buried in the notes (265), but *Spiritual History* sustains the point that "Pym remains most of the novel at the onefold, though he undergoes experiences that *should* transform his way of seeing" (194).

In sum, *Spiritual History* negotiates between the Scylla and the Charybdis of the pure too little and the empty too much. The notes, devoting seven pages to the first five of text, for example, indicate breakthrough, rather than excess, allowing the text to stake out territory from the start. Fresh scrutiny arises from historical vistas that include the relevance of Nostradamus and Agrippa and the discovery that the Blemyae, Himantopedes, Sciopods, and Philli on Richard of Holdingham's map of the South Pole match the creations of Dr. Seuss. *Spiritual History* exhibits an unerring sense of proportion and transition, and the physical features of the book, notwithstanding the lack of a sorely needed bibliography, are attractive, reflecting credit on the issuing press. The tough-minded conclusion startles the tender-minded: "To grasp the ice . . . as a revelation of the groundless ground is to find oneself unmoored, undone, distributed in the all, not attached to any particular thing" (219). The interest in "Romanticism on both sides of the Atlantic" (4) adds to the boom in Anglo-American studies and establishes a long Romantic period. When readers finish this book, they will anticipate Wilson's next. His star rises, or, to shift the metaphor, the new planet of his scholarship has well begun to swim into the ken of specialists and of non-specialists alike.

32. Emerson, Romanticism, and Intuitive Reason: The Transatlantic "Light of All Our Day", by Patrick J. Keane

University of Missouri Press, 2005.
Pp. xv+ 555. $54.95

In *Emerson, Romanticism, and Intuitive Reason*, Patrick J. Keane engages "primarily with Emerson's part in the dialogue between British Romanticism . . . and American Transcendentalism" (2). Thus he calls Transcendentalism (echoing Emerson's "Circles") a "dawn risen on [the] mid-noon" of Coleridgean-Wordsworthian Romanticism (2-3). And he casts Milton's "power *to inspire*" (Emerson's words and emphasis) to play a strong supporting role in this 570-page setting of Coleridge's "intuitive Reason" as the protagonist of both British Romanticism and American Transcendentalism. Keane's preference for *intuitive Reason* over synonyms such as *Imagination*, *Spirit*, and *the Vision and the Faculty Divine* (to borrow a phrase from Wordsworth's *Excursion*) reveals an understanding that British Romanticism opened Emerson's "conduit to German idealism" (2). *Emerson, Romanticism, and Intuitive Reason* focuses on that idealism thoroughly, to the point of making Romantic Anglo-America, however provocatively or aptly, almost a colony of Romantic Germany.

Keane clearly delineates Emerson's Germano-Coleridgean affiliations. Whereas Kant's *Critique of Pure Reason* concludes that "only from the unification" of understanding and intuition "can cognition arise," Coleridge "saw not mutual dependence but apparent demotion, and preferred Milton's *privileging* of Intuition" (57). "Thus, knowledge of the *noumenal* world, prescinded from in the first *Critique*, becomes the main region of Coleridge's spiritualized Reason" (59). Emerson absorbed Coleridge's Miltonic Kant from University of Vermont President James Marsh's edition of Coleridge's *Aids to Reflection* and from his Aunt Mary Moody Emerson. From Fichte's *Ich*, moreover—and here Emerson and Aunt Mary part company—comes Emerson's notion of self-reliance as "all-determining" (63).

The main idea of Coleridge's *Aids to Reflection*—namely, "That which we find within ourselves, which is more than ourselves, and yet the ground of whatever is good and permanent therein, is the substance and life of all other knowledge" (as quoted in Keane 70, 274)—first resonates in Emerson's 1834 letter to his brother Edward (Keane 46-52). For Coleridge, "philosophy would pass into religion, and religion become inclusive of philosophy" (*Biographia Literaria*, as quoted in Keane 328), but Emerson, in Keane's view, remained unwilling "to clearly distinguish the self from God" (328). "To represent [God] as an individual," declared Emerson, "is to shut him out of my consciousness" (as quoted in Keane 331). Thus Emerson proved much more German-idealist in temperament than Christian-theological in tendency, for, to the Unitarian who told him, "I must have an object out of and above myself," he replied, "[I]f we would but look into ourselves, we should find *there* all we needed" (as quoted in Keane 345).

Keane tends to underplay his own, twofold acknowledgment that the "arc can swing from an idealism verging on solipsism to pantheism" and that "the mind," besides exerting "an imperious supremacy," "at times passively receives, or modifies, or co-creates" (238). To his credit, Keane recognizes that "the 'realist' and immanent rather than the 'idealist' and metaphysical aspect of Transcendentalism" underlies Emerson's 1845 prophecy that "after this generation, mysticism should go out of fashion for a very long time" (as quoted in Keane 391). Still, *Emerson, Romanticism, and Intuitive Reason* slights Romantic Anglo-America's conviction that experience and faith constitute a juxtaposition less violent than at first appears.

Readers may want to supplement Keane's secular view of Locke with the surprisingly Christian, though scarcely idealist, Locke delineated by W. M. Spellman, John Yolton, and Jeremy Waldron. And readers may want to extend Keane's awareness of Emerson's transatlantic connections to such purely Anglo-American spheres of influence as emerge from Dee E. Andrews's *The Methodists and Revolutionary America, 1760-1800: The Shaping of an Evangelical Culture* (2000) and from Barry Hankins's *The Second Great Awakening and the Transcendentalists* (2004). The experiential, empirical dimension of Arminian, free-will evangelicalism, as opposed to Calvinism's quasi-idealist, anti-experiential bias, stiffened Romantic Anglo-America's twin imperatives—namely, *Trust in Experiment!* and *Test Religion!* Keane emphasizes how "German hermeneutics" and "the Within and Without and Above of the Romantic dialectic" explain the "Unitarian-Transcendentalist fusion-distinction of Self and God" but *not* how "the Protestant inner-light tradition" does so (348). Keane's emphasis on Emerson's intuitive Reason means that this book takes little notice of such near influences as the Anglo-American concept of the "spiritual sense." That said, however—and herein lies the main point of this review—Keane's synthesizing powers prove magisterial.

Keane's mastery of scholarly dialogue—his bibliography fills twenty-four pages—runs scant risk of reinventing the wheel. Gian N. G. Orsini's study of Coleridge's idealism and David van Leer's of Emerson's, it is true, go missing. Nonetheless, Keane completes a conversation—featuring Barbara Packer and Alexander Kern—that harks back to Transcendentalist Henry Frederic Hedge—and that links Coleridge to Kant, Schelling, Fichte, and Jacobi and all these, in turn, to Emerson.

Keane corrects Phyllis Cole's confusion of "Kant's reason with Coleridge's Miltonic alteration" thereof (64). Keane expands the 1979 suggestion of Joseph Doherty that Emerson's vaunted optimism signals his "achieved equilibrium" rather than his "complacent equanimity" (399). Over the objections of David Porter and Julie Ellison, who take a dim view of Emerson's "Threnody," Keane praises the elegy's "*full* trajectory" from loss to compensation (472-511, especially 473; Keane's emphasis). Taking full notice of "the rich and ambiguous legacy of Emersonian self-reliant individualism," Keane advances beyond the arguments of Maurice Gounaud, Charles E. Mitchell, and David M. Robinson that Emerson's self-reliance augurs his creative engagement with the world (273-320, especially 287-9).

Keane's "exploration of elective affinities, family resemblances, and analogies," as well as of direct influences, deploys Thomas McFarland's "paradox of originality," whereby "profound indebtedness" *enhances* originality whenever "the creative receiver takes only what tallies with his own thoughts" (8-9, 20, and passim). Keane's linking of the Gospel of Thomas—"If you bring forth what is within you, what you bring forth will save you"—with the Divinity School lecture—"That which shows God in me, fortifies me"—represents *Keane's* originality (321-54, especially 333-4). Equally independent of secondary precedent is Keane's emphasis on Emerson's attempt to "reconcile" his "Coleridgean-Germanic vocabulary with the language of the New Testament" (Keane 334): "Jesus Christ," Emerson presumes to say, "was a minister of the pure Reason . . . . The Understanding can make nothing of [the Sermon on the Mount]" (as quoted in Keane 334).

Keane, personally attracted to the "master light" (Wordsworth's language) of Emerson's "intuitive Reason" (3 and passim), remains "skeptical of the grandiose, perhaps obscurantist, even delusional" character of Emerson's idealism (3 and passim). Emerson's sweeping declaration that "There is no doctrine of the Reason which will bear to be taught by the Understanding"

(*Nature*, as quoted in Keane 51) brings to mind the shrinking of Blake's Thel from the senses, and from the dust and heat of experience. Keane, for his part, registers Emerson's idealist excess.

Keane quotes Andrews Norton—"[Emerson] announces his own convictions as if . . . they were necessarily indisputable" (63)—and Margaret Fuller: "[Emerson] raised himself too early to the perpendicular and did not lie along the ground long enough to hear the secret whispers of our parent life" (478). Keane cites Thomas Carlyle, who, despite his admiration for Emerson, found him "somewhat moonshiny" (as quoted in Keane 93). Keane suggests, even more trenchantly, that Walt Whitman's *Leaves of Grass* not only paid homage to Emerson's idealism ("This head is more than churches or bible or creeds") but also resisted the bodiless abstraction thereof: "The scent of these armpits is aroma finer than prayer" (as quoted in Keane 351). Keane, finally, adduces James Russell Lowell—"all creation is duly respected [by Emerson] / As parts of himself—just a little projected" (347)—and D. H. Lawrence: "'Shall I not treat all men as gods?' [Emerson] cries. If you like, Waldo, but we've got to pay for it, when you've made them feel that they're gods. A hundred million American godlets is rather much for the world to deal with" (321). Thus Keane makes hay out of what Richard Rorty says, that Emerson "was not a philosopher of democracy but of private self-creation" (322). Keane foregrounds Rorty's conclusion, that Emerson's "America was not so much a community of fellow citizens as a clearing in which God-like heroes could act out self-written dramas" (322).

Keane confronts the ultimate indictment of Emerson's idealism, that it foreshadows Hitler's. Just as Emerson observes (in "Self-Reliance") that "Good and bad are but names very readily transferable to that or this; the only right is what is after my own constitution, the only wrong is what is against it," so too (in conversation) did Hitler declare (with similarly ominous dollops of antinomianism), "If I live my life according to my God-given insights, then I cannot go wrong, and even if I do, I know I have acted in good faith" (as quoted in Keane 273, 275). Keane points out that in his personal copy of Fichte's writings Hitler drew a line beneath Fichte's claim that "God and I are one," as well as beneath Fichte's answer to how Jesus held sway over his followers: "Through his absolute identification with God" (277). A. Bartlett Giamatti, as Keane remembers, grew uneasy over the Nietzschean, as well as Hitlerian, implications of Emerson's concept of "Power" (280). However, in Keane's view Emersonian "Power" resembles Blake's "mental fight," or Mohammed's "greater jihad" (internal striving, as opposed to the lesser jihad of external "holy war" [Keane 281]). Thus, despite "the ambiguous legacy of Emersonian individualism," Keane endorses George Kateb's description of Emerson's individuality as "impersonal," and hence salutary (Keane 278-9). Emerson himself, as Keane observes, proved capable of acknowledging the weakness and vulnerability of extreme idealism; the death of Emerson's son, Waldo, after all, leveled this "perpendicular" father, as "Threnody" makes poignantly clear:

> For this losing is true dying;
> This is lordly man's down-lying,
> This his sure but slow reclining,
> Star by star his world resigning.
> (Lines 162-5, as quoted in Keane 493)

If, as Keane implies, Emerson's idealism went around the proverbial bend, the cause, in Keane's estimation, lay in Emerson's too-hierarchical approach to "polarities," or to what Blake and Wordsworth, respectively, called "Contraries" and "contrarieties." Emerson "seized on the pivotal Coleridgean distinctions" whereby "Reason is superior to Understanding," the Organic to the Mechanic, Genius to Talent, Imagination to Fancy, Symbolism to Allegory, and Whole to Part (Keane 119). For Emerson, as for Coleridge, "the inferior term in each case" stays "limited to the reception of the objective world, the external realm perceived through the senses, whereas the superior terms pertain to the subjective world, the realm of ideas" (Keane 119-20). Keane adds, "When it came to Wordsworth's contrast between Intuition and Tuition, Emerson clearly privileges the first term—rather like Blake in preferring infernal Energy to angelic Order, or early Nietzsche the Dionysian to the Apollonian, or Yeats the Antithetical to the Primary" (138). Even where Emerson grants privilege to neither term, according to Keane, he seeks to "reconcile" them (Keane 3), or to advance their "tendency to re-union" (Coleridge's phrase, as quoted in Keane 154). Emerson fails to realize, thereby, that whoever tries to "reconcile" such binaries as "the Prolific" with "the Devouring," to refer to Blake again, "seeks to destroy existence" (*The Marriage of Heaven and Hell*, Plate 16).

Keane emphasizes that, at their best, Emerson's "Polarities" eschew rigid hierarchy and facile reconciliation and that they evoke, thereby, the not-*so*-idealistic mood of Coleridge. Coleridge, in a passage purloined (Keane forbears to say so) from Schiller's "reciprocal action" between *Stofftrieb* and *Formtrieb*, observes, "In all subjects of deep and lasting interest, you will detect a struggle between two opposites, two polar forces, *both of which are alike necessary to our human wellbeing & necessary each to the continued existence of the other"* (as quoted in Keane 154; emphasis added). Emerson's concept of complementarity, like Coleridge's in the passage just quoted, stops well short of predictably dissolving halves into wholes: "*An inevitable dualism bisects nature, so that each thing is a half*, and *suggests* another thing to make it whole; as, spirit, matter; man, woman; odd, even; subjective, objective; in, out; upper, under; motion, rest; yea, nay" (as quoted in Keane 267; emphasis added).

Keane's phrases "symbiotic balance" (289) and "mobile dynamic" (125) precisely characterize Emerson's trademark polarities—namely, "Freedom and Fate" (268), "Solitude and Society" (289), and "Conservatism and Reform" (289). M. H. Abrams's definition of Blake's concept of marriage as "the sustained tension, without victory or suppression, of co-present oppositions" (*The Norton Anthology of English Literature*) applies to Emerson's not-*so*-idealist mood. *This* Emerson rests content with "Alternation" and "contradiction" between the co-present oppositions that beset anyone who lives in "the world / Of all of us,—the place where in the end / We find our happiness, or not at all!" (see, respectively, Emerson, as quoted in Keane 289, 349; and Wordsworth, *The Prelude* [1850] 11:142-4).

Readers of *The Wordsworth Circle* will surely rejoice that Wordsworth steals Keane's Emersonian show. Keane, it is true, concentrates on Wordsworth's *influence*. By drawing out the "Kantian-Romantic," as distinct from Lockean-empirical, implications of Wordsworth's "little heard of" theme that "The external world is fitted to the mind," Keane corroborates Emerson's idealist reading of Wordsworth, for whom "the Mind of Man" was "the main region" of his "Song" ("Prospectus," lines 41, 63-66, as quoted in Keane 43, 374). Keane acknowledges that Wordsworth's empiricism ("The mind is fitted to the external world") tempered Emerson's idealism. Nonetheless, Keane contributes to Wordsworth studies *per se*. In fact, Keane sheds light on such an assortment of Wordsworth's works as "Rob Roy's Grave" (42), "Prospectus" (142 and passim), "Nutting" (219), "Expostulation and Reply" (241-4), "Ode to Duty" (324-5), the Preface to *Lyrical Ballads* (462), "Laodamia" (512-7), and *The Prelude* (passim).

Keane's reading of *The Excursion*, in particular, reinforces this great poem. As one might expect, Keane delineates the Wanderer's idealism, his "power to commune with the invisible world" (*Excursion* 9:86, as quoted in Keane 216). Keane understands as well, however, the Wanderer's blend of spirit with *nature:*

> Sensation, soul, and form,
> All melted into him; they swallowed up
> His animal being; in them did he live,
> And by them did he live; they were his life.
> (*Excursion* 1:207-10, as quoted in Keane 131)

The subtitle of Keane's book quotes the Wordsworth poem that best unifies his argument, for the Intimations Ode's "Light of all our Day" serves to epitomize Emerson's idealism, and Keane respects the poem's empiricism, too (he quotes Pater's brief for "external influences" in the final stanzas [Keane 238]). Keane backgrounds, to begin with, the Ode's importance to Emerson's personal life. As a means of coping with the death of his first wife, Ellen, for instance, Emerson fused the Ode with Milton's *Paradise Lost* (Keane 323), and he regarded Waldo as the "mighty prophet" of whom Wordsworth had written (Keane 244). In the end, Keane finds the Ode ingrained in Emerson's art. Wordsworth's "seer blest" and the "transparent Eyeball" of Emerson's *Nature* must henceforth resonate together (Keane 110, 363). Keane's entire book, from one point of view, constitutes a thick description of this single work by Wordsworth. Keane's assessment of the Ode as "the greatest poem of its length in English (except *Lycidas*)" (485) matches Emerson's judgment. The Ode, observes Emerson, occupies "the highwater mark which the intellect has reached in this age. A new step has been taken, new means have been employed. No courage has surpassed that, & a way made through the void by this finer Columbus" (as quoted in Keane 474).

In sum, although short books are generally better than long ones, and although this one tends toward repetition, honorifics like *storehouse, compendium,* and *labor of love* obtain. Even Keane's asides on Plotinus, Bernard of Clairvaux, George Herbert, Napoleon, Blake, Shelley, Keats, Byron, Robert Browning, Thoreau, Melville, Nietzsche, Yeats, Frost, Woolf, and Stevens justify the hefty price of this volume. Telling quotations (such as this from Cyrus A. Bartol) abound: "Pantheism is said to sink man and nature in God, Materialism to sink God and man in nature, and Transcendentalism to sink God and nature in man" (as quoted in Keane 384). Professor Emeritus Keane earlier authored an excellent book on Coleridge and a fine study of Yeats. Eleven years in the making, *Emerson, Romanticism, and Intuitive Reason* adorns a distinguished career.

33. *Text as Process: Creative Composition in Wordsworth, Tennyson, and Emerson,* by Sally Bushell

Charlottesville: Univ. Press of Virginia, 2009. Pp. xi + 302.

Reading, like seeing, is selective: this review offers the broad perspective of a reader chiefly experienced in placing poets like Wordsworth, Tennyson, and Dickinson in their historical contexts. Uninitiated in the discipline of manuscript studies, I fought it for a chapter or two but then went along for a bracing, though not uncritical, ride. By the end, I too saw that the letter *S* in Dickinson's manuscript of "The Sea said 'Come' to the Brook" (Amherst College Library, Special Collections, Set 11, A432/431; qtd. Bushell 234) corresponds to a breaking wave, though I still sometimes wonder whether this text-as-process is just plain text. Even for skeptical browsers in "creative composition" theory, this book's somewhat counterintuitive stress on manuscripts as always already literary wears well, and does not finally represent too much of an un-tempered, or intemperate, stretch. Its willingness to acknowledge manuscripts as also preliminary, and perhaps even as in some sense subordinate, after all, to published or completed forms, constitutes a welcome, commonsense component of its methodology.

Bushell plainly states what is at stake for her and for any other "compositional critic" (160). "On the one hand," she declares, "I want to validate [the] process [of poetic composition] as an object of analysis in its own right and . . . for its difference from the published or completed text" (32). Thus she aims to change our thinking about poets' first thoughts or rough drafts, which in her view can prove to be as good as, and perhaps even (if I may take the next step, that she at times seems ready to take) better than their second thoughts or published work. In light of this point, we might well ask why we would ever again need to teach revising to students (some of whom are, or could one day be, poets). But whether or not a poet's rough draft surpasses what follows it, Bushell demands that we take in both. "I am arguing," she writes, "for critical integration and movement across and between *avant-texte* and text, seeking an enlargement of the definition of literary studies to include this material" (32). Thus, like French *critique génétique* (which she recapitulates with the aid of Michael Groden), Bushell's work scrutinizes not so much the "teleological movement from early stages to finished product" as "a textual field that extends backwards and forwards between avant-texte and text" (qtd. Bushell 35).

In quest of other precedents for her method of reading (besides that of *critique génétique*), Bushell surveys such schools of thought as biblical scholarship on recension or emendation and Elizabethan copy-text theory (she skips medieval manuscript culture despite its primal role in the instability and variability of all texts). While noting the rivalry between claims for the final manuscript version (Fredson Bowers) and the first published text (Philip Gaskell), she is drawn to Jerome McGann's editorial watchword that—in her words—"social forces and communal activity . . . bring the text into being" (12). Like McGann, she moves away from what she calls "the previously dominant view of the author's fixed intention as the ultimate model of authority" (12). Thus her brand of reading seems best suited to the nineteenth or even eighteenth century and after (though her survey skips the eighteenth century, too), when many manuscripts survive to provoke debates over "grounds of intentionality and questions of authority" (11). Citing Siegfried Scheibe, Hans Zeller, and Gunter Martens, Bushell argues that each transmitted version of a text is in theory equally valid and hence that "text as process" may be integrated "into the edition" (27). But she prefers *critique génétique* because it weighs "the critical status, or use, of such material" (27). She takes cues from Peter L. Shillingsburg's concept of editing as "a form of literary criticism" (qtd. Bushell 14) and also makes good use of his distinction between "the intention to do," which is "conclusively recoverable from the signs written," and "the intention to mean," which is "inconclusively recoverable through critical interpretation" (qtd. Bushell 54). To parry German and French denials of "individual creative origins" (6), she paraphrases John Searle and J. L. Austin, who argue—again in her words—that "language is a kind of act" and that "all action is intentional (though not necessarily involving conscious intention)" (53).

Bushell revives intention, then, as a motivating force capable of being inferentially reconstructed from "acts on the page" (50). Thus her methodological mix highlights a practicality that might be called Anglo-American in character. To be sure, whether or not *Text as Process* really counts as "the first study of this kind" (2), it pioneers "a new subdiscipline . . . (in Anglo-American studies at least)" (2) because Bushell's sophisticated cross-Channel importations add explanatory breadth to the savvy of her homegrown pragmatism. Nevertheless, her oscillations between the axioms of "creative composition" theory (each version is equally valid; *avant-texte* is at least as important as text) and the nuts-and-bolts of "creative composition" behavior ("acts on the page") tilt finally toward the latter. Against German and French insistences that a work does not represent an author's intention, yet perhaps with something of New Criticism's focus on a work as an author's *fulfilled* intention (vs. misguided preoccupation with an author's "reasons for writing" [15]), she retains what she calls "a distinctive Anglo-American model" whereby "the core intentional structures of the creative mind (the 'author'), even if a kind of delusion, are a necessary delusion for creative process and one worthy of study" (6). She wittily observes that "even those who write *against* intention" (e.g., Michel Foucault, Roland Barthes) have "the intention of doing so" (49). Bushell's greatest strength, in any case, is arguably Anglo-American in tendency. Together with her flair for generalization, her ability to break down a general proposition into specific instances makes her close reading of draft materials qualify as a viable, none too abstract or theoretical, kind of literary criticism.

Sometimes her close readings turn into hair splitting. In her chapter on Wordsworth, Bushell announces: "Reading the text in a state of process becomes a kind of puzzle in which words on the page signify a sequence of actions, of rapidly changing small-scale acts that can be reconstructed" (93). With regard to Wordsworth's line "While on the perilous edge I hung" (the original version of 1850 *Prelude* 1.336), she painstakingly tracks the steps of revision as the poet adds *alone*, crosses out *edge*, and writes in two alternatives: *ridge* and *cliff*. His process, she observes, goes as follows: "prior intention (I intend to cross the word out); intention-in-action (I am about to cross the word out); bodily movement (pick up pen/place on paper); action (physically make a line through the word)" (92). I find the distinction between "prior intention" and "intention-in-action" virtually invisible. The whole reconstruction of Wordsworth's act of crossing out, for me anyway, verges on self-parody, as Bushell almost admits. "It would be tedious," she confesses, "to undertake this level of microanalysis of intentional acts at any great length" (92). She underscores, however, that it is "helpful . . . to see that the narrative process for written composition is capable of being broken down to this extent" (92). Not every reader will grasp how or why it is helpful.

Manuscript microanalysis, at times, can squint at motes and miss the light they float in. Bushell concedes that "we cannot access the all-important initial point of composition, which in this case produced the line 'While on the perilous ridge I hung alone'" (92). We *can*, however, see something of how composition grows from the passage that precedes it (it does not come from nothing). Also, there is considerable difference between noting the significance of added or changed words and reconstructing the micro-steps of making a particular deletion. Bushell is at her best, I think, in the former kind of critical activity (as in her chapter on Dickinson).

What does Bushell really tell us about Wordsworth? First of all, her analysis of his MS JJ notebook links its early *Prelude* passages to its fragmentary "Essay on Morals." "While the prose piece," she writes, "argues for the need to act upon habit to good effect, the poetic draft describes and exemplifies the desired process. Whichever text was entered first, each bears upon the other" (80). This connection, though scarcely surprising, is successfully made.

Bushell maintains, moreover, that in MS JJ "the physical layout of words on the page enhances the meaning of the words" (90), as in

> . . . how my
> bosom
>   beat
> With expectation[.] (qtd. Bushell 90)

In Bushell's view, the fact that "a certain kind of meaning" exists "on *this* page as a unique object" (90), whether or not Wordsworth intended it, makes for literary-critical hay. One might ask in what sense meaning exists on a page apart from any reader's interpretation of it (a crucial question simply begged here), and Bushell hardly persuades me that physical layout makes this "bosom / *beat* / With expectation."

More convincingly Bushell argues that Wordsworth's "programmatic intention" to compose an epic both helped and hindered his creativity "as a writing poet" (80). Much of his verse, she shows, was "stimulated by his evasion" of his *magnum opus* ambition (80). Since the *Prelude* drafts in MS JJ (DC MS 19) "run forward from the back of the [MS JJ] notebook," she concludes that he thus tried to overcome "the psychologically difficult stage of first composition" (86). Maybe, on the other hand, he was just "hiding" what he had not finished, or was just saving the notebook's first part for something else.

Above all, Bushell helps to explain whether Wordsworth's poetry came direct from his mind (à la Mozart) or was generated on paper (after the manner of Beethoven). The answer—both—will astonish only those still under the exclusive sway of "Romantic poetry as unpremeditated outpouring." Discussing the *Prelude* drafts in MS WW (DC MS 43), Bushell shows that "the lack of change in the 'Arabian Tales' piece seems to support the Wordsworthian ideal of written words as mere 'transcription'" (107). In *The Excursion*, similarly, as indicated by Bushell's assessment of its *avant-texte* as "a large central mass of unsituated material," Wordsworth wanted, if not to elide the poet as writer, then "to envisage long poem composition as some kind of 'spontaneously' self-generating structure" (116). By contrast, a point that seems to me to be well worth reinforcing here is that Wordsworth's work toward *The Excursion* discloses what Bushell's scrutiny of DC MS 70 says it does. His *struggle* with a "prosaic moment of introduction" and "the establishment of character" makes for *highly wrought* style (108). Thus, even in rough drafts, his poetry can become almost lapidary, almost more crafted than inspired.

Turning from Wordsworth to Tennyson, Bushell notes that a Tennyson first draft "looks remarkably 'clean' on the page" (133). With the aid, again, of the distinction between Mozart and Beethoven (in Klaus Hurlebusch's theory of aesthetic production), she maintains that rather than following Beethoven-like "construction," his poetry derives from Mozart-like "reproduction" (133). It could be, instead, that Tennyson's chaotic jottings are simply gone, but Bushell contends, consistently and persistently if not convincingly, that his love of clean pages led him "to externalize process and work in a receptivity-dominated way" (123). In this vein, Bushell reminds us, Tennyson persuaded his publisher to print "trial books," "choosing to read the words in print not merely to prepare the published text but as an active [if neat-freakish] part of the creative process" (125).

Bushell's Tennyson chapter, moreover, takes tantalizing notice of his Trinity Notebook 17, which, like the notebooks of Paul Valéry, features drawings "between passages of written text" (128). Bushell's linking of these drawings to the verbal imagery in the texts illustrates "the relationship between word and image for the creative process" (126). She does not fully spell out what she thinks the notebook reveals about Tennyson's word/image connection, but I gather that even his necessarily outward-oriented visual images can appear as inward in their origin as his words can seem spontaneous in their effect.

Bushell revisits the much-mooted question of why Tennyson's Arthurian idylls "do not appear in the final published whole poem in the same order as that of first publication" (144). As she notes, the standard view of this re-arrangement is that the final order emphasizes "the linear progression toward the kingdom's downfall" and hence the pessimistic direction of the poet's thought (144). Bushell demurs. Drawing on the concept of idylls as vignettes and on Friedrich Schleiermacher's and Hans-Georg Gadamer's hermeneutic circle (understanding through the relation of parts to whole and vice versa), she reasons that the poem's "cyclical model of... repeated return" is "far more positive than the steady movement toward decline and collapse" (144). In particular, she concludes, Tennyson's relocation of "Guinevere" to a penultimate position in *Idylls of the King* demonstrates that the queen "has been 'false' throughout in order to be 'true' to her emotions" (151). Thus the poet's repositioning tempers any pessimistic reading of his idylls' final form, and this optimistic interpretation of "Guinevere" is buttressed by Bushell's upbeat reading of Enid's song (from "Geraint and Enid") as it appears in Trinity Notebook 30 and "within the final published version" (160-7, esp. 166).

Bushell also confronts the charge that Tennyson simply "translates" Sir Thomas Malory's prose into the poetry of the *Idylls*. To answer this charge, Bushell presents "The Holy Grail" as it appears in Harvard Notebook 38. Yes, she admits, Tennyson does his own prose version of Malory and then transforms that into verse. But in this case, she argues, the nature of the creative act is not necessarily a "lesser" phenomenon just because "the poet chooses to create a process-within-a-process in the form of 'self-translation' across forms" (141). She also contends that "*all* poetic creativity involves such acts" (141). Whether or not poetry was once prose, and whatever the degree of Tennyson's selfhood in his writings, Bushell's study of this draft material (136-41) skillfully unfolds his *integration* of a prose plan into *consequent* poetry. His updating of legend, therefore, emerges from her discussion as all the more timeless and alive.

Emily Dickinson's work is the ideal quarry for compositional criticism. During her lifetime, only ten of her 1,789 poems appeared in print, and they did so against her will. Except for fair copies in the first eight of her forty fascicles or manuscript books, all of her lyrics were poems in process, with changes entered on the manuscript page. Bushell resists the widespread tendency among Dickinson scholars "to distort the nature of the unpublished material" by assuming that it achieves the status of a published collection (174). She reminds us that the poet's groupings are "held in multiple, loose, separate bifolium sheets or single leaves" and so "are always subject to potential regrouping" (175). Bushell's insistence on valuing draft material for its own sake turns out to be just what Dickinson studies need at present.

Unlike other specialists in Dickinson's manuscript material, Bushell seeks not so much to survey "a number of alternatives to the word to be replaced" as to explore "a semantic field that generates meaning out of itself" (210). Dickinson's manuscripts, she notes, suggest "an almost physical resistance to rejection" (184). For instance, she writes, "When [Dickinson] does cross out a word, she usually does so not by drawing a line through it horizontally but by a less harsh diagonal across the page to include the word, with the line often made in pencil and rarely in ink" (184). In decoding Dickinson's religious-looking crosses (as distinct from her crossings-out), Bushell finds that they help to make the poet's text "layered and palimpsestic, with one word constantly disappearing below another.... This makes it possible for the poet to *return* to a text repeatedly but not to have advanced it teleologically" (195). Consequently, Bushell argues, "being anti-teleological" is "a fundamental part of the kind of poet [Dickinson] wants to be" (176-7).

In Dickinson's texts Bushell finds "suspended deletion, allowing for the unresolved alternative" (187), and hence "not 'revision' so much as creative optionality" (197). Her options, Bushell states, are concerned not "merely with suspending meaning, or with 'not choosing' between variants" (203), but with the vitality of options. She writes that "the creation of options in one part" leads to their creation "in another, so that optionality becomes an active part of the creative process" (203). Although few readers of even the subtlest literature can always "choose not choosing" (life is too short), Bushell holds that no word of Dickinson's is to be replaced. Each is to remain in play.

Yet at the same time, Bushell discovers stability among Dickinson's variants for each poem, for while half of her text "contains multiple versions" of diction, the other half is a "fixed frame" of syntax (198). Thus Bushell's Dickinson composes by means of "juxtaposed stability and instability" (198). Bushell's acknowledgment of Dickinson's steady word order, as distinct from her English major's yen for the poet's interchangeable words, guides us through the vertiginous world of Dickinson's chosen un-choosing. Bushell's method here, thankfully, is balanced. It does not exacerbate, too much, the postmodern migraine of relentlessly verbal hare-chasing.

As Bushell notes, it has long been recognized how uncannily and "directly" Dickinson "anticipates the complex twentieth-century redefining of the nature of understanding" (210). Bushell adds aesthetic nuance to this philosophical emphasis on the poet's un-decidability. For her, it is "a poetic device," not "an ontological state" (210). Moreover, as a welcome sign of Bushell's attention to historical context, she acknowledges that Dickinson's openness "*also* emerges from a far more ancient, self-enclosed sense of spiritual identity, behind which lies the presence of God as supreme Author" (211). Thus it is not as though Dickinson foresaw Gadamer's concept that the "dialectic of experience has its proper fulfillment not in definitive knowledge but in the openness to experience that is made possible by experience itself" (qtd. 210). Rather, Dickinson's un-decidability functions as a mark of her religious humility.

As Bushell concludes from her reading of such a theoretically prescient, yet surprisingly traditional, poem as "No Other can reduce Our Mortal Consequence," "a deeply self-conscious awareness of the limits of self-conscious awareness" informs Dickinson's poetic works (214). Here is Bushell's transcription of Dickinson's four-stanza version of this lyric (Houghton Library, Harvard, MS 97a), which—Bushell argues—voices not so much "a Gadamerian understanding" of "a life lived . . . in relation to time" as "the Last Judgment" in "the world beyond" (211-12):

> No Other can reduce Our
> Mortal Consequence
> Like the remembering it be Nought -
> A Period from hence -
>
> But Contemplation for
> Cotemporaneous Nought -
> Our Mutual Fame - that
> haply
> Jehovah - recollect -
>
> No Other can exalt Our
> Mortal Consequence
> Like the remembering it exist -
> A period from hence -
>
> Invited from Itself
> To the Creator's House -
> To tarry an Eternity -
> His - shortest Consciousness –
>   (qtd. Bushell 211)

I cannot help but note that Bushell's grounding of Dickinson's openness in a religious worldview nicely confirms my less manuscript-oriented, yet similarly religion-aware, findings in *Experience and Faith: The Late-Romantic Imagination of Emily Dickinson* (2004; paper 2008).

To help summarize her argument, Bushell invokes the philosophy of Martin Heidegger and his privileging of the made object. Anticipating, in effect, Wallace Stevens's "Anecdote of the Jar," Heidegger once wrote, "The making . . . lets the jug come into its own. But that which in the jug's nature is its own is never brought about by its making. Now released from the making process, the self-supporting jug has to gather itself for the task of containing" (qtd. Bushell 217). Bushell, however, privileges "the making process" (219). She wants "the juxtaposition and cross-interpretation of two radically different kinds of literary meaning: the self-sufficient meaning of the text as a work of art, and the meaning of it in the flux of its coming-into-being" (219).

Thus, though differing with Heidegger on the importance of made vs. making, Bushell finds in his philosophy a framework for rounding off her enterprise, as though the discipline of manuscript studies, when all is said and done, should enter into dialogue with phenomenology and ontology. Heidegger might indeed have been describing Bushell's understanding of poetic composition when he wrote, "[T]he possible is drawn into the actual, arising out of the actual and returning to it" (qtd. Bushell 224). Just as Dickinson famously dwells in possibility, Bushell conceives of textual process as just such a realm to live in. Whether or not Heidegger's stress on actualization fully explains manuscript production, as Bushell implies, she deploys his key term, *Dasein*, as her means of epitomizing her rationale for studying texts that precede a printed text: "[C]reative process could be *both* apparently teleological, directed toward a clear goal . . . and, at the same time, part of a larger, always open-ended, process of *Dasein* for the person engaged in it" (227). Heidegger observes that "as long as any *Dasein* is [whether *Dasein* ready-to-hand, present-at-hand, or becoming], it too *is already its 'not yet'*" (qtd. Bushell 224). In Bushell's paraphrase, "*Dasein* directs itself toward part of itself to reconsider and reinterpret anew" (225), and Bushell suggests, in this spirit, that imagination directs itself toward ever-emerging draft materials. Heidegger cares not so much about self-renewal or self-reinterpretation through manuscript production as about the ephemerality of being (always shading into non-being), but Bushell's appropriation of Heideggerian authenticity works well enough for her conclusion, providing its provocative, not to say violent, juxtapositions of forms and ideas.

For all its merits, the flaws in this book are large enough to be sometimes distracting. A bewildering proliferation of the kinds and variations of intention—programmatic, contingent, final, unfulfilled, revised; accidental and unconscious intended meaning; consciously intended unintentionality—makes the head swim, and ache (62-8). Chapter 3, moreover, is overly schematic. Unwieldy sentences, scattered throughout, bounce off the frontal lobes, e.g., "In the case of textual self-extension the mediation of body with the world also appears to the writer to occur to prepare the way for the mediation of consciousness with the world through language" (231). Sometimes this book relies too heavily on other secondary sources; its discussion of Wordsworth's preference for orality over writing (100-4), for instance, goes no further than has Andrew Bennett, who highlights Wordsworth's "inevitable paradox of a writer writing about his poetry as speech" (qtd. Bushell 104). Repetitive at times, the book introduces theories (e.g., Searle's on 52-3) only to reiterate them when applied to a poet (e.g., to Wordsworth on 90-1); in fairness, this arrangement ensures that readers interested only in Wordsworth, let us say, can learn all that the book has to tell us about him from chapter 4. In general, I would have liked to see a little less process-analysis of draft materials alone (this is where Bushell's heart lies, though) and even more of what she *also* promises—namely, "critical integration and movement across and between *avant-texte* and text" (best illustrated, perhaps, in her *Idylls* discussion).

But the book is still worth reading. Even if Bushell's style and procedure do not always please her readers, her content will certainly instruct them. While she admits that she could not afford to reproduce as many manuscripts as she wanted to use (264n.65), and while the cost of doing so—even if some are available online—might well restrict the growth of "compositional criticism," Bushell has laid out a reasonable compromise. She well describes some draft materials and judiciously selects eighteen illustrations that form the focus of her most sustained discussions; thus she advocates "an editorial tension between allowing material to speak for itself and presenting that material in a form that readers are able and willing to respond to" (169). She sensibly compromises, too, by striking a careful balance between *just* reproducing manuscripts vs. *interpreting* them. A courteous scholar, Bushell does not write for "compositional critics" alone.

Seldom taking her approach too seriously, and often entertaining opposed ideas, she brings her "multiple audiences" (8) with her, for the space of this book, at least, "backwards and forwards between *avant-texte* and text." She asks, forthrightly, "Is genetic criticism a theory of criticism or just helpful advice, something like: keep in mind that manuscripts can also contribute to the understanding of literature?" (28). Just when her readers may well be formulating their own versions of Charles Lamb's "Disenchantments of an Original MS," she quotes Lamb's conclusion, "I will never go into the workshop of any great artist again" (75). Bushell's adaptation of Euro-Continental methodology to Anglo-American habitat beckons even skeptical old lay readers like me into that very laboratory, there to test text-as-process theory on fresh objects of practical literary analysis ("there is much more to be done" [237]).

34. *Seeing Suffering in Women's Literature of the Romantic Era,* by Elizabeth A. Dolan

Aldershot and Burlington: Ashgate, 2008. Pp. vii + 249, 7 illustrations.

Emily Dickinson's Approving God: Divine Design and the Problem of Suffering, by Patrick J. Keane

Columbia and London: U of Missouri P, 2008. Pp. xiii + 256.

Elizabeth A. Dolan's *Seeing Suffering in Women's Literature of the Romantic Era* and Patrick J. Keane's *Emily Dickinson's Approving God: Divine Design and the Problem of Suffering* prove complementary: taken together, these two broadly historical, fully interdisciplinary critical monographs define a standard theme of Romantic Anglo-America. Dolan's focus on a range of immediate historical contexts—namely, Romantic-era science, psychology, and politics—balances Keane's on the theological tradition from the Book of Job, through the long Romantic Movement, to the "turn to religion" in post-9/11 academia (compare Fish). Dolan's mastery of medical theory matches Keane's of theodicy (a term coined by Leibniz in 1710). Dolan's view of pain as a secular phenomenon accompanies Keane's perspective on suffering as a variety of religious experience, though the Romantic-era version of theodicy, in Keane's view, forms only a rear-guard "defense of divine holiness and justice in respect to the existence of physical and moral evil" (*OED*). Dolan's Mary Wollstonecraft, Charlotte Smith, and Mary Shelley shine in the light of Keane's Emily Dickinson, and vice versa; Dolan's emphasis on her trio's physical suffering supplements Keane's fascination with Dickinson's spiritual agony, and vice versa.

Dolan's book makes its case at the expense of Romantic-era male writers (e.g., 95, 102, 213). Smith seeks to "move beyond the Keatsian 'sole self' not to transcendence, but to a sympathetic world" (45). This view of John Keats as ethereal overlooks Judith Page's not-*so*-recent presentation of social sympathy as the goal of *all* Romantic-era writers. "In contrast to the portrait of the male melancholic literary genius composing alone in his study," writes Dolan, "Smith's vision of female melancholic genius depends on a sympathetic interaction with another person" (43). This distinction ignores Thomas McFarland's meditation on the importance to William Wordsworth's art of his one-on-one relationships and even of his communitarian sensibility. Wollstonecraft, Smith, and Mary Shelley "do not ask—as does John Keats at the end of his transcendent reverie—'Was it a vision, or a waking dream? . . . Do I wake or sleep?'" (Dolan 219; compare Keats, "Ode to a Nightingale" [1819], ll. 79-80). Instead, adds Dolan, they "ask other seeing subjects, 'Do you see me? What does the world look like to you?'" (219). This contrast properly takes Keats for anything but a reciprocal seer but leaves out Jack Stillinger's demonstration that at every turn, including in the Nightingale Ode, the poet suspects transcendence.

The book's trio of authors "contradicts the [male] idealists' notion that reality is inextricable from an internal vision" and "deflates the [male] fantasy of transcendence, tethering vision to the material world" (215). Such a writer as Wordsworth, however, can surely still see things as they are. His *Prelude* (1850), after all, anchors even "transcendent power" in "sense, conducting to ideal form" (14.75-76). If the men in *Seeing Suffering* do not exactly exhibit fright or flight (their oxytocin weakened by testosterone), then the women of this book certainly tend and befriend (their oxytocin fully enhanced by estrogen [compare "UCLA"]). Dolan's men suffer from idealism/ idea-ism, if not solipsism/narcissism. Margaret Fuller's estimation of Ralph Waldo Emerson—namely, that "he raised himself too early to the perpendicular and did not lie along the ground long enough to hear the secret whispers of our parent life" (Emerson 605)—leaps to mind. Ironically, though, William Blake and William Wilberforce provide Dolan's project with her most compelling Romantic-era examples of what she otherwise implies is an exclusively female mode of "seeing suffering" and writing about it (2-3, 5, 8, 9-10, 21, 39, 159, 165).

These reservations aside, Dolan propounds fresh insights. She points out that, unlike Anne Elliott in Jane Austen's *Persuasion* (1818), and despite Dr. Thomas Gisborne's praise of women for their stoicism, Smith seldom mentions fortitude and rarely seeks to mitigate either suffering or loss (30-31). Dr. Thomas Young's theory of color vision/color blindness supplies the context for Smith's use of color as a metaphor for happiness/despair (40). The Reverend Richard Polwhele's prudish strictures against female botanizing dramatize Smith's boldness in classifying plants according to their seven (!) reproductive parts (108-12). Romantic-era theories of the body in pain shed light on Mary Shelley herself, distinct from her self-projections in her prose and prose fiction, as "the child whose birth killed her mother, the mother who birthed three children who died, the woman who lost another child in a miscarriage that nearly killed her, too" (153). This body equates to "the physical seat of a death-inducing sexuality" (153).

Dolan emphasizes Mary Shelley's legacy from mother Wollstonecraft, and connects for the first time the careers of all three writers, reconfirming how distinctly the late eighteenth century hums along the Romantic era's larger arc. Wollstonecraft's *Wrongs of Woman* (1798) does not so much fictionally continue her *Vindication of the Rights of Woman* (1792) as build on didactic children's literature, the episodic form of which inspires the later book's multiple portraits of marginalized women (195-213). Dolan's gender-based framework establishes the thematic depth, and perhaps even the formal structure, of prose and prose fiction from Wollstonecraft to Mary Shelley, with Smith's achievement the highlight of this sociologically sophisticated canon of Romantic-era identity.

Above all, Dolan breaks ground in historical, interdisciplinary criticism. Whereas Romantic-era philosophies of perception associate the eye with visual evidence *and* internal vision, grounding *and* un-tethering the imaginations of Wordsworth, Keats, and company, Dolan's important but hitherto neglected context of medical science comprehends the Romantic-era eye in exclusively physical, disturbingly vulnerable terms. As she paraphrases Dr. Arthur Edmondston, "the eye is the organ most likely to express suffering (as in tears), but also to suffer pain itself' (6). At the risk of under-reporting the *whole* truth about Romantic-era understanding that keeps oppositions in play, Dolan grants privilege to the *first* terms of the period's dialectical continuums: her provocative, counterintuitive study in Romanticism raises materiality over transcendence, and empiricism (or visual evidence) over idealism and internal vision. By subordinating the both/and logic of *les belles-lettres* (the period's major poetry) to the either/or logic of *les bonnes-lettres* (the period's prose and didactic prose fiction) she purchases much clarity at the expense of some subtlety, throwing into relief the late-eighteenth-to-early-nineteenth-century trend toward realism, however harsh. Her thesis that an "unusual emphasis on the physical nature of looking and of being seen . . . does particular cultural work in the Romantic era" (1) applies convincingly to the early-to-mid-period triptych that this labor of love honors for its reciprocal seeing and proposed palliation of suffering.

In *Emily Dickinson's Approving God*, the second book here under review, Keane argues that Dickinson, like Ivan Karamazov, "was no atheist but a challenger who, in her own oblique way, never ceased asking the same questions: Why does evil strike so meaninglessly? Why do the innocent suffer? How can a purportedly omnipotent and loving God approve of such an apparently random, brutally violent process?" (72). Just as for Karamazov no "divine resolution" can justify "the tears of a single tortured child" (72), so too do answers elude the persistent interrogations of Keane's quite uppity Dickinson. She would agree with Charles Darwin's 1860 letter to his friend and fellow scientist Asa Gray, for whom evolutionary biology and divine design somehow stay commensurate:

> I had no intention [observes Darwin] of writing atheistically. But I own that I cannot see as plainly as others do, and as I should wish to do, evidence of design and beneficence on all sides of us. There seems to me too much misery in the world. I cannot persuade myself that a beneficent and omnipotent God would have designedly created the Ichneumonidae [assassination wasps] with the express intention of their [larva] feeding within the living bodies of Caterpillars, or that a cat should play with mice. (Darwin 2:105, qtd. 79-80)

Dickinson, for her Darwinian part in this mid nineteenth-century dialogue between science and religion (which drags on to this day) signals her acknowledgment of, and her horror at, cat-and-mouse cruelty or "Nature, red in tooth and claw / With ravine" (Tennyson, *In Memoriam* [1850] 56.15-16): "The Cat [writes Dickinson] reprieves the Mouse / She eases from her teeth / Just long enough for Hope to tease— / Then mashes it to death—" (*Poems* #762, qtd. 80). Thus, for Dickinson as for Darwin, the game of cat and mouse images truth, however bald and cold, and whether natural or divine. For both the scientist and the poet, this model of existence demands the theodicean's inquiry, for just as Darwin struggles to reconcile the fact of such suffering with belief in God as loving and powerful, so too does Keane's Dickinson. This Dickinson, however, far from throwing up her hands and taking refuge in agnosticism (as Darwin does), neither lets God off the hook nor, any more than wrestling Jacob, lets Him up off the mat: "I will not let thee go," vows Jacob, "except thou bless me" (Gen. 32.26).

Dickinson's challenge of God, based in part on her acceptance of Darwin's science, which Keane amply demonstrates, recalls Job's even more than Darwin's, as Keane also points out. This initiative of hers dwells even more in the theodicean's province of the theological realm than on the cusp of evolutionary biology. Post-Darwin, perhaps, theodicy becomes old-fashioned, for his science, to apply Ockham's razor to this astringent mode of theological understanding, explains suffering well and simply, if depressingly, as natural selection's inevitable fallout. Like Gerard Manley Hopkins, however—witness his *Wreck of the Deutschland* (1875) and his "terrible sonnets" sequence (1885-89)—Keane's Dickinson writes poetry at least residually theological in both form and content, paradoxically deriving much of her originality from being a "behind-the-times" poet of theodicy. As she would put it, "Retrospection is Prospect's half, / Sometimes, almost more—" (*Poems* #995, ll. 7-8). Despite, or in part because of, how Darwin's science calls her religious frame of reference into doubt, and even if her poetic theodicy should feel somewhat less developed than that of Hopkins, the art of Keane's Dickinson abides, nonetheless, in this suffering-themed tradition of emotionally intellectual God-talk.

This Dickinson thinks, specifically, that the opening movement of theodicy's questioning/answering dialectic suffices for the odyssey of her latter-day, late-Romantic-to-pre-Modern spiritual life, and perhaps even constitutes for the age of Darwin the only viable version of this most skeptical subcategory of traditional theology. By Keane's implication, theodicy-inclined artists before Darwin well wrought their fully worked out explanations of suffering: their literary—that is, their substantially religious but scarcely glib, pious, hermetic, pat, or formulaic—expressions of generic theodicy remained at once intellectually honest and satisfyingly complex or aesthetically open-ended. Unlike, say, either the author of the Book of Job (c. 450 BCE) or John Milton in *Paradise Lost* (1674), on the other hand, such a post-Darwin but still theodicy-intoxicated poet as Keane's Dickinson accepts unavoidably fragmented, yet undertakes deliberately fragmentary, theodicy. Her challenge of God never receives an answer either directly from him in the form of theophany (compare Job 39-41) or indirectly from him through the vatic/apotheosizing voice of her Late Romanticism (compare the alternating of divine authority in *Paradise Lost* with Milton's godlike utterance throughout this sometimes proto-Romantic epic). For Keane's age-of-Darwin Dickinson, systematic religious accounting for suffering would seem necessarily glib, pious, hermetic, pat, or formulaic, and hence both intellectually dishonest and single-mindedly unsubtle or aesthetically closed-off (would certain passages from *In Memoriam* occur to Dickinson in this regard?). This Dickinson, however, has her cake and eats it, too, for, by leaning from closure toward inquiry, she becomes at once the essential theodicean and the aesthetic experimenter.

This Dickinson completes, if not the questioning *and* answering dialectic of theodicy, then what consummate artists like her have always built—namely, bridges from past understandings of the human condition to future perspectives on it.

Keane's Dickinson reasons that the exclusively human Jesus's suffering speaks well for him and appeals as a comfort to sufferers throughout the ages ("Nobody knows the trouble I've seen, / Nobody knows but Jesus") but yields no satisfying solution to the theodicean's problem. For her, "Christ's suffering and death registered more powerfully than the resurrection," and even "the resurrection was to Dickinson testimony of the humanity of Jesus," for, as she proclaims in just eleven of her breakthrough words, "'*Twas Christ's own personal Expanse* / That bore him from the Tomb—" (*Poems* #1543, qtd. 93; emphasis added). This Dickinson's Jesus not only parallels Friedrich Nietzsche's crucified Christ (this Christ is the only true Christian, says Nietzsche) but also echoes Arthur Schopenhauer's suffering Jesus as the emblem of existential humanity (93). "To be human," Dickinson writes, "is more than to be divine, for when Christ was divine, he was uncontented till he had been human" (*Letters* #592, qtd. 93). Thus, at the same time that she seems to acknowledge (with John's gospel) that Jesus existed "before Abraham was" (John 8.58) and so counted as God, she implies (a) that Jesus no longer qualifies as divine and (b) that she prefers him in his human form. The more modest concept of Jesus as God's agent flunks Dickinson's scientific test, for, to use Keane's words, she "raises a possibility never dreamed of" even by liberal theologian Henry Ward Beecher—that is, that (in the words of Dickinson) "Darwin had thrown 'the Redeemer' away" (*Letters* #728, qtd. 36-37). Since in Dickinson's final judgment Jesus proves neither God nor God's surrogate, his suffering only complicates, and perhaps even renders futile, the religious as opposed to scientific approach to the problem. Keane makes clear that Dickinson's sympathetic portrait of Jesus as a sufferer comes as close to finished theodicy as perhaps she ever gets but still depicts, from her late-Romantic vantage point, no complacent extreme of theological closure.

The not so much discarded or dead as deadening God who haunts Dickinson's 1,789 poems is by Keane's account the inscrutable Calvinist Deity whom she "alternately believed in, questioned, quarreled with, rebelled against, caricatured, even condemned, but never ceased to engage" (36). In one sense, this Dickinson agrees with Thomas Jefferson's view that the all-too-cat-like God of Calvinism ranks as a "daemon of malignant spirit," and hence reeks to high heaven (Taylor 804 n59, qtd. 210). As she confronts her tormentor-God, Keane's Dickinson becomes more "dismayed or denunciatory," less thankful or inspired (40). On the other hand, she scarcely embraces Jefferson's conclusion, "It would be more pardonable to believe in no God at all" (Taylor 804 n59, qtd. 210). If this Dickinson does not quite believe in the Calvinist God, she brings her case before and against him, appealing to his nobler nature. Such bold, if not blasphemous, poems as "'Heavenly Father'—take to thee" turn back on God his own prejudgment of human beings as guilt-ridden dust, worms, and embodiments of iniquity (*Poems* #1461 in Keane 157; compare Gen. 3.19, Job 25.2-6, and Exod. 20.5). According to Paul's theodicy, the "whole creation" has been "groaning until now," but this divine delivery from suffering fails to assuage Dickinson, whose "bitter addendum" to Paul's rhetorical question "If God be for us, who can be against us?" ripostes: "but when he is against us, other allies are useless" (*Letters* #746, qtd. 74; compare Rom. 8.22, 31). Keane sums up flatly, but suggests, nonetheless, that Dickinson's God strays so far from solving suffering as to constitute the problem: "Dickinson's omnipresent deity is personal, though more likely to be an antagonist than a friend, exercising his power unpredictably and often cruelly" (74).

The proof text (or pretext) for Dickinson's guarded (and hence in Keane's terms admirable) kind of theodicy is a poem "less hopeful than many readers . . . would seem to prefer . . . a poem resistant to any facile conception of either a painless natural teleology or a providential Design" (130):

> Apparently with no surprise—
> To any happy Flower
> The Frost beheads it at its play—
> In accidental power—
> The blonde Assassin passes on—
> The Sun proceeds unmoved
> To measure off another Day
> For an Approving God (*Poems* #1624)

"By the breath of God," declares Job, "frost is given" (37.10), but, if Keane's Dickinson thinks of the luminously beautiful "blonde Assassin" as divine in origin, she also takes a dim view of God/frost as a *pale* rider/*ash* blonde—that is, as "an agent of the destruction of beauty" (129, 140). This Dickinson remains appalled that God would commit or approve of such waste or carnage. Whereas Jesus's theodicy emphasizes the metaphorically human fruit that comes from the metaphorically human death of a grain of wheat in the ground (John 12.24), Dickinson's exercise in theodicy can find no divine purpose in the literal, natural death of "any happy Flower" (28). "By making the symbolic 'victim' of violence floral rather than human," Keane writes, Dickinson takes a cosmic view, rejecting such human-centered theodicy as (a) God is punishing people's sin, (b) people are exercising the divine gift of free will, or (c) people must suffer as part of God's plan of ultimate redemption (28). In fact, in a thicker description than even Clifford Geertz could manage—namely, the 53 pages of Keane's 223-page text that feature this 36-word lyric—Keane suggests that Dickinson ends up spurning theodicy, or that "Apparently with no surprise—" gives up on God. Keane's close reading brings Dickinson's word *accidental* from its root-theological connotation of fortunate fall (*ad-cadere*, to fall) to its fast-developing, nineteenth-century denotation of random, meaningless chance (121; one thinks here of the "Crass Casualty" in Thomas Hardy's "Hap" [1866], line 11). Thus Dickinson's poetry includes more of Blake's "dull round" or of Wallace Stevens's "malady of the quotidian" than of any coherent plan, "genuine dialectical change," or "Kantian or Darwinian purposiveness without purpose" (140).

Adding detail to Richard Gravil's argument that Dickinson's relation to her high-to-late-Romantic precursors and contemporaries remains more dialogical than subversive (3; but see Diehl), Keane suggests that Dickinson, too, sings a song of *Romantic*-era suffering—shades of *Dolan's* emphasis—albeit one at once not as secularized as, and even darker than, theirs. For example, at least twice alluding to Wordsworth's "Elegiac Stanzas" (1807), Keane's Dickinson develops Wordsworth's "poetic realization of the inevitability and universality of loss and suffering mingled with hope" (190). The stubbornness of her theodicean's questioning, however, distinct from the insouciance of any pre-to-post-Darwin theodicean's solution, marks Dickinson's Late Romanticism as less hopeful and more tragic than even Wordsworth's darkest and most theodicy-toned song of Romantic-era suffering in "Elegiac Stanzas." Just as Darwin read, yet could not share, the benign theism of Wordsworth's *Excursion* (1814) in which "darts of anguish" "*fix* not" in the Wanderer's flesh, so too does Keane's Dickinson part company, in effect, with the Wanderer's bland stoicism (186). "Heavenly Hurt," in Keane's close reading of "There's a certain Slant of light," wounds Dickinson deeply and permanently: "We can find no scar, / But internal difference— / Where the Meanings, are—" (*Poems* #258, ll. 5-8, qtd. 193). Despite being interested more in analogy and "mutual illumination" than in "direct influence" (3), Keane compares the inquiries of

Dickinson's poetic theodicy to corresponding works by Blake, Wordsworth, Shelley, Keats, and Emerson, with the indication that her theological rigor grows more impressive than their merely theodicy-*like* substitution of hope-without-an-object for God (compare Samuel Taylor Coleridge, "Work without Hope" [1825], l. 14). Readers of this journal will relish the resonance of Keane's emphasis on Dickinson's poetic theodicy within what Czeslaw Milosz has called the "Romantic crisis of European culture"—namely, "the dichotomy between the world of scientific laws—cold, indifferent to human values—and man's inner world" (qtd. 118n1). Dickinson, as Keane writes, sings "the dark undersong of Romanticism"—that is, "the cleavage between the human and the natural" (125)—but he would undoubtedly add that the cleavage between the human and the divine precisely makes her Romanticism even more three-dimensional than Milosz's concept of it is.

In sum, despite differences between Dolan's interest in social justice and Keane's in God's, the two together describe a near-tragic arc of Romantic Anglo-America. Although Dolan connects Qoheleth's teaching that "wisdom increases sorrow" to Smith's discovery that "sorrow heightens intelligence" (30-31; one thinks here of Germaine de Staël's Smith-like theory of tragedy), there is nothing biblically comedic even among the most utopian results of the Dolan-reported Romantic era's meditation on suffering. There is something quite tragic, in fact, about Dolan's chronological endpoint in Mary Shelley's body-centered trauma. Although Keane hears religious overtones even in Dickinson's preference not to complete theodicy (compare authority-defiance in Melville's "Bartleby the Scrivener" [1853]), there is little biblically comedic about Keane's reading of Dickinson's poetry in the near-tragic context of the Book of Job. This Dickinson's failure to elicit divine response suggests tragedy insofar as tragedy implies a godless universe. Although the pessimism analyzed by both scholar-critics paradoxically entails the "Gaiety" that "transfigur[es] all that dread" and gloom (compare Yeats, "Lapis Lazuli" [1936], l. 17), Dolan and Keane alike resist the view that Romanticism equals untroubled faith. Both know that not "every flower / Enjoys the air it breathes" since even Wordsworth qualifies this "faith" of his by whistling in the dark that "*I must think, do all I can,* / That there was pleasure there" ("Lines Written in Early Spring" [1798], ll. 11-12, 19-20; emphasis added). Dolan's case for Smith's Job-like "ability to think rationally in the midst of great emotion" (33), above all, coordinates with Keane's for Dickinson's poetry as the upheaval of her thought—that is, as her impassioned as well as intelligent stab at the all but God-denying problem of physical and moral evil.

REFERENCES

Darwin, Charles. *The Life and Letters of Charles Darwin.* Ed. Francis Darwin. Vol. 2. New York: Basic Books, 1887. 1959. Print.
Dickinson, Emily. *The Letters of Emily Dickinson.* Ed. Thomas H. Johnson and Theodora Ward. Vol. 3. Cambridge: Harvard UP, 1958. Print.
———. *The Poems of Emily Dickinson.* Ed. Thomas H. Johnson. Vol. 3. Cambridge: Harvard UP, 1955. Print.
Diehl, Joanne Feit. *Dickinson and the Romantic Imagination.* Princeton: Princeton UP, 1981. Print.
Emerson, Ralph Waldo. *Emerson's Prose and Poetry.* Ed. Joel Porte and Saundra Morris. New York and London: W. W. Norton, 2001. Print.
Fish, Stanley. "One University Under God?" *The Chronicle of Higher Education.* 7 Jan. 2005. Web. 8 Feb. 2011.
Gravil, Richard. *Romantic Dialogues: Anglo-American Continuities 1776-1862.* New York: St Martin's P, 2000. Print.
McFarland, Thomas. *Originality and Imagination.* Baltimore: The Johns Hopkins UP, 1990. Print.
Milosz, Czeslaw. *The Land of Ulro.* Trans. Louis Iribarne. New York: Farrar, Straus, Giroux, 1984. Print.
Page, Judith. *Imperfect Sympathies: Jews and Judaism in British Romantic Literature and Culture.* New York: Palgrave Macmillan. 2004. Print.
Stillinger, Jack. *The Hoodwinking of Madeline.* Champaign: UP of Illinois, 1971. Print.
Taylor, Charles. *A Secular Age.* Cambridge: Harvard UP, 2007. Print.
University of California Los Angeles. "UCLA Researchers Identify Key Biobehavioral Pattern Used by Women to Manage Stress." *Science Daily* 22 May 2000. Web. 8 Feb. 2011.

Reviews, Fourth Series:

Miscellaneous Books

35. *Emily Dickinson's Experiential Poetics and Rev. Dr. Charles Wadsworth's Rhetoric of Sensation: The Intellectual Friendship between the Poet and a Pastor,* by Mary Lee Stephenson Huffer

Lewiston, NY: The Edwin Mellen P, 2007.

Mary Lee Stephenson Huffer's study celebrates the intellectual marriage between the renowned clergyman Charles Wadsworth (1814-82) and the even more renowned poet Emily Dickinson (1830-86). According to standard psychobiographies, Wadsworth and Dickinson's sister-in-law, Susan Huntington Dickinson (1830-1913), wife of Austin, elicited Dickinson's tragic theme of star-crossed love. Without denying the importance either of "Sister Sue" or of Dickinson's pessimistic take on matters of the heart, Huffer's approach pins down both the hopeful aspect and the healthy optimism of her passionate, not always pained, expressions of devotion to the minister, whom she called her "dearest earthly friend." In fact, this re-focus on Wadsworth favors "the marriage of true minds" over the only partially explanatory paradigm of pure, yet unfulfilled and somewhat sentimental, romance. Huffer's model facilitates a less chaste, as well as a more cerebral, interpretation of Dickinson's love poems than does reading them merely as case studies in the psychology of the lovelorn.

To be sure, proof of Wadsworth's presence in Dickinson's imagination remains elusive. Nevertheless, circumstantial evidence of their clandestine correspondence exists. Did they enclose sermons and poems in their letters to one another? Regardless, the sermons of "My Clergyman" formed a definite part of Dickinson's reading. Huffer's method appeals to the simple and seemingly self-evident, yet neglected, truth that his and her texts jibe. The influence of Dickinson's poems on Wadsworth's sermons could create matter for a separate volume. Meanwhile, Huffer's emphasis on verbal echoes, as well as on conceptual parallels, goes the other way. This study demonstrates that the homilies contextualize not just the love poems but the lyrics in general.

Wadsworth's sermons, in Huffer's estimation, gloss the poet's love for this world, on the one hand, and her yearning for a world elsewhere, on the other. First, the methodological strain of Dickinson's language intimately derived from, and eminently built on, the preacher's oscillation and coalescence of sight with insight. Accordingly, her hunger for life looms large in her "experiential poetics" (Huffer's term). To illustrate this point, one need only quote certain familiar phrases: Dickinson's imagination, "inner than the bone," thrusts her poetic personae "out upon Circumference" of the universe. Huffer's fourth and fifth chapters, moreover, break new ground, revealing that the "intimations of immortality" (to borrow William Wordsworth's words) recorded in Wadsworth's sermons explain (to cite John Keats's idea of heaven) the "finer tone" of experience found in Dickinson's equal hunger for eternity. Thus, to accent the poet's difficult, yet fascinating and somehow accessible, idiom, she, like the preacher, desired the world because she could not precisely know it, and she, like the preacher, found otherworldliness intriguing because she did not precisely *not* know it. Huffer's scholarship, above all, resonates with Dickinson's conviction that "Earth is Heaven— / Whether Heaven is Heaven or not."

Just as stories of Dickinson's other friendships have produced acute, enduring criticism, so too does this scholar's concern to establish the intellectual as well as emotional character of the poet's relationship with Wadsworth get down to the serious business of generating cohesive, cogent, and close readings of her works. As re-introduced through this clear guide, Dickinson's poetic personae propound anew their double perspective—that is, their counterintuitive combination of natural models with spiritual metaphors—in "the world / Of all of us, the place in which, in the end, / We find our happiness, or not at all!" (Wordsworth's *Prelude* [1850]). In consequence, her lyrics appear to proceed from hope against hope to hope on the rise. Huffer's monograph underscores Dickinson's injunction to "dwell in Possibility—." By Huffer's implication, indeed, these well-known words signal the poet's signature imperative not only to cultivate gleams of another existence but also to "gather Paradise" in the here and now. The Wadsworth-lodestar of Dickinson's proliferating meanings pulls her art into bold relief, and perhaps even radiates "out upon Circumference" of language.

The intellectual dimension of biographical criticism might seem, at first, narrowly aimed. Huffer's work, however, actually explores the broad historical circumference of Dickinson's sermon- and Wadsworth-centered circle of signification. Besides drawing on the preacher's "rhetoric of sensation"

(Huffer's phrase), this methodology brings a range of experience-conscious, experience-laden theologies to bear on the poet's mix of stances. Huffer's duo of letters, *bonnes* and *belles*, occupies the ground between British empiricism, by way of Scottish common sense philosophy, and the First and Second Great Awakenings of the American world. Such an otherwise diverse group of sources as Jonathan Edwards's prose, the Westminster Confession (to which Presbyterian Wadsworth subscribed), conservative Congregationalism (to which young Dickinson belonged), and liberal Unitarianism augment this study's frame of reference.

Just as Huffer's concentration on Wadsworth's prose proves innovative for Dickinson studies, so too does this willingness to "spread wide" the "narrow hands" of research (to adapt Dickinson's image) prove welcome. As a result, Huffer's preacher and poet appear to have invoked the religious about science and the scientific about religion. They compounded *how to know* with *what to believe*, or, to re-state the conundrum, they *trusted in experiment*, on the one hand, and *tested doctrine*, on the other. The skepticism for which Dickinson's art receives praise emerges from this large viewpoint as more constructive than either destructive or deconstructive. In the spirit of Friedrich Nietzsche's dictum "Truth has never yet clung to the arm of an inflexible man," this Dickinson nicely contrasts with either/or-inclined combatants in early twenty-first-century culture wars. Keats's *Negative Capability* also comes to mind: "the condition of being in uncertainties, Mysteries, doubts, without any irritable reaching after fact & reason." Or, as Dickinson herself puts it best, "Experiment escorts us last— / His pungent company / Will not allow an Axiom / An Opportunity—." On Dickinson's pilgrimage of life, as well as of art, she kept company, as Huffer allows, with Experiment personified and, as presences not only in the heart and imagination, but also in the mind and soul, with persons like Wadsworth.

"The lady whom the people call the *Myth*," Mabel Loomis Todd's famous but misleading label for Dickinson, looks in Huffer's terms not so reclusive, after all. Huffer's core belief, for one thing, rings true—that is, that Dickinson paradoxically chose solitude for the good social reason that through epistolary experience in the privacy of her room she could plumb relationships more deeply than through perhaps banal face to face encounters in her parlor or her town. One recalls, in this regard, the mutual esteem of dramatist George Bernard Shaw and actress Ellen Terry. Shaw answered those bemused by his strange, yet rich and curiously palpable, affection— which entirely consisted of his twenty-five years' worth of correspondence with her—as follows: "Let them remember that only on paper has humanity yet achieved glory, beauty, truth, knowledge, virtue, and abiding love." In any case, perhaps because Dickinson sublimated her longing, she developed in tandem with the minister her own way of knowing, believing, and imagining all things—namely, the carefully epistemological procedure and the tentatively hopeful eschatology of her binocular vision. Or perhaps because the obscure object of her desire and the joy of her desiring abided in the upheavals of her thought, her creative expression *raged* for the knowledge of natural things, however sketchy, and *cried out* for confrontation with spiritual truth, however "slant." Huffer's good offices summon the growing number of the poet's literary addressees to sessions of sweet silent thought at her surprisingly congregational imagination's altar.

36. *Miles of Stare: Transcendentalism and the Problem of Literary Vision in Nineteenth-Century America,* by Michelle Kohler

Tuscaloosa: The University of Alabama Press, 2014.

With a rare combination of thoroughgoing erudition and playful close reading, Michelle Kohler redefines Ralph Waldo Emerson's consequence for the American scene. First, Kohler argues that Emerson assigns "the imagination's tasks to the eye" (5). Then, she shows how such "American seers" as Frederick Douglass, Nathaniel Hawthorne, Emily Dickinson, William Dean Howells, and Sarah Orne Jewett "critique, mock, ironize, fracture, reverse, or otherwise seek to work through the contradictions and equivocations within" Emerson's "transparent eyeball" metaphor (5, 206). Kohler demonstrates that Emerson's originality stokes his influence: what makes him great—his all-seeing eye—accounts for the difference he makes, especially through disagreement, to generations of American writers. A milestone in American studies, *Miles of Stare* establishes a focused but flexible outlook on the difficult fascination of American literary vision.

Kohler's case rests on the signature subject and predicate of Emerson's *Nature* (1836): the transparent eyeball sees all. Emerson, she forthrightly states, "is as vested in locating this experience in the material world as he is in transcending the material world"—that is, his omniscience does not just climb to a world beyond, as in *trans-scandere*, but sees all here, as in *trans-parere* (25). Kohler acknowledges that not even Emerson believes he can "see all" all the time. She astutely points out, however, that the Emerson of his later, more skeptical essays, such as "Experience" (1844), can yet "behold," "as it were in flashes of light" and without presuming to "make" the world, "what was there already" (qtd. in Kohler 40). This "dramatic reappearance" of what Kohler aptly calls Emerson's "poetic epistemology" illustrates, with satisfying complexity, how perennially his resilient sensorium honors precisely "what is manifest" (40, 51, 136).

In Kohler's narrative of Emerson's philosophical development, his eye both departs from and improves upon Kant's Reason and Coleridge's Imagination. Kohler's decisive placement of Emerson at the crux of a uniquely American high-cultural history discloses, importantly and surprisingly, how—by "simply perceiving rather than creating"—his "faculty of vision" turns "the inwardness of European romanticism" outward (18, 23, 26). Thus, in her version of what is distinctive about Emerson, his all-seeing eye reveals all he needs to know on earth and more than what suffices not just for his proper mode of sensory proceeding, but for that of his wide circle as well.

Kohler's seers take their bearings from Emerson but write against him and morph his blithe correspondences of spiritual insight and natural sight into their own inimitable juxtapositions of obscure yearning and flawed, vexed perception. Languishing in a "horrible pit" with "no ladder" (Douglass's images), Douglass finds Emerson's "aerial omniscience" unattainable and arrogant (68). Hawthorne's "feebly transparent" eye sees darkly, stays "limited to exterior, distant views of others" (80, 86). In *The House of the Seven Gables* (1851), Hawthorne prefers the occluded vision of provincial Hepzibah—her "dim optics" (Hawthorne's phrase)—to the all-knowing but aggressive observation, the panoptical intrusiveness, of daguerrotypist Holgrave (103). And just as Emerson's trademark trope exchanges loftiness for clear-sightedness, so do the novels of Howells and Jewett "resist transcendence" (140). Howells, however, in a belated mode, "writes to generate seeing rather than sees to generate writing" (151).

Throughout Kohler's book, she discusses the poem she quotes in her title:

> I've known a Heaven, like a Tent—
> To wrap it's shining Yards—
> Pluck up it's stakes, and disappear—
> Without the sound of Boards
> Or Rip of Nail—Or Carpenter—
> But just the miles of Stare—
> That signalize a Show's Retreat—
> In North America—
> (Franklin 257)

Paraphrasing Dickinson's deliberately anti-Emersonian words, Kohler asserts that "North America is typified by—and typically figured by—the blank stare of perplexed, abandoned viewers, who expected the ongoing revelation of 'Heaven' but find only their own objectless vision" (1). Kohler associates "a Heaven" with the evanescence of an evangelical tent revival, the hype of a circus, and other passing spectacles of quasi-transcendent desire such as a medicine show (125, 181). In her particularly well-sustained assessment of "I watched the Moon, around the House—" (Fr593B), the moon—"what humans are not"—epitomizes the speaker's vast distance from Emerson's subject-object coalescence (106–11). Kohler's five other authoritative critical analyses shed further light on Dickinson's challenge to Emerson's visual confidence. So "keen" is the poet "to skewer the Emersonian eyeball," indeed, that her lyrical self-projections can "cast transparency as emptiness," "a hollowed-out field of vision" where she can barely "see to see" (106, 136; Fr465). Thus, according to the best of Kohler's chapters, the stunned, disillusioned daze of Dickinson's nihilism replaces Emerson's relentless, point blank gaze, and the strangely salutary slant of her truth-telling not only punctures his guileless, wide-eyed wonder, but also repeals false lures of far worse kinds, American or other.

Kohler's less amplified but no less telling examples of attenuated post-Emerson seeing—Melville's "divergent visions," Thoreau's meager glimpses of palpable "absence," Harriet Jacobs's "tiny apertures" of circumscribed sight, and Sarah Winnemucca's stark estrangements of "visible world and written word"—complete her take on American poetic epistemology as rearguard (42, 46, 50, 169). Whereas, for Sacvan Bercovitch, American "texts move sequentially, and inevitably, from initial doubt or crisis toward possession, conclusive meaning, or the resolution of difference, separation, and paradox," Kohler's American sampler reels from omniscience to bafflement, "confronting loss, transience, or absence" (117, 105). This interpretation of mid-to-late-nineteenth-century literary vision as pre-Modern complements Stanley Cavell's classic perspective on the transcendentalist movement as pre-Modern, too (188-9). If Emerson's foundational paradigm abides as a "pivotal" form of indigenous brilliance (Kohler's key term), it devolves into crepuscular vision (her substantial conclusion).

Kohler deftly reintegrates Emerson's achievement with his impact. In her judgment, his legatees *see through* transparency—that is, they not only rely on his visual acuity for a stay against confusion; they also expose his visual ebullience as a source of confusion. In Kohler's comprehensive view, accordingly, Emerson's all-seasons brand of omniscience remains a force for American authors to reckon with, however dissonant or faintly they may ring their changes upon his sense-based method. Above all, perhaps, Kohler's investigation of discordant responses to the Sage of Concord captures a neglected aspect of Emerson's effect on the Myth of Amherst: he proves not so much the cause of her anxiety as the inspiration of her demurral.

37. *The Comedy of Redemption: Christian Faith and Comic Vision in Four American Novelists,* by Ralph C. Wood

Notre Dame: University of Notre Dame Press, 1988. Pp. xiii + 310 pp.

"In the fiction of Flannery O'Connor and Walker Percy, of John Updike and Peter De Vries," writes Ralph C. Wood in *The Comedy of Redemption: Christian Faith and Comic Vision in Four American Novelists,* "there resounds, however distantly, this same Good News: that we do not flail in a void, that the universe has a final floor, that we are upheld by sheer grace, that we stand on Christ the solid rock, that all other ground is sinking sand" (285). This sentence, the final sentence of the book, typifies Wood's forthright, fresh perspective.

Wood begins by acknowledging that, even for theologians, there is truth in tragedy: Reinhold Niebuhr, teaching that human misery derives from life's contradictions, concludes that "all things human" are inevitably caught in a "dialectical bind" (7, 21). Thus Niebuhr's theology scarcely goes "beyond tragedy," and Wood counters Niebuhr's implication that the good will only "ultimately" prevail: "Evil," Wood argues, "is already—and not just 'finally'—under the dominion of God" (9). Comedy, for Wood, derives from the hope and joy announced by the Gospel to the world. Although he admits that "laughter's deep eructations" can spring both from "the vitality of the world's ongoing process" and from "a distinctively human protest against the metaphysical contradiction implicit in self-conscious existence," Wood emphasizes that the deepest comedy, distinct from the black-humor dramas of Beckett and Ionesco, the chthonic theories of Bergson and Langer, and, for that matter, the "tragicomic opposition between the Nay of judgment and the Yea of mercy," is "the unilateral and uncompromising comedy of God's grace" (28, 31).

The theologian of this divine comedy, this "comedy of redemption," is Karl Barth, "a humorous and happy theologian not in spite of his Calvinism but because of it" (35). God, far from being a mere "world-principle self-developing and self-evolving in infinite sequence," is the gracious Person who decided both to create the world and to redeem it (35): Barth, like Calvin, emphasizes God's sovereignty. Unlike Calvin, Barth rejects "double predestination" for the elect minority and the rejected majority: "God is never of two minds but always of one" (36); and to make God the dialectical deity of darkness and light, wrath and mercy, and damning and saving would be "to seek divine justification for the human either/or" (38). Evil, for all its "terrifying effect in the world," is essentially unreal, for, though it tyrannizes over humanity, it has no sovereignty over God: it is "the shadow-side of God's good creation" (42-43). The "impossible possibility" of sin does occur; but while God does not compel us "to accept his acceptance of us," he "sovereignly, and of his own gracious accord, rejects our rejection of him" (47). For Barth, then, grace is radically prevenient, but, though his theology is Christocentric, it is not antihumanistic. He deplores combinations of the Gospel with other things, e.g., "church and state" or "faith and reason": and what God achieves in the Jews and Jesus "stands in history but does not stem from history" (66); but "what happened once for all," as Barth puts it, "possesses in what now happens on earth a correspondence, a reflection; not a repetition but a likeness" (68). It is therefore proper, as Wood puts it, "to detect secular similitudes of God's grace at work in the world" (68): one looks, specifically, for "extracanonical and extraecclesiastical" witnesses to or parables of the Gospel (70); and Barth finds such a parable, most notably, in the "wondrous imbalance" whereby Mozart "heard the harmony of creation to which the shadow also belongs but in which the shadow is not darkness" (73).

Wood finds other such parables in the works of O'Connor, Percy, Updike, and De Vries. While I recommend what Wood has to say about De Vries as "humorist of backslidden unbelief" (230-51), about Updike as "ironist of the spiritual life" (178-206), and about Percy as both "Catholic existentialist" and "satirist satirized" (133-77), I focus on O'Connor.

"Grace must wound," O'Connor wrote, "before it can heal." By exploring her biography, her regionalism, and her Catholicism, Wood traces O'Connor's progress from "a baleful desire to lash modernity for its unbelief, and thus to depict this late stage of human history as uniquely damned and devoid of grace," to a discernment that "the Kingdom of Heaven is not borne violently away by frustrated atheists; it is gratuitously given to the unsuspecting children of God" (81-82).

O'Connor's "synergistic theology," her conviction that "the ultimate issue of our lives depends on our own reception or rejection of God's grace" (90), runs counter to Wood's Barthian taste, and he is equally troubled by the dualism in her fiction: "O'Connor the Christian writer does not always discern that God's resounding Yea always precedes and follows his devastating Nay" (100). Wood emphasizes, however, that "in her better fictional moments" O'Connor "acknowledges the glad Pascalian truth that we seek God only because—in Israel and Christ—he has already found us" (100).

Those moments include, most notably, the stories dealing with "the irony and paradox" of Southern racial relations (106). In "The Artificial Nigger," the miserable Sambo figure (with its implication of vicarious suffering) heals the rift between Nelson and Mr. Head, and the grandfather, in particular, realizes that "he was forgiven for sins from the beginning of time." In "The Enduring Chill," the ceiling stain that has "looked down" upon Asbury Fox since childhood descends, in his adulthood, as the dove of the Spirit, and it conquers his false pride. In "Revelation," an elongated cloud above the setting sun images a mercy that cleanses Ruby Turpin of *her* pride: the vision of an eschatalogical community includes—only because of grace and not because of her works—even a woman who, at a particularly low point of her sin, dreams of all "inferior" people "crammed in together in a box car, being ridden off to be put in a gas oven."

One wishes for more close reading from Wood. One squirms, a bit, at his judgment of O'Connor from a Barthian perspective to which, after all, she was under no obligation to subscribe: he thinks that her satire is often "truculent" or "bilious" and that, whenever it is so, it amounts to an unfortunate "misreading of the Gospel's undialectical comedy of grace" (100, 126).

Finally, however, one entertains Wood's audacious point of view. Against the charge that O'Connor explains rather than dramatizes what mercy means, Wood offers a defense that, without necessarily pleasing literary critics, is staunchly consistent with his general argument:

> Yet it is not only literary clarity that O'Connor seeks to provide. Authorial judgment is necessary for a profounder reason. The bestowal of divine mercy, being transcendently given and humanly unearned, cannot be narrated in strictly literary terms. The grace of God—as surprising gift rather than earnest acquisition—comes as an action *upon* a character even more than it is a movement *within* a character. (117)

Without at all denying "the intrinsic value" of works of art and "culture in general," Wood seeks nothing less than "the knowledge of God" (76}.

Under the guise of paraphrasing Barthian theology, he sometimes preaches (e.g., "Whether in the most miniscule personal acts or in the most grandiose corporate structures, we refuse to trust the God who from the foundation of the world has entrusted himself to us," 46), but through his own distinctive theological discourse, he convinces us of Barth's importance. To sum up much of what Wood argues and to illustrate his own grace and flair, I let him speak for himself at some length:

> Faith is the humble and humorous acknowledgement that we can escape God's grace no more than we can walk out of our own shadow or select our parents. It is the replacement of the tragic claim that we are more sinned against than sinning with the comic confession that we receive infinitely—*infinitely*—more than we give.... Not so much in tragic art, where culture regards itself most somberly, but in the laughter that refuses to take the world's sadness as final may we discern secular parables of the Good News. There we shall find repercussions of the tidings that God himself has acted to make the world's sin ultimately unserious. Amidst a laughter neither grim nor silly, we can overhear something of the Gospel's own rejoicing. We shall detect—sometimes clearly, often obscurely—the same turning which Barth catches in Mozart's music. We shall hear a laughter which moves painfully past a great mound of misery, and yet finally around a comer which, because God in Christ has turned it, the world shall never turn again. (53, 79)

This full-scale interrelation of comic theory, theology, and fiction is more than the usual bland, cautious, and "objective" writing of the academic world.

Wood's perspective is the fresher for his debt to Warren Carr, longtime pastor of the Wake Forest Baptist Church in Winston-Salem, North Carolina. "Karl Barth," writes Wood, "is the intellectual inspiration behind this essay in the theology of culture, but it was Warren Carr who first convinced me that eschatological grace issues in a very earthy humor and joy" (xiii). Such tribute not only reveals the origin, but also explains the verve, of a book that we can cherish: *The Comedy of Redemption* is the fully matured result of a quarter-century of teaching by a Baptist Southerner with keen theological intelligence.

38. *The Story of Joy: From the Bible to Late Romanticism,* by Adam Potkay

Cambridge: Cambridge University Press, 2007. Pp. xiii + 304.

Although studies of love/*eros*/*agape*/*philia* abound, Adam Potkay's *Story of Joy* ranks as the only full-scale, complete, thoroughly researched, and clearly written account of this primal passion. Potkay accomplishes for joy/*joie*/*jouissance*/*gioia*/*Freude*/*alegria*/*gozo*/*chara*/*chairo*/*laetitia*/*gaudium* what Martha Nussbaum, Philip Fisher, and Andrew Stauffer have done for anger. He traces "the historical evolution of a single key word" and hence practices "cultural philology" (viii). Thus he "range[s] more widely than scholars often do in our specialized age" (xi). He addresses statecraft, psychology, philosophy, religion, literature, and art in the West.

Potkay has written two other books on similar themes in the 18th century: *The Fate of Eloquence in the Age of Hume* (1994) and *The Passion for Happiness: Samuel Johnson and David Hume* (2000). *The Story of Joy* makes distinctions and establishes continuities between the 18th and the 19th century and from the Bible to the present. Potkay unites his scholarly narrative by frequent reference to the chief paradox of joy: its rich, strange blending of "perfect concentration" with "self-dispersion" (9). This conundrum, Potkay demonstrates, takes a variety of religious, erotic, ethical, Romantic, and modern forms from Continental Europe to Anglo-America. British Romanticism constitutes "the rock" on which Potkay's comprehension stands (xi).

With regard, first, to religious joy, Potkay uses Jack Miles's *God: A Biography* (1996), which argues that "God's face" in the Hebrew scriptures "changes from invulnerable warlord to [a] husband-lover" who announces "a new order of national if not cosmic joy" (35). Then John 15:11— "These things I have spoken to you, that my joy may be in you, and your joy may be full"—emerges from Potkay's study as joy's chief proof-text (see also Luke 6:23). John's gospel, however, "has as its dark side hostility towards those outside the circle of relationship and love" (30). Potkay's Augustine, reconfiguring the Johannine triad of love, joy, and exclusivity, proved even less communitarian than John did, and the Cistercians, Franciscans, Dominicans—and Dante—followed suit. They all found joy in "the contemplative life" (42-5).

Potkay's Aquinas, on the other hand, as a way to resolve the Johannine triad, located joy within "the ethical life" (46). Concluding like Aristotle that "joy results from an act of justice" (46), Aquinas showed how joy works in the world. Thus, according to Judaeo-Christian joy (whether biblical or post-biblical), the emotion can be alternately, if not simultaneously, deep or inward (as in John's gospel) and embodied or palpable (as in Aquinas's ethics). A sermon (1646) by William Cradock, quoted by Potkay (40), illustrates the latter. Cradock exults that "whole Christ from top to toe is mine" like the "union . . . between a man and his wife."

After religious joy, "the second great semantic field for 'joy' in the West" is erotic *joie*, which, paradoxically enough, "in part depends" on the former (50). Such 12th-century Provençal love poets as Gottfried von Strassburg, Jaufré Rudel, and Bernart de Ventadorn ambiguously praise a lady or the Virgin Mary (or both), and such 13th-century Sicilian and Tuscan poets as Guittone d'Arezzo continued to balance this "joy of desire" with this "joy of reflection" (54-64). Potkay argues, however, that their "elegant insouciance" yielded to the "dark shadows" of asceticism that Dante and Petrarch, during the 14th century, cast over "joy" as "an erotic dynamic" (61). Pierre de Ronsard, demystifying such spirituality, preferred *jouissance* (enjoyment, possession, sexual climax) to Petrarch's more religiously reflective than frankly sexual (if sufficiently erotic) *joi/joie*. As Ronsard writes, "Petrarch had no authority / To impose his law on me, / Nor on any who came after him, to make them / Desirous for such a long time without being able to get undressed" (Potkay 67).

"Ronsard's best-known anti-Petrarchan hero on the Elizabethan stage," Potkay concludes, "is surely Mercutio, the earthy counterpart to Romeo, initially the Petrarchan lover" (68). Romeo, in Potkay's reading, "gets to know both the joy of expectation and of possession" (68). Samuel Taylor Coleridge's notebook poems of unhappy love, according to Potkay, carry "the lingering light" of Petrarchan tradition to its abstracted extreme (51). Potkay finds here little joy of even the expectant kind, to say nothing of joyful possession (51-4).

Potkay's arc from Martin Luther to Robinson Crusoe resumes the story of religious joy. Where emphasizing the Protestant version thereof as more joyless than joyful, *The Story of Joy* comes close to abandoning the main theme of the book. Potkay writes well about "common Protestant pessimism" in

Edmund Spenser, John Donne, John Bunyan, and Daniel Defoe (73-94, esp. 77). One wonders how such dour, one-note authors could ever have entered the multi-vocal canon of either *belles-* or *bonnes-lettres*. Did they *so* exclusively reflect neo-Augustinian astringency, anti-Pelagian stricture, *ängst*, depravity, reprobation, fury, carnal repression, separatism, psychomachia, inwardness, and hardship?

Potkay's take on the Northern European Reformation, like that of James Simpson in *Burning to Read* (2007), feels revisionist. Far be it from *The Story of Joy* to credit the part of Luther's faith that yields "pleasure, food, gladness, peace, light, art, truth, wisdom, freedom, and an abundance of other good things" (Luther's words in "About the Freedom of a Christian" [1520]). Potkay's Reformation highlights, instead, urgency, anxiety, fear, trembling, bondage, sin, indebtedness, and militancy. Perhaps the pendulum needs to swing back (does the revisionist characterization of Protestantism have more to do with Northern climate than with Christian inflection?). True, Potkay acknowledges that Calvinist/Arminian debates "loom large in Protestant theological controversy" (87). Accordingly, he touches on Donne's "attempts to reconcile" joy and joylessness, "free will and election" (86, 254). He observes, moreover, that "Crusoe's progress of the passions is, finally, an arc from common joy in self-preservation to spiritual joy in deliverance from sin" (93). Still, an even stronger awareness of the Calvinist/Arminian dialectic that contrasts joylessness (as a sign of the Spirit's absence) with joy (as a sign of the Spirit's presence) would have lent additional religious nuance (more of joy's story) to Potkay's otherwise always subtle cultural and literary criticism.

Potkay writes well, too, about the secular ideal of ethical joy, upheld by Anthony Ashley Cooper, the third earl of Shaftesbury. Whereas for the Christian, "the ethical life is never an end in itself, but a duty enjoined by God ... and subordinated to the love of God," Shaftesbury argued that "the practice of moral virtues is an end in itself, attended by a joy that ratifies that end" (96). Thus resisting Thomas Hobbes's view that joy consists in "personal ascendancy over others," Shaftesbury developed both Aristotle's idea that "no man is just who does not take joy in acting justly" and Marcus Aurelius's principle that "gladness" or "good cheer" comes from helping others (97, 100-01). Shaftesbury's Christian opponents countered forcefully. Jonathan Edwards, William Warburton, Edward Young, John Brown, Samuel Johnson, Edward Moir, and William Cowper, among others, preached that "eschatological hope alone" affords what Young's *Night Thoughts* (1742-46) names as the "Rich Prelibation of consummate Joy" (96, 105-06, 109-11).

William Wordsworth's Romantic joy, Potkay maintains, applied the secularized ethical joy of Shaftesbury (and of William Godwin) to "the poorest of the poor," who "had hitherto remained under the radar of English moral sense philosophy" (120). Potkay persuasively rereads "The Old Cumberland Beggar" in the context of Shaftesbury's emphasis on 'the ethical importance of joy'" (123-8, esp. 125). On the other hand, Potkay contends that Wordsworth's joy "lies not so much in acts of benevolence as in facets of being itself: breathing, circulating blood, sensing, feeling pleasure, sustaining life" (121). What Potkay regards as the philosophical power of Wordsworth's Romantic joy to "connect" and "integrate" (134) counts, too, surely, as the religious power of his joy to do so. *Re-ligio*, after all, means to tie things back together again.

What Potkay labels Wordsworth's "philosophy of joy" (137) coexists with what one might denominate his "religion of joy." As Potkay admits, Wordsworth's joy boasts the grace to "redeem" his readers (beginning certainly by the mid 19th century [134]). Potkay knows that Frances Ogle, in 1840, saw Wordsworth as "wresting an idiom of spiritual renewal from Protestant Christianity" (135-6). Potkay, however, gives short shrift to such Protestant analogues to, or Protestant sources and beneficiaries of, Wordsworth's Ro mantic joy. Potkay discusses Wordsworth's "deep enthusiastic joy, / The rapture of the hallelujah" (1805 *Prelude* 13.261-2) in a Spinozan context of philosophical reflection (132-3). These evangelical words for joy, however, whether otherworldly or earthly (or both), mean more than just "Spinoza's [exclusively pantheistic] joy in the underlying oneness of things" (132).

"In Coleridge and Wordsworth," Potkay writes, "we find a joy that's either Christian or, if apparently naturalistic, readily available for Christian appropriation" (162). Friedrich Schiller, William Blake, Percy Bysshe Shelley, and Joseph Smith, on the other hand, comprise "Romantic-era poets of joy" who "cannot be recuperated for the orthodox Christianity upon which they nonetheless depend" (162). Schiller's "Ode to Joy" evokes Shaftesbury's praise for "an equal, just, and universal friendship" of "love, gratitude, bounty, practiced with increasing joy" (168). For Schiller, however—and hence for Blake, Shelley, and Smith—joy "becomes the banner not only of social and cosmic incorporation, but also of individual deification" (171). Potkay regards Blake as "post-Christian" because Blake rejected "just about all institutional and doctrinal Christianity" (172). Potkay's formulation that Blake emphasized "mutual forgiveness and, with error behind us, mutual bliss" (172), however, might qualify as centrally, particularly, especially, or unusually Christian.

That said, Potkay offers astute explications of "The Clod and the Pebble" and *Visions of the Daughters of Albion* (1793). Moreover, he draws a highly explanatory distinction between Blake and Shelley—namely, that Oothoon's "bliss *on* bliss" becomes Shelley's "full fusion in bliss" (180). Potkay's interpretation of *Prometheus Unbound* (180-6), equal to the subtlety of Shelley's "evanescent style" (184), manifests Shelley's insight that joy lies "(just) out of reach of representation" (185). Thus, as though Shelley were more recoverable for orthodoxy than Schiller and Blake, or even than Mormon founder Smith, Potkay builds on Robert Ryan's argument that Shelley found "value" in historical Christianity "as the imperfect symbol of . . . forgiveness . . . and imaginative freedom" (180). A more than merely attenuated theistic joy abides as the mythopoeic payoff of Potkay's cultural and philological approach to Shelley.

If Joseph Smith "brought the desideratum of joyous activity to its theistic limit," then an "atheistic vision of human exaltation" characterizes the works of Friedrich Nietzsche and of William Butler Yeats, and perhaps even of Richard Wagner (193). For this triumvirate, "tragic joy" (Nietzsche's phrase) "marks the satisfaction of either a desire for death or the will to live more intensely in the face of death—or both" (193-4). Whereas Beethoven's "sublimely comic" *Fidelio* (1805-06; revised 1814) presents "self-sacrificial marital love and the revolutionary liberation of humanity" (199), Wagner's *Tristan und Isolde* (1865) sings tragic hymns to death, night, adulterous love, hollow marriage, and the "impersonal universal will behind the phenomenal world" (201, 204). Yeats, "a Nietzschean prophet" in Potkay's view, celebrates "the joy of cyclical destruction as well as recreation" (209). Yeats asks, in "The Gyres" (1938), "What matter though numb nightmare ride on top, / And blood and mire the sensitive body stain? . . . / What matter? Out of Cavern comes a voice, / And all it knows is that one word 'Rejoice'" (213).

The Story of Joy measures the distance separating the biblically comedic "Rejoice evermore" of I Thessalonians 5:15 (see Potkay 86), on the one hand, from the troublingly paradoxical Modernity of Yeats's tragic gaiety, on the other. Potkay makes clear his serious doubts concerning tragic joy. He writes, "Thinking through the blitzkriegs and death camps that followed hard upon Yeats's death raises questions about the virtue and efficacy of the tragic vision" that, unlike Aristotle's, pursues joy, as distinct from cultivating pity and fear (194). Potkay, to say the least, finds disturbing "the memoir of a Holocaust survivor trying to make sense of having been made to sing Beethoven's 'Ode to Joy' in the latrines of Auschwitz" (195). With arresting understatement, Potkay faces up to the implications of his subject matter: "[Yeats's] superimposing a tragic metaphysics onto European geopolitics . . . may seem, in retrospect, little short of criminal" (217). Whereas Potkay's Blake endorses violence "for the sake of the future" (Orc's "fiery joy," for its part, is revolutionary), Yeats's joy, in Potkay's estimation, seems only destructively reactionary (213). Potkay's judgment deserves ample quotation: "The slippage from a metaphysical to a purely physical understanding of 'annihilation'—that is, the relation of German philosophy to Nazi atrocity—is more than enough to quell any appetite for destruction. . . . [T]he tragic perspective, even as an affirmation of life and value in the face of their destruction, carries with it no necessary moral content, no radical understanding of good in relation to evil. For such an understanding, we need, if not an ethics of divine or civil disobedience, then something like the classical-ethical frame of happiness" (219). Here Potkay comes full circle to his beginnings in 18th century scholarship. His neo-18th-century perspective provides much salutary insight into Romanticism and Modernism.

In his conclusion, Potkay laments that terms of passion, of whatever kind, especially joy, waned in the 20th century (224). For one thing, "that Beethoven's setting of Schiller can incite ultra-violence as readily as 'world-feeling'" informed Anthony Burgess's 1962 novel, *A Clockwork Orange* (221). For another, mass marketing reduced joy to "mild pleasure" (223). Randall Jarrell's ironic poem "Next Day" (1965) depicted a woman in the soap aisle of the supermarket "moving from Cheer to Joy, from Joy to All" (223). Joy among evangelical Protestants, according to otherwise evangelical-Protestant-friendly Catholic conservative Richard John Neuhaus, has become "forced" (224).

Under the circumstances, *The Story of Joy* calls for renewal of the right kind of joy—namely, "on the road to nowhere," unyoked to "some master narrative of progress or growth" (227). The proper erotic joy comes as "the prolonged desire more desirable than any immediate gratification" (228); one thinks of the almost ethical appeal of John Milton's words for sex before the fall, "sweet, reluctant, amorous delay." Proper ethical joy conforms (simply enough) to the bumper-sticker command to "practice random acts of kindness" (229). Proper religious joy features playfulness (here Potkay draws on John Huizinga's concept of being "'apart together' with others, intensely absorbed 'outside and above the necessities and seriousness of everyday life'" [229-30]). Potkay ends with a fitting account of the film *American Beauty* (1999), describing the "post-secular" figure of Lester Burnham (Kevin Spacey) who progresses from "the joy of unsatisfied desire" to "several minutes of ethical delight" (231-5).

Potkay's sweep, then, turns majestic. To be sure, *The Story of Joy* occasionally reflects the necessarily cursory nature of any useful survey. Neck-snapping abruptness, for instance, mars a single page [196] on which Potkay includes both "a brief exposition of [Arthur] Schopenhauer's metaphysics" and—whew!—"a glance at [Immanuel] Kant." Nevertheless, Potkay's asides alone prove (almost) worth the price of his book. Even his dog Cookie's joy well serves Potkay's purposes (8). Coleridge's "Dejection: An Ode" reminds Potkay of the at least as intriguing versions of joylessness expressed by Felicia Hemans, Emily Dickinson, and Louise Bogan (153).

Potkay, to his great credit, respects counter-examples, counter-traditions. For instance, the conclusion reached by Michel de Montaigne and by John Locke, that happiness feels amoral (242), strengthens Potkay's argument. Wordsworth's Romantic joy, moreover, feels all the more deeply powerful because of Potkay's simultaneous acknowledgment of Wordsworth's "solitary anguish," his sense of "tragedy," and, to use the poet's own words (quoted by Potkay), his "joy perplexed" by "all that is at enmity with joy" (264).

In sum, going so far as to adduce a line from a rock lyric that he wrote as a young man ("We'll succumb to the joy of being twenty years old" [238]), Potkay comprehends comic and tragic joy on his pulses and *Liebestod* in his bones. Grounding the primacy of joy in scientific reality, as well as in cultural and literary history (see, for example, Potkay's epitome of object-relations psychology [14-15, 240, 244-6]), *The Story of Joy* constitutes Potkay's best book yet. Its attention to the role of religion in the narrative of a neglected Western key-word comes as both a welcome surprise and an unusual development in the brash young discipline of cultural philology. May this mature scholar's fourth monograph soon appear. Announced in *The Story of Joy* as a book-length work in progress and already entitled *Wordsworth's Ethics* (263), it will further explore Wordsworth's "writings on joyful life" and should provide a much-needed complement to Laurence S. Lockridge's less joy- and obligation-related (his more meditation- and mysticism-oriented) *Ethics of Romanticism* (1989).

Epilogue: From Credo to Credit

May God us keep
From Single vision and Newtons sleep
—William Blake to Thomas Butts,
November 22, 1802¹

That is what I call living by ideas: when one side of a question has long had your earnest support, when all your feelings are engaged, when you have all around you no language but one, when your party talks this language like a steam engine and can imagine no other—still to be able to think, still to be irresistibly carried, if so it be, by the current of thought to the opposite side of the question, and, like Balaam, to be unable to speak anything but what the Lord has put in your mouth.
—Matthew Arnold, "The Function of Criticism
at the Present Time" (1864)²

Over the years, critics have often split Romanticism into polarities such as emotion vs. reason and experience vs. faith, and subsequently favored one over the other, ranking emotion and experience above their opposites. For Brantley, these great antinomies are not oppositional so much as conversational, perpetually shifting in their mutually inclusive relationships, with one side constantly shaping and generating the other.
—Eric G. Wilson, *Review 19*,
October 15, 2013³

"The first principle of a British system," Bill Bryson writes, "is that it should only *appear* systematic" (Bryson's emphasis).[4] Is that because "set-ups of an organized whole, compounded of parts," fall short of "ways to develop, or developments of a way" *(OED* definitions of "system" and "method," respectively)? Perhaps, for, to extend this distinction in a bi-national direction, "method rather than system" can serve as a prescription for the best behavior of the English-speaking world in particular. And another generalization that may well hold up is that this *aqua vitae* of critical thinking can enhance for the world at large just how to consider, to feel, and to imagine, and perhaps can even brace everyone for how to live: strenuously. So: does procedure, no matter how messy, prove more reliable than principle, however neat?

*

To answer historically, as well as affirmatively: mid-19th-century religious sage and pre-eminent social reformer F. D. Maurice diagnoses "system" as a disease of individual citizens and of whole nations.[5] By way of hoping for the miracle of dispelling *rigor mortis* from the body politic, Maurice isolates "coherent, independent, subordinate, and derivative principles" as the systemic germ that not only infects psychological wellbeing but also blights social progress. He thinks a system threatens private and public health by closing off the fresh air of conversation. He feels it consigns personal and general welfare to the hermetic

---

[1] Donald Ault's study of William Blake's "visionary physics" recognizes the role of the imagination—not just in Blake's scientific thought, but in Isaac Newton's. Blake to the contrary, Newton was scarcely as afflicted with "Single vision" as readers of Blake might think. Blake's ten words, quoted above, come from lines 86-87 of "With Happiness Stretchd Across the Hills," a poem included in his letter to Thomas Butts. Quotations of British and American writers, unless otherwise indicated, are from Damrosch et al., eds., and Baym et al., eds.

[2] Adams, ed., 583-95, esp. 587.

[3] "Brantley's greatest service to Dickinson studies and to Romantic studies in general," Eric G. Wilson adds, "is in disclosing the 'double-ness' of the Myth of Amherst and—by extension—of several of her transatlantic forebears, such as Wordsworth and Emerson."

[4] Bryson 141. Bill Bryson adds: "But having said that, I have come to appreciate with the passing years that being unsystematic gives life a richness and unpredictability that endows even the simplest undertakings with an air of challenge and uncertainty. . . . Once you have spent ten minutes with a map of Paris, you will understand arrondissements forever. . . . [T]he only way to understand the layout of London is to spend years studying it" (Bryson 143).

[5] Quotations in the paragraph above, and in the one after that, come from A. Dwight Culler's discussion (158-59) of F. D. Maurice's distinction between method and system. Thus Maurice's *The Kingdom of Christ* (1838) makes its mark on issues relating to the high-to-late Romanticism of the English-speaking world.

perdition of kneejerk, predetermined responses to discrete, unstructured data and assorted, variable circumstances. Thus Maurice encourages personal and collective expectoration of the system, which he defines precisely (if somewhat negatively) as "that which is most opposed to life, freedom, variety."

Through the welcome release of contrast, Maurice specifies the right medication: he administers "method" as the porous, anything but sealed-up poultice for what ails people systematically. He stipulates method as a curative power—that without which "life, freedom, variety cannot exist," but with which—however effortful the expectation—people may thrive on desire for things "about to be" salutary (Wordsworth, *The Prelude*, 1850, 6:606-08). Maurice applies malleable, one-at-a-time, grass-roots, and inductive procedures as handy adjustments to human conditions. Whether or not his Victorian optimism is misplaced, or perhaps even a little forced, his hopefulness remains desirable, appealing, and his emphasis on method can yet provide the minimum adult daily dosage of diversity.

The prototype of Maurice's kind of wisdom is the joint, concerted flexibility of his virtually American, as well as his really British, birthright. British empiricism, with its sense-based method; British and American Methodism, with its contribution of the spiritual sense to the experience of transatlantic revivalism; and the poetic method/poetic faith inter-identification achieved by Anglo-American Romanticism—all comprise the composite, primordial payoff of methodical efficacy writ large. At the risk of fondness for threesomes of isms, yet as though prophesying the propitious, methodizing influence of Maurice's own tactical love of lists, the transatlantic trio of empiricism, evangelicalism, and Romanticism sounds out a resonant chord of complex harmony. The trio's off-notes of scientism, enthusiasm, and "egotistical sublimity" (solipsism) notwithstanding, the Anglo-American species of philosophical, religious, and literary experience celebrates perceptual robustness, upholds moral choice, and projects kaleidoscopic change, diverting subjectivity outward (Keats, to Richard Woodhouse, October 27, 1818).[6] And thus having moved on from a sustained aural metaphor—the music of the trio—to the more accustomed brief for visual dominance in empiricism, the quasi-Trinitarian mystique of the three-part inventories shifts back down to the twofold leitmotif of seeing-believing.

---

[6] John Keats distinguishes between "the wordsworthian or egotistical sublime" and another kind of "poetical Character." The former is pure self, whereas what Keats aspires to—despite how he fundamentally admires Wordsworth—is the poet who "has no self." "When I am in a room with People," Keats concludes, "then not myself goes home to myself: but the identity of everyone in the room begins [so] to press upon me that I am in a very little time an[ni]hilated—."

To be sure, this logic, too, requires a triad. An Anglo-American Romantic writer, after all, is according to the collection's understanding a third force working with, and against, empiricism and evangelicalism. And for that matter, consistent with the big picture of how life happens in the instability between entropy and chaos, or between general relativity and quantum mechanics, it is no wonder that "a fourth [or a fifth or a sixth] dimension of a poem" occurs.[7] Nevertheless, the collection entertains the expectation that an indigenous, bi-native, English-language both/and may modify, and perhaps even obviate, the Germany-to-Britain direction of Friedrich Schlegel's admittedly influential logic, and so explores empirical/evangelical interaction as nub, not rub, for a richly and strangely multiple effect on both sides of the Atlantic.[8] This modestly but productively ambidextrous procedure of Romantic Anglo-America can go so far as to furnish the hope-against-hope of the world for natural-and-spiritual abundance, for self-and-soul-food combination in the here-and-now. Please remember, after all, that the slash between "both" and "and" also joins these words, so that the time-honored unitary criterion of aesthetics and of reality alike stays paradoxically part of the polyverse's double-ness, and perhaps even poses whether or not the famous truth of indeterminacy is untrue. Be that as it may, and back to the *terra firma* of Maurice: he clarifies for present purposes how "method rather than system" is no mere intellectual slogan but comports and consorts with both/and logic of especially the empirical/evangelical kind. Thus, consistent with how "[c]reativity arises as the result of the intersection between two quite different frames of reference," the method of Anglo-American Romantic imagination may or may not be chartered—but is uncharted—and thereby accounts for the palpable quality of open-endedness in the bi-national aesthetic at its freest (please recall the second epigraph of the prologue).

Perhaps a relatively recent dispensation of "method rather than system"—beyond the shores usually hugged by the series—can even clinch the wider pertinence of the watchword. Twentieth-century Continental Eu-

---

[7] Abrams, 2012. Apart from its sound, its meaning, and its form, the "fourth dimension of a poem," according to M. H. Abrams, is "the act of its utterance," which helps readers practice "interpretive tact" as good-will guessers at an author's intention. This book, published when Abrams turned one hundred (he died in 2015), proceeds from the wise heights of a distinguished career of "doing things with texts" (another of his titles). The paragraph above is owing to conversation with Mikesch Muecke, Gregory L. Ulmer, and Miriam Zach, none of whom bears responsibility for whether or not the proverbial Scotty was in this instance able to beam the discussion up.

[8] For the historical, Germany-located understanding of both/and logic—and for how Friedrich Schlegel's compares with that of Romantic Anglo-America—please recall the discussion throughout the prologue, but especially in the second and fourth footnotes.

ropean philosophical ethicist and profound public intellectual Emmanuel Levinas—in experiencing the faces of other people, one by one—managed to escape the hegemonic system of totalizing impersonality, and of navel-gazing self-mastery, from Plato to Hegel to Heidegger (Bakewell; Large; Mensch; New; Rees). Intriguingly, at the same time as New Critics (if not, indeed, somewhat before their time, as though he could have influenced them) Levinas rediscovered what any rising generation of young minds might profit from finding out: freedom through ambiguity. Most notably, Levinas maintained awareness of good-and-evil simultaneity, and shrank from ever trying to reconcile these two sides of this civilization-blowing binary opposition. Consequently, Levinas drew on the literary value of "divine comedy": to keep goodness free and inviolate, yet engaged, and to "get out of the tragedy" of Nazi-member Martin Heidegger's perpendicular philosophy of abstract "being," wherein, Heidegger wrote, "to think is to confine yourself to a single thought."[9] Levinas's new ethic of philosophy, shading into religion and literature, accessed others and otherness, in effect through "method rather than system." His procedure of cultural analysis, in which the good-vs.-evil conundrum stays crucially at stake, is a historically significant, still-timely analogue to the way in which Anglo-American Romanticism kept empiricism and evangelicalism in play, celebrating the aesthetic value of resisting the no-solution solution of fused finality.

On the one hand, to the extent that human brains seek order, human beings yearn for unity. Single-vision minds can range as effectually as Walt Disney's, which beguiled multitudes with the commercial never-never-land of a not-so-easily dismissible everyman's transcendence: "up through the atmosphere, up where the air is clear."[10] Single-vision minds can also appear as in-

---

[9] In the sentence above, Simon Critchley's paraphrase of Emmanuel Levinas's ethical philosophy is quoted (Critchley 73, 141). Martin Heidegger's words in the above sentence are quoted in Bakewell, 2016, 42. Edward Mendelson's quotation of Sarah Bakewell's important book is judicious (Mendelson 10-11). Maurice Merleau-Ponty's avoidance of the self-mastering pitfalls of Heidegger makes Merleau-Ponty prominent in Bakewell's pantheon, but she also goes to the very heart of Levinas's significance: "For Levinas [Bakewell writes], we literally face each other, one individual at a time, and that relationship becomes one of communication and moral expectation. We do not merge, we respond to one another." Bakewell herself fell under Heidegger's spell in her early 20s, and still feels "re-enchanted" by his philosophy from time to time, yet struggles "to get free," concluding that Heidegger's single-thought fixation is "the very opposite of what thinking ought to be. Thinking should be generous, and have a good appetite."

[10] As silly as such doggerel may sound, its form of transcendence is so widespread that it can scarcely be rejected out of hand. A Walt Disney who commands respect, by the way, is depicted throughout John Lee Hancock's 2013 film, *Saving Mr. Banks*.

genious as those of Hegel (idealist) and Marx (materialist), for both of whom, thesis and antithesis drive toward synthesis.[11] Among poets, no matter how negatively capable, the "blessed rage for order" can vent perhaps even more vociferously than among other people, because "determination at the core"— poet C. D. Wright's label for the synoptic breakthrough that assures "poetry's endurance"—can be even more important than "esemplastic" (flexible) imagination (Stevens, "Key West," 1934, 51; Fried 23; Coleridge, *Biographia Literaria*, 1817, chapter 14). The "Great Old Modern" Robert Frost—scarcely an artless, or a necessarily single-minded, writer—reached sharp-eyed understanding, broke through into a clearing, nonetheless.[12] If Frost feared that neither "look[ing] out far" nor "look[ing] in deep" would finally work as a way of knowing or believing, then, still, he fashioned signature personae who, whether nobly or foolishly, "kept watch" for an elusive, yet beckoning, wholeness, and who sustained, thereby, the integrity of their mutual motivation.[13] Belief in variety jibes imperfectly, at best, with the equally human propensity to cleave to one meaning, or to hear one voice. Phrases like "infinite access to manifold otherness," therefore, may occlude how human nature, in the lurch, prefers the one to the many.

On the other hand, a corollary of "method rather than system" can be quite liberating: human beings also yearn for diversity and, engaged as they are in suspense, may relish the process of trial and error, and even of hit or miss (Schulz). The English professor can appear methodical whenever he or she enjoys the professor's bonus of moderating class discussion. Since, by the breathing model of "better living through criticism," that professor can stay receptive most of the time, wisely passive enough to think one way one day, and another way another, he or she can learn, too.[14] The both/and logic of an

---

[11] Harold Bloom's latest book provides another of his excellent ways to take refuge from too much dialectic. Thanks go to him, every day since 2005, for a 2005 correspondence about the series.

[12] Witness the last stanza of Robert Frost, "Neither out Far Nor in Deep" (1936): "They cannot look out far. / They cannot look in deep. / But when was that ever a bar / To any watch they keep?" In an anti-Romantic vein, Randall Jarrell observes that "it would be hard to find anything more unpleasant to say about people" (Leithauser 42), but, in answer to Jarrell, Brad Leithauser queries, along Romantic lines, "Isn't [Frost] saying that, as seekers after the truth, we're to be commended for our immoderate appetites, rather than damned for our modest achievements?" Thus "Great Old Modern" (Leithauser's moniker) admits of Romantic interpretation.

[13] "Neither out Far Nor in Deep" is consistent with Blake's twofold perception: "More! More! Is the cry" of Man; and "less than All cannot satisfy" (Blake, *There Is No Natural Religion*, 1788, Plate b7).

[14] The above quotation comes from A. O. Scott's title. Leon Wieseltier seconds Scott's view "that an experience of art is akin to a conversion experience, that an encounter with art con-

amateur aesthete need not be such an open-ended process-ride as to paralyze him or her, when the time for action arrives. But—to return to Bill Bryson—this American-born British citizen would surely concur in "method rather than system" as not just a British, but an Anglo-American, watchword. That is why the epilogue essentially elaborates on Bryson's serious subtext and spins his quip not just in a bi-national, but in a historical, direction. The first principle of an Anglo-American system of the 19th century, too, is that it should be not just a principle, but a procedure, and should only appear systematic, yet by no means be any system at all but, rather, a method. Thus philosophy, religion, and literature from the Enlightenment to the Romantic era of the English-speaking world do not so much set up an organized whole compounded of parts, as find ways to develop ways.

Can the cumulative validity of the collection eliminate the scourge of single vision—or remedy that tragic "malady of the quotidian" which is sleep-walking myopia (Stevens, "The Man Whose Pharynx Was Bad," 1921, 18)? It would be a long shot, but "method rather than system" does square with the both/and logic of *bonnes*-and of *belles-lettres* alike. Slowly but surely describing the arc from John Locke to Emily Dickinson, *Transatlantic Trio* is betting its life on that not-unreasonable hope. Or, to put the case more modestly, altogether in keeping with "method rather than system," the collection sustains the following fragile hope. May these pages relieve the pressure of steam-engine language that threatens to derail politics stuck in either/or!

If such a wishful thought amounts only to a tacit, intermittent optative among the essays and reviews, then perhaps even closer to the surface of this new assemblage ascends, nonetheless, a nearly overt refrain: black-or-white perception equates to dogmatic slumber with eyes wide shut. Both/and logic, by contrast, banishes either/or, and whispers, or whistles in the dark, throughout the collection. Does the anthology glimpse from left field (without disregarding the unitary criterion as old as Aristotle's *Poetics [ca.* 330 BCE]) polysemy as the staple of art? Do these twenty-one essays and seventeen reviews of eighteen books presuppose such multiple meaning in literature as Stevens's "thirteen ways of looking at a blackbird"—or in criticism as thirty-eight perspectives (and counting) on Romantic Anglo-America (Stevens, "Blackbird," 1954)? Perhaps, for well-founded paradox—"The contradictions have been so many," William Empson exults—can replace "looking at": not just with "look-

---

fers not only ravishments but also obligations, that a sense of the beauty of existence entails a sense of the gravity of existence" (Wieseltier 38). Wieseltier quotes "the severe and startling words that conclude a renowned sonnet Rilke wrote in 1908, after an encounter with an ancient marble torso in the Louvre: 'You must change your life.'"

ing into," but with searching under, above, and all the way around.[15] That said, the collection is primarily careful to counteract fixed ideas, and the systems that produce and preserve them, by emphasizing the humbly methodical, yet reliably open-ended, "two-mindedness" of literature, above all.[16]

To pause over just what else both/and logic might signify: does it go so far as, first (Levinas notwithstanding) to reconcile contraries? Probably not, though John Milton appears to have believed so, concerned as he was with how the Satan-vs.-Jesus duel and the Adam-and-Eve dual will resolve themselves into "ultimate harmony" among the "unities of creation" (Shoaf xi). The harmony of a Ralph Waldo Emerson or of a Dickinson, however, in the Charles Darwin-haunted absence of any such confident Christian eschatology, appears subtler than, if in some ways still comparable with, Milton's. Ultimate harmony, after all, is system rather than method, whereas the historical, interdisciplinary method of close reading favors the oxymoronic logic of complex harmony in the here-and-now. Accordingly, one side of what Emerson calls the "double consciousness" of fate and freedom or of what Dickinson terms the "Compound Vision" of finite and infinite "constantly shapes and generates the other" (please recall the third epigraph to the epilogue) without irritably reaching after "the unities of creation" (does "unities" undermine the unity of Milton's poetry?).[17] The duel/dual pun works in the 19th century, as well. The best and worst of all possible Romantic-era worlds were by no means without hope, yet did not so much envision harmony or unity as experience oscillation onward: from conflict to a measure of cooperation (as though both/and logic were a dynamic of, and for, the earth).

Romantic Anglo-America, if not Anglo-American Modernism, dramatizes temporality and spirituality in the sublunary setting. On the ground of experience, the "less" of temporality morphs into the "more" of spirituality (to evoke Mies van der Rohe). And by the same token of both/and interchangeability, the "less" of spirituality modulates, on that same constant ground, into

---

[15] Lukas 12-14. David Abram, too, proves apropos. David Lukas observes: "Abram rightly cautions that we have become so accustomed to staring at flat representations (billboards, televisions, computer screens, printed pages) that we have become thoroughly trained to look *at* the surface of, rather than *into* the depths of, the living world around us" (Lukas's emphasis). Wordsworth, for his part, retrains us to "see into the life of things" (Wordsworth, "Tintern Abbey," 1798, 49). William Empson's poem—"Let It Go," 1940—is quoted in Coutts iii.

[16] In 2015, Andrew O'Hagan argued for "two-mindedness" as the distinguishing mark of William Shakespeare's characters. "Shakespeare," O'Hagan writes, "is always various, always interested in two-mindedness, and never knowingly blunt in showing his characters' motivations."

[17] Emerson, "Fate" (1852), in Whicher 351; Dickinson, "The Admirations—and Contempts—of time—" (Poem 830, 9).

the "more" of temporality, too. Choose one, or both, to be content. On a horizontal, yet no less intriguing, axis than the vertical, and in line with a four-decade development of how the two poles of a binary are indeed forever shaping and generating one another, the collection traces the Romantic-era decline of any special reference to "a world elsewhere" (Shakespeare, *Coriolanus*, 1609, III.iii.167). But the anthology also acknowledges how this very earthiness makes the broadly experiential, spiritual as well as natural vision an all the more religiously, as well as philosophically, searching procedure of Romantic Anglo-America's world-oriented, yet no less faithful or conscientious élan. On a good day of reading between the lines and of parsing the primary meaning of these thirty-eight shorter pieces, their readers' increased faculty of redoubled insight may even come to rival a William Wordsworth's! Thus the *omnium gatherum* of forty sections (counting prologue and epilogue)—a 20-20 hindsight!—may even henceforth bear witness to the "double consciousness" or "Compound Vision" of context and of text alike, and hence of the numinous as well as quotidian exchange of Anglo-American subject vs. object.[18]

The "method rather than system" for which the collection stands, then, strengthens the "ability to hold two opposed ideas in the mind at the same time, and still retain the ability to function."[19] Readers may the better monitor swaying from the tough-minded, "empirical" poetic experiment to the tender-minded, "evangelical" poetic faith of the Anglo-American Romantic world. And readers may also the more promptly register how Romantic Anglo-America resists the stasis of synthesis by keeping contraries interpenetrating. Such sessions of sweet silent thought may help academic and non-academic audiences pass the F. Scott Fitzgerald "test of a first-rate intelligence"—and achieve better living through the both/and of criticism, as well as of art and of life. Such an outcome, devoutly wished, would license thinking, for that "method rather than system" would heighten concentration without undue regard to either aptitude or training.

*

"A book that does not contain its counter-book," Jorge Luis Borges writes, "is considered incomplete" (Rose, ed., xi). That goes for a collection, too, perhaps even as though its author could be Pope Leo X and Martin Luther rolled into

---

[18] Robert B. Ray's title comes to mind—though "Brantley X 40" would step over the line.
[19] Fitzgerald 69. F. Scott Fitzgerald adds, less famously, "things are hopeless . . . make them otherwise."

one. Accordingly, the reviews fully quoted in the appendix do not just provide evidence for increasingly favorable reception of the six books of the series, but represent the various strains of resistance to those volumes. Moreover, a similarly truth-seeking air suffuses both/and self-assessment throughout much of this segment, which thereby seeks, in the long run, to buttress and complete the intellectual and methodological credo of the previous subdivision. This epilogue, in consequence, does not just take the pulse of the series' relentless self-consistency, accentuating the positive, eliminating the negative, and reaffirming the whole, but includes an undermining, nagging, yet different and maybe refreshing line of auto-subversion. Speaking not just in the appendix, but at the outset of this longest subsection of either the prologue or the epilogue, a voice of skeptical counter-interpretation will now have its say, acknowledging the contingencies of the argument and recognizing the uncanny simultaneity of "not precisely knowing / And not precisely knowing not" (Dickinson, Poem 1347, 1-2). Experience, after all, not only goes somewhere, but also hovers along the way—takes time for "Wonder—" (Dickinson, Poem 1347, 2). To begin with, the next paragraph gives composite, devil's-advocate utterance to recurring doubts; accentuates the negative; and in doing so, may strongly appeal to those for whom the tingling excitement of suspenseful exploration beats the numb ho-hum of "normal science" anyway (Kuhn).

Mr. Brantley, you have developed a perspective on the 19th-century inheritance, but each century works a combination of science and religion from the previous century, back into whenever, since what humans seem to do is acknowledge the natural world even while aspiring to the preternatural or supernal. What you do not appear to realize, at times, is your special pleading on behalf of John Wesley and Methodism, when, in fact, the entire spectrum of Judeo-Christianity certainly, and all religions probably, adjusted in the same flexible way, as religions must, if they are to survive in their changing cultures. This is the great lesson of the Catholic and Protestant missionary alike. The number of Anglican "scientific" treatises is something you do not even touch. Yet, for instance, the Boyle lectures of the Royal Society were always a combination of science and religion, and most of the lecturers were also divines. In other words that you will not like, Mr. Brantley, human beings cannot abandon either reason or superstition completely, or when they do, they would become Nazis or ISIS on the one hand, and scientists and hollow men on the other. Your Romanticism, too, is a case of special pleading, without sufficiently recognizing how the Romantic Movement can remain quite separate from the cult of sensibility and sentimentality it inherited; nor do you even mention the para-Methodist, yet ever-relevant, poetry of James Thomson, Edward Young, William Collins, and the Graveyard School. Perhaps we skeptics are just asking you to tone down your rhetoric of "subtlety" and "brilliance," even if only to allow for the partiality, in both senses, of your totalization of two centuries and two countries.

Until all is said and done in the series, that dramatic monologist's digest of objections will take hold here, for friendly opposition instructs. Has an essay or a book in the sequence ever discussed a context or a text that did not succumb to the empirical-evangelical, Anglo-American pattern? Well, come to think of it, yes, it has, if not exactly in the collection, then in the most recent book, *Emily Dickinson's Rich Conversation: Poetry, Philosophy, Science* (2013, 2015). To make the point briefly, the latest tome concedes (as though its author could change his mind like Matthew Arnold in epigraph two) that Emily Dickinson's "On a Columnar Self—" (Poem 740) puts to the test any prior claim that her primary voice "is either empirical or evangelical" (Brantley, 2013, 2015, 79-83). The lyric "can sound as formally superior to sense-impressions," whether natural or sense-analogized to the spirit, "as any rationalist/idealist Romantic-era work, English-language or other." More such divagating analysis is on the way, as a component of any series installments that may yet come: the both/and emphasis of historical, interdisciplinary criticism should, by definition, not be monolithic. Future contributions will temper admiration for the subject matter. The opposite of what is being argued, after all, might just be the case, perhaps even at any given time.

Can human minds rest in the mystery and doubt perhaps too glibly—or even somewhat disingenuously—relished throughout the collection? Except for the greatest or sickest, no, they cannot. And here is something else that the series has not taken seriously enough. Neither John Keats's negative capability nor that of any other good poet reaches irritably after fact and reason, but scholars find "truth" and "certainty" and have been known to reduce a word or two to just one single, convenient meaning (though not usually scholars of "natural methodism," surely). As much as inner open-enders might pooh-pooh the resolution-drive of a Hegel or a Marx, secret synthesizers lurk in the hearts of men and women, as well. If that shift of mood (from the previous segment and from the series in general) should denote palinode, then so be it. Who can deny his or her yearning for unity on some days? To see empirical vs. evangelical emerging into harmony (poetry) looks a lot like synthesis just now. So the possibility of works that do not evince both/and exists, however barely.

That said, the epilogue still promotes that logic, as arch among "the better angels of our nature." Poetry strengthens that trait, thereby eliciting the reader's "Poetic Genius" (Blake, *All Religions Are One*, 1788, Principle 4). Criticism, if its analysis proves sufficiently scrutinizing, reflects that dual function. New Criticism plumbs "the richness of ambiguity" (the patented phrase yet rings). And historical, interdisciplinary criticism, too, promulgates liberating paradox.

The Latin origin of the word *ambiguity* is *ambi-agere*—to wander uncertainly. Many 18th-to-19th-century Anglo-American writers of *bonnes-* and of *belles-lettres* take up such roaming; or they do whenever they are on their best, most aesthetically daring behavior. Then, they turn arbitrarily; crisscross; pass by; drift away; weave along; travel on "no set path" to "no true way."[20] But other such authors search for something, they know not what; fear, like Dickinson, that they are "looking oppositely / For the Site of the Kingdom of Heaven—" (Poem 1077); keep on looking, anyway; drive into the unknown; find someplace accidentally; and arrive somewhere on purpose. Both/and logic carries the implication not just of tentativeness or open-mindedness, but, if not of resolution exactly, then of understanding how those who come down hard on one side or the other can be wrong or dangerous. Now even both/and can focus on one side of a dichotomy, as when an otherwise "Compound Vision" parent means "Get out of the street!" or an otherwise subtle general casts the die and storms the main gate. But even the latter case of such logic need not lose sight of the other side, if only because understanding the enemy (as Homer and Vergil knew) is important. So, in their capacity as both/and logicians, humans possess the power, though not the magic, "to repeal / Large codes of fraud and woe" (Shelley, "Mont Blanc," 1816, 80-81; Shelley's language may refer to the church and Napoleon alike).

Even when a writer appears more of a pilgrim than a seeker, he or she can resist all-too-human synthesizing and preserve in a state of readiness the freedom-arsenal of both/and authority. As occasion rises, and if only through the kinetic potential of oscillation onward, people can all reject, presumably the authors and critics among them in particular, the hyper-explanatory formularies of single-vision con-artistry and tyranny. "The specter of enthrallment to single-minded perception," L. J. Swingle writes, "haunts Romantic literary art" (Swingle 49). Whereas the Romantic skeptical mode reaches "a free space between the claims of competing ideologies," Victorian (and Modern?) skepticism does not succeed in re-discovering that "creative power of

---

[20] Jones 103-04. The paragraphs above are indebted to Jeremy B. Jones, a Western Carolina creative writer. His memoir includes an early-21st-century version of a perennial literary stance especially characteristic of the Romantic era.

our distinguishing human nature" (Swingle 188). "Instead," as Swingle concludes, post-Romantic skepticism "risk[s] falling either into a state of almost metaphysical paralysis or into a state of perverse activity that seems antagonistic to humanistic impulses." All the more dramatic a contrast along the Romantic-to-post-Modern arc of skepticism is how the high-Romantic "literary artifact is designed [through skepticism] to move the reader, in company with the artist, toward a free mental space beyond or between enthrallments through simultaneous invocations of competing enthrallments" (Swingle 52). That legacy of freedom, albeit with the possibility of morphing into gridlock or fascism, remains the birthright of post-Romantic generations, however difficult it may be, at any given time, to claim that inheritance.

Shelley himself, as much pilgrim as seeker, is a case in point of political freedom, and, Byron's reputation for being "mad, bad, and dangerous to know" notwithstanding, so is Byron: none other than his good friend Shelley called the freedom-fighting grandson of a wicked lord "The Pilgrim of Eternity."[21] Perhaps even when a writer "finds a way home and the solace of a base," he or she can still practice both/and logic, if only as a disciplined exercise against, or alacritous check on, fixed ideas (Jones 104). T. S. Eliot, despite how dyed-in-the-wool his shades of single-mindedness can appear, nonetheless qualifies as another such author, if only within the realm of a religious rather than a political possibility. And as demonstrated by her by no means entirely non-political conversation with President Barack Obama in autumn 2015, Marilyn Robinson ranks high as a no less open-minded writer for being a deeply religious thinker.

An especially high-Romantic example of a seeker/pilgrim is Blake, whose unforgettable stanza from the preface to *Milton: A Poem (ca.* 1808) sounds the tocsin of religious as well as political freedom:

> I will not cease from Mental Fight,
> Nor shall my Sword sleep in my hand:
> Till we have built Jerusalem,
> In England's green & pleasant land[.]

"Till we have built Jerusalem" signals definitive conclusion not so different from John Bunyan's *Pilgrim's Progress* (1672) to which Blake refers. But even

---

[21] Shelley, "Adonais" (1821), line 264. Note well the title of George Gordon, Lord Byron's *Childe Harold's Pilgrimage* (1812-1818)—though Byron might have interpreted himself differently from Shelley, since Byron referred to his Childe Harold as one of the "wanderers o'er eternity" (3.669). Lady Caroline Lamb's description, above, of Lord Byron, remains delicious.

though the last two lines of the stanza envision such an outcome (the eleven words elevate Britain's not-so-secret national anthem) not even the climax realizes it. And the first two lines, in which the quest for an evangelical, here-and-now destination, like the hunt for an empirical solution, is in process (think: "Onward, Christian soldiers"), are characterized by the clash of contraries. Or by the aroused, yet still mid-battle heat that augurs progress, if any—is the speaker huffing and puffing?—by fits and starts that the pilgrim/seeker may or may not ever see through to completion, since he or she is left, at present, only with Mental Fight.

Just as such a covert reading of Blake's lines can limit how they ring with goal-reaching confidence, so the collection comprises salty as well as sweet trail mix for ramblers as well as pilgrims. Both types of sojourners can join the multitudes contained within each person in the universe "which is not one" (Irigaray). Whether or not the substance of all things considered is twofold, their relations, given both/and dynamic, are manifold. Kant said as much. At one extreme, compulsion to synthesis would yield distortion, or too much clarity; or *rigor mortis*, or nothing but stasis. At the other pole, however, life is just too short for infinite meaning (endless though gist is) and readers must at some point politely pass by the abyss of proliferation, for the most formalistically inclined must bring art and criticism, and art and life, to some kind of rounding-off.

So, despite how everyone's inner English major is the only "person" with the luxury of pure both/and—never coming prematurely home—that very sumptuousness (a nice Keatsean or Dickinsonian word) can nonetheless usher nine-to-five selves into the delicious in-between (Keats, "Ode on Melancholy," 1819; Dickinson, Poem 1404, 7). *Transatlantic Trio*, accordingly, shuttles between the Herbert tribute and "Locke and Wesley," or between the dialogue written with Diana R. Brantley and "Wesley and Edwards." The distinction between conversation and dialectic—and the preference for the former—suggest that a Wordsworth or an Emerson could scarcely have unified contraries through synthesis of any kind, whether idealist or materialist, even if such an author had wished to do so. Dialectical strategy proves ultimately inimical to aesthetic versatility. The writers who have attracted the attention of the series refuse to sleep, until Jerusalem is built. But they never sleep, for they never finish building, and they maintain a watch all the more faithful for being alert: "I will stand upon my watch, and set me upon the tower, and will watch to see what he will say unto me, and what I shall answer" (Hab. 2:1; KJV).

That sets up the following question: how best to epitomize the rise and progress of—or to pinpoint the form and function of—empiricism and evangelicalism in Anglo-American Romanticism? The answer is, first, by summarizing how empirical philosophy and evangelical faith interacted: British empiricism linked the external to words through ideas of sensation, as though perception were mediation; and British and American evangelicalism linked the external to words through ideals of sensation, as though grace were perception. The experiential procedure of knowing and of believing need signal no stand-off, despite how insistently a Kant might call science vs. religion irreconcilable. Nor were empiricism and evangelicalism individually superseded by their merger into a form of higher truth, as Hegel would have said of any thesis/antithesis set. (He portentously called such truth "The Speculative Idea of Absolute Knowledge.")[22] Instead, the natural and spiritual kinds of "epistemology" talked richly, yet down-to-earth, to one another. The collection's cover image of a railroading handcar, and such other images as a weaving shuttle, suggest a back-and-forth that gets somewhere, or produces something, as opposed, say, to the repetitious up-and-down of a yo-yo.

To be sure, the twain of empiricism and evangelicalism would seem never to meet, or, if never to say never, then hardly ever. For instance, if inner empiricists must see for themselves and be in the presence of the things they know, then they may put air quotation marks around "presence," which may sound religious but is not necessarily so. Exclusively sense-based emphasis, on balance, would seem to preclude religious implications. And if inner evangelicals, too, must see for themselves and be in the presence of the things they know, then by the same token of parity with, as well as contrast to, the empirical, they may put air quotation marks around "see," which may sound scientific but is not necessarily so. The spiritual sense can appear superior to the physical eye, despite being metaphorical. Nevertheless, however inexorably the spiritual sense may grow merely sense-analogized to the physical senses, no longer continuous with them, 18th-century evangelicalism remained as experience-oriented as that century's empiricism. This religiously as well as philosophically enlightened approach to both nature and spirit shared points of this-worldly contact as well as of theoretical similarity. Thus the empirical/evangelical interface, a strangely but wonderfully widespread phenomenon of seeing and of witnessing alike, constituted a close-enough encounter not so much of the third kind, from elsewhere, as of the first order, right here.

---

[22] Brantley, 2013, 81-82. G. W. F. Hegel and Søren Kierkegaard are compared, along the lines of the paragraph above, in Hannay; Leib.

A here-and-now philosophy and a world-leaning religion, at any rate, were not in a stand-off or at an impasse but, as separate and different spheres, one secular, the other not, stood off from one another, circling warily, yet energetically overlapping from auspicious moment to moment. Empiricism and evangelicalism spoke to one another from the bi-local, bifocal standpoint of their most intimate proximity in all of history. The one reported on seeing things, the other on witnessing presences. Both did so within their shared frame of experiential reference. On their bi-national ground, faith in experience and experiential Faith commingled, and then flowed on.

An enigmatic, a serious as well as playful, "unity" of resonant double-ness resulted. In the summer of their relative contentment, the sides of the dichotomy sustained an Anglo-American exchange both multipurpose and explanatory, both subtle and accessible, and both complex and satisfying. The paradigmatic pair of contraries not only appealed to, but was also quintessential in, an English-speaking world that is not even yet quite gone. Nor are the non-empiricists and the non-evangelicals among Anglo-Americans necessarily likely to allow this folk and popular, as well as elite, duality of culturally presiding antinomies to disappear or be entirely absent from the individually and collectively bi-national DNA.

On compartmentalized days of the 21st century, neither outer nor inner empiricists/evangelicals have much to say to one another, and this opposition constituted much of what was quirkiest about Anglo-American Romanticism. In advance of a planned book that will ask if the road of a critical Wessex-Yoknapatawpha runs through to Modernism, reaffirmation of just how empiricism and evangelicalism together fostered Romanticism appears nonetheless called for. Romantic Anglo-America wrote neither the first nor the last chapter of literary history to make artistic hay out of science vs. religion. Each age of art aims for that goal. Romantic Anglo-America, however, was both the first and probably the last literary revival to do so in such great homage to a wide and full range of high-to-low-brow culture, and vice versa. Locke, for instance, came down to Wordsworth and Emerson not just through Wesley and Edwards, but through the general readers for whom Wesley annotated Locke's *Essay;* to whom he distributed it; and to whom he tipped his hat, for telling him a thing or two about life (Brantley, 1984, 103-28; Brantley, 1993, 7-42). Bonneletristic prowess of empiricism initially, and of evangelicalism medially, proved pivotal to belletristic mettle ultimately.

If not exactly for purposes of deliberate cooperation, then certainly with the vital effect of creative clash, or "solution sweet," the empiricism and evangelicalism of the transatlantic *Zeitgeist* brought forth the low-to-high-brow drama of Anglo-American Romanticism (Keats, "The Eve of St. Agnes," 1820, 322). The interactive mood of both/and logic did not so much favor knowing over believing, or vice versa, as blend these two coping mechanisms, not just to soften the distinction, but to effect trade that sweetens the former and savors the latter. Whether or not the duality of Romantic Anglo-America translates too readily into all the "stupendous antagonisms" of the human experiment—body/mind, fact/fancy, concrete/universal, *Stofftrieb/Formtrieb*, Dionysus/Apollo, yin/yang—the antiphony nonetheless re-sounds, from the not-so-distant past.[23] To quote William Faulkner: "The past is never dead. It's not even past" (Faulkner, *Requiem for a Nun*, 1950). And to invoke Samuel Beckett—"Ever tried. Ever failed. No matter. Try again. Fail again. Fail better"—the collection, at best, fails better than the books in the series and, at worst, fails again (Beckett, *Worstward Ho*, 1983). Yet all who will ever scan these contents may audition the transatlantic trio and become its impresarios—insofar as the collection plays complex harmony for those "with ears to hear" (Mark 8:18; KJV; an echo of scripture colors the appropriately scripture-like criticism, "still crazy after all these years," of an all-but-scriptural canon). The both/and logic throughout the folk/hymn-singing, as well as popular and elite, mix of cross-national culture contributes to the English language an individualized and expressive, yet interactive and audience-attuned, idiom of in-the-world truth, on the one hand, and of out-of-this-world transformation, joy, love, grace, and hope, on the other.

That last sentence takes account of Terry Eagleton's *Hope without Optimism* (2016). His cultural criticism deploys Catholicism and Marxism in order to land hope somewhere between the immanent and the apocalyptic (it is worth remembering, in this connection, that Karl Marx called religion not just "the opium of the people," but "the heart in a heartless world"). For Eagleton, as for Kierkegaard, Abraham was a genius of expectancy, as opposed to a mundane, banal optimist. From the standpoint of the collection, accordingly, the likes of Emily Dickinson dwelt in their own not-entirely-non-Abrahamic religious possibility. Theirs remains a legacy of hope-against-hope, at least, and, at most, of full-blown "hope that can never die, / Effort, and expectation, and desire, / And something evermore about to be" (Wordsworth, *The Prelude*, 1850, 6:607-09). And that strangely more exquisite than merely indeterminate "something" is "about to be" every bit as good as, say, "a blessing" in a "gentle breeze" (Wordsworth, *The Prelude*, 1850, 1.1).

---

[23] Eric G. Wilson discusses Ralph Waldo Emerson's phrase "stupendous antagonisms" as a categorical name for Romantic Anglo-America's binary oppositions.

To be sure, the notion of a unified field theory of English-language Romanticism may not appear to jibe with that of both/and logic. Nevertheless, at least with regard to their synoptic view of British Romanticism, Gene W. Ruoff and L. J. Swingle find that its very self-similarity inheres paradoxically in the explanatory double-ness of distinct but contiguous historical periods:

> Probably when our unified field theory of British Romanticism finally arrives, the materials will be somewhat nearer at hand than either the distant past of Milton or the far future of Joyce. . . . Thinking about British Romanticism primarily in connection with the eighteenth century may not taste quite so sublime to our intellectual palates, but perhaps our taste has become a bit depraved.[24]

And as for Anglo-American Romanticism, the collection sketches out just how 18th-to-19th-century empiricism and evangelicalism gloss what is most instructive and affecting about, distinct from what is most self-expressive and mimetic in, Romantic Anglo-America at her creatively intersecting best ("integrated but diversified field theory," anyone?).

In the explicitly historical view of the collection, the British and American relationship qualifies as special because an 18th-to-19th-century philosophical and religious reciprocity, back and forth across the Atlantic, undergirds a 19th-century transatlantic dynamic between poetic method and poetic faith. Harold Bloom's monograph (1992, 2006) on "the American religion" during the 19th century reinforced the series' growing understanding of both the staying power and the westering direction of Anglo-American religion.[25] Richard Gravil's volume (2000, 2015) concerning "Anglo-American continuities" of "Romantic dialogues" encouraged the series' stress on comparable and intertwining stripes of Romanticism in both countries. But neither what Gravil ultimately consigns to British Romanticism—tentativeness, doubt, indirection, failure, and compromise—nor what he finally ascribes to the American Renaissance—self-reliance, perfection, and ultra-Romantic liberation—need feel all that exclusive to, or dispositive of, either discrete national literary dispensation. In any bi-national strategy for studies in Romanticism, it is not

---

[24] Gene W. Ruoff and L. J. Swingle thus introduce a special issue on British Romantic fiction.
[25] "Anyone who writes books for well over half a century," Harold Bloom observes, "is likely to believe that one work in particular is a neglected child. . . . I regard that waif as *The American Religion* (1992, 2006)" (Bloom, 2015, 34). The waif of the series, incidentally, is *Anglo-American Antiphony* (1994).

a question of the victory of one side over the other, however intentionally or unintentionally Bloom and Gravil may (in the titles here referred to) be tilting either/or. And in pursuit of what happened to this particular strain of Anglo-American literature in the 20th century, it may well be worth keeping in mind what William Butler Yeats declared of himself and his fellow early-20th-century writers: "We were the last Romantics" (Yeats, "Coole Park and Ballylee," 1931, 41; Baker; Bornstein).

For a variety of reasons, from political and psychological commonalities to parallel senses of humor, Anglo-American ties have stayed strong, despite how the two countries are famously "separated" by a common language.[26] However, granting that, and in light of the collection, the British and American Romantic Movement reflects empirical heart religion. The investigations have delineated that near-oxymoron as a central paradox of that literary strain. The triangle of empiricism, evangelicalism, and Romanticism hums on both shores. And that bi-national Romanticism reacts to, accommodates, incorporates—and engulfs—that empiricism and that evangelicalism.

For anyone for whom evangelical *bonnes-lettres*—however empirically tinged—bears on *belles-lettres*, Helen Vendler's 2015 depiction of literary critics as "evangelists, plucking the public by the sleeve, saying, 'Look at this,' or 'Listen to this,'" leaps off the page.[27] Thinking back over her long career, Vendler describes herself as "a critic rather than a scholar, a reader and writer more taken by texts than by contexts." Without such an "incomparable critic" (Charles Simic's honorific), "the beautiful, subversive, bracing, and demanding legacy of our poets [Simic adds] would remain largely unknown." Vendler's I. A. Richards-like determination to weigh and sift each mood of a poem means that "commentary"—or "aesthetic criticism" (Walter Pater's stock-in-trade)—labels her writing about literature better than "systematic scholarly exposition" (Simic's conclusion). Scholars enamored not just of texts, but of

---

[26] A forthcoming issue of *Symbiosis: A Journal of Transatlantic Literary & Cultural Relations* is edited by Chris Gair and guest-edited by Matthew Scott. The issue selects papers from the Tenth Biennial Symbiosis Conference (July 2015) at the University of Essex.

[27] All quotations in the paragraph above are in Charles Simic's review of Helen Vendler, *The Ocean, The Bird, and the Scholar: Essays on Poets and Poetry* (2015). Vendler embodies what Adam Kirsch calls for. As a watchword for all critique, Kirsch recommends the chief courtesy of Randall Jarrell's—namely, "the intelligent admiration of art" (Kirsch 33). The Vendler-like willingness to express frank appreciation for a work of literature, together with respect for its author's intention, yet without diminution of close analysis or of attention to substance, and without too many bells and whistles of research, is all too lacking, according to Kirsch, in today's critical climate. M. H. Abrams's "interpretive tact" comes to mind, as well, in this general regard.

contexts, though, can also be Vendler-Evangelists. This fine how-do-you-do may be especially true of those specialists for whom contexts rival and rank as texts (for language is never dull) and for whom the empirical as well as evangelical context of Anglo-American Romanticism offers a difficult, fascinating perspective on *les belles-lettres* of the English-speaking world.

Such a historical, interdisciplinary criticism seconds a central value of Vendler's approach—the endeavor to probe, and thence to italicize, the author's point of view. Such inductive reading safeguards against the subjection of *les belles-lettres* to top-down theories of predetermined interpretation, e.g., class, race, and gender grids. Does the collection superimpose its own grid? And does "Dickinson the Romantic" fall short of the inferential standard? And are the seven readings of Dickinson conditioned by the understanding of Wordsworth and of Emerson elsewhere in the gathering? If so, and even if not, readers would do well to consult, in addition, a rising generation of scholars (Anderson; Barbeau; Bennett; Boyles; Campos; Cragwall; Dabundo; Farrell; Franke; Freedman; Harvey; Hsu; Jesse; Leader; Lee; Leigh; Roberts; Snow) whose historical, interdisciplinary criticism features religion, too, and also many of the same major authors' intentions respected by the series.[28]

Should further installments in the series rein in its combination of historical, interdisciplinary criticism and New Criticism? For reasons of both/and logic of which Blake and Arnold would approve, the answer is: not necessarily. Bonneletristic predilection for context and belletristic yen for text ask give-and-take despite any extreme of rag-and-bone-shop sleuthing on one hand or of poem-*qua*-poem privilege on the other. And if that observation risks "language over substance" and repeats, then so be it, for the anthology has nonetheless earned its stripes in commending both/and in the *bonnes/belles* tug. Can the eloquent, heartfelt words of Blake and Arnold keep watch over any context/text détente achieved by the collection and recharge that balance wherever it may flag in the author and among readers? Yes, for, however dubiously efficacious epigraphy may be, what Arnold implies is true enough,

---

[28] Thus Stanley Fish's pivotal essay has proved seminal indeed (though it is not necessarily cited by the scholars listed above). Marilyn Gaull has edited a special issue of *The Wordsworth Circle* (summer 2014) and Roger Lundin of *Religion & Literature* (summer 2014) devoted, respectively, to various historical contexts of Wordsworth's *The Excursion* (1814), including the religious, and to Dickinson's religious imagination. Two essays of the collection, "Wordsworth's Art of Belief" and "The Interrogative Mood of Emily Dickinson's Quarrel with God," form parts of these issues. What Gaull calls "Romantic Religion" is clearly a topic for renewed discussion. For the philosophical emphasis in the rising generation of historical, interdisciplinary critics: Deppman; Noble, Deppman, Stonum, eds. For the Anglo-American aspect: Pace and Scott, eds.

that as though agency were divinity, authors and readers are alike made free "if so it be"—a big if—that they can change their minds in life, as well as in scholarship. Whether or not metaphors buried in words like "recharge" and "flag" comprise weak tea, the rhetoric nonetheless works sufficiently well for rounding-off purposes if—another triumph of hope over experience?—expectation of the continued play of ideas in academic and public conversation is hereby met.

To be sure, the close reading aspired to by "Old Historicism," perhaps especially when allied to the scrutiny invented by the even "older" New Criticism, updates with difficulty. Historical, interdisciplinary criticism, after all, need appear no more praiseworthily inductive than, say, Gregory L. Ulmer's eminently applicable critical theory need seem culpably deductive, for if the series can sometimes wax as "theoretical" as Ulmer's body of work, then the latter can often beat the former at its own game of pragmatics (Brantley, 1994, 261, 305n.2; Ulmer). Nevertheless, as Wallace Stevens would have it, "death is the mother of beauty" (Stevens, "Sunday Morning," 1915, 88). That is, if reading context closely in order to read text closely, and vice versa, should ever seem moribund, then this collection can nonetheless now conduct a séance for that old-time, good-enough reading.

Are *bonnes* and *belles* alike worthy to be read, whenever both kinds of writing are as well understood as, say, a Billy Collins poem? Perhaps, for the main measures elected even by a Wordsworth or a Dickinson include a sufficiency of user-friendliness, notwithstanding how notably such belletristic authors also assume the truth of Blake's view: "what is not too Explicit is the fittest for Instruction because it rouzes the faculties to act" (Blake, to the Rev. Dr. Trusler, August 23, 1799). Another close-reading tip or two arises, in turn, from the text's context, if only from the more dual than dueling criteria of *bonnes* as well as *belles*, e.g., subtlety and accessibility, or complexity and satisfaction.

And now abides "the sustained tension, without victory or suppression, of co-present oppositions": M. H. Abrams's apt formulation of both/and logic captures the experience/faith enigma not just of Blake, but of numerous other luminaries of English-language Romanticism.[29] Their galvanizing

---

[29] Abrams et al., eds., 1974-1998, 2:60. M. H. Abrams's interpretation of Blake's concept of marriage, as in Blake's phrase (and title) "the marriage of heaven and hell," is that marriage is a metaphor not of reconciliation, but of truce. Abrams's ten words, quoted above, have haunted the series ever since the spring of 1986, when Abrams's ingenious formulation energized a survey course in British literature at the University of Florida. Despite the three words ending in ion—which, in such excess (i.e., thirty percent of the words in the phrase) usually

arc comes down to the free play of the mind, the ludic congruency of tradition and the individual talent, whereby optimism goes deep and grows wise, whereby hope follows hope, and whereby the key opposition of optimism vs. hope makes for tense but confident anticipation.[30] The late-Romantic phase of English-language *bonnes*-and-*belles* turns out more redolent of empirical truth than productive of joy with grace. But the poetry of Emily Dickinson, who never forgets that

> Love—is anterior to Life—
> Posterior to Death—
> Initial of Creation, and
> The Exponent of Earth—
>
> (Poem 980)

may well stay more exhilarating and stimulating, nonetheless, than vertiginous and short-circuited, thereby holding its charge of science vs. religion.

Whatever the fate of Romantic Anglo-America's empirical and evangelical model during the era of Modernism, the collection can yet inhibit (only rarely inhabits?) an inherited or acquired monomaniacal propensity or two. Will *Transatlantic Trio* exert such effect on its author, who looks back from his height of age, though not of wisdom, on what, if anything, it all means? Whatever the answer, the twinned but not identical perspectives of empiricism and evangelicalism—in the alembic of a bi-national imagination—kept many writers limber, and saved one or two from the fixed idea. Perhaps even William Blake, on occasion, was tempted by single vision, or Matthew Arnold by steam-engine language, but, happily for all concerned, both men bequeathed to their posterity the paradoxical wherewithal, the double vision in the best sense, whereby anyone might avoid the problem of either/or.

Will these thirty-eight increments of a long-running argument live up to their promise of celebrating rather than reconciling contraries? As "punctuated equilibria" of a critical "evolution," they may, for the pieces not only

---

bounce off the frontal lobes—these words nonetheless lodge in the mind. Abrams's phrase models precision, leaving scant doubt about just what both/and logic means. Shozan Jack Haubner's Zen-description of Leonard Cohen's vision as "the union of contrary things—and their separation again, and the struggle in between" also comes to mind.

[30] It is not just a matter of favoring hope over optimism, *à la* Terry Eagleton. Rather, optimism vs. hope constitutes a binary opposition, and hence an instance of both/and logic, particularly explanatory within the realm of Anglo-American cultural poetics, especially including its most religious manifestation of *les bonnes-lettres*.

Epilogue: From Credo to Credit

apply both/and logic to, but also find it in, contexts and texts alike (Stephen Jay Gould's presiding metaphor proves apropos). May the aggregated analysis of Romantic irony in the Anglo-American style of its efficacy leap from these pages to the collective mind of readers willing for the "double consciousness" of an Emerson or the "Compound Vision" of a Dickinson to "un-cloister" them on the "hot, dusty" road of their experience![31]

What next? A further dynamic of critical deliberation is at stake. In his 1975 poem, "Coming Back to Poetry," Michael M. Cass can impel willing readers to begin. His life/art opposition can cross paths with the collection:

> Once I fell from death into poetry,
> When I was given Homer and Herrick
> And when I pried myself open to Blake.
>
> Then I fell from poetry into life.
>
> (Homer war and Herrick love
> And Blake imagination,
> They waked me to my waking.)
>
> Now scratching cautiously on this paper
> I may be opening a chasm,
> May fall from life back into poetry.
>
> I'm worried.
>
> God knows
> (and Blake)
> Life is where I'm supposed to be.

These lines, after paying due homage to the canon and its autonomy, come down on the side of life. The Anglo-American Romanticism sampled throughout the collection, too, makes up a world apart, yet absorbs force from, and radiates energy back to, the world.

Both/and vitalizes Romantic art, for example, in the logic of Wordsworth's I/thou ethic, forming the focus of David P. Haney's classic study

---

[31] Emerson, "Fate," 1852; Dickinson, Poem 830, 9; Milton's language, above, comes from his *Areopagitica*, 1644.

and of Adam Potkay's recent volume. Haney compares Wordsworth's and Levinas's ethics. Potkay contrasts Wordsworth's emphasis on personal relationships—growing out of the poet's better-known love of particular things—with the depersonalized norms of John Stuart Mill and Jeremy Bentham. The more recent of the collection's two essays on Wordsworth begins to relate Wordsworth's "reflections of morality" to evangelical ethics (Wordsworth, *The Prelude*, 1850, 11:373). "Wordsworth's Art of Belief" suggests how his faith-and-works logic looms as large in his poetry as Dickinson's doubt/faith conundrum does in hers.

Perhaps not even choosing just one side of the empirical/evangelical dichotomy precludes both/and logic. The paradoxical confluence of philosophical and religious language at, or near, the heart of Wordsworth's poetic practice is one thing. But rich-and-strange sea-change double-ness obtains, as well, in the sharply delineated narrowness of his empirical idiom alone, e.g., sensationalist epistemology vs. scientific method, or soft-core/hard-core sense-based emphasis. Wordsworth's exclusively natural passages highlight some subject/object interaction, on the one hand, and some Isaac Newton-descended distinction between light-as-particle and light-as-wave, on the other (Brantley, 1984, 137-44). And it may also be time for someone to explore, perhaps even building on *Wordsworth's "Natural Methodism"* (Brantley, 1975), what, if any, practically critical both/and dividend accrues to an exclusive, thorough concentration on Wordsworth's religious language per se. Not just his faith-and-works duality, but his predestination/free-will duel, might just constitute much of what dramatizes his language and perennially brings it to life. Any such flair of his that might again come to the fore, at any rate, would heighten the aptness of "religion and literature" as a rubric for reading the works of a paragon of the often still supposedly entirely secular-humanist Romantic phenomenon.

For anyone for whom evangelical *bonnes-lettres* bears on Romantic *belles-lettres*, Jonathan Roberts's 2016 point that Wordsworth expands on Wesley's conversion narrative by "magnificently" remaking and "sublimely" realizing it—and by making it available again "as an imaginative experience to us, his readers"—leaps off the page.[32] Roberts does not engage the series, but Wordsworth works with quite a few more details of Methodism than Roberts appears to think he does. Roberts reveals how Wordsworth's concept of religious experience lands in the turn-of-the-twentieth-century sociological and theolog-

---

[32] Roberts 793. Jonathan Roberts notes that Wordsworth makes similarly expansive use of conversion narratives by Paul the Apostle, Augustine of Hippo, and John Bunyan.

ical writings of such well-known and unknown authors as William James, John Trevor, Joseph H. Jones, Charles Buck, John Petty, Edwin Diller Starbuck, and Richard Maurice Bucke. But Roberts's insistence that the phrase "religious experience" is anachronistic in Wordsworth's time is belied by such books of the series as *Experience and Faith* (Brantley, 2004, 2008), which locates "experience," used religiously, and "religion," used experientially, in writers from Wesley to Dickinson. That said, Roberts's welcome consideration of "Wordsworth on Religious Experience" is the place to begin reconsidering Wordsworth's poetic faith and its influence. Roberts's perspective ranging from Wordsworth's "Tintern Abbey" (1798) through his 1805 *Prelude* to his "Ode: Intimations of Immortality" (published 1807) identifies much pertinent poetic evidence to conjure with. Roberts's religion-inflected hint of Wordsworth's both/and logic—Wordsworth's version of "the one life within us and abroad"—parallels the specifically evangelicalism-tinged grasp of Wordsworth's faith/works conundrum (Coleridge, "The Eolian Harp," 1796, 26).

"When a writer is dead," W. H. Auden observes, "one ought to be able to see that his various works, taken together, make one consistent *oeuvre*" (Auden, "Writing," n.d.). Every work of a writer can feel proleptic, as well as retroleptic. "Retrospection" usually amounts to just exactly "Prospect's half"—these words by Dickinson are discussed in the prologue. To round out the portrait of Dickinson is an intellectual, emotional, and imaginative dialogue between her and her soul mate muse, Charles Wadsworth—the prologue introduced the Rev. Wadsworth as an Orpheus-for-the-Bible. Comparison between Dickinson's poems and Wadsworth's sermons may even pinpoint her arrival at, and not just her quest toward, her experience of faith, without diminution of both/and logic. Such an exploration might end up featuring, for instance, her Arminianism and her Calvinism, and might come down on the side of modifying the previous preoccupation of the series with the former stripe of her evangelical heritage (Brantley, 2004, 2008, 116-64; Eberwein, 2006). Meanwhile, and in the further interests of the full picture, the prologue has already emphasized Dickinson's faith in experience, more than her experiential Faith, and has invoked her poetic use of the scientific method.

"Every work of a writer," Auden concludes, "should be a first step, but this will be a false step unless, whether or not he realizes it at the time, it is also a further step." The prologue and the epilogue have not just offered the master key to all these reprints and to the books, but opened the door to more investigation. The description of "natural methodism," forty-plus years on, has thickened. Charles Lamb's oxymoron proves where a Romanticism that familiarizes the unfamiliar and de-familiarizes the familiar enters literary history.

What about the similarities and differences, finally, between Anglo-American Romanticism and that of, say, France or Germany? The question has arisen in the books. Suffice it to say, here, that the discrepancies are intriguing. Were France and Germany more cohesively "literary" than America, where Mark Twain and Bret Harte squared off against Emerson and Dickinson? To say little of variations between Anglo-American and European religion, the one primarily Protestant, the other often Catholic, the disparity between the epistemology of sense perception in Anglo-America and that of deduction in France or of intuition in Germany may show rather stark. The contrast may be too broad (and metaphor in any language is sense-based) but the premise of greater particularity in English-language *belles-lettres* remains worth exploring. The bibliography on the vernacular of natural and spiritual experience in Romantic Anglo-America vs. the idiom of rationalism in Romantic-era France or of idealism in Romantic-era Germany literally speaks volumes about the stand-off between an Anglo-American aesthetic of the concrete and a Continental European aesthetic of the abstract.[33] All this remains a further testing ground for how urgently, or how competitively, Anglo-American Romanticism exercised its spiritual as well as natural, broadly experiential vision.[34]

---

[33] Recent discussions of such issues are in Bennett; Hazareesingh. A Romantic-era account of differences is in Staël. Johann Wolfgang von Goethe's sympathetic portrait of "Werther the Evangelical," on the other hand, is in Tantillo 69-118. And a good French version of both/and logic, without regard to what subject matter occupies the two poles of any given opposition-set, finds embodiment in Louise Dupin (1706-1799), who, according to contemporary testimony, conducted her salon along the following lines of her conversational prowess (her salon secretary was Jean-Jacques Rousseau): "She must have enough spirit to praise what another condemns, and to condemn what another praises, without appearing at all contradictory" (from the Dupin exhibit on display at Château Clemenceau, June 15, 2016).

[34] Another historical clarification needs to be made: Immanuel Kant's "invention" of Aesthetics in his Third Critique, on Judgment of taste (beauty and the sublime), with the imagination as mediator between Pure and Practical Reason, Necessity (Understanding) and Freedom (ethics). Kant sees poets not just as maintaining the tension between, but as opening a further dimension beyond, the science/religion impasse. Hannah Arendt, accordingly, saw Kant's judgment as the best hope for a public sphere in the time of totalitarianism. Kant's promotion of imagination to Faculty status is ground zero for German Romanticism, and parallels Anglo-American Romanticism insofar as this poetic, too, forms a triangle with science and religion. Thus Romantic Anglo-America does not just recognize the different metaphysics between empiricism and evangelicalism, their irreducibility one to the other, but intimates their resemblance, however faint, at the creative intersection between faith in experience and experiential Faith. Debt is acknowledged, here, to correspondence with Gregory L. Ulmer.

The post-9/11 "turn to religion in academia" (Fish) has so far included quite a few younger scholars (as in ten of the fourteen identified a few paragraphs back) who have made use of the series (whether they agreed with its approach or not). Four of the six books in the series were "doing religion and Romanticism" before it became fashionable, around 2001, and it is good to have company now. Here is an all-seasons invitation, a not-so-quixotic, double-barreled hope-against-hope. First, may readers of the collection, in their sessions of sweet silent thought, wrestle with, and take pleasure in, the experience/faith paradox of 18th-to-19th-century transatlantic poetics! And second, may at least a few of those fellow interpreters come to publish insights, important and surprising, into Anglo-American letters, *bonnes* and *belles!*

Anglo-American Romanticism, then, does not just restage a duel between, but reenacts a cooperation of, philosophy and religion. Wordsworth's "natural piety" brands this poetic faith. His will to find a way to "natural methodism" (Lamb's equivalency) is the will to keep believing. But such paradoxical crediting stays so far from abandoning empiricism that—shades of John Wesley!—it not only tests religious dogma, but also trusts in scientific method. And such a Blake-to-Nietzsche-like "trans-valuation of standard criteria" (Nietzsche's concept) or reverse-order drill—lo and behold: a religion of science and a science of religion!—may free Wordsworth and his visionary company—however intermittently, forlornly, or belatedly—even to re-value testing through science, trusting in faith, and springing from hope.

Specifically, what Ralph Waldo Emerson would call the "stupendous antagonism" between the sense-based reason of empirical philosopher John Locke and the spiritual sense of evangelical preachers John Wesley and Jonathan Edwards heightens the drama of English-language Romanticism, which, in turn, calls the plays of aesthetics through a "fine mental chaos" indeed (British Romantic comic novelist Thomas Love Peacock, qtd. in Swingle 71). As a result, faith in experience yields to experiential Faith, and vice versa. First, the great principle of empiricism, that one must see for oneself and be in the presence of the thing one knows, obtains, as well, in its seeming opposite: evangelical faith. Then, this prime set of interlocking antinomies—this subset of science vs. religion—waves catnip at the "Poetic genius" that William Blake thinks is everyone's birthright, and which, on Anglo-American shores, at least, gets a buzz-on from empiricism-*cum*-evangelicalism. And finally, of all the ways that Romantic Anglo-America's contraries converse, debate, interact, clash, coalesce, and interpenetrate, the intellectual/emotional brouhaha of empiricism vs. evangelicalism is the most kinetically at hand. As a pro-genitive case in point, Wordsworth's "natural methodism" constitutes a not so much synoptic as bifocal version of this empirical evangelicalism. Ultimately, the high-Romantic poetry of the English-speaking world offers as its stock-in-trade the empirical philosophy and the evangelical faith of the 18th century to a brave new westerly world: an Emerson's "double consciousness" of fate and freedom and an Emily Dickinson's "Compound Vision" of finitude and infinity. Thus the broadly experiential, spiritual as well as natural vision of Anglo-American Romanticism proves sufficiently binocular to distinguish this embodiment of art for its both/and logic of apprehension, its oscillating, yet onward and renewing, quality of beholding.

In sum, double consciousness, if not the paradoxically often fungible poles of binary oppositions, can supply palliatives for the chronically limited scope, the usually "single vision," of Western culture's either/or blinders, thereby answering the chief indictment from Blake's prophetic correction of humankind. Can the both/and logic of art and of life parry the thrust of man-unkind? Perhaps, for Matthew Arnold's "free play of the mind" puts lockstep out of step and out of fashion. Can "sustained tension, without victory or suppression, of co-present oppositions" strike a balance dynamic enough for contraries to meet, exchange their perspectives, and reach out, not so much for reconciliation or synthesis as for détente or rapprochement? Perhaps, for such back-and-forth, like a railroading handcar or a weaving shuttle, gets on with it and makes something, constituting the give-and-take result of a uniquely engaging poetic.

*

This segment hazards self-reference. An autobiographical earnest may be ill-advised when writing with the goal of scholarly understanding. For the first time in either the prologue or the epilogue, however—or, for that matter, in most of the collection—I switch to the first person. Much of what and how I think—like most of who I am—derives less from the evidence on which my formal arguments stand—and less from the logic of their assumptions—than from people.

My mother's admonition rings in my ears. "It is not for you to say whether you have done well." But it is for me to celebrate how other long-standing influences, too, are always telling. Thus acknowledgments that aspire to the condition of memoir can also seal a lifelong labor of love.

My late parents, Rabun and Elizabeth Brantley, undergird me yet. My father, though a college president, and my mother, though a voracious reader, were practical. Their experience-validated view of the world championed the scientific career of my older brother, Bill, as well as my triangulation of empirical philosophy, this-worldly faith, and the expressively realistic function of Romantic-era literature.

Bill, just completing his fiftieth year as a physics professor at Furman University, in Greenville, South Carolina, talks literature better than I talk physics. Despite his busy schedule, he attended my Bible as literature class, which I was presenting to my fellow retirees in Hendersonville, North Carolina, during the fall of 2014. And he does his best to keep me up to speed in science.

Our parents' more than sixty-year commitment to church-related institutions of higher education amounted to a mission. Virginia Intermont College, in Bristol, Virginia, succumbed to fiscal pressure in 2014 (Smith 117-20). Lee, Bill, and I spent our boyhood years there. Pictures of Diana's and my daughters and grandsons, taken in December, 2015, in front of the president's house, now boarded up, follow, along with the last photograph of Lee and assorted other images relating to these acknowledgments. Allusions to Shakespeare and the Bible shaped the conversation in our boyhood home. Literature came to have a religious valuation for Lee, Bill, and me.

Lee Brantley (1933-1956)

A favorite phrase from Wordsworth—"the unimaginable touch of Time"—comes to mind (Wordsworth, "Mutability," 1822, 14). If a poet cannot imagine that trace, then who can? On March 23, 1956, on Elizabeth's birthday, and toward the end of his senior year as an English major at Washington and Lee University, in Lexington, Virginia, Lee died in an automobile accident, just after he had turned twenty-three. The sudden, violent death of one so young remains unimaginable: "We were cast out of orbit, each of us drifting into our own time and space, occasionally feeling the gravity of one another's pull."[35] More than sixty years later, I am barely able to write about the circle-breaking experience of our family: he who, as it seemed to us, "could not feel / The touch of earthly years," so eternally youthful in spirit was he, did (Wordsworth, "A Slumber Did My Spirit Seal," 1800, 3-4).

On September 30, 1955, as I was beginning sixth grade at Thomas Jefferson Elementary School, in Bristol, Lee had written to me, from Lexington, a letter in which he offered what I all too glacially realized was sage advice:

> Reading everything you can get your hands on will be the most valuable thing you can do toward getting a good education. It is important to read more and more advanced books as it is easy to drift and follow the paths of least resistance. The harder books will often contain the most enjoyable reading.

The letter is gone. I copied out this passage, however, and kept the fifty-five words, all that remain of a mind from a time when we seldom recorded life. Then eleven, I was too young to understand what Lee meant by "enjoyable." Even now, "enjoyable" might seem a strange term to describe such experiences as reading *In Memoriam*, written in reaction to the death at age twenty-two of Tennyson's friend Arthur, and Emerson's "Experience," written in reaction to the death at age five of Emerson's son, Waldo. Such works lead me back to the untimely death of one who had been in life a mystery of experience and sophistication to a younger brother just beginning to grasp the possibilities of the written word.

---

[35] Kushner 112. David Kushner refers to the kidnapping and murder of his eleven-year-old brother, Jonathan, in October, 1973. "The pain" of such a death, Kushner observes, was so "great" that "sharing stories, laughs, memories," was impossible—for the next forty years. Montaigne comes to mind, where he writes that after the deaths of her seven sons and seven daughters, Niobe's "waterfall of tears," turned to stone, "represent that bleak, dumb, and deaf stupor that benumbs us when accidents surpassing our endurance overwhelm us" (in Bakewell, 2010, 164).

Epilogue: From Credo to Credit

Frater ave atque vale. In honor of a military as well as English-majoring young man whose capability handled two and a half years at the United States Naval Academy, in Annapolis, Maryland, please allow me to quote Tennyson's poem of that Latin title. The elegy, conversing with Catullus's on his own brother's death, commemorates the loss of Tennyson's brother, Charles, and sings the more affectingly for its discreet indirection, its mere hint of its own solemn origin through its achingly delicate, yet quite deliberate, echo of Catullus's primal grief:

> Row us out from Desenzano, to your Sirmione row!
> So they rowed, and there we landed—"O venusta Sirmio!"
> There to me through all the groves of olive in the summer glow,
> There beneath the Roman ruin where the purple flowers grow,
> Came that "Ave atque Vale" of the Poet's hopeless woe,
> Tenderest of Roman poets nineteen hundred years ago.
> "Frater ave atque Vale"—as we wandered to and fro
> Gazing at the Lydian laughter of the Gorda Lake below
> Sweet Catullus's all-but-island, olive-silvery Sirmio!
> 1880   1883

The invocation of Catullus's "hopeless woe," though, does evoke Tennyson's. The changes rung on the mourning vowel "o" re-set for the Victorian twilight and for our time (so much in need of Tennyson's combination of tough mind and musical voice) love's old sweet song of not just "deeply distressing," but "humanizing," "world-sorrow" (Wordsworth, "Elegiac Stanzas," 1807, 36; Hopkins, "No Worst, There Is None," 1885, 6).

In Thomas Gardner's equally paradoxical, bittersweet prose poem on his brother's death, he shores fragments against his ruin. Signature phrases from a cloud of virtual witnesses to his grief—Pound, Bishop, Whitman, Dickinson, Stevens, Thoreau, Woolf, Howe, Robinson, Frost, Eliot, Cavell, Wright, and Wittgenstein—lodge in Gardner's mind, and lend incandescence to his moments as they pass. Or so his prose testifies. Such a record of what authors have personally meant to their readers might relieve a troubled profession: an experimental and timely (2007) gathering of essays by accomplished scholars regarding just how Dickinson's "healing power" has restored their very souls is another welcome case in point (MacKenzie and Dana, eds.). Gardner's elegy brought me back to Lee's richly experienced youth. A prime Dickinson scholar demonstrates how we do not yet have to let anything go.

Gardner—whose memorial tribute stands out as nature writing, illustrating a near-religious quality of meditation—confesses that, at many stages of grief, not even Jesus's weeping at the tomb of Lazarus can console us. But Gardner knows that even the toughest-minded of all the writers considered by him over the course of his distinguished career—Emily Dickinson—found room in her poems for the human Jesus, who suffers with humankind. Gardner understands that ink spilled about faith may be spilled in vain as far as those who do not feel faith are concerned, and for whom testimonies, therefore, can ring hollow. Hardy's persona in "The Impercipient," 1898, for instance, wants to believe what he hears from worshipers he admires, yet he cannot. But Gardner's report, like Tennyson's elegy, comes through as experience, as in *ex-peritus*, to see peril and come out of it, and as the true voice of passion, as in *pati*, to suffer or endure.

Lee knew how art instructs: through the pleasure of "thoughts that do often lie too deep for tears" (Wordsworth, "Intimations Ode," 1802-04, 205). On February 24, 1956—his twenty-third birthday and my twelfth—he gave me *Ivanhoe* (1820) and *Kenilworth* (1821) by Sir Walter Scott, and this first introduction to "serious" reading began, for me, "the fascination of what's difficult" about literature of the Romantic era (Yeats, "Fascination," 1920). The series in general and the collection in particular happen to fulfill the odyssey of study foretold by one who died even younger than Keats, yet who recognized—with Keats—that emotionally demanding works are paradoxically all the more "enjoyable" for that. Lee learned from Keats—as English professor father Rabun, fresh from the farm, had learned during his 20s, as well—to "burn through" *King Lear* (1606), because tragedy, "Gaiety transfiguring all that dread," recreates spectator-participants as much as Levinas says comedy does (Keats, "On Sitting Down," 1818, 7; Yeats, "Lapis Lazuli," 1933, 17). Reading, Lee knew, goes beyond such a simple pleasure as letting the words wash over the mind: reading, indeed, pushes the mind. Interpreters fight the good fight of art vs. life: Lee's precocious example of complexity and paradox yet instills poetry as *vade mecum*, a "momentary stay against confusion," and, if so it be, as earnest of wisdom, grace, and joy (Frost, "The Figure a Poem Makes," 1949).

On July 16, 2000, my Jonathan Edwards-reading mother, Elizabeth, "a high-toned old Christian woman" on her death bed at age ninety-two, looked up from her Bible and said to me, two hours before she died, "You are my work in progress" (Stevens, "A High-toned Old Christian Woman," 1923). I was fifty-six at the time. I can hear her, now, saying, "I'm not done with you." The debt to my parents as first teachers is fraught: their love boasted an element of toughness. I hasten to express, with more efficiency, a variety of thanks to my school teachers and teaching colleagues.

Willard Hamrick, at Wake Forest University, immersed me in the Hebrew prophets. Judson B. Allen and John A. Carter awakened my inner English major. Elizabeth Phillips showed me how the close-reading rigor of New Criticism discloses the brainy but playful multitudes contained in Emily Dickinson. At Princeton University, D. W. Robertson, Jr., introduced me to the historical, interdisciplinary criticism that I have practiced ever since, but which began in academia with his pioneering and bold, if fairly controversial, approach to Geoffrey Chaucer in context. Carlos Baker directed my dissertation on "Wordsworth and the Evangelicals" and encouraged me to think it might someday be a book; his later development of group biography, Emerson and his circle, encouraged me to think of authors in mutually explanatory clusters.

Edwin Graves Wilson instilled in many his love of Romanticism (the frontispiece shows him doing just that). The legendary teacher, also known as "Mr. Wake Forest," grew up during the Great Depression, yet notes the bittersweet nature and the joys of that time. "I've always been a rather hopeful and optimistic person," he declares. "That is not to say that the Romantic poets were naïve or without pain and anguish. But it is to say that there is something idealistic and something very compassionate and heroic about Romanticism." This view permeates my work, for, without oversimplifying intellectual problems, Wilson's Romanticism senses "something evermore about to be" true, good, and beautiful, and, without underestimating spiritual dilemmas, reimagines faith, hope, and love.

The indispensable support of three English Department colleagues at the University of Florida proved particularly unwavering in the early days. Aubrey Williams believed in, and impelled me to revise, arguments only dimly implicit in the manuscripts he read. T. Walter Herbert, Shakespearean extraordinaire—and the grandson, son, brother, and father of Methodist ministers—shared his encyclopedic knowledge of the Methodist Movement and painstakingly assessed my work (the collection includes my memorial tribute to him). Melvyn New, walking the walk of oppositional, true friendship, yet challenges—and yet inspires—me through the example of his discipline and fervor. His thorough reading of the prologue and of the epilogue came in the nick of time (and the appraisals of parts of those essays by Jessica Brantley, Burt Fishman, Thomas Fulton, Samantha Harvey, Mikesch Muecke, Carol Claxon Polsgrove, Gregory L. Ulmer, and Miriam Zach were also crucial).

My wife, Diana, instructs me, above all. In fact, she embodies the ideal teacher, as John Leonard's December 27, 1978, column in *The New York Times*, "Private Lives," establishes, and as her poetic tribute to her own teacher indicates:

The Craft
(For Christine Croft, with thanks)

> Real teaching fields mystery,
> Tosses out the first topic,
> Rounds the bases for discussion, coolly
> > Draws the pure perimeter of the field.
>
> Real teaching clothes personae,
> Masks ephemeral in ageless,
> Plays the role until we learn it, broadly
> > Sets up challenge to its master.
>
> Real teaching can be but shown.
> We recognize in it both kinds of play,
> Determine to infer the rules, studiedly
> > Game for its touch.

Diana well knows, because she shares in, the rewards and punishments of writing. She also embodies the ideal reader. Her skeptical counter-interpretation haunts the collection.

The collection is dedicated to our daughters, sons-in-law, and grandsons. Gabriel, 10, David, 7, Rabun, 5, and Leif, 3, grow in Lee's shadow. May they enjoy difficult fascination! Oh, yes, they will "pause a while from letters, to be wise," and, on occasion, they should. But let them think critically at play as well as at work. And may they learn that lesson here!

*

The prologue and the epilogue, then, have traced a shading of poetic and critical method into poetic and critical faith. The prologue identifies the assumptions and defines the terms of a lifetime's approach to the literary *Zeitgeist;* distills contexts and suggests texts of the Anglo-American Romanticism regarded here as mainstream; and typifies a special perspective on the special relationship between the

United Kingdom and the United States. That bi-national composite is a uniquely space-time complex of philosophical, religious, and literary distinction. The epilogue, in turn, reaffirms the series-to-date, and perhaps even addresses what remains at stake. That is, whether or not historical, interdisciplinary criticism, perhaps even if it cannot yet lead to "better," more examined, "living," can yet negotiate the creative "intersection between two quite different frames of reference" (Scott; Koestler). The difficult—and long—fascination with what, if anything, "natural methodism" can still mean, comes down to this: What, if any, broad application might the scholarly narrative have? One possibility: The backgrounds to, and samples of, Anglo-American Romanticism model such flexible both/and that the hitherto tacit but now explicit credo of "method rather than system" resists the blandishment and stands up to the prevalence of either/or. And another: Empirical evangelicalism adds such an ethical as well as epistemological dimension of otherness to the sometimes exclusively inward faith of Romanticism that Romantic Anglo-America leaves to her posterity an ever-claimable legacy—an available, savory, and sweet antidote to soul-sick solipsism.[36]

> Richard E. Brantley
> Professor of English, Emeritus
> University of Florida
> January 3, 2017
> Epilog House
> 200 Pace Cemetery Road
> Zirconia, NC 28790
> brantley@english.ufl.edu

---

[36] Consider German Romantic theologian Friedrich Schleiermacher's definition: "Faith is neither knowledge nor action; it is a trend of feeling, or a trend of the undividable self-consciousness." These words depart momentously and ominously from the Book of Hosea (faith as knowledge) and the Book of Amos (faith as action). The discussion of Schleiermacher's *Der Christliche Glaube* (1830-31) in Van den Berg 21-22 proves apt. If Anglo-American Romanticism and this historical, interdisciplinary critic are so "inveterately convolved" as conjointly to commend "natural methodism," and if that is a good thing, then those (identified in the previous segment) who fostered a cumulative, ongoing project in bi-national cultural poetics may take the credit (Wordsworth, "Yew Trees," 1815, 8). And if such observer-participant criticism is a bad thing—that is, solipsism—then those same worthy influencers bear no blame at all. Of course, critics of all stripes are notoriously tempted to remix and remake the literary object in their own images. Still, for just one example of the proper balance, Cynthia Ozick's criticism, like her fiction, is "a liberating model of engagement with identity" (Giles Harvey 57; Ozick). "Her commitment to Judaism," Giles Harvey concludes, "sharpens her powers of discrimination and inoculates her against the dubious allure of the universal."

Works Cited

Abram, David. *Becoming Animal: An Earthly Cosmology.* New York: Vintage P, 2010.

Abrams, M. H. *Doing Things with Texts: Essays in Criticism and Critical Theory.* New York: W. W. Norton, 1991.

_____. *The Fourth Dimension of a Poem; and Other Essays.* New York: W. W. Norton, 2012.

Abrams, M. H., et al., eds. *The Norton Anthology of English Literature: Third, Fourth, Fifth, and Sixth Editions.* 2 vols. New York: W. W. Norton, 1974-1998.

Adams, Hazard, ed. *Critical Theory Since Plato: Revised Edition.* San Diego: Harcourt Brace Jovanovich, 1992.

Anderson, Misty G. *Imagining Methodism in 18th-Century Britain: Enthusiasm, Belief & the Borders of the Self.* Baltimore: The Johns Hopkins U P, 2012.

Ault, Donald. *Visionary Physics: Blake's Response to Newton.* Chicago: U of Chicago P, 1974.

Baker, Carlos. *The Echoing Green: Romanticism, Modernism, and the Phenomena of Transference in Poetry.* Princeton, NJ: Princeton U P, 1984.

Bakewell, Sarah. *At the Existentialist Café: Freedom, Being, and Apricot Cocktails.* New York: Other P, 2016.

_____. *How to Live—or—a Life of Montaigne in One Question and Twenty Attempts at an Answer.* New York: Other P, 2010.

Barbeau, Jeffrey W. "Romantic Religion, Life Writing, and Conversion Narratives." *The Wordsworth Circle* 47.1 (Winter 2016): 32-39.

Baym, Nina, et al., eds. *The Norton Anthology of American Literature: Fifth Edition.* New York: W. W. Norton, 1998.

Bennett, Kelsey L. *Principle and Propensity: Experience and Religion in the Nineteenth-Century British and American Bildungsroman.* Columbia: U of South Carolina P, 2014.

Bloom, Harold. *The American Religion: The Emergence of the Post-Christian Nation.* New York: Simon and Schuster, 1992, 2006.

———. *The Daemon Knows: Literary Greatness and the American Sublime.* New York: Spiegel & Grau, 2015.

Bornstein, George. *Romantic and Modern: Revaluations of Literary Tradition.* Pittsburgh, PA: U of Pittsburgh P, 1977.

———. *Transformations of Romanticism in Yeats, Eliot, and Stevens.* Chicago: U of Chicago P, 1976.

Boyles, Helen. *Romanticism and Methodism: The Embarrassment of Enthusiasm.* London and New York: Routledge, 2016.

Brantley, Diana. *Phases: A Book of Poems.* Ames, IA: Culicidae P, 2011.

Brantley, Richard E. *Anglo-American Antiphony: The Late Romanticism of Tennyson and Emerson.* Gainesville: U P of Florida, 1994.

———. *Emily Dickinson's Rich Conversation: Poetry, Philosophy, Science.* New York: Palgrave Macmillan, 2013, 2015.

———. *Experience and Faith: The Late-Romantic Imagination of Emily Dickinson.* New York: Palgrave Macmillan, 2004, 2008.

———. *Locke, Wesley, and the Method of English Romanticism.* Gainesville: U P of Florida, 1984.

———. *Wordsworth's "Natural Methodism".* New Haven, CT: Yale U P, 1975.

Bryson, Bill. *The Road to Little Dribbling: Adventures of an American in Britain.* New York: Doubleday, 2015.

Campos, Isabel Sobral. "The Haunted House of Nature—Immanence's Infinity." *The Emily Dickinson Journal* 25.1 (2016): 57-82.

Cass, Michael M. "Coming Back to Poetry." *World Order*, Summer 1975.

Coutts, Marion. *The Iceberg.* New York: Black Cat, 2014.

Cragwall, Jasper. *Lake Methodism: Popular Literature and Popular Religion in England, 1780-1830.* Columbus: Ohio State U P, 2013.

Critchley, Simon. *The Problem with Levinas.* Oxford: Oxford U P, 2015.

Culler, A. Dwight. *The Poetry of Tennyson.* New Haven, CT: Yale U P, 1977.

Dabundo, Laura S. *The Marriage of Faith: Christianity in Jane Austen and William Wordsworth.* Macon, GA: Mercer U P, 2012.

Damrosch, David, et al., eds. *The Longman Anthology of British Literature: First Edition.* 2 vols. New York: Longman, 1999.

Deppman, Jed. *Trying to Think with Emily Dickinson*. Amherst: U of Massachusetts P, 2008.

Dickinson, Emily. *The Poems of Emily Dickinson: Reading Edition*. Ed. Ralph W. Franklin. Cambridge, MA and London: The Belknap P of Harvard U P, 1999.

Eagleton, Terry. *Hope without Optimism*. New Haven, CT: Yale U P, 2016.

Eberwein, Jane Donahue. "Outgrowing Genesis? Dickinson, Darwin, and Higher Criticism." *Dickinson and Philosophy*. Marianne Noble, Jed Deppmann, and Gary Lee Stonum, eds. Cambridge: Cambridge U P, 2013.

———. "'Where—Omnipresence—Fly?': Calvinism as Impetus to Spiritual Amplitude." *The Emily Dickinson Journal* 15.1 (2006): 96-100.

Farrell, Michael. *Blake and the Methodists*. New York: Palgrave Macmillan, 2014.

Fish, Stanley. "One University under God?" *The Chronicle of Higher Education*, January 7, 2005.

Fitzgerald, F. Scott. *The Crack-up: With Other Uncollected Pieces, Note-books, and Unpublished Letters*. Ed. Edmund Wilson. New York: Directions, 1945.

Franke, William. *Secular Scripture: Modern Theological Poetics in the Wake of Dante*. Columbus: The Ohio State U P, 2015.

Freedman, Linda. *Emily Dickinson and the Religious Imagination*. Cambridge: Cambridge U P, 2011.

Fried, Daisy. Review of *The Poet, The Lion, Talking Pictures, El Farolito, A Wedding in St. Roche, The Big Box Store, The Warp in the Mirror, Spring, Midnights, The Fire & All*, by C. D. Wright. *The New York Times Book Review*, February 7, 2016.

Gardner, Thomas. *A Door Ajar: Contemporary Writers and Emily Dickinson*. New York: Oxford U P, 2006.

———. *Poverty Creek Journal*. North Adams, MA: Tupelo P, 2014.

Gaull, Marilyn. "Wordsworth and Science." *The Oxford Handbook of William Wordsworth*, 599-613. Eds. Richard Gravil and Daniel Robinson. Oxford: Oxford U P, 2015.

Gaull, ed. *The Wordsworth Circle* 45.2 (Spring 2014).

Gould, Stephen Jay. *Time's Arrow, Time's Cycle: Myth and Metaphor in the Discovery of Geological Time*. Cambridge: Harvard U P, 1987.

Gravil, Richard. *Romantic Dialogues: Anglo-American Continuities, 1776-1862*. New York: St. Martin's P, 2000, 2015.

Haney, David P. *William Wordsworth and the Hermeneutics of Incarnation*. State College: Pennsylvania State U P, 1993.

Hannay, Alastair. *Kierkegaard: A Biography*. New York: Cambridge U P, 2001.

Harvey, Giles. "The Fanatic." *The New York Times Magazine*, June 26, 2016, 32-35.

Harvey, Samantha C. *Transatlantic Transcendentalism: Cole, Emerson, and Nature*. Edinburgh: Edinburgh U P, 2013.

Haubner, Shozan Jack. " Rites of Passage: So Long, Jikan [Noble Silence] Leonard Cohen." *The New York Times*, December 9, 2016, D9.

Hazareesingh, Sudhir. *How the French Think: An Affectionate Portrait of an Intellectual People*. New York: Basic Books, 2015.

Holmes, Richard. *The Age of Wonder: How the Romantic Generation Discovered the Beauty and Terror of Science*. New York: Pantheon, 2009.

Hsu, Li-Hsin. "'The light that never was on sea or land': William Wordsworth in America and Emily Dickinson's 'Frontier' Style." *The Emily Dickinson Journal*, 25.2 (2016): 24-47.

Irigaray, Luce. *This Sex Which Is Not One*. Translated by Catherine Porter, with Carolyn Burke. 1977. Rpt. Ithaca, NY: Cornell U P, 1985.

Jarrell, Randall. *No Other Book: Selected Essays*. New York: HarperCollins, 1999.

Jesse, Jennifer. *William Blake's Religious Vision: There's a Methodism in His Madness*. Lanham, MD: Lexington Books, 2013.

Jones, Jeremy B. *Bearwallow: A Personal History of a Mountain Homeland*. Winston-Salem, NC: John F. Blair, 2014.

Kant, Immanuel. *The Critique of Judgment*. 1790. James Creed Meredith, trans., 1952. New York: Oxford U P, 2007.

Kirsch, Adam. "Discourtesies." *The New Republic*, October 21, 2002, 32-36.

Koestler, Arthur. *The Act of Creation*. 1964. Reprint. New York: Penguin P, 1990.

Kuhn, Thomas. *The Structure of Scientific Revolutions*. Chicago: U of Chicago P, 1962.

Kushner, David. *Alligator Candy: A Memoir*. New York: Simon and Schuster, 2016.

Large, William. *Levinas' Totality and Infinity*. London: Bloomsbury, 2015.

Leader, Jennifer L. *Knowing, Seeing, Being: Jonathan Edwards, Emily Dickinson, Marianne Moore, and the American Typological Tradition*. Amherst: U Of Massachusetts P, 2016.

Lee, Maurice. *Uncertain Chances: Science, Skepticism, and Belief in 19th-Century American Literature*. Oxford: Oxford U P, 2012.

Leib, Erin. "Both/And." *The New Republic*, February 11, 2002.

Leigh, David J. "Cowper, Wordsworth, and the Sacred Moment of Perception." In *The Fountain Light: Studies in Romanticism and Religion*. J. Robert Barth, ed. New York: Fordham U P, 2002.

Leithauser, Brad. "Great Old Modern." *The New York Review of Books*, August 8, 1996.

Leonard, John. "Private Lives." *New York Times*, December 27, 1978.

Lukas, David. *Language Making Nature: A Handbook for Writers, Artists, and Thinkers*. Big Oak Flat, CA: Lukas Guides, 2015.

Lundin, Roger, ed. *Religion & Literature* 46.1 (Summer 2014).

MacKenzie, Cindy, and Barbara Dana, eds. *Wider than the Sky: Essays and Meditations on the Healing Power of Emily Dickinson*. Kent, OH: Kent State U P, 2007.

Marx, Karl. *Critique of Hegel's Philosophy of Right*. In Geoff Dyer, "By the Book," *The New York Times Book Review*, June 30, 2016.

Maurice, F. D. *The Kingdom of Christ: or, Hints Respecting the Principles, Constitution, and Ordinances of the Catholic Church*. 1838. Reprint. New York: D. Appleton & Co., 1843.

Mendelson, Edward. "To Be in the World." *The New York Times Book Review*, April 17, 2016, 10-11.

Mensch, James R. *Levinas's Existential Analytic*. Evanston, IL: Northwestern U P, 2015.

New, Melvyn, ed. *In Proximity: Emmanuel Levinas and the Eighteenth Century*. Lubbock: Texas Tech U P, 2001.

Noble, Marianne, Jed Deppman, and Gary Lee Stonum, eds. *Dickinson and Philosophy*. Cambridge: Cambridge U P, 2013.

O'Hagan, Andrew. "Macbeth without Evil." *The New York Review of Books*, December 17, 2015.

Ozick, Cynthia. *Critics, Monsters, Fanatics, and Other Literary Essays*. New York: Houghton Mifflin Harcourt, 2016.

Pace, Joel, and Matthew Scott, eds. *Wordsworth in American Literary Culture*. Foreword by Stephen Gill. Basingstoke and New York: Palgrave Macmillan, 2005.

Potkay, Adam. *Wordsworth's Ethics*. Baltimore: The Johns Hopkins U P, 2012.

Ray, Robert B. *Walden X 40*. Bloomington: Indiana U P, 2011.

Rees, William. "Levinas at Large." *TLS*, October 14, 2015.

Roberts, Jonathan. "Wordsworth on Religious Experience." *The Oxford Handbook of William Wordsworth*, 693-711. Eds. Richard Gravil and Daniel Robinson. Oxford: Oxford U P, 2015.

Robinson, Marilynn. "President Obama and Marilynn Robinson: A Conversation in Iowa." *The New York Review of Books*, November 5, 2015.

Rose, C. D., ed. *The Biographical Dictionary of Literary Failure*. Introduction by Andrew Gallix. Brooklyn, NY, and London: Melville House, 2014.

Ruoff, Gene W., and L. J. Single. "From the Editors." *The Wordsworth Circle* 10 (Spring 1979): 130.

Scott, A. O. *Better Living through Criticism: How to Think about Art, Pleasure, Beauty, and Truth*. New York: Penguin P, 2016.

Schulz, Kathryn. *Being Wrong: Adventures in the Margin of Error*. New York: Ecco P, 2011.

Shoaf, R. A. *Milton, Poet of Duality: A Study of Semiosis in the Poetry and the Prose*. Gainesville: U P of Florida, 1993.

Simic, Charles. "The Incomparable Critic." *The New York Review of Books*, August 13, 2015.

Smith, Mary Lou. *Virginia Intermont College: One Hundred & Thirty Years*. San Bernardino, CA: CreateSpace: Independent Publishing Platform, 2016.

Snow, Heidi. *William Wordsworth and the Theology of Poverty*. Burlington, VT: Ashgate Publishing Company, 2013.

Staël, Germaine de. *Germany*. Notes and Appendix by O. W. Wight. 2 vols. 1813. Reprint. Boston: Houghton Mifflin, 1869.

Swingle, L. J. *The Obstinate Questionings of English Romanticism*. Baton Rouge: Louisiana State U P, 1987.

Ulmer, Gregory L. *Electracy: Gregory L. Ulmer's Textshop Experiments*. Eds. Craig J. Saper, Gregory L. Ulmer, and Victor J. Vitanza. Aurora, CO: The Davies Group, 2015.

Van den Berg, J. H. *The Changing Nature of Man: Introduction to a Historical Psychology*. New York: Dell Publishing Co., 1964.

Vendler, Helen. *The Ocean, the Bird, and the Scholar: Essays on Poets and Poetry*. Cambridge, MA: Harvard U P, 2015.

Whicher, Stephen E. *Freedom and Fate: The Inner Life of Ralph Waldo Emerson*. 1953. Reprint. Philadelphia: U of Pennsylvania P, 1979.

Wieseltier, Leon. "Critic without a Cause." *The Atlantic*, March 2016.

Wilson, Eric G. Review of *Emily Dickinson's Rich Conversation: Poetry, Philosophy, Science*, by Richard E. Brantley. *Review 19*, October 15, 2013. http:www.nbol-19.org.

Images

Rabun Lee Brantley (1903-1999)

Aerial view of Virginia Intermont College (VIC)

President's Home

Grandchildren at the President's Home, VIC

Justine, Leif, Rabun, David, Gabriel, and Jessica

Lee Brantley in Navy attire

President Elizabeth Davis, of Furman University, honors William H. Brantley upon his completion of fifty years as a professor of physics.

Elizabeth Brantley (1908-2000)

University of Florida President Fuchs and Richard Brantley

Diana Brantley

Appendix:
A Range of Responses

These ninety-six chronologically ordered, excerpted or complete, favorable or unfavorable replies to my seven volumes will appeal to researchers. This host of witnesses to my lifelong vocation has the last word of the series-to-date. Others, though, might have a further say on this long-standing topic.

Wordsworth's "Natural Methodism" (1975)

1. This is a book I have always wanted and needed—a full-scale, complete, thoroughly researched, clearly written account of Wordsworth's relation to the major Protestant tradition in British history. **—Harold Bloom**, reader for Yale University Press

2. This is a book for mature students: It makes considerable and constant demands on the reader but its cogent and scholarly interpretations provide a rewarding "new look" at Wordsworth. **—Peter Derwent**, *The Cumberland Evening News* (February 1975)

3. Brantley's study is meticulously researched. His notes range in citation through all major works either directly or peripherally related to his topic. Names of scholars now forgotten by many contemporary critics (Lane Cooper, Emile Legouis, Abbie Findlay Potts, Edith Batho, et al.) vie with the giants of our own day (e.g., M. H. Abrams, Harold Bloom, Northrop Frye). In addition, all classical writers who had any possible influence on Wordsworth's ideas are examined and elucidated. Unquestionably, the notes alone constitute a useful and significant contribution to Wordsworth scholarship. . . . Recommended to all students interested in Wordsworth—and in the Romantics in general—at all levels. **—Anonymous**, *Choice* (September 1975)

4. Using the Evangelical sequence of chastening of natural pride and guilty passion in order that the humbled spirit, fearful of retribution, may properly fear God, Brantley reads the critical passages of "The Prelude" to indicate the poet's growth in awe, sensitivity of conscience, and awareness of a great and mysterious power. . . . Within the given frame, the contention fits; but it does give the poem something of the atmosphere of "Crime and Punishment" rather than that of a great and liberating experience of the beauty, power, and mystery of nature as it reveals itself to a youthful consciousness. . . . Brantley's book is consequential and will, if not turn the tide, reshape the sands of criticism over which it flows. —**Ruth M. Adams**, *The Review of Books and Religion* (October 1975)

5. The book is praiseworthy in its attempt to approach the complex issue of Wordsworth's religious views with methodological rigor. Its insistence that matters theological deserve the serious and sustained intellectual attention that we commonly grant to matters philosophical should have a salutary effect on Romantic scholarship. —**Gene W. Ruoff**, *Western Humanities Review* (Autumn 1975)

6. This helpful and important analysis of Wordsworth convincingly broadens the focus of scholarship in this phase of English literary history. Professor Brantley holds that the "presiding ideas" of Wordsworth studies have ranged across such issues as ethics, epistemology and ontology to the origin and character of his poetic style and subjective imagery. The general argument is that this has been done by minimizing the orientation of Wordsworth within an influential and definable English religious tradition. "The most distinctive features of Wordsworth's literary practice can best be understood in terms of his pervasive Evangelical idiom" (p. xi). This may contradict some undergraduate reading of his poetry as fascinating and inspiring empiricism, strike some specialists in romanticism as a marginal comment and yet occur to some historians and theologians as an illumination of another dimension of early nineteenth-century religious thought. Professor Brantley has made his case clear, documented it superbly both from Wordsworth's own writings and the contexts from which they came, making a valuable contribution to students of the romantic tradition, literary historians and analysts of the vitalities of modern religion.

Nearly a third of the book is devoted to "Wordsworth's Spiritual Biography." Careful attention is given to the influence of his early "Christian household," the formative influence of the Cambridge tradition of dissent, the congenial spirit he enjoyed with Wesleyanism and the Great Awakening, as well as the specific impact made on him by such personalities as John Wesley, William Wilberforce, Francis Wrangham and Isaac Watts. The biographical analysis is not a recitation of precious data but a "remythologizing" of Wordsworth's Christian heritage and outlook. This study of the man and his development should remarkably deepen Coleridge's comment on Wordsworth in a letter of 1798: "he loves and venerates Christ and Christianity... I wish he did more" (13).

"Wordsworth's Theology of the Spirit" comprises the largest segment of this study, providing explication of Wordsworth's role as a bridge between Anglicanism and Evangelicalism. Going far beyond the commonplace that Wordsworth's poetry "abounds in religious imagery," Brantley develops through his own exegesis as well as significant secondary studies a portrayal of the poet's religious insight as "a composite Watts and Wesley, or like an embodiment of both the Puritan and the Evangelical strains in a spiritually awakened England, or like a prophet of the intimate God and the apotheosized Man" (p. 77). From the vantage points of strength, weakness, crisis and contentment, Wordsworth is understood as experiencing the implications of "the indwelling Spirit," "the Christ in us," "perfection," "aspiration," and "the experience of infinity."

Climactic to this study of Wordsworth's self-understanding is the book's fourth chapter, "Wordsworth and the Book of Nature." His experience of the Divine Sublimity is not understood in the earlier deistic sense, in simply aesthetic terms, nor in the Coleridgean fashion. Wordsworth's natural theology is not intentionally apologetic nor reducible to the categories of traditional doctrine. As "the book of nature," it is for "the religious man" who "reads with a spiritual eye to unseen levels, and he learns, therefore, what morality is, what hopes can be" (p. 159).

Wordsworth's vision of God and man as well as of himself as a poet in a time and tradition when this inner experience was essential may not be as clear as in his day. However, this fine scholarly work has delineated historically and theologically a religious mode that demands constant and careful attention. —**Ralph Hjelm**, *Church History* (December 1975)

7. The title of this book comes from a phrase used by Lamb and the work is an attempt to present "biographical and poetical evidence for William Wordsworth's indebtedness to Evangelical Anglicanism." Dr. Brantley notes

the poet's contacts with Wilberforce and he mentions but does not dwell on Cookson of Forncett, uncle to Wordsworth, who brought up Dorothy and was a definite Evangelical. What is more important, he does not consider the Cambridge influence on Wordsworth at a time when Simeon was in his earliest and most controversial years at Holy Trinity.... Moreover, much of his supporting evidence is derived from Wesley, who was hardly the best source for Evangelical *Anglicanism*.... Then there is note 14 (p. 193) where we are told that "Clarkson's Evangelicalism can be seen, for example, in his participation with Wilberforce in the fight against the slave trade"—as if this were an Evangelical monopoly!... Indeed, the whole of the section on *The Excursion* shows what the author apparently cannot see, namely, Wordsworth's traditional middle-of-the-road, good-works, un-doctrinal Anglicanism. In other words, what we have always thought him to be. Even where the parallels between this, that and the other sort of Evangelicalism seem possible, these are not proven and are sometimes unlikely.... To see a real Evangelical, he would have done well to read Cowper before embarking on Wordsworth.
—**Arthur Pollard,** *Church Society* (1976)

8. "**It** circulates a good deal among Quakers, who are wealthy and fond of *instructive* Books. Besides, though I am a professed admirer of the Church of England, I hope that my religious sentiments will not be offensive to *them.*" Thus Wordsworth of his newly published poem *The Excursion,* wryly hoping for profit as well as glory but acknowledging, too, one of the more prominent strands of criticism from his reviewers. The unorthodoxy of his sentiments had been evident in earlier volumes, but in this it was felt by Lamb ("a sort of liberal Quakerism...a kind of natural methodism") and Jeffrey ("the mystical verbiage of the Methodist pulpit") to border on religious heterodoxy, and it drove Montgomery, that pillar of Calvinist orthodoxy, into fits of indignant commination which sorted uneasily with his wild enthusiasm for the poem in other respects. This is ironic: modern criticism tends to find it a dull repository of Christian platitudes and would perhaps prefer not to find it at all. We cannot wish to turn the clocks back but may still sigh over a lost intensity and the conviction, stressed *ad nauseam* by Jeffrey, that the poem was of a piece with the *Lyrical Ballads* and the *Poems in Two Volumes.*

Two trends in modern Wordsworth studies fall into sharp focus. The first is the conviction that any ideas we may elicit from his greatest poetry are of epistemological rather than religious interest (close analysis has clarified our understanding of Wordsworth's relationships between self and nature, subject and object); and the second a new concentration on the early poems, partly a result of the important textual studies now in progress. For example, there are now at least four substantially independent versions of *The Prelude*, and the implication is that it's a case of the earlier (and the shorter) the better—the more pure and characteristic. The Wordsworth of today is a young poet, largely untutored and certainly un-Christian in the institutional sense, struggling to embody his very individual experiences of man and nature.

Richard E. Brantley challenges both these trends, arguing that the baptism of Wordsworth's imagination took place not after but well before the so-called Great Decade, and that in consequence nearly all his poems take their impulse and direction from a consistent spiritual striving, a striving for sanctity as Wesley and the Evangelicals understood it. There is a good deal of evidence of the poet's coming into early contact with Evangelical doctrine, both before and during his period at Cambridge. Much of it has been noticed before, particularly by Ben Schneider in *Wordsworth's Cambridge Education*, but Brantley gathers and reinforces it, with some persuasiveness. Wordsworth himself, however, is almost silent on the issue, and, for all our research into the milieu, it remains a matter of indifference whether and to what extent he was seriously influenced. It may be significant, for example, that he numbered among his close friends John Mathews, son of a Methodist preacher, and Francis Wrangham, an admirer of Wesley and the Congregationalist Phillip Doddridge, but his letters to them are almost wholly literary in content, urbane and often amusing. Brantley is resourceful in his arguments, but many of them are less persuasive than he would like them to be. Much is made, for instance, of the letter Wilberforce received with his presentation copy of *Lyrical Ballads*, in which Wordsworth is described "a Fellow-labourer in the same Vineyard." It ought somewhere to have been acknowledged that the letter was written by Coleridge and not Wordsworth. Again, Brantley points out that Dorothy, in her letters to Catherine Clarkson, referred twelve times to Thomas Clarkson's *Portraiture of Quakerism*. This is true, but in most cases she was merely enquiring what became of the first volume, which they had not received. Similarly Wordsworth's criticisms of a local preacher (in a letter to Beaumont) might have helped us to understand his theology, had he not begun his next paragraph: "I have talked much Chit-chat." Niggling criticisms, perhaps, but they do show what feeble straws we have to clutch at. I should add, too, that these points are made by Brantley with very little sense of chronology.

But influence may be a subtler thing than that, and it is surely helpful to be reminded that in parceling out Wordsworth's intellect we may have under-stressed a religious dimension in his vocabulary and, more important, in the forms of his experiences. Here the argument is specific: we are asked to think in terms of conversion, baptism, covenant, guilt and punishment, and amazing grace—familiar terminology in the writings of Wesley and his followers. Such concepts, it is claimed, help us to understand both individual poems and passages, and the whole structure of Wordsworth's spiritual biography as recorded, though not in chronological order, in *The Prelude*. The poet's "conversion," then, occurred in 1788 during his morning walk at Hawkshead when

> I made no vows, but vows
> Were then made for me; bond unknown to me
> Was given, that I should be, else sinning greatly,
> A dedicated Spirit.

His fall from grace was, of course, during the period of his interest in the French Revolution, after which, through the mediation of Dorothy and Coleridge, he reestablished his covenant with God. Other episodes have subsidiary roles in the same scheme. It looks too simple, and indeed it is; but some of the local argument is sufficiently impressive to define analogies between Wordsworth's experiential religion and the Evangelicals'. Brantley is at his most persuasive when dealing with a few specific problems, such as the balance all Arminians must find between a passive receptivity to grace and active spiritual striving. This has an exact counterpart in Wordsworth's

> balance, an ennobling interchange
> Of action from within and from without,

in the paradox of his "wise passiveness," and in the tentativeness with which he sometimes ascribes causes to his experiences:

> Now *whether* it were by peculiar *grace*,
> A leading from above, a something given,
> Yet it befell that, in this lonely place,
> When I with these untoward thoughts had *striven* ...
> I saw a Man before me unawares

—where the vocabulary of religion is clearly employed. An equally plausible case is that of the young Wordsworth's "chastisement," in the form of his father's death, for his impatience while waiting for the horses that would take him home from school *(The Prelude,* 1805, Book XI); arguably a guilt and punishment situation, and "impatience" was a favorite vice among the Evangelicals. But the same cannot be said—it has been argued many times—of the stolen boat episode or of the bird-nesting passage, in both of which the poet is at pains to suppress the notion of guilt in order to allow the experience all its haunting complexity. Narratives of sudden conversion, such as those published by Wesley in *The Arminian Magazine,* have their counterpart in the Hawkshead passage mentioned above, but the analogy is far more difficult to sustain, relying on a gross exaggeration of the youth's activities immediately preceding the walk:

> In a throng,
> A festal company of Maids and Youths,
> Old Men, and Matrons staid, promiscuous rout,
> A medley of all tempers, I had pass'd
> The night in dancing, gaiety and mirth.

Harmless enough, one would have thought; but the old men, who, we are told, "perhaps look upon the maids rather than the matrons," are transformed into "dirty-minded greybeards"; and the

> Slight shocks of young love-liking interspers'd

become, with eloquent absurdity, "the rising flame and straight wick of passion and sexuality."

Perhaps this is unfair: Wordsworth had, you see, mentioned "tapers glittering," and this Brantley reads as an emblem. He devotes a chapter to the topic, finding Christian Renaissance emblems in abundance in the poems, and pointing out, too, similar images in the writings of the Evangelicals. Occasionally a neglected phrase or two is illuminated, but this method is indiscriminate: we are asked, for instance, to think of the passages describing the man drowned in Esthwaite *(The Prelude,* Book V) as emblematic of baptism, a notion that ignores completely the poet's own interpretation of the event in the lines immediately following. Most of all, it simply dismisses those directions to interpretation that we call style, and the argument is not challenging but evasive. It is odd that Brantley's main text is *The Prelude* since he starts with a criticism of *The Excursion—*but that, I suppose, is the point: several attempts have been made to prove that the poet of *The Prelude* really did write *The Excursion;* this book wants us to believe that the author of *The Excursion* also wrote *The Prelude*. It is worth believing, but needs more sensitively adduced evidence than this. —**Michael Baron,** *English* (Spring 1976)

9. Virtually all of the many recent studies of Wordsworth can be spoken of—without any grave injustice—as elaborating arguments already disseminated, reinforcing positions staked out by predecessors, their claims to novelty rarely amounting to more than the filling in of detail or shading for a portrait already sketched. But Richard Brantley's *Wordsworth's "Natural Methodism"* is clearly a work that runs against the grain, one that hopes by its undeniable originality of approach to revise received opinion in the most fundamental way.... Because of Brantley's uncompromising commitment to his position, he leaves us with the sense that we have seen one line of investigation carried to its ultimate limits.
—**Alan Grob**, *The Wordsworth Circle* (Summer 1976)

10. This book performs a genuine service in suggesting the importance to Wordsworth's life and poetry of the "Evangelical" tradition, defined broadly to include analogous movements within Anglicanism as well as Dissent.... One is grateful for the sheer scholarly abundance of new sources and analogues to which this book draws attention, especially in the notes.
—**Bishop C. Hunt**, *English Language Notes* (September 1976)

11. This well-crafted piece of criticism argues persuasively that eighteenth-century evangelicalism had an important (and heretofore improperly appreciated) influence on Wordsworth's work.... Brantley deserves to be read not only by literary critics, but also by historians of the English religious scene and by latter-day practitioners of "theopoetic" and "intermediary theology." —**Charles I. Wallace**, *Religious Studies Review* (January 1977)

12. Wordsworth's relationships with Christianity have evoked the interest, and often uneasiness, of his family, acquaintances, and critics from early points in his career. John Sterling gave perhaps the most succinct, if not the clearest, comprehensive evaluation of the matter: "Wordsworth is not a Christian. He is nothing but a Church of England pantheist." The judgment has not been enough for posterity, which has continued discussion and debate—often as parts of book-length studies (such as those of Abrams, Batho, Benziger, Fairchild, Ferry, Hartman, Inge, Jones, Moorman, Piper, Potts, Rader)—of the poet or his intellectual background. The narrower subject of the poet's affinities with Evangelical Christianity has attracted attention in its own right at least from the time of publication of *The Excursion,* parts of which Charles Lamb called "natural methodism"; but the attention has seldom been close, and Elizabeth Geen's article "The Concept of Grace in Wordsworth's Poetry" *(PMLA* 67 [1943]: 689-715), although more concerned with orthodoxy than Evangelicalism, remains a virtually unique example of readily available extended treatment, founded in rigorous examination of the poet's language, of Wordsworth's reference to a concept central to Evangelical thought. Abrams's *Natural Supernaturalism* (New York, 1971) broadly examines the poet's relations with Protestant and Evangelical tradition within a sweeping treatment of nature and spirit in many English and German Romantic writers and philosophers. Two closely related but more narrowly centered studies have appeared recently. One is Frank McConnell's *The Confessional Imagination* (Baltimore, 1974), which traces (with some overlapping of Abrams) connections between *The Prelude* and Augustinian and Protestant confessional narrative. The other is *Wordsworth's "Natural Methodism,"* which derives from a 1969 Princeton University doctoral dissertation, undertaking the potentially useful task of presenting "biographical and political evidence for William Wordsworth's indebtedness to Evangelical Anglicanism" [please note: *political* is a misreading of *poetical;* Robert M. Ryan later emphasized the political aspects of Wordsworth's religious concerns—REB].

Brantley's "Introduction" and first chapter argue for the need for recognition of association between Wordsworth and Evangelical tradition and describe historical and biographical circumstances making likely the poet's knowledge of such religious developments, finding in the poet a much greater consistency of allegiance to Evangelical views than has been discerned by previous students, and concluding that "Wordsworth's identity as a poet . . . derives from a religious ideal of service, an ideal imbued with a zealous didacticism unlike anything to be found in the work of other major Romantics . . ." (p. 36). The second chapter, "Wordsworth's Spiritual Autobiography," discerns among various passages of *The Prelude* an account of the poet's boyhood progress "from pride to humility and thence to new heights of religious experience" (p. 42) and presents a background discussion of the centrality in Methodist and Puritan autobiographical narrative of humility and conversion (the central event of the lives of such narrators)—the poet's conversion being the spiritual dedication described in *The Prelude* IV as an event of the poet's first summer college vacation (1788). The next, and longest, chapter, "Wordsworth's Theology of the Spirit," discusses *The Prelude, The Excursion,* and a number of shorter works as religious poems in which the poet "developed his narrative patterns and borrowed his most characteristic themes from what he absorbed of the doctrinal configurations in spiritual theology" (p. 141)—particularly configurations of an Evangelical cast. The concluding chapter, "Wordsworth and the Book of Nature," treats Wordsworth's "spiritual reading of nature." An accumulating weight of information about contemporary Evangelical Christianity and the poet's use of terms common in this religious vocabulary—"grace" (although Geen is seemingly not mentioned), "joy," "covenant," "extraordinary call," and the like—heighten awareness of an important and, as the author claims, neglected, aspect of Wordsworth's historical context and poetic language. . . .

Few experienced readers of Wordsworth would require more than minor qualification of the phrasing of a thesis that Wordsworth's poetry was an effort to "*re*mythologize his Christian heritage and that he thus participated, as did the Evangelicals, in the revival of Christian myth and morality" (p. 2), or that most of his work is evangelical in the sense that through it he urgently "sought to minister to the good of the soul and thus to improve the spiritual welfare of his readers" (p. 36). The primary problem is that the author, despite his own occasional claims to the contrary, throughout confuses these purposes and qualities of poetic service with comprehensive ambition of doctrinal service: the poet is sometimes said to resemble, but is normally treated as being in fact, an Evangelical witness. . . .

. . . [A] crucial event of the poet's spiritual life in *The Prelude*, we learn, was his "call" by the Spirit, or "covenant/conversion," or "covenant resolve," or the like, of 1788, following which "his career during the 1790's (except, perhaps, for the period of his French experience)" was that of one "signally included" in the number of "Evangelical laborers in the English vineyard of God's kingdom" (pp. 97-100). . . . The poet's actual words are

>   I made no vows, but vows
> Were then made for me; bond unknown to me
> Was given, that I should be, else sinning greatly,
> A dedicated Spirit. On I walk'd
> In blessedness, which yet endures.

Of this we are told that "the poet promises . . . to keep his 'vows' and covenant 'bond' 'else sinning greatly'" (p. 98). Since an Evangelical "bond" cannot be "unknown," nor experienced without intellectual awareness of past deficiency—hardly the reference of "else sinning greatly"—clarification is required, but it is not forthcoming. An implicit admission of earlier sin is nonetheless discovered in Wordsworth's description of the festivity attended by his persona during the night preceding the "covenant resolve"—a party which, even if attended, as Brantley claims, by youths who "show no sign of putting on the New Man of holiness," is unlikely to serve many readers adequately for an emblem of Original Depravity. The basic excitement of such passages, from this perspective, of course, lies in the interplay between relevance and thorough irrelevance of Evangelical doctrine....

... In a letter to Landor of January 21, 1824, Wordsworth makes certain distinctions—and they are a necessary foundation of any study of religion in Wordsworth's thought and art—about relations between language, poetic suggestion, doctrinal concept, and the Christian community:

I cannot ... accede to your objection to the "second birth" [in *Laodamia*], merely because the expression has been degraded by Conventiclers. I certainly meant nothing more by it than the *eadem cura*, and the *largior aether*, etc., of Vergil's 6th *Aeneid*. All religions owe their origin or acceptance to the wish of the human heart to supply in another state of existence the deficiencies of this, and to carry still nearer to perfection whatever we admire in our present condition.... I have little relish for any other [books than those treating of religion]—even in poetry it is the imaginative only, viz. that which is conversant [with], or turns upon infinity, that powerfully affects me, ... but all great poets are in this view powerful Religionists....

Such discriminations play no functional part in the principles of organization of this book.

The scope and range of philosophical complexities that impinge on an investigation of the Wordsworthian poetical evangelism and its doctrinal ties are best indicated by Abrams's *Natural Supernaturalism*. McConnell's study, although often hasty in reasoning and more limited in sweep of contemporary religious background than Brantley's, contains useful and sympathetic insights into relations between language, thought, and religious commitment in Wordsworth.... **—Mark L. Reed,** *Modern Philology* (August 1977)

13. This is the first full-length study of a significant but largely neglected dimension of Wordsworth's work and cultural background, a study whose relevance is clear and undeniable, and which will surely force reconsideration of what most influenced the poet in his readings and contact with his contemporary milieu. **—Vincent Newey**, *Modern Language Review* (October 1977)

14. Emphasizing as he does the consistent spiritual idiom and symmetry of Wordsworth's poetry in a "neoapostolic" age, Brantley has done much to correct T. E. Hulme's simplistic notion of Romanticism as being "spilt religion" and opened a fresh avenue of inquiry to one of its major figures. Whether he has given us "the basis for a synoptic criticism" (p. xi) of Wordsworth, however, remains to be seen. **—Robert Lance Snyder**, *Criticism* (Fall 1977)

15. Wordsworth is no longer regarded as a pantheist but rather as a Christian—some even say an Evangelical. We have already seen his influence on the Tractarians through [John] Keble, his unabashed admirer. Aubrey de Vere, who knew him well, believed him to be an orthodox Christian, increasingly so as he grew older [Paraclita Reilly, *Aubrey de Vere: Victorian Observer* (Lincoln: U of Nebraska P. 1953), 39-40]. He was evidently introduced to evangelical writings through his sister Dorothy and what he called a "bond of connection" with [William] Wilberforce because of his liking for the *Practical View*. Richard Brantley's view of the poet, which can be seen in his title *Wordsworth's Natural Methodism*, had also been Charles Lamb's view of Wordsworth. Hannah More, who had been disgusted by the young Wordsworth's radicalism, was overcome by the revelation of a very different man in *The Excursion*. Thomas De Quincy informed Dorothy of Wordsworth's visit to Hannah More and announced that her brother "has made a conquest of Holy Hannah" [Jones, *Hannah More*, 225]. **—Herbert Schlossberg,** *The Silent Revolution & the Making of Victorian England* (Columbus: Ohio State U P, 2000), 214

16. Frederick Gill emphasized Romanticism and Methodism's common faith in the doctrine of the wisdom of the heart, citing Wesley and Coleridge's celebration of a spirit of enthusiasm which manifested itself both as personal revelation and communication: 'an internal ecstasy or "fullness", representing the divine "overflowing" by its "communicativeness", "budding and blossoming forth in all earnestness of persuasion"' [Frederick C. Gill, *The Romantic Movement and Methodism*, 175]. Gill was not, however, concerned to explore the more contentious nature of this discourse. Richard Brantley's later study of *Wordsworth's Natural Methodism* made an emphatic claim for the spiritual and stylistic affinity of Wordsworthian and contemporary evangelical discourse. His thesis is supported with reference to those who, like Archbishop William Hutton, observed that 'the age of Wesley and Whitefield introduced what may be called a new romanticism in religion, just as the Lake School, half a century later, may be said to have destroyed the classic tradition of the older poetry' [cited in Brantley,

Natural Methodism, 176, fn. 28]. Brantley also notes how E. H. Sugden, early editor of Wesley's *Sermons*, drew a parallel between the internal emphasis of Wordsworth and Wesley's visionary inspiration. He saw their common emphasis on the 'indwelling spirit of God' as helping to refine 'enthusiasm', and, in Brantley's words, 'establish an honorific sense for the pejorative term' [cited in Brantley, *Natural Methodism*, 72 and 176, fn. 28]. . . . Richard Brantley's remark that Wesley's 'love of all Christian thought steadied the momentum of his Methodism' implies that his alertness to ideas conferred a stabilizing objectivity to balance the subjective emphasis of his religion of the heart' *[Natural Methodism*, 3]. . . . In *Wordsworth's Natural Methodism*, Brantley remarks on the 'pervasive Evangelical idiom' of such phrases as 'the indwelling Spirit', 'the Christ in us', 'perfection' etc., which express the concepts of spiritual renewal central to religious revivalism [xi and chap. 3]. Such language is applied to the revelatory character of Wordsworth's transformative 'Spots of Time' experiences, recorded in the early books of *The Prelude*, which express in similarly visionary terms the inspiring and chastening impact of spiritual power. . . .

However, even Brantley seems anxious to disassociate Romantic writers from 'enthusiasm'. . . . This study [Helen Boyles, *Romanticism and Methodism*] gives critical emphasis to Wordsworth as the Romantic writer who (besides self-declared 'enthusiast' William Blake) was most often accused of being Methodistical, despite having made few explicit references to Methodism in his writings. . . . [Jean-Pierre van Noppen's *Transforming Words: The Early Methodist Revival from a Discourse Perspective* (Brussels: Peter Lang, 1999)] emphasizes the need for a closer attention to Methodist linguistics for the insight that it can provide into a speaker's principles and temperament. This has prompted my investigation . . . of John and Charles Wesley's linguistic choices and strategies, and what they reflect of the bothers' complex relationship with enthusiasm. . . . A linguistic focus also seems appropriate for an analysis of the innately communicative aspect of 'enthusiasm' which, in its religious origins, is closely identified with the Word (of God). — **Helen Boyles**, *Romanticism and Methodism: The Problem of Religious Enthusiasm* [London and New York: Routledge, 2017), 6, 9, 40, 87

Locke, Wesley, and the Method of English Romanticism (1984)

17. Richard Brantley's *Locke, Wesley, and the Method of English Romanticism* could well contribute a new chapter to our understanding of the religious roots of Romanticism in English. Written against the background of contemporary critical developments and everywhere exhibiting a sensitive and thoroughly informed grasp of the relevant scholarship, Brantley's study presents a solid and convincing case for Wesley's centrality to the entire Romantic program.... The great virtue of Wesley's view of experience was that by locating the religious in the empirical it suggested a new way of overcoming the traditional split between the natural and the supernatural and indeed enabled others to envision the terms of their reunification. **–Giles Gunn**, reader for the University Press of Florida

18. This is a careful and convincing discussion that shows in detail how Wesley mediated the empirical philosophy of Locke, and how through his own amalgam of feeling and experience he provided an important conditioning climate, in what E. D. Hirsch calls "les bonnes lettres," for "les belles lettres" of English Romanticism. Brantley's study makes it henceforth necessary to include the evangelical Wesley with traditionally literary and philosophical writers among the significant precursors of the Romantic movement as a whole. **–Thomas McFarland**, reader for the University Press of Florida

19. This book reflects a growing application of rigorous standards of scholarship to the field of Wesley studies. At the same time, it indicates a growing awareness among scholars of the importance of Wesley both within and beyond the scope of denominational studies. **–Richard P. Heitzenrater**, *Perkins Journal* (Spring 1984)

20. Brantley states his case persuasively, coherently, and with a clarity of style. His work breaks exciting new ground for an interdisciplinary method to integrate various aspects of English culture in the eighteenth and nineteenth centuries. In addition to his masterful investigation into the evangelical influence upon English Romantic poetry, Brantley provides a critique of Wesley's own thought and language that opens new vistas for the study of Anglican evangelicalism.... This work is a significant contribution to knowledge and demonstrates the lively interchange of Christian fervor and poetic sensibility. The Conference is pleased to honor a book which not only reflects high standards of scholarship but represents a significant dialogue between Christian theology and literature. **–from the Conference on Christianity and Literature Book Award Citation**, *Christianity & Literature* (Fall 1984)

21. According to social historian W. E. H. Lecky, John Wesley's conversion "meant more for Britain than all the victories of Pitt by land and sea"

(p. 103). And yet, Richard Brantley argues in his very valuable *Locke, Wesley, and the Method of English Romanticism*, Wesley has been ignored. Literary scholars have dismissed Wesley, Brantley tells us, as an "unenlightened anachronism" (p. 16), and as a result, the extent of Wesley's intellectual influence, especially in terms of English Romantic poetry, has not yet been fully evaluated. If what Brantley says is true (and I think it is), *Locke, Wesley, and the Method of English Romanticism* may well add a new chapter to English literary criticism's sourcebook on romantic poetry. . . .

Although *Locke, Wesley, and the Method of English Romanticism* is hardly a biography, in these middle chapters Brantley is so good at catching Wesley's character that he almost makes his subject breathe. Here Wesley moves with cloak and book amidst the Cotswold circle of intellectual friends, most of whom were women, discoursing on Locke and theology. Demonstrating an appealing feminism, Brantley writes that "the women in his life were of more than passing interest." But it was hardly a question of "simple addiction to gallantry"; rather, Wesley loved women as "intellectual equals" (p. 116). With similar charm, Brantley claims for Wesley not only feminist, but also proto-romantic democratic sympathies, quoting the Wesley scholar Herbert to describe Wesley as a man who "when a poor man thanked him for a favor always removed his hat" (p. 117).

Brantley tries to rewrite critical history directly by showing how good readings could be made better (and I have no doubt that they will be) by including Wesley. The method is strategically sound and the attempt valiant but less successful than one would hope.

Notwithstanding the fourth chapter's vulnerability, Brantley's *Locke, Wesley, and the Method of English Romanticism* may be considered excellent for its scholarly integrity, for its superbly conceived argument, and for its original thesis that Wesley's mediation of Locke's naturalism informs natural supernaturalism, the central dialectic of romantic poetry. Here at last is new happy hunting ground for romantic and eighteenth century scholars. Or has a whole new planet swum into view? —**Lisa Low**, *Kritikon Litterarum* (1984)

22. Richard E. Brantley amply justifies his view that John Wesley's conception of human experience—including his idea of conversion and the consciousness of salvation, owed much to Locke's epistemology. He convinces first by his evidence of Wesley's "Lockean connection"—his abridgment of Peter Browne's *The Procedure, Extent, and Limits of Human Understanding* (1728), which Brantley takes to be "a theologizing of Locke's *Essay*". Browne,

Bishop of Cork and Ross, was not so substantial a figure as to account for Wesley's interest unless, as Brantley contends, Wesley had first of all recognized the Lockean bias of much Dissenting interpretation of human cognition. The book goes on to examine Wesley's philosophical theology and again is convincing in its argument that this is based on evidence (of the senses as well as of reason) which precedes conviction. So far so good.

It is when Professor Brantley goes on to write of Wesley's intellectual influence, and of the parallel interpretation of human experience in Wordsworth, Coleridge, Shelley, and Keats that we find ourselves unable to join him on his personal critical expedition. It is as if a contemporary critic took it upon himself to examine the influence of Freud on contemporary theologians and then made the leap to a specific connection between this and the much vaguer influence of Freud on modern poets. There is always a general effect of the *Zeitgeist* in any age, and Locke, after Descartes, dominates eighteenth-century feeling, as eighteenth-century feeling throws its shadows over developing romanticism. But, useful though it may be to relate Wesley to a more expansive imaginative vision than that of his own age, it is pointless to try to make specific or even generalized comparisons between men whose preoccupations and understanding of the nature of revelation were so substantially distinct. . . . The second part of this book reads too much like jottings on loosely related topics to be more than a starting-point for general speculation; it is interesting in itself, but scarcely a secure foundation for the tracing of influence and conscious imitation.

Nevertheless, there is a way in which Wesley can be connected with the emerging spirit of Romanticism—not largely, through his philosophical and theological views, but more particularly, through his and his brother's idea of the influence of poetry, and of hymnody especially, on the feelings of ordinary men. . . . The great hymns of the eighteenth century are lyrics, and they are more powerful in their emotional effects than most literary lyrics of the same period, though curiously, in their popular appeal, nearer to folk poetry and ballad than to the conscious creations of art. **–Rachel Trickett**, *TLS* (December 21, 1984)

23. It is customary to regard John Wesley as the father of an emotionalist Christianity which set itself against the brittle rationalism of the eighteenth century. It is equally commonplace to view Romanticism as the poetic source of modern unbelief. Wesley turned religion into a mindless matter of the heart—so runs the usual argument—while the Romantics sought solace not in Christian faith but in nature or even in poetry itself. In this learned and daring book, Richard Brantley brilliantly undermines these simple-minded assumptions. He demonstrates that, far from being an antirational pietist, Wesley had a deep sympathy for the most advanced ideas of the Enlightenment, and especially for the philosophy of John Locke. Brantley also shows that the Romantic poets were hardly the secularists they are often made to seem. However great their skepticism, they were men obsessed with transcendent reality and imbued with a Wesleyan insistence that it is mediated through concrete experience. The effect of Brantley's book is spiritually and literarily explosive....

Brantley does not naively conflate the God revealed to Wesley in Jesus Christ with the nameless power whom Shelley addresses in "Mont Blanc." Yet Brantley does demonstrate that the work of the poet and the theologian cannot simply be set at odds. The empiricist faith achieved through the Wesleyan revival filled the air that the Romantics breathed. This theological milieu gives their work a tone and quality that must be called religious in the specifically Wesleyan sense. They heard the same inner voice of immediate revelation, though transposed into a different key, that Wesley heeded when his heart was first "strangely warmed" at the chapel in Aldersgate Street on May 24, 1738.

Locke, Wesley, and the Method of English Romanticism is a scholarly book in the best sense of the word. Brantley has mastered a massive amount of learning—theological, philosophical, literary, historical—but never tries to impress the reader with his erudition. On the contrary, he relegates to modest footnotes what must, in fact, constitute many years of painstaking work. It is not surprising that the Conference on Christianity and Literature (an interdisciplinary society allied with the Modern Language Association) has given Brantley's treatise its outstanding book award for 1984.... Brantley's rigorous concern to establish a right understanding of revelation and reason makes him one of the most distinguished products of the Wake Forest tradition. —**Ralph C. Wood**, *Wake Forest University Magazine* (February 1985)

24. Brantley's book is undeniably important; it has something to say, and it will be read by historians as well as literary critics. Historians are often inclined to think of Methodism as a merely social event, intelligible in terms of its social causes and social consequences. Brantley forces us to regard it as an intellectual event. Religion, after all, is not just something that men do; it is also something that they think. It has intellectual origins and intellectual consequences. With the lone exception of Bernard Semmel, historians have long been reluctant to listen to the Methodists and take their arguments seriously. In the textbooks Methodism is dismissed as consequence of social distress or disordered mass-psychology. It is hard to understand why historians should treat Methodism and Puritan thought so differently, ignoring the one and studying the other to death. Methodism's status among historians is best illustrated by the uncritical respect that is still extended to Ronald Knox's *Enthusiasm*. For all its merits, Knox's work is little more than a fluent exercise in Catholic propaganda. Methodism appears as another stage in a long, sad tradition of heresy that stretches from Montanus to Father Divine. Brantley places Methodism in its proper historical context. He studies it in terms of its contemporary origins and consequences and never asks us to ignore the fact that Methodism is an eighteenth-century development.

Whether Brantley is right or wrong in seeing Methodism as the source of English Romanticism, is a question for specialists in English literature to decide.... What will be more valuable for historians, is the lengthy analysis that Brantley gives us of Wesley's thought.... No less than Voltaire's, Wesley's thought reflected the philosophical orthodoxy of his age. As a result of Brantley's work, it will be more difficult to repeat the old cliché that Methodism is in some significant sense a reaction against the Enlightenment. **—Frederick Dreyer**, *Albion* (Spring 1985)

25. Brantley proves that Wesley drew heavily on Locke, but Wesley's influence is another matter.... Brantley's contribution is sound, insofar as it presents Wesley as a child of the Enlightenment, not a retrograde pietist. **—D. G. Paz**, *Religious Studies Review* (July 1985)

26. The chief importance of this illuminating study is its bridge position as an interdisciplinary study. Brantley brings to Wesley studies a fresh sense of Wesley's indebtedness to Locke and [Peter] Browne, and particularly to the pervasiveness of this interest throughout Wesley's historical development. He brings to the study of English Romanticism an unusual knowledge of John Wesley's thought and its influence. In both areas Brantley has made a basic contribution. **—Thomas A. Langford**, *The Journal of the American Academy of Religion* (September 1985)

27. Those who take the time to work through the sometimes difficult prose will find it a provoking experience in the best sense of the term. Besides the persistent basic argument, one-line sub-theses abound, tempting the reader to test new ways of looking at the thought patterns of the period. Such is the value of critical intellectual inquiry, whether it be in philosophy, theology, or literary criticism, and this work contributes to (and should provoke thoughtful responses from) each of these disciplines. **—Richard P. Heitzenrater**, *Church History* (Fall 1985).

28. The strongest evidence for Brantley's case is of course Wordsworth, and Brantley adds authoritatively here to his *Wordsworth's "Natural Methodism"* (1975). He agrees with Colin Clarke that Wordsworth's struggles with the strangeness of perception caused some of his finest poetry.... Brantley shows in some detail how the center of "Tintern Abbey" is "fully consistent with and sharply reminiscent of the Wesleyan and quintessentially English form of natural religion whereby God is seen to be present in, but not equivalent to, the text and the texture of his second book."

Almost we are persuaded that "Wesley is the one figure who comes near being the model for Wordsworth's ability to convey to an increasingly widespread audience a complex message creative in its tension between 'the language of the sense' and otherworldly glimpses of 'the light that never was, on sea or land.'"

Brantley's book is both precise in its detail and provocative in its assertions, or as Brantley himself says he is trying to be, "both judicious and creative." However, a "unified field theory" will need to be more inclusive than this. **—Mark T. Smith**, *The Romantic Movement: A Selective and Critical Bibliography for 1984* (1985).

29. Richard Brantley's book is not only a carefully researched and well-written essay in the history of ideas but also an intriguing case study in the sociology of knowledge. The author shows how John Wesley transmuted John Locke's sensationalist epistemology into a method of religious illumination and of transcendentalist poetic expression. **—William T. Bluhm**, *The Eighteenth Century: A Current Bibliography* (1985)

30. Besides its provocative thesis and cogent demonstration, Brantley's richly learned book is distinctive for its critical-theoretical awareness, implicit throughout and explicit in the postscript, which reminds us only too well of how far literary scholarship has advanced since Frederick C. Gill essayed the same subject, in *The Romantic Movement and Methodism: A Study of English Romanticism and the Evangelical Revival* (1937; reprinted 1954). **—Frank Jordan**, *The English Romantic Poets: A Review of Research and Criticism*, 4th edition (1985)

31. In its effort to correct received opinion about eighteenth- and early nineteenth-century English literary culture, the motives of this project are admirable in more ways than one. Like Donald Davie's recent work, *Dissentient Voices* (1982), Brantley's book seeks to establish terms for describing a specifically English Enlightenment in the eighteenth century, and, again like Davie, he looks to philosophically minded Protestant thinkers to do so. Also laudable is the effort to revise Basil Willey's influential representation of how the "Locke tradition" carries forward to the nineteenth century, for Willey tends to bypass important theological mediations of Lockeanism. Brantley argues effectively that intellectual historians have laid too much stress on one line of English associationism, that of Hartley and Lord Kames, at Wesley's expense. Many readers will also profit by Brantley's more general insistence on Wesley's cultural and intellectual influence through the romantic period and beyond. **–James Chandler**, *The Journal of Religion* (January 1986)

32. Brantley perceptively analyzes the intricacies of the philosophical thought of Wesley and establishes the reciprocal relationship between Wesley's Methodist faith and poetic creation in the eighteenth century. Brantley's work is a triumph of interdisciplinary research and justifiably deserves the recent award from the MLA Conference on Christianity and Literature.... Brantley's book demonstrates that historical criticism is opening new avenues to the study of Romantic thought. **–James C. Villalobos**, *The Huntington Library Quarterly* (Winter 1986)

33. *Locke, Wesley, and the Method of English Romanticism*, 1984 winner of the annual book award of the Conference on Christianity and Literature, is as ambitious as its title portends. A study in the history of ideas, it is really two books. The first is a carefully and thoroughly documented, convincing argument that John Wesley, often stereotypically associated with the enthusiasm that appears to be unthinking feeling in Methodism, was deeply influenced by his careful and rigorous study of the philosophy of Locke and Locke's followers in such a way as to make him at least partially adopt elements of British empiricism as well as some general tenets of the British Enlightenment. The second book, less thoroughly illustrated and consequently less convincing, posits that Wesley's "philosophical theology" permeates in varying degrees the epistemological assumptions and poetic practices of Blake, Wordsworth, Coleridge, Shelley, and Keats, if not Byron. **–John Greenfield**, *South Atlantic Review* (May 1986)

34. The hasty survey of the Romantics is particularly disappointing given Brantley's initial ambitions. Yet the text and bibliography reflect years of reading. He glides from Asimov to Augustine, Calvino to Copleston, Sagan to Saussure. Above all, Brantley is steeped in Methodism and the literature it spawned. He is compelling on Wesley, and it is chiefly for this learned devotion that one welcomes his book. **–Richard Fadem**, *Philosophy and Literature* (August 1986)

35. Professor Brantley's book, which won the 1984 CCL Book Award, is, in many ways, bold and adventurous; it makes claims about a John Wesley-English Romanticism nexus that will astonish some. . . . We have something to think about. . . . Readers not thoroughly familiar with Wesley's intellectual training and reading will emerge from this orientation convinced, I think, that Brantley is onto something: that there is a reason, if not to reassemble our notions of the intellectual milieu that helped shape Romantic literature, at least to enrich the context in which we think about the poets and their writing. . . .

The importance and strength of this study notwithstanding, some readers may find a number of objectionable features. For example, occasionally the methodology, usually solid and admirable, slips into a facile strain. . . .

To object that this book should do more with the poetry might be tantamount to saying that Blake's miniatures should have been bigger. Better, perhaps, to express gratitude to Professor Brantley for making us better informed about John Wesley's theology and for giving us the opportunity to think closely about what may be an important addition to the constellation of Romantic influences. **–Howard H. Hinkel**, *Christianity & Literature* (Summer 1986)

36. One hopes that Brantley is now engaged on a definitive study of this topic whose importance and wide ramifications he has here convincingly demonstrated. No one is more qualified by learning and enthusiasm (in its broader sense) to do the work. But it will be a better book if he considers not only the kinship that existed between Romanticism and the Wesleyan revival but also the natural enmity that was recognized by both sides. It seemed to most of those involved that these two powerful movements of the spirit, emerging from the Enlightenment with radically different views of human nature, were joined not in an alliance but in a *kulturkampf*, in what could be described as a contest between art and religion at a time when people knew the difference. Romanticists might like to think that all the genius was on one side, and yet in this war for British hearts and minds the Methodists and Evangelicals won decisively. We need to have a clearer idea of how and why they prevailed, and Brantley's continuing investigation is likely to provide us with one. —**Robert M. Ryan**, *The Wordsworth Circle* (Summer 1986)

37. L'ouvrage est remarquable tant par ses résultats que par sa méthode. Il ouvre le lecteur 'continental' à un monde et à une forme de pensée qui lui sont malencontreusement trop souvent inconnus. Il fait appel à un type de recherche à la fois pluridisciplinaire, portant sur une relativement longue période et offrant des synthèses particulièrement bien documentées qui proposent une manière très séduisante d'apprôcher l'histoire de la pensée. Le lecteur 'continental' regrettera seulement que l'a se soit limité au mode anglo-saxon et n'ait pas montre en cette occasion combien le romantisme anglais différait, de par des racines mêmes, des romantisme allemand et français, mais combien aussi le méthodisme et ses avatars revivalistes avaient eu du succès, en France en particulier, précisément à l'époque romantique. —**J. D. Kraege**, *Études Théologiques et Religieuses* (1986)

38. Intellectual affinities are easy to describe; intellectual genealogies are more difficult to establish. Brantley accepts the challenge without flinching. —**Richard P. Heitzenrater**, *Church History* (March 1987)

39. [This] study is certainly a valuable storehouse of material. A great national figure must both leave impressions on future generations and share many features with his countrymen. The most interesting parts of the argument, however, have a generality which inevitably weakens their application. —**Roger Sharrock**, *Notes & Queries* (September 1987)

40. The great virtue of this book is that it points to connections that have not been noticed before. Some of Brantley's examples may be unconvincing and his claims for the importance of Wesley himself and his influence on Romanticism may be inflated. But if the book directs further attention to Wesley and his influence on the Romantics, its effect will surely be salutary, for Brantley has indeed established that Wesley's importance was more than cultural and religious, and that students of English Romanticism have much to learn about their subject by exploring it against the background of Wesley's thought. –**Ronald A. Sharp**, *JEGP* (Fall 1987)

41. I risk the criticisms that come to all who combine genres, who mix metaphors, who cross disciplines, who refuse to be confined to the questions addressed by a single metaphor of mind or discipline of inquiry because I have been inspired by historian/literary critic Richard E. Brantley. His key insight into the secret of the theology that fueled the eighteenth-century New Light movement known as the Evangelical Revival is this: It brought together into shared space the Enlightenment project (the scientific method and rational empiricism) with natural and revealed religion. **–Leonard I. Sweet,** *Quantum Spirituality: A Postmodern Apologetic* (1991)

42. Most of the discussion about the influence of Methodism has been over Wesley's avowed mission field—the poor people of England. Controversy abounds over the movement's influence with the masses, which is natural when the main question dealt with is the presence or absence of revolution—in other words the Halévy thesis and its critics.... But the cultural influence of the Methodist movement may have been far more significant than its ability to enhance or to neutralize the revolutionary fervor of the populace. By the first third of the nineteenth century more than 63 percent of Methodists were classified as artisans, a group which encompasses many well-paid people. About thirteen percent were composed of people in middle class occupations—merchants and manufacturers and the like—and a significant number of them were quite well off.... To some degree, then, these are people who are actors in the shaping of English culture, and not just passive reflectors of it....

... The founder of the movement, despite his sense of call to minister to the poor and unlettered, was himself an Oxford graduate and a teaching fellow, and he did not lose his academic interests when he began preaching in the countryside. Recent scholarship on Wesley's ideas and their influence provide important new knowledge of the later significance of the Methodist movement. Richard Brantley has studied Wesley's ideas in relationship to the philosophy of Locke, and concluded that the Lockean emphasis on experience as the source of knowledge is a major component of Wesley's theology and subsequently of the romantic movement in sensibility. Locke's theory of knowledge formed the intellectual grounding of the Wesleyan movement, lending to it the conviction that true knowledge came from sense perception along with reason. Thus the senses and the intellectual components of the process together make real knowledge possible. "Locke's rational empiricism (i.e., his epistemology of sense perception attended by induction and deduction) directly informs the religious 'epistemology' whereby Wesley claimed the saving faith he felt was his." Brantley believes that because of their prejudices over the last two centuries students of the Enlightenment have ignored Wesley entirely, regarding him as a kind of obscurantist anachronism, and this accounts for the fact that his role in the intellectual history of the times is so little appreciated.... In another work Brantley elaborates on why Locke was so important for understanding Wesley: "Although empiricism is 'natural' and evangelicalism is 'spiritual,' the great principle of empiricism, that one must see for oneself and be in the presence of the thing one knows, applies as well to evangelical faith. Each of these two methodologies operates along a continuum that joins emotion to intellect; each joins externality to words through 'ideas/ideals of sensation,' that is, through perception or grace-in-perception or both. While empiricism refers to immediate contact with and direct impact from objects and subjects in time and place, evangelicalism entertains the notions that religious truth is concerned with experiential presuppositions and that experience need not be nonreligious" (*Coordinates of Anglo-American Romanticism*, 1-2).

Moreover Brantley shows how the natural experiential emphasis of Locke combines with the spiritual experiential emphasis of Wesley to provide the "central dialectic" of the romantic poets. "Not only does the almost religious quality of their emotion relate to Wesley's emotional faith, but a Wesleyan blend of 'spiritual sense' and a posteriori reason forms part of what they all retained from the century and the place in which all of them were born" (*Locke, Wesley, and the Method of English Romanticism*, 25).

Blake, Wordsworth, Coleridge, Shelley, and Keats—apart from their consciously-held theological convictions or lack thereof—formed a continuation of the Lockean-Wesleyan fusion of experience and ideas, and this explains the improbable Romantic juxtaposition of the mundane and the otherworldly. "Romantic tension in England at least is both partially reconcilable and fully understandable along clear lines of Wesley's philosophical theology" (Ibid., 129). "Wesley's thought and expression, in other words, together form not only a heuristic way in, but also a close analogue to, the works of Blake, Wordsworth, Coleridge, Shelley, and Keats. Coleridge stands closest to this quintessentially native context: in his method are especially explicit signs of the Wesleyan method 'in the air' that all these poets breathed. In addition to Zeitgeist, then, and in addition to heuristic/analogistic criticism, is the question of influence. This question is answered affirmatively thus: Blake, Wordsworth, Coleridge, Shelley, and Keats owe something of their theory, and much of their practice, to the relation between John Wesley and John Locke. This mix, then, is English Romantic method" (201).

If Brantley is right, any examination of the Wesleyan influence on English culture must consider both the romantic writers that followed him and those on whom they exerted influence. . . . It was largely due to Coleridge's influence that later English theologians rejected the common continental theodicy and retained sin in their theology (Pym, *The Religious Thought of Samuel Taylor Coleridge*, 54). Coleridge interpreted history as theodicy, incorporating human experience into the biblical framework (De Paolo, *Coleridge*, chapter 5). When he read in his brother-in-law Robert Southey's *Life of Wesley* the Methodist founder's belief that the internal evidence in the individual's soul convinces the person of the presence of new spiritual life, Coleridge added this marginal note, dating it 1 May 1820: "I venture to avow it as my conviction, that either Christian faith is what Wesley here describes, or there is no proper meaning in the word" (quoted in Prickett, *Coleridge and Wordsworth*, 105). **–Herbert Schlossberg,** "The Cultural Influence of Methodism: Religious Revival and the Transformation of English Sensibilities in the Early Nineteenth Century," *The Victorian Web: Literature, History, and Culture in the Age of Victoria* (1998)

43. It is largely because of [Wesley's] role as the mediator of Locke to contemporaries and followers that Brantley, in effect, endorses Southey's judgment quoted earlier by calling [Wesley] a "founder of the Religious Enlightenment": "Wesley's intellectual influence surpassed that of all other intellectuals of his century, for he popularized as well as contributed to almost any field that one can name." *[Locke, Wesley, . . .,* 224.] Brantley also stresses the influence of the Massachusetts clergyman and theologian Jonathan Edwards as cofounder with Wesley (215). Wesley routinely digested and published the writings of people whose thinking he admired, and he did so with Edwards's work—omitting the Calvinist portions. **–Herbert Schlossberg,** *The Silent Revolution & the Making of Victorian England* (Columbus: Ohio State U P, 2000), 323.

44. [According to Henry D. Rack's *Reasonable Enthusiast: John Wesley and the Rise of Methodism,* [1989], Wesley reflected the culture of the Enlightenment, including, for example, Wesley's use of Lockean terms in explicating the role of religious experience as a source of knowledge. . . . Richard E. Brantley's study of *Locke, Wesley, and the Method of English Romanticism* (1984) [first] argued that John Wesley's modification of Locke's epistemology, by which Wesley allowed for religious experience and certain religious affections as genuine sources of human knowledge, laid an intellectual foundation for the work of the English Romantic poets. Brantley had focused on Wesley and the leading poets of the Romantic period. A more recent study by Phyllis Mack, *Heart Religion in the British Enlightenment* (2008), views the phenomenon of Methodist "heart religion" as a function of popular religious culture, utilizing hymns, pamphlets, tracts, and other literature as indications of the spirituality of common people. Her work focuses on the tension between the exuberant religious experiences of the Methodists, on the one hand, and the Methodist insistence on self-discipline, on the other. In their own ways, both Mack and Brantley reflect a growing consensus among interpreters of the eighteenth century that early Romanticism does not need to be seen in opposition to the Enlightenment. **–Ted A. Campbell,** chapter 2, "The Origins and Early Growth of Methodism, 1730-91," in *The Ashgate Research Companion to World Methodism* (2016), William Gibson, Peter Forsaith, and Martin Wellings, eds.

45. In the Postscript to his *Locke, Wesley, and the Method of English Romanticism,* [Brantley] states his view that English Romanticism's 'religious passion' should be acknowledged, but insists that it is nevertheless 'not "demonic"', since it is 'sufficiently commensurable with intellectual criteria to be less than enthusiastic'" [206]. Enthusiasm is here clearly seen as something distinct from rationalism and, by implication, is a label which would degrade the authority of what Brantley has acknowledged to be a spiritually inspired English Romanticism. **–Helen Boyles,** *Romanticism and Methodism: The Problem of Religious Enthusiasm* (London and New York: Routledge, 2017), 6

Coordinates of Anglo-American Romanticism: Wesley, Edwards, Carlyle, and Emerson **(1993)**

46. An interpretative monument, showing the heavy links joining the thought and literatures of America and Great Britain in the nineteenth century. In truth the argument could be extended far beyond Emerson and Carlyle. . . . The writer has wrestled with complexity and pinned it to the page in a clear, simple prose. . . . I doubt anyone in English studies today in this country knows the ties between John Locke and evangelical Christianity better than he does. **–Samuel F. Pickering**, reader for the University Press of Florida

47. A highly useful contribution to the effort to recognize complex connections between seemingly diverse and even contrary modes of eighteenth- and nineteenth-century thought. Vigorously, with much supporting evidence, Brantley takes us into intellectual territory that is relatively unexplored. —**L. J. Swingle**, reader for the University Press of Florida

48. A work of exceptional intelligence and often brilliant insight. Richard Brantley deploys his triangular knowledge of English and American literature, philosophy, and theology to provide a refreshingly different view of the terrain. —**Leonard I. Sweet**, reader for the University Press of Florida

49. Richard E. Brantley's project in *Coordinates of Anglo-American Romanticism* seems altogether worthy. He sees Locke as founder of the empirical method, sees Jonathan Edwards and John Wesley as heirs of Locke, and both of them as exemplars of the empirical/evangelical nexus, this despite their differences, the Calvinism of the one and the Arminianism of the other. Then he takes up Carlyle and Emerson as followers of the empirical-evangelical strain. Certainly there are elements of empiricism in evangelicalism; the insistence on the experience of personal conversion, and the conviction of salvation by faith. But evangelicalism means a lot more than the merely experiential. It has to mean, essentially, the grounding in the Gospel. . . . Both Carlyle and Emerson do preach. And ever since John Holloway's *Victorian Sage* (1953), we have understood the preaching to be a secular substitute for the pulpit. It is a misrepresentation to call it "evangelicalism." —**Ruth ap Roberts**, *Philosophy and Literature* (October 1993)

50. In *Coordinates of Anglo-American Romanticism*, Richard E. Brantley describes the "simultaneously rational and sensationalist reliance on experience" that is the common intellectual ground of Wesley and Edwards, and in a later generation, Carlyle and Emerson. Brantley argues that Emerson's development was guided by "key Lockean tenets," and in an extended treatment of *Nature* he traces the Lockean "emphasis on perception" characteristic of the English empiricist tradition. —**David M. Robinson,** *American Literary Scholarship: An Annual* (1993), Gary Scharnhorst, ed.

51. John Wesley's adroit suppression of Edwards's emphasis on Original Sin and his heightening of Edwards's emphasis on the sensation of religious affections are surmised by Richard E. Brantley in *Coordinates of Anglo-American Romanticism.* Also in contrast to Edwards [and also bringing a British perspective to bear on the North American colonial scene], Nancy Rutenburg contends in "George Whitefield, Spectacular Conversion, and the

Rise of Democratic Personality" *(AmLH* 5:429-58), Whitefield represented himself as having reconciled humility (self-abasement) and power (self-exaltation); this portrait of a regenerated and revolutionary self, textualized through his sermons, functioned as a model for [American] national selfhood. —**William J. Scheick,** *American Literary Scholarship: An Annual* (1993), Gary Scharnhorst, ed.

52. Brantley's sense of the centrality of Locke, Wesley, and Edwards to the British and American intellectual world gives his interpretation a distinctive tone. His application of the concept of "Romanticism," a term most often used in literary study, to religious thinking distinguishes this analysis as well. The strength of his work is in its synthesis of methods and its identification of a common and enduring cultural orientation in Anglo-American society. Precisely because Richard Brantley takes a decisive stand on these issues of historical approach and historical patterns, moreover, he raises further, provocative questions about the dynamics of culture and the ways intellectual life may best be explored. His interdisciplinary method expands the literary canon and encourages close reading of religious texts. His cross-cultural perspective demonstrates the possibilities of studying international intellectual communication. —**Anne C. Rose,** *Critical Review of Books in Religion* (1994)

53. Brantley is most convincing and insightful in his description of the Wesley and Edwards connection where he finds, through a subtle analysis of Wesley's abridgments of selected works by Edwards, that the American Puritan was a formative influence on the British divine.... Linking Wesley and Edwards to Carlyle and Emerson, however, proves to be a more daunting task.... Overall, this study presents an interesting theory of influence that, although somewhat unevenly argued, is engaging and thought provoking throughout. —**Leon Gougeon,** *Journal of the Early Republic* (Spring 1994)

54. Richard Brantley, a professor of English at the University of Florida, has written an ambitious book: he is concerned with the links between two eighteenth-century figures, John Wesley and Jonathan Edwards, and also with the ties that bind two nineteenth-century figures, Thomas Carlyle and Ralph Waldo Emerson. In addition, he hopes to show that the later two writers were influenced by the earlier two, that "Carlyle and Emerson reflect an Anglo-American philosophical theology most notably expressed by Wesley and Edwards" (p. 3). In making his case, Brantley puts himself at the center of his argument, using the first person singular throughout: "I seek both to demonstrate what ideas Wesley and Edwards hold in common (each is Lockean as well as religious) and to show how the two provide an interdisciplinary framework for interpreting the Anglo-American pairing of the late Romantic writers Carlyle and Emerson" (p. 4). The task, needless to say, is daunting; the extent to which Brantley succeeds is open for debate.

The point to be stressed is that Wesley and Edwards represent, in Brantley's opinion, the "twin pioneers of transatlantic revivalism" and that both "appropriate Lockean empiricism for religious methodology" (p. 8). Building on "the pioneering argument of Perry Miller that Edwards is a Lockean," Brantley goes on to say that "the labels *empiricist* and *sensationalist* are particularly apt for Edwards in his eighteenth-century context" (p. 9). But Edwards, it would appear, thought little of Wesley, while Wesley made ample use of Edwards. Although Edwards "referred to Wesley just once, and disparagingly," we are told, "Wesley rejoiced in Edwards." Therefore, writes Brantley, "I seek to establish the intellectual as well as emotional sense in which they should be linked" (p. 10). And this he does by analyzing Wesley's abridgment of Edwards's *Religious Affections* (1746). But we are also informed that the edition of the *Affections* that Wesley used was itself an abridgment by one William Gordon, so that Wesley's edition is two steps removed from the original text.

Not to be diverted, Brantley maintains that by analyzing an abridgment that is based on an abridgment, "I characterize Wesley's distillation of Edwards and hence Edwards's influence on Wesley" (p. 11). He does not, however, stop here. "By an abridgment," he writes, "I mean a bridge indeed. It is the intersection of the thought of Wesley and the thought of Edwards" (p. 15). Moreover, although Wesley was an Arminian and Edwards a Calvinist, their differences need not be stressed. "The abridgment contains," Brantley insists, "what they share . . . the Locke-inspired emphasis on the experiential" (p. 16). A "close reading" of the abridgment, we are told, will "facilitate what is difficult" without diminishing the contents: "I want to abstract, without diluting, the complex empiricism of Wesley and Edwards" (p. 34). Moreover, a close reading of the text, which is "saturated with Lockean language," should convince the reader that Wesley and Edwards were determined to "modernize" Christianity, which, indeed, is their major achievement. "And by so modernizing Christianity," Brantley maintains, "Wesley and Edwards lay the intellectual as well as emotional groundwork for religious expression not simply in the Anglo-American Enlightenment, but in the Anglo-American world of the nineteenth century as well" (p. 36). . . .

"The next step," Brantley insists, "is to complete the connection between the abridgment and American as well as British literature." This step, which he calls "a logical one," provides the theme to which the second half of the book is devoted. "For the remainder of this book," he writes, "I look for the mature expression of this Anglo-American character in the vital synthesis and complex entity of nineteenth-century British and American letters, for the abridgment, as I have approached it, provides access to Carlyle and Emerson" (p. 41). Carlyle, we are told, is "descended from the empirical/evangelical dialectic" (p. 43). . . . Indeed, the key to Carlyle's "romanticism" is to be found in the "philosophical theology shared by Wesley and Edwards" (p. 73). More than that, his romanticism can be "most precisely described as Anglo-American in that its 'spiritual sense' rivals the methodological efficacy of Wesleyan-Edwardsean philosophical theology" (p. 75). The extent to which Carlyle's "transcendentalism" is derived from Kant and the German idealists, or his "romanticism" from Goethe and Schiller, is a secondary matter. "His original ideas," we are told, "have more to do with his various English-language origins, empiricism and evangelicalism among them, than with German sources" (p. 45).

Brantley's discussion of Emerson runs along similar lines. Emerson, we are told, "is both a transcendentalist and an empiricist": "Thus I situate Emerson on the empirical ground of evangelical faith" (p. 77). . . .

. . . Brantley has decided that Emerson put Edwards on a high plane. "For Emerson to have admired Edwards's writing," we are told, "his admiration of Edwards's thought must have been great indeed" (p. 93). The expression "must have," of course, should be noted; for there is very little evidence that Emerson read Edwards in any depth at all.

Finally, we are asked to accept that Wesley's influence on Emerson was profound. "It might even be said," writes Brantley, "that, also like Wesley, who was literally the rival of Franklin, Emerson was an effective *evangelical* preacher." Great admiration for Wesley can be found in Emerson's journal, we are told. One finds his "experiential identification with John Wesley, or, at least, with what Wesley stood for" (p. 74). Because Emerson wrote in his journal (26 April 1834) that "a religion of forms is not for me: I honor Methodists who find like St. John all Christianity in one word, Love," Brantley concludes that "Emerson resembles Wesley" in numerous ways, especially in the "territorial boldness" of his preaching. "Just as 'the world' was Wesley's 'Parish,'" writes Brantley, "so New England was Emerson's" (p. 95). . . .

. . . Indeed, Brantley's argument builds to a resounding climax with a single sentence of extraordinary dimensions. In summing up *Nature*, he writes: "Its empirical themes of the tabula rasa, the physical senses, sense-based reason, the understanding, the waking consciousness, inductive method, radical skepticism, subject-object interaction, and nature-culture coevolution, and its evangelical themes of warm exhortation, personal conversion, immediate revelation, the religious affections, practical charity, moral action, spiritual perfection, and millennial expectation, are joined through its empirical-evangelical themes of Berkeleyan immaterialism, theistical natural religion, the doctrine of proportional analogy, and, clearly, not least, the doctrine of the 'spiritual sense'" (pp. 117-18).

As he brings his book to a close, Brantley tries once again to show that the philosophical theology shared by Wesley and Edwards "applies to Carlyle and Emerson" (p. 145). . . . Although Brantley offers no concrete proof that either Emerson or Carlyle ever read the abridgment, he nonetheless makes extravagant claims for it: "This important British version of an important American work lends its authoritative perspective to an empirical-evangelical vision of intellectual history, religious culture, and literature in the English-speaking world, for common to the sensibilities of England and the United States is the single, though twofold, tradition of empirical philosophy and evangelical faith" (p. 150).

We must ask ourselves, however, to what extent the abridgment is a "British version" of an "American work." We are told at the start that while Wesley and Edwards "never consciously cooperated with one another," a "special relationship between the Englishman John Wesley and the American Jonathan Edwards" was established. We are also told that this "relationship" had directly to do with matters that were important for "both England and the United States" (p. 7). . . . [Brantley] shares with other American scholars the need to impose an "American" identity on colonial times. Unwilling to detach the colonial from the early national period, he proceeds as though they were one and the same.
–**Norman Pettit,** *The New England Quarterly* (June 1994)

55. Combine a devout Arminian, a transcendentalist, and two Calvinists (one a prophetic evangelical, the other disaffected although never entirely separated from Calvin's presence), and what have we? A strange, anomalous mixture, hardly the ingredients expected to blend smoothly in a satisfying scholarly study. Richard E. Brantley, however, manages to construct an intriguing relationship among four major figures of the late eighteenth and early nineteenth centuries. . . . He provides a strong case for a commonality between American and English Romanticism and a number of fresh insights into the works of these important men, especially their roots in Lockean sensationalism and their clear empirical methodology.... Nevertheless, many modern evangelicals will find it difficult not to part company with some of Brantley's conclusions, and Calvinist readers in particular will detect an Arminian bias. **Norman M. Carson**, *Christianity & Literature* (Summer 1994)

56. What is new here is the inclusion of John Wesley as the fourth member of a group which, according to Brantley, established the coordinates of Anglo-American romanticism. Wesley is vital to his argument, which seeks to set up a broad schema for what he sees as an international culture that can best be understood by using the combined approaches of literature, philosophy, and religion.... Whatever view one may take of his argument, Brantley's book is important for the premises on which it is based: that there is and has long been an Anglo-American culture worthy of study, and that the religious beliefs of writers are important and demand consideration in any analysis of their works. One can only agree. The transatlantic book trade has flourished for at least two centuries, and the passage of ideas in both directions provides a fruitful area of study. So too do the religious views of both British and American writers, for they form a significant part of the meaning of their works. Brantley is right to base his book on these premises. **—Donald A. Ringe**, *American Notes and Queries* (July 1994)

57. Despite its tendency to avoid recognizing conflict, this is a quirky book—as suits a study that unselfconsciously elevates John Wesley, father of Methodism, as the heretofore unrecognized progenitor of a joint British and American literary tradition. Brantley is certainly on to something: The relationship between British and American literature is richer than is typically understood, and the basis of that relationship in the eighteenth and nineteenth centuries was heavily indebted to similar ideological perspectives in the two countries. Yet to say that two literatures are related is not to say they are the same. **—Stacy L. Spencer**, *Nineteenth-Century Prose* (Fall 1994)

58. Brantley explains cogently that "Locke would separate the Spirit from natural operations," while "Wesley and Edwards do not."... Although lucidly written, the section on Edwards and Wesley may prove heavy going for literary readers not used to theological discussion. They will feel more at home in the ensuing sections on Carlyle and Emerson, though Brantley's treatment of these two writers remains somewhat philosophical and theological.... The section on Emerson is in my opinion the most interesting because the most complex.... Brantley concludes by extending the application of his argument, sometimes drawing too many writers into his net.... The survey of Americanist scholarship to reinforce his argument seems superfluous, but the extracts from the Carlyle-Emerson correspondence are valuable. The book's argument is consistently strong and interesting, and with some exceptions mainly convincing. —**Robert Langbaum**, *The Wordsworth Circle* (Autumn 1994)

59. Brantley skillfully demonstrates how eagerly Wesley adapted the New World theologian who would have seemed the polar opposite. ... By stressing Wesley's intellectualism, Brantley leaves one guessing at the Methodists' subsequent intellectual flabbiness—what Sidney Ahlstrom called simply their anti-intellectualism—though it is a signal service merely to establish the conundrum.... Brantley's transatlantic emphasis offsets the still prevalent emphasis on exceptionalism in American literature and history. The book sometimes focuses too intently on arcane differences among scholars without succinctly explaining either their views or the importance of their interpretations, but it does not commit the same sins when discussing Wesley, Carlyle, and Emerson directly, all of whom can be seen in some new light here, both individually and collectively. —**Jon Butler**, *American Literature* (Spring 1995)

60. *Coordinates* *of Anglo-American Romanticism* has several purposes, most of them achieved, by means of the author's extensive scholarship, extraordinary command of his eighteenth-century materials, and pertinacity of argument. Of these purposes, the one most polemically announced, and proclaimed in the book's title, is to re-establish "Anglo-American literature" as a "valid concept", now that the "adolescent insecurity that demanded independence from tradition" has been shed (p. 1). Pursuing this claim, Brantley reaches the conclusion that Carlyle's and Emerson's "friendship, having much to do with the Anglo-American sensibility shared by Wesley and Edwards, virtually founded Anglo-American literature" (p. 141). But precisely what such a literature is or how Carlyle and Emerson are its founders remains obscure. Certainly we are here a long way from the Edwards who hoped that "the sun of the new heavens and new earth... shall rise in the West", revealing "America a brighter type of heaven", and from the Emerson who wished to "extract the tapeworm of Europe from the brains of our countrymen". —**R. W. (Herbie) Butterfield**, *Modern Language Review* (Spring 1995)

61. This is a new and important study of Anglo-American romanticism. The presence of Wesley and Edwards in this book indicates that Brantley's theological interests are again very much in the forefront of his study, and indeed it is into the currently flourishing area of literature and theology that his scholarship most readily falls. . . . In pursuing his thesis, Professor Brantley sees himself very much at odds with the approach to America's cultural history which is concerned above all to insist on the distinctiveness of the national culture. In this tradition, American transcendentalism has its roots in America's own religious past—not in German or English or Scottish philosophy. Professor Brantley probably has the better case in this general argument: American culture has long been secure enough to be able to acknowledge its European debts. And he demonstrates that the specific network of parallels and relationships involving Edwards and Wesley, Emerson and Carlyle, is tight indeed. . . . In the book's conclusion, the empirical-evangelical continuum is seen by the author, in almost evangelical spirit, as all-embracing in terms of time as well as space. Even Mrs Thatcher's youthful Methodism gets a mention. One's final impression remains that of a challenging book, simultaneously reductive and widely ranging. **—Andrew Hook**, *Notes & Queries* (June 1995)

62. We should welcome Richard E. Brantley's particular vision of Carlyle's debt to the methodologies of John Wesley and Jonathan Edwards. *Coordinates of Anglo-American Romanticism* is a scholar's book: its logic is thick and its arguments dense. One especially appreciates Brantley's intimate acquaintance with Wesley and Edwards. Indeed, it is this very acquaintance that shadows Brantley's persistent argument that Carlyle, among others, had the "empirical-evangelical sensibility" (5) in the tradition of Wesley and Edwards. Such a thesis is provocative, if not revolutionary. . . . Unfortunately, Brantley does not have time and space to ponder as he marches through and past Carlyle's ever-changing vision. . . . No matter. Brantley's central thesis, the essential "Anglo-American Romanticism of Carlyle," which joins "empiricism to heart-religion [evangelicalism]" (75) and thus addresses the dilemma of a Romantic becoming a Victorian, leaves us with a great deal to think about. Our debt, then, is not to the substance of Brantley's arguments, but to the provocations they create. *Coordinates of Anglo-American Romanticism* is a book well worth reading, both for what it does and does not say. There are quibbles that could be made, such as putting in italics Carlyle's essays as if they were books, or the misdating of *Sartor Resartus*, or the use of corrupt texts as authority. Yet such defects are more than compensated for by the uniqueness of Brantley's vision(s). The book is handsomely presented by the University Press of Florida, which adds to its appeal. **–Rodger L. Tarr**, *Carlyle Studies Annual* (1995)

63. Brantley's evaluation of Carlyle's early essay, "Signs of the Times" (1829), is particularly effective, but there is a Johnny, or rather Richard one-note tendency in his constant search for "empirical," "evangelical" and Wesleyan overtones in Carlyle's thought. . . . While Brantley is not alone in looking beyond German influences for keys to Carlyle's thought, those profound influences cannot be ignored in considering Carlyle, yet that is precisely what Brantley has done in *Coordinates of Anglo-American Romanticism*. **–D. J. Trela**, *Victorian Periodicals Review* (Winter 1996)

64. This reorientation . . . constructs the bridges that link the religious, philosophical, literary, and national-cultural traditions [Brantley] discusses. Kenneth Burke, in an essay on Emerson and prophecy, remarked that the roots of the word "pontificate" lie in the construction of a bridge, a pons, between various positions and even, in the case of Emerson, between this world and the next. What I find chiefly attractive in the pontifications of Brantley's text is its insistence on the worldly significance of the religious footings he establishes for these writers. Despite his obvious investments in evangelical methodism, he finds occasion to criticize the political directions that abridgments between real world politics and enthusiastic religion by Carlyle, Emerson, and their readers sometimes facilitate. Like Christopher Lasch, Harold Bloom, and other recent commentators, Brantley reminds us that modern culture in the United States and England is rooted in religious soil. Better than Lasch or Bloom he carefully establishes and analyzes the specific intellectual and theological sedimentations upon which Anglo-American culture in particular rests, for better or for worse. I wonder, however, why the empirical evangelical tradition of Anglo-American romanticism should be limited to the small group of figures he here considers. In particular what does this abridgment of religion, philosophy, literature, and politics suggest about a figure like Frederick Douglass whose personal and professional relation to the religious and experiential worlds was especially rich and vexed? What stake do the vast numbers of non Anglo-Americans have in this culture and these traditions? Can this study shed light on the rhetoric and power of the evangelical right in contemporary United States politics? The most significant contribution of Brantley's abridgment of religious, historical, and literary study may be that it leads to these and many other questions. **—John Michael**, *Studies in Romanticism* (Fall 1996)

65. Brantley's brief for linking the British and American experience in a common sensibility is fervent. . . . Brantley's scholarship is both broad and deep; his manner perhaps more earnest Victorian than heady Romantic. **—Frank Jordan**, *The Romantic Movement* (1997)

66. Reading Wesley's and Edwards's philosophical theology becomes a useful and illuminating historical and heuristic context for reading Carlyle and Emerson. A fine, and stimulating, addition to Brantley's typical exegetical mode, now focused less on "method" than on bridging. **—Robert F. Gleckner,** *The Romantic Movement* (1997)

67. Considering that Calvinism is, in Wesley's own words, "the direct antidote to Methodism," it is not surprising that most studies of eighteenth-century evangelicalism have avoided overlapping discussions of the individuals who served as their respective mid-century American and English representatives. The exceptions are notable, if sporadic, beginning in the early 1960s with Albert C. Outler. In an edition of Wesley's writings, Outler goes so far as to claim that the Great Awakening as led by Jonathan Edwards was a significant source for Wesley's own revival in England (*John* 16). Edwards himself, Outler further argues, "always minus his 'Calvinism,'" contributed significantly to the evangelical aspects of Wesley's Methodism (16n54). After Outler critics such as Charles Rogers, Gregory Clapper, Frederick Dreyer, and Richard E. Brantley have variously taken up the subject; the first three focus predominantly on theologically or philosophically based differences, whereas Brantley instead looks at their epistemological similarities.

. . . Rogers infers that Edwards, in a position clearly more antinomian than Arminian, would disapprove of Wesley's doctrine of perfection because it puts too great emphasis on the believer's personal powers over God's sovereignty. . . . [Clapper points to] a tension between Wesley's practical, outward-oriented theology and Edwards's antinomian tendency (evident especially in the "Personal Narrative") to concern itself precisely with the formative powers of mystical-intuitive "inner experience" to the neglect of the world-oriented aspects of spiritual life. . . . [For Dreyer the differences are] "not so much theological as metaphysical. Wesley is an empiricist in his basic assumptions and Edwards a rationalist. The former is preoccupied with the world of perception, the latter with the world of necessary relationships." . . .

As an alternative to this wholly metaphysical version of Edwards, it is certainly appealing instead to consider him in epistemological terms that seem more commensurate with present taste, as Brantley does in *Coordinates of Anglo-American Romanticism: Wesley, Edwards, Carlyle, and Emerson.* Why indeed discuss any theologian's influence (in this case into the nineteenth century) in terms of largely obsolete dogma, including discomfiting ideas such as innate depravity and irresistible grace? [The footnote to this sentence, Bennett 257-8, reads as follows: In *Varieties of Religious Experience*, William James had already begun to feel a similar uneasiness and expressed it in political terms: the cruel and arbitrary "monarchical type of sovereignty" of Puritan America's God seemed "positively to have been required by their imagination. . . . But to-day we abhor the very notion of eternal suffering inflicted; and that arbitrary dealing-out of salvation and damnation to selected individuals, of which Jonathan Edwards could persuade himself that he had not only a conviction, but 'delightful conviction,' as of a doctrine 'exceeding pleasant, bright, and sweet,' appears to us, if sovereignly anything, sovereignly irrational and mean." He goes on to argue that as a culture we dispense with any belief system whenever it ceases to follow the perceived direction in which the culture is tending—in America's case, of course, the movement from monarchy to democracy.] Brantley seeks not difference but synthesis of Wesley's and Edwards's shared Lockean epistemologies and their combined influence on nineteenth-century Anglo-American thought. He argues convincingly that experience is one of the most powerful connections between the seemingly irreconcilable empirical ("natural") and evangelical ("spiritual") epistemologies: in both traditions "one must see for oneself and be in the presence of the thing one knows." On this basis Wesley, Edwards, Carlyle, and Emerson seek finally to "theologize empiricism" by balancing faith with reason, myth with scientific fact, and through an inclusive "both/and" philosophical approach to theology, "they share the simultaneously rational and sensationalist reliance on experience as the avenue to both natural and spiritual knowledge" (1).

By taking this line, Brantley explicitly chooses to emphasize the "aesthetic-epistemological" over the "ontological" Edwards (9-10). Curiously while he argues for Wesley's and Edwards's "both/and" philosophy of empirical evangelicalism, he limits his own treatment of Edwards to epistemo-

logical concerns. One consequence of this choice is that the argument does not fully do justice to the fact of Edwards's Calvinism and its central role in shaping his attitude toward experience and its formation of individual identity. More attention to Edwards's theology would, of course, lead away from a synthetic vision and enter into serious and possibly irreconcilable differences between the two figures, or everything that the differences between Arminianism on the one hand and antinomianism on the other would entail.
—**Kelsey L. Bennett,** *Principle and Propensity: Experience and Religion in the Nineteenth-Century British and American Bildungsroman* (Columbia: U of South Carolina P, 2014), 31-34.

Anglo-American Antiphony: The Late Romanticism of Tennyson and Emerson (1994)

68. Brantley's best book yet. It is wonderfully lively and informative, and actually provides a conspectus of much of the current, ongoing scene in academic literary criticism. Brantley is hugely erudite and full of a quiet humor, and he writes in a clear, concise style. —**Harold Bloom**, reader for the University Press of Florida

69. Both the empirical and the evangelical influences [are] convincingly presented and illustrated, and I am willing to believe, on the basis of the argument, that the poetry and the prose do indeed find a unity, if not a significant closure, in the tension. The attitudes toward death (a theme dominant in Tennyson and strong in Emerson) . . . emerge more clearly here than in most of the other criticism I know on these writers. —**Robert Detweiler**, reader for the University Press of Florida

70. Brantley spends part of his introduction in a survey of Romantic theory, creating something like a catalogue of names (19-23), and his conclusion places his critical approach—a history-of-ideas approach involving the synthesis of empirical and evangelical positions—in comparison to the three current approaches of feminism, New Historicism, and deconstruction (245-61). Thus, besides the readings of the individual works, there is a scholarly background framing the discourse. . . .

The claim is not that Tennyson is a Wesleyan Christian, nor indeed an orthodox Christian of any kind, but that his "religious imagination" is shaped by the theological positions of his day and background so that his heterodoxy is best understood through a consideration of the Lockean and Wesleyan tradition.... Brantley's words mean that I will have to consider the text [of *In Memoriam*] again....

Let me repeat that this is a valuable book. It traces the synthesis of two sides of the Victorian age—one religious, one this-worldly—in the literary works. And Brantley insists that it is a synthesis, not just a juxtaposition. The volume offers good specific readings, based on but going beyond the published criticism. Within its period it will be a significant study for an understanding of the times and the works. And for readers of this journal, it records the influence of a Christian culture on literary works in interesting ways. — **Joe R. Christopher**, *Christianity & Literature* (Winter 1994)

71. Richard Brantley's use of "antiphony," and his structuring of chapters with further musical titles like "Themes and Variations," "Introit," and "Recapitulation and Cadenza," an imaginative and ingratiating idea, give his book a more personal touch than it otherwise might have had as he investigates "the triangle of philosophy, religion, and literature [in] a case study of the sociology of ideas" (23). He aims to achieve antiphony on several levels by his lengthy discussion of empiricism and evangelicalism, experience and faith, as they are unified into a synthesis in the works of his two authors, concentrating upon Tennyson's "In Memoriam" and five of Emerson's major essays. By broadening his consideration of writers to include Blake, Wordsworth, Coleridge, and others, he establishes his claim to being an intellectual historian as well as a critic.

Tennyson's classic seems a natural choice for study. Its view of a harsh Nature for the first half of the poem is well grounded upon the poet's knowledge of science, and its later expressions of faith seem hard won. The chapters on "Empirical Procedures," "Evangelical Principles," and "Philosophical Theology" are solid and sensible elaborations of the poem's troubled journey from doubt to belief....

Though the selected Emerson essays are far superior as works of art to Tennyson's poem, Brantley has a more difficult time in his exposition of their contents. A few stanzas of "In Memoriam," strategically quoted, display the best side of the poet, but short quotations from Emerson's prose rarely give a sense of his excellence. Likewise, having to restrict each of several chapters to discussion of a single essay, rather than to themes from a single work, put the author at some disadvantage. But he offers a skillful summary of Emerson's thought, particularly in the chapters on "Self-Reliance" and "The Over-Soul." Again, the chapter on language method is interesting for what it says of Emerson's theory of language and its limitations....

A great deal of time, perhaps too much, is expended in recapitulating the work of other scholars, but, on the other hand, Brantley displays a real breadth of scholarly reference. He has read and absorbed much, and he offers excellent quotations and paraphrases on critical opinion in order to agree, build upon, or diverge from it. And, in the handling of his texts, his "philosophically theological method of close reading" (273) often yields substantially rewarding results. **—Douglas Robillard**, *Journal of the Early Republic* (Fall 1994)

72. Brantley's leading idea (one might say his *idée fixe*) is that a distinctive and pervasive Anglo-American experiential sensibility developed out of the philosophy of Locke and the theologies of Wesley and Edwards. These three thinkers are commanding presences for Brantley and, he claims, for the most significant English-language writers of the romantic period. . . . *Anglo-American Antiphony* is a work of large ambition and large defects, a work that simultaneously fascinates and frustrates. However, the goal it aspires to—a therapy for the "sickness unto death" (that is, the divided self)—is so needed that even a flawed attempt to attain it is welcome. **—Steve Gowler**, *Church History* (June 1995)

73. The antiphony referred to in the title of this volume relates not, as the innocent reader might at first suppose, to England and America, or even to Tennyson and Emerson, primarily, but to the "antiphonal, nonunisonary 'unity' of resonant doubleness" which Richard Brantley finds in the coexistence of empiricism and evangelicalism within Anglo-American culture. Tennyson and Emerson are both taken as exemplars of this quality. As virtual contemporaries, working in cultures profoundly affected by the inheritance of Locke's empiricism, and by the Lockean Edwards and the Edwardsean Wesley, they create their own antiphonal commentaries upon broadly similar questions of faith and hope.

Direct comparison between the two writers is in fact almost wholly absent from this book. Instead, each is examined in terms of their empirical-evangelical antiphony, as each independently addresses such challenges as the conflict of science and religion, the meaning of death, the absorption of Lyellian geology. Tennyson is explored under such headings as "empirical procedures," "evangelical principles," "theodicean impulse," and "language method." Only the last of these is used again for Emerson, but the separate discussion of the two writers is so consistently concerned with their marriage of spiritual insight and spiritual vision that a comparison in depth is achieved by implication. This discussion of each is enriched by generous and genial reference to the critical scholarship on the two writers, and an impressive range of contemporary theoretical disputations. Some four hundred scholars and critics appear in the list of works cited, including almost every recent commentator on Emerson or Tennyson and virtually all of the major (as well as many minor) combatants in the current disciplinary wars. Brantley's approach is so critically erudite that very few readers will be familiar with all of the perspectives he manages to find room for in an impressively collegial (but by no means neutral) colloquy.

The work is presented as the completion of a tetralogy addressed to the examination of this empirical-evangelical model of Anglo-American culture. This sustained inquiry began with *Wordsworth's "Natural Methodism"* (1975), in which John Wesley's theology was used to gloss Wordsworth's Romanticism, and Wordsworth's "view of a nature that warms the heart, informs the mind, and provides a standard of value for the actions of men" was persuasively treated as showing him working in "alliance with a prevalent mode of thought and feeling." In *Locke, Wesley, and the Method of English Romanticism* (1984) Wesley's adaptation of Locke's empiricist epistemology was used to elucidate the marriage of natural observation and imagination in Romantic poetry. An exploratory symbiotic essay on "The Common Ground of Wesley and Edwards" (1990) developed the challenging argument that the Arminian John and the Calvinist Jonathan are even closer empirically than they are evangelically, and the Atlanticist dimension of this argument was then elaborated in *Coordinates of Anglo-American Romanticism: Wesley, Edwards, Carlyle, and Emerson* (1993). The present book offers a surprisingly wide-ranging set of variations on the theme established more systematically in the earlier works....

Brantley's Tennyson is a less riven or driven character than that of other readers. His poem is not divided between its skepticism and its affirmation, lurching helplessly between "sense-based reason . . . and spiritual sense." Rather it interrelates science and religion because "fundamentally . . . it finds no irremediable controversy between empiricism and evangelicalism." The book's argument for Tennyson's empiricism is supported, of course, by Tennyson's receptivity to inductive science, of which his knowledge was, Brantley claims, deeper than either Coleridge's or Carlyle's, enabling him not merely to incorporate the data of Lyell's *Principles* but (as Jerome Buckley suggests) to articulate fully the disquieting implications of human evolution which Lyell leaves implicit. Its claims for his "evangelicalism" are, to me, less persuasive.

Brantley's Tennyson is better informed biblically than mine, and his lyrics make more telling allusion to scriptures than the one I read each year (I am, by the way, grateful for Brantley's ears and eyes, as he is for those of Christopher Ricks and other generously acknowledged commentators) but he is much less troubled by biblical/scientific rifts. His evangelical warmth—"And like a man in wrath the heart / Stood up and answered, I have felt"—is not immediately answered, as in my text it is, by "No, like a child in doubt and fear." In this reading, the sister's sunny and "literal creed" is privileged over the brother's doubt. The opening quatrains of the prologue suggest "a harmonious or at any rate unproblematic, relationship between science on the one hand and experiential faith on the other." This *In Memoriam* reaches an empirical-evangelical synthesis where mine is a drama of moods punctuated by periodic shipwreck.

Contrariwise, mine can enjoy picturing evolution in industrial terms, where "Life is not as idle ore, // But iron dug from central gloom, / And heated hot with burning fears, / And dipt in baths of hissing tears, / And battered with the shocks of doom / To shape and use," while Brantley's Tennyson, in these same lines, "recoils at the violent means employed by evolutionary reality." My section 95 is a quasi-erotic experience of reunion with Hallam, leading to the apotheosis of the honest doubter in 96, facing the spectres of the mind, where Brantley's section 95 is a spiritual revelation leading to the religious affirmation of 106 ("Ring out the old, Ring in the new") as "the high water-mark of the empirical-evangelical continuum in British if not Anglo-American literature." All in all, I find Brantley's reading of *In Memoriam* unsettling. If sometimes unconvincing, it is refreshingly uncoercive, since it allows at many stages for contrapuntal voices and radically different Tennysons.

Much the same may be said of the treatment of Ralph Waldo Emerson. The book sets out, specifically, to challenge the notion of Emerson as one who experienced a fall of some sort from freedom into fate, or aspiration into acceptance of "the fated limitations of human power." Instead, "From the beginning to the end of Emerson's prime his specific aim if not his accomplishment was to unite empiricism with evangelicalism." This formula, incidentally, neatly differentiates Emerson from Coleridge, though rather at the risk, it seems to me, of conflating his career with that of Jonathan Edwards. Troubled by the Emerson that others (Nietzsche, for instance) find most engaging—the one who creates the antinomian excesses of "Self-Reliance"—Brantley finds in the same essay a reassuringly scriptural Emerson for whom Self-Reliance is typed in John Wesley, soul-brother, and sect-founder.

Perhaps because it is a sequel to *Coordinates of Anglo-American Romanticism*, where the Emerson-Carlyle connection is primary, the work does not ask whether Emerson can be profitably or realistically considered without continuous and specific reference to Coleridge and Carlyle, whose styles and substances constantly obtrude in the quotations offered. Interestingly, however, the search for an empirical Emerson invites another (unstated) comparison. This Emerson, in which *Fate* and *Experience* are not sequels to but part and parcel of the Emersonian prime is as Melvillean as Melville himself. Whether one believes in him, altogether, is not the point. Brantley makes room, as he does in discussing Tennyson, for a variety of hecklers from other critical perspectives, including that of Yvor Winters (Emerson had "the gift of style without the gift of thought") and those for whom his work begins in sentimental optimism and ends in contradiction. The idea that *Experience* (1844) and *Fate* (1852) demonstrate that the optimism of *Nature* (1836) and *The American Scholar* (1837) is "well-earned" will not persuade everyone. But the Emerson on offer here is a quintessentially Romantic figure, and a major one, who reconciles the ideal and the ordinary through what Abrams [with reference to Blake] calls 'the sustained tension, without victory or suppression, of co-present oppositions.'"

Anglo-American Antiphony ends with a critical-theoretical skirmish, or "cadenza" in Brantley's term, in which a spirited but genial argument is made for a revival of "humanity, if not humanism" in English studies, based upon a methodology which values "nature- and spirit-grounded proliferation of meaning" over "language-centered subversion of meaning." Brantley, clearly, is *au fait* with rather than at home in the post-Derridean world of critical theory and practice. His selection of Emerson and Tennyson for this study is impelled in part by a genetic sense of relationship to their tradition (as a descendant of "four generations of Waldo Emerson Brantleys") and in part by an admiration of their "unembellished, lucid, and revealing styles." Writing works which are "sufficiently pluralistic . . . to avoid the closure of too much order," and modern enough to avoid the univocal, the unplayful, Tennyson and Emerson nevertheless speak with conviction: "putting the weight of their lives behind the words they speak." Rather a good mission statement, one might feel, for a dissenting academy. —**Richard Gravil**, *The Wordsworth Circle* (Autumn 1997)

74. Richard E. Brantley has devoted his scholarly life to exploring the religious dimensions of Romantic literature and [he] brings to bear an impressive expertise whenever he addresses the subject. . . . It needs to be said nonetheless that Professor Brantley and I read the British Romantic writers quite differently and have come to different conclusions about the religious significance of their work. Rather than indulging the pleasure of reviewing the broad areas of agreement that I share with Brantley, . . . it would be more interesting and fruitful . . . to indicate how we differ in our understanding of the religious character of British Romanticism. . .

Brantley's primary interest is in religion, while mine is politics. . . . A politically alert critical perspective does not prevent or substitute for a religious commitment, necessarily, but it must be content to watch its religious preferences competing with other self-assured versions of truth and codes of conduct. . . . I concede that Calvinism and Arminianism may serve as synechdoche for permanent or recurrent tendencies in the religious imagination . . . . The Romantics would have agreed with the basic Arminian insistence that human values must govern any proper description of the relationship between God and His creatures, a relationship that should be morally comprehensible, ethically defensible, and socially useful. But since these humanist principles can be traced back in the Judeo-Christian tradition as far as the Pentateuch, it is not clear to me what purpose is served by describing them as "Arminian." . . . Percy Bysshe Shelley's "threefold theme of charity, mercy, and forgiveness," which Brantley identifies as an Arminian strain in the poet's thought, can be traced more simply and more persuasively to the Bible, a book that Shelley read with passionate attention all his life. . . .

Brantley has at times reminded me of an enthusiastic usher forcefully escorting to the front pews those who would prefer to observe the services from the church door. . . . Brantley and I agree that Percy Shelley is the central protagonist in the Romantic campaign for religious reformation, . . . but one ought to acknowledge . . . that the poet finally despaired of purifying Christianity . . . .

When Brantley detects in Romanticism "the doubt/faith dialectic of the Protestant tradition," he does not take the doubt seriously enough to allow for a genuine dialectic. . . . He likes to think of religious doubt as a healthy Protestant (even Methodist) instinct rather than as a possible prelude to or synonym for atheism. . . . What he wants, he says, is an Hegelian synthesis, a mechanism by which the Romantics' "contradictions merge into a higher truth that comprehends them, and through which their opposites are continuously unified." This search for a higher, reconciling truth is, I think, the essential difference between my vision of Romanticism and Professor Brantley's.

Contradictions are, for me, what makes British Romanticism an especially exciting intellectual movement, in art as well as in religion. . . . One hears in [the Romantics] the true, uncompromising, unsynthesizable doubt/faith dialectic that inspired the Romantic Reformation. To turn from Shelley's allegory to Blake's, using the energy generated by the conflict between authoritarian Urizen and antinomian Luvah, the artist-prophet Los struggles to forge a merciful, imaginative, socially redemptive religious vision. But such a vision requires the perpetual vitality of an intractably irreligious Luvah, an antithesis powerful enough to resist any Hegelian *Aufhebung*.... It is not as Christians but as heretics and apostates and maverick mystics that the Romantics continue to exert a powerful religious influence on their readers. **–Robert M. Ryan**, *Christianity & Literature* (Autumn 1999)

Experience and Faith: The Late-Romantic Imagination of Emily Dickinson (2004, 2008)

75. In *Experience and Faith* Richard E. Brantley accomplishes a rich and deep recontextualization of Emily Dickinson's mind and art. Focusing on her experiential approach both to fact and to faith, Brantley moves from "the village to the world" in tracing out the poet's weblike connections with major figures in native as well as transatlantic nineteenth-century religion, literature, and culture. One of his most surprising discoveries is Dickinson's dialectical testing out of a private religion of the heart, stiffened by the tradition of British empiricism and cushioned by John Wesley's redactions of the difficult theology of Jonathan Edwards. Both of these formidable intellectual explorations are done with knowledge and grace. This is a scholarly yet personal study of the entire Dickinson corpus, packed with fresh close readings of major poems and animated by a philosophical thrust that demonstrates an admirable sensitivity to the creative heft of the past as well as a lively sense of the complex present. **–Barton Levi St. Armand,** reader for Palgrave Macmillan

76. With considerable wit and passion, Richard Brantley puts his impressive learning to work in *Experience and Faith*. By situating Emily Dickinson within the Wesleyan tradition and an Anglo-American context, he provides us with a refreshing way of rethinking the connections between Dickinson's poetry and her religious thought and experience. **–Roger Lundin,** reader for Palgrave Macmillan

77. [Roger Lundin's *Emily Dickinson and the Art of Belief,* 1998, 2004] argues that Dickinson is not only the greatest American poet but also, despite what she often perceived as her own "failure" at conversion, one of the finest religious thinkers of her day. This thematic critical biography sweeps away many former assumptions and generalizations about the Calvinism of Dickinson's family and community. No longer harshly Puritan, the Congregationalist Church of her time merged with the prevailing Whig culture of New England to create a genteel, rational, restrained alternative to the "undiluted" Calvinism of Jonathan Edwards and his age. "It was an ideal faith for men of the rising professional class," men like the poet's father Edward Dickinson, and "it would prove to be a superb foil for Emily Dickinson," according to Lundin. Like Nietzsche, but with a very different tone, she confronted head-on the possible loss of God in an age dominated by scientific materialism and advancing secularization.

Richard E. Brantley's *Experience and Faith: The Late-Romantic Imagination of Emily Dickinson* (Palgrave) builds on Lundin's arguments. Brantley's main contribution is to explore how correspondences of Dickinson's work to evangelical Protestant philosophy, notably that of John Wesley's Arminianism, and other philosophical influences complicate her position between late Romantic and modernist poetics. "British empiricism and free-will evangelicalism," he argues, "contribute to the play of her late-Romantic imagination, for the scientific and technological prowess with which her poetic personae commit themselves to natural religion yields . . . to their Protestant witness and . . . Romantic hope." The "complexity and intrigue" of these personae, which distinguish them from "the despair and nihilism of Modernism and Postmodernism, derive from the dynamic of suspense through which their faith in experience shades over into their experience of faith." —**M. Jimmie Killingsworth,** *American Literary Scholarship: An Annual* (2004), David J. Nordloh, ed.

78. Brantley's first of two planned volumes on Emily Dickinson celebrates and analyzes her poems, letters, and prose fragments in a densely packed, erudite, and personal study that reflects his dialogue with past and contemporary thinkers. He says that Dickinson looks beyond the near influences of the Civil War and Charles Darwin and draws from her philosophical, religious, and literary heritage: "her Anglo-American triangle of empiricism, evangelicalism, and Romanticism hums through her career." Informed by John Locke, John Wesley, Jonathan Edwards, and 18th- and 19th-century empirical philosophy, Brantley says, "the broadly experiential, spiritual as well as natural epistemology of the Anglo-American world explains Anglo-American Romanticism in general and Dickinson's poetry in particular." Discussing more than 150 poems, he ranks "On a Columnar Self—" (Fr740) as "a signature lyric or miniature poetic manifesto of Dickinson's Late Romanticism." Asserting that her lyrical excellence remains unequalled, he says her "chief virtue lies in her tough-minded search for truth," and her "transcultural art represents the most invaluable resource that the Anglo-American heritage can provide—namely, optimism earned from experience." He concludes, "She out-thinks, out-believes, and out-imagines her Romantic precursors and coevals, as distinct from out-disbelieving the Moderns, or out-deconstructing the Postmoderns." --**Barbara Kelly,** *The Emily Dickinson International Society Bulletin* (November/December, 2005)

79. Richard E. Brantley's *Experience and Faith* is a wide-ranging consideration of Emily Dickinson's poetry, letters and prose fragments in the context of transatlantic Romanticism. The book is a thematically arranged exploration of Dickinson's evangelical experientialist method. Brantley uses three broad themes in his approach to Dickinson's work: "experimental trust" (chapter two), "nature methodized" (chapter three), and the "Romantic to Modern arc" (chapter four). Brantley situates these thematic concerns within deeply informed readings of Locke, Wesley and other nineteenth-century empiricists. I'll return to these thematic considerations after first briefly describing the contextual ground within which he explores them.

Dickinson deployed a "method," Brantley writes, rather than a "system" because, in A. Dwight Culler's words, we must distinguish "between system and method, two words which many people take to be synonymous but which seem to [F.D. Maurice, in *The Kingdom of Christ*] 'not only not synonymous, but the greatest contraries imaginable: the one [i.e., system] including that which is most opposed to life, freedom, variety; and the other [i.e., method] that without which they cannot exist.' . . . The terms are, indeed, useful for making distinctions throughout the century (8)." I think most readers will be struck by the appropriateness of the distinction as regards Dickinson in particular, but also by the wide applicability of the distinction across the nineteenth century. This, in short, is how Brantley justifies his transatlantic contextualizing approach to Dickinson: "Dickinson's modest, non-totalizing practice of method . . . defines her Late-Romantic imagination on the broadly experiential, skeptical yet testimonial, common ground between British empirical philosophy and free-will evangelical religion" (8).

Indeed, Brantley reminds us that, in Robert Langbaum's words, "The essential idea of Romanticism is the doctrine of experience" (10). But Dickinson is not a passive experiencer: she is a powerfully interrogative or, to use Brantley's preferred term, evangelical poet. "She makes clear" that "natural, spiritual, and aesthetic . . . experience constitutes her and her readers' sole mode of knowing, believing, and imagining" (10-11). Dickinson is by turns "tender-minded" and "tough-minded," an opposition Brantley returns to throughout *Experience and Faith*, but it is always these empirical considerations that motivate her work. Thus her work is based on "experiential faith"—"a seemingly absurd, oxymoronic, and self-contradictory phrase that, like waging peace, or well-known secret agent," is nonetheless "essentially true" (20)— and "religious epistemology" in the spirit, in Christa Buschendorf's words, "of American pragmatism inaugurated by Emerson" (21). Indeed, throughout his book Brantley uses Emerson as a sounding board or basso continuoso against which he tests the Romantic resonance of Dickinson's poetry.

For Brantley the spirit of pragmatism is important since, unlike post-modernist approaches to Dickinson's work (which he eschews), pragmatism does not dodge "issues of transcendence" (26). This is a key point in *Experience and Faith*, for it allows Brantley to take strong positions based on his own experience of reading Dickinson, rather than wallow in the impersonal, foundationless linguistic Sisyphism of post-modern criticism. This, then, is a brief précis of Brantley's approach; time now to turn to a synopsis of his thematic exploration of Dickinson's work.

In his second chapter, "Experimental Trust," Brantley again first foregrounds the importance of John Locke's empiricism, especially via the transatlantic evangelist and founder of Methodism, John Wesley. As Brantley points out, a number of books by these and similarly minded writers were in the library of Edward Dickinson, the father of the poet (21). The poet's grandfather and father both stressed the importance of the "cultivation of the female mind," a very Lockean idea, and insisted "that sons and daughters alike should receive a more scientific than strictly human education" (37). Thus "[s]choolgirl Dickinson breathed in empirical air" (39).

Overall, Brantley finds in Dickinson a preference for the applied over the pure, for praxis over theoria. He specifically reads the poet's work for leaps of experimental faith as regards a variety of scientific fields, for example medicine. "[E]ven when she invalidated a doctor's nostrum, she did so in an open-minded, receptive spirit of trial and error, or of scientific cooperation with her doctor-partner in the search for a cure" (48; see also *Letters* [Cambridge, 1958] 1:171-72). This is an example of Dickinson's trust in the scientific method, but her "experimental trust" has another, spiritual aspect: she is always retrospective, so that after a family friend died "she wrote to Elizabeth Holland . . . that 'living Fingers that are left have a strange warmth'" (49; *Letters* 3:685). This line echoes Keats' famous line, "This living hand now warm and capable" (49), and demonstrates that for Dickinson the personages of the dead live on in her imagination.

"Dwell[ing] in possibility" (a line Brantley quotes many times), the poet displays an optimism towards the power of the burgeoning industrial revolution in such poems as "Force Flame" (Poem 963 [all references are to the Franklin edition], quoted on page 52). Dickinson embraced all the sciences with "subtle, sense-related complexity" (55), but wrote particularly compelling poems using images and language from astronomy, biology, geology and the new challenge of evolution. Brantley seems especially sensitive to Dickinson's animal poems, for example Poem 359, which he says "celebrates the scientific sense in which the speaker and the bird share common ground" (71). What strikes me, though, is that Brantley himself, though apparently a lover of the natural world and thus deeply sympathetic to Dickinson's bios-themed poems, may not have spent much time in a lab. In discussing Poem 1181, "Experiment escorts us last— / His pungent company / Will not allow and Axiom / An Opportunity—" (quoted on page 71), he finds "pungent" to connote "sweaty, overwrought" and to be unflattering (71-72). But anyone who has spent any time in a chemistry lab instantly understands the word "pungent" to be a straightforward empirical observation regarding the aroma of such a place. Acidic, astringent, sulfuric—a chem lab's experimental results are "pungent company" indeed but are nothing like those of a "sweaty" and "overwrought" gymnasium, which is what Brantley seems to be thinking of here. This is a minor quibble, though, in an otherwise fascinating ramble through Dickinson's themes of experimental trust. What I was struck by, in rereading the many poems Brantley presents, is Dickinson's resistance to the fetishization of charismatic mammals; she prefers birds, bees and bugs, and the God of small things.

Chapter three, "Nature Methodized," is Brantley's foray (though even he never uses these terms) into a climatocritical and ecocritical reading of Dickinson. He discusses her "atmospheric conditions" and "perspective on the seasons" (81) and "her preference for spring and for summer" (85). Climatocriticism, a recent sub-discipline of ecocriticism that reads for images of weather and climate change, is a perfect approach to Dickinson, whose poetry abounds with storms. "The Wind begun to rock the Grass," for instance, is a brush with death and destruction; in Brantley's terms of experience and faith, it is a kind of "there but for the gust of God go I" thanksgiving, since the storm brewing in the first line "overlooked My Father's House" in the penultimate one (Poem 796, quoted on page 89).

Again, the wealth of biology in Dickinson's poetry is ripe for a deep-ecological exegesis. Brantley, for some reason, steers clear of an explicit reading in this respect, though the spiritual force he finds in her work makes his book important reading for ecocritics. "Four Trees—upon a solitary Acre—", for instance, is a perfect example of Dickinson experiencing the world as an interdependent entity, for "Without Design / Or Order, or Apparent Action—" the parts "Maintain—" the whole (Poem 778, quoted on page 93). In Dickinson's "Four Trees" we're seeing a witness to the God of nature at work and the poem is an emblematic example of Dickinson's "natural religion" (102-103).

In chapter four, "Romantic to Modern Arc," Brantley locates Dickinson within that historical arc as both forward- and backward-looking; she is "Janus-faced," as the author states in several places. She is skeptical of received opinion, but her skepticism is "[k]inetic, not deadening" (118). She evokes an "art of belief" that recognizes "the split between science and religion" (143). It seems to me that she bridges this split, if not precisely attempting to heal it. This is the "Compound Vision—" that "Reorganizes Estimate" (Poem 830, quoted on page 136).

Throughout *Experience and Faith* Brantley uses the famous "Negative Capability" passage from a letter of Keats much in the way he uses Dickinson's line "I Dwell in Possibility," that is, as a resonator against which his various thematic strings sound. And as sounding boards, the two ideas seem to me to harmonize beautifully. But I've always been puzzled, and here more than ever, at the elision of the final fragment of that famous, wandering sentence of Keats'. What the "poet-doctor" (174) wrote was that what "Shakespeare possessed so enormously" was "Negative Capability, that is, when a man is capable of being in uncertainties, mysteries, doubts, without any irritable reaching after fact and reason—Coleridge, for instance, would let go by a fine isolated verisimilitude caught from the Penetralium of mystery, from being incapable of remaining content with half-knowledge." But Brantley (and most everyone else, for that matter) leaves out everything after "reaching after fact and reason" (see, for example, page 13). What of "the Penetralium of mystery," this curious word that is unique in its usage in English (the rare penetralia being the standard spelling)? It seems that the Penetralium would only bolster Brantley's case here. The Penates were the gods of the hearth at the heart of the home; what could be more "naturally religious" than their "mysterium tremendum" (174)? Moreover, "being incapable of remaining content with half-knowledge" suggests the motor of skeptically imaginative curiosity that drives Dickinson and that Brantley so longs to share with us.

But share he does, especially in his final two chapters. He finds in Dickinson a poet of "hopeless love"—not hopeless from despair but in "manifoldness" (196) and irreducibility. That he saves this idea for the end—rather than letting it drive the book from the beginning, rather than making plain his own "hopeless love" for the poet at the outset—seems backwards to me. True, I think Brantley wants to mirror Dickinson's "Janus-faced" looking. But in his Acknowledgments, Brantley writes that he hopes "to cast a wide net, if only to catch a few in it" (iv). I'm not so sure his net is "wide," but it trawls very deep in the waters of transatlantic Romanticism. Nearly every paragraph of the book is loaded with quotes, from the primary sources, the Romantic writers themselves, as well as contemporary and historical critical commentary. And I wonder if this is a problem in "catching" readers: we don't actually get much of Richard E. Brantley until the final two chapters of the book. In short, I think the book might have been organized differently to greater effect. Having said that, I think this fascinating and deeply learned contribution to Dickinson studies deserves to be widely read—especially, as I indicated earlier, by ecocritics. There is much food for thought here, there is much scholarly legwork done here; in a couple hundred pages Brantley has distilled an era and captured something essential about Emily Dickinson. Whether we agree that hers was truly a "Late-Romantic imagination" or not, this book performs an invaluable service. —**Brian Clark**, *Consciousness, Literature and the Arts* (December, 2005)

80. In the context of what we now call transatlantic romanticism, J. Hillis Miller wrote some time ago of each work being a "node or intersection in an overdetermined network of associations, influences, constraints, and connections" and that "Each [intersection] must be patiently untangled and interpreted for itself" (in *Theory Now and Then* [1991], 225). Richard E. Brantley's newest study of the poetry of Emily Dickinson indeed patiently untangles and respectfully interprets the various points of association and connection in Dickinson's poetry between a British evangelicalism in the theology of John Wesley and a philosophical experiential tradition following from Locke. Brantley's method of combining religious and philosophical forms of knowledge to read Dickinson's poetry is helpful, in his words, for "sharpening [the] argumentative edge in Dickinson studies" (5) as well as more generally "hold[ing] that philosophy, religion, and literature figure in the special relationship between the United Kingdom and the United States" (175).

Thus, *Experience and Faith* covers much ground, not only in the author's wide reading and fine close readings of Dickinson's own poetry and letters, but also in his interactions with the theological and philosophical underpinnings of both Britain and America as influential for American poetry. *Experience and Faith* follows from Brantley's previous studies in transatlantic comparison, with particular reference to the religious, philosophical and literary climate of what he has called Anglo-American romanticism.

Brantley's method is far-reaching and deeply personal. *Experience and Faith* is both for the general reader—Brantley writes that the forty-eight sections may be read as one argument or as stand-alone sections from which to browse—as well as for the critic, as it resituates Dickinson in terms of historical and theological criticism rather than contributing to psychological or political readings. The first chapter, "Distinguishing Mode," sets up the twin axes on which Brantley's argument relies (namely, free-will evangelical theology and British empiricism) as indicative of Anglo-American romanticism generally and Dickinson's poetry in particular. In this short chapter Brantley gestures to his own as well as others' critical assessments of Dickinson that he explores more fully in chapter five.

Chapter Two, "Experimental Trust," examines the first intertwining between experience and faith where he argues that sensationalist epistemology and scientific rationalism are vital to an understanding of Dickinson's imagination. This chapter roots Dickinson's poetry both "in the world but not (quite) of it" in its relation to medicine, the Industrial Revolution and the biological and physical sciences. It also offers a helpful reading of Wesley's views on women's education and Dickinson's own education in the sciences.

It is chapter three, "Nature Methodized" (with its dual understanding of scientific method and Methodist theology), where Brantley's arguments and readings are most skillful. Brantley reads Dickinson's often-neglected nature poetry as indicative of the "central paradox of her 'naturalized imagination' and her 'poetic faith'" where "rich phenomena shade over into strange noumenon" (80). By reading nature through an empiricist lens and then reinvesting this with the mystery of faith, Dickinson poetically unites the seemingly contradictory categories of experience and faith. Following from Wesley's own "philosophy of experience" situated at once "within, as well as outside, nature," Dickinson's poetry evinces a "religion of nature" that is at least "ambiguous as to whether the natural and the supernatural can, or should, be reunified" (103). Brantley, like Dickinson, "dwells in Possibility" and both opens up and out the potential for both ecological and faith-informed readings of Dickinson in this chapter that will resonate beyond "the lady whom the people call the Myth."

The fourth chapter, "Romantic to Modern Arc," takes a step back from direct examination of experiential faith and faith in experience to focus through these categories on Dickinson's place both in relation to the High-Romantics and her Modern and Postmodern imitators. Brantley here again "dwells in Possibility" by treading a fine line between literary periods, preferring to read her imagination as Late-Romantic in that it has more in common with British High-Romantics than with the mode of Continental or Anglo-American Modernism. He therefore prefers to read her art as multiply informed: "*Modernist Romanticism* and *Romantic Modernism* largely denominate it. While *Romanticism* amply informs it, *Late Romanticism* labels it" (160). Establishing how her poetry both looks backward (and insinuating it also gazes across the Atlantic) as well as anticipates later writers' concerns, such as "out-rag[ing] Woolf and out-freez[ing] Frost" (163), Brantley clearly places Dickinson as bridging the gap between the Romantic and the Modern.

The final two chapters, "Practical Conspectus" and the Conclusion, are where Brantley as Dickinson devotee emerges from behind his academic argumentation and very personally professes his own faith in experience and hope for an experience of faith. Restating his thesis, Brantley writes: "Dickinson's expression validates, as opposed to ironizing, or seeing through, the empirical/evangelical dialectic of Anglo-American Romanticism, which she invites her reader to participate in, as well as to observe" (211). Brantley himself takes up this challenge directly; whereas the last four chapters had observed this empirical/evangelical dialectic, here he participates in it. The ordering of this penultimate chapter seems out of place, as Brantley's own descriptions of faith in experience and experiential faith are vital to his own Methodising where he uses Dickinson as "suggest[ing] . . . a way of overcoming the split between the natural and the supernatural and envision[ing] the terms of reunification" (188). These personal reflections as well as the review of Brantley's earlier work in transatlantic Romanticism would have been more helpful at an earlier point in the book, providing the context in which to read Brantley's own re-contextualization of Dickinson.

The idea of "Anglo-American Romanticism" brings me to my own penultimate point. As Brantley notes, "the perennial reciprocity on each side of, and back and forth across, the Atlantic between positive and negative poles of philosophical and religious values, and not the victory of one side over the other, makes the Anglo-American relationship special in the realm of literature" (175). Such observations, unfortunately, are rare. Brantley neglects to interrogate this hyphen between Anglo and America, a point that would have helpfully added to a theorizing of the transatlantic. It seems that at times in his efforts to display the various nodes and intersections between experience, faith, Britain and America, that rather than disentangling these intersections and arranging them in a manner that helps his reader to trace their interactions and implications, Brantley himself gets entangled in their paradoxical and multiplicious nature. This, of course, could simply be due to Brantley's efforts to "dwell in Possibility" as well as the nature of his wide-ranging study which testifies on every page to the author's familiarity with British and American Romanticism as well as with current-day criticism, theory, religious milieu, and pedagogy.

Additionally, more first-hand interaction with Wesley's own writings would, I imagine, be welcomed by readers. Brantley does include perceptive moments of reading Wesley (especially Wesley's abridgments of Edwards's works), but on the whole Brantley's interaction with him is simply as a way into Dickinson's imagination. A single chapter on Wesley would have been welcome to establish how Wesley espoused both a free-will evangelical as well as experiential theology through his writings; this, in turn, would have enabled Brantley to locate more precisely the exact modes of comparison between Wesley and Dickinson where the comparison is not exactly a Bloomian notion of "anxiety of influence" but also more specific than *"this* is somehow like *that."* —**Ashley Hales**, *Symbiosis: A Journal of Anglo-American Literary Relations* (2006)

81. In this ground-breaking, learned and passionately argued book, Richard Brantley places Emily Dickinson within the Anglo-American literary culture of late Romanticism on the basis of the Lockean-empirical aspects of her thought interacting with Arminian-evangelical Christian faith. He takes us back to the root meaning of "re-ligio" as a tying together of disunified forces, and he does so by a process of associative and analytic thinking that links Dickinson not only to Emerson but also to Jonathan Edwards, John Wesley, William Wordsworth, Gerard Manley Hopkins, and Alfred Lord Tennyson to establish the intellectual and emotional bases for her hard-earned optimism. He also posits significant links in approaches to religious faith between Dickinson and her "dearest earthly friend" (L807), the Rev. Charles Wadsworth.

Watching with admiration how gracefully this poet's "image-EYE-nation" and "image-ination" traversed "the broadly experiential common ground between sensationalist epistemology and testimonial heart-religion," Brantley envisages her standing there "resolutely, yet resourcefully, after the manner of wily Odysseus, or of resilient Jeremiah, or of both" (180, 184). She emerges as the preeminent practitioner of Keatsian negative capability in her ability to cope with mysteries and doubts.

Although dividing his introduction, seven chapters, and conclusion into relatively brief sections for ease of reading and to allow readers to browse through this study in search of particular themes, Brantley presents a complex and challenging analysis grounded in his earlier books, especially *Locke, Wesley, and the Method of English Romanticism,* and looking forward to a planned book further devoted to Wadsworth. Allusions to British and American poets and spiritual or philosophical figures proliferate, with the reader expected to grasp how Dickinson partook in a literary-intellectual continuum running from the eighteenth century through the twentieth. As a newcomer to the Dickinsonian critical conversation, Brantley displays his wide and respectful reading through frequent references to commentary on her writings—at times, perhaps, too much so for clear exposition of his own views. Fortunately, he provides frequent reprises of his argument and justifications for his approach, which resists modernist and post-modernist readings in favor of a sophisticated history-of-ideas methodology that shows how "the broadly experiential, spiritual as well as natural epistemology of the Anglo-American world explains Anglo-American Romanticism in general and Dickinson's poetry in particular" (10).

Probably the least controversial aspect of this study will be Brantley's placement of Dickinson in an empirical tradition that subjected both science and religion to demands for sensory demonstration and experiential conviction. Edward Hitchcock's influence on Amherst and Mount Holyoke educational culture can be recognized in her many scientific references and her demands for proof. Chapters Two, "Experimental Trust," and Three, "Nature Methodized," deal with empiricist tendencies in Dickinson's approaches to both nature and faith. Also well known is her immersion in the evangelical religious culture of the Connecticut Valley during the Second Awakening, though Brantley's understanding of her religious options and choices may puzzle as well as surprise readers acquainted with Roger Lundin's *Emily Dickinson and the Art of Belief* and James McIntosh's *Nimble Believing* or with Sewall's, Wolff's, and Habegger's biographies—all of which situate her in a New England more than Anglo-American theological context.

Scholars of Dickinson's religious environment tend to characterize the post-Puritan religious culture of Dickinson's formative years in terms of an Arminianized Calvinism that softened the fundamental Calvinist dogma asserting depraved man's total dependence on God for salvation by allowing for a person's cooperation in the work of salvation through exercise of free will. What is unusual here is the contrast Brantley draws between Calvinism, which he considers rigidly anti-experiential, and Arminianism, which he represents by contrast as flexible, experiential and better adapted to scientific and philosophical empiricism. Themes Brantley identifies with Arminianism include Dickinson's tendencies toward "individualism, progress, breadth, exaltation, joy, love, and presence—in a phrase, prophetic heart religion" (139). Yet one wonders how the "New England way" of Puritan and post-Puritan Congregational churches, with their demands that every candidate for admission to the church demonstrate personal experience of saving grace, can be regarded as "anti-experiential"—even if many of those professions of faith came to seem formulaic. Most surprising, for those of us accustomed to thinking of Arminianism as a heretical current within Calvinism from its origins in seventeenth-century Europe (when the Pilgrims' pastor, John Robinson, debated its champions at the University of Leyden) until it gradually seeped into New England practice in the eighteenth century against the formidable intellectual resistance of Jonathan Edwards, Brantley places Edwards himself within the Arminian camp. Thus, in recognizing Dickinson as Edwardsean in religious disposition, he aligns her with optimistic tendencies toward assertion of free will. Brantley's characterization of Edwards seems to depend rather heavily on John Wesley's abbreviated edition of some Edwards publications (those oriented toward revivalism rather than the late-life treatises on "Original Sin" and "Freedom of the Will"); and Wesley's Methodism enters into this discussion as an inspiring force in Dickinson's late Romanticism, even though little evidence emerges of her direct acquaintance with Methodism either in England or the United States. George Whitefield's mediatorial role between Edwards and Wesley might be considered here, as would that of Nathaniel W. Taylor, a key transitional figure within the Neo-Edwardsean theology of antebellum New England. Taylor, under whom Samuel Fowler Dickinson studied briefly, strongly influenced the dominant religious culture of the poet's youth, which Lundin identifies as Whiggish New School Calvinism; but he gets mentioned here only once in passing. The term "evangelical" takes its root from proclamation of the Gospel and active efforts to spread religion—tendencies powerfully characteristic of the revival-oriented piety fostered in the Connecticut Valley and exemplified by Edward Hitchcock, Mary Lyon, Abiah Root, Abbie Wood, Charles Wadsworth, and even at times Susan Gilbert. Even though Dickinson's letters and poems reflect no such missionary zeal, Brantley treats her as evangelical. Overall, however, he proves himself an attentive, appreciative reader and arrives at conclusions about her that do not depend on classification within any particular category of belief or doubt. "Even when she feared that Experiment would not be Faithful and that natural religion would be unavailing," he writes, "her poems of her climate rarely either renounced her faith in experience or abandoned her hope for an experience of faith" (155).

If this sounds like the characterization of a figure poised between Romantic and modernist or even post-modernist intellectual and artistic tendencies, Brantley devotes most of Chapter Four, "Romantic to Modern Arc," to securing her place as a figure of her own time. Recognizing a tendency for today's critics to "emphasize the forward-looking visage of her Janus-face," Brantley argues for the opposite position—even while admitting with disarming humility the ease with which he could make the opposing case if not already finding it so well defended (141). Grounding her intellectually in a Lockean/Edwardsean/Wesleyan tradition originating in the eighteenth century, he represents Dickinson as an exceedingly sensitive, visionary reflector of her age and argues that "the empirical/evangelical dialectic of her Late-Romantic art constitutes . . . a richer lode than does either the postexperiential tendency of her pre-Modern mode or the antiexperiential bias of her Postmodern intimations" (158). Perhaps because Romanticism was itself so open to contradiction and doubt, his argument persuades.

This is the book of a mature and accomplished scholar of Anglo-American Romanticism, and its ample notes and citations bear ample evidence of painstaking research. Yet it is also an often lyrical declaration of love for Emily Dickinson, whose "wise hopefulness," Brantley declares, "braces a physical sense of truth and fills Spiritual Sensation with grace and joy" (206). He sees that art as a challenge to literary criticism, especially currently fashionable practices, and responds with his own distinctively personal blend of close reading, intellectual history, and confessional fervor. In his introduction and especially his conclusion, Brantley reasons thoughtfully on the critical methods Dickinson's art demands and the importance of venturesome, experimental thinking such as hers for our own academic and religious environment. He has given us a wise, deep, yet friendly, exploratory, and unpretentious book that ought to have great influence on studies of Dickinson's religious thought even as it inspires curiosity about its promised sequel. **–Jane Donahue Eberwein,** *The Emily Dickinson Journal* (2006)

82. ***Experience*** *and Faith* might have served as the title of any book published by Richard Brantley in the past three decades. He has now completed five books, and promises a sixth, devoted to a single line of argument—that British and American Romanticism derives much of its essential character from a dialectic between empirical psychology and evangelical faith, a dialectic that originated in John Wesley's efforts to unite the two. Confident that his own faith was based firmly on a personal experience of God's reality, Wesley appropriated Locke's sensationalist epistemology to provide intellectual support for that confidence. For Wesley, Brantley says, "The great principle of empiricism—that is, that one must see for oneself and be in the presence of the thing one knows—functions, as well, in evangelical faith" (168). This empirical evangelicalism, Brantley argues, provides the dominant "intellectual and emotional context of Anglo-American Romanticism" (168).

Pursuing the argument advanced in his earlier studies of the British Romantic poets and of Carlyle, Tennyson, and Emerson, the present book examines the "natural/spiritual dialectic" (18) that informs the inconsistent religious sentiments expressed in Emily Dickinson's verses. Reading widely and attentively in the poetry and letters, Brantley examines more closely than other critics have done the variety and subtlety of Dickinson's metaphysical explorations, documenting the skepticism and hope, the hesitancies and exuberances that follow from her testing of religious traditions against the facts of her own experience. Brantley's most informative and persuasive chapters demonstrate the poet's alertness to new developments in science, an interest that informed the tough-mindedness that she brought, along with an instinctive natural piety, to her consideration of every aspect of nature from storms to insect life. In her effort to balance scientific knowledge with religious aspiration, she was at one with her post-Darwinian contemporaries in their search for a faith that could not be subverted by experience.

Given his admirably careful attention to the poet's conflicting sentiments of faith and doubt, one is a little disappointed when Brantley's analysis imposes upon her the same theological framework he has employed in his studies of other writers, detecting in her writing the pervasive influence of Wesley and the Arminian tradition that Wesley refined. Indeed, the present book is as much concerned with Brantley's "cumulative project" (22)—his effort to demonstrate the dominance of the Wesleyan influence in British and American Romanticism—as it is with Dickinson.

Having read and reviewed other books by Brantley, I have often sensed a logical inconsistency at the heart of his usual mode of argument in this matter. For example, when he writes that Dickinson's interest in medical science was "in the spirit of Wesley" (48), the implied syllogism goes something like this: Wesley was interested in medicine; so was Dickinson; ergo, Dickinson owed an intellectual debt to Wesley. The Wesleyan influence on Dickinson is not documented specifically but attributed vaguely to "the complex process of cultural osmosis" (166-7). Since for Brantley nearly everything good and positive in Anglo-American thinking, or in the modern history of Christian thought, is in the spirit of Wesley, the attribution ceases to have persuasive force as intellectual history.

Brantley concludes the book boldly with a public profession of his own Arminian faith and a tribute to Dickinson for having helped strengthen it. The book reveals itself as a work of Christian apologetics, intended to lead his readers toward a spiritually richer life, with Dickinson's "kerygmatic power" providing aid and comfort on the journey. The conclusion of Brantley's personal religious pilgrimage is announced as a commitment to the kind of moderate evangelicalism represented in this country by the Baptist Christian Fellowship [a liberal-evangelical spin-off from the Southern Baptist Convention, and joined by such laity as Jimmy Carter].

Brantley is a conscientious scholar. He has read Dickinson's poetry carefully; part of the pleasure he provides in this book derives from his generous quotations from her collected works, many of them texts not usually anthologized. He has immersed himself in recent criticism of Dickinson and takes account of it here dutifully and, in the main, respectfully. His emphasis on the Arminian tradition in theology usefully complicates American religious history, which has focused exclusively on its Calvinist Puritan origins. And he continues to adjust and enrich our understanding of John Wesley's wide-ranging cultural influence. Brantley's concluding confession of his personal faith may damage his credibility as a critic and historian in the eyes of some readers. He understands that. There is no such thing as disinterested criticism; all literary theorists are in the business of recruiting disciples to one metaphysics or another, and Brantley claims as much legitimacy for his Wesleyan/Arminian reading of Dickinson as that claimed in recent years by "the unholy alliance of nihilism, unbelief, and aporia," specifically "the paralyzed skepticism of hard-core Deconstruction" (195, 141). Brantley defends

his territory with tenacity. He remains a stubbornly independent voice in literary scholarship, insisting that his fellow scholars and critics rethink and refresh the questions they ask about the origins and meaning of Romanticism.
—**Robert M. Ryan,** *The Wordsworth Circle* (2007)

83. In his exceptional work, Richard E. Brantley's examination of Dickinson's epistemological milieu is a major contribution to both Dickinson scholarship and to nineteenth-century studies. Taking seriously the profound influence of the religious and philosophical currents surrounding Dickinson, Brantley argues that she synthesizes a natural/spiritual dialectic founded on British empirical philosophy and free will evangelical religion (8). Thus, Dickinson emerges not as a poet of rampant unbelief who embraces an amorphous spirit of Nature but as a mind grappling with the major pre-Modern epistemological shift that necessitates a faith in empirical procedures. Brantley's work traces the triangulation of empiricism, evangelicalism, and Romanticism that surrounds Dickinson's mind and art. First, the Scottish Common Sense school and the empirical philosophy of John Locke permit Dickinson to "plumb the mystery that underlies" her faith in experience (77). Then, Brantley suggests that an ascending Arminian evangelical faith, rather than Calvinism, grounds Dickinson's emphasis on free will and heart religion (139). Finally, Romanticism itself evolves in Brantley's study to a movement thoroughly grounded in nineteenth-century evangelical revivals. Dickinson "reimagines Romanticism . . . neither battening on the irony of irony nor believing in unbelief" (189). Brantley argues that Dickinson's "faith in experience strengthens her experience of faith" thus ending the "empirical/evangelical dialectic of Anglo-American Romanticism" (15; 159). She takes her place at the apex of Late Romanticism because her healthy skepticism and religious doubt destroy neither her faith nor her knowledge; instead, her faith is enriched and her knowledge deepened.

Brantley's first chapter—a preview of more fully developed studies later in the volume—analyzes the mix of religion and philosophy informing Dickinson's frame of reference. This chapter, "Distinguishing Mode," establishes the influences of John Wesley, Jonathan Edwards, and George Whitefield within nineteenth century Anglo-America and, more directly, on Dickinson's spiritual and intellectual formation. Brantley traces how these three religious figures, particularly, introduce British empiricism to the American scene. Chapter Two, "Experimental Trust," begins the true labor of the volume in bringing to the foreground the influence of Locke and the Scottish Common

Sense School on nineteenth-century Anglo-America, from the British High Romanticism of Wordsworth to the later sermons of American preacher and Dickinson's "dearest earthly friend," Charles Wadsworth. Brantley traces the empiricism grounding life in mid-century Amherst as well as within Dickinson's development as an experimentalist particularly under the influence of Edward Hitchcock at Amherst Academy and, later, in her knowledge of the theories of Charles Darwin. This background provides an understanding for Dickinson's faith, poetic practice, and personae rooted in a sense-based scientific method.

"Nature Methodized" unveils Dickinson's religion of nature that dances between a study of phenomena and a trust in the mysterious. Brantley accomplishes this through a study of Dickinson's treatment of the seasons, Indian summer, storms, flowers, trees, insects, birds, mammals, and the sun within a host of poems (80). Brantley's treatment of these subjects and his readings of her poetry support one of the major assertions of the volume, that she places her faith more in a Wesley inspired spiritual experience than a more Calvinistic one (93). Thus, her faith is viewed as much more orthodox (90), though Brantley suggests that Dickinson, at least at times, maintains a separation in her mind and art between the natural and the supernatural (103). While they inform each other, Dickinson sees them as more dialectically distinct and either impossible to reconcile or, more likely, in no need of such reconciliation.

Whereas Chapter Two highlights Dickinson's connection to an earlier Anglo-American philosophical and religious tradition, Chapter Four, "Romantic to Modern Arc," highlights Dickinson's Late-Romantic imagination. Brantley suggests that the radical skepticism of Dickinson "recommends a doubting method both tough and tender in that it feels both philosophically and religiously experiential" (118). Experience is at once both natural and spiritual. And this is what makes Dickinson firmly and fully a Late-Romantic in intellect and sensibility, for she never fully slips into the Modern or Postmodern fascination with undecidability. Brantley's readings in this chapter of Dickinson's milieu and poetry are particularly strong and convincing. Thus, it is in this chapter that Brantley most overturns the generally accepted recent scholarship on Dickinson. While he also traces Dickinson's trajectory toward the Modern, he argues that she resists the urge to dwell in suspicion, for she holds nature and spirit in constant dialectic. Not only does this chapter establish Dickinson as a poet (if not the poet) of her time, it also remaps the philosophical and religious terrain of nineteenth-century Anglo-America.

The concluding chapters of Brantley's study review and reinforce the arguments set forth in his earlier chapters and emphasize the evangelical revivalism and empiricism at the heart of Anglo-American Romanticism. Further, in Chapter Five, "Practical Conspectus," he posits that "Dickinson mediates between the empirical procedures and the evangelical principles of Romantic Anglo-America" (187). In his refreshingly candid conclusion, Brantley lays bare his own religious and methodological grounding—in Methodism and in historical, interdisciplinary criticism—and calls for an intellectually honest critical methodology as well as a more sophisticated and open theorizing. Brantley's study shows that many recent critics have ignored, in both content and method, an entire geography of the spiritual in Dickinson studies. He brings together a deep knowledge of Dickinson scholarship and Anglo-American studies of eighteenth and nineteenth century cultures, along with the strongly philosophical and theological grounding. While at times readers might wish for a more supple, less dense prose style, in positioning Dickinson and her work within the emerging Arminian-evangelical theology and increasingly experience-based culture, Brantley deftly contextualizes Dickinson's poetics and her faith and makes a significant contribution to Dickinson studies. —**Lynda Szabo,** *Christianity and Literature* (2007)

84. Brantley is as unable as any scholar to pinpoint exactly where Dickinson's dialectic fits into definitive groupings of Romantics, but he does set the stage for declaring her a true Late-Romantic (10-16). . . . Brantley sees a kind of tug-of-war between the Calvinism of Dickinson's upbringing (which she ultimately rejected) and the Methodist Arminianism filtered down to her through Carlyle and Emerson (20). Brantley is correct when he asserts that Dickinson placed great faith in her experience (27), applying an almost scientific approach to translating that faith into the personae that populate her poetry as he "emphasize[s] . . . her free-will, evangelical principles" (29). He sees that the Reverend Charles Wadsworth greatly affected Dickinson's outlook . . . . . Wadsworth was a significant force in Dickinson's life for a time and whether she reacted against him or in response to him, he is a figure who cannot be ignored. . . . I do not agree that the concept of "dwell[ing] in Possibility" . . . is the same as Negative Capability, in which the poet must accept things as they are, even if he cannot explain, change or understand them. While Negative Capability can be applied to many of her poems, it is not so appropriate in this poem, where the narrator is aware of her process. . . . Brantley quotes so many scholars and poets within his discussion . . . that his own voice is lost.... Brantley is right to note that often, Dickinson's birds are literal and metaphoric at the same time (98-99). He misses the opportunity, however, to relate Dickinson's birds to her "methodized Nature" as he concludes that "Dickinson accepts birdsong apart from purpose" (101).... Brantley knows that "birdsong operates as Dickinson's quintessential expression of naturalism" but he needs to see that naturalism as more than "bearers of the secrets of God" or even a force that drives her nature poetry (101-2), for Dickinson's birds are a reflection of her Self....

Brantley is correct to underscore the religious language that permeates much of Dickinson's N/nature poetry but I would argue against him that rather than acting as a substitute for religious faith or Christianity (110), her use of this language enhances her belief that God's glory is found in his creations rather than in the doors of man-made churches, where religion is supposed to be found and Nature is shut out.... As her Anglo-American affinities are enumerated for the reader, Brantley makes the excellent point that "She holds natural knowledge to be at once a ground and a continuing ingredient of faith. She holds that faith ... consists of such knowledge" (126). Wesley's embracing of science, Wordsworth's seeing into the life of things, Emerson's transparent eyeball, even up to Tennyson's struggle with faith and doubt, all appealed to her because they were influenced by the Spirit of God (127) and spoke to her own empirical sense. The conflagration of the spiritual and physical in Dickinson's poetry allies her, for Brantley, with the Late-Romantics' poetic vision.... Brantley seems to see her as a pre-Modern seer, taking her Late-Romanticism further than any of her literary peers. He does make it clear that her pre-Modern mode does not replace nor out-do her dialectic of Anglo-American Romanticism.... What is significant here is the positive association made between Dickinson and Wordsworth, whose influence on her is much too neglected. The current interest in Transatlanticism will reflect more on the connections between Dickinson and her British counterparts during the next decade or so; Brantley does make a strong contribution to that reflection here as he notes not only religious ties between the two but a sense of empiricism that is shared (171-6).... [Brantley] verges a bit too close to a personal, emotional response to his subject, but Brantley does have a valid argument in saying that "Dickinson's imagination culminates the philosophical, religious, and literary strain of Romantic Anglo-America" (191).... He would have benefited from relying less on secondary scholarship and putting more stock into the connections he makes between the works of Wesley, Edwards, Locke, Emerson, etc. and Dickinson. The deep-seeded influence he insists Charles Wadsworth had on Dickinson may be more apocryphal than actual, but to see Emily Dickinson as a Late-Romantic, following the tradition of Wordsworth, Coleridge, and Keats, using empiricism to find faith in experience and experience in faith is a useful point of departure for continuing a conversation that may well have no end. —**Marci L. Tanter**, *European Romantic Review* (January 2008)

Emily Dickinson's Rich Conversation: Poetry, Philosophy, Science (2013, 2015)

85. [This book] explores the function of hope in Dickinson's poems and looks to place her in a broad cultural context. Brantley teases out the implications of a succinct central perception by treating that perception as a pebble tossed into the pool of late-19th-century transatlantic culture. His departure from familiar stylistics and his challenging, yet entertaining mode of analysis make for delightful reading. —**Paul Crumbley,** reader for Palgrave Macmillan

86. Brantley provides us here with a witty, energetic, and buoyantly inclusive examination of Emily Dickinson's intensely creative engagement in an intellectual dialectic ranging from John Locke's time to ours. Brantley establishes Dickinson as a bold, realistic, yet hopeful thinker as he engages in a graciously lively critical conversation that is sure to quicken appreciation of her dialogical art. —**Jane Donahue Eberwein,** reader for Palgrave Macmillan

87. For decades now, ever since the publication of *Wordsworth's "Natural Methodism"* in 1975, Richard E. Brantley has rigorously sounded one of Romanticism's deepest mysteries: the relationship between physical experience (the exquisite vitalities of the senses) and metaphysical faith (those visions of realms beyond—but somehow in—space and time). Whether studying how Wordsworth tried to square the empiricism of Locke with his yearning for the ideal worlds "evermore about to be," or how Dickinson struggled to reconcile her ecstatic love of nature with her evangelical heritage, Brantley has deepened our understanding, as A. O. Lovejoy and M. H. Abrams did before him, of the great oscillations of the human condition, those "stupendous antagonisms"—in Emerson's fine phrase—that we are forever trying to reconcile, or at least place into productive conversation.

In looking back to this august critical tradition, one based firmly on the history of ideas, Brantley was also gazing ahead (as his studies of both Wordsworth and Dickinson intimate) to the recent scholarly interest in transatlantic romanticism. In particular, Brantley has unearthed vital connections between Wesley and Jonathan Edwards, and between Emerson and Carlyle as well as Tennyson, showing how powerful ideas crossed the great ocean, with mutually illuminating results.

Brantley's latest book interweaves these two ongoing concerns: the dialogue between experience and faith, and the conversation between England and America. In the first half of the book, Brantley shows how Dickinson's commitment to the sensual world—its storms, flowers, and birds—inspired her to read, quite systematically, the leading scientific texts of her time. In fact, borrowing a distinction made by E. D. Hirsch, Brantley usefully demonstrates that a full understanding of Dickinson's "belles lettres," her literary output, requires an engagement with the "bonnes lettres"—the philosophy, science, and theology—in which she immersed herself.

It turns out that Dickinson was "rich in conversation"—her phrase—with Locke, Wesley, and Charles Wadsworth, among others, from whom she learned a "natural methodism" that heartily endorse[d] sense-based reasoning" and "up-to-date knowledge of empirical philosophy and of science" (43). Attuned to physical experience and experiment, Dickinson adopted a "tough-minded tone" in her expressions of the geology, astronomy, medicine, and biology of her age, particularly in her interpretation of Charles Darwin.

Brantley's interdisciplinary readings of Dickinson's poetry are enlightening, not only in showing how this compellingly dialectical poet oscillated "among the incandescent prospects of this world" but also in providing fresh scientific and philosophical contexts for understanding her poetry. Especially fruitful are his readings of "Experiment escorts us last," "On a Columnar Self," and "Apparently with no Surprise."

Yet Brantley's greatest service to Dickinson studies and to Romantic studies in general is in disclosing the "double-ness" of the Myth of Amherst and—by extension—of several of her transatlantic forebears, such as Wordsworth and Emerson. Over the years, critics have often split Romanticism into polarities such as emotion vs. reason and experience vs. faith, and subsequently favored one over the other, ranking emotion and experience above their opposites. For Brantley, these great antinomies are not oppositional so much as conversational, perpetually shifting in their mutually inclusive relationships, with one side constantly shaping and generating the other. Dickinson, Brantley argues, doesn't choose between experience and faith; she places them into dynamic dialogue that "allows experience its fighting chance against . . . faith, notwithstanding this poet's nostalgia for, nay her love of, her evangelical heritage" (34).

While the first part of this book studies Dickinson's exciting, complicated efforts to balance experience and faith, the second part shows how she grapples with the depressing aftermath of exuberant experience: with those terrible losses—of loved ones and of hope—that left her in "excruciating" "disillusionment and disaffection" (17). What Brantley finds is that the "post-experiential," "late-Romantic" Dickinson unflinchingly faces earth's inevitable tragedies, and still discovers hope, often in the deepest darkness. Her resiliency is Wordsworthian, drawing from his own "post-experience sounding 'hope that can never die'" (104). In her poetry of aftermath, such as "They say that 'Time assuages'" and "The Soul has bandaged moments," she "recounts the twofold experience of holding despair at bay and keeping hope-against-hope, though not quite hope full blown, alive" (104).

In the end, Dickinson's experiences of the failure of experience (to grant vitality, creativity, and joy) only reconfirmed her faith that if held open and expectant, the senses could gather what one requires to live. Rejecting both nostalgia for a better time and blind optimism for a brighter future, Dickinson realized that "Knowledge Avenue" and "Aftermath Byway" intersected one another (158). For Dickinson, Brantley reminds us, thirst teaches water, just as sorrow instructs joy: you can't know what one is without the other, and the more extreme the encounter with one, the more intense the experience of the other. This potent middle path is properly one of melancholia, in the mode of Wordsworth and Coleridge, both of whom embraced the darkness as an invitation to the most powerful light.

This book gives us a newly riveting Dickinson, a capacious, complex, and supple poet who could out-do Darwin in staring at the earth's chaos but who could also, at the core of the turbulence, channel Wordsworth's undying sense that order would prevail: not the rigid orders of the logicians or the philosophers, but the more aesthetic structures of the heart, always attuned, even when saddest, to beauty, which, as we know from Keats, can only exist if it's already dying. Remarkably, given his past achievements as a historian of ideas and a literary critic, this is Brantley's best book yet. **—Eric G. Wilson,** *Review 19*, October 15, 2013

88. Richard Brantley's mellifluous prose, with its considered doublets, often conveys a sense of one concerned with the *mot juste*—but knowing that one word is rarely *juste* enough, ... Of Locke, Wesley, Wadsworth, and Darwin, the apparent odd man out (his parish being obviously less global) is perhaps the one dubbed "My Clergyman," the Rev. Charles Wadsworth, whose emotional and intellectual importance to Dickinson is persuasively argued in this volume (their marriage of minds is treated in a third appendix) and whose sermons (there were 1,125 pages of them) provide some telling analogues to Dickinson's experiential poems especially when the clergyman is using natural science as illustrative matter or arguing through metaphor in his sermons. . . .

Emily Dickinson's Rich Conversation is a carefully contextualized exercise in an intellectual biography of one who, in Harold Bloom's somewhat surprising judgment, "had the best mind of all our poets," and if it does not wholly persuade this reader of that high claim—after all, Bloom also imagines Emerson to be an original thinker—nonetheless it amply justifies the "rich conversation" motif that runs through the book, whether in her deployment of multiple personae in her poems (somewhat more various than Lord Byron's but used for similarly vicarious ends) or in the assemblage of "co-dialogists" who assembled daily at her imaginary "seminar table" (8). . . .

In Part 2, the chapters "Gaining Loss" and "Despairing Hope" celebrate her presciently pre-Modern (Hardyesque?) pessimism, her somewhat Wordsworthian calculus of loss and gain (a joy that *something* yet survives, and survives without renouncing fidelity to experience) and the "sumptuous Destitution" in which (quite as much as Philip Larkin, who strangely, is not mentioned in this book), she builds her poetic mansion. The paradoxical chapter titles wittily make the point through their two substantives: the first substantive "Loss," is itself not without gain, and the honesty Brantley finds in this late-Romantic poetry is shown by the insistence that such profitable "Loss" accompanies rather than yields to despairing "Hope."

In *Emily Dickinson's Rich Conversation*, Brantley demonstrates triumphantly, through his generous and engaging consideration both of Dickinson's range of personae and of her innumerable interlocutors, living or dead . . . . Richard Brantley is a superbly gifted critic and (if one may use that term) a master of Dickinson's oeuvre: might I beg that he make more allowance in his next volume for those readers who sometimes find that her less triumphant poems, and the reverence with which they are treated, put them in mind of the story of the emperor's new clothes, or to put it bluntly, that allowances are made for Dickinson that are made for no other poet? . . . **—Richard Gravil,** *The Wordsworth Circle* (Autumn 2013)

89. Brantley's erudite, spirited study envisions Dickinson as the moderator of a seminar, in dialogue with both dead and living precursors and contemporaries—a select society . . . . Brantley tracks Dickinson's progressive thinking along an arc of intellectual, literary, and cultural history from Anglo-American Romanticism, evangelical idealism, and experiential faith; through sense-grounded reason, evolutionary biology, knowledge-based skepticism, tough realism, and empiricism; leading to pre- and post-Modern pessimism that foreshadows and influences current writers and their work. Dickinson's often oscillating stance may be compared to Keats's "Negative Capability: being in uncertainties, Mysteries, doubts, without any irritable reaching after fact and reason"; that is, remaining open to imagination and new thought. Although Dickinson's empirical voice coexisted with her "stubbornly persistent evangelical vernacular," Brantley argues that her empiricism, "her faith in experience, trumps her evangelical yearning." He concludes that in her aftermath poetry she balances pessimism with optimism, turns loss into gain, acquires wisdom, and entertains hope. He references 123 Dickinson poems from the Franklin edition and provides selected close readings.... Engaging other Dickinson scholars, Brantley's well researched study includes 97 pages of three appendices, informative notes, works cited, and two indexes. —**Barbara Kelly,** *The Emily Dickinson International Society Bulletin* (November/December 2013)

90. Brantley's emphasis on Dickinson's "dialogical aesthetic" makes this book a significant contribution to scholarship. Other valuable aspects of the book include situating the poet in an Anglo-American rather than strictly New England context; locating her in an empirical tradition in which experience and experiment tend to eclipse faith; and revealing her as a poet who is less an eccentric recluse than she is an individual mentally interacting with a community of authors and intellectuals. Although his focus is on the history of ideas, Brantley also comments on numerous poems, most interestingly, to this reviewer, those displaying the poet's knowledge of astronomy, geology, evolutionary biology, and steam technology. Summing up: Highly recommended. Graduate students, researchers, faculty. —**D. D. Kummings,** *Choice* (March 2014)

91. Richard Brantley's erudite and affectionate book brings a lifetime of scholarship on Dickinson and the wider context of Anglo-American empirical and Romantic traditions to bear on his reading of the poet.... The newcomer to Dickinson might find the sheer range of references and allusions in the introduction slightly baffling, especially when set alongside Dickinson's characteristically complex and opaque poems.... Brantley's generosity toward the community of Dickinson scholars as well as the community of 18th- and 19th-century poets and intellectuals amongst whom he situates Dickinson shines throughout his volume. . . . Readers conversant in Dickinson studies and familiar with the intellectual terrain of 18th- and 19th-century England and America are likely to find this book engaging and rewarding. First-time readers might be forgiven for feeling a little at sea when dropped into the midst of Brantley's own rich associations . . . .

For those willing to enter into a generative and associative conversation, however, this is a good read and worth perseverance because Brantley's knowledge resembles Dickinson's in its breadth, wit, and generosity. The book's organizational structure is typically Romantic connective and web-like rather than logical and progressive. Brantley acknowledges that his "leaps across space and time may seem anachronistic" as he reads Dickinson alongside Charles Wadsworth, John Wesley, John Locke, and Charles Darwin and situates her among late Romantic geniuses such as Ralph Waldo Emerson, William Wordsworth, and Alfred Lord Tennyson, to name just a few (69). . . . Hopkins, Browning, Shakespeare, and Miss Piggy feature on just one page (19). . . .

One of the most illuminating strains of Brantley's argument focuses on Dickinson's treatment of aftermath or post-experience, which in her case, as with Wordsworth and Tennyson, often translates into the literature of mourning. Brantley compares her work with Wordsworth's "Lucy" poems and presents equally insightful points of contact and dissonance in relation to Tennyson's *In Memoriam*. Here, Dickinson's complex and lively thought-processes spin a web of cultural and intellectual references that show her poetry to be profoundly important to the major intellectual movements of the 18th and 19th centuries. If anyone still believed in the intellectual isolation of the Myth of Amherst, this book would destroy that belief.

Brantley claims to illustrate Dickinson's "art of knowledge as distinct from her 'art of belief'" (5). The latter is Roger Lundin's phrase, and while I appreciate Brantley's desire to distinguish his recent work from those studies more intently focused on religion (including his own earlier work), the real strength of this book lies not in the distinction it draws between empiricism and religion as influences on Dickinson but in the way it fleshes out the continuities between empiricist and late Romantic thought. These continuities lie predominantly in the area of experience, specifically sense-experience. Brantley shows how Locke, Darwin, and Wesley people Wadsworth's prose and hence directly influenced Dickinson. Brantley presents Dickinson as a candid friend of pragmatism, also acknowledging (though perhaps slightly underplaying) the way she cast her ironic eye on the "twig of Evidence" (Fr373), at which, he says, "she can never stop plucking" for material knowledge (26). Her irony is not a barrier to engagement—quite the opposite—but it is often her slightly unfriendly starting point. However, Brantley brilliantly elucidates the importance of empiricism to Romanticism, comparing Dickinson's Romantic imagination with that of Wordsworth, Tennyson, Emerson, Percy Shelley, and John Keats. Brantley also draws links with William Blake, though these are through similarities in temperament rather than influence. Readers of this book might feel as if they have entered midway through the conversation. This may frustrate some but, for many, it will be a conversation they do not want to leave. —**Linda Freedman**, *The Emily Dickinson Journal* 24.1 (2015)

92. Richard Brantley's *Emily Dickinson's Rich Conversation: Poetry, Philosophy, Science* addresses the poet's engagement with many contexts in one magisterial study emerging from his years of reflection upon the poetic and belletristic (and "bonne-lettristic") texts of the 19th century in his previous books on the Romantics and Dickinson. Brantley dispenses with generic differences not in order to emphasize the material context of Dickinson's compositions, like Virginia Jackson and her followers, but because he hears in Dickinson's words a central node of the various conversations of the "unified poem" that constitutes "the arc from Romantic to Modern." His book is divided into two main sections, "Gathering Experience" and "Extending Experience." The first part situates the dialogue between faith and experience in Dickinson's conversation with thinkers from Locke to Charles Darwin but especially with John Wesley and (the other pole of Anglo-American evangelical thought) her "dearest earthly friend" Charles Wadsworth. This dialogue, Brantley argues, "formed a vital . . . part of her informal education in both the philosophy and the science of her day." The second part of the book takes up Dickinson's "poems of aftermath"—poems describing the survival of some tremendous event as reflecting a "hard-won optimism" grown out of empirical science. In all, the book reads as the mature reflections of a long-time student of the period and of literary writing, musing about the shift in the center of the dynamic cultural conversation from the spiritually centered discourse of Romanticism to the empirically centered discourse that has dominated since the beginning of the 20th century. —**Dan Manheim**, *American Literary Scholarship 2013* (2015)

93. Two metaphors dominate Richard Brantley's intriguing *Emily Dickinson's Rich Conversation*—experiment and conversation. The book is itself a kind of experiment. Whereas in a previous book—*Experience and Faith: The Late-Romantic Imagination of Emily Dickinson* (2004)—he had looked at the way Dickinson had brought to a point of culmination what he called Romanticism's "philosophically religious agenda," a merging of rational empiricism or sense-based reasoning and natural and revealed religion, in this book he "background[s] the religious and foreground[s] the philosophical and scientific concerns of her personae" (36), in order to see as clearly as possible the way "her faith in experience and in experiment talked with, tempered, tested, and talked back to Experiential Faith" (164). Playing off of Roger Lundin's *Emily Dickinson and the Art of Belief* (1998), Brantley brings to the fore Dickinson's empirical, model-driven approach to reality, her inductive "art of knowledge," in order to ask whether his previous version of Dickinson's "constructive skepticism," working through doubt and the testing of initial perceptions towards truth, still holds, even without the theological underpinnings that drew this approach to reality into existence. (The answer is yes.) I'm reminded of an artist deliberately bringing forward a new aspect of perception by deliberately muting another, in order to see reality in a fuller light, further down the road—an experimental approach to reading and thinking clearly drawn from Dickinson, who writes, in a poem central to Brantley's analysis, "Experiment escorts us last." As this book convincingly demonstrates, this method of thinking—what Wallace Stevens calls "the mind in the act of finding"—is the final truth Dickinson passes on to her readers.

Brantley illustrates the role of experiment or a sense-driven examination of reality in Dickinson in two ways. In the first half of the book, he refers to a core distillation of the mind's engagement with reality ("Experience is the Angled Road / Preferred against the Mind / By—Paradox—the Mind itself—") and then reads a number of poems which put this paradox (that the mind seeks ever-deepening encounters with experience in order to check and deepen and strike against its initial takes on the truth) into play. The strongest of these is Dickinson's encounter with the Northern Lights in "Of Bronze—and Blaze—," a poem which, in Brantley's account, immediately brings to mind Stevens's "The Auroras of Autumn" and Yeats's "The Circus Animals' Desertion." (More on this later.) Dickinson, as Brantley convincingly shows, moves here from a humbling of the mind before sublimity to an overreaching exaltation of her own inner splendors—she calls this an "infection"—to a chastened return to the earth and her eventual death, a complete enactment of a sense-driven, experience-checking approach to reality, knowingly performed.

In the second half of the book, Brantley examines what he calls Dickinson's poems of "aftermath" or "post-experience"—poems in which the notion that the mind and heart are deepened through being checked by experience is put under enormous pressure. The poems he examines here are among Dickinson's most well-known ("Before I got my eye put out—," "After great pain, a formal feeling comes—," "There's a certain Slant of light"), and I found his argument that these poems of "reduced circumstances" are finally acts of chastened, experience-driven "enlargement" to be quite convincing. "I see thee clearer for the Grave," Dickinson wrote to a lost lover in a poem Brantley doesn't cite but could have, exactly spelling out the terrible costs and gains of this process.

It seems to me that once this is understood, we are poised to move beyond the book's this-world focused experiment and make a second observation, one that Brantley rules out of this book but will perhaps discuss in a follow-up—which is that Dickinson applies this same approach to reality and its impossible-to-fully-comprehend truth to other "Reportless Subjects," among them the divine. "Behind Me—dips Eternity— / Before Me—Immortality— / Myself—the Term between," Dickinson writes, not so much keeping these framing terms out of bounds as inviting us to record their pressure on her work in the space between them. And that that pressure is almost inevitably recorded as a chastening and a loss, a post-traumatic experience of diminishment and inner enlargement, is something that Brantley's work here allows us to understand, as in, for example, these lines of lament and growth:

> A Grant of the Divine—
> That certain as it comes—
> Withdraws—and leaves the dazzled soul—
> In her unfurnished rooms—

The second metaphor driving this book is conversation. In her unfurnished rooms, we might say, deprived of the most basic tools by which we orient ourselves in the world, the dazzled soul finds herself surrounded by voices—in Dickinson's case, the voices of poets and scripture, but also, Brantley shows, the voices of philosophers and scientists. Dickinson made a home for herself in the world, he claims, by conversation, engaging with the (often prose) voices of precursors and contemporaries, making poems by, as we do in conversation, responding to and carrying forward what's already been put in play. Testing, trying out, playing with, supporting, exemplifying—this is what we do as we attempt to make out where a conversation's initial exploratory wave might take us. Conversation, for Dickinson, becomes "a laboratory of free mental play," with her conversational partners being sometimes known, sometimes deduced, sometimes speculatively proposed, and sometimes simply anticipated, as in my hearing Stevens and Yeats tugging at her voice earlier. In each case, the conversation metaphor lets Brantley hear into her work in a more focused, intense, and provisional way—creating what the poet Susan Howe called *My Emily Dickinson*, a figure experimentally drawn to the surface when other voices are put near hers and allowed to resonate. It's a productive, provocative, Dickinson-like way to read, the approach allowing us to test out new ways of hearing her voice.

Building on an argument detailed in a number of his earlier books, Brantley suggests we listen to Dickinson's work as if it were in conversation not only with the "exemplars of Anglo-American Romanticism . . . Blake, Wordsworth, Coleridge, Shelley, Keats, Carlyle, Tennyson, and Emerson" (7-8) but also with the rational empiricism of John Locke which reached her through John Wesley's "Locke-inflected influence" on Charles Wadsworth, the clergyman she called "my dearest earthly friend" (11). Dickinson, he proposes, could have picked up Locke as a conversational partner through Wadsworth's sermons, though he is careful to note that we have no record, until late in her life, that she had access to them. The idea that Wadsworth sent her sermons and she sent him poems and letters in reply is speculative—Brantley calls the evidence that she read his printed works "circumstantial but strong" (188)—but it does allow him to hear deeply into certain tones of her voice. Wadsworth, who wrote in a sermon that medicine and other arts of knowing are based "upon the first principle of experiment and induction" (58, 78) could well have given her the push to apply those principles to her Jacob-like wrestling with God. If so, Dickinson could have developed, in her poetic exchanges with him, a drive to know for herself what was "naturally and spiritually true" (37), but a drive that pushed beyond his "with a greater tough-mindedness" (38) into an "interrogative mood" comfortable with "hurling open-ended and near-blasphemous interrogatives at the God not so much of orthodoxy, whether Calvinist or other, as of nature in the rawness of its violence" (84) as presented to her senses. Whether her "tough-minded lyrics" speak directly back to Wadsworth's exhortation to seek to know with one's own eyes and ears and senses, putting it this way and testing such an approach out, lets us hear, under her various and often contradictory tones, a constructively-skeptical faith in action, driving towards a kind of inner incandescence (going "White— unto the White Creator—") in that place of "internal difference— / Where the Meanings, are." Brantley lets us hear a Dickinson who puts sagacity and knowingness aside, stepping into the free play of considering and speculating, of plucking and clutching and laying aside—which is to say, into the world of conversation and experiment. He gives us a Dickinson who would walk attentively with us through the riddle of experience:

> This World is not Conclusion.
> A Species stands beyond—
> Invisible, as Music—
> But positive, as Sound—
> It beckons and it baffles—
> Philosophy, dont know—
> And through a Riddle, at the last—
> Sagacity, must go— (372)

—**Thomas Gardner,** *Religion & Literature* (Spring 2016)

94. Richard E. Brantley's *Emily Dickinson's Rich Conversation: Poetry, Philosophy, Science* (2013, 2015) belongs to a longstanding scholarly effort of locating the convoluted literary and cultural relations between Dickinson and her Anglo-American male contemporaries and precursors, and is undoubtedly one of the best efforts so far.

In the past, critics such as Gary Lee Stonum, Harold Bloom, and Joanne Feit Diehl have shown how Dickinson's poetry differs from the male literary tradition, or even forms an antagonistic relationship with the male-dominated Romantic convention. Later feminist readings by critics such as Margaret Homans, Helen McNeil, and Mary Loeffelholz emphasize the deconstructive nature of her poetry that undermines the binary structure in the writings of her fellow male writers. Despite the perceived ambivalence in Dickinson's relation to the male-dominated literature, recent scholars such as Robert Weisbuch and Inder Nath Kher place Dickinson squarely within the Anglo-American Romanticism of her time. More recently, scholars such as Richard Gravil and Brantley explore the intertextual relationship between Dickinson and her Romantic precursors closely.

As Gravil in *Romantic Dialogues: Anglo-American Continuities, 1776-1862* (2000, 2015) remarks, Dickinson is "the most bookish poet in the poets of

Anglo-American tradition," whose poetry "is in a strict sense unreadable without some awareness of the precursor text or texts on which many of her major poems are meditations" (188). Brantley's *Emily Dickinson's Rich Conversation* testifies to this "bookishness" of Dickinson by probing her transatlantic connections with a number of thinkers, philosophers, scientists and writers. As a sequel to *Experience and Faith: The Late-Romantic Imagination of Emily Dickinson* (2004, 2008), the fifth installment of the series and one of the very first books to locate Dickinson's poetic influences in "the empirical philosophy, evangelical religion, and Anglo-American Romanticism of her recent past" (3), Brantley's latest book continues to examine Dickinson's Anglo-American literary roots by shifting its attention from "politics, sex and religion" to her intellectual engagements as well as poetic approaches (24); by doing so, this book illuminates one's understanding of Dickinson's transatlantic "meditations."

Brantley uses one of the most enigmatic poems of Dickinson—"Experiment escorts us last" (Fr1181) as a prime example to place her poetry in the literature of both *les belles-lettres* and *les bonnes-lettres*, illustrating brilliantly how Dickinson's poetic "experiment" is not only literarily-minded but also philosophically- and scientifically-informed, and that her relationship with her male precursors is more "dialogic" than "subversive" (85).

Dickinson's works are not only examined in a wider transatlantic framework, but also positioned in a broader historical and interdisciplinary context, stretching from eighteenth-century thinkers such as John Locke (British empiricist) and John Wesley (British Methodist) to Dickinson's contemporaries, such as Charles Wadsworth (American evangelist), William Wordsworth (British Romanticist), and Charles Darwin (evolutionary biologist) in the nineteenth century, a select group of male figures that Brantley calls Dickinson's "Royal Society" (29). Brantley's analysis is most intriguing when it comes to the striking parallels and associations made through systematic juxtapositions and close-up comparison between Dickinson's poems and works of these "Royal" members in her literary society, especially the sections on Dickinson's relationships with Wadsworth, Wordsworth and Darwin.

A particular emphasis is placed on Dickinson's correspondences with Wadsworth. Their intimate friendship is described as being largely philosophical and literary—what Brantley calls a "marriage of minds" (187). Brantley's meticulous cross-examination of the associations between Wadsworth's comments on and references to modern sciences, such as steam technologies, geology and astronomy in his sermons, and Dickinson's use of metaphors such as gems and steam engines in a number of poems, including "The Day that I was crowned" (Fr613), "She went as quiet as the Dew" (Fr159) and "I like to see it lap the Miles" (Fr383)—provides a fertile ground for further research on the connections between these two writers on a level both intellectually compelling as well as emotionally stimulating.

The book further offers a nuanced reading of Dickinson's poems about loss and death by presenting her as a more hopeful, Wordsworthian poet (see also Brantley's "The Wordsworthian Cast of Dickinson's Romantic Heritage" in *Wordsworth in American Literary Culture*, edited by Joel Pace and Matthew Scott). As Brantley puts it pertinently, Dickinson "drowns her sorrow in joy" (159). Her "natural methodism" and "hope-against-hope" serve as a continuation of as well as departure from Wordsworth's "hope-after-hope" (34, 149). According to Brantley, Dickinson is a late-Romanticist rather than a Victorian or pre-Modernist, whose poetry is, peculiarly, "closer to Blake's than to Stevens's" (5).

Dickinson's Darwinian thought offers another highlight to the book. The potential impact of Darwin's evolutionary biology on Dickinson, for Brantley, complicates Dickinson's Wadsworthian and Wordsworthian, Evangelically and Romantically inflected poetry. Scholars such as Nina Baym, Hiroko Uno and Robin Peel have shown how Dickinson adopts scientific methods to address poetic problems. Brantley continues the scholarly dialogue by seeing how the discipline of science, perceived as "natural philosophy" in the nineteenth century, provides a gateway to one's deepened understanding of some of Dickinson's pre-Modern pessimism.

Brantley's reading further resonates well with the critical views of Jane Donahue Eberwein, Peel and Joan Kirkby on the affinities between Darwin's scientific theory and Dickinson's poetry. Brantley countenances the empirically-minded and evangelically/scientifically-sustained optimism of Dickinson, observing that "Dickinson's personae of aftermath yet 'dwell in Possibility—'" (149).

What makes such an interpretation of Dickinson most appealing is the way the book teases out and explains the ambivalence in Dickinson's oscillation between the late-Romantic and the pre-Modern mode of thinking. According to Brantley, Dickinson's poetic vacillation does not signal her "indecisiveness." Instead, she is methodical with her poetic experiments. Dickinson's ambiguity results largely from her empirical and pragmatic approaches, the philosophical and scientific influences of which shape her as a poet of hope, love and faith based upon senses, reason and natural experience. Brantley illustrates how "the Myth of Amherst held to the truth of imagination" (68) by portraying Dickinson as a poet of combination—combining both physicality and spirituality, of sensual experiences and thoughts, joy and regeneration as well as despair, mourning and death. Her embrace of multitudes is manifested in her intellectual "oscillation." And through the process of Anglo-American "cultural osmosis," she conducts her "lyrical pragmatism" (25).

A glimpse at the book's footnotes reveals Brantley's vigorous involvement in the critical dialogues among Dickinson scholars. The abundance of notes and biographical information is a valuable asset. The careful scholarship provided in these footnotes not only draws a lucid picture of how the author's mind is at work, but it also proves an indispensable reservoir for future directions in Dickinson and Transatlantic Studies. The frequent cross-referencing and evocation of contemporary literary criticism as well as eighteenth- and nineteenth-century literary, scientific and philosophical texts further testify to the fruitfulness of interdisciplinary crosspollination in these fields. If readers are wary of getting trapped or lost in the labyrinth of numerous obscure allusions and unfamiliar literary terms in the book, they might seek comfort in the largely and straightforwardly progressive and chronological arrangement of the chapters. The appendixes similarly serve as good supplements and points of departure for a better grasp of the sometimes corrugated metaphorical routes presented in the book's mapping of Dickinson's transatlantic connections.

Oscillation, one of the key concepts in the book, also characterizes the linguistic style of the book, and in the best possible way. The recurrence in Brantley's writing of a subtle and yet constant semantic and philosophical vacillation equals (and mirrors) Dickinson's sophisticated poetic twists and turns. The tonal swing that Brantley detects so well in Dickinson's experimental shifts between sense and thought, faith and doubt, hope and loss, Britain and America, also forms a basis for the fundamentally conversational mode of the book.

By investigating the transmission of thoughts through Anglo-American empiricism, evangelicalism and evolutionary biology and their profound impact upon Dickinson, the book promises intriguing and persuasive results. Its interdisciplinary approach, encyclopedic knowledge, and all-encompassing scope have a far-reaching effect upon Dickinson criticism and Transatlantic Studies alike. Undeniably, *Emily Dickinson's Rich Conversation* is a challenging book for its stylistic density and intellectual intensity. However, along with its scholarly attention to details, this book also yields tremendous pleasure for poetry lovers and researchers alike. This is a book that delivers infinitely more than it modestly proposes. For readers of Dickinson, the book is certainly one of the most inviting and engrossing conversations to be had. —**Li-Hsin Hsu,** *Symbiosis: A Journal of Transatlantic Literary & Cultural Relations* (April 2016)

Transatlantic Trio: Empiricism, Evangelicalism, Romanticism, Essays and Reviews, 1974-2017

95. In his carefully crafted prologue and epilogue to *Transatlantic Trio*, Richard Brantley lays out the core argument that has guided a lifetime of scholarship. His primary subject is Romanticism; his central claim is that "the rival traditions of empiricism and evangelicalism come together" to form "one great poem." Brantley's aim throughout his career has been to define the dynamic interplay of scientific and religious thought that shaped artistic and intellectual culture throughout the English-speaking world during the eighteenth and nineteenth centuries. One consequence of this claim is the necessity of developing a method for reading the intertwining discourses of religion and science as components of a poem in the making. Doing so is no small challenge, but one that Brantley welcomes, as it offers him the opportunity to identify what he views as an extraordinary imaginative and spiritual vitality running through even the thorniest debates. In the epilogue to *Transatlantic Trio*, Brantley refers to this approach as "scripture-like criticism" that makes rich use of quotation and allusion to reveal a pervasive cultural "double consciousness" that prizes the sustained tension of both/and logic over the either/or impulse to resolution. Brantley's unique gift is his ability to illuminate "a complex harmony of ideas-over-time" that finds poetry in the rich conversation he presents as uniting artists and thinkers ranging from John Locke and John Wesley to William Wordsworth and Emily Dickinson.

Brantley's trio, made up of empiricism, evangelicalism, and Romanticism—as spelled out in his complete title—may be thought of as a productively unresolved dialectic whereby Romanticism draws energy from the conflicting imperatives of faith and experience. In a revealing epigraph to his prologue, Brantley quotes Arthur Koestler on the generative power of opposing points of view: "Creativity arises as the result of the intersection of two quite different frames of reference." For Brantley, the "different frames of reference" are experience/empiricism/science, on the one hand, and faith/evangelicalism/religion on the other. He unites the clashing polarities at the very beginning of his prologue through the incisive chiasmus, "faith in experience and experiential Faith," that crystallizes the mutually beneficial cross-pollination that he views as the driving force of Romanticism. "British empiricism and transatlantic revivalism," he writes, "strike sparks off the literary imagination of a bi-national Romantic Movement." The poem, then, that Brantley reads across two centuries is his metaphorical celebration of these conflicting voices: "just as an antiphony is 'an opposition of sound'—'the answer made by one voice to another'—so empirical philosophy and evangelical faith alternate, or converse, in Romantic Anglo-America (*OED*)." Brantley goes so far as to argue that "'the harmony produced' by that 'opposition of sound,' . . . can appear on the same page of, and perhaps even as the single voice of, Anglo-American Romanticism (*OED*)." Such language clearly reflects Brantley's interest in presenting the great central poem of Romanticism as forward looking, and not merely a record of artistic triumph consigned to the past. He is at his most ambitious when he proposes that Romanticism is not content "just to make poetry new, but to pass it on, and perhaps even to prepare the ear of readers, however unwittingly on all fronts, for the taught pleasures of the Modern-era dissonance to come." At the heart of Brantley's life's work lies his conviction that Romanticism has a crucial role to play in our present moment.

The beauty of Brantley's method derives from its insistence that the both/and logic he advocates will yield creative responses to opposing fields of reference only when each pole of the opposition commands equal respect. In his epilogue Brantley applies this principle of generative opposition to his own scholarship, in effect stepping behind the thought processes that have guided his entire project to question his procedure by subjecting it to self-scrutiny that must of course be serious if it is to be productive. As in the prologue, he judiciously sets the tone for the assessment to follow by means of meticulously selected epigraphs. In this instance, the three quotations build upon each other. He begins with a William Blake quotation that cautions against the dangers of "Single vision" that Blake equates with "Newtons [*sic*] sleep." The Matthew Arnold passage that follows defines the noble goal of "living by ideas" as dependent on the ability "to be irresistibly carried . . . by the current of thought to the opposite side of the question," even when your "side of the question has long had your earnest support." Brantley's third epigraph trains attention on his own work by drawing from Eric G. Wilson's positive review of *Emily Dickinson's Rich Conversation*, Brantley's 2013 book on Dickinson. Wilson's conclusion that the "great antinomies" that "have often split Romanticism into polarities" become for Brantley "not oppositional so much as conversational" is indeed an accurate formulation of what Brantley does, but one that also has the potential to reduce Brantley's procedure to an all too tidy, if not smug, algorithm—once it is viewed oppositely. In the spirit of severe self-scrutiny Brantley in effect turns Wilson's words on their collective head to show how even within the most complimentary assessments a sufficiently attentive author can sense the germ of his own complacency.

To insure that his own work meets the standard he most admires in the thinkers and artists who have long been his subject, Brantley departs from what he describes as his own tendency toward "relentless self-consistency, accentuating the positive, eliminating the negative, and reaffirming the whole" to interject an entirely "different and maybe refreshing line of auto-subversion." The key question he directs to himself in his epilogue is whether or not "human minds [his own included] rest in the mystery and doubt perhaps too glibly—or even somewhat disingenuously . . . ." This willing contemplation of his own potential for superficiality ultimately leads to the most devastating of his admissions: "Who," Brantley wonders, "can deny his or her yearning for unity on some days? To see empirical vs. evangelical emerging into harmony (poetry) looks a lot like synthesis just now." Having confronted his own fears and thereby shown respect for what Jorge Luis Borges has described as the "counter-book" that each complete book must contain (qtd. by Brantley), Brantley dedicates the remainder of his epilogue to rebuilding the foundations for his argument.

The steps Brantley elaborates as most central to his method now concentrate on the emotional, affective dimension of the more narrowly intellectual approach he sketched in the prologue. His first move is to affirm the importance of ambiguity as an antidote to the allure of complacency that threatens his own scholarship as much as it does the visionary aspirations of the Romantic writers he studies. Working from the Latin roots of the term—he translates *ambiguity* as "to wander uncertainly"—Brantley gives particular emphasis to uncertainty as an essential byproduct of Romantic writers' determination to "search for something, they know not what." "Both/and logic," he argues, "carries the implication not just of tentativeness or open-mindedness," but the "understanding" that "those who come down hard on one side or the other can be wrong or dangerous." Brantley's next move is to present active and unceasing vigilance as the best defense against the inclination to seek final answers and succumb to single-mindedness. "The writers who have attracted the attention of the series refuse to sleep, until Jerusalem is built," but, of course, he notes, "they never sleep, for they never finish building." Here again Brantley directs attention to the forward-looking, future-oriented

component of Romanticism. "Dialectical strategy," he reminds us, "proves ultimately inimical to aesthetic versatility." Continuous resistance to dialectical closure as brought about by the vigilant pursuit of an uncertain future yields the creative dynamism Brantley finds most admirable in Romantic writers, and it provides the standard he applies equally to his own published works. Brantley concludes his epilogue by asking the one question guaranteed to provoke resistance and intensify vigilance: "What next?" He concludes with a summary of his primary aims expressed in admirably plain language: "The prologue and epilogue have not just offered a master key to all these reprints and to the books, but opened the door to more investigation." We leave the epilogue with the sure sense that Brantley is already moving into the future.
—**Paul Crumbley**, reader for Culicidae Press

96. *Transatlantic* *Trio: Empiricism, Evangelicalism, Romanticism, Essays and Reviews (1974-2017)* is the fruit of a distinguished scholarly career spanning over four decades, the rich harvest of one of the thinkers who inaugurated the field of Transatlantic Romanticism. Richard Brantley comes full circle by returning to the subject of his first book, *Wordsworth's "Natural Methodism"* (1975). In *Transatlantic Trio* he offers illuminating collected essays that widen the scope of his argument to show how "natural methodism" is *the* central framework for scholarly understanding of Anglo-American Romanticism. Brantley's theological focus is as important as it is overlooked, with few scholarly exceptions. The role of religion in Metaphysical poetry has been well documented by scholars, but studies of the poets and thinkers who came after them have not paid enough attention to this aspect. Brantley picks up the motif where it runs threadbare, weaving a continuous pattern that runs across nations, the Atlantic, periods, and disciplines into a tapestry that connects Locke, Edwards, the Great Awakening, Wordsworth, Keats, Emerson, and the late Romanticism of Dickinson. Like the Metaphysical Conceit's poetic yoking of opposites, "the faith in experience and experiential Faith" of Romantic verse is able to connect the seemingly separate spheres of Lockean empiricism and Cartesian innatism. Brantley triangulates this opposition by considering how Romanticism bridges the two.

"Can this transatlantic trio," queries Brantley, "of sense-based method, the spiritual sense, and the poetic fancy resonate in today's oversimplified, anti-intellectual climate of polarized either/or"(45)? These essays speak to the way Enlightenment, Romantic, and Victorian thinkers created a Venn diagram out of an opposition that still nibbles at the soul (to paraphrase Dickinson) of today's postmodern world: science vs. religion. Of the many strategies the Romantics offer us to overcome the Manichean duality that runs rampant today are the flexibility of method over the rigidity of system as well as the multiple perspectives of "both/and logic" over the singular vision of "either/or logic." In terms of literary criticism and history, these methods show us the benefits and necessity of moving beyond the single-nation formulations of Romanticism towards a comparative approach. By examining transatlantic influence and literatures as hierarchical, scholars of Transatlantic Romanticism have unwittingly embraced the very duality they are trying to deconstruct. Brantley's methodology levels these fields to remove the competitive poetics and politics that emerged in the wake of the American Revolution and still maintains a foothold. His application of these strategies to present-day Western thought expands this book beyond a work of criticism to a philosophy that overrides the binary coding of a digital age. He ties "the transatlantic trio of empiricism, evangelicalism, and Romanticism together" in new and compelling ways: the collected essays and book reviews are tesserae that together form a mosaic, a more complete scholarly picture of Anglo-American Romanticism than previously existed. The book ends with a powerful autobiographical epilogue that testifies to the transcendent methods of Anglo-American Romanticism to help us make sense of not only the 18th-to-21st centuries, but also of our own lives, the antiphony of internal and external worlds that composes our thoughts and the "music of humanity." —**Joel Pace,** reader for Culicidae Press

About the Author

Richard E. Brantley is Alumni Professor of English, Emeritus, at the University of Florida, where, from 1969 to 2011, he taught courses in Romanticism, the History of Criticism, and the Bible as Literature. He hibernates in Gainesville, Florida, and rusticates in Zirconia, North Carolina. He gladly teaches, and gladly learns from, his fellow retirees. He still explores the realistic, yet hopeful, give-and-take between science and religion during the long Romantic Movement from roughly 1770 to 1870. *Transatlantic Trio* shows him warming to his subject at every crucial stage of its development.

Cover Key

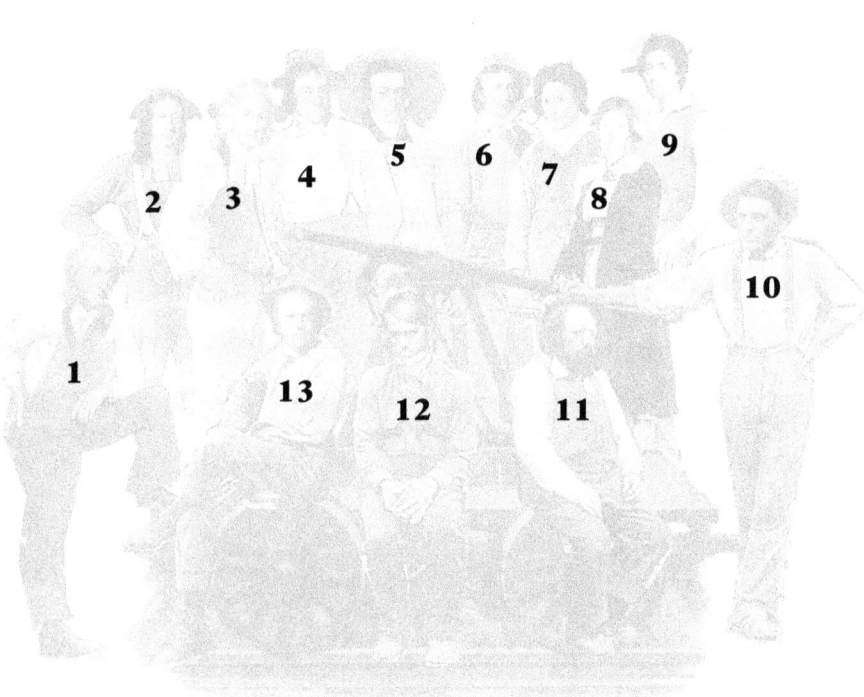

Key

1. John Locke
2. John Wesley
3. Jonathan Edwards
4. William Wordsworth
5. Samuel Taylor Coleridge
6. John Keats
7. Percy Bysshe Shelley
8. Emily Dickinson
9. George Gordon, Lord Byron
10. Ralph Waldo Emerson
11. Alfred, Lord Tennyson
12. Thomas Carlyle
13. William Blake

www.ingramcontent.com/pod-product-compliance
Lightning Source LLC
Chambersburg PA
CBHW060407300426
44111CB00018B/2845